DORIS STOKES
C·O·M·P·E·N·D·I·U·M

VOICES IN MY EAR

MORE VOICES IN MY EAR

INNOCENT VOICES

WHISPERING VOICES

WITH
LINDA DEARSLEY

BLACK CAT

First published in Great Britain as individual
volumes by Futura Publications, a Division of
Macdonald & Co (Publishers) Ltd
London & Sydney

Reprinted 1988 under the Black Cat imprint by
Macdonald & Co (Publishers) Ltd
London & Sydney

Macdonald & Co (Publishers) Ltd,
3rd Floor, Greater London House,
Hampstead Road, London NW1 7QX

a member of Maxwell Pergamon Publishing Corporation plc

ISBN 0-7481-0917-7

Photoset in North Wales by
Derek Doyle & Associates, Mold, Clwyd
Printed in Hungary

Contents

Voices In My Ear	5
More Voices In My Ear	223
Innocent Voices	433
Whispering Voices	613

Voices In My Ear

Doris Stokes and
Linda Dearsley

Chapter 1

It was still dark when I woke up. Out in the night a bell was clanging. Shouts and running footsteps echoed from the street below, and the sky through the gap in the curtains was a strange reddish black.

Then I heard my father's voice. 'My God Jen, there's a fire round at Tom's!'

Muffled conversation floated up the stairs. There was a scuffle of hurried activity; boots creaked across the floor, clothes rustled, voices whispered urgently. Then the front door slammed, two pairs of feet clattered on the pavement. Brisk footsteps crunched quickly away – and there was silence.

I lay still, listening. In the next bed my older half-sister Edna was sleeping peacefully, blonde hair fanned across the pillow. Dad had gone, Mum had gone, Edna would sleep through a hurricane. Carefully I pushed back the sheets and slid out of bed. I tiptoed across the room and stopped. Edna didn't stir. No-one would ever know.

Tugging my coat on over my nightie I crept downstairs. Stretching tall, I lifted the latch, softly opened the door and then I was out and racing down the shadowy street, barefeet pounding over the cold cobblestones.

It wasn't far. Tom only lived round the corner, but at night the familiar streets were transformed – empty and dark with terrifying pools of blackness. There was smoke in the air as I ran dodging shadow and by the time I turned the corner there was a fire engine pulled up outside Tom's house. Crowds of people were standing in the road, the pavement was running with water and busy figures hurried to and fro.

My eyes were stinging and the smoke was tickling my

7

throat, but I hardly noticed. I was so eager to see what was going on. Making myself as small as I could I wriggled into the crowd, squeezing and pushing through the legs, and the adult voices went on above me as if I wasn't there.

'Yes, an invalid ... always sleeps downstairs ...'

'... that paraffin lamp right by the bed ... daft ...'

'... knocked over ... easily done when ...'

Then someone gasped. At the same time, a great shove brought me to the front of the crowd, just as two of the neighbours bearing a homemade stretcher appeared in the smouldering doorway. There was a strange silence. Uncomprehending, I craned my neck. Then as the stretcher bearers passed a gas-lamp I saw the thing they were carrying. A dreadful, charred blackened thing – scarcely recognizable as a human body. I stared, horrified yet fascinated, then I raised my eyes and froze.

Walking along beside the stretcher was Tom. Real and solid, not a hair singed. And yet there was his body on the stretcher. Burned and black. What was happening?

Puzzled and frightened I watched as the three of them – the two stretcher bearers and Tom walked away down the street. Then I turned, as a man opposite turned – and I was staring straight at my father.

'Doris!' Amazement then anger flashed across his face. He strode through the crowd and clipped me smartly round the ear. 'What are you doing here? Get yourself back to bed my girl. *This minute!*'

I ran. I tore round the corner as fast as my legs would carry me, tears streaming down my face. The shadows, the darkness, I didn't even notice them as I belted along. Something enormous, something terrifying had happened that night but I didn't understand what it was.

I was still sobbing when my parents came home. They found me huddled at the bottom of the stairs, tear-stained and snivelling.

'Now my girl,' said my father, 'you shouldn't have come out. It's not a thing for any child to see ... Poor Tom.'

'But father,' I gasped, 'he isn't dead.'

My father looked impatient. 'Don't be ridiculous. He was burnt to death.'

I shook my head, 'No daddy he wasn't, I *saw* him.'

And my father paused and stared at me, a strange expression on his face. His eyes didn't leave mine. Then he said softly, 'Did you Doll? Did you really see him?'

'Yes I did Dad,' I insisted, 'he was walking right beside them.'

It was all too much for mum. 'That girl will be in a mental home before she's finished,' she snapped, 'and you encourage her in these silly notions Sam.'

But my father just ruffled my hair, told her Doris was all right and sent me to bed.

He knew I was different. Looking back I'm sure he was a natural psychic. He hadn't had any training, followed no philosophy except his own, but all the same he used to know things instinctively. I'm sure he realized he wouldn't have very long with us and he tried to teach me, prepare me for what lay ahead in the few short years we spent together. At times I got so angry with him. I thought he was such a strict father, but I was too young to see what I see now – that all the time I was learning valuable lessons that would influence me all my life.

Mind you, I don't think even father realized the full implications of this strange gift I was born with. Certainly I didn't have a clue. As far as I was concerned I was just plain little Doris Sutton from Grantham.Sometimes odd things happened to me which I suspected didn't happen to other people, but I pushed them away, refused to think about them. I wanted to be like everyone else – and, apart from this other faculty, I was.

The gift wouldn't be suppressed however. It was as if my whole life was planned round it. I ignored it, forgot about it, denied it, yet no matter what I did this peculiar, sometimes frightening ability would surface again when I least expected it and eventually I'd discover I'd been following my destined course all along.

I still don't understand why it's happened to me. I was born an ordinary Lincolnshire girl. I wanted a husband, a nice home, children. Those were my greatest ambitions. If I'd thought about a career at all, I'd have loved to be a a nurse – but with my scant education that seemed way out of reach.

If some old gypsy had gazed into her crystal ball or read my tea leaves back in those Grantham days and told me that I had a gift which would help thousands of people, from the poorest old age pensioner to famous celebrities and millionaires; that one day I'd appear on TV, film and radio programmes, I'd have roared with laughter. What me? Doris Sutton? I couldn't *do* anything. I had no special talents. Even my dearest friends couldn't imagine me as a dancer, singer or actress and I was never a great beauty. Yet bit by bit, year by year, the pattern quietly built up – and that's exactly what happened.

I was born in Grantham and by all accounts was a weak, sickly baby. The doctors told my parents I couldn't live and I was christened in a silver sugar basin belonging to a Salvation Army Captain because they thought there wasn't much time. Against all the odds however, I survived.

I realize now we must have been desperately poor. Father was a blacksmith, but he suffered badly with his chest from being gassed in the First World War. He was a tall, bald man and he always wore a muffler round his neck to protect his chest. It can't have been much help. By the time I was six he had to give up work altogether. He used to get ten shillings a week sick benefit and my mother used to take in washing to help out.

She was a small, wiry woman with beautiful thick black hair and she was a marvellous washer. She could put her hands into almost boiling water. When she did the washing up she'd fill the sink with soda and steaming clouds of water and she'd scrub away for ages. She pulled the dish cloth through every handle over and over till the china was sparkling; her washing was out of this world even though she didn't have a washing machine.

Our house was a typical two up and two down, with cold water from the pump in the yard and an outside loo. We didn't have a garden, but mother used to fill the house with ferns in pots.

When I was very young we had oil lamps, I loved them. I looked forward to the long winter evenings when the coal fire and the lamps were lit and father would tell us stories about what he did in the war.

Friday night was 'cleansing night' as father used to call it. My half sister Edna and I were bathed in the tin bath in front of the fire and then father would wash our hair with his own shampoo. He used to boil up coconut chippings he bought from the chemist and massage our heads with the dreadful smelling concotion. The stench was awful. Edna and I squirmed and complained, but father never took any notice.

'Better smell, than lice in your hair child,' he'd say – and we never did have lice.

He was the guiding light in our family. Mother was very practical when it came to housework. She kept the place, and us, spotless – but for everything else she leaned on father. He was the one with ideas.

Sunday was a very important day. We used to go to Sunday school in the morning and afternoon, and in the evening mother would either take us to Evensong or to listen to the Salvation Army in the market square. It was a matter of pride to my parents for Edna and I to be neatly turned out in smart Sunday clothes, like the other children. Unfortunately, they couldn't afford it but father came to the rescue.

He used to go round the market on Saturdays and pick up remnants of material. What a performance when he came back. Edna and I would stand giggling on the kitchen table while father, a mouthful of pins and a large pair of scissors in his hand, walked round us draping the material, pinning and cutting, pinning and cutting. The results might not have been high fashions; but we were always tidy for Sunday school.

Another of father's brainwaves resulted in Edna and I becoming the first children in Grantham to wear fur hats. He'd picked up some scraps of fur from somewhere and converted them into two little hats. He pinned an Australian badge on Edna's because her father had been Australian, and his own Lincolnshire Regiment badge on mine.

Food was often a problem but in those days people helped each other. We were just as likely to sit down at a neighbour's table for tea as our own. It might not be a substantial meal, but mother tried to fill us later with supper of bread soaked in hot water and condensed milk. The important thing was to share.

I remember one night when I was still so small I had to stand on a stool to reach the kitchen table. Edna and I were both in our nighties ready for bed and mother was dishing up our supper, when there was a knock on the door.

Father went to open it, being nosey, I ran after him. I stood in the doorway hanging onto his brown corduroy trouser leg, staring open mouthed at the people outside. There was a man, a woman with a baby and two small children pale and ragged.

'Good evening brother,' said the man.

'Good evening brother,' my father answered.

'I'm just on my way to the spike,' the man went on, 'but I don't want to take my family in. If I do they won't let them out again, and we're walking to try and find work.'

'Bring them in brother,' said my father. It didn't even cross his mind to turn them away.

The first thing he did was take our suppers away from us and divide the mixture into two more bowls so the other children had a share. The man went away and I asked my father what the 'spike' was. 'None of your business,' said mother sharply.

Father interrupted her. 'No the child wants to know,' he said. 'It's the workhouse Doris.'

That night Father slept on the sofa, mother, the woman and the baby slept in the double bed, the smallest of the children was put in my crib and the other child, Edna and I were in Edna's single bed.

Next morning we were eating our usual breakfast of bread in milk and water when the man came back to collect his family. We all rushed to the door and there he was carrying a paper sweetie bag.

He came inside and put the bag on the kitchen table. 'Thank you brother,' he said, 'I haven't got much but these are for the children.'

Father opened the bag and took out two large walnut whips. Our eyes lit up. We only saw chocolate at Christmas or birthdays. This was a wonderful treat. We snatched out greedily but father stopped us.

'Wait!' he ordered and taking out his penknife he sliced the whips in half, so that there was a piece for each child.

'But they were bought for us,' Edna and I wailed. 'It's not fair.'

'Quiet,' he said. 'In this world you must learn to share. Only in that way will we get back any semblance of normality.'

I didn't know what he was talking about. It was only words to me, yet I never forgot them.

I spent a lot of time with my father. He used to take me for long walks in the country and talk to me about the birds, the animals and all the different plants. He never talked down to me. He treated me like an adult – but an adult without as much knowledge as him. He explained which plants you could eat, which plants made good remedies for common ailments, which plants you had to stay away from because they were poisonous. I used to listen spellbound.

He had a knack of slipping little lessons painlessly into the middle of a story; so that I'd hardly realize he was trying to teach me something. One night after our ritual bath and hair wash, I remember my father took me on his knee to tell me a story. The plot unravelled and then he said, 'So remember Doris, it doesn't matter if you haven't got any money so long as you have good manners. Good manners can take you anywhere in the world, you can mix with any type of person. Always respect the others person's point of view. Never be frightened of anyone so long as you're speaking the truth, but always remember that courtesy and good manners are God's money.'

I don't know if it was relevant to the story. I've forgotten the story but I'll never forget his words.

He was a kind man generally, but if I did anything wrong or tried to deceive him I was in trouble. It was impossible to get away with it because father always *knew*.

Like the time I stole a balloon. I had to pass a new Woolworths store on my way to school and it was such a fascinating shop my friends and I used to walk in the back door, through the store and out the front door just for an excuse to look round. The shelves were open, slanting slightly downwards and laden with lovely things.

The loveliest were the balloons. They'd recently brought out a new line. Bright yellow, covered in tiny spots; they were the prettiest things I'd ever seen. They were 1d each and several of the children had them. I would have sold my soul for one of those balloons.

I begged and begged for a penny to buy one, but it was no use. My parents simply didn't have a penny to spare. I've known my mother and father debating whether to get a penny packet of tea or make do with the old tea leaves till pay day; in order to let me have the penny to pay my dues at Girl Guides. Father thought it was important for me to go to Girl Guides. Balloons however, were not on his list of priorities.

Day after day I passed that tempting counter. The more I thought about it the easier it seemed. It would be so simple to stretch out my hand as I went past, pick up a balloon and carry on walking. No-one would know. And so, one morning that's exactly what I did. I scrunched the balloon tightly in my hand until I was out of the shop, then I stuffed it in my pocket.

It was in my pocket all day. I didn't dare take it out in case someone saw it. After school I raced home, hurried up to my bedroom and took it out. It was beautiful. I laid it on the bed to admire the brilliant yellow, then I started to blow it up. That was when my father appeared in the doorway.

'Where did you get that balloon Doris?' he asked.

I was terrified. 'I found it,' I muttered quickly. Solemnly he picked it up and examined it carefully.

'This has never been on the floor,' he said at last. 'Where did you get it?'

'I found it Dad,' I said.

'No you didn't Doll,' he said quietly, 'you stole it!'

Those soft words were worse than an angry shout. My heart seemed to stop beating. 'It's only a penny balloon father, only a penny balloon,' I gabbled.

'A penny or a hundred pounds my girl, stealing is stealing,' he said. 'Get your coat on.'

I thought he was going to take me to the police station. Dumb with fear, I did as I was told and he led me down the street by the scruff of my neck. Not a word was spoken. The streets were already dark, the gas lamps had been lit and I kept my head down in case we passed someone I knew. Did little girls go to jail? I was wondering. Was it true you only got bread and water to eat? When suddenly father pulled me into Woolworths.

He dragged me right back to the toy counter, and asked to see the manager. Then he took out the balloon. 'This is my daughter,' he explained, 'she stole a balloon on her way to school. Now I've brought her back. Will you thrash her or shall I?'

The manager looked embarrassed and I was trembling. 'I don't think that's necessary sir if she's brought it back.'

'She didn't, *I* brought her back,' said my father, 'I told her she had stolen.'

'Yes well, I don't think it's necessary now.' The manager glanced uneasily from me to the curious shoppers hovering round.

'Oh but it is,' said my father. And there and then, in the middle of Woolworths he put me across his knee and spanked and spanked my bottom until I yelled.

'Never be tempted to take something that doesn't belong to you,' he told me,' everything is known.' And with him around, it was.

He had an instinctive, clairvoyant quality that helped him recognize and understand the same in me. My mother noticed it too, but she didn't understand. She often said darkly. 'There's something strange about our Doris,' and would stare at me disapprovingly. I didn't know what she meant. I couldn't understand what I'd done wrong.

I know the episode of my seeing Tom walking about unharmed after he'd been burnt to death worried her quite badly. The next morning when I came down to breakfast she tried to persuade me I'd either imagined it or made it up. I wouldn't be shaken. I stuck to my story so adamantly that, in the end, she realized I was telling the truth or what I thought was the truth. It only confirmed her worst fears – that I was going mad – so she took me to the doctor.

I don't know what she said to him. I was sitting beside her in the surgery swinging my legs, deep in a daydream. The dull adult talk went back and forth over my head. Then suddenly the doctor sat back in his chair and roared with laughter.

Mother was distressed. 'But doctor,' she insisted, 'she actually *believes* this.'

The doctor only chuckled and grinned at me. 'Well it doesn't do her any harm, does it,' he said. And mother had to be content with that.

No more was said, but afterwards I often noticed mother watching me when she thought I wasn't looking, trying to detect further signs of madness. She was always chivvying my father for 'encouraging' me. I learned not to mention anything slightly doubtful that I saw. I didn't want to get dragged to the doctor again.

No-one ever knew about my secret friends. The children I played with whom no-one else could see. I was about six or seven when they first came. I'd been very ill with impetigo and rheumatic fever …

Once again the doctor told my parents I couldn't live. It was very serious and there was nothing more they could do for me. The fever grew worse. I tossed and turned restlessly getting hotter and hotter, the hours merging into delirium.

I must have reached a crisis in my illness, because the next thing I became aware of was my mother sobbing and our young curate kneeling beside the bed. 'Into thy hands oh Lord receive the soul of this child,' he prayed solemnly.

I felt too detached even to wonder who they were talking about. Then from somewhere in the shadows I heard my father, 'No! She'll *not* die.' He sounded almost angry I thought, as I drifted back to sleep.

From that moment on father devoted himself to curing me. He'd stood by and let the doctors do their best, now he was going to take over. He scoured the fields for special plants and herbs and brewed up two concoctions, one of herbs and one of coal tar. My head had been shaved and father rubbed his concoctions into my scalp three times a day. The neighbours might have scoffed but slowly, to everyone's amazement, I began to recover.

I was weak for months afterwards. Mother was advised to make me sit still and conserve my strength. I wasn't to walk far. I soon got fed up with that. They used to wheel me round in a pushchair like a baby! On fine days they'd take me 'up the garden' – a dusty cinder path flanked by allotments that led to the railway – and leave me there for a couple of hours to take the air. They did it with the best intentions, but I got very bored sitting there alone.

Then one sunny afternoon I was parked on the path as usual, listlessly watching a butterfly flutter round the cabbage rows, when I realized someone had come up behind me. I looked round in surprise, to find a little girl standing there.

'Hello,' she said, 'I'm Pansy.'

I gawped at her. She was fascinating. Her skin was black! and shiny like father's boots. She had brilliant white teeth tight curly hair and the loveliest dress I'd ever seen. It was like a long wrap printed in gorgeous bright blues. I'd never seen anything like it in Grantham before and I'd never seen anyone with black skin either. I thought Pansy was wonderful.

She was a bright, cheerful girl. We laughed and chattered and after a while a couple of her friends, two little boys came over to join us. They were just ordinary boys with white skin, not black like Pansy's but they were fun too. Soon we were all playing a noisy game of I Spy.

It never occurred to me to wonder why they weren't at school like the other children. When you're very young you accept things without question.

I was completely absorbed in the game. It was my turn. 'I – spy – with my little eye ...' I looked round quickly for something really difficult but all I saw was old Mrs Rush passing the end of the path. She waved.

'Hello Doris,' she called. 'Feeling better?'

I nodded and, smiling, she went on. I watched her walk away, shopping bag swinging. I don't know why, there was no reason for her to have remarked on my friends, but in that moment I knew with absolute certainty she couldn't see them.

Later that afternoon mother came to fetch me. She was

pleased to find a rosy cheeked, smiling child, instead of the bored, restless girl who normally waited impatiently to be taken home.

'Enjoyed the sun Doll?' she asked as she took the brake off my pushchair.

'Yes mum,' I said. She turned me round and we set off briskly down the path. Suddenly I was hungry and eager for tea. I felt much better. I didn't mind coming to the garden if there was someone to play with. Maybe Pansy would be there tomorrow. I twisted in my seat to wave goodbye, but when I looked back the path was empty. My friends had vanished.

That was when I knew I couldn't tell mother. I couldn't tell anyone. They'd think I was mad.

I realize now my friends were spirit children, yet at the time I didn't even wonder about them. They were as real and solid to me as the members of my family. Where they came from, why they came were questions that never entered my head. I was simply glad to see them when they came.

After a while I realized they only visited me when I was alone. At first I met them at the 'garden' and later, once I was up and about again, I saw them in my bedroom. The hours passed very quickly when we were together. We chatted and giggled over childish things. They loved looking at my books and sometimes, if I was stuck over my homework, Pansy would help me. I was hopeless at Maths whereas Pansy was very quick with figures.

I'm sure mother was suspicious. Once after a particularly noisy game I went downstairs for tea to find mother eyeing me warily. 'Who were you talking to up there?' she asked. 'I heard you chattering away.'

I looked down at my plate. 'I was playing with my dolls mum,' I muttered. She glared at me disbelieving. Then lips, folded in a thin line, she hacked more slices off the loaf. She knew I was holding something back but she could never get to the bottom of it. She didn't even need to say the words, her thoughts were as plain as if she'd spoken aloud. 'End up in a mental home one of these days.'

As I grew older I sometimes wondered myself. My secret

friends were always so conveniently there when I needed them. If I had a row at school, I'd walk home brooding silently and then fly up to my room thinking. 'I don't care if Marjorie Allen doesn't want to know me any more – Pansy does.'

When I opened my bedroom door – there was Pansy sitting on the end of the bed in her beautiful blue dress.

Sometimes, particularly if mother had been going on at me, I'd feel uncertain. 'Is it me?' I'd think 'Am I just making them up in my head?' I knew I had a good imagination, the teacher at school said so when she marked my essays. Yet my friends were so real. Playing with them was completely different from making up a story for English lessons.

At other times I was sure. One day for instance, after wandering home from school with some classmates, I found Christopher in my room. 'Hurry back to the garden,' he said urgently, 'they've buried some drowned kittens but one of them's not dead.'

I ran back to my schoolfriends and told them. They hooted with laughter. They weren't surprised to hear that a litter of kittens had been drowned. In those days of the depression people couldn't afford vet bills. Kittens were drowned and buried at the allotments. No, what they couldn't understand was how I knew and why I thought one kitten had survived.

'I can't tell you how I know, I just know that's all,' I insisted. They joked and scoffed but in the end I was so intense, they trouped back to the garden with me just to prove me wrong.

We stood in the centre of the path and listened. Everything was quiet. Then suddenly we heard a feeble miaow. There was a pause, then the cry came again. A little further along I saw a patch of newly turned soil, the sound seemed to be coming from that direction. Racing over I dropped to my hands and knees and scrabbled frantically at the earth. The kittens were buried just beneath the surface. One of them, a tiny tabby scrap was trapped in a pocket of air between the bodies of its brothers and sisters – and it was alive.

I dusted it off, tucked it gently into my coat and proudly took it home. My friends were impressed and I was very pleased with myself.

'Haven't we got enough mouths to feed?' asked father when I showed him, but he let me keep the kitten. I called her Polly.

Chapter 2

When I was eleven we moved house. We left our tiny two up and two down for a house in Turner Crescent with a bathroom *and* a garden front and back. Never had I known such luxury. I'd have had a bath every day if mother had let me.

For days before the move mother was sorting out cupboards and putting things in boxes, while I wandered from room to room getting in the way. Then one morning I came downstairs to find the handcart outside.

I couldn't keep still for excitement. We didn't have much furniture and soon the house I'd known since I was baby had disappeared. In its place were four bare walls, a home no longer.

I skipped outside again. The other children in the street were clustered round watching father and some of the men loading up. Women stood in doorways keeping an eye on things and mother bustled around looking important. Our family was the centre of attention.

At last we'd finished. Mother slammed the door, the handcart creaked and our belongings were trundling down the street, closely followed by the children.

Grantham was a small place in those days and Turner Crescent wasn't far away. It didn't take long for our procession to reach the new house. Father proudly opened the door and I bolted inside, ignoring mother's scolding.

It was a marvellous house. There was a little garden in front, a big garden at the back and it looked out over Halls Hills – the local beauty spot. Best of all it had a bathroom with a proper bath – solid cast iron and gleaming white.

For the first time I had a bedroom to myself. Edna hadn't come with us. She'd gone to a wealthy family nearby as a sort of live in maid. I missed her company but I certainly enjoyed having my own room.

We were very happy at Turner Crescent. Father was in his element. He loved gardens and now he had the chance to keep his own. It was his pride and joy and I was always being warned not to tread on the flower beds.

He pottered about out there every day. He grew most of our vegetables and a few flowers for mother. I don't think he'd been so happy in years. On summer Sunday evenings, his work done; he liked to sit outside with his penknife, two big hunks of bread and some corned beef left from lunch. I used to sit at his feet and he'd carve off a chunk of bread and put a piece of meat on it for me. We'd sit there for hours, sometimes talking, sometimes in silence, just looking at the garden and the countryside beyond.

It was at Turner Crescent that one of my dearest wishes came true. On my way to school I used to pass a shop called 'Sharples'. Displayed in 'Sharples' window was the most beautiful dress in the world. It was deep blue velvet, the deep, pure blue of the sky on a summer's day and the collar and cuffs were trimmed with gold braid.

Every day I used to stand and gaze at it longingly. Then I'd run home and say 'D'you know the thing I want most in this world? If I could have that blue velvet dress I'd never ask for anything else ever again.'

My parents didn't seem particularly impressed with this idea which would, in the long run, save them money at Christmas and birthdays. 'Blue velvet dresses cost a lot of money,' father used to say. 'We'll have to see Doll, won't we?'

Then on the Friday before Whitsuntide I came home from school and the first thing I saw was a big bag with 'Sharples' on it. It was lying on the couch under the window. I didn't dare go near it, didn't dare even hope for fear I'd be disappointed.

'Don't you want to know what's in that bag?' asked father coming into the living room. I just stared at him dumbly, too apprehensive to answer. He laughed. 'Go on, you can open it.'

I dived to the couch, ripped open the bag and there in

all its glory was my blue velvet dress. I started unbuttoning my cardigan but mother stopped me. 'No,' she said firmly, 'You don't put that on till Sunday.' She looked warningly at father. 'Don't be silly Sam. She's got to learn.'

So the dress was put on a hanger and hung up in my room. I had to be content with gazing at it every day. I couldn't wait till Sunday, but when I woke up with butterflies in my stomach – it was raining.

'No,' said mother, 'You're not wearing it in the rain and that's that.' I argued. I cried. I pleaded; but it was no use. I wasn't allowed to put my dress on. I still had to go to Sunday school though.

By the time I got back from afternoon Sunday school however, the rain had stopped. I was all of a twitter again. 'Please, please,' I pestered, until in the end my parents gave in. Father polished my black ankle shoes. Mother found a clean pair of socks and I was ordered into the bathroom to scrub my neck until it shone.

When I came out the dress was put on. It fitted perfectly and I stared down at myself in wonder. I twirled round. The effect was dazzling. In vibrant blue I was a fairy queen. 'It still looks a bit like rain Sam,' Mother warned.

'Never mind,' said father, 'she can take a coat.' He carefully turned my coat inside out so that people wouldn't see how shabby it was, put the coat over my arm and off I went.

I hurried straight to Wyndham Park about ten minutes walk from our house. On Sunday afternoon the park was full of strollers and I wanted to be seen. It was the most wonderful experience of my life. I walked round and round that park, every path every shady walk – and nobody in this world was finer than I, I held my head high, nose in the air and strutted happily. To my mind everybody was looking at me and thinking 'What a wonderful dress!'

Eventually I couldn't help noticing the clouds were getting low and dark, so reluctantly, I went home. I took off my new dress as carefully as if it had been made of tissue paper and put it back on its hanger.

'Well Doll?' said father when I went back downstairs, 'Was it worth it.'

'Oh yes father,' I assured him, 'It was wonderful. I felt like a queen?'

'Then you're a very lucky girl,' was his only comment.

Not long afterwards I noticed that mother was getting very fat. Her stomach was swelling like a balloon and she got tired and out of breath quickly. In those days nobody mentioned pregnancy to children, so I was never told the cause. I wasn't even particularly curious. It happened gradually over several months, to me mum was getting a bit tubby that's all.

Then one day I came home from school and she wasn't there. Father explained that she'd gone into hospital. He took me along to see her. Children weren't allowed in, so he held me up outside the ward to wave through the window. I could see mother at the end of a row of ladies in bed, and I waved madly. She smiled and lifted her hand.

'There you are,' said father setting me back on my feet, 'and there might be a surprise for you later on.'

I was pleased. I liked surprises.

But the days went by and there was no surprise. Mother came home, thin again and pale and she sat around a lot looking miserable. Then suddenly she was taken back to hospital.

I discovered afterwards that mother then in her late forties had had a still born baby boy. The difficult labour caused a rupture and she needed further treatment.

Naturally at the time I didn't know what was wrong; but I was getting used to mother being in hospital. I don't think I was worried. Father told me she was getting better and I believed him.

She must have been away a couple of weeks when father called me into the living room. He was looking serious and I wondered if I'd done anything wrong. 'Your mother is coming home soon,' he said. I sighed with relief. I wasn't in trouble after all.

'She's been very poorly and she's got to have extra milk and eggs to build her up,' he went on. There was a long pause, 'I'm afraid we've all got to make sacrifices to buy things like that Doris – and I've got to sell your blue dress.'

Nice little girls in books would have said,, 'Yes of course

father. Anything to make mummy well.' But I wasn't a nice little girl in a book. I was an ordinary child with an ordinary child's selfish lack of understanding – and I threw a tantrum.

I flung myself on the floor. I kicked and I beat my fists and I screamed at the top of my voice until my face was scarlet. Strangely enough, my father didn't belt me as he normally would have done at such behaviour. He knelt down at my side and over my screams he said, 'Listen to me Doll. What was it you said to me the night you came back from Wyndham park, when I asked you was it worth it?'

'I don't know! I don't know!' I yelled defiantly.

'Well I remember,' he said, 'You said to me. "Father I felt like a queen". Now let me tell you something my girl. There are millions of people in this world who go from their cradle to their grave and never know one day or one hour when they felt like that. Nobody can take that away from you. Remember that. Nobody.'

I took no notice. I wanted my dress and that was all that mattered; but the dress was sold. Mother came home and gradually grew strong. The subject of the dress wasn't raised again. It wasn't until years later that I realized father had been absolutely right. To this day the sight of blue velvet brings the memory of that marvellous feeling flooding back.

The months slid into years. Life went on as before. With Pansy's help I won a scholarship to the grammar school – which had been father's dearest wish for me. We were a happy family. We weren't well off but we had enough. I never doubted that our pleasant life would go on for years.

If father was becoming thin and drawn I didn't notice it. I was wrapped up in my life, new school, new friends, everything was exciting. Like most children I took my parents for granted.

Then one Friday evening I came home from school and went to clamber on father's knee as usual, when mother stopped me. 'Don't bother your father. He's not well.'

I looked at his face and saw deep tired lines across his forehead.

'It's alright Doll, it's alright,' he said wearily, 'I want to talk to you.'

Obediently I sat down beside him.

'Have you remembered all the things I've taught you?' he asked. 'Do you remember the walks we took in the country? How I showed you what herbs were good for you, what roots to eat. Nobody need starve Doris, God has seen to that. Above all, do you remember that bitter lesson I taught you when you took that balloon?

'No matter how hard up you get and there will be times in your life when you'll think "why?" always hold your head up high. If you've only got three ha'pence to jingle in your pocket and you've got good manners you'll be able to go anywhere. But never never be tempted to take something that doesn't belong to you.'

I wriggled uncomfortably. That was when I was only eight, I thought, and I was spanked and sent to bed without my supper. Why bring it up now? And I changed the subject as quickly as possible.

But at midnight the next night he was rolling in agony, sweat pouring down his face. Mother rushed out of the bedroom, hollow eyed and frightened. 'You'll have to fetch the doctor Doris,' she said her voice trembling. 'As fast as you can.'

Black terror swamped me. I'd never seen father so ill. My whole secure world was crumbling round me. I put on a coat over my nightie, stuffed my bare feet into wellington boots and rushed out into the night.

Dr Allan lived in a wide tree-lined street and by that time all the lights were out. It was pitch dark and eerie – but for once I wasn't afraid. I was too scared for my father to worry.

I was almost sobbing when I reached the doctor's. I hammered on the door and, to my relief, Dr Allan took one look at me and came out at once.

Father was rushed to hospital that night.

The next few days were bewildering. I was sent to school as usual. There was little news. Children weren't allowed to visit patients in hospital; but mother went every day. When I asked her how father was she'd only say. 'He's poorly Doris, don't bother me now.' Yet the neighbours kept popping in and they were crying.

At playtime on Thursday I was racing into the playground with the other children, when suddenly an overwhelming urge to see my father stopped me in my tracks. I could almost hear his voice calling me. I knew the rules, knew I wasn't allowed out of school, knew I wasn't allowed into the hospital. Yet I couldn't help myself, I had to go to my father, he wanted me.

Without a word to anyone I turned, went straight to the cloakroom, took my coat from the peg and left. I ran through the empty streets dreading I might meet a policeman who'd ask why I wasn't in school, but I reached the hospital without incident. At the reception desk I told them my father's name and they directed me to his ward. No-one tried to stop me until I actually reached the ward and found the sister blocking my path. 'Are you Mr Sutton's daughter?' she asked. She was tall and forbidding in her crisp starched apron and cap.

I was so terrified she'd send me away I couldn't speak. Silently I nodded. 'Well your father's very ill child,' she said, 'he's had an operation.' She paused her eyes saying more, and looked me up and down. 'I think it would be good for him to see you though.'

He was lying propped up in bed, his face a sickly yellow white. His eyes lit up when he saw me, but I was puzzled. He looked ill yet I could see something else. He looked as if he didn't belong to us any more.

'Hello Doris,' he said smiling, 'you knew I wanted you didn't you?'

'Yes dad.' I pulled up the chair close to his bed and held his hand.

'I'm glad you've come Doll. I'm not very well.'

'Never mind dad,' I said soothingly, 'you'll soon be well now you've had this operation. You'll be home in no time.'

'No girl,' he spoke softly, his eyes direct as ever, 'I'm not going to come home any more. I want you to promise me one thing. I know you're only 13 but your mother's very easily put upon. Promise me you'll always look after your mother.'

I stared down at my hand, tightly holding his on the crisp white sheet. The tight tense feeling I'd had inside, ever since they'd taken him into hospital, got worse.

'You're not going to die, are you dad?'

He was matter of fact as ever. 'Yes I'm afraid I am girl, but don't say die. That's a word I don't want you to use. Just say I've gone a little way ahead and I'll always be there if you need me. Remember that. You've got a tough furrow to plough girl; but all you've got to do is put out your hand and I'll be there to take hold.'

I stared at him then. He wasn't making any sense at all. How could he hold my hand if he was dead? He was talking nonsense. I was almost relieved. His face looked a little feverish, he must be delirious. That would explain all this morbid stuff.

The ache in my chest subsided and I promised I'd take care of mum till he came home, then I started entertaining him with funny stories of what I'd been doing at school. It wasn't long before the sister came to tell me it was time to go.

I kissed his cheek and left him.

The next morning Miss Brown, the headmistress was taking our lessons. The room was absolutely quiet, she was so strict we didn't dare even whisper. In the silence no-one could mistake the sound of footsteps clicking down the corridor. Abruptly they stopped and I looked up to see a woman standing outside the half glass door. I knew at once she'd come for me and the band tightened round my chest.

Miss Brown went outside. She stood talking to the woman for a few moments. Then she came back, her face serious. 'Doris come here dear.'

My body went very stiff and heavy as I walked to the front of the classroom. Miss Brown put her arm round my shoulders. 'You must go home my dear. Your mother needs you.'

I couldn't speak, I'd burst if I tried. I simply nodded, picked up my books and walked silently out of the classroom.

I stumbled blindly home. By the time I reached the gate

tears were streaming down my cheeks. I didn't care who saw me. I didn't care what happened. All I could do was cry and cry; there seemed to be no end to the tears. Nobody had said the words but I knew. My father was dead.

Our life disintegrated after that. Mother was terribly upset, but worse still, she didn't know what to do. Father had always looked after her. Without him she was adrift and aimless. At first Aunt Sally, father's sister came to take charge.

She made all the arrangements for the funeral. She said there was no sense in having father home first. We could meet the hearse as it came from the hospital on the way to the cemetery. I thought it was a terrible idea. I would mean that father's coffin would drive through the streets without any flowers on. I couldn't bear that.

I plagued and pestered my mother until she agreed to have the wreaths delivered the day before the funeral. Then at 7.30 the next morning, I trudged up the hill to the hospital with two square cardboard boxes; the type they used to put wreaths in. Piled one on top of the other, they was so big I couldn't see over them, but I didn't care. I wasn't going to have my father's coffin come through Grantham flowerless.

Aunt Sally went home after the funeral and things became worse. People kept calling round and asking if they could have things. My father's tools, his gardening equipment, bit by bit our property was walking out of the house. I remembered what my father had said about mother being put upon so I spoke up; but she wouldn't listen to me. She didn't seem to care.

Then we discovered she couldn't afford to keep the house on any longer. We had to move into two wretched little rooms. The next blow was that she couldn't afford to let me stay on at the grammar school – the uniform and books were more than her tiny budget could stand. So it was back to council school which I had to leave at fourteen with no qualifications. My dream of being a nurse seemed to have died with my father.

Life became unbearable. I missed my father terribly and

mother had become unapproachable. She was sunk in depression. She didn't talk to me except to scold and she hardly noticed what went on around her. I expect she was very tired. She took in as much washing as she could manage and whenever I saw her she was up to her elbows in soapsuds.

I wasn't too keen on my new school and, to make matters worse, there was an awful man who lurked near our flat and tried to grab me as I went past. I didn't know what he wanted, but the thought of him made my flesh creep. I used to run whenever he came near; but I was haunted by the fear he'd come up soundlessly behind me, or might be waiting silently in the shadows on the stairs.

It was a grey, dismal time. The happy days when father was alive seemed like a dream. I think mother felt the same way. She wrung her hands helplessly; unable to make any decisions on her own. We got under each other's feet in our two tiny rooms, yet when she heard a house had become vacant at a reasonable rent she didn't know what to do. She diddled and daddled and we got nowhere.

Finally, although I was only thirteen I decided I'd better do something myself. I sat on the end of my bed wondering where to start. 'What would you have done father?' I thought in despair. And suddenly, as if he was answering me the idea came in a flash. 'Go and see the landlord, right away.'

It turned out that the landlord, Mr Golding, was also an estate agent and auctioneer and had known my father, an auction addict, for years.

The clerk behind the counter raised his eyebrows as I walked in. 'I've come about a house,' I said, nervously.

'What, for you child?' he asked.

I nodded. 'Will you tell Mr Golding that my name is Sutton and I've come about a house for my mother and I,' I said.

Rather doubtfully, the clerk went off to find his boss and a few moments later Mr Golding himself came out. 'Did you say your name was Sutton?' he asked, a puzzled expression on his face. I nodded. 'You mean you're Sam Sutton's little lass?'

'Yes I am,' I said.

He stared at me for a second or two, then led me into his office. 'Now then,' he said, sitting me down on the chair opposite his big desk. 'What's the trouble lass?'

He was patient and sympathetic and he was the first adult for ages who actually listened to me. Once I got started I couldn't stop talking. The story was a bit jumbled but everything came pouring out. I even found myself telling him about the awful man who tried to get hold of me. When I finished there was a long silence. It was very quiet in the office without my chatter. I wondered whether I'd said too much and ought to go. Suddenly Mr Golding went round to his desk and took out a key and a rent book. He put them into my hand. 'There you are,' he said, 'it's your's. Move in as soon as you like.'

I ran back to the flat in triumph, brimming with pride at my great courage. The next day mother and I were installed in a house again.

Once the excitement of the move had worn off I found I was in an unusually thoughtful mood. Father seemed close to me. Sometimes his presence was so strong I'd look up expecting to see him standing behind me, but of course the room was empty. I kept remembering that flash of inspiration about the house and the last conversation I had with my father. He'd implied he'd still be near me even after his death, that he'd help me when I was in trouble. Could he really have known he was going to die? Was he trying to explain something to me, something I still didn't understand? I couldn't get it out of my mind.

Finally I had a word with Maggie Smith. Maggie was a young acquaintance of mother's. She was a kind-hearted, cheerful girl but mother didn't wholly approve of her because she was interested in 'they spiritualists'. I knew mother would be cross, but Maggie was the only person who could give me any information on the subject.

She suggested I went to a seance and offered to go with me. I was very scared. I didn't want Maggie to think I was a baby, but the minute I'd arranged to go I wanted to back out. As the days passed I had nightmares where I was chased by great ghosts, white sheets flapping; and my waking moments were filled with vague worries about selling my soul to the devil.

Maggie, however, looked forward to the adventure. When I met her outside our house on the appointed evening she even appeared to be excited. I'd been so nervous I couldn't eat my tea and mother had wondered grimly whether I was 'sickening for something'.

Maggie led me up some rickety stairs leading to a small loft room over a pub. The room was bare except for a table and some wooden chairs and the only other people there were old ladies. They looked harmless enough I thought suspiciously and I was relieved to see no candles or cobwebs.

I wondered fearfully when the medium would arrive. I knew what mediums were like. They had long dresses and fat hands with rings on every finger. So I was surprised when one grey haired old lady, identical to the rest stepped forward and asked us all to take a seat.

She said a short prayer, then lifted her head and stared at the ceiling in deep concentration. I started trembling. What was going to happen? Would there be thunderbolts, disembodied voices, or ghostly hands appearing out of the air? There was a long silence. Then her gaze came down from the ceiling and rested on me. 'You dear.'

'Me!' I squeaked in alarm.

'Yes. I have a man here who says his name is Sam.'

Overcome with shock and shaking in every limb I dimly registered that she was telling me the name of my mother, my sister and the street where we lived.

'That's not Sam Sutton is it?' she asked after a while. The invisible person she seemed to be talking to obviously said 'yes' because she said, 'Sam, I can't believe it,' and tears began trickling down her face.

I struggled to understand what was happening. Was my father in the room? If so, why couldn't I see him? Why couldn't I hear his voice?

'My dear I know your father,' said the medium, 'though I've not seen him for years. He used to lodge with us before he was married.'

I couldn't stand all this talk of my father. Just thinking

of him too much still brought tears to my eyes. My throat was tightening and as the medium passed on with a message for someone else, I tugged Maggie's arm. 'Come on, let's go,' I whispered.

I could tell she wanted to stay. Her eyes were wide with amazement as she listened to the messages and she was hoping the medium would come to her next. But good natured as always, she led me outside when she saw I was upset.

'Well – what did you think?' she asked as soon as we were on the pavement again.

I shook my head. 'I don't know,' I said, 'I don't know what to think.'

Nevertheless I was impressed enough to rush in and tell mother as soon as I got back. I thought she might want to go. Perhaps we could go together some time.

I should have known better. She went beserk. 'I've told you before about they spiritualists,' she shouted angrily, her face red, 'I don't want you mixing with them. Your father's dead and that's the end of it and the sooner you realize he's gone, the better.'

I'd never seen her so cross. I was sent to bed early – something that hadn't happened for years and I wasn't allowed to go again.

But the incident often sprang into my mind despite mother's warnings not even to think of it. I didn't know what to believe, but I couldn't help wondering how that lady knew my father's name was Sam.

Chapter 3

Despite my early fears I settled quite well into the council school. I'd always enjoyed my lessons and the weeks went by quickly. During the last term, the class was urged to think of career possibilities ahead. Most of the girls had some idea. They were going into service or a shop, but my mind just went blank. I couldn't be a nurse and nothing else appealed.

I was lucky. A young teacher had taken an interest in me and seeing me more despondent as the end of term approached, she stayed behind after lessons one afternoon to find out what was wrong. 'You can't be a nurse till you're 18 you know,' she said when she heard my story, 'and then you might not like it. Why don't you try for a job as a ward maid. That way you'll see what hospital life is like and if you still want to be a nurse you can study in the evenings.'

I thought it was a wonderful idea. Better still, her sister was Theatre Sister at Lincoln County Hospital and would be able to find me a vacancy. The only problem was mother. I didn't know how she'd feel about me living away from home. Lincoln was too far away for me to go backwards and forwards every day.

I needn't have worried. Mother was so glad I was being practical at last, and probably so relieved there was another income on the way, she didn't raise any objections. So at fourteen years old I was despatched to Lincoln for my first job.

Soon I was scrubbing floors, emptying bed pans, fetching and carrying. I'd never worked so hard in my life, but I loved it. I felt I was helping if only in a small way, to heal the patients and for the first time I was just 'Doris'. Not that odd child. Plain Doris the same as everyone else.

Weird things didn't happen to me any more. I was on the go from the moment I got up till the moment I crashed exhausted into bed and fell instantly asleep. It was obvious I couldn't study in this environment, I was too tired to do anything but sleep. On the other hand I was quite content as I was.

I'd been there about a year when mother had a fit of wanting me back home. She was lonely without me, she said, I was too far away and she needed my help. I felt torn. I didn't want to leave the hospital, but if mother really needed me, I must go. Reluctantly I said goodbye to my friends in Lincoln and went home.

There was very little work in Grantham. The local hospital had no vacancies. There was nothing for me to do. I ended up running errands and helping with housework around the town. It was dreary work and I thought there was no future in it, but I was wrong. Gradually I progressed.

I was often in houses far grander than my own, seeing a life style quite different from mother's. At times like that my father seemed very close. I could imgaine him standing just behind my shoulder and almost hear his voice say 'Watch Doris. Learn something from this,' and I did. Soon I knew how to lay a table, how to receive guests, how to behave, how to look neat and smart. It gave me more confidence in myself and eventually I was getting work as a children's nanny.

I was very happy. When I'd dreamed of being a nurse, I'd planned to specialize in children's nursing. Nanny was the next best thing. I looked after the children in my care as if they were my own.

I was twenty when war broke out. My life had opened up and I was enjoying a hectic, lively time. There were boyfriends, and dances and long conversations with the girls about love and the latest fashions. The declaration of war set the young people buzzing with what they were going to do.

The airforce was the newest of the services. It seemed daring, glamorous romantic and we joined up in droves.

With several of my friends I went along to be a WRAF, eager to put on that muted blue uniform and do my bit. I had no idea what the work entailed; so I was quite surprised when they asked me what I wanted to do. I hadn't realized I'd have a choice. I hesitated, and in that instant my father seemed at my shoulder again. 'Learn something ...' Yes that's what he would have said had he been alive.

'I'd like to learn to ... to drive,' I blurted out. Funny really because it had never occurred to me before.

They sent me to Port Talbot in Wales where I rapidly became an experienced driver. Soon I was chauffeuring officers all over the place, as well as servicing the car and changing wheels whenever necessary. I'd never been so far from Grantham, or had such a responsible job. Everything was so new and exciting, I couldn't dread the war. I was enjoying myself.

I was changing day by day. I grew independent, confident – tougher than ever before. The shy, nervous girl who'd forced herself to walk into Mr Golding's office had disappeared ... and yet, just when I thought she'd gone for ever, reminders of the old days came crashing into my new life.

We were always broke in the WRAF, always looking for cheap entertainment. One night one of the girls suddenly said, 'Let's go to the spook show' – our nickname for the local spiritualist church. The very mention of it brought all the old fears and mother's dire warnings flooding back.

I wasn't keen but the others were enthusiastic. It was only sixpence to get in and they thought it would be fun. I had no alternative. If I didn't want to be left out I'd have to go with them.

It soon became regular entertainment. We sat at the back of the church giggling and whispering and I convinced myself the whole thing was nonsense. Time and time again the different mediums would come to me and say, 'One day you'll be doing this,' a prediction which caused greater hilarity. The girls would nudge me, roll their eyes and we had to bite our lips to keep from laughing out loud.

On the walk back they'd tease and joke, and to squeeze every bit of fun out of the evening I'd hurry into the billet, wrap a towel round my head, turban-style and walk amongst them proclaiming, 'I can see into the future ...' in a deep spooky voice. Then I'd make up predictions for them – saying the first thing that came into my head about their boyfriends and families.

Usually they'd say, 'But that's *right* Doris!' and I thought they were playing me along. 'Oh if you believe me you can knit fog,' I'd retort.

But it wasn't always a laughing matter. It could be very disturbing. Once, on night duty, I had to collect some very senior officers from the station and drive them out to an airfield. A special raid was about to take place and the press had been invited to watch the take off.

Dawn was breaking. Everything was very still as the first light touched the sky, and the bombers lay like black shadows on the ground. We stood at the edge of the field, mist rising from the grass and waited.

Suddenly sunshine flooded the horizon, a clamour of birdsong filled the air and trucks of airmen began spilling onto the runways. In the midst of the scurrying figures, my eye fell on a young rear gunner. He climbed from a truck and started walking unhurriedly to his plane and as he walked he was whistling. 'The Lord's My Shepherd.'

The high sweet notes carried clear and piercing across the field and something raw, grated painfully inside me. For no reason at all I began to cry.

The boy got into his plane and, as it taxied round for take off and drew level with us, he put his thumb up. Solemnly we returned the signal, but I was half blinded with tears.

He was perhaps eighteen years old and I knew, with absolute certainty, he wouldn't come back.

An hour later I was off duty but I didn't go to bed. I couldn't settle. I went to the briefing room and hung around getting in the way, until finally one of the chiefs said, 'What the hell's the matter with you? What do you want?'

I felt about two inches high but I had to ask. 'I was just wondering if C for Charlie's come back,' I said.

'No,' he snapped, 'she's pranged,' and he walked away.

I fled to the bathroom, locked myself in and broke my heart. I hadn't even spoken to that boy. I didn't know him but I couldn't stop crying. It wasn't just grief for the tragic waste of a young life that made me sob, it was the horror of knowing ...

Even this incident wasn't enough to make me take psychic power seriously. Once the shock had worn off, I put it out of my mind as an odd coincidence and I was soon back to my 'I can see into the future' games.

Shortly afterwards I caught a nasty tummy bug. I had such severe pains in my stomach they sent me to the military hospital for tests and observation. They were afraid it might be appendicitis.

The pains came and went but I wasn't allowed out of bed. I got very bored. One afternoon just before tea I noticed everyone was clustered round a girl further down the ward. Unable to get up and see what was going on, I called out, 'What're you all doing?'

'SSh,' someone said, 'we're getting through to the spirits.' They moved aside and I saw the girl had a case on her bed with cut out letters of the alphabet arranged in a circle on the lid, and an upturned glass. They were quite engrossed, but I wanted someone to talk to.

'Well I can tell fortunes,' I shouted impulsively. That attracted their attention. A few of them drifted back, someone found a pack of cards and they looked at me expectantly. I didn't have a clue what to do. I'd never even been to a fortune teller before so I hadn't the faintest idea how to make it look convincing.

I shuffled the cards around and cut the pack frequently, chatting all the time saying the first thing that came into my head. They seemed to enjoy it. 'That's good,' they'd say, 'How d'you do it?' and I'd say nonchalantly, 'Oh it's simple.'

Our circle was finally broken up by the arrival of the tea trolley. I took my cup and settled down quietly with a book, but a few minutes later the nursing sister came over. 'I understand you tell fortunes,' she said.

I laughed, 'Oh no sister, it was only a bit of fun.'

'But they all say you're very good,' she insisted. 'Will you do mine for me?'

'Honestly sister, I can't do it,' I said.

'Just try,' she pleaded.

So I went through the cards again, shuffling and cutting and they didn't mean a thing to me. They were just playing cards. I chatted a bit, putting on as good as show as I could. Finally when I'd finished, the nurse surveyed me curiously.

'Most extraordinary,' she said. 'My sister got married last week and you've just told me her married name and the address of her new house. How *do* you do it?'

I was stunned. She was obviously telling the truth. The frightening thought that I really did have some kind of power struck me for the first time. I must have done something to tell Sister those things – but what? Perhaps some people would have been pleased. I found the idea horrifying.

Mother's dark warnings and hints of madness that had haunted my childhood were firmly rooted in my mind. Such 'unnatural' affairs should be avoided at all costs. 'That's what comes of meddling with things you don't understand.' I told myself sternly, 'no more fortune telling,' and I wouldn't do it again, no matter how the girls begged.

A few weeks later, almost as if in punishment for my meddling, mother was taken ill. I felt guilty about being so far away, unable to help. The fact that Edna was close by didn't even occur to me. She'd left home so long ago I always thought of mother as my responsibility. Anxiously I applied for and was granted a compassionate transfer to Grantham.

The homecoming was better than I'd expected, Mother, probably encouraged by having her family round her, made a remarkable recovery and I discovered I was billeted with a Mr and Mrs Stanley Webb. I was delighted I knew Wyn and Stan very well, I'd worked for them as nanny to their small daughter Sandra before I'd joined the WRAF.

I was returning to friends. They welcomed me back and

little Sandra, now four, threw her arms round my neck. I hugged her happily. She hadn't forgotten me.

Once I'd caught up on the latest events in Grantham however, I realized homelife wasn't quite as rosey as I'd imagined. Edna lived nearby and, in my absence, Edna had turned into an elegant, willowy blonde. I tried not to be jealous but it was difficult. I was tall and inclined to be heavily built and while my hair was nice and thick, it was a very ordinary light brown beside Edna's film star locks.

To make matters worse she was now engaged to an airforce Pilot Officer. He'd bought her an impressive ring which she flashed proudly from her third finger. He took her to dinner with Wyn and Stan at a posh hotel called the Angel·and worst of all, when he was on duty I had to call him 'Sir'.

Mother of course, was delighted that Edna had landed a PO and continually sang her praises. 'Knows how to make the most of herself that girl,' she'd explain with satisfaction and then eye me critically.

I told myself I didn't care as I babysat while they dined at the Angel. I am happy for them, I thought, as I visited mother or walked Sandra in the park while Edna whisked off to the country. Nevertheless, I was absolutely green.

It's no excuse of course, but when Frank Clark, a pleasant good-natured American airman, asked me out, I jumped at the chance. He was a Captain too!

'Where would you like to go honey?' he asked innocently and my answer was ready before he'd finished the question. 'The Angel.'

I didn't feel guilty about the expense because the Americans seemed so rich. Frank for instance, used to make my eyes pop out by complaining that our white £5 notes were 'Silly little bits of paper', and he'd try to get rid of them as quickly as possible.

I was genuinely fond of Frank. He was polite, happy-go-lucky, marvellous with mother and we never quarrelled. When he asked me to marry him I was thrilled. It was so romantic. I didn't know much about love but I liked being with Frank, we got on well together – surely that's what they meant by love?

He bought me the most beautiful five diamond engagement ring. I'd never seen anything so splendid. I couldn't stop spreading my fingers to admire my hand. Now when Edna flashed her ring, I could flash mine right back.

Mother was quite beside herself with happiness that both her daughers had captured officers'. Wyn and Stan approved wholeheartedly, and in due course Edna got married and I began planning my own wedding.

I think I would have had a happy marriage with Frank. It wouldn't have been a passionate match, but it would probably have been a contented one. If things had been different I expect I'd be an American Grandma by now.

But then one evening I came home and realized I'd run out of cigarettes. The shops were closed and the next day was Sunday. I knew I couldn't get through the weekend without a smoke.

I asked Wyn if she'd come to the pub with me to buy some. In those days, nice girls didn't go into pubs alone – but Wyn didn't feel like it. She hadn't been well for some time.

'Why don't you try Auntie Lawson's in the market place,' she suggested. 'She'll probably be open.'

'Auntie Lawson' as she was known to everyone in Grantham ran the town's only milk bar and she often stayed open late. I turned round and raced up to the market place, not even stopping to change out of my battle dress. I got there just as Auntie was slamming the door.

'Hello Doris, you're just in time. I was going out. What would you like?' I followed her back into the shop and paid for the cigarettes. We chatted while she locked up again. She was off to the Black Bull – a pub where they still sold spirits – to see if she could get a drop of whisky for her husband who had a bad chest.

I wasn't doing anything that evening. Frank had a long spell on duty, so I walked along with her for the company. We soon met up with a friend of Auntie's and the three of us ambled up the road swopping gossip. Further on, we came to a pub I'd never noticed before and Auntie and her friend decided to go in.

'Come on Doris,' said Auntie. 'Come in and have a drink.'

'Oh no I couldn't,' I said, 'I'm still in battle dress.' It wasn't exactly flattering to large figures and it was considered improper dress for social occasions.

'Oh just have one,' said Auntie persuasively. 'No-one'll see you here.'

So doubtfully I went in, and immediately wished I hadn't. The place was full of servicemen. I was mortified to be caught in my battle dress in a crowded place like this. Embarrassed, I fixed my eyes on Auntie's back, as I followed her through the crush, looking from neither left or right, with the vague idea that if I didn't look at anybody, nobody would look at me.

Suddenly my foot hit something hard and I was pitched violently forward. 'Clumsy airforce!' said a voice close by.

Red faced, I turned round. A good looking paratrooper with curly brown hair was sitting behind me, legs sprawled out. I'd tripped over his feet. 'You'd be in a bad way without us Sergeant,' I retorted sharply and pleased with my quick answer, I hurried to catch Auntie.

We were sipping our drinks listening to Auntie's account of Mr Lawson's illness when the paratrooper appeared at our table.

'Can I buy you a drink?' he asked sitting down beside me.

'No thank you,' I said politely, 'I've already got one.'

He wasn't put off. 'What's your name?'

'Doris,' I said.

'That's nice. I'm John.'

'She's engaged you know,' Auntie cut in.

John smiled at her. 'I was only asking her her name, not to marry me.'

Auntie sniffed.

John didn't seem to notice the frosty atmosphere. He chatted easily to me as if he'd known me years, and soon I found I was responding. He knew I was engaged, I reassured myself, so I wasn't deceiving anyone.

Eventually I finished my drink and looked at my watch. I'd been out ages, Wyn must be wondering what on earth had happened to me …

'I must be off now Auntie,' I said. I turned to John,

'Goodbye.' He stood up when I did. 'Can I walk you home?'

I stared at him, not sure whether to admire or be irritated by his cheek. I ought to say no, that was quite obvious, but there was something about him … I didn't want to.

'Look I'm engaged to a Captain. One of my CO's – d'you undertstand that?' He nodded. 'Well you can walk along with me as long as you remember that.'

He grinned and escorted me to the door. As we walked out into the night, I could feel the disapproving eyes of Auntie and her friend on my back.

It was strange, within half an hour of meeting John I was going against my friends, risking criticism, maybe even my engagement, just to be with him. There was nothing rational about it, just a peculiar feeling that this was right. I knew I should get rid of him. I knew it wasn't fair to lead him on, but somehow I couldn't say the words.

We stood talking outside the Webb's gate, reluctant to part, until in the end I was afraid Wyn would come out looking for me. I must have been away hours.

'I've got to go,' I said desperately.

'Well can I see you again?'

A bleak, miserable feeling came over me. 'There's no point is there?' I said. 'I'm engaged,' and for once the statement didn't make me glow.

'It can't do any harm just seeing each other once more,' John pleaded.

'It's pointless.'

'Look I'm on duty tomorrow, but if I wait here on Monday night will you come out?'

'There's no point!' I insisted and breaking away from him, I ran down the path. As I got to the front door I heard him call, 'See you Monday then,' and as I slammed the door behind me, I caught a glimpse of an infuriating wave.

This is ridiculous, I told myself in the silence of the hall. Thoughts were racing round my head and I was totally confused.

'Is that you nanny?' Wyn's voice floated from the dining room.

I opened my mouth to answer and realized I was shaking.

Sunday and Monday crawled by. My thoughts kept going

back to John. I relived Saturday night over and over again in my mind. Suppose he really did come on Monday, what would I do? But he wouldn't come, he mustn't come, I didn't want him to. And yet, part of me knew I'd be very disappointed if he didn't.

I twisted the engagement ring round and round on my finger and there was no pleasure in watching the diamonds catch the light.

Monday evening when I got back to the house it was pouring with rain. There was no sign of John. He's not coming, I told myself. Just as well. I went into the kitchen where several war workers, also billeted with the Webbs, were having tea. I fiddled with a slice of bread, but I wasn't really hungry. Their chatter began to get on my nerves.

'I think I'll go and bath Sandra and put her to bed,' I said, abandoning the bread and swallowing the rest of my tea. No-one looked up. They were used to me slipping into my old job when I was off duty.

Just then Stan came in. He sat down at the table with us and piled his plate with bread. 'Who's the 8th Army sergeant waiting out there in the pouring rain?'

No-one answered, but I almost choked on my tea.

'Is he waiting for you Dorothy?' he asked one of the pretty war workers.

She shook her head, 'No I don't know any 8th Army sergeant.'

I stared down at my plate, feeling my cheeks burn redder and redder. Stan couldn't help noticing.

'He's not waiting for you is he nanny?' he asked in amazement.

'I told him not to come,' I mumbled. Stan knew and liked Frank Clark.

'Well you get out there and tell that poor boy. I'm ashamed of you.'

Scarlet and disgraced, I dragged my coat on and hurried outside. He was standing by the gate, his army greatcoat dripping, curly hair plastered to his head. Illogically I was angry with him; for coming, for coming late, for letting Stan see him, for getting me into trouble.

'I told you not to come,' I hissed.

He took my arm as if we'd been courting for months. Even his eyelashes were wet. 'We can't talk about it here, you'll get soaked,' he said, 'come to the NAAFI for a cup of tea.' Before I realized what was happening he was leading me through the shiny streets.

We sat in that scruffy NAAFI drinking cup after cup of awful NAAFI tea for the whole evening. We couldn't stop talking and, somewhere along the line, John asked me to marry him and I said yes. I hadn't gone off Frank. I just knew now that Frank and I were wrong and John and I were right.

'What about Frank?' I said at last.

'Don't worry about him now,' said John, 'we'll sort it out later. We'd better get married as soon as possible because I'm on standby – I could be dropped at any time.'

Perhaps he thought I might have married Frank while he was away if we waited, but whatever the reason it was all right with me.

Tuesday evening, instead of going to the Webbs' I went to mother's. She was up to her elbows in washing as usual, and she didn't seem to be listening as I tried to tell her about John. The bits she did hear she treated as a joke. That was partly my fault. I was always larking about and often even when I was serious, people still thought I was joking.

Finally I gave it up as a bad job and went to see Mr and Mrs Aires next door who were friends of mother's. 'I can't seem to get through to mum,' I told them, 'but I've met this sergeant and I want to marry him. We want to get married as soon as possible.'

They were a bit stunned. 'But I thought you were …'

There was a silence. 'Well you're old enough,' said Mr Aires. I was 24. 'If you're sure … Look why don't you bring him along to see us, and in the meantime we'll have a word with your mother.'

Wednesday evening I took John to meet the Aires. They were marvellous. Old Mr Aires took the place of my father and fired a lot of questions at John. Did he realize what he was doing? We hardly knew each other etc etc. John reassured him on every count. Yes he'd thought it over, yes he knew what he was doing, yes he'd take good care of me.

At last Mr Aires was satisfied. 'Well you'd better get on with it then.'

He and his wife had managed to explain things to mother, but she hadn't taken it well. She'd been fond of Frank and she was disgusted that I planned to throw over a Captain for a Sergeant. She passed the message on that she had no wish to meet my new fiance.

The next day, as John was stationed at a camp outside Grantham, I went to the registry office to arrange our wedding. John had written down his number, date of birth, full name – all the details I would need and still didn't know – and gave me the money for a special licence.

'Is your fiance in the forces?' the registrar asked. I said he was. 'Is he likely to be sent abroad at any moment?' I nodded. 'Well in that case we can rush it through. You can get married on Saturday.'

Now with the wedding fixed, I had to break the news to Edna and Wyn and Stan. I had no more luck than with my mother. They simply didn't believe it. 'But I am,' I insisted. 'I'm getting married on Saturday.'

'Yes of course you are dear,' said Edna ironically. 'You met him last Saturday and you're getting married this Saturday. Will you be having twins the Saturday after?'

It was hopeless. I could see this was going to be the strangest wedding in Grantham, with no guests because no-one would believe it was taking place. I don't care, I said to myself, John and I love each other, that's all that matters.

Fortunately there were just a handful of people who did take us seriously. Mr and Mrs Aires who agreed to act as witnesses, and dear old Auntie Lawson who said we could use her upstairs room for our wedding night. After that it was back to the Webbs' for me and back to camp for John, until we found somewhere to live.

It was a very odd wedding day. I didn't want to get married in uniform; but fortunately I had a very nice three piece costume (we call them suits now) which looked smart. All it needed was a hat. So bright and early on

Saturday morning, I went into Grantham with my wages in my purse to buy a hat.

I'd quite forgotten that with the war on, clothes had gone up tremendously in price. I found the perfect hat. A beautiful maroon, dipping over one eye and with a feather. Very Bette Davis. I preened before the mirror, delighted with my reflection.

'Shall I charge it Miss Sutton or will will pay cash?' asked the assitant.

'I'll pay cash,' I said grandly – and to my horror all that was left of my wages afterwards was 2d!

The other problem was an overcoat. It was January and very cold. I badly needed an overcoat to slip over the costume, but I had nothing suitable. On the other hand I knew Edna had a beautiful coat.

As soon as I got back, I asked her if I could borrow it. She sighed deeply. 'Oh come on Doris, it's time this joke was over with.'

'It's not a joke,' I said firmly, 'I'm getting married at 3.00.'

'All right. Have it your own way. Borrow the coat, it's all yours. Hope you enjoy the wedding.'

I had a slow, lingering bath, wandered downstairs in my dressing-gown for roast beef sandwiches for lunch, and then went up again to dress. The hat, the overcoat and the costume went very well together and as I glided past Edna and Wyn I could see doubt come into their eyes for the first time.

The registry office was only five minutes' walk away and I was early. There was no sign of John. My God, I thought, he's not going to turn up. there were so many people about I didn't want to be seen lingering alone outside the registry office, so I stood in a shop doorway next door. The minutes ticked by and I felt sick. Maybe I'd imagined the whole thing. Maybe he didn't love me, maybe he was playing a joke …

Then suddenly amongst the crowd I could see a brand new red beret bobbing along. I dived into the street towards it and there, handsome in full dress uniform, was John. I flung myself against him and hugging and smiling we walked into the registry office. Half way up the hall we both stopped at exactly the same moment, said 'Are you sure?' at exactly the same time, and of course burst out laughing.

I don't remember much about the ceremony except that I was shaking so much John had to hold my hand with both of his to get the utility ring on my finger. When we walked outside there was my sister and Wyn with Sandra in her pushchair. I heard Edna say, 'My God Wyn, she's done it!'

Wyn said, 'Yes but isn't he good-looking.'

In a dream I introduced John, then we walked home with Mr and Mrs Aires who'd made a wedding tea for us.

Mother of course, was nowhere to be seen. I slipped next door and found her at the sink in her old 'epen', she never said apron, always 'epen', an old Lincolnshire word. 'Are you not coming to have some tea with me on my wedding day?' I asked quietly.

Even her back was disapproving. 'I don't want to meet him,' she said and folded her lips tightly.

I'd known what to expect. After all these years I knew mother like no-one else, but even though I was prepared for it, it hurt. Silently I went back to the Aires. 'Is she coming?' asked Mrs Aires. I shook my head. I didn't trust myself to speak.

Mrs Aires put down the tea-pot and left the room. The rest of us made bright conversation, until some time later Mrs Aires returned, dragging a disgruntled mother behind her. Still in her old epen.

Well mother had some wedding tea with us, but she completely ignored poor John. We were relieved when it was time to go.

There was still one unpleasant thing to do and that was tell Frank. I hadn't wanted to tell him before the wedding, because I couldn't bear him to try and talk me out of it. I knew I'd treated him badly but I couldn't help it. I couldn't marry him. After meeting John it was impossible.

I phoned him from Auntie Lawson's and explained what had happened, but he wanted to come round and speak to us.

It was very embarrassing. I think Frank's ego had suffered the biggest blow. I didn't say much. We sat round the table and John did most of the talking. Finally, he pushed that beautiful ring, now back in its box across the table to Frank. 'I'm very sorry mate – but that's the way it is.'

Frank, good natured to the end, looked at the ring, then pushed it back. 'It's no use to me. Let her keep it.'

He left shortly afterwards and we were alone, properly alone for the first time since we'd met.

Chapter 4

Twelve noon on a warm September Sunday. Bees were buzzing through the late roses in the garden and the air was thick with sunshine. Everything was very quiet, very still – and then I heard it.

Far away a low humming. It grew louder and louder, closer and closer, until the morning was filled with the roar of hundreds of engines and suddenly the sky was black with planes.

I stood at the window, my baby in my arm, looking up. Somewhere in that teeming mass of aircraft was my husband. So this was it. After all the false alarms the drop was on and John had gone.

I had no idea where he was going. It was only later I found out it was a place called Arnhem.

I'd fallen pregnant almost immediately after our marriage, which delighted us both. We loved children. We wouldn't have minded half a dozen. It did make the problem of accommodation more urgent however, so knowing mother had some spare rooms in her house I tried to talk her round.

She wouldn't hear of it at first. She couldn't forgive me for jilting a Captain, but gradually she softened. I think the news that she was about to become a grandmother had a lot to do with it, and of course the more she saw of John the more she accepted him. She still thought we were mad, but once she got to know John she couldn't dislike him. Nobody could.

Several weeks after the wedding we moved into the top two rooms of mother's house and we furnished them ourselves. We were tremendously happy. John had a sleeping out pass, which meant he could come home for

the night, as long as he was back at camp for reveille at
6.00 am. He had to walk five or six miles to get there and
I'd get up to cook bacon and eggs if we had any or
porridge if we hadn't at 4.30 in the morning so that he'd
be back on time.

Throughout the spring and summer rumours of a drop
flew round the camp. No details, except this was going to
be a big one. We had several false alarms. Twice the men
were confined to camp and twice nothing came of it. I was
on tenterhooks the whole of the pregnancy.

Once after we'd said goodbye and John had gone, a
friend of mine came racing to the house. 'Quick,' she
shouted, 'they're all down at the Granada Cinema!' I said,
'Who are?'

'The Paratroopers!'

I was enormous with the baby by now; but I ran down
the road after her. We arrived at the cinema just as the
paratroopers were filing out. They'd been brought into
town to see a film. We weren't allowed to speak, but we
smiled at each other and waved and then the men were
taken away in trucks.

Each time we met again was joy, yet it only prolonged
the torture, the uncertainty. I was more fortunate than a
lot of young wives however, for John was with me
throughout my pregnancy. He was even with me in the
ambulance when my labour pains started, though he was
called away at midnight.

It was a difficult birth, but I forgot all the pain when, on
Bank Holiday Monday, in the morning my baby son was
put into my arms. He was beautiful. A bit red perhaps at
first, but with wisps of soft blond hair and huge violet eyes.
Not blue, violet.

I cuddled him happily and suddenly I felt terribly tired.
My eyelids were so heavy I couldn't hold them open, and
the last thing I thought before I fell asleep was 'what a pity
John can't be here to see his son.'

Then that afternoon an incredible thing happened.
Refreshed after a sleep and a cup of tea, I was back in the
ward with the other mothers. One of them was standing by
the window watching the visitors when she called to me,

'Doris, your husband's coming up the drive, but he's got his arm in a sling and plaster all over his nose!'

Unsure whether to be delighted or horrified by this information, I crawled out of bed and waggled to the window. There was John, just as she'd described him.

Apparently he'd been riding in a truck when it overturned, badly spraining his wrist and grazing his nose. They'd sent him home to recover.

And so I had John with me for the first six weeks of our baby's life. We called him John Michael after his dad and there was no prouder father than John. Whenever the weather was fine, we used to take the baby out in his pram with John pushing. I couldn't get near it! Often we bumped into friend's of John's and they'd pull his leg a bit. 'Left hand drive, left hand down a bit Jack,' they'd tease, 'back it up, three point turn.' And John would just beam proudly at them and carry on.

Then on Friday September 15, he arrived home at lunchtime. He'd been given the afternoon off. 'Now don't worry love, you won't be seeing me for five days or so. There's a drop in the air but I'm not on it. I'm going out by boat, so once they've got away I might be able to get back.'

We spent the afternoon together and before he left he had a bath. I didn't notice till afterwards that he left his dog-tags behind. Once again we said goodbye and once again I watched him walking down the street, and thought, 'Is this the last time?'

Saturday passed quietly. I went to bed as usual and fell into an uneasy sleep. It must have been about 2.00 when a sharp click woke me. I sat up in bed and the noise came again. It sounded like a stone hitting my window pane. I padded across to open the window, and there was John in the street. 'John!' I cried wondering whether I was still dreaming. 'Ssh!' he warned.

I ran downstairs to let him in and we tiptoed back to the bedroom. 'The drop's on,' he whispered, 'and I'm afraid I'm on it.' Apparently, so many men had failed to return from their half day off they needed everybody they could find, and John ended up going with a different platoon in a different company. As soon as they'd discovered what

was happening, John and several of the men married to
Grantham girls had sneaked home for a last farewell.

We had three precious hours together. John got back
into bed with me, we put John Michael between us and our
last minutes as a complete family flew past. I didn't want
morning ever to come, but all too soon the first light was
creeping into the sky. Reluctantly John got up and pulled
his boots on. I clung to him. I couldn't bear to let him go,
yet I couldn't beg him to stay or let him see my tears. It
wouldn't be fair. He had no choice.

We kissed, he cuddled John Michael and then he tiptoed
outside. On the landing he paused, 'if you see the planes
go over at 12.00 tomorrow love, you'll know I've gone,'
and then he was creeping downstairs.

I ran to the window and watched him walk away, fixing
his image in my mind. That slim figure, that curly hair,
that much loved husband I might never see again. I stood
there, my feet turning blue on the cold lino, until he
disappeared in the smudgy half light at the end of the
street.

And the planes did go over the next day and I knew my
husband had gone.

Then came that awful waiting time that all wives and
mothers with men on active service went through, when
we didn't know if our men were dead or alive. What made
it worse was that Arnhem was such a big operation, such a
big disaster. It was constantly reported on the radio. I and
the other wives with men out there used to gather round
the radio, compulsively listening to every broadcast and it
was agony. We heard of complete chaos, how the Germans
were waiting, how they shot our men as they parachuted to
the ground, how communications between the allied
forces had broken down and nobody knew what was
happening.

It was torture, yet we had to hear everything. We
formed a sort of wives' club and met at each other's houses
to listen to the radio, speculate on our husband's chances
and have a little weep. One day I was so miserable I said,
'You know if I had to choose between my husband and my
baby I'd choose my husband. You can always have another

baby, but you can't have another husband.' I didn't realize at the time what a terrible thing that was to say.

I don't know how I'd have got through those awful days without John Michael. He was a little piece of John and he was a marvellous baby. I know every mother thinks her baby is the most wonderful baby in the world, but my John Michael was special. He wasn't a bit of trouble. He never cried, even though there were many nights when I lay awake worrying till 4.00 in the morning, then fell into an exhausted sleep and slept right through his morning feed.

He never made a fuss. He'd just lie in his cot gurgling to himself and playing with his toes until mother came banging into the room saying. 'Are you still asleep? What about the baby's feed!'

Then one day a letter arrived to say that John was missing. They'd let me have more information when the situation was clearer. I was frantic. I thought I'd die of suspense. The constant wear on my nerves, the violent swings from hope to despair were driving me mad. Anything must be better than this endless worrying.

Of course all our neighbours knew the story and every development, and one morning one of them stopped me in the street and suggested I go to the spiritualist church. Apparently they did something called 'psychometry'. I'd never heard of it; but I was assured they could tell whether a missing person was dead or alive by holding an object belonging to them.

It sounded exactly what I wanted. I was convinced that knowing the truth, however awful, must be better than this uncertainty. I decided to go along. I couldn't tell mother obviously, so I just said I was popping out to visit a friend and would she mind baby sitting. Then, tucking John's dog-tags into my pocket, I hurried off to the Labour rooms where the Spiritualists church held its meetings.

There was a lady standing at the door with a tray and I was asked to place my article and a shilling on it. I handed over the dog-tags and the coin and went in and sat down.

At first it was very nice. There was a church service with singing and prayers and I got quite weepy with the atmosphere. Then the medium came onto the stage with the tray of objects, and I went rigid in my seat. I didn't take my eyes from her as she picked up object after object. Some of them she placed against her forehead and then she'd start to talk about them and desribe their owners. All over the audience people were saying, 'Yes, that's right,' and my heart thudded harder and harder in anticipation and fear.

At last she came to the dog-tags. I held my breath as she picked them up and lay them on her palm. She sat quite still for a moment or two, then she said, 'I'm sorry to have to say that the owner of these discs is definitely in the spirit world.'

I gasped. The hall swam around me, everything started spinning and I was falling dizzily into darkness ...

When I came round I was lying on the floor. There was a crowd of people standing round and the chairman of the meeting was kneeling beside me, fanning my face with a newspaper. 'Nothing's been proved, nothing's been proved,' he said over and over, as I struggled to sit up.

'Are you all right dear?' Hands helped me up, arms supported me out into the air and they clucked round in concern. My mind was still whirling with the thought 'John's dead. He's dead. I won't see him any more,' and I wanted to brush all these people away. I wanted to be alone.

Eventually I managed to persuade them I was better and they let me go. I don't remember walking home. I was in a daze. I noticed nothing around me, I might as well have been walking through thick grey fog. If my baby hadn't been waiting for me I don't think I'd have gone back. I don't know what I'd have done. I couldn't drown myself because I was a strong swimmer, maybe I'd have wandered into the fields and gone on walking till I dropped.

I don't know how long it took me to get there, but when I did get home I went into the kitchen where mother was sitting with John Michael's pram beside her, walked straight past without a word and went upstairs to my bedroom. I sat on the bed absolutely numb. It seemed so unreal ...

There was a bellow from downstairs, 'Doris! What about this baby of yours?' Very slowly, because my feet felt like lead, I went back down. 'What on earth's the matter with you?' asked mother staring at my white face and completely forgetting I'd meant to keep it a secret, I told her what had happened.

She sighed impatiently. 'Oh nonsense. I've told you before. Dabbling with that will drive you mad. You don't know what's happened to John yet. Now will you see to this baby.'

I suppose I must have bathed my baby and fed him and done all the usual things; but I honestly don't remember any of it. The next thing I was conscious of was laying him in his cot in my room. I stood looking down at him and for the first time, I cried. Tears splashed onto his face and, as I wiped them off, I sobbed, 'Oh John Michael what are we going to do without your daddy? Will I be able to bring you up the way he would have wished?'

I was sobbing and talking to him and wiping away the tears with my handkerchief, when suddenly from nowhere I heard a voice. The most beautiful voice which seemed to fill the room, 'My child,' it said. I looked round in alarm but there was no-one there, 'My child I've come to tell you your husband's not with us on this side of life and on Christ's birthday you will have proof of this.'

There was silence. Frightened, I picked up John Michael and cuddled him close. Mother's right, I thought, I'm going round the twist. That's all my baby needs. No father and a mental mother.

Then the bedroom door flew open so sharply I thought it was mother bursting in and there stood my father. My mouth dropped open. He looked as real and as solid as he did when he was alive. The years rolled back and I was thirteen again.

'Dad?' I whispered.

'I never lied to you did I Doll?' he asked.

'I don't think so,' I said.

'I'm not lying to you now. John is not with us and on Christmas day you will have proof of this.' Then as I watched, he vanished.

With John Michael still in my arms I sat down heavily on the bed. I was stunned but not frightened. How could I be frightened of my father? I rocked backwards and forwards turning it over in my mind. Surely I hadn't imagined it. It must be true. When I'd last seen my father I wasn't even grown up let alone married, yet he'd known John's name. It must be right. John was alive!

I felt utterly convinced. A little later when the baby was asleep, I went downstairs with a dreamy smile on my face. 'Oh you've cheered up a bit,' said mother.

'Yes, it's all right now,' I said happily, 'John's alive.'

She gave me one of her looks, but refrained from saying anything.

The next day I rang John's Company office, and told them I knew my husband was alive. 'We hope you're right,' they said, but three days later I had a letter from the War Office to say that my husband had died of his wounds and as soon as the grave numbers were sorted out, they'd let me know where he was buried.

I rang the Company Office again and I said, 'You've made a mistake. It's not my husband,' and they were very sweet.

They said, 'We hope it isn't dear'; not actually adding 'humour the girl', but obviously thinking it.

The same note was in other people's voices when I told them John was alive and I suppose I began to have a few tiny doubts. So just to check, I went to see an old lady who had a reputation as a marvellous reader of tea leaves.

She made a pot of tea and we drank it very solemnly, then she told me to swirl the dregs round three times and turn the cup upside down on the saucer. I did as I was told and she peered at the tea leaves intently. She told me a lot of things that weren't particularly interesting and then she said. 'I can see the letter "J" here and a man sitting on the end of a bed. It's a queer bed, it's made of wood and there's another of wood above it. He's blind and he's holding his head, but he'll be all right. Whoever this "J" is he's alive and he'll come back.'

I was overjoyed. My father had been right. Dimly I heard her say 'and that'll be 3d.' I'd have given her a hundred pounds if I'd had it.

I returned home absolutely unshakeable in my conviction that John was alive. Mother was getting seriously worried by now. John's mother, my mother-in-law from London had also had the bad news from the War Office and she came to Grantham to share her grief with us. She was very disturbed to find the widow, and mother of her grandchild wasn't grieving.

She and mother got together in the kitchen with a pot of tea to discuss the matter. 'I don't know what to do with her,' mother said. 'She's had a letter to say he's dead, he's died of his wounds and she's got another letter – haven't you our Doris? – to say that second week in January she's going onto widow's pension ... Now what more could you want than that?'

'I don't care what you say,' I said stubbornly, 'John is alive and will be coming home.'

Mother-in-law tutted. 'I think she ought to go into hospital you know. I don't wonder at it, it's driven her a bit peculiar. I'll take care of the baby.'

So they sent for the doctor. Fortunately it was a woman doctor who knew me and John Michael very well.

She refused to be drawn on the subject of whether or not I was peculiar and she assured them I was a fit mother. 'Whatever happens to Doris,' she said, 'she'd never harm that baby. She cares too much about him for that.'

So I didn't go into hospital and mother-in-law couldn't take John Michael. Every day I went down to the post office to see if there was a letter for me. I made a thorough nuisance of myself. 'Are you sure you haven't lost any letters?' I was always asking, 'I know I should have had a letter from my husband.' But there was nothing.

The weeks went by and as Christmas approached I was certain I'd hear something. Mother shook her head in despair of me, but I remained convinced.

Night after night I went to my friend Dorothy's house to listen to the radio. She had a sophisticated set, powerful enough to receive Lord Haw Haw's programme from Germany. It was mainly anti-British propaganda, but at the end of the broadcast they read out names and messages from men who'd been captured and were now prisoners of war. I always hoped to hear news of John, but his name wasn't mentioned.

At last Christmas Day arrived and I woke early full of excitement. Christ's birthday – they'd promised, there had to be news today. It was a real Christmassy Christmas morning. Snow had fallen in the night and frozen on the ground. The Salvation Army band was playing carols at the end of the street and I sat in bed listening to the music and giving John Michael his morning feed.

Suddenly over the familiar tunes came the sound of footsteps crunching across the snow. I didn't need to go to the window. It was the postgirl, I knew it. Gently, I laid John Michael in his cot, grabbed my dressing gown from the hook and raced downstairs, tying it as I ran.

She was hurrying up the road, and when she saw me on the doorstep she trumphantly waved a letter in the air. 'You knew there was something for you Doris didn't you?' she laughed, 'here you are. Merry Christmas!'

There on the doorstep, my fingers shaking, I ripped open the envelope and tore out the official letter. 'Dear Mrs Stokes ...' I skimmed impatiently through the formal lines until I came to the precious words. John was alive! Suffering from head injuries which had caused temporary blindness; he was now recovering in a P.O.W. hospital in Holland.

He was alive! He'd be coming home!

Drunk with joy I ran back up the passage yelling at the top of my voice. 'Mother! Mother! John's alive! He's alive and he'll be coming home. I knew it – he's alive!'

Chapter 5

Now I knew John was safe and recovering, I was able to relax and enjoy my baby properly. He was the most beautiful baby, he really was. With his blonde curls, enormous violet eyes and long black lashes, people were always stopping me in the street and saying, 'Isn't she lovely,' despite the fact I'd dressed him in blue.

'It isn't a girl – it's a boy,' I'd say indignantly, but of course I was delighted that people admired him.

He used to do the most extraordinary things. At four months old he insisted on taking his feed from a cup. Always the same cup, a large white tea cup with red roses. He used to clutch it in both hands and tip his head right back, until the rim of the cup was resting on his face, leaving a big milky ring. It looked so funny the neighbours used to come and watch, and sometimes they'd bring their relatives as well.

'Could my sister see your baby take his milk from a cup,' they'd ask, 'she doesn't believe it.'

John Michael wasn't in the least put out by his audience. He'd chuckle and gurgle and hold out his arms to his admirers, a real extrovert. Young as he was, I swear he had a sense of humour and knew when he made people laugh.

One night I'd brought him downstairs for his ten o'clock feed. Mum and her friend, old Mrs Scothen, were sitting by the fire having a glass of beer and after I'd fed John Michael I sat him in his pram with his dummy and joined them on the hearth. I wasn't keen on dummies, but John Michael had started sucking the red tassels on his pram cover and I was worried the dye might come out.

Suddenly Mrs Scothen looked past me and started

laughing. 'Well if I die tonight I've seen everything now. Will you look at that boy of yours!'

We turned round there was John Michael sitting in his pram, his hands laced across his stomach, and the dummy on his head, teet pushed in so the loop stood straight up. We all burst out laughing and John Michael laughed with us till the tears rolled down his cheeks.

At other times he was a serious old soul. He'd lay and stare at you with those huge solemn eyes, as if he could see what you were thinking.

'Eee you've been on this earth before you have,' Mrs Scothen used to say to him. 'My word Doris, if you have another half a dozen kids when John gets back you'll never have another one like this.'

Mention of John always brought a sharp pang. I was very conscious that John Michael was getting bigger every day and John wasn't here. Our baby had hardly seen his father. Would he know him when he came home?

Sometimes I felt sure there were memories still lodged in his mind of that first six weeks with his daddy. I often sang to him, but he didn't take a bit of notice unless I sang 'Lilly of the Lamplight'. It was the paratroopers song that John whistled while he pushed the pram all those months ago. As soon as he heard that tune, John Michael would kick his legs and wriggle until I held him upright on my lap – then he'd dance away on my knee.

By the New Year John Michael was a strong healthy baby, my pride and joy. I dressed him up in blues and yellows and took him everywhere with me. He was never any trouble and everyone loved to see him.

Early one evening after visiting friends, I lifted him out of his pram and took him upstairs for his bath. Bathtime was always fun. He had a rubber duck and a fish to splash in the water, and afterwards he sat on my knee wrapped in a fluffy white towel and we played 'peep boo'.

Tonight he sat in the water, kicking his legs gleefully while I lathered him all over. His pink baby skin was warm and glowing and the steam had turned his hair into damp little curls. He looked good enough to eat.

Suddenly, bent over the tub, soap in my hand, I froze.

The back of my neck began to prickle and at the same instant, the voice was in the room again. Soft and beautiful, coming from nowhere. 'He's done his time on earth,' it murmured. 'He's got to come back to spirit.'

The soap dropped into the water and I stared at John Michael in horror. They were talking about my baby. My baby! Shocked, I scooped him up still dripping wet and held him tight. The voice had gone. The room was silent. It was a mistake. I must have imagined it. My mind was playing cruel tricks.

Trembling with fear, I laid him on the towel and checked his body carefully. His eyes were clear and bright, cheeks rosy. He was alert and cheerful, the picture of a healthy baby. You could have used him to advertise baby food. There couldn't be anything wrong with John Michael.

Yet that night I took him into bed with me. I couldn't let him out of my sight. It was a hallucination. I was tired, I'd imagined the whole thing I told myself. But like a dark cloud, the thought kept coming back that I'd heard that voice before and it had been right.

The next day I took John Michael to the doctor. 'Now look Doris,' she said at last, 'I know you've had a lot to put up with, but there's nothing wrong with John Michael. He could do with his foreskin clipped, I'll make an appointment at the hospital, but that's nothing. It only takes a couple of minutes. He's a healthy boy.'

Comforted, I took him home. That voice was definitely my imagination this time.

The appointment came through quite quickly, and the night before we were due at the hospital I put John Michael into his cot earlier than usual. I felt weary myself that evening, so I lay down on the bed to wait for him to fall asleep. My mind started drifting. I thought about John and the letters I'd written him, the photographs I'd sent. I thought about the appointment the next morning and the things I had to do when I got up. Everything was jumbled and relaxed. Then for no reason my mind seemed to lurch forward, and a picture popped into my head. It was me, pushing the pram up the hill to the hospital. In my mind's eye a whole series of pictures unfolded like a film. I saw myself walk into the hospital, saw the sister come up to me and admire my baby. I heard her say, 'Make yourself comfortable in the waiting room. It won't take a minute. I'll bring your baby back in a moment or two.'

I saw myself waiting and waiting. The minutes ticked by and nothing happened. I was getting more and more anxious. I could see the worry on my face. Then I saw the door open and the sister came in – but she was alone. She wasn't carrying John Michael. 'Now Mrs Stokes,' she said, and there were tears in her eyes. 'You've got to be very brave. I'm terribly sorry. I'm afraid your baby's dead.'

'No!' I screamed out loud. Panic stricken I jumped off the bed. The pictures stopped. I was still here in the bedroom and John Michael was in his cot. I rushed over to him. He was sleeping peacefully, a happy smile on his lips, but I snatched him up and held him so tightly I could feel his heart beating.

That night was agony. I tossed and turned in desperation. There could only be two explanations of these peculiar warnings. Either I was going mad or my baby was ill and I was going to lose him. Insanity was infinitely preferable of course, but if I was insane I'd lose my baby anyway.

First thing next morning I phoned the hospital and cancelled the appointment. 'I'm afraid my son's got a bit of a cold,' I lied. The nurse was sympathetic.

'Never mind Mrs Stokes,' she said. 'Keep him wrapped up and we'll make an appointment for next week.'

We made the the appointment for the following Monday and, in the meantime, I started on a crazy round of visits to child specialists. I took John Michael to every specialist I'd heard of. I even took him to Nottingham, but no-one could find anything wrong with him. They all said the same thing. 'This is a fine baby. Nothing to worry about with him.'

But I was worried. The next Monday I cancelled John Michael's appointment again, and the following Monday I made another excuse. I just couldn't bring myself to take him along for that minor operation.

All that day I felt guilty about the lies I was telling. I put him to bed and sat by his cot, wondering how long I could go on avoiding the issue. If I cancelled the appointment too many times, the hospital would get suspicious. Perhaps they'd even send someone to check. The problem was getting too big for me to cope with.

I leaned against the side of the cot, my forehead wrinkled, wondering what to do. And then, I felt somebody watching me. I looked up quickly and gasped. My father was standing just inside the door.

'Doll,' he said softly, 'you know this isn't right. John Michael should be with us. He has to come back. At quarter to three next Friday I'll come for him and you must hand him over to me. Don't worry. I'll take good care of him,' and he vanished. One minute he was as solid as the furniture, the next I was looking at empty air.

I burst into tears. I didn't want to believe it. I'm mad, I'm mad, I told myself. How can a perfectly healthy baby die? 'It's pointless, he's not even ill. You're imagining it all,' whispered a voice in my head. 'But this has happened before and it came true,' another voice hissed back. On and on they argued, backwards and forwards until I wanted to scream. I felt I was being torn in two by hope and despair. Yes, I must be going insane.

But the next day, when white-faced and red-eyed, I put John Michael in his bath, he started to scream and draw up his legs in pain. Afterwards he refused his feed and I sent for the doctor.

'This often happens when they're teething,' she said after she'd examined him, 'don't fuss yourself so Doris. The strain's got on your mind. He's got a cold and a slight temperature that's all. Give him glucose and boiled water when he wants it.'

I kept him by the fire all day and tried to get a little glucose water down him, but he wouldn't touch it. By evening I decided he wasn't well enough for his bath. I didn't want him getting cold, so I just sponged his hands and face. Then I fetched a clean nappy, tugged open his dirty one and found blood.

My hands turned to ice. This was it. Fearful and angry I

called out to mother and thrust the nappy at her. 'I knew!
I just knew!' I cried. 'Fetch the doctor.'

But the doctor wouldn't come. She sent back a message.
'Tell Doris to stop panicking. It's just the cold going
through the child.'

I sat up all night with John Michael. As mother's house
was cold, I kept the living room fire going, dragged the
sofa close and lay my baby on it. Then I sat on the floor
beside him, my face close to his. The whole world was very
quiet and still. The firelit hours ticked by, unreal as a
dream. Now and again in a spasm of pain crossed John
Michael's face; but in between he smiled and played peep
boo. He never cried once.

As soon as it was light I sent mother to ring the doctor
again; but though we waited quite a while, no-one came. I
was furious. I was trapped in a nightmare and I couldn't
wake up. I knew my baby was slipping away from me, but I
couldn't make anyone understand.

I hadn't wanted to leave John Michael for a second but I
had to do something. Angrily I stormed out to the phone
myself. 'Either there's a doctor at my house in ten minutes
or I take my baby to the police station,' I snapped. 'My
baby's *dying* I tell you.'

The doctor obviously thought I was being melodramatic
again. Too busy to come herself she sent a locum, but by
now John Michael's condition had deteriorated so much
anyone could see he was ill. His face was pale and sunken,
his eyes glazed and dull. He didn't want to play, but he
never murmured when the locum examined him.

'I'm afraid he'll have to go into hospital right away,' the
locum told me at last. He went off to make the
arrangements and someone ordered a taxi to collect John
Michael and I.

Mother was in a terrible state. Though she scolded and
moaned and was endlessly practical about everyday
matters, she was really very soft hearted. She couldn't cope
in a crisis, couldn't face serious matters. Now she wrung
her hands and sobbed. She couldn't possibly come to the
hospital she said. She couldn't bear it.

Fortunately old Mrs Scothen had come in to help, and

she said she'd go with me. She packed up the few bits and
pieces I'd put out to take, and bustled round trying to get
mother and I to sip a cup of tea. Then all at once the taxi
was outside.

I put on my coat, wrapped another thick blanket round
John Michael for it was bitterly cold, and opened the door.
The icy blast hit me immediately. After the long sleepless
night and the strain of getting a doctor, the light and cold
air made me dizzy and I stumbled.

'Give John Michael to me Doris,' said Mrs Scothen
noticing the slip. 'I'll carry him.'

'No Scottie, you won't,' I said firmly, 'this'll be the last
time I ever carry him.'

They operated on him right away. It was an exploratory
operation they said. In those days nobody told you much
about what was wrong or what treatment was needed.
With the war on, they were so short staffed I heard that
the surgeon was 83 years old.

The next day, Thursday, when I went up to see John
Michael, they said he was a little better. One of the nurses
told me he kept holding out his hands, as if he wanted
something. Did I have any idea what it could be? Instantly
I remembered the tiny white fluffy rabbit he held in one
hand, and the rattle he held in the other, when he was in
his cot. He used to have the time of his life banging them
against the cotside. I rushed home to fetch them, and
when I put them in his hands he seemed to know what
they were. There was no happy banging, but he gave a
little smile and seemed more content. It was a good sign I
decided.

That evening for the first time since Monday, I felt
hungry and was able to eat a corned beef sandwich with a
cup of tea. I was ready to clutch at any straws and now I
thought I saw a glimmer of hope.

First thing Friday morning I told mother I'd call in at
the doctor's surgery on my way to the hospital. 'I want to
know what's the matter with John Michael,' I said, 'and
what they did in that operation.'

I was sitting in the waiting room, pretending to read a
battered old magazine when the cleaning girl popped her

head round the door. 'Is there a Mrs Stokes here?' I said that was me, 'Well there's a policeman come to see you,' she informed me, eyes wide.

My heart dropped to the bottom of my shoes. I rushed outside and bumped into a dark uniform figure in the hall. He looked rather nervous. 'I've been to your house and your mother said you were here,' he said, 'you've got to get back to the hospital right away. Your baby's taken a turn for the worse.'

I couldn't face it on my own. That long, grey, anxious walk seemed impossible unless someone came beside me. I knew it was no good asking mother, she'd have hysterics, so instead I ran round to my Aunt Sally's. She dropped everything to come.

The ward was quiet and solemn when I walked in and the nurses didn't meet my eyes. I rushed to the small wooden cot in the corner that was John Micheal's, and as soon as I saw my baby, I knew. His little face was grey and shrunken, his plump, healthy body wasted. The change in four days was incredible. I could hardly recognize my glowing rosy son of a week ago.

The last hope was shattered. I was certain now of what I'd known all along but refused to accept. I was going to lose my baby.

I didn't leave his side again. Hour after hour I sat by the cot, my hand through the bars, holding onto the tiny sick arm that had once been dimpled, willing my strength into his frail little body – and feeling him slipping away.

Hours later I saw his face turn paler still. Quickly I stood up and bent over the cot. I could feel him going. I had to cuddle him one last time. Gently, gently I picked him up – and he weighed nothing, my beautiful baby who could take his feed from a tea-cup.

I held him as tightly as I dared, hardly taking my eyes from his face, memorizing everything. The soft baby smell, the pale silk hair, those long, long lashes. I must store it all in my mind. Time stopped. I gazed for hours, or maybe only seconds and when I raised my head, my father was standing on the other side of the cot.

He didn't say a word. He looked steadily at me and then

silently held out his hands. I clutched John Michael more tightly, but still my father held out his hands. There was a long pause. I just didn't have a choice. Slowly, reluctantly, I passed my baby across, and at the very instant father took my son in his arms, I looked down and saw my little John Michael was dead.

When I looked up again my father was gone. The spell was broken. Tears were streaming down my face and terror, panic, pain were flooding through me. 'Nurse! Nurse!' I screamed, but even as they came running it was too late. And in the middle of the confusion, as they tried to prise the lifeless body from my arms, I realized I was facing the ward clock – and it was just gone quarter to three.

Chapter 6

My son had rather a spendid funeral. The padre of the paratroop regiment came to help with the service and an escort of six paratroopers lined the path to the church door.

It was a raw, bitingly cold day. Snow lay on the ground, iron grey clouds hung low over the church roof and stinging snowflakes whirled about us, as our procession crunched through the bleak churchyard. In the centre was a little white box, heartbreakingly small. I hardly took my eyes off it. My baby, my beautiful baby was gone. Blockage of the bowel they'd said – and in his place, a white box.

'We think of those who are absent,' said the padre at the service, 'particularly this tiny child's father who's away fighting for his King and country ...' But I was full of hate. What did I care about King and country?

And then we were in the churchyard again, with snowflakes flying like bullets and an enormous black hole in the ground ringed with ice and that tiny white box being lowered slowly down. I had to force myself to stand there. I wanted to rush forward to stop it, to scream at these stupid people, 'Don't put my baby down there! He'll be so frightened, so cold!' Because even though I'd seen my father take him, I still didn't understand.

Then when it was over the young vicar came across and put his arm round my shoulders. 'God's will be done,' he said and I could have hit him. I wanted to lash out, spit in his face. 'God!' I thought, 'don't talk to me about God. I don't want to know a God like that. Five months ago I went through agony to bring that boy into the world and here I am in agony, watching him go out. For what? But fury and grief got choked up together and I couldn't say a word.

I know what they mean by the expression 'living hell', because during those months after John Michael's death I lived through it. Spring came but I didn't notice it. I didn't see how it could ever be Spring again for me. They were long bleak days without colour, only endless tears.

I couldn't bear to stay in my room in mother's house so I moved back with the Webbs. I got a job in a munitions factory and threw myself into the work, threw myself into anything that would stop me thinking. Afterwards I'd go out with the girls and get rather drunk.

It made no difference. Eventually the time would come when I had to go home to my lonely room and walk past the empty cot and the pram that I refused to part with. I used to lie awake, and the need to hold my baby in my arms was like a physical pain. I used to think about him in that dark hole in the ground and I was sure he must be cold. Night after night, I had to fight a terrible urge to go and dig him up to see if he was all right. I knew it was wrong, it was a wicked thought but all the same I had to force myself to stay in bed.

Then one night after I'd been crying for hours I thought I heard a gentle voice murmuring in my head. I stopped sniffing to listen and I realized I was hearing a poem. I've never fogotten it. 'In a baby castle just beyond my eye, my baby plays with angel toys that money cannot buy. Who am I to wish him back, into this world of strife? No – play on my baby, you have eternal life. At night when all is silent and sleep forsakes my eyes, I'll hear his tiny footsteps come running to my side. His little hands caress me so tenderly and sweet, I'll breathe a prayer and close my eyes and embrace him in my sleep. Now I have a treasure that I rate above all other, I have known true glory, I am still his mother.'

I couldn't remember ever having heard that poem before, but now it comforted me. I could just imagine him in some beautiful place happily playing and for the first time in weeks, I turned over and slept peacefully. After that, whenever I felt tears coming into my eyes I whispered that poem to myself an felt better.

Somehow I managed to compose a letter to John,

breaking the terrible news. I was almost afraid to post it. Supposing he thought it was my fault, supposing he blamed me? But I discovered later he never received that letter. He flew to England thinking all was well.

Then in glorious May, came VE day, and I woke up to find a friend banging on the Webbs' front door. 'John's home, John's home!' she yelled as soon as I opened it. I was instantly alert. 'Where? Where? I cried.

'England, but we don't know where exactly yet,' she said.

Of course I dragged her inside and excitedly she told me what had happened. John, just arrived in England, had phoned a neighbour of mother's who had her own private phone, to let us know he was back and would be home as soon as possible. My friend looked at the floor. There was something else. John hadn't received any of my letters. He hadn't heard about John Michael, so the neighbour had told him. It must have been a dreadful shock.

The day dragged by. I couldn't eat, couldn't settle to anything. I was so excited and nervous I couldn't keep still. Stan reckoned it would take a day or two at least for John to reach Grantham. If it took longer than that I thought, I'd be worn to a skeleton with nerves.

You could almost taste the excitement in the air that day. People were rushing about the streets, laughing and shouting, building bonfires, hanging bunting and flags from the lamp-posts. When night fell the fires were lit and people danced in the road.

I didn't feel like dancing but as I lay in bed listening to the singing outside, I was almost happy. I drifted off to sleep.

The next thing I knew the door bell was ringing and mother's voice was bellowing. 'Doris, John's home! He's here!'

Apparently, as soon as he'd heard about John Michael, John had gone straight to his C.O., who'd put him on the first train home – but not knowing I was back with the Webbs, he'd gone to mother's.

Mother woke the house. Doors banged, everybody tumbled out of bed. There were excited exclamations and then I heard that dear, familiar voice in the hall. John!

Slowly, I tied my dressing-gown round me and picked up

my hair brush. My heart was racing. I was longing to see him, yet I couldn't walk out of that door. No, I thought, he's been blinded, he's got a head wound, he's been through so much. How can I tell him what happened? Will he blame me?

'Doris! Doris! Where are you girl?' Mother sounded agitated. 'Don't you understand. John's here!'

But I daren't go down.

There was silence for a moment or two. Then the stairs creaked and footsteps thudded across the landing. The bedroom door opened slowly – and there he was.

'John!'

He was just the same. The curly hair, the slim figure, the smart uniform. We both stood transfixed, gazing at each other and then I saw his eyes drop to the empty cot.

'Baby … baby isn't here,' I whispered.

'I know,' said John and then he was across the room and we were in each other's arms weeping together.

'There'll be other babies,' he said at last stroking my hair.

I shook my head. 'But they won't be John Michael.'

'No,' he said, 'they'll never replace John Michael.'

Meanwhile downstairs everyone was going mad with excitement. John must be starving they decided. So at 1.00 in the morning they raced around fetching bacon and eggs – all strictly rationed, and cooked an enormous, magnificent pan of food.

'Come on down you two,' Wyn called from the foot of the stairs, 'there's time for that later!'

And so we walked into a family party. No-one was tired. They laughed and chattered while John ate his breakfast, firing dozens of questions at him without waiting for replies. Then John remembered the chocolates and cigarettes the Red Cross had given him, so we sat around smoking and eating chocolate – another great luxury – while the Webb's dog chased its tail and barked for joy.

The Webbs kindly let us stay with them until we got our first house – from good old Sam Golding, and we tried to put our lives together again. It was wonderful to have John back, but because he looked well; two arms, two legs

and handsome as ever, I didn't realize how badly wounded
he was. As the months went on I noticed his co-ordination
seemed slightly wrong, he often bumped into things and
he was unusually clumsy. He'd liked a drink occasionally in
the past, but now half a glass of cider made him dizzy.
Then Sam remarked to me, 'he can't remember anything
for two minutes together Nanny,' and it was true. At last I
realized that John was still a sick man.

His memory and his concentration were unreliable.
Poor John, he tried so hard at a variety of jobs, but he
could never keep them for long. He was a loyal, steady
worker, he always did his best, but in the end that quirky
memory let him down. He could never quite understand
what went wrong. Often he was humiliated and angry with
himself because his mind wouldn't work the way it used to.

To make matters worse, I couldn't seem to fall
pregnant. Month after month went by and nothing
happened, and the more time that elapsed, the more
desperate I became. Then the woman opposite us adopted
a little girl from a local children's home. Of course that set
me off. 'Oh let's adopt a child John,' I begged, 'if John
Michael had lived and we hadn't had any more we'd still
have had him to keep.'

'If it'll make you happy lovey,' said John.

We made enquiries from our neighbour and then went
to see the Children's Officer. I explained that I didn't want
a boy because I couldn't put another child in John
Michael's place, but we'd love to give a home to any little
girl.

It was arranged for us to visit the Home every Saturday
to get to know a little girl called Monica. She was three
years old, and if we all got on well, we were told we could
adopt her.

She was a lovely little thing. She had long blonde hair,
brown eyes and a sweet nature. I knew it would be easy to
love her and I was sure we could make her happy. I was
pleased it was so straightforward.

But a funny thing happened. Every time we visited
Monica, there was a pathetic little boy hanging round. He
followed us everywhere. He was about 2 years old and he'd

been brought to the home in a shocking state. He could hardly stand up because he had rickets and malnutrition. There were sores on his skinny legs and his nose was always running. Whenever I turned round, there he was gazing silently at us with enormous blue eyes. Before I knew it I was wiping his nose and John was lifting him on his knee.

Somehow, to this day I'm not exactly sure how it happened, we went along to adopt Monica and ended up with little Terrence John.

Mother was against the whole thing, naturally. We couldn't afford it, she said. If it happened and we had one of our own that was different, but to take on someone else's child was ridiculous. Well we needn't think we were taking him round to her. She wouldn't have that child under her roof.

Then we brought Terry home and suddenly there were sweets, suddenly mother just happened to be passing our door more frequently than ever before, and obviously had to drop in to say hello. Before long she was spoiling Terry unashamedly. He soon learned that if he couldn't get what he wanted from us, he only had to ask granny.

Terry responded well to family life and good food. His bones grew straight and strong, his thin body filled out and the sores on his legs cleared completely. I loved him dearly and yet – he was mine but he wasn't mine. I still mourned John Michael.

I think John felt the same way, but with him there was something else. The things he'd seen in the war, the strain of adjusting to his injuries, of accepting limitations where before there were none – all combined to make him depressed and restless. He was searching for something, but he didn't know what.

So one day when he found me weeping over some baby clothes of John Michael's, he suggested we go to the Spiritualist Church. He must have been thinking it over for weeks. 'Even if it does nothing else love, it might give us peace of mind,' he said.

Secretly I doubted it. I thought I'd seen enough of spiritualism and I wasn't impressed. On the other hand

John needed some sort of help that I wasn't able to give. Then again, in my grief my thoughts always went to those strange appearances of my father. I was quite certain I'd really seen him and as added proof, I knew that what he'd said had come true – but he was dead. I couldn't understand it, but the more I puzzled over it the more the hope grew – if my father was somewhere near, then surely John Michael must be too.

And so once again, I found myself going back to a Spiritualist Church. Strange how at the time I didn't notice the pattern, I failed to see how all paths led me to spiritualism, no matter what course I took.

We began attending services on Sunday afternoons when Terry went for a walk with his granny. I was surprised to find that though we didn't get any evidence of an after life, the actual service was very comforting. The philosophy seemed to be more about learning to live life than about death, and we certainly needed some advice at that stage. Our lives were very difficult in just about every area at the time, financially, emotionally, physically, yet the services gave us new strength to face our problems.

Occasionally we travelled further afield. Our search had given us a new interest – almost a hobby and though it was frustrating when the messages weren't for us, it was never dull.

News of unusual events spread fast on the psychic grapevine and now and again, if we could find the money to get there, John and I would go to a seance or a demonstration we'd heard about. We were disappointed many times. I came to the conclusion that even if they were out and out fakes, there were quite a few deluded people about. In fact I might have dismissed them all as phoneys had I not had one incredible experience that forced me to think again.

We heard that Helen Duncan, a materialization medium – a medium who made spirits materialize – was holding a seance in Manchester. We were sceptical but always hoping to be proved wrong, and so though John couldn't come that day in cold December I went along.

Helen Duncan has long since passed over, but I shall

never forget that seance. It started quite normally. The room was darkened with just a single red light burning, yet the dim glow was bright enough for everyone to see the medium quite clearly.

Silence fell, Helen Duncan concentrated deeply and then appeared to go into a trance. This was quite routine, and by now I'd seen it happen several times, yet there was something electric in the air. Something strange and tense that I'd never noticed before.

As we watched a thin silvery mist began to creep from the medium's nostrils and her middle, yet she remained motionless in her chair as if she was asleep.

'Ectoplasm,' someone whispered behind me. Gradually the flow increased, until mist was pouring from the medium and a wispy cloud hung in the air in front of her. Then like fog stirred by a gentle breeze, it began to change shape, flowing and swirling, building up in places, melting away in places.

Before our eyes the outline of a woman was being carved in mist. Hair and features began to sharpen and refine. A small nose built up on the face, then a high brow, lips and chin, until finally the swirling stopped and she stood before us, a perfect likeness of a young girl in silvery white – and she was beautiful.

My mouth dropped open and I couldn't tear my eyes from this vision. I was seeing it, yet I couldn't believe it. Dimly I was aware that the woman next to me had gasped and clasped her hands to her mouth, but before I could register the significance of this the girl began to move.

The audience watched, riveted as she drifted across the room and stopped right in front of my neighbour.

'I've come to talk to you mother,' said the medium in a light, pretty voice quite different from the one she'd used earlier. The girl spoke to her mother for several minutes, explaining that she still visited the family and knew what was going on and listed a few personal details as proof.

Then unexpectedly, she turned to me. 'Would you like to touch my hand?' she asked.

Dumbly I brushed the slim, pale fingers held out to me, and then in astonishment took the whole hand. It was warm! I don't know what I'd expected. Something damp, cold and unsubstantial I suppose – but this was incredible. I'd touched a warm living hand.

Suspiciously I glanced at the medium but she was still slumped in her chair. It was impossible. It must be a fake and yet how could she have done it? Nonplussed I sank back and stared at the girl, quite speechless.

She smiled as if she could read my thoughts, then she raised her arm and out of the air, a rose appeared in her fingers. Gently she placed it on my neighbour's lap.

'Happy Christmas mother,' she said and then slowly moved back and began to shrink, getting smaller and smaller, fainter and fainter, until she disappeared through the floor.

No-one stirred. We all sat motionless as if hypnotized. The only sound was the woman next to me quietly sobbing. In her hand a deep red rose, still beaded with dew – in December.

Dear God, I thought, how marvellous to be able to do that.

It was only later I discovered that Helen Duncan was one of the greatest materialization mediums who ever lived and I was very privileged to have seen one of her seances.

The episode of the rose was a very rare and special thing. I'd seen it with my own eyes. Either I'd been conned, or anything, absolutely anything, was possible.

We went to our weekly services with renewed hope after that.

Then one Sunday, for some reason we had to go to the evening instead of the afternoon service, so we took Terry with us. He was about four then and quite well behaved. We sat at the back, settled Terry with crayons, a colouring book and comics and he played quietly.

There was a visiting medium that evening, a man called Walter Brooks from Yorkshire. His messages were quite routine and we listened politely until suddenly, he pointed directly at us.

'I want to come to the lady and gentleman at the back.' John and I looked at each other in surprise. 'There's a man here who says his name is Sam.'

I shot off my seat as if I'd been stung. 'That's my father!'

'Well he says he's got John with him and John wants to send his love to his brother Gerry – no sorry, wait a minute. Not Gerry, *Terry*.'

I gasped and John gripped my hand. At last, after all this time there was proof. Walter Brooks had never seen either of us before. There was no way he could have known my dead father's name, my dead son's name or my adopted son's name. 'John wants to send his love to his brother Terry.' When little John Michael died there'd been no thought of another child, so how could he know there was now a brother unless he was still close to us?

It was a wonderful thought. I don't think anyone who has not suffered a tragedy can understand the joy of knowing your loved one isn't lost completely. When you know that somehow, somewhere they live on, life takes on new meaning, it's not futile any more.

Suddenly I looked at Terry, happily crayoning his picture-book-house scarlet and he was mine. For the first time he was my son, because John Michael had called him 'brother'.

Spiritually we were much happier but there were still problems. John's health was fading. Since he'd come back from Arnhem, he couldn't bear to be shut in. He hated talking about his war experiences, but he explained to me that after he was wounded he was picked up by some allied soldiers and they were given shelter in a cellar by a kind and very brave Dutchwoman.

John was blind and helpless, so he had to stay in the cellar while fierce fighting went on outside. Day after day he sat in the dark, relying on the others to tell him what was going on. Every time the door opened he had no way of knowing whether a friend or enemy was about to walk in.

Then came the news that the Dutchwoman had had her head blown off by a sniper and all he could do was sit and wait in the dark like a trapped animal.

Eventually there was a twenty-four hour armistice for the wounded to be handed over to the German's for medical treatment. John was amongst them, but he could never forget those long, tense days in the cellar.

After trying several jobs in Grantham he managed to get work with an engineering firm. It was quite well paid but he grew unhappier by the day. The dim, noisy factory made him claustrophobic and he was desperate to get out. Instead of getting used to the conditions, as time went on his tolerance got lower.

He grew pale and nervous and I knew he couldn't stand it much longer, but what could he do in the open air? He was no longer strong enough for building work. Then I had an inspiration. 'Why don't you try gardening John,' I said. 'It doesn't pay as much, but we'd manage and I'm sure you'd be happier in the open.'

John agreed. Not long afterwards he got a job as a gardener with Major and Lady Turner at Little Ponton, a village a few miles from Grantham. With the job went a tied cottage.

It was a pretty place and I was thrilled when he took me to see it. Small and stone-built, it had massive gardens front and back. How lovely, I thought, John can grow fruit and vegetables and we can sit in the garden on warm summer evenings enjoying the peace and fresh air. Much better for Terry too, to grow up in the country.

But when I stepped into the stone flagged hall I had the weirdest feeling, as if someone was standing on the stairs watching me. I turned round but there was no-one there. I shrugged and told myself my imagination was working overtime again. There was no reason to mention it to John. He was happy with the job and the cottage and it was vital that he left the factory. I didn't want to spoil it for him.

We moved in and soon enjoyed a different way of life. The country was a mystery to us town folk and it was fun to learn. We had an outhouse in the back garden, where there was a cooper for boiling your clothes and also I discovered, for boiling a pig. Not that I had any intention of doing that.

Our neighbour was a motherly woman called Mrs Briggs who helped us tremendously, though she often laughed at my squeamishness. 'Why Doris there's nothing like really fresh pork,' she'd say and chuckle at my shudders.

Indoors, I could never quite be rid of the eerie feeling that there was someone else there. I realized that first experience in the hall hadn't been imagination after all, but it didn't worry me now. I'd heard enough at the Spiritualist Church to know I needn't be frightened of unseen visitors.

Yet after a while it became irritating. One night John and I were listening to the radio in the living room, when the door opened and a sleepy Terry trailed in rubbing his eyes.

'Daddy, Mummy, will you come and tell this old lady to go out of my room.'

'What old lady love?' I asked.

'The old lady who's looking cross at me,' he said.

John and I exchanged glances. 'You must be dreaming Terry,' said John. 'Come on let's all go and look together.' Taking Terry by the hand, we led him back upstairs.

The room was quite empty, but as soon as I stepped over the threshold the familiar prickly sensation of being watched tingled down my spine. I ignored it.

'Well she's gone now Terry,' I said brightly, 'I expect you *were* dreaming. Come on, jump into bed and I'll tell you a story.'

Back downstairs, John was still inclined to think it was a dream, but I wasn't so sure.

'You know I think I'll ask Mrs Briggs if anyone else has had trouble in his house,' I said, and so the next day, I told her the whole story.

'You know dear I wouldn't be a bit surprised if it wasn't her come back,' she said at once, and went on to tell me about the previous tenant of our cottage. I never did find out her name so I called her Old Polly, but apparently she was an extremely materialistic old woman who was always boasting about what she had.

'There should have been some money you know after she died,' said Mrs Briggs, 'but the family never found it.'

'Well if there is, it must be in Terry's room,' I said.

I think I was right. A few days later I was working in the kitchen when I heard a terrific crash upstairs. Terry was playing in the garden, John was at work and I wondered what on earth it could be.

Mystified, I went to investgate and for some reason

made straight for Terry's room. In those days we had
marble wash stands with Victorian jug and bowl sets in the
bedrooms, and I was surprised to see that Terry's soap
dish, which I'd placed neatly beside the bowl earlier that
morning, was lying on the floor by the fireplace. Somehow
it had slipped off the washstand and 'fallen' right across
the room.

Puzzled, I bent to pick it up and in doing so, found I
could see right up the chimney. Instead of an empty black
flue, I could make out a sack and some paper bundles.
'Old Polly's money,' I thought instantly and at the same
moment felt eyes boring into my back. I knew the room
would be empty if I turned round.

'It's alright Polly,' I said, straightening with the soap dish
in my hand, 'we don't want your money'; and replacing the
dish firmly on the marble top I went back downstairs.

We never did investigate the contents of the chimney.
Whatever was up there didn't belong to us, besides we'd
antagonize Polly even more if we did.

After that Terry slept with what we called his 'Christmas
light' burning. It was a light bulb painted red, which gave
the room a pretty rosy glow. It looked nice but it didn'
help.

We had no idea then that red lights attract physical
phenomena and the combination of the light and my
latent psychic powers must have been irresistible to the
unhappy Polly – a woman so materialistic in life, she
obviously had the attitude that if she couldn't take it with
her, then she jolly well wasn't going.

We lost count of the times the living room door would
open late at night and Terry's pyjama clad figure would
appear. 'She's there again,' he'd say indignantly, 'and she
keeps saying. 'It's up the chimbley. It's up the chimbley,' I
can't get to sleep.'

But when John and I went to his bedroom there was no
sign of Old Polly. I never did see her, though she got at me
in other ways.

One Sunday morning John was helping me turn the
feather mattresses and as we stripped the dirty linen off
the beds, I was piling it on the landing, ready to take

downstairs for washing. Finally I popped my only pair of nylon stockings on the top – they were very scarce, you had to save a lot of coupons to get them – and returned to put the last clean sheet on the bed. When I went back to the landing, seconds later, my nylons had gone.

'John have you must moved my stockings?' I called.

'No. Haven't seen them.'

Terry was in the garden riding his tricycle. No-one else could have touched them.

I searched the whole house for those stockings and I never saw them again. What's more, I didn't have enough coupons for another pair, so I had to make do with an ugly lisle pair. I was furious. I was convinced Old Polly was behind the disappearance.

Peace reigned for some time after that and we were lulled into thinking Old Polly had left us for good. The weeks went by, Christmas approached and I set to work one evening on our Christmas pudding.

John was listening to a comedy on the radio, so I spread some newspapers over the dining-room table and brought my ingredients and mixing bowls in to enjoy it with him.

I was beating eggs when Mrs Briggs arrived. She'd been into town and brought me a small bottle of brandy and a bottle of stout for the pudding.

'There you are girl, I got them,' she said lining up the bottles on the table beside me. 'It'll be lovely and rich. I hope you're going to save me a bit when it's finished!'

We chatted for a moment or two then she said, 'Had any more trouble lately?' she loved to hear our ghostly stories.

'No,' I said. 'Old Polly's been quiet for a while now, thank goodness.'

But the words were hardly out of my mouth when the bowl of eggs was torn from hands and hurled across the room. Instinctively I dived after it, did a flying tackle and caught it before it hit the ground.

'You can just stop that Polly!' I yelled furiously and slammed the bowl on the table. She'd already cost me a pair of stockings; she wasn't spilling my eggs as well.

I looked up to see a pale Mrs Briggs edging towards the door. 'Oh girl I don't like this,' she muttered, 'I'm not coming here any more.' Before I could stop her she hurried away.

She never would come indoors again. We were still friends. We chatted on the doorstep or in the garden and she still liked to hear of Old Polly's exploits, but I could never persuade her inside. She didn't want to witness them.

Old Polly wasn't to bother us much longer. We'd forgotten how heavy gardening work could be. The autumn and spring digging was too much for John, and eventually he had to admit he couldn't manage it. The cottage of course went with the job, and so sadly we had to pack up and move back to Grantham. Despite Old Polly, we'd enjoyed living in Little Ponton.

Yet it was amazing how quickly we picked up the threads of our old life again. Within two or three weeks of returning to the town, it was as if we'd never been away.

Gradually we became committed to the church. John joined the church committee, and if any visiting medium needed to sleep overnight in Grantham we often had them to stay with us. We built up a circle of new friends and we fell into the habit of attending Sunday evening services, then having a cup of tea at the home of one of our friends afterwards.

One evening quite a few of us were gathered in a friend's kitchen drinking tea and discussing the paranormal. Somebody produced a ouija board, and within seconds everyone was gathered round the table turning the glass. By this time I'd lost my fear of supernatural things and I was as eager to join in as the rest of them. But an odd thing happened. Whenever I touched the glass it wouldn't move. Nothing happened at all.

To my disappointment they soon got fed up with me spoiling it for the rest of them, and they wouldn't allow me near the glass. I retired to the corner and had to be content with watching. Even that was difficult. There were so many heads bending over the table I couldn't see the board at all. I could only hear the questions they were asking.

'What's my grandfather's name?' said someone.

'George,' I muttered from my corner.

The speaker turned to look at me, 'How did you know Doris?'

'Know what?'

'That my grandfather's name was George.'

'I didn't know,' I said.

'Well you just gave the right answer.'

I shrugged my shoulders. 'I just said the first thing that came into my head. I guessed.'

They turned back to the board, but I guessed the answer to the next question and that was right too. I wasn't purposely trying to interrupt them, it was just that for some reason every time they asked a question, the answer sprang into my mind and I couldn't help repeating it out loud.

Eventually they were so intrigued they left the board and gathered round me, firing questions. I laughed and protested, but even I was surprised and pleased at the way my answers were right. I kept thinking I'll get it wrong in a minute, but I didn't.

They were delighted with my newly discovered talent, and when it was time to leave they made me promise I'd have another go the following week.

The whole thing escalated. Word spread, and the next Sunday there were more people packed into the kitchen to see what it was all about. I rapidly became the weekly entertainment. Strangely enough I'd been shy as a girl, but now though I was a bit nervous before I arrived, I found I enjoyed the fuss and attention.

I soon realized my answers were coming from a voice in my head, and if I was quiet and paid attention, the voice sometimes said things without a question being asked. When that happened I repeated the words out loud and they were usually relevant to one of the people gathered there. In fact I was doing what I'd seen the mediums on our church platform doing.

'You'll be doing this one day ...' Across the years came the words spoken to me by those Welsh mediums when I was in the WRAFs. Funny I'd never thought of them since. I'd taken it as a joke, but now ...

'You know you should join a developing circle,' someone was saying, 'I think you have a gift dear.'

Developing circles were often set up by established mediums, to train young people who thought they had a talent in that direction. A few years ago I wouldn't have dreamed of going near one, but now mother's warnings were far behind me. If spirits were only people like my father and John Michael, how could I possibly be frightened of them?

John was enthusiastic about the idea. He'd found a philosophy he could live by, and if I could use it to help other people he thought that was wonderful. So I got in touch with a local circle and went along. It was a great disappointment.

I was shown into a private house and, to my horror, I found a room of cranky old dears clucking admiringly about a bossy medium. There was a large circular table in the centre of the room and after they'd welcomed me to their group, the medium instructed us to sit down and silently open our minds to the spirit world.

The room went very quiet. I peeped round the circle and noticed they'd all closed their eyes and wore intent expressions. Hastily I shut my eyes too, and as the seconds passed I started to relax.

Suddenly a chair scraped back. My eyes flew open instantly and I saw a large grey haired woman opposite, stand up. 'Me Big Chief Sitting Bull,' I was astonished to hear her announce, in a slightly deeper voice than she'd used earlier. 'What pretty shoes you have on lady.'

I slid down lower in my seat in embarrassment. It was so obviously untrue, such obvious nonsense I wondered why she was making such a fool of herself. Surely the medium would be angry? But no. To my amazement the medium listened gravely, her head on one side and then solemnly thanked Big Chief Sitting Bull for coming!

I couldn't understand it. I knew it was phoney, what were they trying to achieve? The large woman sat down again, smiling smugly and the room fell silent. I shifted on the hard wooden chair and tried to concentrate on the part of my mind where the voice came from. Soon I was drifting away.

'You – young woman!'

I jumped, my mind crashing back into the room. The medium was glaring accusingly at me. 'Yes you! Uncross your legs. You must keep both feet on the ground to earth the power and you must hold your palms upwards, like this, to receive the power.'

What on earth was she talking about? She made me feel like a human light bulb. Bewildered, I uncrossed my legs and awkwardly arranged my hands in the position she'd demonstrated. It was hopeless. For the rest of the evening she watched me closely to make sure I didn't change my posture, and I had to concentrate so hard on not crossing my legs, I couldn't hear the voice at all.

Walking home through the dark streets afterwards I felt completely discouraged I'd never heard so much rubbish in my life. If that's what you have to do, I thought, I'll never be a medium in a hundred years.

I didn't go back.

I obviously wasn't going to become a medium through 'formal' training, but our friends who came to the kitchen meetings weren't bothered. Those meetings became so popular they overflowed into the hall and up the stairs. People were tightly squeezed into every inch of space, yet the following week even more would turn up. In the end we couldn't cope with the numbers and we persuaded the church to let us borrow the hall for our meetings.

On the first evening I remember looking down from the platform at all the expectant faces turned towards me, and an eerie shiver ran down my spine. This was exactly what those mediums had prophecized I'd do and without ever intending to make it come true, events had almost been *arranged* so that I'd fulfil that prediction. I had an uncomfortable feeling my life had been taken out of my hands.

The work snowballed. Soon other churches were inviting me to come and speak at their meetings and I travelled around quite regularly, always accompanied by John and Terry.

The more practise I had, the more experienced I became at distinguishing the voices. At first it seemed to me like one voice speaking inside my head, but after a while I realized it was outside me, and then that it wasn't one voice but different voices. Soon I was able to tell if they were male or female, old or young.

I repeated what the voices said to me. It seemed the natural thing to do and it pleased my audience; but gradually I came to feel I didn't know enough about what I was doing. I wasn't interested in going back to a developing circle, one bad one had put me off for good. Instead, I started reading as many books on spiritualist philosophy as I could get my hands on, particularly the teachings of Silver Birch.

There was little time for reading during the day. John's earnings were so uncertain I had to work to help support the family. I did anything, scrubbing floors, chamber-maiding, driving, anything that allowed me to bring Terry. Later when I got home there was the house to clean, the washing and ironing to do and the meals to cook. The day was so hectic I fell into the habit of sitting alone for ten minutes after John and Terry had gone to bed, to unwind quietly. Sometimes I just sat, enjoying the peace, at other times I read my philosophy.

One night I flopped as usual into our newest, most comfortable chair, a high backed, winged style, in black leather. I was too tired even to fetch my book from the table. I leaned back and closed my eyes, enjoying the silence. Then I heard a voice. 'I will teach you,' he said, 'sit here, every night when the house is quiet and I will teach you.'

I didn't know it then, but I'd found my guide. It wasn't until years later that I learned his name – Ramonov is the nearest I can come to the pronunciation. I knew nothing about him but he was always there to help me. Every night I sat in the leather chair that became known as Ramonov's chair and Ramonov would talk to me. Usually he told me a little story, almost a parable and I would think about the meaning as I scrubbed dirty floors the next day. Ramonov rarely interrupted when I spoke at meetings, but if I got in a mess or several voices tried to communicate at once and I was confused, he'd break in and help.

Finally when I was twenty-nine I decided to take my credentials. They're a sort of exam set by the Spiritualist Union, and if you pass you become a recognized medium entitled to work in any Spiritualist church.

I had to go to Nottingham – sufficiently far from my home town to ensure I knew no-one, then I had to speak to a meeting of complete strangers, dotted here and there with anonymous examiners from the Spiritualist Union. I was so nervous I was hardly conscious of what was happening. The meeting was a blur, I've no idea what I said, I was only aware of my heart thudding and my sticky hands, but afterwards there was applause and someone came up and congratulated me. I'd passed.

Incredibly, here I was, Doris Stokes – the medium.

Chapter 7

I thought I was marvellous. Now a young, fully qualified medium, I got so used to people telling me I was wonderful, I believed them. It takes a long time to learn humility. I didn't yet understand that it wasn't me doing these marvellous things for my grateful audience, it was something outside me. So I revelled in the praise and became quite big-headed.

Financially John and I were better off than before. Not through my medium-ship, the churches I spoke at could only pay my travelling expenses – but through the Ministry of Pensions. I'd become so concerned about John's condition that I wrote to the ministry, to tell them I was sure John was much worse than they'd first thought. They arranged for a thorough medical examination and it was discovered that John had had a metal plate put in his skull; but unfortunately the depression in the bones had now sunk too far and it would be impossible to operate. There was nothing they could do for him, but at least his pension was upgraded and he was officially a badly wounded ex-serviceman.

We were able to buy an old banger of a car, with the extra money, which was a great help. I was travelling quite a lot at weekends, always accompanied by John and Terry and it had been so dreary trailing about on buses and trains.

One Saturday evening we were invited to a meeting in Boston, Lincs, over fifty miles from home. The church president and his wife, Fred and Madge Davis were a friendly couple, and they asked us to stay the night with them to save us driving back when we were tired.

They lived in a very large house. Downstairs, three

reception rooms had been knocked into one to create a church hall, and the Davis' living rooms were over the top.

They'd obviously gone to a lot of trouble. The church was beautifully decorated with flowers and it was packed. When I took my place on the platform I saw John squeeze into the last empty seat at the back. We were ready to begin. Fred Davis introduced me and we launched into the service without a hitch. The singing was beautiful and the scent of the flowers wafted up over the rostrum. I felt very happy, I wouldn't have missed this for the world.

The service over, I stood up to begin the demonstration and as I walked to the front of the platform, I noticed an elderly man wandering down the aisle. I stared pointedly at him but he just stared straight back at me. 'What a ruddy cheek coming in at this time,' I thought in my young, arrogant way, 'fancy interrupting the great Doris Stokes.'

'Would you mind sitting down please, so I can continue,' I asked him irritably, but he didn't budge. He stood quite still, staring stupidly. I began to get impatient. 'Look you'll have to sit on that bench, there aren't any chairs left but would you please *sit down* so I can get on.'

And still the man didn't move. I began to get angry. The president had got up out of his chair and was peering over the rostrum, and the audience were giving me puzzled looks. The man was clearly disrupting the meeting. Was he deaf or something? I opened my mouth to make a cutting remark, when suddenly I heard Ramonov at my side. 'Be very careful,' he said, 'he's only just taken his transition.'

I was so inexperienced and tactless I leant straight over the rostrum and said, 'Do you know you're dead?' Little gasps sounded all over the hall and I realized for the first time that nobody else could see him.

'Don't be so bloody silly,' he said.

'But you *are*,' I insisted. 'What's your name?'

He said his name was Joe and he lived at a pub called the Carpenters Arms. I turned to Fred Davis, 'D'you know Joe who lives at the Carpenters Arms?'

He gasped. 'Yes.'

Joe in the meantime was staring round the hall, a

bewildered expression on his face. 'They look just like my flowers. I can't understand it. I can't be in that spirituism church. I never go in there.'

I repeated this remark to Fred. 'But Doris. He was here at 11.00 this morning. He always brings us flowers from his allotment, but he never comes inside the church. He doesn't believe in it.'

'Well he'll have to believe it now,' I said, 'he's here.'

The conversation went on and Joe told me how he spent his time. He worked his allotment in the morning, went back to the pub for lunch, tidied up the kitchen and washed glasses for his daughter. 'Then I go for a bit of a lay down,' he went on. 'I get up about 6.00, read the evening paper, has my bit of tea then I go into the bar and wash glasses again.' He paused and looked round at the audience, 'I wish you wouldn't keep saying I'm dead. Ask Eva there, she knows me.'

I turned to the woman he'd pointed at. 'Are you Eva love? She nodded. 'Well,' I said to Joe, 'what about Eva?'

'I met her this morning coming out of the market and we sat on a form together. She told me her ankles were swolled.'

I repeated this to the nervous Eva. 'Yes,' she whispered, 'that's right.'

While we were chatting to Joe, two officers from the church slipped away to the Carpenters Arms to find out what was going on. They asked the landlord, Joe's son-in-law if they could speak to Joe.

'Yes,' he said, 'he'll be in the kitchen having his tea.' He led them into the kitchen, which was empty. 'That's funny. Me father-in-law hasn't come down for his tea yet. I think I'd better go and call him.' He went upstairs, but a few seconds later he came racing down, his face as white as milk.

'I think me father-in-law's dead!'

'I'm sure he is,' said one of the officers, 'he's in the church talking to our speaker!'

By now all hopes of completing the meeting had been abandoned. Ramonov tuned in again, and told me I'd have to take Joe back to the pub where he'd be collected. I explained this to Fred and we closed the service, then he, John, Kelly, one of the officers, Joe and I walked out into the high street.

Joe was quite happy to lead me to the Carpenters Arms, where he felt sure he could prove he was as alive as I was. We left the high street and threaded through dark, cobbled lanes until we reached a pub standing on a corner. There was a door at the side, probably leading into the yard and as I glanced at it, I saw the shape of a man appear. His body was in shadow but there was a faint luminous glow around him.

As we drew nearer, he turned towards us. 'Come on Joe, let's be having you.'

Joe stopped in his tracks. 'Is that you our Tom?' he said softly. 'Nay, can't be, ye've been dead nigh on ten years.'

'That's what I keep trying to tell you Joe,' I said. 'That's what's happened to you.'

He looked up at a lighted window where the curtains were drawn, which must have been his bedroom. 'D'you mean to tell me girl that my body's laid up there and I can just walk away with our Tom.'

'Exactly,' I said.

A slow smile spread across his face. 'Well that's all right then,' and he walked over to the shadowy figure that was Tom. As he drew level, the glow spread, shone around him and they both disappeared.

I turned back to the others who'd been silently watching me, probably wondering what on earth was going on. 'It's all right now,' I told them. 'He's safely over.'

It was one of the strangest experiences I'd had.

Oddly enough, not long after that, I found another meeting being taken over by an elderly man. It was a Saturday evening again, but this time in Rotherham. The meeting had been quite routine and the demonstrations fairly simple, until suddenly all the voices were drowned out by a thick Yorkshire accent.

'My name's Jim,' he said, 'and I want to talk to Eve, my niece.' I located Eve in the audience. I turned out that Jim had been killed the previous Tuesday. They hadn't even held the funeral yet, but Jim was anxious about his possessions and he spent some time instructing Eve what to do with them.

When he'd finished I asked him what had happened to him. 'Well I was working in me garden till about 9.30 lass, then I went down to the Swan for a jar. I were on the bloody crossing when the fool hit me.'

He left with a last instruction for his niece. 'Me tatters want lifting but don't let our Denis do it. He doesn't know one end of bloody fork from t'other.'

I happened to be staying a few days in Rotherham because I'd agreed to do some individual sittings for the church, so early the following Monday afternoon I was working in the vestry. I was doing a sitting for two ladies, when suddenly Jim's unmistakable voice butted in again.

'I've come to tell you it's all over lass,' he said. 'They've just pushed box in.' I glanced at my watch. It was 2.30. I explained to my sitters what had happened and we asked the church officials to check with Jim's niece whether this message was correct.

They came back with the news that the funeral had started at 2.15 that afternoon, and it would have been close to 2.30 when the coffin was cremated.

Spontaneous cases like those of Jim and Joe were thrilling. I'd lost all trace of fear, and by now it seemed quite natural for me to talk to spirits – particularly as there was nothing 'spooky' about the conversations. They were like earthly telephone conversations. With the fear, I'd also lost the sense of being a bit odd, a bit different from other people. I realized now that I was an ordinary wife and mother like millions of other women, but just as some of them were also brilliant cooks, gifted artists or wonderful athletes, I too had a talent. I'd been born with ears that could hear sounds other people couldn't hear and eyes that sometimes saw things other people couldn't see.

I enjoyed being a medium but it wasn't always easy. After each demonstration of 'clairaudience' as hearing voices was called, I ached round my middle and felt rather tired. Ramonov told me in one of my 'lessons' that this was because the spirits draw their energy to communicate from my solar plexus. It sounded rather nasty to me.

Another problem was that occasionally in the middle of
a meeting, when the voices had been coming through loud
and clear, they'd suddenly stop. The audience would be
staring up at me expectantly, waiting for me to speak and
nothing happened. I couldn't hear a thing. It was very
unnerving.

The trouble was that I couldn't choose who I spoke to. I
had to wait until someone in the spirit world wanted to
communicate with someone in the audience and if no-one
wanted to get through, nothing happened. I had no
control over it.

I still attended other medium's meetings of course, to
learn as much as I could about my work and I noticed that
some of them never suffered this problem. The messages
would flow impressively without interruption. 'Will I ever
be as good as that?' I wondered.

I was very excited after one of these meetings to be
introduced to a top medium who'd been demonstrating.
They seemed like gods to us young ones then, and if they
actually spoke to you, it was like being picked out by the
King or Queen.

'When I'm working I lose contact sometimes, but you
never lose contact do you,' I said admiringly.

He smiled. 'Yes I do,' he said, 'but I'll teach you a trick of
the trade.' He lowered his voice. 'When you go to a church,
arrive a little early. They'll take you into a committee room
or ante-room and there'll be people in and out talking to
each other. Keep your ears open and you'll hear little bits.
I usually go to the bathroom just before the meeting starts
and scribble everything down on a scrap of paper and put
it in my hymn book. Then if I lose contact, I've got
something to help me.'

I was tremendously impressed. What a wonderful idea.
What a difference it would make. Yes it was cheating, I
supposed, but not *bad* cheating. Ramonov had always told
me to speak the truth. Well the information itself would be
true, wouldn't it? And I closed my conscience to all other
arguments on the matter.

My next big meeting came round and I was anxious to
do well in front of all those people so, as I'd been advised, I

arrived early. Sure enough I overheard scraps of several conversations and I dashed to the bathroom to jot them down on a piece of paper. Then I slipped the paper between the pages of my hymn book. I was ready.

Out on stage everything went well. Messages came through thick and fast and the audience buzzed with appreciation. I began to feel exhilarated. I pushed myself harder, strained to hear the faintest whisper that might mean the end of years of searching to someone sitting out there. On and on it went, better and better, and then suddenly, for no reason at all, nothing. In the middle of a message for a pleasant, middle aged lady, the line went dead.

I faltered. How could it possibly happen now of all times? Thank goodness I'd learned that trick of the trade. Calmly I opened my hymn book and the blood drained from my face. The paper had gone.

Panic rising I struggled to finish the message with odd scraps I remembered from my notes, but of course I got them all jumbled up and it was a complete muddle.

'Thank you dear,' said the woman in a slightly puzzled voice, as I limped to the end – but I hardly cared because the next moment the voices blasted back.

I completed two more messages successfully, then I was surprised to hear Ramonov cut in and the other voices died away. What was going on? 'Now,' said Ramonov, 'we will go back to Mrs ...' and he called her by her name which I hadn't got, 'and you'll apologize to her and tell her that the last part of her message didn't come from the spirit world.'

I felt about six inches high. I hesitated, but there was complete silence and the audience was staring at me, waiting for me to speak. I knew that Ramonov wouldn't let me go on till I'd apologized.

'Mrs ...' I said with difficulty.

'Yes dear?'

'I'm terribly sorry. I've got to tell you the last bit of your message didn't come from spirit. That was me.' My face was scarlet and I could hardly look at her for shame.

She smiled. 'I thought it was strange. You'd been so good up till then.' She was very nice about it.

The tension eased, I sensed Ramonov leave and the voices came back. I was able to finish the meeting without further problems.

Admittedly I was shaken, but I still hadn't learned my lesson. At the next big meeting where I wanted to impress I did it again and the same thing happened. My notes mysteriously disappeared, and Ramonov wouldn't let me go on. He forced me to own up. I was so embarrassed, felt so small I never ever dared do it again.

To this day if I lose contact I just say, 'Can't hear a thing. Would you like to sing a hymn or something?' until something comes through. Then I say, 'Right! We're away!'

It takes great confidence, great guts to do that. When you're standing up in front of hundreds of people who've perhaps come a long way, at some expense, expecting to hear you perform miracles, it's terribly difficult to say, 'Sorry I can't do it at the the moment,' and sit down again.

People have been lynched for less. The only thing you've got to show for your work as a medium is your reputation, and if you fail to produce the goods on just one evening, several hundred people will go away and tell their friends you're a fraud, you're no good. So much is at stake it's not surprising even the most genuine of mediums are occasionally tempted to 'fill in'.

Unable to do this myself now, and too young to have built up the necessary confidence to deal easily with the odd lapse, I became very discouraged on the rare occasions it happened. One night I went home in despair after a partial 'failure'. I flung myself miserably down in Ramonov's black chair and tuned in to him.

'D'you think I'll ever be any good at this Ramonov?' I asked, and in reply he told me one of his stories.

'Picture to yourself a mountain and upon the top of this mountain there stands a shrine,' he said. 'Now I tell you my child, everyone of us has come this way before you. None of us can say we'll ever reach the shrine on the earth plane, but as long as you keep aiming for it, that's all that matters.

'You will set off up the pathway and it will all seem easy

and you'll think what's all the fuss about? I can do it. Then you will come to a place which will be filled with many people of many colours and many creeds, and you will stop and you will ask, what are they doing here. You will be told this is the half way house. Now nobody will blame you if you decide to stay there, but by the same token your development will stay there.

'Now the second half of the climb, for every step you take – you will fall back six. You will fall and bruise your knees, but I say again, every one of us has trodden the same pathway before you. We cannot promise you roses all the way. We cannot even promise to remove the stones from the pathway. What I can promise is that I will always be there to take your hand when you have to climb a stone, and always say to yourself, "One day I will reach the shrine." '

He paused to let it sink in, then he continued, 'Now picture to yourself a rose tree. And I say to you my child, go pick for me the most perfect rose you can find. Where would you go to pick it?'

And I said, 'The top I suppose.'

'Exactly,' he said, 'so you will have to reach yourself and in the process you will get pricked and torn. True my child, you could pick me a rose from the bottom of the tree with no effort but I wouldn't want it. It would be imperfect.

'Then picture the apple tree laden with fruit and I say to you, go pick for me the most perfect fruit you can find. Where again would you go?'

And I said, 'Well I think I'd have to climb the tree.'

'Exactly,' he said, 'effort all the time. You could take a basket and fill it with no effort from the apples on the ground, but this we do not want.'

His meaning was quite clear. I had to aim for the top. I might not get there, but I certainly wouldn't get there if I didn't try!

Chapter 8

Most of the time I loved being a medium. I was very conscious of it and I'd 'tune in' to show off my skills at the slightest excuse.

It was tremendously exciting. I knew so little about the subject and my own powers that every day was an adventure. I was always wanting to try something new, to see what I could do. Among our friends at the church, John and I soon realized there were several people who felt the same way and so we formed our own 'home circle' to explore the unknown.

Every week four of them, Mrs Atherton, Mrs Wright, a man we always called the Major and a young airman, came round to our home for an evening of psychic experiments.

We soon discovered I could go into deep trances and when that happened, Ramonov would talk to them through me. I was unaware of what he said, so occasionally they'd record the session and play it back to me afterwards. It was mostly philosophy, spoken in a beautiful English that was quite beyond me normally, peppered with long words that I had to look up in the dictionary.

These episodes were very popular with the members of the circle, but I didn't like them. They used to scare me. As I went into the trance my head would spin and the room would go round as if I was having gas – then everything would go black. 'The next thing I'd be aware of was John's voice saying 'Here's your cup of tea love,' because Ramonov would tell them when I was returning and warn John to have a cup of very sweet tea ready for me, to replace the energy he'd used. That was the only time I could drink tea with sugar in and, even then, it would take ages for me to feel normal again. I'd know I was in my sitting room and that the other people were there having tea and biscuits, but it didn't seem real. It was a sort of dream world.

We usually sat with the curtains drawn and just a red light burning during these meetings, because we'd heard that's what happened at seances. What we didn't realize, was that for some reason red lights attract physical phenomena.

We first became aware of it when at the end of one session Mrs Wright and I looked down to find our necklaces lying neatly in our laps, and Mrs Atherton discovered the invisible hairnet she always wore had been removed and folded tidily across the back of her neck. None of us had felt a thing.

Ramonov told me that John Michael had paid us a visit and this was his way of making his presence felt. After that it happened quite frequently and, although Mrs Atherton got a bit fed up with replacing her hairnet, we weren't really bothered. I thought it was an endearing childish prank.

Still we kept our red light burning. Then one evening the Major suggested we try table levitation. 'I think we have sufficient power with you here Doris,' he said. He and John hunted round the room until they found a suitable table, a small round wooden one that wasn't too heavy.

The six of us drew our chairs round it and sat with our hands spread flat on the top. We fell silent, all concentrating on lifting the table. Nothing happened. The clock on the mantelpiece ticked away and, as the minutes passed, I began to get edgy. This was daft sitting here doing nothing I was a medium, and when I worked I liked results.

Just as I opened my mouth to suggest we try something else, I felt a sudden upward pressure under my hands. The table lifted slightly and moved to one side.

'Somebody's lifting it!' shrieked Mrs Atherton.

The Major felt she was looking at him. 'I can assure you madam I am not,' he said affronted.

'And I'm not,' I said, 'I'd be afraid to.'

The pressure subsided and the table settled down again. Mrs Atherton looked relieved. She wasn't enjoying this experiment at all. Our hands were still flat on the table however, and without warning it lurched upwards again, rising a good 18 inches off the floor.

'Somebody is moving this table,' Mrs Atherton insisted nervously. 'Look Mrs Atherton,' I said as the table drifted back to the ground, 'I can vouch for myself. What about you John, are you moving it?' 'No,' he said.

Slowly I went round asking each one in turn if he or she was responsible. They all denied it strongly, but Mrs Atherton refused to believe them. I think like me, she was feeling rather frightened and didn't want to believe them.

'Oh *somebody's* lifting it,' she said emphatically.

The words were hardly out of her mouth when the table rose sharply, almost angrily and tilted on its side until the top was resting on Mrs Atherton's tummy. We didn't have a fitted carpet in the sitting room, just polished lino and slip rugs. Unfortunately Mrs Atherton's chair was standing on one of the rugs.

While we struggled to keep our fingers in place, the table lurched forward again, aiming directly at Mrs Atherton's middle and she, her chair and the rug were propelled smoothly backwards over the lino. We watched, eyes bulging, as she was pushed screaming and kicking across the room, the door flew open, she disappeared into the hall and the door closed shut behind her. There was silence.

I sprang up and turned on the main light with trembling fingers. 'I don't know enough about this,' I told the others shakily and rushed into the hall.

Mrs Atherton, her face grey, was wildly struggling into her coat.

'Mrs Atherton are you all right?'

She gasped at my voice, turned a pair of stricken eyes on me as if it was all my fault and ran out into the street, her coat buttons done up the wrong way.

She never came back and I can't say I blame her.

I closed the front door and walked slowly back down the hall. There in the corner, an innocent looking group, was the table, the chair and the rug. Quite motionless. I gave them a wide berth as I returned to the sitting room, and John and the Major had to bring them back later. That was the last time I tried levitation.

Mrs Atherton wasn't the only friend we lost through odd happenings at our home. Another was a man called Tom Wingfield, who was also learning to be a medium.

One evening he called at the house very excited because he'd learned something new. 'My guide's taught me how to hold back the power. No matter how good the medium is I can stop them getting through,' he boasted.

I was immediately determined he wasn't going to do it with me. This was a challenge I couldn't turn down. I tuned into Ramonov. 'We're not having that are we? I asked silently and Ramonov agreed.

'All right Tom,' I said, 'we'll try it.'

Tom proudly took a deep breath and flung out his arms. 'Right,' he said triumphantly, 'now try to get through!'

I closed my eyes and concentrated hard on the 'psychic' part of my mind. I didn't hear a thing. Surely Tom couldn't really be blocking it? Then without warning, a strong breeze from nowhere whirled through the house. I opened my eyes to see the curtains plastered to the ceiling, the light bulb spinning on its flex and the china ornaments on the mantelpiece rattling up and down.

'There must be a window open somewhere,' said Tom hanging on to his fluttering tie. Instantly the breeze died away.

'Close any window you like,' I said.

So he and John painstakingly went through the whole house, shutting every window and door. Finally, satisfied they'd excluded every draught, they came back to the sitting room. The window was already shut, but for good measure they closed the door as well. We were practically airtight.

'Right Tom,' I said. 'Everything's closed. It's a fair trial agreed?'

'Agreed,' he said. He took another deep breath and flung out his arms. 'Go on then.'

I tuned in. Immediately the curtain billowed more

violently than ever, the light bulb whirled, the ornaments rocked fit to fall off the shelf, and even the rugs on the floor started lifting. Tom gaped at the wind-swept room, then frantically went through the motions of glancing at his watch.

'My, is that the time? My Missus'll kill me. Sorry, I've got to go.' Like Mrs Atherton before him he rushed out into the street, never to call again.

The experiences weren't always frightening. Sometimes they were strange and wonderful. On another occasion, our home circle had arrived early and Terry was still up. Dressed in pyjamas, he was sitting in his little armchair having milk and biscuits. Normally we wouldn't have started until he was in bed, but tonight the young airman immediately announced that he was in contact with John's father.

Old Mr Stokes had died the year before and John was very upset. Unfortunately we couldn't afford for all of us to go to London for the funeral, so John had gone alone. He went to see his father before the coffin was closed and slipping an object into his father's hand, he'd mentally said, 'If you ever come back dad, bring this with you as proof it's you.'

He'd never told anyone what that object was. Not even me. If any medium managed to tell him correctly what it was, it would be proof indeed.

Anyway the airman rambled on saying nothing of value, but it obviously made John send up a thought to his father. Suddenly Terry said, 'Look Daddy, there's something on the floor!'

We all looked but could see nothing. The lino was bare. Terry carried on pointing to an empty space and was so insistent he could see something I said, 'What is it lovey? What does it look like?'

'It's a round medal,' he said. 'It's blue with gold on it.' And without warning John burst into tears. Apparently it was a christian spiritualist badge he'd put into his father's hand before the coffin was closed. Round and dark blue, with a gold cross on the front.

Unusual events weren't confined to the times we chose

to contact the spirit world. Sometimes they chose to contact us, and not always at convenient moments.

About a fortnight before Easter one year, I spoke at a meeting in Newark and got through to a man whose wife was in the audience. Apparently he'd recently died and was worried because his wife was having trouble getting the insurance money. The woman confirmed this, and her husband proceeded to tell her through me, the name of the office, the name of the street it was in and the name of the man she should see to get the problem sorted out.

This message wasn't particularly unusual and over the years I'd had so many communications like this, I thought no more of it.

The night before Good Friday, John and I went to bed as usual. John was tired and trying to sleep, while I read a few chapters of my book by the light of a tiny bedside lamp. Suddenly there was a terrific knocking on the headboard. I knew it wasn't John, but phenomena like this didn't worry me any more. 'Goodnight friends, God bless you,' I said absently and turned over the page.

Seconds later the knocking sounded again, so violently it woke John.

'What's that, what's that?' he mumbled.

'It's only the spirit people,' I said.

'Oh,' he turned over. 'Goodnight friends, God bless you.' He settled down to sleep again.

The next moment there was another great hammering, then the keys on the piano which we'd moved into our bedroom because there was no other space for it, started jangling wildly all by themselves – despite the fact that the lid was closed.

John sat up angrily. 'Will you put that bloody book down and see what they want? I'm trying to get some sleep!'

Reluctantly I lowered my book, I was tired too and I didn't want to work. 'Does anybody want me?' I asked hoping they didn't.

Immediately I heard a man's voice that was vaguely familiar. 'I'm sorry to disturb you,' he said, 'I've come to thank you for what you did for my wife at Newark and to tell you there's a parcel in the post for you. You'll get it in the morning.' He was gone.

'Somebody's having us on,' I told John. 'They said there was a parcel in the post for us in the morning – but tomorrow's Good Friday. We won't get a delivery then surely.' But at least the crashes had stopped and we were able to sleep.

Eight thirty the next morning there was a knock at the door and Terry, who could now reach the catch and loved opening doors, ran to answer it. A few moments later he raced back with a package wrapped in brown paper. 'There's a parcel for you mummy. Go on open it, open it! Can I help?'

John and I exchanged glances over his head as we helped him untie the string. There had been a delivery after all! I folded back the brown paper to reveal a beautiful embroidered table cloth and a letter. I read it quickly. It was from the woman in Newark. She thanked me for the message I'd given her which had been very helpful. She'd gone to see the man her husband had mentioned, at the address he'd given her and the problem had been solved. She was getting her insurance money after all and she hoped I'd accept the tablecloth as a token of thanks. I was touched and I treasure that table cloth to this day.

Over the years, as we learned more about spiritualism and met more of the people involved, we became interested in another section of the work – healing. As well as mediums there were many gifted healers, and one of the greatest who became a friend of ours was Harry Edwards. He became very well known in his lifetime, books were written about him and he had many spectacular cures.

John was told several times by mediums that he had the gift of healing, but this seemed so ridiculous compared with the marvellous and obvious talents of Harry Edwards, that he did nothing about it. What he didn't realize was that even though his gift may not be a great one; it was valuable in its own smaller way. I'd noticed myself when I had a headache that John only had to place his hands round my forehead for a few moments and the pain would be soothed away – but still he refused to take it seriously.

Eventually the matter was taken out of his hands on yet

another occasion when we were in bed, John asleep and me reading. I was busy during the day, my mind was rarely relaxed enough then for the spirits to contact me spontaneously. I was also going through a phase of finding it difficult to sleep and I'd read for hours before dropping off. I suppose that's why they chose late at night to get in touch.

Anyway John was snoring happily and I was deep in my book, when I gradually became aware of the uncomfortable feeling that someone was watching me. I glanced uneasily at John wondering if he was ill, since he'd been wounded he'd had a couple of queer 'turns', but no. He was sleeping peacefully. I shrugged and returned to my book but the feeling persisted. Someone was staring at me.

Then out of the corner of my eye I saw movement. I looked, and gasped. There in the open doorway was the most astonishing sight. A Red Indian. I did a double take and hastily stared down at my book. 'Now Doris you've gone too far this time,' I thought. 'It's ridiculous.' But when I cautiously raised my head again he was still there.

I couldn't tell you what he had on the lower part of his body but his chest was bare, he had long black hair, a band round his head and a white feather standing up at the back.

I nudged John violently. 'John! Wake up!'

'UUUUg ...?' he groaned.

I nudged him again. I was a little frightened. I wasn't at all keen on having a Red Indian in the bedroom. 'John. Please wake up – there's an Indian in the doorway!'

'Oh well let him alone, ay.' He snuggled deeper under the blankets. Although he believed in my voices, John was a bit sceptical about the things I saw late at night. He thought I made some of them up because I couldn't sleep.

I shook him hard, 'But John *there is* an Indian in the doorway.'

Reluctantly he sat up with a resigned 'here-we-go-again' look on his face. 'Well ask him what he wants.'

Obediently I asked.

'My name is Red Dawn,' said the Indian, 'I'm your husband's healing guide, and I've come to tell him it's time he started his work for spirit. If he wants proof, I was killed at the battle of Blackwater Creek in 1876 and he can verify this.'

I relayed the message to John who was staring doubtfully at the doorway, which to him was silent and empty.

'Your husband doesn't believe I'm here, does he?' said Red Dawn.

'No, I'm afraid he doesn't.'

'Well ask him if he'd like proof.'

I asked and John said, 'Oh I'm all for that.'

So Red Dawn asked him through me to close the window and draw the drapes, he didn't say curtains as we would have done. John did this. Then Red Dawn asked him to close the door. John walked sarcastically towards it. 'Is your friend in or out?'

'Would you come in please?' I asked Red Dawn and John said, 'After you Claude,' and closed the door. 'Right now what?'

He was told to get back into bed. 'I am going to prove to John that I am here,' said Red Dawn. 'I will send some psychic breezes.' He walked to the end of the bed and instantly a gale tore through the room. The curtains lashed across the ceiling, the eiderdown flew into the air and we hung on to the top of it while the bottom whipped around our feet, and our hair streamed out behind us. The whole room was filled with the rushing roar of the great wind. It was terrifying.

'Does he believe I'm here now?' asked Red Dawn.

'Well something is,' said John. 'I hope you know what you're doing girl.'

And at that the wind stopped as if someone had clicked off a switch, and Red Dawn disappeared. Our ears were popping in the silence.

'I think you'd better start healing,' I said to John.

'Oh no,' he said lying down, 'we'll find out about this Blackwater Creek business first.'

The following morning he wrote to the American Embassy to check. Some time later they replied that they'd passed our letter on to the American Legation which we'd never heard of, and sometime after that we had a note from them. Yes, they said, there had been a battle of Blackwater Creek in 1876, and there was now a town called Blackwater Town on the site.

John went to the Spiritualist Church to practise healing.

Chapter 9

People often confuse mediums with fortune tellers and are disappointed when we don't predict the future for them, but this is not our function. Some mediums are clairvoyants as well, but the work of a medium is to pass on information from dead relatives and friends, to prove that they live on in another dimension.

Occasionally if these relatives see trouble ahead, or something to be prepared for, they will warn or advise, which may sound like a prediction, but they never tell a sitter what to do, because we are here to learn for ourselves by our own mistakes.

I had one of these warning 'predictions' myself, and it was very lucky I did. John and I had never given up hope of another baby and despite two miscarriages we were still trying. Nothing happened however, and every now and then my own words, spoken so lightly when John was missing in the war came back to haunt me. 'You can always have another baby.' How stupid, how arrogant of me to assume it was that easy.

In the January when I was 33 and still hoping, we happened to be talking to Walter Brooks, that same Yorkshire medium who'd given us our first message. Now I was a medium too, we moved in the same circles and had become friends.

'Have you just come out of hospital?' Walter suddenly asked me in the middle of the conversation.

'No, don't wish that on me Walter,' I laughed.

'Just a minute, this is serious.' Walter paused, his eyes faraway, then his attention snapped back and John and I were distinctly uneasy. 'Well I'm afraid you're going into hospital – July I think, something to do with your right side. They'll say you're going die, but your father wants you to write this down. It's the name of the person you must ask for. Mrs Marrow. Don't forget it's very important. Write it down John.'

Dazed, John took out his pen and scribbled the name on the back of an envelope and put it in his wallet. 'Mrs Marrow? It sounds like a joke.'

'Yes Walter, thanks,' I said weakly, 'I feel a lot better now.'

'Sorry Doris but your father wanted me to tell you. It's important.'

I'd been feeling perfectly well until that moment, but suddenly my limbs were cold and my body shaky. It was only nerves however. The next day I was fine, and throughout the spring and early summer my health was good. Gradually the warning dimmed and it was only when the month of July leapt out at me from calendars, that I felt a quick jolt of apprehension.

The idea seemed absurd. As spring turned to summer I grew fitter than ever. How could anyone think I was going to die? Yet I couldn't discount it altogether. Look what happened to John Michael.

By the time July arrived I was edgy. I wasn't exactly frightened, my father implied I'd be all right with Mrs Marrow and in any case I wasn't afraid to die. No, if it happened it would be extremely unpleasant and I wasn't looking forward to it.

The sun shone, I went brown and looked glowing. John was convinced the warning had been wrong. After all, mediums do make mistakes sometimes just like everyone else.

But then towards the end of the month I woke in the night screaming in agony. White hot pains were tearing through my stomach. John raced out to fetch the doctor and I was rushed to hospital. The pain was so bad it filled the whole world and I was hardly aware of anything else. Now and again my hearing cleared and I'd catch snatches of conversation but it meant nothing, I didn't even realize who they were talking about.

'Pregnancy of the Fallopian tube.' No hope.' Nothing we

can do,' and from miles away, 'I'm sorry Mr Stokes, your wife is dying.'

I opened my eyes slightly and the bed was surrounded by a beautiful turquoise light. Blue light, I vaguely remembered, the healing power. I looked again and my father and John Michael were standing at the foot of my bed. They were smiling at me and I tried to smile back. If I'm going to die, I thought, all I have to do is go to them. Then the blue light started spinning and other colours whirled into it and I felt myself drawn feet first into a brilliant rainbow spiral. I was rushing down, my father and John Michael a little ahead of me, and beyond them at the end of that tunnel of madly flashing colours was a bright light, so bright I couldn't look at it. Instinctively I knew that if I reached that light I would have passed over. Yet the only emotion I felt was relief. I don't have to fight any more, I thought, it's out of my hands.

Suddenly there was a tremendous jolt and I crashed back to the bed again. The tunnel, my father and John Michael were gone and there was John's voice saying, 'I don't care if she's in Timbuctoo – get her.' Another voice said, 'Well if you think she'll stand the journey to Nottingham.' I was aware of nothing else.

Afterwards I discovered that John had asked who Mrs Marrow was, half expecting to be laughed at and was told she was a gynaecologist. He immediately insisted she treat me, only to be informed she worked at Nottingham hospital. By now he was so convinced that Walter Brooks had been right, he was willing to risk the long ambulance journey to Nottingham, and he had me transferred.

It worked. I survived the journey, to the doctor's surprise and under the care of Mrs Marrow I recovered.

I'm quite certain that if Walter Brooks hadn't given me that message I would have died. In fact I nearly died anyway; but strange as it may sound I'm not sorry. I'd been hearing about, reading about and telling people about what happens when we die, and now I'd had personal experience of at least the early stages. I *knew* there was nothing to fear.

It took me several months to recover completely and,

during the low state that often follows illness, I became fed up with Grantham. John and I were running out of odd jobs in the area and we felt like a complete change of scene. We were still wondering where to go, when one morning I opened the paper and my eye instantly fell on an advertisement for a disablement village in Lancaster. Called Westfield, it had been specially designed for disabled and war wounded people. I showed John who agreed it looked very nice and so we wrote to the address given. Back came an invitation to an interview, and some time afterwards we were allocated a house.

It was a lovely place. At the foot of Lancaster Castle, now unfortunately partly a prison but still picturesque, it was an open, airy cluster of houses separated by grass verges and trees. We were very happy there. We both found work, Terry settled down at school and the request for my appearances at Spiritualist meetings increased if anything.

It was in Lancaster that I experienced the second type of prediction – the encouragement prediction – though it wasn't for me.

One day a distraught young woman came to see me. Her name was Pat and her beloved husband had just died, leaving her with a baby daughter only a few months old to bring up alone. As far as she was concerned she didn't have a future. Her life had ended and if it wasn't for her little girl, she would have liked to die too.

I comforted her as best I could and gave her a sitting. It was fairly routine. I got through to her husband who sent many love messages to his Pat and baby Tracy and gave names of relatives and friends and anniversary dates to prove his identity Then near the end he unexpectedly told Pat to cheer up, life would soon be better and she'd marry again in about two years.

'Never,' Pat insisted firmly, 'I'll never marry anyone else.' But all the same she went home happier than she'd come.

She didn't live far from us and she soon became a regular visitor. She still went through patches of despair and she often felt the need of someone to talk to; and for my part I was always pleased to see her and little Tracy.

At around the same time, a small article was written about me in Psychic News – the spiritualist newspaper – and as often happens I began to receive readers' letters. Among them was one from Monty Spurrier, a young soldier stationed in Germany. He said that he was interested in spiritualism, but he was an orphan and had no-one to discuss the subject with.

I always reply to letters even though it might take me a while to get round to it, and I wrote to Monty inviting him to visit us next time he was on leave in Britain.

My correspondence began to pile up and I fell into the habit of stacking letters for answering on the coffee table beside my armchair. It might not look tidy, but it jogged my memory every time I sat down.

The table was pretty full one afternoon when Pat and Tracy arrived. By now Tracy had grown into a lively toddler with an inquiring mind. She raced into the room on her wobbly legs eager to say hello, stumbled against the table in her enthusiasm and the whole pile slid to the floor in a flourish of paper.

'Oh Tracy. Look what you've done!' cried Pat. 'Come on, help me pick it up or Auntie Dodey won't let you come again.'

Despite my protests, Pat scrambled the sheets together and Tracy picked up a fistful of blue air mail paper and placed it contritely on my knee. It was Monty's second letter.

'Pat,' I said suddenly, 'this is from the man you're going to marry.' Where the words came from I don't know, I'd spoken them without thinking.

'What did you say Doris?'

I repeated it and then went on to tell her about Monty.

'Oh get on with you,' Pat laughed, 'I bet he's 5 ft nothing.' She was a very tall girl and preferred men taller than herself.

Nothing more was said, but I secretly made up my mind that if Monty did come to visit us I'd make sure he was introduced to Pat.

Well of course he did come, and he turned out to be a strapping six footer with a quiet, sensitive personality. He and Pat took to each other immediately and, not many months after I introduced them, they announced their engagement in our house.

Today they're happily married with a small son of their own, but the funny part about it is the first time Tracy met Monty, she called him 'Daddy'.

Our old banger had finally come to the end of the road so I was back to travelling on buses and trains, usually alone now, because we couldn't afford the fares for all of us. I often got paid for these appearances now, however – the princely sum of 2/6d – 12p!

One night I'd been to a meeting that involved two bus journeys. I arrived home very late, soaked to the skin from waiting an hour in the pouring rain for a bus. I was so cold and wet and miserable I was physically sick when I got in.

'Oh Ramonov,' I said later, when I'd peeled off my saturated clothes and sat in a thick woollen dressing gown for our daily lesson. 'Is it worth it? 2s 6d?'

And he said, 'What are you talking about child? We don't count money over here. There are no pockets in shrouds. You can't take it with you. The only money God cares about is what you give of yourself, so you did very well tonight. You gave a marvellous meeting, you convinced the people that there was life after death. So you've had to give part of yourself, but I promise you the energy will be replaced. By tomorrow morning it will be a thing of the past. What you send out is the money God's interested in. Don't worry about money. The spirit world will never see you without.'

And of course he was right.

As the years passed, word spread in the mysterious way it has, and I got more and more requests for private individual sittings. I'd never advertised, but somehow people kept finding their way to my door and letters arrived from all over the country and even abroad. I did as many as I could but what with public meetings at weekends, a job during the week and a house to run, there simply weren't enough hours in the day.

Finally John got so fed up with seeing me rushing exhausted from one appointment to the next after work, he suggested I give up my job. 'Plenty of mediums work full time and manage to live,' he said. 'Why not give it a try for a while?'

I was tempted. It would be lovely to work at home and do the housework between sittings, but John's job was so unreliable. Could we risk it? I thought and thought, then I remembered Ramonov's promise that the spirit world would never see us without money. Right I thought, I'll gamble.

I charged £1 a sitting and soon I had quite a few customers. Local people, visitors from London, even a journalist from Cairo who made a point of coming every year. Some people wanted to visit regularly, but I discouraged it. Unless they needed help with a particular problem I told them once every six months was quite enough, otherwise I got to know too much about them and the information I relayed wouldn't be clear proof.

I know some people criticize mediums for charging anything at all, but when you think about it, even clergymen get paid. If you are working full time at sittings there's no alternative to charging a fee; unless you have a private income tucked away. you have to live.

I soon realized that when people came for their first private sitting they didn't know what to expect. They came for one of two main reasons – simple curiosity, or a blind, searching grief which drove them to seek some means of easing their pain. The grief stricken were the most common.

Mrs Curwood from Blackpool was a typical case. Unknown to me she was in the audience at a public meeting I held. She'd never had anything to do with spiritualism before; but since the death of her husband thirteen months previously she was ready to try anything. She told me much later. 'I just wanted to die. My life was so empty.'

I didn't notice her in the crowd that day and apparently none of my messages were for her, but nevertheless she felt I might be able to help her and she booked a private sitting.

She arrived with her grown up daughter for moral

support, a pale, sad middle aged woman with suppressed hope in her eyes.

The familiar nerves jangled in my stomach. This stranger, so in need, was pinning all her faith on me. The responsibility as always, was terrifying.

I settled her into a comfortable armchair, hoping my tension didn't show.

'Now I must tell you we might not get anything,' I warned. I liked to prepare sitters for possible disappointment because with the spirit world you just can't guarantee to get through. 'I can't promise it'll work,' I went on, 'but if it doesn't it won't cost you anything and we'll try again another day.'

I cleared my mind and instantly I heard a man's voice. It was faint, so I judged he hadn't been over very long. He told me his name was Bert.

'Do you know a Bert?' I asked Mrs Curwood.

She gasped. 'That's my husband!'

'Well he says he wants to send his love to Edie and to Mary who's been a power of strength to you.'

Mrs Curwood nodded. Apparently her name was Edith and Bert always called her Edie, and Mary was a widow she'd become friendly with after Bert's death. Mary had indeed helped her tremendously in coming to terms with her loss.

Bert went on to describe his funeral, which he said he'd watched, including the number of people present, thirteen. He sent his love to Keith his first grandson, mentioned the date of their wedding anniversary and also the fact that Edith had had a stillborn child.

Edith confirmed that all this was correct.

Bert's voice faded a little after the effort of these details. I'd noticed before that the longer someone had been over and the more they communicated with a medium, not necessarily me, the stronger and louder their voices became.

There was a pause, then Bert came back.

'He's talking about meeting Catherine,' I explained to Mrs Curwood. 'He says she passed in her sleep four months after he did …'

'Yes, that's his mother-in-law.'

'Oh and now he's mentioned David, your unmarried son still at home. He says he's been a great blessing to you.'

'That's true,' said Mrs Curwood. 'Without David I don't think I'd still be here.'

Then he mentioned meeting Grenville again.

'Grenville, Grenville, I don't think I know anyone of that name,' Mrs Curwood said slowly, forehead creased as she tried to remember.

'She doesn't know Grenville dear,' I said to Bert. 'Are you sure that's the right name?'

Indistinctly he muttered it was, but by now his voice was so weak I could barely hear it.

'He's getting so tired I might be mishearing him,' I explained. 'We'd better stop there.'

It was a pity the last message had been unsatisfactory, but Mrs Curwood was delighted. Her face radiant, she pressed my hand, 'It was wonderful, wonderful.'

I sighed with relief. Thank goodness I'd been able to help.

I hadn't heard the last of Edith Curwood. A few days later she contacted me triumphantly. 'I've remembered Grenville! He was a friend of my husband's in Wales many years ago before we were married. Grenville died in his teens!'

Puzzling details often fell into place after a sitting. A similiar thing happened with Mrs Sedgwick also from Blackpool. I was able to give her many accurate family names, including that of her grandson Mark. Then there was mention of a grand-daughter called Kathleen, but Mrs Sedgwick didn't have a grand-daughter.

Three weeks later, her son phoned her from Australia. 'Mum, you've got your grand-daughter at last! D'you like the name Kathleen?'

Sometimes spirits gave pet or nicknames, rather than their christened name, so that they were only recognizable to close family members.

During a sitting for Mrs Berry of Oldham her mother came through to me, introducing herself as Gerty Seward.

'Mother's real name was Martha Ann,' said Mrs Berry,

'but the family always called her Gerty and Seward was her maiden name, she hadn't used that for years.'

To anyone else it sounds a small, trivial point; but to the sitter it was genuine evidence. There was no way I could have checked or researched so many personal details.

People often asked me why the messages weren't of more importance. After several conversations with Ramonov, I came to the conclusion that the spirit world wanted only to prove its existence and to reassure the bereaved, not to alter our destiny. What's more, the sitters themselves were perfectly content with 'trivial' details. I could see for myself what a difference it made to them and I was glad I could ease their grief. After all, I understood exactly what they were going through – I'd been there myself.

I was still doing public services at weekends, and for a long time our life was smooth and settled. This is what I was meant to do, I thought, work as a full time medium. The pattern was set for the rest of my life, or so I thought. In fact there was an extraordinary change just around the corner.

I was forty-two and speaking at a service just like any other when it happened. Everything went well. I got some very good messages through and I was pleased. Afterwards I fetched my coat, and as I walked out I passed behind two old dears who were chatting over a cup of tea.

'Isn't she good,' said one.

'Oh she's not genuine,' the other assured her, 'she must have looked up names in the telephone book or something. She was much too good to be genuine.'

I felt sick. Speechless with shock I blundered past them into the street. I'd never heard people say such things about me before – but just because I hadn't heard them didn't mean they weren't said behind my back. I was shattered.

Perhaps it had all been an illusion, perhaps everybody thought I was a fraud. I thought back over the meetings I'd attended, the times I'd forced myself out in the rain and the cold, the times I'd literally waded knee-deep through snow to some remote hall. Had they been doubting me all along? Were they really laughing behind my back?

To this day I don't know why that chance remark affected me so deeply. I couldn't shrug it off. I was more than hurt. In just a few seconds, my confidence had been torn to shreds.

I walked straight into the next phone box I came to and rang the Royal Albert Hospital where John worked as a porter. 'Are there any vacancies?' I asked the Matron.

'There's always vacancies,' she said. It was a mental hospital, never very popular with staff. I started as a trainee nurse the following week.

I cancelled my public meetings and private sittings and vowed I'd give up mediumship for ever. Looking back, it was an extraordinary extreme reaction. John couldn't understand such a violent change of heart, but then I couldn't expect him to. I didn't understand it myself.

I wasn't unhappy. At forty-two here I was fulfilling my life-long ambition, and I was very proud when I passed my exams and became a fully fledged State Enrolled Nurse at forty-six. Who says you're too old to change at forty? It's never too late to do what you want, if you want it badly enough.

I should have realized however, that it was impossible for me to give up mediumship. I didn't choose to be a medium, I was a medium. I couldn't give up being myself. I stuck to my decision about public meetings and private sittings, but I was soon working again – for the nurses.

Little by little they found out who I was, and soon persuaded me to have a 'quick try' as a special favour. Word spread through the hospital and soon I was getting away with murder. Our mini demonstrations took place in the staff bathroom because it was quiet and comfortable, and in there we were still technically 'on duty'. The other nurses used to ask the Sister, 'If we do Stokes' work can she come into the bathroom after tea?' and invariably the answer was yes, because the sister liked the demonstrations too.

There was only one person who would have nothing to do with these sessions – and that was Nurse Burney. She was an elderly widow who'd stayed on after the nurse's retirement age of fifty-five. A sweet, kind, deeply religious woman, she didn't believe in what I did, but she never ridiculed it. She'd just walk quietly away when the other nurses asked me to work for them. I respected her for it.

One night after work, I was up late finishing my chores in the kitchen, long after John and Terry were in bed. Eventually I cleared up, turned out the light, walked into the sitting room and stopped dead.

A strange man was standing by the fire, his back to me. My goodness, I thought, someone's escaped from the prison. I stepped silently backwards, hoping to withdraw before he saw me. I was too late. He turned.

'My name is Alec Burney,' he said.

I was still thinking of prisoners, but something about the name struck a chord. Burney, Burney – like *Nurse* Burney?

'Burney's husband?' I said.

'Yes,' he said. He went on to tell me he was worried about his wife because she was having a particular money problem, and he wanted to advise her how to sort it out.

'Will you tell her what I said,' he asked at last.

How on earth can I mention this to Burney, I thought, but he looked so worried I promised I would. He nodded and disappeared.

I stared at the empty space beside the fire, wondering what I'd let myself in for. Burney probably thought of me along the same lines she thought of witches, deluded perhaps, and slightly wicked. She probably wouldn't even listen. I sighed and started upstairs to bed. Oh well, I thought, the opportunity will present itself somehow.

Two days later we were both on duty together and I happened to walk into the bathroom as Nurse Burney was folding a new cap.

'Hello Burney,' I said.

'Hello Stokes,' she replied smiling at me in the mirror, but not looking round. It was a complicated business getting those caps right.

I slowly washed my hands and watched her shaping the starched white peaks. Satisfied, she carefully placed it on her head and picked up the hairpins to hold it in place.

I've got to tell her somehow, I thought, but I didn't know what to say. I dried my hands in slow motion and having no possible reason to delay longer, started to walk towards the door. Half-way there I stopped.

'It's no good, I've got to say it.' I turned back and said very quickly before I could change my mind. 'Burney your husband came to see me last night. His name is Alec and he is worried about you because you're having this problem. He says you're not to get upset because it'll turn out all right.'

Burney had let go of her cap only one side pinned, and it was standing upright on her head. It looked hilarious but she didn't notice. She was staring at me open mouthed.

Afraid I'd upset her. I hurried from the room, but seconds later she was at the door calling me back.

'What did you say nurse?'

I repeated it. 'I'm sorry Burney,' I added, 'but I promised your husband I'd tell you and I've done it. Now it's up to you entirely.'

'But I haven't even told my kids I'm having this trouble,' she said breathlessly, 'I'm the only one that knows.'

'Yes. And your husband,' I said.

She was obviously shocked, but when she'd had a little time to think it over she asked me to her house to do a sitting. Although I'd officially given them up I was glad to do it, and Alec Burney was able to advise her.

She never did take part in those bathroom sessions, but I think she viewed them in a different light after that.

On another occasion I was walking down the corridor with a newly married nurse, on the way to the cafeteria for a cup of tea, when I heard a woman's voice say, 'She's having twins you know.'

'D'you know you're having twins?' I asked the girl. She certainly didn't look pregnant.

'Indeed I'm not!' she said indignantly. 'Who told you that story?' I shrugged and said no more, but a few weeks later she discovered she was pregnant and sure enough it was twins.

After that it was standing joke. 'Don't walk down the corridor with that Stokes,' she used to tell the other nurses, 'she'll have you pregnant before you turn round!'

They tried to give the patients the best facilities they could at the Royal Albert. There were bright, pretty rooms, frequent changes of clean clothes and plenty of fresh air and sunshine when the weather was fine. They had a new sports field laid and would have liked a spanking new sports pavilion to go with it, but unfortunately they couldn't afford it. £3,000 was needed and the hospital didn't have the money.

Then someone suggested we try to raise it ourselves, starting off with a garden fete. The idea was greeted enthusiastically. Everyone was keen to run a stall and volunteer their particular talents. Nurses who could cook, nurses who could make stuffed toys, nurses who could collect jumble; they were all eager to help. The suggestions became more and more inspired. 'Oh and we can have a fortune teller,' cried Staff Nurse, 'Stokes can do that can't you Stokes.'

I said I'd think about it. I wasn't sure whether I should or not, so I asked Ramonov. I still had my lessons with Ramonov who never tried to persuade me to go back to public meetings. He'd taught me that what I did with my life was my responsibility, and he never gave advice unless I asked for it.

On the subject of fortune telling, he felt it would be right for me to accept this time as it was for a good cause, and said not to worry about the 'predictions', just to work as I normally did as a medium. He even told me that if I needed a crystal ball as a prop, a Mrs Lee who was president of the Spiritualist Church in Grantham had one.

I phoned Mrs Lee and she did indeed have a crystal ball which she was prepared to lend me. We had another car now, so we were able to drive down to Grantham to collect it.

On the day of the fete, dressed in long flowing costume complete with big loopy ear-rings, I settled in my tent, the crystal ball and a pack of cards spread on a table before me. Outside a large brightly painted notice proclaimed that Madame Durenda saw into the future.

The 'fortune telling' was a great success. I play acted

with the crystal and the cards, but didn't really use them. I
didn't know how. Instead I did my usual sittings. No one
seemed to mind.

The afternoon flew past, and I got so engrossed in my
work I was surprised when Matron appeared in the tent
flap. 'Nurse, how long are you going to be?' she asked,
'everybody's gone off the field and there's still a queue of
people sitting outside your tent!'

She had to turn most of them away, but at least we raised
a lot of money towards the pavilion.

The next day Terry, who was now a grown young man
and able to drive, was going to take the crystal ball back to
Grantham for me. I brought it into the sitting room ready
for him to collect and on impulse decided to have a quick
look at it, to see if I could see anything. I lifted it out of its
box, laid it on its special square of black velvet and gazed
into the clear crystal. To my surprise a tiny colour picture
appeared. I could see our car, a bright yellow Ford,
standing empty and deserted in a country road, beside a
clump of trees. Nothing else, but that picture made me
uneasy. Why was the car deserted?

'Terry, I'd rather you went on the train,' I said putting
the crystal ball back in its box. 'I don't feel happy about
you using the car today.'

'Oh don't fuss mum,' he said, 'I'm a good driver and
besides, I can't be bothered hanging round waiting for
trains. Don't tell me you're taking that crystal ball stuff
seriously!'

There was no stopping him.

Several hours later, driving down a country road, the
car started making a terrible clanking noise. The big ends
had gone. Terry had to abandon it where it stopped, by a
group of trees exactly like the spot I'd seen in the crystal
ball, and get the train home. To add insult to injury, he
had to take another train journey to collect the car when
it'd been repaired.

I know mental hospitals aren't very popular and it's
difficult to recruit new staff, but the staff who do join
usually stay and become extremely dedicated. The work is
increasingly rewarding. I know during my first week I was

appalled and distressed by the sad cases I saw, especially the brain damaged children. I thought I'd never stand it, was sure I'd have to ask for a transfer to an ordinary hospital; yet as the weeks went on I found I'd grown to love those poor, broken people. From nowhere came compassion and unexpected pleasure.

I'd walk into a ward after a short spell off duty and their faces would light up when they saw me. They might not get my name right, there were all kinds of touching attempts 'Tokes', 'Stoker', but they knew who I was.

I would probably have stayed at the Royal Albert until my official retirement at fifty-five if it hadn't been for an injury with unexpected consequences.

We had a difficult girl called Irene, who like so many mental patients could summon up almost superhuman strength when she was in a temper. One night as we were trying to get her to bed, she became violent. She lashed out at sister and I, and attempted to bite Sister's arm. Quickly I leant across the bed to grab her hands and she kicked out viciously, catching me a heavy blow in the throat. It felt as if my head had been torn from my body. I staggered backwards clutching my neck and gasping for breath.

Blood was streaming from my mouth and nose, I was choking, coughing and drowning in it. Irene stared at me in wonder, and then she started to cry.

They rushed me to the doctor. I was in an awful state. The kick had ruptured my thyroid gland so badly it had to be removed and I was put on 'Thyroxin' tablets for life. Yet even this dreadful injury was a blessing in disguise. The operation revealed a growth in my throat which needed to be removed immediately. If Irene hadn't kicked me, it might not have been discovered until too late.

I was away from work for quite a time after the operation, but it never occurred to me to give up my job. John was now an auxiliary nurse at the hospital and we enjoyed being in the same field. I was looking forwad to going back.

When I returned, I couldn't speak properly, I had difficulty with swallowing and I tired easily, so they started me on light duties – the quiet wards and the old ladies home. I was progressing nicely. I ambled happily through each day, glad to be back with my old friends.

Then late one morning, they discovered they were a nurse short on Copeland Ward, where the difficult patients, including Irene were kept. It turned out I was the only SEN available and after much to-ing and fro-ing with the Nursing Officer, they decided to send me.

Unfortunately the Sister on Copeland Ward was at lunch and wouldn't be back till 2.00, so meaning to be kind, they told me not to report to Copeland until she arrived. I expect they thought I'd feel safer with the Sister there as well, but this decision meant I had an hour to sit and brood.

The more I thought about it, the more nervous I became. What would I do if Irene was in a temper? She might go for me again. Would she remember the last time? I hadn't seen her since …

By 2.00 I was in a nervous state. I rang the bell outside Copeland – it was a security ward and always locked – and shakily reported to Sister. Nurse Metcalfe was already on duty, she told me, a good, experienced nurse; so there was nothing for me to worry about. But of course I was worried.

I went into the day room where Nurse Metcalfe was sitting beside the door, and took my place. We had to sit on either side of the door where we could see all the patients at once.

'How's Irene?' I asked.

'Fine,' said Nurse Metcalfe, 'It's Jennie Lee we've got to keep an eye on this afternoon.'

Jennie Lee was huge – sixteeen stone of solid woman with the mind of a child, and she was clearly in a mood. She stamped sulkily around the room, knocking other patients out of her way, kicking at chairs and thumping her fists down on tables. As we watched, she hurled a large armchair aside and crashed towards the curtains, grabbing one in each hand.

'Jennie Lee!' shouted Metcalfe. 'You pull those curtains down and I'll have your guts for garters!'

At that, Jennie dropped the curtains, turned round and

stared menacingly at us. Her eyes narrowed, her head
sunk lower into her enormous shoulders, she let out a
bellow of rage and came charging across the room,
scattering patients in her path.

'Quick Stokes! Get out the way!' cried Metcalfe, leaping
from her seat. But I couldn't move. I stared at the huge
bulk rampaging towards me and I was paralysed. This is it,
I thought. I can't move. I'm finished as a nurse.

'Stokes!' shouted Metcalfe desperately, but the next
second Jennie reached me. She skidded to a halt in front
of my chair, then suddenly her expression changed. 'Ah –
nurse Stokes has come back,' she said happily and
plonking herself down on my lap, she wrapped her arms
lovingly round my neck.

Under the sixteen stone of woman, I felt my stomach
flip over.

Nothing more was said and the next morning I was back
on the quiet wards, but the incident worried me. I'd
reacted very badly in a crisis, my nerve had gone and it was
only pure luck that I wasn't injured for a second time. My
whole future as a nurse must be in the balance.

The day passed quietly. After work I went straight home
and ran a bath. Thoughtfully I unbuttoned my uniform,
and as I did so I felt something in the pocket. I put my
hand in and, to my horror, brought out the drugs I should
have given the patients before I left.

I was frantic. It was a serious mistake to make and if the
night Sister found out she'd be furious. How could I have
forgottten? John was home thank goodness, and he drove
me back to the hospital. The sister hadn't yet been round
to see the patients fortunately, so I doled out the drugs
and hurried away before she saw me.

No harm was done, but I lay awake worrying all night. I
knew it was more than an ordinary mistake. How could I
forget the drugs the moment after they were given to me?
I went over and over it in my mind. Sister had taken the
drugs from the drug cupboard as usual and handed them
to me to give the patients. I put them in my pocket,
walking into the ward and then – what? Had I been called
away? Had something distracted my attention? I couldn't

remember. It was very peculiar and disturbing. Supposing it happened again?

The next day my shift didn't start until after lunch. John had been on duty during the morning and he popped home at mid-day for a quick coffee and to run me back in the car.

It was pouring with rain and we were going to collect another nurse called Stevie who lived round the corner. I ran to the car, watched the water bouncing off the windscreen as we drove along and spotted Stevie waiting for us under the shelter of a shop awning. John braked beside her and as it was only a two door car, I went to get out to let her in. I leant forward, my fingers on the doorhandle and suddenly my body locked. Just as two days ago I'd frozen before Jennie Lee, so I'd frozen again. I was completely paralysed.

John was speaking to me and Steve was knocking on the window but, to my horror, I couldn't move a muscle. I couldn't even tell them what was wrong. There was an awful moaning noise coming from somewhere, it went on and on, louder and I thought who on earth is that? Then I realised it was me.

By now John and Stevie had seen I was really ill. Stevie jumped into the car from John's side and they hurried me home to wait for the doctor. Later that afternoon I was taken to hospital.

They said it was tension paralysis and there was little they could do. There was nothing organically wrong, it was all in my mind. They could only calm me with powerful drugs in the hope that when the tension eased, my muscles might unlock.

I wasn't particularly happy with the diagnosis. It was all very well saying it was a mental problem, but it certainly felt physical to me. They didn't seem to realise I was trying as hard as I could to lift my legs, to walk, but nothing happened whatsoever. I found it difficult to believe my mind was causing the problem when I was willing myself as hard as I could to move.

I was eight weeks in hospital, during which time I improved. They got me talking again, or rather stuttering, moving my arms and even walking a bit, but as soon as I arrived home the paralysis came back. It seemed the condition was caused by the responsibilities of my real life. My nerve was gone and outside the sheltered world of the hospital I couldn't cope. The doctor shook his head and said I'd have to learn to live with it.

I was prescribed six or seven pills three times a day, and I suppose I must have been in a drugged stupor most of the time. I used to sit in the kitchen which was at the front of the house, wearing an apron with a big pocket, for all my pills, waiting for the neighbours to call in to do things for me.

I was very bitter. I fell out with the spirit world and closed my ears when they tried to talk to me. I felt they'd used me badly to allow my life to be ruined like this. Ramonov tried to get through but I blocked him out. I wanted nothing to do with any of them.

Time passed and the hate built up. I felt doomed to end my days in a kitchen chair. I couldn't even have a conversation with anyone, yet my mind was active, a prisoner in my useless body. The only parts I could move were my arms. Any attempts at speaking came out as unintelligible stammers. I was seething with frustration.

Day after day I raged inside, and one morning I was so overcome with self pity, I forgot to set up the psychic block in my mind. Why, why, why has this happened to me, I was thinking for the thousandth time. Me who's travelled all over the country in bitter weather, spent half my life waiting on railway platforms. Why should the spirit world have allowed this to happen to me, after all I've done for other people?

Suddenly I heard Ramonov's voice interrupt sharply, 'Why should it not happen to you? D'you think you're one of God's favourite people because you do the things you do? You've forgotten the most important word we've ever taught you. Trust.'

'And what good will that do me,' I retorted bitterly, 'the doctor says I've got to learn to live with this.'

'Oh yes,' said Ramonov, 'and what are you going to do about it?'

'What can I do about it? The doctor says I've got to accept it.'

'Remember this,' said Ramonov, sternly, 'failure is not falling down, it's failing to get up when you've fallen down. Trust in us, trust in God, do what we tell you and within a year we'll have you back on a public platform.'

The idea was ludicrous. I couldn't even speak let alone address a public meeting, but I was so miserable and bored anything was better than this half life.

'All right,' I said grudgingly, 'what shall I do?'

'Well to start with, you can go and throw away those drugs.'

My hand flew protectively to the pocket in my apron. My drugs! I needed them, I couldn't manage without them. Besides how could I throw them away – I couldn't walk? But Ramonov's voice was in my ear the whole time repeating 'Trust in us, you can do it, you can do it,' over and over again.

'All right,' I thought in the end, always one to accept a challenge. 'I will.'

Clumsily, I rocked myself backwards and forwards until I fell out of the chair. Then I crawled and stumbled across the kitchen, pulled the door open, dragged myself painfully inch by inch up the stairs on my hands and knees, and at last collapsed exhausted on the bathroom floor.

'You can do it, you can do it.' Ramonov was insisting in my ear as I lay resting. 'Trust in us, you can do it.'

Slowly I gripped the edge of the sink, heaved myself upright and emptied my apron pocket down the lavatory pan. With great effort, I pulled the chain and watched my vital drugs flush away.

Then I slithered back to the top of the stairs and stopped. The steps stretched away below me – impossibly steep and dangerous. I'll never get down there. But Ramonov wouldn't leave me alone. 'Come on, you can do it. You can,' until in the end I half slid, half fell from top to bottom. At last I dragged myself back to the safety of the kitchen and somehow hauled myself into the chair. I was exhausted. Utterly drained and breathless and yet for the first time in weeks, rather pleased with myself.

John nearly had a fit when he found out what I'd done. He wanted to get the doctor back to prescribe more pills, but I wouldn't let him. I was going to do this myself – with Ramonov's help of course.

From that day on I progressed. It was a terrible struggle. Without tranquillisers I panicked and couldn't get my breath, and I choked on my food so much I was afraid to eat. A sudden loud noise made me freeze, and once I badly burned my arm because the milkman knocked unexpectedly, just as I was taking a tray out of the oven. Yes it was agony, but with each day that passed I clawed myself back to normal life.

I pushed myself to try new things and the more I tried the easier it became. I started walking again. First with tottering steps around the house, and then though I trembled and shook uncontrollably, the length of our street.

That was the turning point. Once I'd broken the barrier to the outside world I forced myself to go out every day, and that was how I met Mark. He was a blond, blue-eyed toddler who was looked after by his grandmother while his mother was at work. Often he was playing in his front garden as I stumbled past and I'd stop to talk to him. I stuttered away in my funny, squeaky voice, but of course Mark didn't notice anything odd, he was only a baby. I couldn't be self conscious with him.

Then one day he trapped his finger in a toy gun and his grandmother, remembering I'd been a nurse, rushed him round to me. To my amazement, I freed him and dressed the wound without a tremor.

After that they came to see me frequently and when one morning his grandmother fell ill Mark was brought to me. From then on I took care of him.

I'm convinced he was the reason for my complete recovery. I sang him songs, took him to places I'd never have dreamed of going on my own and I was forced to find words in shops and on buses because he depended on me.

Dear little Mark, he brought colour and humour back into my life. I learned all over again that special knack children have, of turning things around and making you see them in a different light.

One wet Saturday afternoon Mark brought his cousin Jeremy round to play. Jeremy was 7 – three years older than Mark and his complete opposite in colouring – dark haired with big brown eyes and long black lashes. They crawled about the floor setting up the model farm, making such a pretty picture, brown head touching blond as they bent over the toys in total absorption, that I tiptoed to the armchair to watch them.

'And that's the ghost,' Jeremy was saying to Mark.

'There aren't any ghosts,' said Mark, 'at least not ghosts with white sheets and things are they Stokey?'

'No dear.' We'd had many a discussion on this subject.

'Well if they don't wear white sheets they're not ghosts so what are they?' asked Jeremy.

This was a bit beyond Mark. He fiddled with the plastic animals. 'I don't know but there are ghosts and Stokey can talk to them,' he insisted.

Jeremy snorted. 'Go on!'

'Yes she can, she can. She talks to them.'

Jeremy laughed derisively. 'You can't can you Stokey?'

'Yes,' I said.

His eyes opened wide. 'How d'you mean?'

'Well Jeremy,' I said, 'everything that lives cannot die; flowers, animals, people, there's no death. Everything living still lives on in another world.'

There was a long silence while he digested this, then he said, 'And you can talk to them?'

'Yes,' I said.

He turned back to the farmyard and the game went on. I picked up the newspaper and glanced through it. It wasn't often I had a chance to read during the day. I dipped into the pages luxuriously, only half an ear tuned to the boys. Suddenly there was a light touch on my knee.

I looked up. Jeremy was standing there, his huge brown eyes studying my face solemnly.

'And you can *talk* to them?'

'Yes,' I said.

He gazed at me in awe. 'I say – you're never lonely are you?'

Within a year, exactly as Ramonov had promised, I was ready to speak on a public platform again. 'Come on, you know you can do it now.' Ramonov insisted.

I didn't want to. It was bad enough talking to one bus conductor let alone 100 people, but somehow I felt I ought to, just once, as a token of appreciation to Ramonov for all the help he'd given me. Funnily enough after all I'd been through, the idea that some people might think I was a phoney seemed completely irrelevant. It was the reason I'd given up in the first place, and yet now it didn't seem to matter at all.

Word got out that Doris Stokes was in circulation again and a meeting was arranged. It was only a small, local affair; but for hours beforehand I was a stuttering, trembling wreck. I'll never do it, I thought, I must be mad to try, I'll be a laughing stock. Yet the moment I stood on that stage my nerves vanished. I spoke perfectly.

Afterwards, as the applause rang in my ears and people crowded round to tell me how much I'd helped them, I was hooked. I was finished as a nurse, there was no question about that, but I could still do worthwhile work – as a medium. These people needed me and I needed to be needed.

Chapter 10

It was wonderful to get to work again. I slipped back into public meetings and private sittings like a fish into water.

I still had attacks of nerves and I couldn't trust myself to drive any more, but with Ramonov's help I was leading a useful life.

All over again I felt the tremendous need for my gift, and I was ashamed to think how close I'd come to throwing it away, just because someone upset me.

One of my first new cases was an RAF sergeant named Hugh Drummond. Apparently I'd given him a brief message from his late wife at a public meeting, and later he asked me to do a sitting for him at his home. He lived in Lancs, but he was convinced the sitting would work better if I were surrounded by his dead wife's things, I agreed.

I could feel his grief the moment he opened the front door. A small, thin man, he looked lost and alone and I was desperately sorry for him.

'She died of cancer six months ago,' he told me brokenly, leading me into the living room which he still kept as immaculately as his wife could have wished. 'We walked through life together as one ...'

He asked me to sit down and without thinking, I made straight for an armchair near the fire. I put my handbag on the floor beside me, and was just straightening up, when a woman's voice said in my ear. 'That's my chair.'

'Oh,' I said aloud, 'I'm sitting in your wife's chair.'

Mr Drummond stared at me. 'Why yes. How did you know?'

'She just told me.'

Open mouthed, he sank down opposite me and the sitting began.

I raised my left arm. 'Your wife says all that's missing is her little dog who used to cuddle in the crook of this arm. She says the dog's called Pindy.'

'Cindy,' corrected Mr Drummond, 'but you're right. She's a little pug bitch, she's being looked after by relatives now because I'm out all day, but she always sat there with my wife.'

The woman went on to say she was worried because her husband carried her rings around his pocket and he might lose them. Would I ask him to wrap them in tissue paper and put them in safe place.

At this Mr Drummond sheepishly drew a bumpy envelope from his pocket. 'Nobody knew I carried these. I used to take them with me to spiritualist meetings thinking they might help me get a message.'

His wife then directed me to look in a glass cabinet containing ornaments. I saw the one she meant, and went over and knelt on the carpet before it, peering through the sparkling clear doors. The little figures were arranged neatly in dust-free rows on the glass shelves and they looked perfect.

'I can't understand this,' I said to Mr Drummond. 'Your wife is telling me to look in here for something broken which she cried over, but I can't see anything broken.'

Silently he joined me, opened the cabinet and took out a miniature Dresden doll. The small finger on the right hand was missing.

'Yes she had a good cry when she discovered this. It got broken on the way home from one of our tours abroad.'

We went back to our seats and Mrs Drummond gave me many names, some of them still living friends and others long passed relatives. Her husband semed quite happy with this; but I was still unsatisfied because I hadn't yet got her christian name.

Then right at the end of the sitting it came. 'Gay,' I said out loud, 'Gay by name and gay by nature.'

Hugh Drummond was delighted. 'Yes. Her real name was Gladys but I never called her that during all our years together. To me she was always Gay.'

I was pleased the sitting went so well, but beyond that I

didn't give it another thought. The weeks passed, I met dozens and dozens of new people and I forgot all about Hugh Drummond.

It must have been nearly a year later when my sitter arrived promptly at the arranged hour. A thin man with a sleepless look and something vaguely familiar about him, but before I could work out what it was a woman's voice angrily interrupted my thoughts. My eyes widened as I listened to her. She was using very strong words indeed.

The surprise must have showed on my face, because the man asked if there was anything wrong.

'No, not with me dear,' I said, 'but your wife Gay's just been talking to me. She says you've been considering taking an overdose haven't you?'

The man crumpled visibly, and I suddenly remembered this was the same Hugh Drummond I'd visited at his home all those months before. I sat him down and gave him cup of tea.

Slowly he admitted he'd recently suffered depression and thought of taking pills. He was lonely without his wife and wanted to join her.

'Your wife is very anxious about you,' I stressed. 'She says that is not the way. You must not do it. She's waiting for you and if she's gone on she'll make sure of being there to meet you when your time comes, but you must wait till your time comes, or you will regret it.'

Hugh nodded resignedly and, as I looked at him, I realized that I had to give him some fresh evidence. I'd told him his wife's name was Gay, but I could have remembered that from our last sitting.

'Have you got a middle name?' I asked Gay.

Back came the reply. 'May' which Hugh confirmed. She then went on to give several anniversary dates, including one very important one at the end of July.

'July 31st would have been our silver wedding anniversary,' said Hugh, 'my wife set great store by that date.'

Gay then described some of her personal possessions and jewellery that Hugh had given to their 21-year-old daughter Diane.

'Tell him I've met William Greenwood,' she said next.

Hugh shook his head. 'No I can't recall a William Greenwood.'

Gay laughed, 'Tell him it's Sgt Bill Greenwood.' I duly repeated it and Hugh's mouth dropped open.

'No – that's incredible. He was a physical training instructor colleague of mine in Germany. I haven't heard from him for years. Surely he's not dead?'

Gay insisted he was, and proceeded to name other RAF friends from Penang. Singapore and Germany who she'd met on the other side. She also mentioned Hugh's brother Andrew who'd died after a short illness a few months before, together with the name of his wife Renee and those of his three children.

Finally she said she'd had a miscarriage many years ago. Hugh confirmed this.

'This was a son, now called Peter,' I said, 'and she says you must stop worrying about who Peter could be.'

This last bit seemed rather obscure. 'Does that mean anything to you?'

'Oh yes,' said Hugh. 'Minutes before she died she called out "Peter". It was quite audible to the family and I, and they asked me who Peter was, but I couldn't answer. Even though it's a common name, none of our friends or relatives is called Peter. I've often wondered since, who it could be she remembered as she lay dying. Now I know.'

Hugh left, all thoughts of overdoses forgotten, but I did hear from him again a week or two later. He wanted to let me know that Bill Greenwood had died of a heart attack five years before.

Not long afterwards, another man contacted me out of the blue. He said his name was Dr Per Beskow and he was taking a course run by the religious studies department of St Martin's College, Lancaster. Could he come and talk to me?

'Well yes of course,' I told him, rather surprised. Although I'd had favourable comments from individual clergymen, rabbis and even muslims, most churches disapprove of spiritualism. Nevertheless I was always willing to state our case for anyone open-minded enough to listen.

Dr Per Beskow turned out to be a Swedish University Lecturer on religion. He was a thin, precise man with receding hair, glasses, and spoke fluent English with a charming Swedish accent. He explained that the members of the course had been split into groups and assigned to study Quaker, Jewish, Muslim, Buddhist and Spiritualist communities in the area. He, together with four students had been allotted spiritualism and a colleague at the college had suggested he have a word with me.

John made us a pot of tea while we talked. It soon became clear that Dr Beskow was highly sceptical; but being a conscientious man he would tackle his investigation methodically and fairly. Instinctively I liked him and respected his views.

'John and I will give you all the help we can,' It told him finally. 'Just let us know what you'd like us to do.'

He certainly did. Over the next weeks we worked closely with him and his group. They came to public meetings and talked to members of the audience, they attended church services, they spoke to people who'd had sittings and they had sittings themselves.

Dr Beskow was quite startled with his. I spoke to his late father and two other recently deceased relatives. They gave me minute details of his childhood in Sweden, including the name of a Stockholm street where he'd lived in the early 30s, and then said that He'd been offered two jobs, the most recent one not to his advantage.

'That's extraordinary,' said Dr Beskow, 'I was offered a second job only yesterday.' What's more, he later decided it wasn't suitable.

One of his students was particularly impressed with his own sitting too. I was able to tell young Brian Gardner the name of his dog Charlie, the name of his sister Nancy, the name of his closest friend, Sam and the fact that his Uncle Herbert had died in tragic circumstances. The last part about Uncle Herbert he couldn't accept, but when he checked with his mother later, he found it was quite correct.

It was hard work, but at the end of it I was satisfied we'd given Dr Beskow and his students a good insight into Spiritualism.

'We've certainly been in touch with something that can't be explained by scientific studies,' he admitted cautiously and invited John and I to the end of course summing-up; where each group would give a talk on their investigations.

Intrigued to know what conclusions he'd come to, we went along. all the talks were interesting, but we waited eagerly for Dr Beskow's. At last he stood up. He shuffled his papers and looked round the audience, possibly trying to locate John and I. He took a deep breath.

'Spiritualists don't believe,' he announced firmly. I groaned and dropped my head in my hands. After all these weeks, all the work we'd put in, all the explaining ... I glanced at John to see his reaction, but the next words pinned me to my chair.

'They *know*!'

And I looked up at the platform to see he was grinning broadly in our direction. We had got through to him after all.

It wasn't only non spiritualists who found their way to my door. Life-long believers came as well. Frequently, married couples make a pact that whoever passes first will come back to communicate with the other, and so the surviving half heeds a medium.

Connie and Reg Maddox, both members of a spiritualist church in Birmingham had made just such a pact. Only months before he died, Reg had told his wife, 'I'll prove my survival in my own time with a medium of my choice.'

I hadn't met either of them before. But a year after Reg's death Mrs Edwards, a friend of the Maddoxes' from the same church came to me for a sitting. Poor woman only had about 10 minutes to herself then an unusual thing happened. The voice faded and I had a sudden mental picture of a group of people. The impression sharpened and I counted them. There were eleven figures clustered in a semi-circle, one standing a little forward from the rest – an elderly man with white hair and glasses.

'My name is Reg Maddox,' he said and then one by one the others introduced themselves, while Mrs Edwards hastily scribbled down the names so she wouldn't forget.

First came Charlie Makin a former vice president of the

Maddoxes' church, then Percy Langley, a medium, Amy Stait the organist who insisted 'Call me Aunt Amy' – which Connie confirmed was one of her catch phrases – Elsie Lees, Johnson, Porter, Harrison, Copeland, Mrs Jenkins and John Butler – all late members of the church.

Once they'd established their presence, the group faded into the background and Reg took over. First he sent his love to Connie, then he said, 'I'd like to be remembered to Mrs Fall who speaks at the church and to my old friend Bill Strickland.'

'Tell Bill we think we know it all, but we've only just touched the tip of the iceberg.'

Then he wished his wife happy birthday in advance, gave his daughter's name, Frances, and his sister-in-law's Pat. He also mentioned seeing the purple cushions with the gold pattern.

I raised my eyebrows at this: 'Have you just bought some purple cushions?' I asked Mrs Edwards.

'No,' she said, 'but I know what he means. My brother brought me some purple and gold cushions from China 35 years ago. They didn't really match anything, so I put them away in a trunk, but a couple of weeks ago I came across them again and got them out.'

This clinched it for her and when she told Connie of the sitting she was convinced that her husband had kept his part of the pact.

On another occasion, our dear friend Harry Edwards told me that National Federation of Healers was holding a Christmas Bazaar, and he asked if I'd go along and do sittings for them to raise money.

Always glad of an opportunity to help the healers, I said, 'Certainly Harry,' but as it turned out I was able to help another spiritualist as well.

Ruth Anderson, the wife of the President of the Federation was going through a spell of doubt and, as we'd never met, she decided an anonymous sitting with me would be a good test.

To me of course she was just a face in the long queue of sitters I saw at the bazaar. Thank goodness I had no idea how crucial a successful sitting was to her; or I might have been so nervous I'd have blocked the vibrations!

It went well from the start. 'I've got a Les here,' I said, 'and he's calling you Ruthie.'

The woman laughed. 'That's my brother and my name's Ruth. Les only called me Ruthie when he was teasing.'

'And there's another man here, Victor. He's stressing it's Victor, *not* Vic and I don't know why but I feel I ought to call him *sir*.'

It turned out Victor was another of Ruth's brothers who always insisted on being called by his full name and he'd been an RAF officer. No wonder I wanted to call him sir!

He went on to talk of many more friends and relatives, then listed the contents of an unread will – all later verified – and the sad fact that Ruth's last brother was ill and hadn't long to live.

'We've got him here with us,' said Ruth, 'we're trying to heal him.'

'Well I'm sorry,' I told her, 'it's not to be. I'm afraid they're preparing for him.'

Sadly this too was correct, but when I met Ruth later and was properly introduced she gave me nothing but thanks.

'I've never heard such evidence Doris,' she said. 'You gave me everything on a plate. Names, what people died of, where it happened, everything. I'll never doubt again.'

I was more glad than ever then, that I'd been able to work at the Christmas Bazaar.

Chapter 11

The case was splashed right across the front page of the Lancashire Evening Post and I felt very sad as I sat down to read it. A young girl, only 17 years old had been found murdered. She was last seen alive, waiting at a bus stop on her way to church, and the police were appealing to anyone who'd passed the bus stop or noticed the girl that Sunday, to come forward.

Poor little lass, I thought looking at the innocent young face in the photograph. What a thing to happen. I continued reading, shaking my head over the dreadful story, when suddenly a voice whispered, 'Shepherd, Shepherd, Shepherd,' and a picture of a field with a building in it flashed across my mind.

I couldn't make any sense of it at all. I knew instinctively the picture was linked to the words and the words to the murder case, but what did it mean? The building in the field bothered me. It was a strange setting for a building which didn't look like a farm building or a house. I didn't know what to make of it.

That evening I mentioned it to Terry. He was an ambulance driver now, and friendly with the police. I thought he might have heard something about the case which would explain this peculiar message; but he was no wiser than I was. All he could do was promise to mention it to one of his police friends, on the off chance it would help.

At the time the police were investigating the most unlikely clues, and in due course they checked mine. Probably to their great surprise, they found a small factory which made agricultural machinery, situated in a field not far from the place where the body was found. The factory was called Shepherds.

They were impressed enough to send Detective Sergeant Woods running for a sitting. At first it didn't go well. I had difficulty getting through to the girl and when I did, she didn't seem able to help us much. 'Brian, Brian, Brian,' she kept repeating and 'bus, bus, bus.'

'Well my name's Brian,' said Det. Sergeant Woods, 'and she was waiting at the bus stop.'

It seemed a reasonable explanation, but as we realized later, it threw us off the scent. Then she said that the man sometimes wore a fawn uniform and sometimes a navy blue one. Well there was an army camp not far away, where the soldiers wore khaki uniforms and blue dress uniforms. The murderer could well be a soldier. The police went off to investigate.

A few days later I was on my way to a meeting, when for some reason I found myself on the wrong train. I ended up at Kirkham where the girl had been murdered. Cross with myself for being so stupid, I walked grumpily into the waiting room to wait for the next train back – and came face to face with a huge head and shoulders poster of the dead girl. It was like bumping into her walking down the street. Shocked, I stared into the young carefree eyes and as I stood there she came to me again. 'My shoes are by the railway line,' I heard her say distinctly.

There wasn't time to do anything about it that night, but the next day I rang the police. They'd just found the shoes – by the railway line as the girl had told me. Det. Sergeant Woods came back for another sitting.

This time it was much more successful. The girl started taking me through what had happened to her and I could almost feel it myself. She'd been waiting at the bus stop she said, and a man had offered her a lift to church in his van. The police were looking for a white Mini, but she insisted that was wrong, it was a larger vehicle, a van either green or blue, and she'd been wrapped in a blanket in the back, before being dumped in the countryside.

Step by step she went through what the man had done to her, and I felt ill. I was the only one, apart from the police, who knew the full extent of her dreadful injuries. They were never made public.

During the sitting I glanced down at my hands and was surprised to see they looked dark blue to me, and although I wasn't holding anything, I could feel the sensation of coins pressed into my palms.

'That's funny,' I said to Brian Woods, 'my hands are blue and I'm holding money. I can't understand it.'

'I can,' he said. 'She was wearing navy blue gloves and left lying in the rain. The dye ran and stained her skin. She was also holding her bus fare. Ask her if this man's married.'

Back came the answer that he was, with two children.

Some time later they caught the man. Married with two children, he was in the process of repainting his green van when they arrested him. His name was Brian Ball and he was a bus driver – wearing a beige uniform in the summer and a dark blue one in the winter.

That experience taught me how difficult it is to solve crimes effectively through mediumship. As Ramonov had said, 'It's effort all the time.' You rarely get the problem solved for you. Instead you get fragments of clues and it's up to you what you do with them. In the case of murderer Brian Ball, we were given his christian name and strong clues to his occupation with the word 'bus' repeated many times and the fact that he wore a uniform in his job and even the colour of the uniform; but our initial wrong interpretation of those facts sent us searching in the wrong direction. All too often you don't understand the significance of the clues the spirit world gives you until after the case has been solved. This seems to indicate that the spirit world is more concerned with proving to us its existence, than interfering with our lives down here.

I have had some spectacular successes however, the best being another murder case.

It started early in the morning when Terry, already on duty, drove into the local children's hospital and found police gathered round. He asked what was going on and was told that three children had been found murdered in the children's ward of Blackpool's Victoria Hospital a few miles away. The police were trying to prevent the maniac striking again.

Certain the police would call on me to see if I could help again, Terry raced home to get me out of bed. Sure enough, at quarter to nine a detective was knocking on the door. Brian Woods had flu and this young man had been sent in his place. He was obviously highly sceptical and his questions were tongue in cheek, but I said I'd do my best.

The children were too young to communicate themselves, so this time Ramonov helped. I began getting a series of words and pictures. First I heard the names of the children and the name of a staff nurse who'd also been stabbed – I didn't even know anyone else was involved. Then I saw a mental picture of sand – sand everywhere and heard a name that sounded like Akmed and more sand.

The sand was very puzzling. Then I remembered that the murders had taken place in Blackpool and thought perhaps the knife had been thrown away on the beach.

'It's not a knife,' said Ramonov suddenly, 'it's a surgical instrument of some kind.'

Instantly it clicked into place. 'Don't look outside, it's somebody in the hospital,' I told the detective. Immediately, as if to confirm I was right, a picture of a car parked in the hospital grounds flashed into my mind.

'He's there now,' I said, 'his car's at the hospital.' I described in detail the car and its location, while the detective scribbled rapidly in his notebook.

Then in my mind, I was walking into the hospital, through swing doors down corridors, but as neither I nor the detective had been to the Blackpool Victoria before, we didn't know where I was being led.

I called Terry. 'You know the Victoria a bit don't you Terry? Where am I going?' I closed my eyes and the walk unfolded again.

'There's a staircase on my right and I can see a notice written up. I'm turning right, and going through some swing doors ...'

'Sounds like you're going to the operating theatre,' said Terry.

In a flash I knew. 'That's where he is,' I cried excitedly, 'he's there now. You'll get him in the operating theatre!'

The detective, quite caught up in the atmosphere, had forgotten he didn't believe in such nonsense. 'Right!' he said leaping up. 'We'll check it out.'

At 10.30 the same morning the CID superintendent rang. 'We've got him Mrs Stokes. He was a surgeon – calmly performing an eye operation when we arrived.'

It turned out his name was Ahmed not Akmed and he was an Arab – a Jordanian – so much for the sand!

Some time after this I received a phone call from an actress named Pat. She was in great distress because her engagement ring and a ring belonging to her late mother had disappeared. She'd called the police, but uncertain whether it was a crime or just carelessness, she'd decided to ask for a medium's help as well. She explained that after a show, she took off her rings and left them on the sideboard while she cooked supper. They seemed to have vanished from the sideboard.

I tuned in immediately and a picture of her sideboard sprang into my mind. Next to the sideboard I could see a big bag full of what looked like pink knitting. Then I heard a girl's name. Teresa.

'Teresa,' I said out loud. 'It's a girl called Teresa.'

'Oh dear,' said Pat. 'She's a relative. She's been staying with me.'

'Well I'm afraid that's where your rings have gone. Out with Teresa in her bag of pink knitting. She's taken them to Newark I think, or Nottingham, the name's not very clear.'

That was where the girl lived, so Pat told the police she thought it was a relative and she'd try to sort it out herself. She and her husband visited Teresa, but the girl swore she'd never touched the rings. She was so convincing Pat came back perplexed.

'I'm sorry Pat it is her,' I insisted later when the actress telephoned. 'I've been talking to your mother. She says the rings definitely went out in the knitting bag and now they've been handed over to Teresa's friend. I can see her in my mind. She's very young with jeans and long dark hair.'

Pat, unable to tackle Teresa further, turned it over to

the police. A detective went down to talk to the girl, but this time told her a medium had been called in and went on to describe in detail everything I'd said. It was too much for Teresa. She broke down completely. 'All right, all right. Yes I did take them,' she sobbed, 'but if you promise not tell mummy and daddy I can get them back.'

A meeting was arranged and, true to her word, Teresa turned up with the rings and the friend she'd given them to. The friend had jeans and long dark hair and was very young, just as I'd described – but 'she' was a boy!

I don't know whether I was getting a reputation for finding lost objects; but shortly afterwards I had a phone call from another distressed woman. Her husband had recently died and as she sorted through his belongings she realized his valuable gold cigarette case was missing. Could I possibly visit her at home to help find it?

I agreed. I'd never set eyes on the woman or her house before; but within minutes of arriving I felt an irresistible urge to go upstairs. 'I hope you don't mind,' I said, 'but I think your husband wants us to look upstairs.'

As if I was being pulled along by an invisible thread I hurried upstairs, across the landing and found myself in a strange bedroom. The woman caught up with me just as I was dragged off again. I was taken straight to the wardrobe, my hand opened the door without hesitation and a dress suit, tucked right at the back practically jumped into my arms. In its pocket was the cigarette case.

I was even asked once to find a missing wife. I was doing a private sitting in Manchester when my sitter asked if I'd be able to help a neighbour of hers. He was a very wealthy man, with a beautiful house and everything that money could buy; but now he was practically suicidal because his wife had left him. One day he came home and she was gone. He had no idea where she was.

I said I couldn't promise I'd get anything, but if this man would like to speak to me I'd do my best. My sitter phoned him but he was too shy to come. Instead he asked if he could put something of his wife's through the letterbox for me to work with.

A few minutes later an expensive nightdress slipped

silkily onto the mat. I held it in my hands and concentrated and soon I heard the wife's real name, as well as the pet name her husband and friends knew her by. She'd gone away with a man and I got his name and the colour and number of his car.

My original sitter phoned through this information and the husband was impressed enough to ask for an individual sitting alone with me. After that we became friends and I said he could phone me if ever he felt suicidal. I hadn't realized however, just how depressed he was. I didn't regret my promise, but I hadn't been prepared for continual phone calls often late at night. Sometimes at 1.30 in the morning he begged me to see him. 'If I can't come and talk to you I'll go on the bottle,' he'd threaten. So I'd slide wearily out of bed, get dressed and sit up talking to him and making tea all night.

One evening he was on the phone when I heard Ramonov speaking. 'I'm going to ring off now,' I cut in abruptly. 'Your wife's waiting to ring you.'

'That'll be the day,' he said bitterly.

'I'm telling you she is,' I insisted and put the phone down.

Twenty minutes later my phone was ringing again. I picked it up, and instantly a jubilant voice sang in my ear.

'You were right. It was her! She rang me!'

And I heard myself reply. 'Yes and she'll come back on September 16th and not before; so you may as well content yourself till then.'

Even her husband found that hard to believe. It seemed most unlikely that his wife would ever return, but the spirit world was usually right. Over the weeks several more phone calls were exchanged. Eventually the wife agreed to meet her husband to discuss their problems, and the date they settled on just happened to be September 16th.

'You'd better get the cleaning lady in to tidy everything,' I told the husband when he phoned to let me know he was meeting his wife in Blackpool. 'She'll be coming home with you tonight.'

'Oh come on Doris,' he said, 'I can't believe that.'

But of course she did.

Chapter 12

Over the years another interesting development of my work began to build up – the job of tracking down 'troublesome' ghosts! People either laugh about 'haunted' houses if they don't live in them, or are terrified of them if they do, but in my experience 'hauntings' aren't usually sinister.

One of my first cases occurred in Lancaster. I received a frantic call very early in the morning from a panic-stricken girl, who said she'd been driven out of her flat by a ghost and could I come over immediately. She sounded so frightened, John and I got out the car at once.

When we arrived we found two or three policemen standing sheepishly on the pavement with a white-faced girl, huddled in a coat and a blanket. None of them had been prepared to wait in the flat, but they led us upstairs to show us where it was. Crowded on the landing opposite the front door, we could hear muffled thuds from within though there was no one else at home.

'I'm not going in there,' said one of the policemen and the rest hung back silently. They weren't either.

I shrugged and opened the door. It was chaos inside. Ornaments, cushions, lamps, fruit from the fruit bowl, everything portable was hurling around the room as if deliberately thrown by furious and invisible hands. I stepped over the threshold and instantly a book picked itself up from the shelf, smashed across the room and hit me hard on the mouth.

I was too angry to be frightened. 'Bloody well cut that out!' I shouted and, to my surprise, everything simply dropped to the floor and a watchful silence settled over the flat.

'All right,' I called to the girl. 'You can come in now.' She slipped fearfully inside the door and stared at the debris with enormous eyes. 'Tell me what happens,' I asked. 'Does it always start in here?'

She said no. Apparently her husband, a baker, left for work very early in the morning and it started after he'd gone. The blankets would be ripped off her in bed and, when she moved out of the bedroom to lie on the sitting room sofa instead, the trouble followed. Today was the worst it had been and she was too frightened to stay there any longer.

'Well I think we'd better start in the bedroom,' I said.

What a sorry state it was in. The bedclothes lay in a heap on the floor. There were containers of holy water everywhere, crucifixes nailed to the walls, garlic strewn about, everything the girl could think of to protect herself from this 'evil'.

I sat down and she perched gingerly on the edge of the bed while I tried to tune in. Instantly an angry woman burst into my consciousness. She was very anxious to communicate and the whole tragic story poured out.

She said she was the girl's grandmother. Several years ago the girl had had an illegitmate baby. She had kept the child and lived with her gran in the top flat of a three storey terraced house. She was still very young and liked to enjoy herself in the evenings, so the grandmother used to baby-sit. But very late one night, when she was still out, the baby started to cry and the sleepy grandmother got up to comfort it. In the darkness she kicked over a paraffin stove and the old woman and baby both died in the resulting fire.

The grandmother paused and I quickly explained what she'd been telling me. The girl turned even paler. 'I don't know what you're talking about,' she said, 'I've never had any baby.'

The grandmother exploded again. This was what she was angry about. Since the tragedy the girl had shut the event out of her mind. She told no-one about the baby, not even the man she later married and now she herself almost believed she'd never had a child.

'That's why your grandmother's doing this. She's trying to attract your attention,' I told her. 'She's determined you shouldn't deny your child.'

'But I never had child,' she insisted.

So I found out the grandmother's name and the baby's name which was Denise I think. 'Look love,' I said at last, 'you don't have to tell your husband, it's entirely up to you, but for goodness sake don't deny your child in your own heart. If you talk to her, and talk to your gran, out loud or in your head, then these things will stop.'

She remained unconvinced and I could do no more. Shortly afterwards I heard she'd moved. I think she'd either refused to take my advice and the phenomena had driven her away, or she was afraid I might one day meet her husband and tell him – which of course I'd never have done.

The next case I was called to was a woman with a young son, who said her flat was haunted. She had a part time job while the boy was at school, and she asked us to meet her at the flat as soon as she finished work. We all arrived at the same time and walked in together.

The place looked quiet and uneventful. The lounge was neat and tidy, the way she'd left it that morning.

'Oh good,' she said looking round, 'it's all right. Please sit down. I'll just go and wash my hands then I'll tell you all about it.'

She left the room and John and I sat on the settee to wait. It was a bright modern home, in a pleasant residential area – not at all the spooky setting you see in film hauntings. Children were playing in the street outside and sunshine streamed through the window.

'What a nice place,' I was saying to John when suddenly there was a piercing scream.

I leapt up, flew to the door where the woman had gone, raced down the corridor, John close behind me, and found her sobbing outside the bathroom. 'Look!' she gasped. 'Just look in there!'

The radiator had been wrenched from the wall and lay on its side on the carpet, face cloths, towels and the bath mat were strewn all over the place, soap smeared the mirrors. It looked like the work of vandals.

The woman was very upset and I made her a cup of tea,
while John checked the building for signs of a forced entry
– in case someone had broken in. He found nothing. The
outer doors were still locked and undamaged. The
windows were not only intact, but also had thick sheets of
polythene tacked over them, a do-it-yourself form of
double glazing and draught excluder. This too was
untampered with. Obviously this was no earthly untruder.

We went back to the lounge for a sitting, and after a
minute or two I was talking to a man who said he used to
live in the flat. He deeply resented the fact that these
people had moved into 'his house'. He kept talking about
'his' carpets and 'his' curtains.

'Well yes, I bought them when I moved in,' the woman
told me. 'I did pay for them.'

Then he kept calling for his daughter Edith. He was
very concerned about her and couldn't rest until
something had been sorted out – something to do with a
holiday. I couldn't quite make out what.

'Do you know his daughter Edith?' I asked the woman.
She said she did. 'Well I think we'd better talk to her. She
seems to be the reason for all this.'

A few days later Edith rang me. It turned out that she
and her family were due to go on holiday when her father
was very ill. She didn't want to go, but her father
absolutely insisted she did, and while she was away he
died. She felt so guilty about it, she'd not been able to go
on holiday since.

This was the reason for the haunting. Her father was
desperately trying to get through to her that he was all
right and it didn't matter that she wasn't with him when he
died. He wanted her to go on having holidays and enjoy
her life. Once I'd explained this to Edith the haunting
stopped.

I had a similar case in London. I was called to a very
large house where a young couple lived with their baby
son. They complained that objects were continually being
moved. They didn't see them go, but they'd put a knife
down in the kitchen for instance and find it minutes later

in the bathroom. The wife also felt a strong presence in the house. Often she'd spin round, convinced someone was standing behind her, but there was no-one there. This had been happening for several months, and by now she was a nervous wreck.

I was thinking about these strange events as I got ready to visit the couple, and as I pulled a comb through my hair I heard a voice say, 'It's in George's room'. It seemed likely this odd statement was connected with the haunting, so I kept it in my mind.

When we arrived the wife made us a cup of tea while we waited for her husband to come home from work, and we sat watching the baby playing in his playpen by the fire.

'Have you got a George here?' I asked.

'No,' said the wife in surprise, 'but we did have. At one time we let rooms to students and there was a boy called George. Why?'

I explained about being told 'It's in George's room'.

'Oh that's the baby's room now,' said the wife and went on to remark that she had a terrible time with her son at night. He was so restless she had to keep getting up to him and bringing him into her bedroom. He wouldn't settle in his own room.

Just then the husband arrived and we were ready to start. First of all I wanted to find the presence. Ramonov had taught me how to do it. You walk through the rooms, backwards and forwards and if there is anything there, you'll come to a place which feels like cold bathwater. As you stand in this spot, an icy sensation creeps up from your feet over your whole body. I never say anything to the others. I just ask them to walk behind me, putting their feet exactly where I put mine and they feel it too.

We checked the whole house, ending up in the baby's room. I felt nothing at all until I approached the cot and suddenly stepped into a patch of chill, freezing air. The wife had been right. There was a presence here.

I called the others and got them to stand in the same spot. 'Oh – it's cold – is there a draught in here?' the wife asked her husband.

'No,' I said, 'we've found your "ghost". We'd better do the

sitting now.'

We trooped back to the sitting room. I tuned in and was soon speaking to the husband's father. Apparently he'd been very much looking forward to the birth of his son's child, as had the whole family, but he'd passed over just before the baby was born. Ever since, throughout the family no-one would mention the little boy without adding, 'Oh, if only his grandad had lived to see him.' Now he was trying very hard to let them know that he *had* seen his grandson and was delighted with him.

'Oh,' said the wife when I explained, 'well I don't mind that. He can come as often as he likes.'

Sometimes hauntings occur when the deceased objects so strongly to the behaviour of his relatives, he can't resist coming back to complain. I remember visiting a distraught widow who was plagued by bangs and crashes in the house and objects moving. Her husband had obviously been a domineering person and still was. During the sitting he admitted being responsible for the disturbances and told his wife: 'Get my bloody photograph out of the sideboard drawer Missus. I belong here.'

And when the photograph was restored to what he considered its rightful place – peace reigned!

I think the most unpleasant 'haunted' house I visited, was in Baker St, London. We were asked to the upstairs flat by two girls, one Italian and one Spanish. They said they were kept awake at night by unexplained noises, the bedclothes were ripped off them in bed and the little daughter of one of them was terrified of being in the house at all.

I could understand why. The minute we walked through the door a shudder went through me. The air felt heavy and oppressive, and as we walked up the stairs I noticed they were painted black. There were no seats in the sitting room, just a sheet spread on the floor, and hideous papier mache masks leered down from the walls.

I felt more and more uneasy. I walked into the bathroom, a long, narrow room, painted dark brown and suddenly the walls seemed to close in, the ceiling crushed down and I had an overwhelming sensation of being shut in a coffin. I could feel a band tightening round my neck and this terrible dark, dark coffin squeezing closer and closer. Gasping for breath, I rushed for the door and threw myself out into the hall.

I was badly shaken. I stood there panting and struggling to compose myself for several minutes, until I was able to rejoin the girls. There was something weird about this house and I didn't like it at all.

Much of the sitting was in Italian and Spanish. When I'm working for overseas people I get family names, places and odd phrases in their native language; but the main body of the message is in English because it's difficult to repeat large chunks of a language you don't understand, and you're certain to make a mistake.

The main message to the girls seemed to be that their relatives wanted them to leave the house but, between communications, other impressions kept crowding in.

Someone had hanged himself in the bathroom, a voice told me. I kept hearing the name Alistair and black, black, black, repeated over and over again.

'There's an impression on this house that's bad,' I said attempting to sort out the jumble. 'Everything's black and I keep getting the name Alistair.'

There was much excited whispering between the girls at this and eventually they told me that the woman downstairs who owned the place was Alistair Crowley's sister – the man who called himself The King of the Witches.

Whether witchcraft had been practised in the flat and that accounted for the black staircase I don't know – but John and I were certainly glad to get out of the place.

Sometimes people don't even realize they share their home with unseen tenants. One evening I was invited to a beautiful old country house, called Beaumont Manor Cote, which was owned by Lesley and Ada Pearce. They were interested in my work and asked if I could give a demonstration for a group of influential friends.

I didn't mind at all and so, on the date we agreed, I walked up a long, long drive to an imposing mansion.

It was one of the loveliest places I'd ever seen. Inside, a

wide oak staircase wound gracefully to the first floor, there was rich red carpet deep as velvet and a mixture of antiques and reproduction furniture.

Awed, I followed Mrs Pearce into the drawing room which was large and elegant and dominated by a gleaming grand piano. Several people stood up and I was introduced to an authoress, a diamond merchant, a psychologist and one or two others. A chair was pulled out for me and we all sat down.

There was an awkward pause. I was waiting for them to ask me to start work and though I didn't realize it at the time, they were waiting for me to start.

'Would you like to see the rest of the house Mrs Stokes?' Ada Pearce asked suddenly, realizing there must be some difficulty.

And because I was nervous and anxious to visit the bathroom, I said yes.

She led me back through the hall and up the lovely staircase. On the bend I met an elderly lady walking down.

'Good evening,' I said politely.

She stopped and smiled radiantly at me. 'Good evening. Do you like this house?'

'Yes it's very beautiful what I've seen of it so far,' I replied and turned to Ada to add something about the marvellous piano in the drawing room, when to my surprise I saw that she'd passed behind me on the wide step and was racing back down again.

Strange, I thought. I'd been under the impression she was going to show me round, but as I had to go to the bathroom I went on up by myself, and found it quite easily.

Coming down again a few moments later I found the old lady was waiting for me.

'I thought you might like to see my nursery,' she said.

'Oh yes, I'd love to.' I enjoyed the excuse to meet children. Obviously Ada was anxious to attend to her guests, and had asked her mother or grandmother or whoever this lady was to show me round instead.

We walked along several thickly carpeted corridors and finally my guide threw open a panelled door and stood back to let me walk in. I stopped in surprise. There were no cots or little beds. All the room contained were floor to ceiling book shelves, and a large period desk. It was a study.

'This is my nursery,' said the old lady proudly.

I stared at her. Until then I'd only looked properly at her face, but now I examined her closely. Her skirt reached right down to the floor and her lace edged blouse with its little collar was not just old fashioned as I'd first thought – it was another century. She was a spirit person.

'Do you stay in the house?' I asked gently.

'Oh no,' she said, 'but I often return because I had some of my happiest days here. My name is Anne Worthington.'

I introduced myself and then, realizing she wasn't my appointed guide and that the Pearces could have no idea where I was, I explained I'd better go back to the drawing room.

There was dead silence when I walked in. Ada was looking white and strained and the others stared at me curiously. I glanced anxiously from face to face, wondering if I'd offended them by being away so long.

'Ada was a bit scared Doris,' said Les at last, 'you saw somebody.'

'Yes I did,' I admitted, 'she used to live here she told me. She must have been a nanny or something, because she showed me what was once her nursery. Her name was Anne Worthington.'

'*Anne Worthington!*'

'Yes I'm sure that's what she said.'

Abruptly Les walked into the hall, opened a big old chest and came back with a faded piece of cloth. He handed it to me.

It was a sampler and embroidered in tiny stitches across the front were the words 'ANNE WORTHINGTON 1776'.

They didn't need much convincing that I was genuine after that, and my sitting went well.

Les and Ada invited me back several times. On one visit Les said,' I'd like you to look at this old chair Doris and see if you can get anything from it.'

He brought over a plain wooden chair with just a single bar backrest, and placed it in front of me. The wood was dark and battered. It was obviously old, but apart from that it looked a pretty ordinary chair to me.

'I don't really do this psychometry lark Les,' I said doubtfully, 'but I'll have a go if you like.'

I put my hands lightly on the chair, and instantly the room swung sideways and I whirled into a peculiar half trance. Part of me was still in the room with Les and Ada and the other part was in a rowing boat on the water.

The other men in the boat were wearing striped jerseys and shiny black hats with ribbons down the back. All around us the water was churned by explosions, smoke stung my eyes and the air smelled of gunpowder.

'I think this chair was made by someone from a ship,' I said above the noise and I gave them a few names which meant nothing. Then a loud voice said in my ear.

'I'm a chippy and I made that chair for the Captain's cabin. 'Then he kept repeating, 'It shouldn't have happened. I was forced to go. I was 19 years old.'

And suddenly everything swung again and I only had one eye. 'I'm blind in one eye,' I told Les and Ada, and apparently tucked one arm into my cardigan. 'My father was a vicar you know.'

Then the noise of the battle died away, the boat and the sea faded and I was back in Les and Ada's drawing room, my fingers still resting on the rough wooden chair.

Les was very excited. Apparently his chair was one of only three known to be in existence. It was made in Hull around 1800 by an apprentice cabinet maker. He was pressed into the navy before he finished the last one and never returned.

It also turned out that Nelson who had only one eye and one good arm in the end was the son of a vicar. Whether the young man had served under Nelson we never found out, but all in all I wasn't too disappointed with my rare attempt at psychometry.

Chapter 13

During our last days in Lancaster, John and I and even Terry were plagued by ill health. John was affected first.

He was still nursing at the Royal Albert Hospital. He enjoyed it very much, but it was hard, often heavy work and since his injuries he'd never been strong. Over the weeks I noticed he was losing weight and he looked exhausted.

'I'm just a bit tired,' he said when I mentioned it and I suppose at first I put it down to overwork and the fact that he wasn't getting any younger. I asked him to ease up a bit and I tried heaping his plate with food and suggesting early nights, but it made no difference. His appetite disappeared and he looked worse than ever.

'I'm all right, don't fuss,' he said when I asked him to see the doctor. 'I've had a hard day.' But he looked frail and ill, and according to that explanation every day was a hard day.

I kept silent a little longer, but then one evening he came home and I was shocked by his appearance. His face was like glass. The skin stretched taut over his cheekbones, almost transparent. A picture of my father in hospital just before he died leapt without warning into my mind, and I was struck by the similarity in those two faces.

'John,' I said. 'You *must* go to the doctor. If you won't go to him, I'll get him to call here. 'By this time he felt so bad he went without protest.

Our doctor was away on holiday and the locum diagnosed exhaustion. He told John to rest at home for a week and call back.

Relaxation didn't help. John got worse instead of better. His skin turned an unhealthy yellow colour and his strength evaporated. He could hardly summon the energy to get out of bed.

At the end of the week he reported to the locum again, and when he came home he went straight to the wardrobe and took his uniform out.

'What on earth are you doing John?' I asked. He was so weak he was almost in a daze.

'The doctor says I've to go back to work.'

I couldn't believe it. 'Over my dead body,' I said. 'You're ill, any fool can see that.'

I stormed to the phone and rang the locum. 'You've just seen my husband and sent him back to work,' I said.

'Yes,' he admitted.

'But he's so weak he can hardly put one leg before the other.'

'Well,' he said, 'I'm the doctor.'

I was furious. 'Just answer one question then doctor. Do you really think he's fit enough to be on a ward with mental patients, where at some point during the day he's going to be entirely alone?'

He hummed and haahed and finally asked John to come back to the surgery the next day – Tuesday.

This time I went with him. Overnight his condition had deteriorated so fast his face was almost brown, I knew there was something seriously wrong. So did the locum. 'Oh my goodness! I'm afraid you'll have to go into hospital Mr Stokes,' he said as John walked in. He gave him a thorough examination. Afterwards, he arranged for John to be admitted for tests on Thursday, and asked me to call at the surgery the next day to collect a letter for the hospital.

I was still too unsteady to drive much from my own illness: so Arthur, the president of our church gave me a lift down to the surgery the next day. Naturally I was worried about John, but no-one had given us a diagnosis of his illness, so I was surprised when I bumped into our old doctor back from his holiday and he put his arm round my shoulder.

'I'm so sorry,' he said, giving me a little squeeze, before continuing down the corridor.

What did he mean? Puzzled and uneasy I went on into the locum's office. 'Sit down Mrs Stokes,' he said. He seemed uncomfortable. He shuffled papers on his desk, fiddled with a pen and didn't quite meet my eyes. 'I'm afraid I've got some bad news for you,' he said at last. 'Your husband's dying. I found a large lump in his stomach. It's almost certainly cancer and in an advanced stage. I'd say he's got 10 days at the most. He'll be better off in hospital.'

I think he said more but I don't remember it. I don't think I spoke a word. I felt completely numb. Surely this wasn't really happening. I must be dreaming it all. I'd wake up in a minute. I walked out of the surgery clutching the letter tightly in my hand.

'What did he say Doris?' asked Arthur as I climbed silently into the car. 'He said John's going to die,' I replied slowly, 'he's got cancer of the stomach and he's only got about a fortnight.'

Arthur was shocked. 'Doris I can't believe it. Surely it's not definite?'

'It seems pretty definite,' I said.

We drove silently home. 'If there's anything I can do, anywhere you want driving, just let me know,' said Arthur as he dropped me off. 'I'll come at once.'

He was being very kind but I couldn't take it in. I wandered inside and found John asleep on the settee. I kept looking at his thin, wasted face and thinking it can't be possible. It was so unreal.

To make matters worse, Terry was already in the same hospital for a minor operation on his foot. How could I break the news to him?'

I stumbled blindly round the house, always coming back in disbelief to John's still body on the settee. Then I stopped, as the first practical idea struck me with a jolt. 'What am I doing, I must ring Harry Edwards.' After all the years of friendship with the famous healer, why hadn't I thought of him to start with?

Checking that John was still soundly sleeping, I dialled Harry's Surrey number. 'Oh Harry,' I said quietly when he answered, 'I am in trouble.'

'What's the matter dear?'

I lowered my voice further, 'I've got to take John into hospital tomorrow,' I said, 'they say he's only got 10 days to live. He's got cancer of the stomach and there's nothing they can do.'

'Now don't panic Doris,' Harry said calmly. 'We'll have a try shall we. Lock the door, take the phone off the hook and sit and hold his hand. You must direct all your power into him and I'll go into my sanctuary at the same time and concentrate from here.'

We were 300 miles apart but I knew if anyone could help, Harry could. I did exactly as he told me. I locked the door, lifted the receiver from its cradle and sat beside John, his thin hand in mine. He didn't even stir. 'If I've got anything that can be used, let it come now and be used.' I prayed silently.

Out of the corner of my eye I noticed a faint blue light creeping into the room. I concentrated harder, willing every ounce of psychic energy I possessed into John. The light was pouring into the room now, deep blue, thicker and thicker until everything was hidden in a beautiful fog. I couldn't see the furniture or any of my surroundings, only the vague outline of John swam in the blue haze in front of me.

I didn't move, I hardly breathed, my whole body contracted into a tight ball of concentration and became one with the blue blur.

I was almost in a trance. Time stopped, but gradually I became conscious of the light diminishing. The colour faded and bit by bit the chairs, the table, the wallpaper came back into focus. I hung onto John's hand until the light had completely disappeared. Then I phoned Harry and, as I picked up the receiver, I noticed over an hour had passed since my last call.

'Yes, I've just this minute come out of the sanctuary,' said Harry. 'We'll have to wait now and pray to God that we've done a bit of good.'

It seemed impossible to wait and do nothing, but I knew Harry was right. I walked restlessly into the kitchen and put the kettle on, more for something to do than because I was thirsty and, as I turned off the tap, I heard John stir.

'I'm just making a cup of tea love,' I called.

'I'll have to go up to the bathroom first,' he said faintly.

'Don't climb those stairs,' I begged, 'you'll wear yourself out, I'll fetch a pail.' He was so weak I couldn't bear him to waste the little energy he had, but of course he protested about the bucket.

'For goodness sake John,' I said, 'I've been a nurse for seven and a half years, d'you think a little thing like that's going to bother me? Don't be silly.' He agreed in the end. Though he wouldn't admit it, I don't think he could face the stairs.

I took the pail into the sitting room and afterwards I was amazed. Sweat was pouring off John and the bucket was three quarters full. I helped him back onto the settee and he fell into an exhausted sleep.

The next day I took him to the hospital and went to see the male sister on duty. 'Well I'm afraid it seems pretty definite,' he said sympathetically, 'but don't worry. We'll see he doesn't suffer.'

Back home again I rang a very good friend. Rosemary in Liverpool and asked if she could possibly come to stay with me for a few days. I was still shaky after my own illness and I couldn't bear to be alone in the house with my two men in hospital. She was wonderful. She packed her things and came on the next train.

On Friday I went to see John and then plodded to the other side of the hospital to see Terry. He was having his operation that day, and I'd decided not to tell him until it was over. Back and forth I went, from one to the other all day.

On Saturday I was all set to repeat the process; but when I got to Terry his foot was in plaster and he was crying.

'Is the pain very bad Terry?' I asked, distressed.

He shook his head. 'No. Sister's just told me about Dad. I've told them they can put me on a trolley and take me to see him.'

It was highly irregular of course, but he made so much fuss that, that night they pushed him from one side of the hospital to the other to see his father. It set the pattern.

Soon he was able to use a wheelchair, and every day he came over himself. We'd get John comfortable in the day room and stay with him till about 10 at night. I was glad that if this was his last illness, at least he had his family round him. It certainly seemed to help. It might have been my imagination, but I was sure his colour improved and his manner brightened.

The following Friday when John had been in hospital just over a week, the phone rang quite early in the morning. I was in the kitchen making toast for breakfast, so Rosemary answered it.

Minutes seemed to pass before I heard her speak, then she said, 'Oh sister, sister!' and it sounded as if she was crying. The butter knife nearly slipped from my hand. 'My God,' I thought, 'has John gone and I wasn't there?' I rushed to the phone and Roesmary said, 'Just a minute sister, here's his wife.'

Numbly I took the receiver. My heart was banging so hard it shook my whole body, and my mouth had gone so dry I could hardly speak. 'Yes?' I croaked with difficulty.

'Mrs Stokes,' said the metallic voice on the line, 'you can come and collect your husband.'

I couldn't grasp what she meant. 'Pardon?'

'We've done all the tests and that nasty old lump has gone, so you can come and collect him.'

'Now?' I gasped.

'This minute if you like,' she laughed.

I dropped the receiver and Rosemary and I hugged each other and cried for joy – then we raced round the house, gathering coats and car keys, and shot off to the hospital driving far too fast.

We found John in the consultant's office, where he was looking at his X-rays. 'D'you think my wife could have a look, she's an ex-nurse?' he asked the consultant. So the plates were held up for me. It was extraordinary. You could see the loop in the intestine where the lump had been – but now it was empty. The lump had vanished. It was a miracle. Thank God for Harry Edwards.

John came home and put on weight and within weeks it was impossible to tell he'd been ill at all. Terry too was soon out of hospital, and walking again on his bad foot.

You'd think we'd had enough ill health in the family to last us several years – but don't they say these things come in threes? Hardly had John and Terry become fit and well again, than I discovered a lump in my breast.

It's the thing every woman dreads, no matter what age, and although as a nurse I *knew*, probably better than most, I should see a doctor immediately, I didn't. I waited. Medical authorities often think women delay seeking professional advice in these circumstances through ignorance, but from my own experience I think it's more than that. The discovery is so horrifying, and it seems so ridiculous that you might be seriously ill when you feel perfectly healthy, that you keep hoping it's your imagination, that next time you check, the lump will be gone. It was three weeks before I would admit that I was deliberately putting it off, and forced myself to see the doctor.

I was sent straight into hospital for an immediate biopsy. That was on the Friday and the test results came through the following Tuesday. 'I'm sorry Mrs Stokes,' said the staff nurse who had to break the news, 'the surgeon's just rung. I'm afraid it's positive and a radical at that.'

It was like a physical blow. I couldn't speak. Nodding dumbly, I got up and hurried to the day room where I picked up my glasses and the newspapers I'd been reading.

'Are you all right Doris?' asked my new friends.

'Yes,' I said quickly, 'I'm just going to the bathroom.' I rushed away to lock myself in. Alone at last I just sat there with my glasses all crooked, tears rolling down my cheeks and the paper upside down on my lap.

After a while there was a knock at the door. The staff nurse had come looking for me again. 'What are you doing?' she called.

'What d'you think I'm doing?' I snuffled.

'Not what you're supposed to be doing in there,' she said. 'Come on, it's not as bad as all that you know. I've got some more news for you.

Reluctantly I wiped my eyes and unlocked the door, and

she told me the surgeon had phoned back. Realizing what torture the wait would be, he said he could do the operation on Thursday – earlier than originally planned – if I was prepared to transfer to Morecambe Hospital.

Naturally I agreed and, as soon as I'd composed myself, I rang John to break the news and then Harry Edwards. Harry was kind as ever. 'Well never mind Doris, we've come through worse than this haven't we? Ask John to let me know what time you go into the operating theatre, and I'll go into my sanctuary at the same time and stay there until your operation is over.'

I had a depressing two days to wait, but even here in hospital I had another psychic experience which was very reassuring.

I'd read many times in spiritualist books of the process of passing over; but I'd never actually seen it myself until that night. I was due to be transferred to Morecambe Hospital the next day and I'd been given a sleeping pill, but it hadn't worked. The dreadful operation was playing on my mind and I couldn't sleep.

I lay propped up on my pillows watching the doctors coming in and out to the old lady in the bed opposite. She was very ill. She was unconscious and there was an oxygen mask over her face. It was obvious she wouldn't last much longer.

Suddenly I heard a gentle voice talking to her. 'Hello lass, it's me, Henry. It won't be long now, don't be frightened.' He continued murmuring reassuring things.

One of the doctors came back and looked at her. 'Oh I think I can go to bed,' he said to the night nurse, 'she'll go through the night.'

'She won't you know,' I couldn't resist putting in.

The doctor frowned at me. 'Oh Mrs Stokes is a medium,' the nurse explained.

'Is she,' said the doctor walking over to me, 'and how d'you know she won't go through to the morning?'

'Her husband's already there talking to her,' I said, 'he says his name's Henry.'

'Well she's not answering is she?'

'She will do when it gets nearer the time. She'll be able to hear him now but not see him.'

Intrigued, the doctor pulled up a chair and sat by me, his feet across the foot of my bed. They brought him a mug of tea and we chatted for a while. Suddenly I glanced across and saw a wisp of mist, like smoke, coming from the crown of the old woman's head. 'It's starting to take place,' I said recognizing the signs from the books I'd read. 'Any minute now she'll see her husband.'

And at that very moment she brushed her hand across her face pushing off the mask and said, 'Oh 'enery. That you Henry?'

'Oh bloody hell,' said the doctor.

As I watched I saw the spiritual body, which is exactly the same as the physical body, even appearing in the same clothes, but lying face down, hovering above the woman. She was chattering away to Henry.

'She's delirious,' said the doctor, but he was shaken.

The spiritual body rose a little higher and I could see it was attached to the physical body by a silver cord, like an umbilical cord. 'I should think it'll be about another twenty minutes,' I told the doctor. Just then the woman stopped talking and settled back, very still. The doctor hurried over and felt her pulse. 'Well it's faint, but she's still alive.'

He must have been convinced by now that she wouldn't last the night, because he sat beside her holding her wrist. The minutes ticked by. After a while the spiritual body rose till the cord was stretched to its fullest extent, then slowly the spiritual body tilted and the cord broke.

'Now she's gone,' I said.

And the doctor, his fingers on her pulse said, 'My God, she has.'

As the cord parted the spiritual body came upright and there was a look of great happiness on her face. A hand came down, that's all I could see, just a hand but I know it was Henry's and the old woman took it joyfully.

'Now look at her face,' I told the doctor and it was incredible. All the pain and suffering had vanished from that tired old physical body and there was a smile on the face. The doctor got out his stethoscope and listened to her chest; but of course it was no use.

When I looked up again, the woman and Henry had gone.

'Well I'm blowed,' said the doctor, 'you were right. You must tell me how you do that sometime,' and he hurried away to make arrangements for the body.

The next day I was transferred to Morecambe Hospital where I had my operation. I was very ill afterwards, but thanks, I'm convinced, to Harry Edwards as well as the surgeon, I made a remarkable recovery. I didn't even need radiation treatment.

The extraordinary thing was I had another 'passing over' experience in Morecambe Hospital, the day after my operation. I didn't realize it because I hadn't yet been out of bed, but I was in an 'L' shaped ward. From where I was I couldn't see that the ward turned a corner, let alone what was round the other side.

Anyway it was visiting time, and all the patients, even those who could get up, were confined to bed until the visitors had gone. John had brought me some flowers and we were admiring them together, when over the top of the blooms I saw a little old lady in a nightdress walk right down the middle of the ward. I'd never seen her before, and she seemed to have come round the corner at the top of the ward. 'You'll cop it if sister catches you out of bed,' I was thinking, when suddenly a radiant smile came over her face as if she'd just seen someone she knew, she threw out her arms and disappeared.

'John,' I said, 'someone's just passed away round there.'

'Where love?' he asked. All the beds we could see were filled with very live patients.

'Round the corner I think,' I said. 'Are there any more beds round there?'

He didn't know and I thought I'd better not create a disturbance during visiting time; but when the visitors had gone I stopped the nurse who was bringing the tea trolley round.

'Are there any beds round there nurse?' I asked.

'Yes, why?'

'Somebody's passed away round there,' I said.

She eyed me suspiciously. 'You haven't been out of bed

have you?'

I looked ruefully down at all my tubes and bottles. 'Chance would be a fine thing.'

She gave me a funny look, left the trolley and went round the corner. A few seconds later she came back almost running, staring at me as if my hair had turned green, as she passed. She went into the sister's office and after a couple of minutes they both came out together. Both of them eyed me warily as they clattered round the corner. Soon the doctor came, heading in the same direction and the sister came back. She paused at the foot of my bed.

'How did you know?' she asked.

'Well I saw her,' I explained truthfully and went on to describe the old lady, including the style and colour of her nightdress.

The sister didn't care for me at all after that. Apparently they hadn't expected the old lady to die. She'd been on holiday when she was taken ill so she didn't have any visitors that afternoon, and the other people in that part of the ward had assumed she was asleep.

The funny thing was, though the sister didn't approve, the other nurses were delighted with my unexpected gift. When they'd bedded down the other patients at night they used to take me into the kitchen, make me a big pot of tea and get me to do sittings for them. I wasn't very strong, so when I'd had enough, I took my sleeping pill and they guided me dozily back to bed. In the end these night sittings were so popular I even had an engagement book!

A masectomy is more of a psychological blow than a physical one, as I found out when I went home from hospital. Physically I was recovering well, but I remained depressed. I felt like a freak and for months afterwards I undressed in the dark.

I didn't think it would affect me. I ought to have gone down on my knees and thanked God that I was cleared of cancer, that I was one of the lucky ones. Instead I moped and felt sorry for myself.

Then I went out and took my first service. I was absolutely exhausted afterwards, and for the first time I didn't stop to think as I undressed. I forgot to turn off the light and, as my clothes fell to the floor, I saw myself in the mirror. Suddenly from nowhere, a song I used to sing as a child came into my mind. To the tune of 'After the Ball is Over' we parodied: 'Old Peg puts her false leg in the corner, hangs up her hair on the wall and then what's left goes to bye byes, after the ball ...' and I laughed and laughed until tears streamed down my face and it was half funny and half sad. But that was the turning point. I learned to accept it, talk about it and even – hardest of all – to laugh about it.

Chapter 14

In 19 … we moved to London and my work snowballed as never before. Life became extraordinary.

As with most important events over the years, it was quite unplanned. John had been advised to give up work. He had heart trouble now and the doctor thought he should retire. He said that considering John's war injuries, it was remarkable he'd managed to work for so long and he'd done very well, but now it was time he had a rest. Terry, being an ambulance driver could work anywhere in the country, so we suddenly found there was nothing to keep us in Lancaster.

Not that we were thinking of moving – but over the months I got more and more requests to work in the London area and I found the travelling very tiring.

In the summer of 19 … I was invited to Stansted Hall, our spiritualist college just outside London, to be the resident medium for two weeks. It was fun but hard work, because the job involved giving lectures, demonstrations and private sittings.

As we were so close, we went to stay afterwards with John's sister Kathleen in London instead of going straight home. I'd imagined I'd have a rest but no, incredibly I was soon in the middle of another assignment.

Kathleen was interested in having a sitting but it would be no use with me, because knowing so much about her and the family, any personal information I gave her would not be clear proof of spirit contact. So I took her along to the Spiritualist Association of Great Britain headquarters in the centre of London, to see if I could get her a sitting with another good medium.

'I'd hardly got through the door before Tom, the

association secretary pounced on me. Would I help him out? Their resident medium had been taken ill – could I do her sittings? What could I say?

Before I had time to stop and think, I was working at the SAGB. One of my most interesting cases there involved a beautiful Jamaican lady. She walked into the room one morning, a striking, elegant woman in a navy blue coat, white turban hat and gleaming black skin that reminded me of my long ago friend, Pansy. She was lovely to look at, but there was something very sad about her.

As soon as I started the sitting I realized what it was. She was a widow. I got through to her husband and he told me it was nearly a year since he'd died from a heart attack. He called her by her pet name 'Birdie', listed his children's names and told me where they lived in Jamaica.

I was passing this on to his wife when suddenly I stopped in mid-sentence. Her husband had materialized behind her chair. A huge, black giant of a man he bent forward, gently lifted the turban from his wife's head and dropped it on the floor. 'Ask her to promise me she won't wear mourning any more,' he said and disappeared.

The woman's hand had flown to her head and she whirled round in alarm but of course, there was no-one there. She stared in horror from me to the hat on the floor.

I didn't want to frighten her any more so I said gently that the spirit world had carefully removed her hat, because they didn't want her to wear it. I wasn't sure about the mourning hat because the turban was white, not black. Anyway the woman was clearly shaken and we finished the sitting shortly afterwards.

I thought that was the end of it, but the following Monday she came to see me again. I hardly recognized her. A radiant beauty in a yellow dress and loose black hair walked into the room like a ray of sunshine. Now she'd got over the shock of the sitting, she was able to explain the significance of the hat. Apparently white is a mourning colour in Jamaica and the day her husband died she'd put on that mourning turban. She'd changed the rest of her clothes since then; but she'd never removed the turban.

She even slept in it. This was the first time for nearly a year she'd gone bare-headed.

Towards the end of my stint at SAGB Tom and I were chatting in the corridor. 'You will come back and work for me again won't you Doris?' he asked.

'Oh I don't know Tom,' I said. 'It's the travelling. All the way from Lancaster to London, with the ill health I've had lately I don't feel up to it.'

'Well why don't you get a flat in London?'

I laughed. 'What will I use for rent? Shirt buttons?' John and I were poorer than ever since his retirement, and London was about the most expensive place to live in Britain.

A man was passing as we talked and, at these words, he stopped and came back. 'Were you talking about a flat?'

'Yes,' I said.

'Well I know one that's vacant.' He went on to explain that he knew of a complex of special cheap flats for disabled ex-servicemen.

The spirit world couldn't have given me a stronger hint that I was to move to London if they'd blazoned the words across the wall. That conversation took place in September, and by January we were living in London.

Soon I was working harder than ever. I was very conscious that apart from John's small pension we had to rely on what I could earn. Our flat was cheap but, as I'd expected, everything else in London was dearer and I was nervous of depending solely on my sittings. Admittedly I was quite well known in the North, but would I have enough customers in the South to provide me with regular work?

I wasn't keen to put it to the test, so when Tom asked me to work for him at the SAGB as a resident medium, I was pleased to accept. It was hard work. Often I'd do individual sittings, group sittings and a demonstration all in one day, working from 12.00 till 8.00 in the evening, four days a week. But at least Tom paid me on a daily basis and it was a steady, reliable income.

The group sittings, naturally were the least popular with visitors. Often people arrived for individual sittings without an appointment, and if we were fully booked they were given a choice of making an appointment or joining a group sitting. Usually they settled for a group.

Despite their relative unpopularity, they were often very successful. I remember one lady in particular who was delighted with her's. Although I didn't know the circumstances beforehand, she had travelled to London for a funeral. Having time to spare, she called at the SAGB to ask for a sitting. At such short notice they told her it was impossible, but she could join a group. She had so little time she agreed and was more than satisfied with the result, because the messages were almost entirely for her, the other five members present hardly got a look in!

She either tape recorded the sitting or took shorthand notes, I can't remember which, but afterwards she sent me a verbatin transcript of the proceedings. This is what she wrote:

MRS STOKES: (explaining what she does to those present who were not accustomed to her). There were 5 others and myself. 'I hear a name and if you know that person please answer that you do. I hear the person talking to me, if I point backwards over my shoulder it means the person is on the other side and if I spread out my hand in front that means they are alive now.'
Pause for concentration for all of us.

MRS S: Does anybody know of someone that has died recently?'

ONE MEMBER: How recently?

MRS S: During this year.

ME: Yes I do.

MRS S: Does the name David mean anything to you?

ME: Oh yes.

MRS S: This man has a young voice. It comes and goes, which means he hasn't been over very long and can't hold it. David is doing well but he finds it difficult.
Did he die suddenly?

ME: Yes.

MRS S: My chest hurts and now my heart; did he have a heart condition?

ME: I don't know.

MRS S: He asks if his car is at home all right.

ME: I don't know.

MRS S: he mentions an inquest.

ME: Yes that's right.

MRS S: David says he remembers going out, coming back, going to the bathroom and nothing more until he found himself here. He came up with you today. He is trying to say your name, it begins with an 'M'. (She tried and tried and kept murmuring Marjorie, Maisie etc but couldn't get it).

Do you know of a relation on this side called Pete?

ME: Yes.

MRS S: Now you are tired David, rest a few moments and I will get someone else's vibrations. She mentioned names, illnesses and various happenings to everyone there. She paused and then said: 'I hear the word antiques.'

ME: David collected antiques and so do I.

MRS S: (Holding up four fingers) Does this mean anything to you?

ME: Yes, David's four children.

MRS S: David has three girls and a boy. Does the name Christopher mean anything?

ME: Oh yes, his son.

MRS S: David says Christopher is not to be blamed in any way. He says he is sorry for what he did, he was doing so well for his children and wanted to do more. I have the name Jane.

ME: Yes, David's daughter.

MRS S: Does anyone know the name Caroline?

ME: Yes, David's youngest daughter.

MRS S: How long has David been over?

ME: Sunday evening.

(The people in the group gasped)

MRS S: It's wonderful David that you can do this. Is anyone helping you? He says yes, Nana.

ME: That's my mother who David always called Nana.

MRS S: David says he wants as little as possible spent on the funeral. His body is nothing, but he'd like anything done for the children. David says you talked to him about Spiritualism and he mocked you and said 'Don't you believe all that hooey Mum' and you said to him 'I shall die before you and you'll be so surprised when you come over and I'll be there waiting to meet you'. He says 'Now I'll be waiting for you mum.'

I see two wedding rings and I also see a divorce in the family. I also hear the name Lor – Lormet or something like that.

ME: Laurette?

MRS S: Yes that's it. David also mentioned the word insurance. Oh dear I'm getting too tired and must soon stop, but how old are you David?

He says young middle age!

At the close the five people gather round me and said they were so glad I had such a wonderful time, but they were all smiling and pleased for me. Note. I was disappointed not to have a private sitting but now I think they all helped greatly, we all being of one mind and they all being so willing to help. I didn't feel so nervous either.'

I made many new friends at the SAGB, some were colleagues, others clients. A typical example was businessman Phil Edwardes. He turned up one afternoon with several friends to watch a demonstration. He told me later they only called in for a lark to see what was going on, but they became fascinated.

I spoke to the mother of one of Phil's friends and among the details I was able to give him, was the fact she disapproved of the shirts he wore nowadays. When she was alive she told me she did his washing and ironing and always made sure he had a white collar, but now he wore coloured and even patterened shirts. Where would it end?

They all laughed heartily at this. The man said it was typical of his mother and absolutely right about the white collars. Afterwards, Phil and his friends booked private sittings.

It was the start of a lasting friendship. Phil visited us at our flat and invited us down to his beautiful home in

Sussex. I did several sittings for him and his family. On
one occasion I suddenly found I was talking to his mother.
I introduced myself to her and asked her to call me Doris
but she refused. She referred to me throughout as 'Mrs
Stokes' and when I asked her name she said 'Mrs
Edwardes'.

Phil was amazed. 'You're so right Doris, that's mother all
over. She was very proper. She certainly wouldn't use
anyone's Christian name until they'd been formally
introduced!'

My horizons were widening every day, but to my
frustration, I realized my health was no longer strong
enough to allow me to make the most of it. The years of
travelling in all weathers, the constant struggle to make
ends meet and several serious illnesses had left their mark.
Much as I enjoyed my work, I began to find the daily trip
through the London crush and the long hours at SAGB a
strain. I cut down my time there from four days to three
and then to two, doing two sittings a day at home on my
'off' days.

Yet ironically I soon found myself doing more travelling
than ever!

It started when a Mrs Beryl Peta Pryor from Gibraltar
came for a sitting while she was in London on holiday. It
was successful but to me, unremarkable. I got many names
through in Spanish, but again I was used to working with
overseas visitors, so it wasn't unusual to me.

Mrs Pryor was impressed however, particularly with a
message for 'Luisa from Filipe'. I told her that Luisa was
very worried about her dog who had terminal womb
cancer. The dog would have to be put to sleep but Filipe
said Luisa mustn't worry, he would look after it.

Apparently Mrs Pryor had known Luisa for several
years; but she'd never mentioned her late husband's name.
On returning to Gibraltar she discovered I was right, his
name was Filipe and Luisa was immensely comforted to
think he'd be looking after her beloved dog.

Word spread in the community on the rock, soon Mrs
Pryor's friends wanted sittings too. Obviously it would be
very expensive for them all to travel to Britain separately;

so they hit on the idea of sponsoring a trip for me in Gibraltar. That way I could do all the private sittings they wanted, and maybe some public ones as well.

It was a tremendous challenge. Not only would it be difficult because it's a Spanish speaking community and the ordinary people, unlike Mrs Pryor might not understand English and I didn't know a word of Spanish, but also because the people are predominantly Catholics and the Catholic Church disapproves strongly of Spiritualism. There were a few spiritualists on the rock, but they kept more or less under cover.

I accepted and fortunately the trip was a success. The first night we held a public meeting and it was packed. Word had got out and we even had the local TV station there.

I'd been a little worried because someone had told me that Gibraltarians and Spanish people talk incessantly, even in the cinema, and I wondered what I'd do if they refused to keep quiet. In the event it wasn't a problem. When I started to work the audience fell so silent they might not have been there.

The voices came through loud and clear and the crowd was able to understand my struggles to pronounce the Spanish names. The most vivid communication was with a young boy who said he'd hanged himself on the rock. As I started to talk of his suicide and called out his mother's name the woman, who was in the audience, went into hysterics.

Her other son, the dead boy's brother came rushing towards the stage.

'Do you want me to stop?' I asked him, but before he could answer she screamed, 'No! No! I must hear!' So I continued.

'Who's Peter? He's talking about Peter.' The boy who'd run down the aisle said, 'I am.'

The dead boy said he'd passed over at 2.00. No-one knew whether this was right or not, so the local TV presenter went back and checked the records and sure enough, the time of death was entered as 2.00.

Finally the boy said that just before his coffin was closed, his mother had come into the room alone, kissed his forehead and whispered a phrase in Spanish and I repeated it as best I could.

At this the poor woman burst into tears. 'Yes, yes that's what I said,.' She sobbed as her son led her weeping outside.

I felt rather bad about the episode and scolded myself for continuing when she was so obviously upset, but as I discovered later I was right to do so. Afterwards her son came to see me. He explained that when his brother committed suicide, his mother went into deep black mourning and couldn't leave the house. Our meeting was the only event she'd attended since his death, but now, after receiving his message she'd come to life again. She started going out and even occasionally, wearing colours. The family couldn't believe it.

Back in England my friends at the SAGB were eager to hear about my trip, and we had many long discussions on the subject of Gibraltar. Work continued much as before, but I was getting increasingly tired. I suffered from cold after cold and in the summer of 1977 managed to catch a particularly nasty one.

I couldn't get rid of it, but there was still the SAGB, my sittings and the teaching circle. I'd by now set up to train young people; and so I dragged myself from one to the other with my red eyes and streaming nose. Summer colds are always the worst I told myself, but then one morning another medium at SAGB looked more closely at me than usual.

'You know Doris you must see a doctor,' she said, 'you're ill.'

'Oh it's just a cold,' I sniffled. 'This hot weather makes it worse.' But in the end I felt so dreadful I took her advice, and not a moment too soon.

'Well I'm not surprised you feel so rough,' said the doctor after he'd examined me. 'You've got pneumonia.'

Forced to stay in bed dosed to the eyeballs with antibiotics, I spent many wheezing hours with nothing to do but think. I'd already cut my attendance at SAGB from four days to two, perhaps the time had come to cut it out altogether, and concentrate on private sittings and public demonstrations. Only lack of financial security had prevented me from taking this step in the past; but hadn't Ramonov once told me the spirit world would never see us starve? All I had to do was trust and it would come right.

As soon as I was well enough to explain, I told Tom of my decision. 'I'm not getting any younger Tom and with all the ill health I've had recently, I can't seem to manage running a home and doing a regular job as well.' He was very sweet about it and said if ever I changed my mind, I could get in touch with him.

I was still very weak. The summer of '77 was hot and dry and our small flat surrounded by concrete was like an oven. I used to get up in the morning full of good intentions but the smallest task, a bowl of washing up or a flick round with the duster, left me limp and exhausted.

I was very lucky with my friends however, and people were always popping in to see what they could do to help. Among them was a young woman from my teaching circle, a honey haired New Zealand girl called Judy Smith.

'What you need Doris is a good rest away from this place,' she said to me one day. 'A friend of mine's got a cottage in Suffolk she often lends me – why don't you come out there for a few days? It's much cooler in the country.'

I protested at first. What about John? What about Terry? But everyone assured me they'd cope and the idea of a shady garden in the quiet of the countryside appealed so much that it didn't take long to persuade me to go.

It was a beautiful place. A large detached cottage with a big secluded garden and an air of serenity that seeped into my bones from the very first day. Within hours I was more relaxed and I could feel my strength returning.

Even here however, I couldn't be entirely 'off duty'. Sittings and work were far from my mind, yet one night an odd thing happened. I still took sleeping pills to help me get a good night's rest, and this particular night I'd taken my pill and Judy sat chatting with me while it took effect.

I hadn't done trance work for years, but suddenly I felt my head spin and my eyes wouldn't focus on the room.

Goodness, I thought, I must have been overdoing it today, this doesn't usually happen. Then all the colours swum together and I can't remember anything else till Judy roused me 45 minutes later.

Apparently I'd fallen into a trance and 'become' Judy's late father. I started rubbing the 'bald' spot on the top of my head the way he used to do and speaking in his slow, deliberate way with a thick New Zealand accent. I spoke of his old nanny, his two brothers, his aunties and a neighbour Violet who he described as a 'Bible Basher'. I talked about his farm in New Zealand, his dogs Blue, Tip, Betty and Butch and reminisced about a bull he once bought for 200 guineas that had no interest in cows but once killed a horse. Finally he said through me, that he was worried about his son who had a bad heart, and to tell his wife not to stand around so much with her bad hip.

Judy was thrilled. She chattered away excitedly, bursting to tell me all the details while I struggled to bring my mind back to the bedroom. I couldn't take in what she was saying. Woozily I grasped that it was something to do with her father Tom being here, but I couldn't make out what.

'All right Judy,' I said sleepily, 'we'll try an experiment.' I looked round the room and a large brass lamp stand caught my eye. 'If you're there Thomas,' I said, 'ping that lamp.'

There was a pause. Judy and I stared at the lamp hardly daring to breathe in case we drowned the possible communication. Then suddenly there came a loud metallic clunk, the unmistakable sound of fingers flicked against brass.

'Well Judy,' I yawned as the sleeping pill began to work, 'you're right!'

The rest in the country was just what I needed. I went home strong and relaxed ready to cope with whatever work came along, and I soon realized my fears about too few sittings had been groundless. Requests flooded in. My diary filled for months in advance and I could easily have broken my rule of only two sittings a day if I'd wanted to. People wrote, telephoned or called to make appointments, or sometimes friends made appointments for them.

One morning Phil Edwardes was giving me a lift through London and, as we drove along the North Circular, he asked if I could give a sitting to some friends of his, a widow and her two daughters. It was the rush hour and heavy lorries were thundering past, but somehow through the noise I heard a man's voice.

'It's Eric they've lost isn't it?' I said to Phil. 'He's an artist.' By now Phil was used to me. He laughed. 'Yes you're absolutely right Doris.'

But Eric was still talking. 'Just a minute. He's talking about an unfinished painting of his granddaughter. Does that mean anything to you?' Phil shook his head. 'Well he says to tell Coral to finish it. He'll help her.'

'Well I know who Coral is. That's his daughter.'

It turned out that this particular Coral was Coral Atkins, a well known television actress who starred in a popular programme called Family at War … She was extremely sceptical, and I discovered later the main reasons she wanted to accompany her mother to see me was to make sure she wasn't cheated.

Phil brought them along to my flat. I recognized Coral immediately, a tiny bird-slim woman with long tawny hair. Phil introduced us and I shook hands with her, her mother and sister Sylvia, and then made them comfortable in our small living room. They were pleasant and friendly; but I could sense a cynical atmosphere. They didn't believe in this at all. Phil just smiled noncommittally and withdrew to a corner.

'My husband was an atheist,' Mrs Atkins explained.

'That doesn't make any difference,' I said as I tuned in and, sure enough, Eric undeterred by the doubting atmosphere came through strongly.

At once my chest began to ache and unbearable tickle burst out into cough after cough. The family gasped.

'That's father's cough,' said Coral.

Apparently Eric had suffered from emphysema (a painful lung condition).

'He had only a quarter of a lung left at the end,' she added.

Eric started talking about the painting again and asked

Coral to finish it for him. Then he mentioned seeing Alice and Bert, who Mrs Atkins was able to place as Eric's parents. Then Michael Hempkin, a friend of Coral's who'd been killed in a plane crash 15 years before. He also said he'd been to Australia to see two relatives and the stained glass windows in the cathedral.

Coral and Sylvia looked blank at this odd piece of information, but again Mrs Atkins was able to explain it. An old uncle, also an artist years ago had designed some stained glass windows for an Australian Cathedral.

Next Eric said he had a message for Phil. 'You made a good job of the statue – thanks.' I raised my eyebrows. 'I'm sure that's what he said Phil but it doesn't sound right.'

'Yes it does,' said Phil, 'Mrs Atkins gave me Eric's bronze statue of Diana that he used to have in the garden. I've cleaned it up and polished it and put it indoors and it looks marvellous.'

Eric continued. He named many more friends and relatives, and gave Coral some private advice concerning the future of a children's home she runs, and the name of a lawyer she should contact about another matter.

By the end of the sitting the three Atkins were mourning no longer, the atmosphere of doubt had melted away.

'It all seems so obvious now,' said Coral. 'You can't feel sad. I'd swear father was with us.'

Chapter 15

People often ask me what the other side is like and of course I'm not able to answer them from personal experience. All I can do is pass on the details I've heard spirit people give their relatives.

Ella Gregsten's husband was particularly helpful. They'd been a devoted couple living in London and soon after her husband died, Mrs Gregsten came to see me.

Mr Gregsten was eager to speak to his wife and he was there immediately I tuned in. He introduced himself as Bernard and asked me to thank Ella for the red roses, and John for the card.

'That's incredible,' said Ella. 'It was Bernard's birthday yesterday, so I put some roses beside his photograph and the only card that came was from his friend John who hadn't heard the news.'

Bernard went on to say that his dressing-gown still hung on the back of the bedroom door, which Ella confirmed, but most of all he was anxious to tell her what had happened to him since his 'death'.

'Death is nothing to fear,' he said. 'I woke up and found myself in a hospital here. Many of my old friends were there. Some held my hands and told me very firmly that I'd passed over.

'It's a beautiful world over here with trees and flowers and halls of music and learning. I'm not lonely but I miss you so much Ella. I shall not go on. I shall stay and help you all I can. I'll wait until you are ready to come over. Then I'll fetch you and we can progress together.'

Time and time again I've heard them say that the spirit world is a real world on another dimension – as real to them as ours is to us. Whether all married couples stay together on the other side, I don't know. Particularly as so many people marry more than once these days. I think it must only be couples who are spiritually suited the real soul-mates – who stay together.

Another thing I'm often asked, particularly by reporters, is to get in touch with a specific person: Elvis Presley, or President Kennedy or some other famous personality they'd like to have a chat with. I have to explain that it's impossible. For a start I can't choose who I get through to, and secondly, spirit people usually only make contact with people connected with them on earth.

Sometimes of course there are surprises. Once I made a journalist's day, by unexpectedly getting a message for escaped bank robber Ronald Biggs.

The journalist who'd interviewed Biggs in South America some time before was having a sitting, with me with a view to writing an article about it. Suddenly in the middle of personal information for him, a man's voice interrupted saying he had a message for Biggs.

'My name's Arthur,' he said. 'Tell our Ronnie to come back and get it over with, it won't be long.

'Ronnie was named for me you know.'

This seemed odd as the man had said he was Arthur, but the journalist got it all down on his tape recorder and promised to check.

Arthur then mentioned Wyn and spoke of Charmaine – Biggs' wife who was living in Australia – getting a divorce.

Afterwards the journalist phoned Biggs. It turned out that his middle name was Arthur, after his uncle Arthur, his sister-in-law was called Winnie, but the bit about the divorce didn't fit. 'Does she know something I don't?' he joked.

Three days later it was in all the papers. Charmaine had been granted a divorce.

I was even called in to help a private detective once. John Sullivan an investigator in Chesham, had a mystery fire at his office. It seemed to have started between floors, but no-one could decide exactly where, and he was not happy with the results.

John came to me for a sitting. Naturally I couldn't

promise to get anything about the fire at all, but he was fortunate that day. His father came through and told me the exact spot where the fire started and that it was caused by an electrical fault. This was later confirmed.

I also spoke to a late friend of John's. He said he was a heavy drinker, who liked classical music, he last worked in Sheffield where he died and he'd been an accountant. John said this was absolutely correct.

A phenomena you hear a lot about when people talk of psychic experiences is the 'out of body' experience. I'd read about them and heard about them; but assumed I'd go through life without experiencing one myself.

Then one night I sat down in Ramonov's chair as usual. I was pretty exhausted. I was going away somewhere the next day to take a weekend service, and I'd been rushing about trying to get the flat clean, finish the washing and ironing and get my case packed before I went.

John was already in bed and quite honestly I felt more like joining him; but I made it a rule to spend a quiet ten or twenty minutes every evening with Ramonov and so I dutifully sat down. My best dressing gown was packed, so I was wearing an old woollen one. I'd put my boudoir cap on ready for bed and my teeth were in the bathroom. I tuned in.

The next thing I knew I was standing on the hearthrug looking at myself in the chair. What a sight! My goodness, I thought, talk about your own grandma! There I sat in this faded dressing-gown, boudoir cap pulled low over my ears and head sunk on my chest. Then I thought I must have passed over! Somebody wake John and get him to come and put my teeth in! But the next second there was a wrench and I was back in my body, my heart banging away and perspiration standing on my skin.

'Don't ever do that again,' I said angrily to Ramonov.

'You have forgotten how to trust haven't you,' was his only remark, but it never happened again.

Around this time I was getting more and more overseas visitors coming to my flat, and one of them in particular became a special friend.

It started with a phone call one afternoon from a

Swedish woman who was living in France. In London for a short stay, she asked if she could come for a sitting.

I looked through my engagement diary and saw I was fully booked for weeks. I was about to say, no I was sorry, when I felt a tremendous impulse to fit her in somehow. She didn't sound tearful or desperate, but something in her voice suggested she was badly in need of comfort.

Perhaps I could shuffle my other appointments, or work on Sunday. However I managed it, I had to see her. We made the arrangements and I wrote her name down in my diary. Ulla Pahlson Moller.

We live in a very complex development and our flat is so hard to find that I usually go out, just before a stranger is due to arrive, to help them find the place. The afternoon Mrs Pahlson Moller was coming I went out on to the landing as usual, just in time to see her walking up the steps. What a nice surprise. She'd brought her little boy with her. I smiled at him. He was a pretty child with typical Swedish colouring of fair skin with white blond hair. I opened my mouth to greet them, but I don't think I got a word out. As I watched, the outline of the child faded and he disappeared. I knew then why it was important I saw Mrs Pahlson Moller.

'Oh my dear, you've lost a child haven't you?' I said when she reached me.

The colour drained from her face. 'Yes I have,' she whispered, her expression alarmed. I realized I'd spoken without thinking and startled her. 'Come inside and have a cup of tea,' I said, 'and I'll tell you how I knew.'

I always feel a special affinity with women who've lost children, because of John Michael. No-one however kind and sympathetic understands what it's like better than another bereaved mother. It's a special kind of anger and despair …

So I told Ulla about my son and showed her the only photograph we ever had taken of him which was standing, as it always does, on the sideboard, and after a few minutes I saw her child again.

He was a beautiful little boy about 5 years old with shining hair and striking blue eyes. He said his name was

Peter and he walked up to his mother, put his hand on her knee and turning his head sideways to look up into her face he said 'love you Esterling, love you.'

'What does Esterling mean?' I asked Ulla.

'It's Swedish for darling, why?'

I told her what had happened and she started to cry – not with sadness but with joy, she was so happy to think her son was so near.

'That's exactly what he used to say,' she explained dabbing at her eyes with a tissue. 'I could never tell him off when he was naughty. He used to look up at me with those big blue eyes and say, "Love you darling, love you!" and I didn't have the heart to be angry.'

Peter, close to his mother's knee the whole time, was thrilled to talk to me. He'd been drowned while playing near water with his friends, he explained. Then he told me his brother's name and the place where they lived in France and he sent his love to his Papa. Not his daddy, as we would say in Britain.

Ulla went away very happy and not long afterwards her husband came for a sitting. He too was so pleased, he asked if I could possibly go to France for a few days to stay with the family and do sittings for Peter's grandparents, who'd also been grief-stricken at his death.

It was the first of several happy visits. The communications from Peter were hardly earth shattering. They were tiny intimate details that would seem trivial to an outsider, but to the family they were proof that their son was a constant, if unseen visitor.

On one occasion Mr Pahlson Moller – Sante – had to go to Copenhagen for a business trip. I was doing a sitting for his grandmother, when suddenly Ulla said, 'Ask Peter what his Papa is doing now.'

I asked and Peter said, 'He's on a sort of train where they sit one behind the other and it's going up and down steep hills.'

'No, no that can't possibly be right,' said Ulla. 'Papa is a banker.' But that night when Sante phoned and she asked him what he'd been doing he said, 'You'll never believe this, but I've been to the fair. I was on the Big Dipper!'

Another time I was doing a sitting for Ulla and Sante together and Peter said, 'Papa's got a hole in his stupa.'

This seemed a bit doubtful to me and I wasn't sure whether to say it out loud, when Sante asked me what I was smiling about.

'Well it sounds most peculiar to me,' I said, 'but I'm sure Peter said you've got a hole in your stupa!'

Sante roared with laughter, slid off his shoe and held up his foot, to reveal a hole in the heel of his sock. 'Stupa is Swedish for sock,' he explained. 'I discovered this hole this morning!'

Some months later I got a phone call from a man named Kevin Arnett. He wanted to come for a sitting, and he asked if I minded if it was filmed. He was making a TV show for an Australian company. I didn't mind at all. If it worked it worked, I explained. It wouldn't make any difference if there was a camera there or not, but I couldn't guarantee success.

It was exciting of course, but not completely new. While I'd been living in the North of England I'd been interviewed on a local afternoon TV programme, I'd done a live phone in for a radio show and, of course, there'd been that TV team at my public meeting in Gibraltar. I was used to the media.

Kevin's sitting did work fortunately. I talked to his father who'd passed over only three months before, and also much to his surprise, the grandmother of the cameraman. She popped in out of the blue, interrupting Kevin's father and the cameraman was so astonished he nearly stopped filming!

I heard later that the programme, which went out on Channel 9, was so popular they wanted to hear more from me. Kevin suggested a live phone-in with me on the phone too.

It's more difficult to get communications over the phone, particularly if a lot of people are waiting to speak on the line, because the vibrations can get mixed up and there's always a danger of giving the message to the wrong person. Still I'd done it before, and I was willing to have a try.

The arrangements were made and at 9.00 one night my telephone rang and Australia was on the line. Suddenly twangy Australian accents were crackling into my tiny hall. The spirit voices poured through and I struggled to get my tongue round the strange names and places. It was difficult, but worth it. As I passed on the messages I heard squeals of delight several thousand miles away.

At last Kevin was back on the line to wind up the show, but his father was there again. 'You've signed another contract with someone,' I said. 'You're going to do more psychic work aren't you?'

Kevin laughed. 'Yes, you're right Doris. I signed a contract this morning with Channel 9 to do more psychic programmes.'

What I didn't realize then, was that his work was going to involve me.

Early the following year he came back to make another film, for Channel 9 this time, and the public reaction was so great I received an incredible offer. Would I fly to Australia to appear on a celebrity chat and variety show – The Don Lane Show?

Me on a variety show in Australia? What a strange invitation. What could I say? The challenge was irresistible.

Chapter 16

9-45 Tuesday June 13th, John and I were nervously buckling our safety belts. Australia! The other side of the world. What a long long way to fly.

I peeped out of the porthole at my elbow. The light was fading fast now, the colours draining from the busy scene. Somewhere in one of those long grey terminal buildings, Terry and the members of my teaching class were watching. Could they see our plane, or did they think we'd taken off already?'

Over our heads the no-smoking sign was brightly lit, and I fiddled with the ashtray in the armrest. 'I'm dying for a cigarette John,' I groaned.

Heaven knows how many I'd smoked already today. I hadn't been able to eat a thing, I'd been so apprehensive. Ever since we'd heard we were going, people had been telling us how difficult Australians were to work for, and that we'd never stand the plane journey.

Well it was done now, I glanced down at the Paddington Bear I'd bought for Kevin, hastily stuffed Wellington boots first, under my seat. Everything was arranged. We couldn't turn back now.

The engines started up and the jet began to move forward along the runway, gathering speed. Through the window, the grass raced past faster and faster. The whine turned into a scream and then we were flying up into the pale sky, the shadowy fields falling swiftly beneath us.

'Well that's it then love,' said John, 'we're on our way.'

A twinge of excitement wriggled along my spine. Australia! This was our greatest adventure so far, and at the time I was only thinking about the distance and the challenge. I had no idea just how great an adventure it would turn out to be.

Several hours into the flight, the first flush of
excitement had gone and distinct disillusion set in. We
simply hadn't realized what a gruelling journey it was. The
sky stretched endlessly around us and we'd long since
grown bored with looking at it. Time was meaningless. We
couldn't eat, we couldn't sleep, we ached from sitting still
for so long and our feet swelled. I must have been mad, I
thought. Quite mad. Our friends were right. This trip'll be
a disaster.

We'd started out on Tuesday evening and didn't arrive
in Melbourne until Thursday morning; by which time we
were like a pair of zombies. Stiff and glassy eyed, we
dragged ourselves to the terminal building where,
through glass doors, we could see Kevin waiting.

He'd brought a Rolls-Royce to whisk us to our hotel; but
we were too tired to appreciate the compliment. The only
thing we vaguely registered was the unexpected greenness
of Melbourne. I'd imagined Australia to be a hot, desert
like place; but all around us were lush green trees.

We reached our hotel feeling like nothing on earth. The
floor seemed to be going up and down under our feet as if
we were still on the plane, and yet when I sank into the
hotel bed I couldn't sleep. A fat lot of use you're going to
be, I told myself sternly, if you don't pull yourself
together, but I couldn't seem to take any notice.

That evening, Kate, the girl from Channel 9 who was to
look after us during our stay, told us that the Don Lane
Show was on, and so we watched it on the huge colour
television in our room. It was hilarious. Don Lane, a suave,
dark haired American was joking with Bert Newton,
co-star, who also had his own radio show.

'Don't stand there!' Bert yelled and Don leapt out of the
way. 'That's Uncle Charlie.' 'Move out the way. It's Uncle
Charlie.' 'It's no good you coming today Uncle Charlie, she
won't be here till Monday.'

Then Kevin Arnett came on and talked about his sitting
with me and the film he'd made in England.

'Will they be watching the show?' Don asked him.

'Oh yes,' said Kevin and so Don waved to us.

John and I burst out laughing. We almost felt they could see us sitting there. They'd made us feel welcome already.

What we didn't realize was that Don and Kevin were coming to see us after the show to take us out to dinner. At 11.30 at night! They took us to a lovely restaurant and a beautiful meal arrived, but to our shame John and I could hardly touch it.

Don and Kevin didn't seem to mind. They explained that I'd be appearing on Don's show on the Monday and the Thursday, and the rest of our fortnight in Australia would be taken up with some interviews, a radio phone-in on Bert's show the next day, private sittings, a church service I wanted to do and sight-seeing.

It sounded marvellous, but right at that moment all I wanted to do was to go bed and I was quite relieved when the meal was over.

I'd heard about jet-lag before of course, but I didn't really understand what it was. I wouldn't have believed that a long flight and a few hours time difference could make you feel ill and bemused for days. It seemed ridiculous but it happened to me. Late that night I crashed exhausted into bed and slept at last – only to wake up at 5.00 in the morning.

I was sitting in a chair, leaden-eyed and weary but unable to sleep, when to my horror a bright, fresh Kate knocked at the door. 'Come on Doris,' she said cheerfully. 'We've got to be at the studio for Bert Newton's phone-in at 9.00.'

9.00? Thank goodness it was radio, not television the way I must have looked. I felt about 100. Somehow I scraped my hair into order and put on some lipstick, then Kate led me down to the waiting car.

Bert was smaller than he looked on television, but I felt I knew him already. 'Hello Bert,' I said. 'How's Uncle Charlie?'

His smile faded and he looked sheepish. 'Oh I hope you didn't mind.'

'No of course not,' I said. 'We can laugh at ourselves. John and I really enjoyed it.'

The actual phone-in is hazy. How I did it I don't know. I

was so disorientated I hardly knew what I was saying. Afterwards they told me it was a success, but I haven't a clue what happened.

The same dreamy state lasted all day. I floated through events as if they were happening to someone else. Back at the hotel there was a press conference and I know I spoke to the reporters, but I've no idea what I said. I only hope I didn't put my foot in it.

Then that evening a strange thing happened. Some people from Channel 9 came round for drinks and with them was Lorraine Bayley, an actress in the popular TV programme the Sullivans, and her journalist boyfriend.

Lorraine was going away for a couple of weeks and would miss me they said, could I possibly do anything for her before she went?

I was pretty muddled by now, but I said I'd try. Luckily it seemed to work. I got through to Lorraine's father Alec and the normal type of messages were coming across, when suddenly the dream state deepened and I slipped into a sort of half trance. Names and street names started pouring out, and I was addressing them to the journalist rather than to Lorraine.

It meant nothing to me but it did to the other people, particularly the journalist. I mentioned Easey Street, a pscyhiatric hospital and many names. Then I was back in the room, surprised to find that the people who'd been standing around chatting were now gathered about me. There was a buzz of excitement in the air and curious eyes were staring my way.

'What happened?' I asked bewildered.

It turned out that two girls, Suzanne Armstrong and Susan Bartlett had been murdered at the address I'd given. I'd told them the girls' names and the names of members of their families.

My hosts must have been a bit taken aback, but the journalist treated it seriously. We're not very well informed about Australian affairs in Britain, so it was unlikely I'd heard of the murders before my visit, and I hadn't had time to research into the case since I'd arrived, even if I'd wanted to.

I discovered afterwards, that the journalist wrote about it and Suzanne Armstrong's sister came to see me at my hotel.

She was a pretty dark-haired girl and I was able to talk to Suzanne for her. I discovered she was looking after Suzanne's little boy Gregory, and Suzanne asked her to regularly show the child her photograph and say, 'This is your mummy.'

Then I saw blood splattered walls and a bath. Suzanne described the house and the cul-de-sac where the murders took place, a white van and the two men who were connected with it. I think the sister passed the information on to the police.

But this was a little later on. In the meantime, I had a relaxing weekend to prepare for the show. We wandered about and were taken sightseeing to Melbourne's botanical gardens. John and I had never seen anything like this beautiful place, where great black swans with red beaks sailed on a looking-glass lake.

Black swans? I thought swans only came in white. Completely fascinated, we bought a loaf of bread to feed them. They seemed pretty hungry. They took whole slices straight from our hands, and when we moved away a black and red procession followed.

Then our Australian guide caught up with us and turned pale as I pushed another slice into a scarlet beak.

'My god don't do that!' he yelled rushing over, 'they'll have your hand off!'

We didn't know they were dangerous.

By Monday I was getting nervous. The Don Lane Show was a variety show. What on earth were people going to make of me when they were used to seeing singers or comedians? And what if it didn't work? 'Trust' Ramonov's voice murmured somewhere in my head, but it failed to calm the jitters.

By the time I got to the studio I was chain smoking. I was introduced to Lesley the producer, and then hurried along to the make-up department. I'd chosen a pretty, long dress to wear on screen and I'd already done my make-up to match it, but no, that wasn't good enough.

Lipstick, powder – everything had to come off and they started again.

I was sitting there smoking frantically when Don Lane came past. He was getting ready himself and still wearing a dressing gown; but he looked as calm and unworried as if he was only on his way to take a bath at home.

'Oh wish me luck Don,' I implored.

'I will if you give me a kiss and a cuddle,' he said impishly and came over and kissed me.

Then he was gone and time speeded up. Far too soon it seemed to me, I was being led behind the set and introduced to a man called Graham, the musical director. 'Your music is "We'll meet again" ' he told me, and though I concentrated very hard I had a strange feeling I wasn't taking it in properly. 'I'll play the opening bars and then you go on and just walk over to Don. Okay?'

'Walk over to Don,' I echoed though I'd already forgotten everything else he'd said.

'Yes, you've got it.'

Then he was gone too, and I was standing alone behind the set, icy cold, terrified, my heart banging against my ribs. I tried to tune in. One by one, I made myself squash each stray thought in an effort to concentrate. I took long, deep breaths and was almost calm when the first clanging bars of 'We'll Meet Again' shot me back to the present. Music crashing round me, I raced forward and suddenly was bathed in hot bright lights. Clapping sounded from somewhere and Don, now in a smart, neat suit, was saying, 'Well here she is … the lady you've been waiting for …'

I sat down beside him and, as my eyes adjusted to the brilliant light, I saw the blackness was packed with people. 'My goodness,' I thought panic rising again. But Don must have sensed it because he started chatting in such a friendly way I relaxed in spite of myself.

He asked me a few questions to start with, then the floor was mine. This was what I was used to. The house lights came up so I could see the audience and suddenly I forgot the cameras, forgot the lights and plunged into my normal work.

A jumble of Australian voices came streaming through

and, as I looked round the audience, I saw a light like a torchlight dancing above a woman near the back. I heard a man's voice trying to say something to her.

'The lady over there – that's it there in the white coat. I've got a man here called Bert.'

She gasped. 'That's my brother-in-law.'

'He says he went over very quickly.'

'That's right.'

'Who's Wyn?'

'I'm Wyn.' And so it went on.

One girl's grandfather came through and made me rather puzzled at first. He said he'd been drowned, but he had a gun.

'I don't know,' I said to the young girl. 'I'm sure it's early morning and your grandfather says he was drowned, but I can see a gun.'

'Yes that's right,' she said, 'he was out duck shooting.'

The messages continued fluently. Poor Don didn't know quite what to make of it. He tried to move me round the audience so that everyone had a fair turn, but you can't do that. I have to go where I'm sent. Then as often happens, some recipients of messages got a little tearful. I'm quite used to it. It's a healthy release of tension and they often write to tell me afterwards that, far from making them sad, the message has made them terribly happy. Of course Don was unprepared for it, and I think he was a little alarmed at people crying on his show.

The audience was so engrossed, I discovered afterwards, that the producer made signals for me to continue and they cut out some of the commercials. Even so it seemed hardly ten minutes before Don was telling me it was time to finish, and thanking me for my work.

Elated I walked off to loud applause, and then rather spoiled the effect by falling down the steps behind the set. For some reason the lights had been switched off at the back and though the audience couldn't see me, they must have heard the terrific crash.

I twisted my ankle, grazed my knee and tore a great hole in my tights. What was that about pride comes before a fall? Muttering to myself I picked myself up in the darkness, and limped back to the room where John and Kevin were waiting and watching the show.

'Oh dear look what I've done! Trust me!' I said staring down at my ruined tights. 'I'd better get out of this long dress before I do any more damage.' I changed into a denim street dress.

We sat together quietly watching the end of the show, me nursing my wounds. Then suddenly the door burst open and Lesley the producer rushed in. 'Come on Doris, they want you back.'

Cigarette half way to my lips, I stared at her. 'I beg your pardon?'

'Come along, they want you back. The audience want you back.'

'But I've got out of my long dress.'

'Never mind, that'll do.' She picked up a red scarf. 'Whose is this?'

'Mine,' I said.

'Right,' she tied it quickly round my neck. 'That'll give you a bit of colour, come on.'

So I went back on set and the audience clapped and carried on. Whether it was because they'd enjoyed my performance, or because they wanted to see if I was all right after the crash, I don't know. But all I could think about was to keep my skirt down, so they wouldn't see the hole in my tights!

The reaction to the Don Lane Show was staggering. Afterwards the studio telephone lines were jammed with over 1,000 calls each in Melborne and Sydney, where the show went out simultaneously. About 500 letters poured into our hotel. The newspapers were clamouring, and people kept trying to get sittings.

There was such a fuss they extended my Thursday appearance, and took off Starsky and Hutch to give me an hour to myself. 'And we didn't do that for Sammy Davis Junior,' joked a television official.

Events became a bit unreal. At times John and I felt caught up in an incredible dream. It was marvellous, but we couldn't quite believe it was really happening.

The next thing we knew Kevin was bursting into our

hotel room with more thrilling news. 'We are going on tour with the Edgeley's,' he cried. 'I can't get over it but they're taking us on tour.'

Apparently Australia's top promoter wanted to send me on a tour of the country holding meetings in the big cities. Kevin was to go along to introduce me to the audience and act as a sort of compere. My stay was extended to six weeks, and two body guards were employed to look after us.

I was to visit Melbourne, Sydney, Adelaide, Brisbane and Perth, but because it was such short notice it wasn't possible to block book halls; so I had to hop backwards and forwards from place to place.

It took a lot of arranging and in the meantime, I offered to hold a church service for the Spiritualist Church in Melbourne; which was something I'd wanted to do since we left England.

It was just an ordinary Sunday service, but when I drew up in the car I thought I'd come to the wrong place. Crowds of people lined the streets. The church was overflowing, every seat had been taken, they were standing in the aisles, against the wall, in the doorways and they'd crammed another 200 downstairs and rigged up microphones so they could listen. The others who couldn't squeeze themselves into the building waited outside.

As I stepped out of the car, the crowd surged forward trying to touch me, kiss me and throw flowers. I couldn't understand it and it was a bit frightening. What did these people want from me? I couldn't hope to give a personal message to all of them. What did they expect. They must be mistaking me for something I wasn't.

Inside the church I went straight to the microphone. 'I'm nothing special,' I explained. 'Please don't get the wrong impression. I'm just the same as you are. I'm no different. I have my faults and my weaknesses like everyone else.' But it didn't seem to make any difference. I was bewildered. What was it these people were looking for?

All over Australia it was the same. I was constantly amazed at the extraordinary reaction I roused. Even buying clothes for instance.

I'd suddenly realized that if I was going on tour I'd need

some more evening dresses – I'd only brought two – one
for each Don Lane Show. I was doing a phone-in
programme when the realization dawned, don't ask me
why, and afterwards I asked the presenter, Mary Harty, if
she knew where I could buy outsize evening dresses. She
promised she'd find me a place.

The next morning our phone rang and Alan our
bodyguard answered it, because I wasn't allowed to answer
the phone any more.

'It's a place called the Wicked Lady, for you,' he told me
after a short conversation.

'Sounds like a nightclub,' I said to John. But it wasn't. It
was a dress shop selling outsize evening clothes, and they
told me that if I would say where my dresses came from, I
could have the first two free. It sounded like a very
generous offer to me, so we went along.

I had a pleasant morning trying on clothes and chatting
to the staff, and I even did a mini sitting in the fitting
room. There was a German lady there and suddenly her
husband started talking to me. I gave her his name and
several bits of family information, before finishing my
shopping.

I thought no more about it until, a little later, a flimsy
jacket that went with one of the dresses got caught in a zip
and tore; so I went back to the Wicked Lady to get another
one. For a moment as I walked in the door I thought
they'd put up a new mirror, because I came face to face
with myself. Then it struck me that I hadn't put on the
clothes that the me in the mirror was wearing, and in the
same instant I realized I was looking at a full length
photograph of myself.. I stopped dead in sheer
amazement. Then for the first time, I spotted the notice at
the top of the picture, 'We dress Doris Stokes,' and I burst
out laughing.

On another occasion I went to buy some evening shoes
and, for a change, John and I went alone. We walked into
the first big store we came to and found ourselves in the
men's department. 'Oh John, you could do with some
more socks,' I reminded him, but before we had time to
say what we wanted, the boy came out from behind the

counter and said, 'It's Doris Stokes isn't it? May I give you a kiss?'

We got the socks but unfortunately there was nothing I liked in the shoe department so went back to the street. Almost at once, two ladies stopped us.

'It's Doris Stokes! Oh we have enjoyed your shows on television and we've bought tickets for your live show.'

'Thank you, I'm glad,' I said a bit overwhelmed. 'You couldn't tell us where there's a shoe shop could you? We can't find one.'

'We'll show you,' they said, and so the four of us set off together. A little further down the road some more people stopped us, and after a little chat they joined us too. Somehow as we went along we gathered more and more people; until eventually about sixteen of us crowded into the shop to buy one pair of shoes. Yet far from being angry, the manager even got the assistant to come out with us, to see us safely across the road!

My first public meeting was in Dallas Brook Hall, Melbourne. There, for the first time I met someone who was definitely not impressed with my work. The master engineer was a pleasant young man, but very tongue-in-cheek about the whole thing. People were mad queueing and paying for tickets. It was all nonsense, he thought.

A little later we saw him again and his attitude was the same. Still, everyone's entitled to their own opinion I thought.

The show started and out on stage everything was going well. The audience at least was appreciative, but when I came off for a short break I discovered that all the clocks, and there were a great many of them back stage, were going beserk. The hands were whizzing round an hour every minute. The master engineer had no time to chat now. He was rushing about trying to locate the fault.

'You shouldn't have taken the mickey out of Doris,' someone in our party joked as he went past, but he wasn't in a laughing mood.

I went back on stage, but when I returned in the intermission the clocks were as crazy as ever, and the poor engineer was almost tearing his hair out. He'd tried everything he knew but he could find nothing wrong.

I went into my dressing-room and stared at the clock. The hands were spinning madly and showed no sign of slowing down.

'If it is you lot up there,' I said, 'stop it now. He's had enough,' and immediately the hands gave a little jerk and then slowed to normal pace.

I doubt if the young man believed it was anything to do with me, but he made no more comments after that.

Back on stage, a great wave of love met me as soon as I stepped out. They were a marvellous audience. Towards the end we'd decided to have a question time so the audience could ask me questions, and this evening a woman stood up and asked if she could have a sitting with me, because she'd just lost her husband.

'That's hardly fair madam,' said Kevin, 'so many people would like sittings with Doris.'

But her husband was there, and so without even trying I was able to give her a few little details, his name and family names which were German because the family was of German origin. Afterwards she wrote to tell me how thrilled she'd been.

Then all at once it was time to say goodbye. I said my last few words as usual, there was a slight pause and then suddenly a tremendous roar burst out. They leapt from their seats, they stamped, they shouted and clapped and whistled. The noise was deafening. 'Good for England!' someone yelled. 'Yes good for England,' someone else echoed, and I just stood there and cried like a baby. I was so proud.

If someone had offered me a thousand pounds to walk off the stage at that moment, I couldn't have done it.

I was appearing at Dallas Brook the next night too, and in the middle of my demonstration, a little boy materialized on the stage. He'd lost most of his hair, there was only a little tuft on the top of his head, but he was a dear, lively little thing. He said his name was Jerad and he was looking for his mummy and daddy.

I described him to the audience and asked if his parents were there, but no-one claimed him.

'Sorry lovely, they're not here today,' I told him, 'you'd better go and play while I get on,' and he disappeared.

The following day we flew to Adelaide where I was orginally to do one show; but the tickets sold out so quickly they had to arrange another three. During the second show, Jerad materialized again, still loooking for his mummy and daddy.

'Has anyone lost a little boy called Jerad?' I asked. This time to his delight, his parents were in the audience.

'How old are you Jerad?' I asked him.

'I'm 5,' he said, 'but I'll be 6 on Friday,' and his parents confirmed that Friday would have been his sixth birthday.

After the show I asked them backstage, and gave them my flowers as a gift from Jerad.

I would have liked to do private sittings while I was in Australia, but sadly it was impossible to meet the demand. One of the newspapers, the Sydney Sun, got round it holding a competition to win a sitting with me. Readers were asked to complete the sentence, 'The moment I began to believe in life after death was ...' and the six winners had a sitting.

Sydney was possibly the most exciting place I visited because I appeared at the famous Opera House, that fantastic modern building overlooking Sydney Harbour. As with all the halls, I'd refused to go and look at it first.

'If I see it you'll never get me out there,' I used to say, I'll get cold feet.' So Kevin used to stand in for me when they were working out the lighting and sound and whatever else they had to do.

It was just as well I had no idea of the size of the Opera House or I might have flown home in fright! When we arrived I saw hundreds and hundreds of people going up the steps; but it didn't click they were coming to see me.

Back stage took my breath away. There were miles and miles of hushed carpeted corridors, then I was led into the number one star dressing room.

I'd never seen anything like it. There was a huge lounge with several settees, a grand piano and picture windows overlooking the bobbing lights of Sydney Harbour, a separate dressing room with a bed, and a separate bathroom. I wandered about open mouthed. It was bigger than my flat back home and this was just the dressing room!

The bed certainly looked inviting but I couldn't even sit down, let alone lie down. All I could do was pace. Kevin practised yoga and, just before he went on stage, he used to stand on his head in his dressing room.

'You ought to try it you know,' he said seeing the state I was in, 'it's a great way to relax.'

'Kevin,' I said, 'if I did that, they'd have to carry me on, on a stretcher!'

When I finally got to the wings I died a thousand deaths. There were so many lighting men and sound engineers, they would have made an audience on their own. What on earth's it like out there, if it's this crowded back here? I wondered nervously.

Mintues later I found out. Kevin introduced me, I heard my cue, walked boldly out and almost tripped over my dress in astonishment. There were seats behind me, seats at the side of me and seats in front of me in a big tiered circle; so that everywhere I looked I saw a sea of faces. I felt like a fly at the bottom of a glass.

Kevin smiled encouragingly and I took a few more steps towards him. This is madness, I was thinking frantically, I can't do this. Then I tuned in and immediately my fears dissolved. As soon as I started to work my mind was blank to everything else.

Time raced by and suddenly it was the end; I was in the centre of a tremendous hurricane of applause, so loud I felt it would lift me to the ceiling. Tears were flooding my eyes all over again.

I did three shows at the Opera House which was a marvellous experience; but the other exciting thing about Sydney was all the famous people who were staying at our hotel. Jimmy Edwards, Eric Sykes, Warren Mitchell, Catherine Grayson; John and I loved to sit in the restaurant and star spot.

One day when I'd been working in the morning and had an appearance in the evening, I decided to lie down after lunch. John was tired too and already in bed; but I'd had my hair done and carefully tucked my fresh curls into a hair net before I dare lay down. Delicate operation complete I was just getting into bed, when the phone rang. Our bodyguard had gone of course, so I picked it up myself.

'Is that you Dol?' asked a vaguely familiar voice.

'Yes,' I said uncertainly.

'This is Dick Emery.'

I nearly collapsed.

'John!' I squealed covering the mouthpiece, 'it's Dick Emery!'

'Who?'

But the voice on the phone was talking again.

'What are you doing?'

'Nothing,' I said bending the truth slightly. I didn't want to admit I was just going to bed.

'Well I was wondering if you'd like to come and have a cup of tea with my wife Jo and I?'

'Oh we'd love to,' I gasped.

'Good. We'll see you in the restaurant then,' and he was gone.

'John! John! Get up,' I cried, dropping the receiver and tearing off my hairnet. 'We're having tea with Dick Emery.'

'Dick Emery?' he was pushing back the sheets in maddening slow motion. 'Yes. That was him on the phone. Come on. Get up, we're seeing him in the restaurant.'

Somehow we dressed. I got my hair back in order and we reached the restaurant in such a short space of time, anyone would have thought we'd been up and dressed all along.

There was no mistaking the broad friendly face of Dick Emery. He stood up as soon as we walked in and gave me a big hug. He was a real gentleman. Such a clever, talented man himself; he took the trouble to try and make us feel important.

'How are they treating you?' He asked over tea.

'Oh everyone's been very good to me,' I said, 'the only thing is, instead of this going out after the show and having champagne, I'd sooner come back to the hotel, have a cup of tea, watch a bit of television and go to bed.'

'Well you tell them dear,' he said, 'you're the star.'

I laughed. 'I'm not a star.'

'Yes you are,' he said, 'I'm a big name in Australia but at the Entertainment Centre in Perth I could only sell 3,000 tickets. You've sold every seat and that's 8,000. You sit there and tell me you're not a star!'

I just laughed. I couldn't really take it in. 8,000 seats? Surely he was exaggerating. I couldn't imagine a hall holding 8,000 people.

Later that night as we were leaving for the show, Dick was in the foyer. 'Hello love, how are you?'

'Oh a bit weary,' I admitted.

He turned to the rest of the party. 'She doesn't want to go out for any meals,' he told them, 'all she wants is to go to her suite and have a nice cup of tea, don't you love?'

'Yes I do,' I said.

'Well that's what she's going to do,' he insisted.

I couldn't get over his kindness.

Strangely enough, considering how well the tickets sold in Perth, I had to have special permission to go there, because I believe that mediumship is illegal there. Even after permission was granted there was still quite a fuss.

A religious society decided to hold a forty-eight hour prayer meeting and fasting because I was coming, and they were so against my work.

I heard about it at quarter to seven in the morning when a reporter phoned to read the story to me and ask for my comments. I was absolutely amazed, but I tried to be fair, 'Well they're perfectly entitled to do that if that's the way they feel,' I said, 'but it's up to all the people of Perth to decided whether they want my work or not. Not just one society.'

And that night, seeing the incredible audience of 8,000 people in front of me, I felt they'd decided. It was an extraordinary experience. I was very conscious of all those people wanting something from me, and that I couldn't hope to satisfy them all if I carried on for twelve hours. In such a multitude – how would I find the right contact? The whole thing seemed too big.

They tried to suggest how I should work. 'Do the front section first, then the back session, then to one side and then to the other side.'

'I'll do my best,' I said. 'But I have to go where I'm sent.' They didn't seem to understand.

Anyway as luck would have it, the first contact was in the front of the hall, but next the light went to the side of the stage. I had to abandon my instructions. 'I've got the name of Kitchin, a lady's voice and she belongs to someone over there,' I pointed to the side.

A girl stood up immediately, 'That's my mother.'

'Who's Margaret?' I asked.

'That's me, that's me.'

At last I was satisfied. In such a big place two people can have the same names and the wrong person sometimes claims the message which can cause all sorts of confusion. 'Well we've got the right contact then,' I said and drowning out the other voices I homed in on Kitchin. But as soon as I did so all I heard was 'tidy kitchen, tidy, kitchen, kitchen tidy.' What on earth was going on?

Kevin saw I was stuck and started to get a bit agitated. He tried to move me on; but I couldn't get past this 'tidy kitchen, kitchen tidy.' I know it sounds most peculiar,' I said at last, 'but all I'm hearing is kitchen tidy, tidy kitchen!'

A great roar of laughter went up over this, but Margaret said: 'That's quite all right Doris, my married name is Tidy.'

Her mother then went on to say that she'd passed with a cerebal haemorrhage, that Margaret was divorced but would marry again, a man named Laurie I think it was, and she also named her grandchildren. Then she said she had a woman with her called Phyllis who'd died of cancer.

Margaret shook her head, 'I don't know a Phyllis.' But her mother insisted she'd met her.

'Well your mother thinks you do dear,' I said, 'maybe you've forgotten.'

The messages went on and when the show was supposed to finish the audience wouldn't let me go. 'She hasn't been over here yet!' came an anguished cry from a neglected section of the hall, so I walked amongst them, going up and down the aisle until they'd had their fair share of attention.

The next morning, after a longer lie in than usual, the phone rang. It was the same reporter who'd phoned the day before for my comments on the religious society. 'I just want to thank you for the message you gave Margaret Tidy last night,' he said, 'I'm Laurie, the man she's going to marry and the Phyllis who died of cancer was my mother. Margaret had met her, but her mind went blank until afterwards.'

Someone wrote after my visit that I appeared before 39,000 people live in Australia, and millions on television. How accurate those figures are I'm not sure; but I do know that throughout my tour I was only heckled once – in Adelaide.

The place was packed and this girl must have slipped in towards the end at question time, because she suddenly yelled from the back, 'Is the devil up there working with you Doris?'

'I don't know dear, I've never met him,' I said. 'Have you?' and with that she slipped out again.

That was the only trouble we had. Everyone gave us so much love.

I'm left with so many precious memories of Australia. Some funny – like the time we flew from Adelaide to Brisbane in a small private jet. The car pulled up on the tarmac and we got out, Mrs Edgeley, Kevin, Clive and Eric, John and I, and climbed into the cramped plane.

First John put his foot on the savouries, then Kevin put his foot on the cakes – thankfully they were covered with cling film – then Mrs Edgeley said 'I wonder where the toilet is? Pilot, where's the toilet?'

'In the cabin madam,' he said.

'Where?' we asked.

'Where that little curtain is.'

We looked and we saw a flimsy little curtain that only came down to your knees.

Not a word was spoken. Silently we all got up, climbed out on to the tarmac again, got back into the cars and returned to the terminal to visit the loos. What's more, throughout the flight Mrs Edgeley and I daren't so much as look at a cup of coffee!

There are some sad memories as well. In Adelaide we were invited to the Premier's house to meet the Premier's wife – Adele Coe.

She was a lovely girl, beautiful in looks and nature. Petite and fragile as a little bird, she had long black hair, dark glowing eyes and she was dying. She had cancer and she knew it.

We had several long conversations, we went to lunch with her again, and she came to our last live appearance in Adelaide. In fact her husband even left Parliament to see the end of the show and then they came back stage.

After we got home Adele continued to write and telephone. Then one Sunday morning, while John had gone for a walk and I was preparing lunch, I happened to glance out of the kitchen door into the hall and there was Adele, standing looking at me, her beautiful black hair falling about her shoulders.

I opened my mouth to speak and she was gone.

No, I thought, it can't be. Not so soon. But I mentioned it to John when he got back, and we decided to wait a little longer before ringing Australia.

Then on the Tuesday I saw her again. Just as before. This time I knew for certain she'd passed over. I didn't like to disturb her poor husband, so I phoned the Edgeley office in Melbourne. 'Yes you're right Doris,' they told me. 'She passed over last week.

I'm so glad John and I were able to visit her in Australia. I know from what she told us in her letters and telephone conversations that I'd taken the fear of death away from her, so if I did nothing else in Australia I know I did something really worth while.

Most of all I remember the tremendous kindness shown to us everywhere. There was Scottie who worked at our hotel in Melbourne. A wiry little Scotswoman with a scarf perpetually tied round her head gypsy-fashion, who always insisted on bringing our breakfast up to us in the morning. She'd stagger in with an enormous tray, because our wrestler bodyguard had jugs of milk and four eggs for breakfast.

'I've made your porridge love,' she'd say, 'they can't

make it here.' She even knitted us two little egg cosies to keep our eggs warm.

Then there was, I'll just call her Ruth, at our hotel in Sydney. She often came to our suite to see if we needed anything, and she always looked rather sad. One night I said to her, 'I think you'd like to talk to me wouldn't you?'

'Oh I know you're terribly tied up,' she said.

'Well I've got a free afternoon on Saturday. Could you pop in for an hour then?'

Well she came, I did a sitting for her and it turned out she had a daughter, a beautiful young girl who'd taken her own life.

Later on we were chatting and I happened to say, 'Oh I hope they don't keep me out too late tonight, we're leaving for Perth in the morning and I've still got the packing to do.'

But when we got back, later than we'd intended, as usual; I discovered Ruth had done all our packing and beside my case was a little parcel. Inside I found a luxurious cigarette lighter, a bottle of her daughter's favourite perfume and a little note to say I'd changed her life.

There were all sorts of touching surprises. One night Alan, our bodyguard, went to the door to put our breakfast card out and came in with two blue carnations that had been taped to the door handle with a card that said, 'Dear Doris, from your favourite writer, Ray.' As I passed reception before a show, there was always some little gift that had been handed in for me, an orchid, a bunch of violets or in one case, a tin of talcum powder from an old age pensioner. From churches carved writing case.

Yes, we were very sad to leave Australia at the end of our six weeks, but we made up our minds that one day we'd go back.

Chapter 17

Back in London I was soon brought down to earth with a bump. It was lovely to see Terry and Matey our ginger cat again and of course all our friends. But it was quite a shock to come from a world of expensive hotel rooms, lavishly cooked meals and chauffeur driven cars to our small flat, a pile of washing and queueing in the greengrocer's with a shopping bag.

I couldn't get delusions of grandeur while I was ironing fourteen shirts!

The excitement was by no means over however. My tour of Australia had a snowball effect, and the following spring I was invited to America and Canada.

John and I flew to New York, where we were to meet the producer of a programme called Mid-day Live, to discuss the possibility of me appearing on the show. I was also to do a radio phone-in on a Canadian radio station, the John Gilbert Show.

The meetings in New York seemed to go well and, while arrangements were being made, John and I went to Canada for one night only, or so we thought at the time. We arrived on the Tuesday and the phone-in was from 9-11 the Wednesday morning.

I took to John Gilbert immediately. He was a warm, sympathetic man and I knew I could work well with him. The phone-in was going splendidly, when suddenly I got a man's name. Alec. No-one claimed him and so I didn't pursue that communication. During the commercial break however, he came back. 'I want to speak to John,' he said very distinctly.

'John,' I said, 'this Alec wants to talk to you.'

His face turned a shade paler. 'My God,' he gasped, 'it's

my father. I hoped it might be, but I wasn't going to give you any help.

Then we were on the air and the message continued. Alec correctly named his children and then told me that his own nickname was Bubs.

'That's incredible,' said John, 'nobody but the closest family could possibly know his nickname.'

I wasn't sure whether I should repeat it, but Alec went on to say that his wife Floss had had a terrible life with him, and how proud he was that his son John had made such a success of his life.

'Remind John about Sheila,' he said, 'that's the floozie I pushed off with.'

'Yes, yes, that's right,' John admitted.

Next I got a young girl on the line and I was stumped to start with. A voice came out with a name that I couldn't even begin to pronounce.

'I'm sorry dear,' I said, 'but I'm hearing some foreign name that I just can't manage.'

'That's right,' she said, 'it's probably Polish and I can't pronounce it either!'

Then her father came through and suddenly I felt a terrific crushing sensation at the back of my neck and in my head. I heard an explosion and smelled a strong tang of smoke.

'My goodness there's been a tragedy here,' I said, 'he's been shot.'

'No,' said the girl, 'he wasn't shot.'

I was puzzled. The sensations had been very strong. 'Well he went over very suddenly,' I said. Then all at once I felt myself being hurled into the air. 'It was an explosion of some kind.'

'Yes,' said the girl, 'a boiler blew.'

Her father was still upset about it. 'Just another five minutes,' he kept telling me, 'she'd made me a cup of coffee and I said I won't be a minute and left the flat to see to the boiler. If only I'd sat down and drunk my coffee. Just think. Five minutes difference between life and eternity.'

The phone calls were coming in thick and fast, and John

Gilbert had no trouble filling the two hour slot. Afterwards we left the studio together, and came face to face with a burly truck driver clutching two steaming cartons of coffee.

'John,' he said, 'that's the best show you've had on. I've sat here and listened to the whole show. I haven't done a bit of work!' and he solemnly presented us with a carton of coffee each.

It seemed so popular with the other listeners too, that John asked me back the next day. The show went just as well, and once again as we left the studio the same truck driver was waiting. Once again he explained that he'd done no work, and this time he presented me with a bunch of flowers.

Finally I was invited back a third time afterwards and I could hardly believe my eyes when that same faithful truck driver came to meet me with a beautiful bouquet.

'The whole show?' I asked.

'The whole show,' he said.

I was quite glad it was time to move on. If I did any more shows he might lose his job!

Requests for me to take part in phone-ins were coming in from all over Canada now. I did one in Ottawa and one in London, though I wasn't very happy about that one. I had a splitting headache that day and I wasn't very pleased with the results that came through. Bill Brady, the presenter reassured me afterwards that they'd had a good response, but I was still rather disappointed.

There was an interesting development to my trip to Hamilton however. While I was there I was doing a newspaper interview. The reporter was a girl named Anne and, after her questions, she asked if she could have a sitting.

It was a routine affair – I got through to her grandfather and she was scribbling it all down, when suddenly a little boy's voice came through louder and clearer than the old man's.

'I'm Jason,' said the little boy.

But Anne shook her head. It didn't mean a thing. 'The lady doesn't know you Jason,' I told him. He wasn't at all put out.

'I was killed you know. My mummy and my sister and I were killed.'

I repeated this aloud and recognition suddenly flashed across Anne's face.

'I know who that is,' she said jumping up, 'just a minute, I'll get the editor.'

It was the chief reporter who came back I think. He explained that I might have stumbled across some details of a murder case, could I do more for them?

I hesitated. I made it a rule that I never got involved in cases unless I was working for the people directly concerned – in criminal cases, either the relatives of the victims or the police.

'I'm sorry,' I said at last, 'I can't. If the police or the relatives ask me to help that's different, as it is it's no-one else's business.'

Some sort of story must have appeared in print however, because it was mentioned again on my next phone-in.

I was to speak on the Tom Charrington programme and on the way Donna, the girl who was looking after us, frightened the life out of me. 'Now don't let him worry you Doris,' she warned, 'Tom Charrington is a real hard nut. Cyncial as they come.'

By the time I got there I was nervous to put it mildly, and when I saw Tom Charrington I felt like turning round and going back. He was very tall with a very stern, austere face. Goodness I thought, how on earth am I to do anything with him.

But there was no getting out of it. So I sat down, and we started; by the first commercial break Tom turned to me, a smile lightened that stern face and he said: 'Jesus Christ,' you're an incredible lady.'

Back on the air again he asked me about the Jason story. I was able to confirm the details he'd read and add that the sister's name was Stephanie. Then as I was speaking Jason's voice came through once more.

'It's me Jason,' he said, 'and I want to speak to Doug.'

I repeated this aloud but it meant nothing at all. There was nobody in the studio called Doug. I shrugged my shoulders and went on to the next communication.

The show ended and, to my great surprise, Tom came over and gave me a smacking kiss. 'You might not believe this Doris,' he said gravely, 'but in twenty years of broadcasting you're the first guest I've ever kissed.'

Dazed, I put my hand to my cheek, not sure how to reply to this great honour, but I was saved by the telephone. It rang and rang and Tom reluctantly took the call.

I saw his face turn serious again as he listened, then he covered the mouthpiece. 'Doris, it's that little boy's grandmother. Will you talk to her?'

'Of course.' I took the phone from him and instantly a distraught voice crackled over the line. 'Jason is my grandson and Stephanie is his sister,' she said, 'please can we come and see you. They found my daughter's body and Stephanie's body, but they couldn't find Jason's and I'm certain you can help. Please can we come and see you?'

I couldn't refuse such a desperate plea. The following Saturday the grandmother, her husband Doug and a policeman came to visit me in Toronto.

I started the sitting but, instead of the young boy's voice I'd been expecting, a woman came across very strongly. It was Sandra, Jason's mother.

As she talked I began to experience some weird and unpleasant sensations. I saw blood spattered all over a bed, felt blows in my face and teeth being knocked right back into my mouth. Sandra then described the location where the two bodies had been found – which the policeman confirmed – and then another location where she thought Jason's body might be.

At that point little Jason butted in again. 'She's saved my blue suit you know.'

And his grandmother began to sob. 'Yes, yes that's true. I've saved his little suit to bury his body in.'

Gently I tried to explain to her that after two years in the water she wouldn't be able to put a suit on Jason; but it didn't matter because he was quite safe and happy and had no need of it now.

As I comforted the elderly woman, it occurred to me that so far the police might feel I'd told them nothing I couldn't have read in the papers. So I tuned in to Sandra again and asked her if she could give me any details the police and reporters didn't know.

She told me about a white station wagon her husband had borrowed, the name of their next door neighbours and the words: Pasadena, Jack, Laurie and Hamilton.

The police inspector looked blank. 'D'you know what that means?' he asked the grandmother.

'Oh yes, most certainly,' she said. 'Jack is her husband's cousin who's in prison for these dreadful murders. Laurie was his wife. They lived at Pasadena, and before this happened Sandra and her family used to go and stay with them. Now they've moved to Hamilton.'

The story of Jason and his family wasn't the only violent case I came across during my visit. Shortly afterwards, John Gilbert asked me if I could do a private sitting for some friends of his.

He brought them to our room one evening, two couples, one of their sons and John himself. John hadn't told me a thing about the case, because he knew I liked to start from nothing; but it soon became clear they were all from one family and their parents came to talk to me.

Suddenly I was looking at another bedroom. There was a woman laid across the bed with blood stains spreading across her body, and her husband was slumped down on the floor beside her where he'd tried to protect her. They'd both been shot.

'This is terrible,' I said in horror, 'they've been shot.'

The family confirmed I was right.

Then the father gave me quite a few names, including the name of the murderer.

The family knew it immediately. It turned out they'd suspected this man all along, but he had an alibi and there was no evidence to convict him.

It sounds as if all my work across the Atlantic was rather grim, but in fact there were many happy moments. One of the nicest things we did was visit Niagara falls. I was doing some live appearances in halls and I had to get a special work permit to work in theatres. They told me it would take a little time to prepare; so we went to see the falls while they got it ready.

It was a sight John and I will never forget. It was winter time. The snow was still on the ground but the sky was vivid blue, and between white ground and blue sky roared this great ice green mountain of water, with cascades of flying spray that caught in the sunshine and made an arching rainbow.

The fall was like a magnet and we walked closer and closer, thrilled by the tremendous power and beauty. It was very hard to tear ourselves away for something as mundane as a work permit.

Back in New York everything had been fixed for my appearance on Mid-day Live. First I did private sittings for the producer and Bill Boggs, the presenter, then the producer asked me if I could arrive half an hour early to rehearse.

I laughed. 'There's no point in rehearsing,' I said, 'you never know what's going to happen.' Somehow I don't think that set her mind at rest.

She needn't have worried. Everything went smoothly on the air, even though there were a few surprises.

First Bill Boggs told the audience about his sitting with me, then a glamorous young blonde walked on to appreciative applause. This was Monique Vanhusen, a famous star in the States. She sat down beside me and Bill said.

'Have you visited psychics before Monique?'

'Oh yes, of course,' she said, 'I go to them often. I think everyone's interested in the future.'

Before I could stop myself I was blurting out, 'Well you're on a dead loss with me love. I don't do that sort of thing.'

She raised her eyebrows. 'Oh really. What do you do then?'

'I'm a medium,' I said, 'I'm an instrument between the two worlds.'

'Oh,' she said looking none the wiser, 'you won't be able to do anything for me then.'

'We'll just have to see.' But even as I said the words, a rapid torrent of French was coming through.

I told Monique. 'Just a minute it'll be translated,' I added. It turned out to be Monique's mother from Belgium. She told me how she passed, which Monique confirmed, then she listed some names.

'Who's Pierre?' I asked.

'I know a Pierre,' Monique said cautiously.

'Who's Jacqueline?'

'My God. That's Pierre and Jacqueline with whom I'm going to stay.'

'Near the Eiffel Tower?'

'Yes! That's right!'

There was more and then at the end, I took hold of her hand and said 'Your mother wants to say happy birthday darling.'

'It was my birthday yesterday,' she gasped, and with that she dissolved into tears and hurried away.

I did some general work with the audience next, then there was a commercial break and afterwards a very handsome boy came and sat next to me.

'This is all a bit strange,' Bill Boggs explained, 'you won't know him. He's our chief reporter but he just wants to see Doris. He'll tell you about it.'

His story was certainly unusual. He explained that he'd been going out on a job, he'd left the TV station with his brief case, got as far as the street corner and stopped dead. He just knew he had to turn round and go back. What he didn't know was why.

Back he came to the station and asked the receptionist, who was upstairs on Mid-day Live. 'Doris Stokes, the British medium,' she told him.

'That's why I had to come back,' he said, 'and here I am.'

Intrigued, I tuned in for him. His grandfather made quick contact and, little by little, a sad story came out.

Apparently the boy had heard voices before and dismissed them. Then on his way home from a party at 4.00 in the morning, he heard a voice say quite distinctly 'Go home now'. Thinking it was ridiculous he walked on, but again, close behind his shoulder, the voice said 'Go home now'. Fed up with strange voices and thinking he might be going mad; (didn't I know how he felt) he decided to sit down on a seat and wait, to prove once and for all it was his imagination. Finally he wandered slowly home, and when he arrived he discovered a tragedy had happened. I won't say what.

At this point his grandfather was very insistent – I repeat his exact words. 'He says don't worry son,' I repeated, 'you'll have all the forgiveness in the world.'

Tears came into the boy's eyes. 'D'you know after it happened I spent the whole week on my knees asking for forgiveness, because I hadn't gone straight home.'

Right at the end I told him, 'You have their forgivenenss and they love you very much.'

And to my surprise he took my hand and kissed it. 'And I love you very much,' he said.

Once again it was time to go home and I left with many promises to return again soon. I had no idea as I made them however, just how soon it would turn out to be.

Only a few months later British D.J. and presenter David Hamilton, invited me to appear on a programme he was doing in Los Angeles. Apparently our Thames Television was putting on a week of programmes in America, one of which involved David Hamilton the whole week.

It was great fun. I did a phone-in on the television and was invited back to do another, and I did a radio phone-in on the main radio station, as well. But the most memorable case I was involved in happened by accident.

John and I were invited to lunch in Beverley Hills Hotel's famous Polo lounge by actress and singer, Kay Stevens. It was a very plush expensive place with celebrities everywhere, and John and I could hardly find our table staring around and muttering, 'Isn't that ...?' 'Surely that can't be ...?'

We settled down for an interesting lunch, but after a while I couldn't concentrate on the conversation round the table. An insistent male voice kept talking to me, demanding to be heard. He mentioned a white house on a hill, the names Vic and Rose, said he'd left in a maroon and white Rolls-Royce and that he'd been shot twice in the head.

I put down my fork. My appetite seemed to have disappeared. This sounded like another terrible murder. Wearily I told the others what I'd heard and asked if they knew anything about it.

At first they thought I might be referring to the murder of a local soap tycoon's family some time ago, but I was sure that wasn't right. The man seemed certain he'd passed within the last few days.

It was quite a puzzle but just in case it might help, our friends took a tape recorder of my 'evidence' to the police. It meant nothing to them.

The next day however, we heard that a sports promoter called Vic Weiss had mysteriously disappeared. A 'red' Rolls-Royce was involved, the man's wife was called Rose and they lived in a white house on a hill.

It all seemed to fit and as far as I was concerned, the news next day clinched it. Vic Weiss had been found murdered in the boot of a maroon Rolls-Royce in a hotel car park. The cause of death so far was unknown.

For once I broke my rule about not helping, unless the police or a relative asked me to. This time I felt sure that Vic himself urgently wanted me to do more. I couldn't barge in uninvited on his shocked widow; so instead John and I drove to the hotel car park where the Rolls-Royce was found. I lit a cigarette, sat back quietly and waited.

Vic came to me almost immediately. He was an angry man. He repeated that he'd been shot in the head twice, once behind the ear and again at the rear of the skull. He said he'd been dumped in the car park by two men, one had waited outside in a green car while the other parked the Rolls.

'Watch my wife,' he kept saying. 'Ask Jerry, Ask Jerry.'

He repeated the name of one of the killers and the words 'River' and 'canyon' many times.

'I loved that Rolls-Royce,' he said, 'I never thought it would be my coffin. Get the bastards! Get the bastards!'

By the end of his communication I felt limp and drained. The evidence and pent up emtion came over so strongly, I felt this man wouldn't rest until his killers were brought to justice.

Again we contacted the police, and this time they took extensive notes and asked dozens of questions. Yet frustratingly, afterwards they wouldn't confirm that my information had been of any use at all.

Still later the same day, the coroner's office came back with the results of the autopsy. Vic Weiss had died from two gun-shot wounds … one behind the ear, the other at the back of the skull!

The story got out and soon it was in the papers in California, New York and London. Once again the same clamour that had started in Australia was beginning in America. The phone didn't stop ringing. Reporters, television stations, radio stations, enquiries from promoters. But by this time I had to go home to fulfill several months of long standing engagements.

'Yes,' I told everyone, 'I'll be back soon.'

But even at home I didn't lose contact with them. The letters are still pouring in, from America, Canada and Australia and time and time again the writers thank me, because the tiny snippets of information I've been able to provide have given them hope and peace.

And really, those letters, when all the fuss and excitement is over, mean more to me than anything else. Of course the trips were fun. Of course they were a thrill, but the best thing of all is the knowledge I've done some good.

I don't try to push what I think is the truth down other people's throats. I simply want to share what I've found – the peace of mind, the hope and the strength to carry on with a life shattered by tragedy.

Chapter 18

I went back to Grantham recently. Thinking about this book and recalling the events of my life, filled me with a great longing to go back to the beginning, to see the places and the faces of long ago.

'Are you going to go to the cemetery?' one lady asked me.

And I said, 'Good gracious no. Why should I want to go there?' She looked shocked. 'Don't you want to see your parents' grave, or John Michael's grave?'

I laughed. 'No. I wouldn't know where to find them. My parents and John Michael aren't in the cemetery.'

I'd obviously offended her and she went away, but I couldn't help smiling. How strange to be shocked that I didn't want to place flowers on graves and do the morbid bit.

But it was a mistake to go back. Grantham seemed so small, so greatly changed. I walked to the street where I was born and there was now an indoor heated swimming pool. The place where we played tag and and the window ledge from which I jumped on to the backs of passing wagons for a free ride had disappeared.

Instead of the gardens, there were open fields and horses grazing.

I leant against the fence, staring at the horses, my eyes filled with tears of disappointment. I'd so wanted to see the rows of cabbages and the cinder track where I'd played with my spirit friends, the place where I'd found the kitten. How weird to think it was all gone. My past was gone. And then suddenly I felt my father's presence very strongly and his old familiar voice said, 'But isn't this much better? Look at all this lovely open space for children to play and horses to graze. It's much better now girl.'

He was with me for the rest of my walk.

And I did find something left untouched. Retracing my steps into town, I came to the old Market Cross where Edna and I had sat picking seeds out of pomegranates; while my father took mother into the pub to celebrate an occasional win on the horses.

Maybe I'm getting a sentimental old thing, but I climbed on that market cross once more and sat there again. And suddenly as I sat there, the scene swam before my eyes, the present slipped away and I was looking at a kaleidoscope of pictures.

There was the old market with gas lamps smoking and cobblestones, and there were people, so many people, there was the stage at Sydney Opera House, television studios in America, radio stations in Canada, they were all there, side by side. Past and present were all one, and I found I was crying again for long ago and the things that might have been.

Then, through it all, came my father's voice. 'Remember Doll, never look back, progress, always progress …'

MORE VOICES IN MY EAR

More Voices
In My Ear

Chapter 1

It was a stormy night. The rain had stopped, but a wind had sprung up and it was getting stronger every minute. Everything was in motion. Tattered clouds were flying across the moon, great black branches tossed against the sky, dead leaves whirled along the gutter and the six of we WRAFs, brave because we were in a group, decided to take the short cut home through the churchyard.

We joked nervously as we approached the path. Beneath wildly plunging trees the silent gravestones stood in rows, now in moonlight, now in shadow. Wet twigs slapped against our hair, strange dark shapes bobbed by the fence and our skirts tangled round our legs making it difficult to walk. The six of us huddled closer together, yet each voice grew a little louder, a little more daring.

'Bet you wouldn't walk across one of those graves!'

'I would too.'

'The spooks'd get you.'

'Spooks!' Molly's voice rose in decision. 'Don't tell me you believe in spooks.'

'Bet you wouldn't stay here all night.'

'No. I've got more sense. I'd freeze to death.'

I listened to them and laughed. You wouldn't have got me staying there all night either and not because of the cold. I wasn't going to let on but the place gave me the creeps. All those gloomy tomb stones. They made me shudder. I glanced across at the church, a pretty stone building in daylight, but now just a black hulk against the sky, and as the moon came out again I stopped in surprise. There were people standing outside the church door. A whole family by the look of it; a man, a woman and two children, just standing there, patiently waiting. What in the world could they be doing? Surely the vicar hadn't arranged to meet them at this time of night.

'I wonder what those people are doing on a night like this,' I said to the other girls.

'What people' asked Molly.

'Those people over there.'

They looked vaguely up and down the path. 'Where?'

'Over there,' I said pointing impatiently. 'Look, standing by the church door. A whole family.'

They peered in the direction I indicated, and then looked back at me. There was an odd pause and then suddenly, without a word being spoken, they all turned round and ran. Bewildered, I stared after them. What had I said? I glanced back at the family, still waiting, their clothes strangely unruffled in the gale. And then my heart lurched violently. Before my eyes they disappeared. They didn't walk away, they just went out like flames in the wind. For perhaps two seconds I just stood there, my mouth open, staring at the empty space and then I hitched up my skirt and ran as fast as my sensible shoes would allow me.

That was in 1943 and looking back now it seems very funny to think that I ran away from spirit people. I'd had quite a job persuading the girls afterwards that I'd made the whole thing up. After all they'd seen my white, terrified face as I hurtled out of the graveyard behind them, and even though I had a reputation for being a bit of a clown they couldn't help feeling I'd been able to see something they couldn't. They looked at me a little strangely after that. It was my childhood all over again. Mother always feared I'd end up mad or, at the very least, a bit peculiar and scolded me if I saw or heard anything that other people couldn't. Sometimes I'd come home from school and tell her that one of our acquaintances had died.

'What were you doing round there when you're supposed to come straight home?' Mum used to demand.

'I did come straight home,' I'd protest.

'Then how d'you know Mrs So and So's gone?'

I'd look at the floor and shuffle uncomfortably. 'I – I just know, that's all,' I'd mumble. I really had no idea how I knew, I just *did* know. So I'd get a clout for failing to come straight home from school and a clout for telling lies, on the grounds that I must be guilty of one or the other, or more likely both.

There was no way of knowing then that I was a natural medium. I didn't even know what a medium was and I hated my 'funny streak'. I wanted to be the same as everyone else. It's only as I've grown older and as my powers have developed that I've come to realize what a wonderful gift I've been given.

Since my last book *Voices in My Ear* was published, I've been overwhelmed by letters from all over the world. I feel quite sorry for the postman who has to struggle up to our second floor flat with such great sacks of mail. Unfortunately it's impossible for me to reply to everyone – I'd be busy from morning till night and wouldn't have time for my work – but I try to read them all and they are very moving. One man working in Germany wrote to tell me that he'd sent for the book after hearing me on the radio. Shortly afterwards he and his wife lost their baby daughter. 'That book,' he said, 'gave us strength to go through what we had to face.'

Another woman wrote to say she had never had any experience of mediums but one day she was in a shop and she turned round and saw a smiling face looking at her from the cover of a book. She picked it up, read the blurb on the back and thought, 'Oh, I don't know. I don't go in for this sort of thing.' But she bought it anyway, took it home and read it from cover to cover in one sitting. It opened a whole new set of ideas for her, she says. The idea that death isn't to be feared, that it's a great adventure to look forward to; the idea that we don't go anywhere alone and when our time comes, somebody will take us by the hand and lead us.

It's strange to think that this ability that used to frighten me so much should have enabled me to help so many thousands of people, even people I've never met. And, I'm very glad to say, people don't run away from me any more.

These days they flock to my door and I have more invitations to visit overseas than I can cope with.

In the spring of 1979 my husband John and I were invited back to New York. We'd been there briefly the year before but this time we were able to get a much stronger impression. On the first morning we left our hotel with our friends Mike and Bill who were looking after us. It was a cool, blustery day, and I looked up at the sky to see if it might rain. My head went back and back as my eyes scanned acres of concrete and glass until, way up above, I could see a thin strip of grey. It was like being at the foot of monstrous great cliffs and the sensation made me feel quite dizzy. Quickly I dragged my eyes back to the ground and then stopped dead in horror. I'd nearly tripped over the body of a man sprawled across the pavement. Clothes awry, one arm flung out beside him, the man was quite motionless.

'Mike, quick we must do something!' I cried, dropping to my knees. 'This man's ill.' But to my surprise Mike hauled me up again and steered me round the body.

'Leave him, Doris,' he said firmly. 'It's drink or drugs. He'll sleep it off. You'll see a lot like him in New York.'

I looked anxiously over my shoulder. No-one else seemed the least bit worried. Pedestrians were stepping over the body as calmly as if it was a pile of litter. John and I exchanged glances. It wasn't like this in Fulham.

There was worse to come. A little further on we came to a doorway where a pathetic creature, hardly recognizable as a woman, sat huddled in newspapers, two or three grubby bags pressed close to her side.

Bill saw me look at her. 'She's a bag lady, Doris.'

'A what?'

'A bag lady,' he repeated and went on to explain that the bag people, men and women, lived rough, endlessly wandering the city streets carrying their belongings in bags. It seemed terribly sad. I know people sleep rough on the Embankment in London, but here they were in the main streets of the city. It was a shock to see these poor bag people in their newspapers lying outside the luxurious shops of New York's famous avenues.

The pace of life was extraordinary. Leaving early one morning John nudged me. 'Look at that!' he said grinning and my mouth fell open in amazement at the sight of a businessman, briefcase tucked under his arm, a cup of coffee in one hand and a hot dog in the other, having his breakfast as he rushed along the road to work. But we soon discovered this wasn't an unusual sight in this city where life seemed to be lived at running speed.

The other surprising thing was the way nobody seemed to go to bed. I was asked to do some radio phone-ins, one for a couple called Peggy and Eddie Fitzgerald who had had their own show for forty-one years, and another for Dick Sommers. The shows didn't start until John and I would normally have been in bed, and in the early hours of the morning when we were ready to leave, our eyelids heavy as lead, listeners were still phoning in and the presenters were still as chirpy and alert as if it were the middle of the afternoon.

I'd gone to New York mainly to do some television shows and some live appearances at a theatre in Greenwich Village. The first television show was a programme called *AM America* and I was to be given fifteen minutes with the presenter to explain what I did. I thought this a big strange as I'm used to working with an audience, but I soon realized they probably didn't know what to expect from me. Apparently psychics in New York are usually more interested in foretelling the future than in contacting people who've passed over. There are some extraordinary variations on the fortune-telling theme (apparently you can even have your dog's paw read!), but confronted with a psychic who had no intention of looking into the future – well they didn't know what to make of me.

I was taken on to a cosy set which was decorated to look like someone's living-room. Comfortable armchairs were arranged around a fireplace complete with brass fender, shovels and pokers. I sat down and the interviewer came over and sat opposite me. She was a very attractive, dark haired girl in smart, expensive clothes. She introduced herself as Janet.

'Well, Doris,' she said, 'I know you don't tell fortunes but can you tell me anything about myself?'

Her voice was pleasant but I could tell she was sceptical and my mouth went dry. It's always more difficult to work when people are sending out waves of doubt but the cameras were rolling and they expected me to come up with something. Heart thudding, I tuned in. Instantly all background noise faded away, my field of vision narrowed until I was only aware of Janet and I heard an elderly woman say, 'My name's Mary. I had a cerebral haemorrhage, you know.'

Janet was watching me calmly, a polite smile on her face. I took a deep breath. 'Well, there's an elderly lady here called Mary,' I said, 'and she says she passed on with a cerebral haemorrhage. Have you any idea who she is?'

The effect was astonishing. The colour drained from Janet's face, the smile disappeared and she turned round accusingly to the television. 'I just don't believe this,' she said.

Oh God, I thought, I must be way off beam, it's obviously not going to work. I was just beginning to panic when I realized that Janet was still addressing the crew. 'Has anybody been talking to her about me?' she demanded.

I nearly fell off my chair. 'They couldn't have done, Janet,' I interrupted. 'I was taken to make-up the minute I arrived and then brought straight here. I haven't spoken to any of them.'

The producer agreed that this was correct.

'So you do know Mary?' I ventured cautiously.

Janet nodded. 'Yes,' she said reluctantly. 'She's my grandmother.'

I breathed a sigh of relief. It was going to be all right. The old lady passed on the names of people in Janet's family and then I felt her lean forward and touch the girl's gold wedding ring. 'This is a new one, you know,' she explained. 'She's taken another wedding ring off.'

'That's right,' said Janet. 'I was divorced and I married again.'

The show went on, more and more details were

accepted by an increasingly bemused Janet until right at the end I said, 'Mary wants to tell you she's got David with her,' and the girl's eyes filled with tears.

'That's impossible,' she whispered. 'Nobody knows about David. Only my mother and myself.'

'And your grandmother, love,' I said gently. 'David's your son, isn't he?'

'Yes,' she said, and threw her arms around me and gave me a big hug.

Fortunes or no fortunes they were obviously satisfied with my work after that, because the following Friday I was invited back again and this time I was allowed to talk to the studio audience. I wasn't so nervous this time as it was my second appearance but to my horror, when I tuned in, all I could hear was a flood of Italian. It was a woman's voice and very emotioinal but I couldn't understand a word of it.

When I work with a group of people I see a small light hovering near the person the message is intended for and on this occasion a bright light was dancing crazily over the head of a young girl at the back.

'I want to talk to you, dear,' I said to her, 'but at the moment I can't understand it. I'll have to get it translated.'

I don't know how it happened, but even as I spoke English words started coming into my head over the top of the unintelligible Italian and I knew someone was translating for this excited latin lady.

The light darted round and round the girl as the woman told me her name and then added in a trembling voice, 'She's my bambina, my bambina.' I repeated this aloud, glad to be able to make a start, but instead of answering, the girl burst into tears.

All around me I could sense a buzz of concern. The producer and presenter were alarmed. It must have looked to them as if they'd made a big mistake. They'd trusted me with a studio audience and in less than a minute I'd upset them.

'It's all right,' I reassured them. 'Do you want me to stop, love?' The girl shook her head. I wasn't at all surprised. People often cry at first due to the overwhelming release from emotional tension, but they usually want to hear more.

The Italian lady was still chattering eagerly to me. She gave the name and occupation of the girl's husband who was sitting beside her. Then she mentioned two other people and said to her daughter, 'I'm very grateful to them for caring for you, but remember, I'll always be your mother.'

At this the girl stood up, dabbing her eyes with a handkerchief and explained that her mother was Italian but she remembered nothing about her. She'd been brought up by her adopted parents, whose names her mother had given.

The long lost mother would happily have talked all night but I could hear a babble of other voices clamoring in the background and finally she was nudged to one side.

Immediately, the light bobbed away to the front of the audience and hovered over a group of four or five people sitting together.

'That's Mabel,' said a voice close to me.

'Is one of you Mabel?' I asked. A grey blonde woman with a sun-tanned face looked up in surprise. 'Yes. I am,' she said. And suddenly there was the strong, sweet scent of orange blossom and I was looking at a mass of swaying orange trees.

I couldn't understand this at all. Was she getting married perhaps, but even that explanation seemed obscure. I stared at the picture in my mind, struggling to interpret the hidden meaning. It was no use. All I got was orange trees. I gave up. 'Well,' I said at last. 'I don't know if this will mean anything to you. I can't work it out but all I can see are dozens of orange trees.'

The woman laughed in delight. 'It's all right, Doris. I live in Florida and you've just given a perfect description of my garden. It's filled with orange trees!'

Between appearances on *AM America* I was doing live shows at the Players Theater, Greenwich Village. I'd been worried about going to New York because people had warned me that they're tough cookies over there. 'You'll have trouble getting through to them.' But in fact they

were lovely – really warm and friendly. I arrived at the
theatre on the first night, to come face to face with two
huge photographs of myself at the front and my name in
lights over the door. *An evening with Doris Stokes.*

John and I couldn't help standing there admiring it and
then John took a picture with his instamatic. It might not
be Broadway, but my name up in lights was an occasion to
be remembered!

I was pleased to see large numbers of young people
every evening who listened attentively to what I had to say
and asked intelligent questions. One night a young man
stood up and said, 'I've just got engaged, Doris.'

'Congratulations!' I said warmly.

'Well, the thing is,' the young man went on, his face
turning pink, 'we love each other very much but supposing
anything happened to my wife or me and the other one
remarried. What happens on the other side?'

This is a difficult point because it seems to vary from
couple to couple.

'It's quite complicated, I'm afraid,' I said slowly. 'It
seems to be that if you marry again and love the other
person just as much as your first partner, but in a different
way, then you might all be together on the other side. But
if you're not lucky in love the next time and the affinity
isn't there, on the other side you will go to the person you
have affinity with.'

At this a tall, blonde woman stood up. 'Well how do I go
on Doris? I've been married five times!' Everyone fell
about laughing, but I could see that she was serious.

'Which one do you love most?' I asked. 'I think it's your
third husband.'

'Why yes, it is!' she said in amazement.

'Well that's the one you'll go to. That's the one who'll be
waiting.'

These sessions used to last for ages and the audience
took such interest in the proceedings that they didn't want
to leave. When the show finished they used to rush to the
stage and the stage door; they gathered in the dressing
room and wouldn't go. The manager got quite cross about
it. One night he said to me: 'Doris, would you please go

home and then I can close the theatre and we can *all* go home!'

Towards the end of the week, however, he'd changed his mind. He was so pleased to have his theatre full every night instead of only at weekends that he asked me to stay on another week. Unfortunately I had to refuse. I had long-standing engagements in Britain and I had to leave.

It was while we were in New York that I became involved in one of the most disturbing cases of my career. Quite out of the blue we got a telephone call from a Detective Sergeant Bob Harris from the 49th precinct, who wanted to know if I would see someone at the police station. He didn't say what it was about, only that he'd come and pick us up.

He arrived at the hotel on Saturday morning, a big, black policeman with a warm smile and an understanding manner.

'I'm afraid you might be shocked, Doris,' he said helping me on with my coat. 'We're going to the Bronx and although it's still New York it's a different landscape entirely from Manhattan.'

'Oh, I'm fairly unshockable by now,' I said confidently – after all, I'd seen the bag people and the drunks on the pavement; I was getting used to the harsh contrast of rich and poor side by side. Yet as the car bounced towards the Bronx, I began to feel depressed. The potholes that seemed to scar the roads all over the city were getting worse and I clung to John as we lurched along. The towering glass sky-scrapers of Manhattan gave way to crumbling grey blocks and grubby shops with gaudy hand painted signs over the doors. Rusting cars tore through the streets, radios blaring. Litter overflowed the gutters spilling onto the pavements. No street corner or doorway seemed complete withouts its group of shabby young men chatting aimlessly. We didn't see a single white face and despite the frosty blue sky and diamond bright sun I felt as if I was on alien territory.

The police station seemed positively welcoming in comparison. At least it was familiar. It was just like walking into one of the television detective films. Dark shirted policemen with guns on their hips strode purposefully around, frayed lino covered the floor, coffee rings circled the desks and the walls were papered with yellowing 'Wanted' posters.

Those posters became unnerving after a while. We stood there in the centre of them, waiting for Bob Harris to show us which office we were to use, and dozens of cold staring eyes seemed to follow us accusingly every time we moved. I turned with relief to one of the few notices that didn't bear a photograph and saw that it advertised a raffle. I brightened considerably. Now raffles I understood. I could relate to a raffle.

'Look, John!' I said. 'Just like at home.' I leaned forward to read the rest of the details and then recoiled in surprise. It was to raise money for bullet-proof vests for the policemen.

'Isn't that dreadful?' I couldn't help saying. 'All the shootings that go on here and the police have to raise their own money for bullet-proof vests!' Then I realized the room had gone quiet and I clapped my hand over my mouth in horror. How tactless of me. What was I thinking of? But the few policemen within earshot just grinned to themselves and went on with their work.

'Right, Doris,' said Bob Harris appearing at my elbow, 'the person you're to work with is in the office. Would you like to come now?'

'Yes, of course,' I said, glad to get away before I got myself into trouble. 'Where can I leave my coat?' It was quite warm in the station and I'd taken off my coat, a treasured fur given to me by my friends in Australia on my last visit. I was immensely proud of it. It was the first fur coat I'd ever had, but Bob Harris eyed it doubtfully.

'I think we'll take it in with us. I don't know how safe it'll be out here.'

I laughed. 'But this is a police station!' Nevertheless he was quite serious, so in we trooped with Bob Harris carrying my coat over his arm.

A small, dumpy black woman with a red headscarf over her hair was sitting alone in the office. She was chain-smoking and the ashtray on the table in front of her was piled high with dog-ends. I could see by her face that she wasn't at all keen on my visit so I asked Bob to stay and take notes. Perhaps his presence would reassure her.

I explained as I always do that I couldn't guarantee anything but it would help if I heard her voice now and then. She seemed to understand so I tuned in and immediately a woman's voice said, 'I'm Helen and I've got May with me.'

'Do you know these people, love?' I asked the woman.

'That's my grandmother and May's my mother,' she replied reluctantly, but even before these few words died away the air to her right seemed to tremble and thicken and as I watched, a little boy materialized. He was a dear little soul with very short dark curls, melting brown eyes and tiny pink palmed hands. He beamed at me and skipped over to the woman's chair.

'There's a little boy here who belongs to you,' I told her.

'Yes, that's right,' she said. The boy leaned close to her, his head on one side.

'I'm Kevin,' he explained proudly. 'I'm six.'

Even as he spoke a picture flashed into my mind. I could see what looked like a rubbish dump with dozens of old cars, abandoned wheels and bits of engine scattered all over the place.

'He was playing on a dump of some kind,' I remarked to the woman and described what I could see.

'No, that's not a dump,' she said. 'It's a place where people park their cars and do their repair work. Kevin used to spend a lot of time there.'

I glanced back at the child. It seemed unwise to let such a little boy wander off alone to a place like that. I wouldn't have allowed Terry to do it when he was small. Suddenly there was a sharp pain round my neck, something was tightening across my throat and my wrists hurt very badly. I gasped and whirled round to Bob.

'This little boy was strangled with piano wire or something similar,' I spluttered.

'Yes, he was,' said Bob.

'And were his wrists tied with wire too?'

'No,' said Bob, 'they were cut.'

I could hardly look at that poor little child. I felt sick. My head was swimming, my eyes misty and as I hung onto the chair wondering whether I was about to faint, the room swirled away altogether. When the mist cleared I was in the place where his body was found.

I was walking down an alleyway between a dingy derelict house and a great heap of rubbish. Rotting boxes and old tin cans slithered down at the slightest movement, rats scuttled amongst the debris and the slimy path was so narrow I had to walk sideways, my back pressed to the wall.

I inched along, wary of rats and then suddenly I was staggering backwards into empty air. Part of the wall behind me had collapsed and I was drawn silently through the opening into the building. It was pitch black inside and an overpowering stench, like the smell of rotting animal carcases, enveloped me. My eyes stared blindly into the darkness and horrors crawled across my skin. Something evil lurked just in front of me; I couldn't see it but I could feel its presence in the soupy air. The wire was at my neck again, my wrists were blazing with pain and the smell grew stronger and stronger until I thought I'd suffocate. Choking for breath I groped desperately for the opening in the wall. I made out a slice of light in the blackness and I rushed headlong for it and then I was out, breathing clean air again, my eyes streaming in the brightness. From far away I heard Kevin's voice say, 'There were four of them, you know,' and vaguely I understood that he meant there were four wires attached to the one round his neck. Then there was a jolt and I was back in the office again.

Bob was scribbling furiously in his notebook. Kevin's mother was still smoking silently, her face expressionless but as she lifted the cigarette to her mouth her hand was shaking. I realized I was trembling so much that my knees were knocking together and I had to clamp my lips tightly to stop my teeth from chattering. I took a few deep breaths to get myself under control.

'Is this – too upsetting for you?' I asked the woman when I'd managed to calm myself.

She shook her head. 'No, because I already know these things.'

'You call my mother Dooly,' Kevin interrupted. 'That's her nickname.'

Dooly confirmed that this was true.

Kevin then mentioned his brother Tony, his sister Gloria and the name Peter.

'Who's Peter?' I asked.

Dooly explained that Peter was her boyfriend. Then Kevin drew closer to me as if he had something important to say. 'Will you tell Gloria the baby's with us?' he said.

I repeated this and for the first time Dooly showed some reaction. 'No, no, I don't know anything about any baby,' she said sharply.

'Are you quite sure about the baby, Kevin love?' I asked.

'Yes,' he said positively. 'We're looking after the baby now.'

Dooly pursed her lips and shook her head, but protesting voices were pouring into the room and the loudest of all was Dooly's grandmother, Helen.

'You just tell her we do have the baby with us,' she said angrily. 'The baby came over tragically while Kevin was still missing.'

I tried again but it was no use. Dooly flatly refused to acknowledge a baby of any sort and we were getting nowhere. In fact the atmosphere was getting hostile. The only thing I could do was change the subject.

'Can you tell me about anything else?' I asked Kevin. So he talked for a while about the trip to an amusement arcade promised him by the people who'd lured him away. He also named a person responsible for the murder and Bob confirmed later that this person was at the top of their list of suspects but the police hadn't yet collected enough evidence to charge them. Kevin went on to talk about his teacher at school who had been very kind to him and then he said, 'I'm almost seven now. I was just six when it happened and the baby was six months old.'

I didn't dare mention the baby again but fortunately Kevin went straight on. 'Mummy never gave me any flowers at my funeral, you know,' he added.

I glanced at Dooly. 'He says you didn't give him flowers at the funeral.'

She shrugged. 'No, well I couldn't afford it, could I?'

I couldn't imagine such poverty. I'd been hard up in my time never in such desperate straits that I couldn't have got together a few flowers for my son's funeral. On the other hand, look at the bag ladies, I couldn't imagine being in their situation either but they existed all right. Quickly I pulled my purse out of my handbag. All I had was a ten dollar bill. I wasn't much good with American money but I felt sure she could get some nice flowers with that. I pressed it into her hand. 'Look Dooly, take this, buy yourself some flowers and put them by the side of your little boy's photo. He'll like that.'

'I haven't got a photograph,' she said. 'The police have them all.'

I turned to Bob. 'Surely she can have one photograph, Bob. You're not working on them all, are you?'

'Of course you can, Dooly,' said Bob. 'I'll go and get one.'

While he was gone Helen came back, still protesting that Dooly knew the baby. She was absolutely determined to get through. It seemed very important to her.

'Look love, you don't have to say anything to me or to Sergeant Harris if you don't want to,' I told her, 'but they are quite certain you know this baby. At least admit it to yourself.'

Dooly stubbed her cigarette violently in the ahstray. 'I don't know what you're talking about.'

'But they are convinced,' I pointed out. 'Sometimes things get a bit confused and I might mishear something or make a mistake but in this case it's quite definite. The message is for you and the baby is connected with you somewhere.'

At that moment Bob Harris came back with the photograph and he caught the end of the conversation. He watched Dooly shake her head in denial once more and he let out a long sigh.

'Are you going to tell Doris or shall I?' he asked wearily. Dooly stared sullenly at the floor.

'All right then, I will. Doris, you're right, there is a baby. Before Kevin's body was found, his sister Gloria drowned her baby, six months old, in a pail of water.'

I struggled to keep the horrified expression off my face and Dooly fiddled with the corner of her headscarf. 'Oh well, yes,' she muttered.

There was an awkward silence. 'Well I think that's just about all you can do, Doris,' said Bob. 'You've been very helpful and there's no way you could have known all the details you've given us, but there was one more thing I was hoping for. One small detail that would clinch it beyond all doubt.'

'Well, I'll try,' I said. 'Perhaps it's something they don't want to talk about.'

I tuned in again and caught Helen's voice as she was fading away. 'What is it, Helen?' I asked silently. 'Can you help?'

And back came one whispered word that made me go icy all over. 'Oh no, I can't say that,' I muttered half to myself.

'Say what, Doris?' asked Bob. 'What is it?'

I hesitated. 'Well, I'm sure the grandmother said witchcraft.'

Bob nodded. 'That's what I was waiting for. It was.'

He led us out of the office but I was so dazed I could hardly take it in. Witchcraft! I couldn't believe it. In this day and age?

In the outer office Bob paused to pick up a sheaf of photographs. 'You were absolutely right, Doris. Kevin was missing for some time and his body was eventually found by an old tramp in a derelict building, exactly as you described. This'll explain why you smelled dead animals.' He handed me a photograph.

My heart seemed to stop as I realized what I was looking at and I gasped in horror. As long as I live I will never forget that terrible picture. It showed Kevin as they'd found him. The poor little mite was hanging suspended from four wires, his curly head slumped forward on his chest, his little arms hanging limp at his sides and on the ground beneath his tiny drooping feet, a circle of mutilated animal carcasses …

I dropped the picture and I must have gone white, because Bob quickly guided me to a chair and handed me a cup of coffee.

'It's all right, Doris,' he said. 'We'll go in a minute.'

We gave Dooly a lift home on our way back to the hotel but I don't think I said a word. That terrible picture kept springing into my mind. When I looked out of the window all I could see was Kevin. Eventually we dropped Dooly outside her house and the car headed back towards Manhattan.

'You know after Gloria drowned her baby I went round to see her,' said Bob. 'I went into her room and although she had a good bed in the corner she'd dragged the mattress off it and was sleeping on the floor. I said, 'Gloria, what have you got the mattress on the floor for when you've got a lovely bed there?' and she said, 'I want to be close to the demons. I want the baby and I to be possessed.' She's in a mental home now.'

'But Kevin ... It was witchcraft – but why?'

Bob shrugged. 'We don't know, but I'll tell you a funny thing. Those people have a belief that if an elderly person in the community is ill or has some infirmity, the soul of a child who is sacrificed will go into the old person and the infirmity will disappear.'

'Oh what nonsense,' I protested.

'Yes, of course,' said Bob, 'but I know the family quite well. Before this happened Dooly was crippled with arthritis, she could hardly walk. You've seen her today, walking perfectly normally. Don't ask me why.'

By the time we reached our hotel I was feeling limp and exhausted. It had been a long day. The horrifying case hung over me like a dark shadow and I felt grubby from the contact with it. I ran myself a deep, hot bath and lay back under the water soaking the nastiness away.

'Aaahhh that's better ...' I sighed as my muscles relaxed. But then gradually I realized it wasn't better at all. In my mind I could hear rats skittering through rubbish and if I closed my eyes I could see that photograph of Kevin as clearly as if it was printed on the back of my eyelids. In fact now I came to think of it I was feeling distinctly unwell. I thought I might faint and so quickly got out of the bath. I picked up a towel, pulled it round my neck and almost screamed with pain.

'John!' I cried, gently probing the searing flesh. 'I think I've been bitten. Would you come and have a look?' It felt swollen and sore. Whatever could have done it?

'Honestly, love … bitten by what?' said John strolling into the bathroom. Indulgently he lifted my hair to look at the place I indicated, and then he froze. 'My god …' I heard him whisper. For there across the back of my neck was a thin red line, a quarter of an inch deep, sore and angry just as if wire had been put round it and tightened …

Chapter 2

There was no doubt about it, I was feeling sorry for myself. I hadn't long come back from America, there was Christmas to look forward to and the prospect of moving into a new flat. Nothing grand of course. It was identical to our old flat in the disabled ex-servicemen's block and only a few doors further along the same corridor but it was being modernized and by the new year it would have a bathroom a luxury I'd almost forgotten. Then in the spring my first book, *Voices in My Ear*, was being published.

Yes, the future was looking marvellous, but instead of feeling happy, I was depressed. Soon after returning home I'd developed a severe pain in my right side. At first I dismissed it as some kind of bug and I was careful to eat plain food and drink plenty of water. The diet didn't help. Instead the pain increased. John, who is a healer, gave me spirit healing every night, which eased the pain considerably but I was still conscious of a grumbling ache every time I moved and a stiff, dragging feeling when I walked.

One afternoon I limped awkwardly back from the kitchen where I'd been making a pot of tea and as I lowered myself gingerly into the armchair a voice said sternly: 'You must go to the doctor, you know.'

I looked round, but of course there was no-one there. Terry was at work and John was out shopping. 'Go to the doctor,' said the voice again, so loudly that I couldn't pretend I hadn't heard. It was a clear warning from the spirit world and deep in my heart I knew that it shouldn't have been necessary. Commonsense should have made me seek the doctor's advice without prompting as soon as I'd realized that in this case John's healing was only going to dull the pain, not cure the problem. I had to admit that I was being silly because I was afraid. I'd had cancer twice before and now any persistent pain that refused to respond to home remedies filled me with dread.

That's the trouble with cancer, even when you're cured. You can't understand what triggered it off in the first place so you can't help wondering whether the same force might be silently at work again. Not that I'm afraid of death, I know there's nothing to fear and as far as I'm concerned they can throw my body into the dustbin like a pile of old clothes because that's all it is. It's just the manner of going that worries me, and as I sat there staring blindly into the fire, the pain sharpening in my side, I couldn't help remembering that my poor father had passed in agony with cancer of the bowel.

Of course I succeeded in making myself thoroughly miserable with lurid picture of me gone and John and Terry wandering around the dusty flat in creased shirts with only beans on toast for supper, when the shrill ringing of the telephone brought me back to reality.

Begrudgingly I dragged myself to my feet and stumbled out into the hallway, banging my toe on a chair leg as it had grown dark while I brooded and I hadn't switched on the light.

'Hello!' I said into the receiver not as charmingly as I might.

'Hello. Is that Mrs Doris Stokes?' asked a chirpy, bright voice.

'Yes,' I said in resigned mood.

'Mrs Stokes, this is the United States Embassy.'

I blinked stupidly at the receiver. 'The what?'

'The US Embassy. We've been asked to trace you by General Omar Bradley. He is a five star General and one of the heroes of the second World War.'

The throbbing in my side and toes ceased miraculously and I was quite speechless.

'The General and his wife are coming to London to attend the unveiling of a plaque at St Paul's,' the voice which I now recognized as American continued, 'and they would very much like you and your husband to take tea with them at Claridges.'

'I'd love to,' I gasped. 'But why me?'

'Apparently they saw you on a television show,' said the voice. 'The David Suskind Show. They were very impressed and wanted to meet you.

'Oh ...'

'They'll be so glad you can come. We'll send you the details by post.'

John walked in as I was putting the phone down.

'Hallo love. Why aren't you resting?'

'I was,' I said impatiently, 'but the American Embassy phoned.' I saw his eyebrows go up. 'They want us to go to tea with General Omar Bradley and his wife.' I could see that he wasn't taking this in properly. He opened his mouth to speak. 'Go and sit down,' I told him. 'I'll put the kettle on and tell you all about it.'

I was amazed at such a response from the David Suskind Show. It was recorded during my visit to New York and I hadn't been at all pleased with my work that day. I didn't feel I'd done a good job.

David had asked me to do a telephone sitting for him before deciding whether to have me as a guest on his show and I assumed he approved of my work because the invitation went ahead. But just before the show started he put his head round my dressing room door. 'I don't want you to be too good,' he said, 'or we shall be accused of collusion.' He was gone before I had a chance to ask him what he meant.

What a funny thing to say, I thought, as I finished combing my hair. Most television people wanted me to be as good as possible, in fact they were usually nervous in case I was a flop and spoiled the programme. I was still puzzling over it when I went onto the set, and a few minutes work left me utterly bewildered.

David gave me a terrible time. As I worked he stood in the audience with a microphone and he kept coming back to the platform, putting his foot on the bottom step and saying, 'Well, how did you do that, Doris? What's the secret?' and questioning almost every message I gave, implying that it was some sort of trick.

I ploughed on but it became increasingly difficult. At one point David was standing next to a young man in the audience and the light hovered between them. The voice was a bit blurred but I could just make it out. The trouble was I couldn't be sure for which of them the message was intended.

'I can hear the name Davis. I think it's Joyce Davis. Do you know anyone of that name?' I asked.

'I know a Joyce Davis,' said the young man guardedly. What they didn't admit was that she was David's wife and she was in the audience, so I was trying to give the wrong message to the wrong person, and of course it didn't fit. So it went on – the waves of hostility from David combining with waves of panic from me, until the voices were obscured in a fog of doubt, and I thought, oh dear, I'll have to pack up, this isn't working at all.

I was just wondering how I could walk off the stage without looking too rude, when a young woman suddenly stood up, took the microphone and said, 'David, why don't you sit down and shut up? You haven't done your homework. You don't know what it's all about. We've come here to listen to Doris. Why don't you let her get on?' And to my horror the rest of the audience joined in shouting, 'Yes, shut up. We want to hear Doris.'

I stood there petrified. The show had come to a standstill and it was my fault. I'd been told that David was a big cult figure in America and I felt sure he wouldn't stand for this sort of treatment. I looked across at him expecting to find him angry, but, suave as ever, no emotion showed. He put his hands over his ears, pretending to be deafened and as the din quietened he said, 'All right, all right, I'll sit down and shut up.'

There was a commercial break just then and the producer came hurrying over. Oh well, I've done it now, I thought expecting the worst but, to my surprise, he asked if I would do the next hour of the show, if David agreed not to interfere. What could I say? I agreed but I was in such a nervous state my concentration had gone. I did the best I could but I was disappointed. I knew I could have done a lot better under different circumstances and I felt the audience hadn't got as much from me as they deserved. Yet strangely enough I received a lot of letters as a result of the appearance and the Bradleys enjoyed it enough to seek me out.

The prospect of tea at Claridges cheered me enough to go to the doctor but, as I'd feared, I was referred to a cancer specialist. He examined me and I could tell he wasn't happy. 'I think we ought to have an X-ray,' he said. 'I'll make an appointment for you at the hospital and you'll have to collect a bottle of laxative the day before.'

This sounded pretty depressing to me and it got more depressing when I received the appointment. I was to present myself at the hospital at 2 pm on Friday and I was to take the laxative at 2 pm the Thursday before – which happened to be just two hours before our tea at Claridges.

'John, I can't possibly!' I cried when I received the letter. 'Can you imagine what would happen?' But cancer or no cancer, I didn't want to put off our visit. If I was seriously ill I might as well enjoy myself while I could. I rang the hospital and explained my predicament to the sister. 'I'd very much like to go to this tea,' I said. 'Would it be all right if I took the laxative at 6.00?'

'Oh yes,' she replied, 'we make provision for people who work during the day but you'll probably be up late at night.'

'I'll put up with that,' I said thankfully and that's the way it was left.

The days passed the tea drew nearer and then the Embassy rang again with another tempting invitation. After tea, the General and his wife would like us to join them in the Royal Box to see *Evita*, the famous musical. Could we go?

In anguish I phoned the sister again. 'Oh dear,' she said when I explained, 'I can understand your not wanting to miss out on this. The only thing I can suggest is that you come out of the theatre in the intermission and take the medicine then. But you must go straight home and you'll be up all night.

'That's all right, sister,' I said rashly.

I had no idea what I was letting myself in for, but it was

worth it. I had my hair done and put on a smart day dress, John wore his best suit and we took a taxi to Claridges. John and I had imagined the tea would involve just us, the General and his wife, but to our surprise we were shown into a large drawing-room full of people.

Our feet sank into drifts of deep pile carpet and we stood there a little awkwardly, awed by the elegant furnishings. Instantly an elderly man in a wheelchair excused himself from the group of people he was talking to and expertly manoeuvred himself over to us.

'Good afternoon. I'm General Bradley. Very pleased to meet you.'

We shook hands. He was a fine old gentleman with silvery white hair, a little frail now perhaps, but his eyes were bright and shrewd and his manner alert. Somewhat at a loss for words, I remarked that there seemed to be a lot of military people present.

'Oh yes,' agreed the General. 'They're travelling with me. We've taken over the whole floor of the hotel.'

Just then his wife Kitty came over. She was breathtakingly slender and as elegant as the room.

'Oh there you are, Doris!' she cried. 'I'm so glad you could come. Come and meet some of the others.'

She introduced me to Sir Winston Churchill's grandson, and to Eleanor Hibbert, otherwise known as Victoria Holt, one of my favourite novelists. Apparently Kitty had been particularly keen for Eleanor to come because one night back home in America, Kitty had been reading one of Eleanor's books, and had become so engrossed in it that she had stayed up to finish it. Hours later the General was taken seriously ill and had Kitty not been awake to attend to him he might have died.

'So you see, if it hadn't been for Eleanor's book I might have lost him,' said Kitty.

We settled down to talk about books while John, who was a paratrooper at Arnhem, had the time of his life reminiscing about the war with the military people. Tea was passed round and though I was only allowed plain bread and butter because of my X-ray the next day, I thoroughly enjoyed myself.

After tea the crowd dispersed, the General was taken away for a rest before the theatre and Kitty asked me if I felt well enough to do a sitting for her. The ache was nagging away in my side as it had been for weeks now, but as long as I sat still and didn't rush about it was bearable.

'I'l gladly try, Kitty,' I said, 'but I can't guarantee good results even when I'm in the best of health.'

'That's all right, I guite understand,' Kitty assured me.

She took me up to her private suite, and Eleanor, who had shown great interest in my work over tea, came along as well to see what would happen.

I think they were quite relieved when I explained I didn't need dimmed lights or candles or any spooky stuff of that sort. 'Just relax,' I told them. 'That's all I'd like you to do.' We sank back in the luxury armchairs, and the silence in the warm room made my eyelids grow heavy. I shook my head impatiently – this was no time to feel sleepy – and then a sweet woman's voice with a soft American accent murmured somewhere near me, 'I'm the General's wife.'

Startled, I stared at Kitty. She was Mrs Bradley and she was still quite definitely on the earth plane.

'The General's wife, dear? Are you sure?' I asked silently. The woman laughed. 'His first wife, Mary.'

I hadn't realized the General had been married before but Kitty confirmed it. 'Well, Mary says she wants to thank you for all the happiness you've given him. The last thing she wanted was for him to be lonely and miserable and it makes her very happy to see what you're doing for him.'

I think Kitty was a little surprised though pleased with this message, but in fact it wasn't unusual. Where there has been real love between a couple, the one who passes first is usually only too thankful to see her partner happy again with someone new. Remarriage doesn't detract from the original love at all and on the other side that love continues, but free of sexual jealousy.

The sitting progressed. The General's brother came back, followed by some of Kitty's relatives. Then a different voice interrupted loudly with the name, 'Wisconsin.'

I knew this was a place in America. 'I'm getting the name Wisconsin,' I explained. 'Do you know anyone there, Kitty, or do you have any ties with the town?'

She wrinkled her forehead, trying to recall any connection. 'No,' she said at last, 'I don't know that place at all.'

But the voice was most insistent, repeating the name Wisconsin and adding that a baby would soon be born there.

Kitty shook her head. 'No, I'm sorry, that means nothing to me.'

I shrugged. 'Oh well, never mind, we must have a crossed wire somewhere. She doesn't know you,' I added to the voice. 'Can you give me any more …'

There was a slight cough behind me and we turned, startled to see that the special sergeant who had been on guard duty outside the open door had come in.

Noiselessly he crossed the thick carpet and bent to whisper something to Kitty. She listened with a puzzled expression on her face at first, but as he finished she burst into peals of laughter. 'No!' she cried merrily.

'Oh yes, ma'am,' said the sergeant smiling broadly and went back to his post.

'Well, Doris, I can hardly believe this,' said Kitty when he'd gone, 'but Specialist Rogers just told me that he's from Wisconsin and his wife's expecting a baby next month! We must be giving our sergeants too much time off!'

After the sitting Kitty and Eleanor went to change for the theatre and I was rather embarrassed when they came back in evening dress, because of course I was still in my ordinary day clothes, but they didn't seem to worry. We made our way down to the foyer where the General's aides were organizing transport to the theatre. John and I were to travel with Lieutenant Colonel Little, we were told, and we went outside on to the hotel steps to wait for him. There was quite a party assembling and a line of sleek black cars glided towards us.

'Look at that, John!' I cried. 'We're going in a cavalcade.'

The first car, a long, low affair that shone like glass with a flag fluttering on its bonnet, stopped beside the Bradleys and while they were being helped inside, another Colonel came over and touched my arm.

'Mrs Stokes ma'am. The General and Mrs Bradley would

be very honoured if you would ride with them in the Embassy car.'

I gazed longingly at the beautiful car. 'Oh John, would you mind very much if I did?'

''Course not, you go. I'll be all right with Lieutenant Colonel Little.'

So I slipped in beside Kitty and almost disappeared up to my neck in pale upholstery. The car whispered away from the hotel and the evening took on a glamorous, dream-like quality. London, during the day when you're pushing through unfriendly crowds and dicing with death from taxis at every corner is one thing, but on a cold night, from the depths of a luxury car, when all the lights are glittering in the darkness and buildings look warm and inviting, it's quite another. What with the flag billowing proudly on the bonnet and the people staring in the windows at us, I felt like royalty.

The feeling was reinforced when we reached the theatre and were dropped at a side door to find the entire cast lined up to meet us. Dazed, I shook each outstretched hand and then followed Kitty along the carpeted corridors to the Royal Box. It was like a small room with a balcony at the front and chairs arranged in rows. We were so close to the stage I almost felt I was taking part in the show. The only thing that struck me was the draught. After about twenty minutes the cold air was swirling round my feet and I began to feel quite chilly. I though of the Queen in those flimsy dresses she often wears to the theatre and my admiration for her increased. She must be frozen at times but she never turns a hair.

During the interval we were led to a softly lit retiring room.

'I wonder if the Queen uses this room?' I asked, looking round at the dressing table where drinks were set out and the plush chairs grouped round a low table decorated with flowers.

'Oh yes, when she comes to this theatre,' I was told.

Drinks were passed round and John meaningfully showed me his watch.

'Do you really have to go, Doris?' asked Kitty as John went

off to find my coat.

'Yes, I'm afraid I must,' I said reluctantly. 'I'd love to see the second half but I've probably stayed out too late already.'

I felt like Cinderella leaving the ball as I tore myself away, and the glamour of the evening disappeared as if it had never been. Within half an hour John and I were climbing the concrete steps to our flat. Matey the ginger cat was running to meet us, complaining loudly that he was hungry, and indoors the bottle of bitter medicine awaited me.

The sister had been right. It did keep me up all night and I arrived at the hospital next day feeling a wreck. Mind you, that was nothing to the way I left, after an enema and a highly unpleasant X-ray. But I was very fortunate. When the results came through the specialist was surprised to find no growth. I didn't have cancer after all. I was delighted and tremendously relieved of course, but still worried. The pain continued to burn in my side. There had to be something wrong.

Eventually a gynaecologist diagnosed that I needed a hysterectomy as soon as possible. The trouble was I would have to wait at least six months to have the operation performed on the National Health and in the meantime I could hardly walk. If I was prepared to be a private patient the whole thing could be over in a couple of weeks. John and I exchanged glances and I groaned inwardly. We'd saved some money to buy furniture when we moved into our new flat, but now ...

'Well, it's more important for you to be healthy than to look at a bit of carpet,' John pointed out and of course he was right.

I don't remember much about my stay in hospital. I know it was run by nuns who were very kind to me, but one strange thing happened that stands out in my memory.

After the operation I struggled to open my eyes. My head felt stuffed with feathers and my throat was dry as sand.

'Don't worry, dear,' said a voice from somewhere above

me as cool hands fluttered near my face, 'we're putting a mask on to give you some oxygen to help you breathe.'

It was water I wanted not oxygen, I tried to tell them, but then I drifted away again and the next time I opened my eyes I felt more comfortable but couldn't remember where I was. To one side I could see a pair of unfamiliar french windows and to the other ... my eyes widened in surprise, a handsome young man in naval uniform.

He stood there beside my bed, so smart with his dark hair and close fitting blue jacket with its gold buttons and braid round the sleeves, and as he smiled at me I recognized him: it was my war time friend Walter Pryce Jones!

But what am I doing in Wales? I thought weakly as I struggled to smile back; I was far too tired to speak. Then I remembered. I wasn't in Wales, I was in hospital in London and Walter had passed over years ago.

Even as the thought slipped through my mind, Walter walked to the foot of the bed, smiled encouragingly at me once more and disappeared ...

Chapter 3

I first met Walter Pryce Jones when I was in the WRAFs
stationed in Port Talbot in Wales. I'd just come off duty
one afternoon and I was waiting for a bus to take me into
town when a little Welsh lady at the bus-stop started
talking to me. She had dark wavy hair and kind eyes.

'How d'you like Port Talbot?' she asked.

'Very much,' I said. 'I've never been to Wales before.'

'And how d'you get on up at the school? Are you
comfortable there?'

Our HQ was in the vicarage and the WRAFs were
billeted in the school. 'Oh yes, we're very comfortable,' I
said. 'They look after us very well. The only thing I ever
miss is a bath. They've only got showers at the school
which are all right, but there are times, when you've been
on duty all night and half the day, when the one thing you
long for is a nice hot bath.'

'Then you must come and have a bath at my house,' said
the lady immediately.

I felt my face burn red. 'Oh, no – I mean – I wasn't
asking …' I was dreadfully embarrased. I'd been
chattering thoughtlessly again and put my foot in it. 'I
couldn't possibly …'

'Of course you could,' said my new friend firmly. 'I'd
like you to. It'd be nice to have some company. My son's in
the navy so I don't see much of him these days.'

And that's how I met the Pryce Jones family. Walter, Mr
and Mrs Pryce Jones' only child, became a great friend.
There was nothing romantic about it, he was going out
with one of the other WRAFs, but he had a marvellous
sense of humour and he could always bring me down to
earth with his common sense when I was in a tizzy about

256

some scrape I'd got myself into. Like the time I was in trouble for disobeying a superior officer ...

I was working as a WRAF driver and one evening when I was on night duty I was asked to pick up one of our officers from the General Hospital and take him to the military hospital. It seemed straightforward enough but when the man came out I noticed he only had slippers on his feet, although it was his arm that had been injured.

'Where are his shoes?' I asked the sister who helped him into the back of the car.

'Oh, they must be at the police station,' she said. 'I think they were round his neck when he hit the tree.'

This seemed rather strange to me, but the man obviously needed shoes, I could see that, so I stopped at the police station to fetch them for him.

When I came out again, the shoes under my arm, I was a little disturbed to see that the officer had moved into the front of the car. Oh well, perhaps he wants a chat, I thought nervously, and got in beside him without comment.

It was 3 am by now and very dark indeed, particularly as the headlamps were taped to allow only half an inch of beam, but I knew the road well and soon we were spinning down the black country lanes. We were making good time, when suddenly I heard the leather passenger seat creak, and an instant later the man lunged at me. He only had one good arm but he could manage well enough with that and he was very strong. He pulled me towards him and as I tried to beat him off with one hand and steer with the other, the car was swerving all over the road.

I can only assume he'd been drinking. 'Oh – look – be careful, sir, we'll crash!' I cried in alarm, but he only laughed and tried to drag me out of my seat. The wheel spun through my fingers, I could see a tree looming out of the blackness in front of us and I was terrified.

Pushing him away with all my strength, I wrenched the wheel round again, my brain racing. The man was clearly enjoying the whole episode. I could feel his breath on my cheek and he closed in again. I'd have to do something, fast. I made an effort to block the fear and anger from my voice.

'We'll have to get to the hospital first, they're expecting

you,' I gasped as sweetly as I could manage. 'We can stop on the way back,' and I gave him what I hoped was a playful kittenish push. It worked. The man chuckled and settled back in his seat, but I had to endure his arm round my shoulders for the rest of the journey.

At the hospital I helped him out of the car and then dashed on ahead up the steps. One was supposed to book oneself in and out of the hospital and, much to the amazement of the sergeant on duty, I booked myself in and then straight out again.

'Hey, just a minute,' he cried, as the officer came up behind me, 'you might have to take him back again.'

'Not me, sergeant,' I said backing down the steps, 'I've had enough.'

At that moment the officer realized that he'd been tricked. 'Hey!' he shouted, stepping towards me. I jumped the last three steps with the officer right behind me.

'Come back here, driver! Come back this minute!' he yelled, but I was in the car. The engine fired, I did a racing U-turn and as I accelerated away the last furious words, 'I haven't dismissed you yet ...' came floating through the window.

'You'll be lucky, mate,' I said under my breath and for some reason I was overcome with the wittiness of this retort and giggled all the way home.

The next day of course I was in a terrible state. I realized I'd done a very silly thing but though I went over and over the events in my mind I couldn't think of any other course of action I could have taken. I was too young to know how to handle the situation. In terror, I went to see Walter, who happened to be home, to ask his advice.

'Don't worry, Doris,' he said when he'd heard my story, 'it's serious on the face of it but I should think that officer would be far too embarrassed to complain about you and even if he did, you need only tell the truth and he'll be in trouble, not you.' Then he burst out laughing at the thought of me wrestling with the wheel and a burly officer at the same time. 'I must say though,' he spluttered, 'you mustn't make a habit of it, but good for you, Doris. I bet you taught him a thing or two!'

I couldn't help laughing myself. Walter was like the brother I never had. He made me feel much better.

Two days after that I was arrested for disobeying an order from a superior officer, but Walter was right. After I explained in great detail what had happened to several officers in ascending rank, the matter was dropped and I heard no more about it.

Several months later I popped in to see Mrs Pryce Jones as I often did on my way back to the billet. Over a big pot of tea she liked to tell me all the gossip of Port Talbot and then she loved to hear my stories of life at the school with the WRAFs. On this particular day as I walked into the hall, the sitting room door was open and I saw Walter in his uniform cross towards the fireplace.

'Oh, I didn't know Walter was home on leave,' I said as I unbuttoned my coat.

'Walter?' said Mrs Pryce Jones in surprise. 'Walter isn't home, dear. Whatever made you think that?'

And I looked again and saw that the living room was quite empty. A terrible pang shot through me. I knew nothing about spiritualism or mediums in those days, but several strange things like this had happened to me, usually with tragic results. Oh God, no, not Walter, I thought in despair and Mrs Pryce Jones must have caught my stricken expression.

'Why, what's wrong dear,' she asked, her mother's face suddenly white with fear. 'What made you think of Walter?'

I forced myself to smile. 'Oh nothing,' I said lightly, taking off my coat. 'Maybe I've got a crush on him and I see him wherever I go.'

A few weeks later I had to go home to Grantham because my mother was ill but I'd only been back a fortnight when I received a desperate letter from Mrs Pryce Jones. Walter had gone. The day I'd seen him in the living room, his ship had been torpedoed and Walter was lost at sea. Mr Pryce Jones had had a stroke only a week before the official letter came through and she didn't know how to break the news to him. Could I come down at once?

I could only get a forty-eight hour pass and the old steam trains were a lot slower than our modern expresses today. Forty-eight hours barely gave me time to get from Grantham to Port Talbot, stay the night and go back again, but of course I went. I was very apprehensive about my task. I sympathized with Mrs Pryce Jones, but if she didn't know how to tell her husband, how could I? And yet in the end, from somewhere, the words came. I remember kneeling by Mr Pryce Jones' chair, holding his hand as the tears trickled down his poor old cheeks, telling him over and over, 'Walter hasn't gone, Mr Pryce Jones. Not really. You will see him again. I know you will. Don't ask me how I know, I just know you will.'

That was the strange thing, even in the days before I was a medium, people used to seek me out in their grief, as if they knew instinctively that I had the means to comfort them. The same thing happened a few years later when my friend Edie was going through a difficult time.

By then I was married, I understood more about spiritualism and I was no stranger to grief. I'd lost my own darling baby, John Michael, at 5 months 2 weeks while my husband John was a prisoner of war.

In those long black days following John Michael's death, I was convinced the sun would never shine again, not for me. But of course it did. John came home, we adopted little Terry and we settled down in Grantham among my old friends.

Edie Clark was one of the best. Small, dark and vivacious, she'd been my friend since we were children together in the same street, and we've remained friends ever since.

In those days there was a marvellous community spirit in Grantham. Everyone helped each other. When Edie, her husband Jack and their three little girls, Joan, Susan and Beryl went on holiday, Edie would get them ready and do the packing on Friday night so that on Saturday morning, all she had to do was give me their door key. I used to look after their dog, collect up the dirty washing, wash it, iron it and put it away. Then I'd go in every day to check that everything was all right and the day before they came home I'd clean the house and get food in for them. It was second nature because that's the way we lived then and of course Edie did exactly the same for me.

Christmas Day was a particularly exciting time. Edie would start first because with three ecstatic little ones waking each other up and bursting to know what Father Christmas had brought them. I expect she was up at the crack of dawn. I'd hear them early on Christmas morning laughing and giggling as they skipped down the street with Edie and Jack strolling behind. Then there would come a thunderous knocking on the door and in seconds our living room was submerged in wrapping paper and happy people as the children exchanged presents from the tree and Jack, Edie, John and I had a glass of sherry.

That was only the beginning. After a while we'd move on to wish a merry Christmas to another friend, where the procedure was repeated, then she would join us and we'd all go on our merry way to the next house and so it went on until by lunch-time we were a very jolly band wandering home to serve the Christmas dinner and if there were a few extra people at the table, what did it matter – it was Christmas after all.

Like me, Edie had known tragedy. Her only son, Tony, had died in hospital during an operation to remove his tonsils. Something went wrong they said. So when her youngest daughter, Susan, had to have the same operation Edie was understandably frantic. I sat with her during the long hours while we waited for the operation to be performed but the staff at the hospital were very good. Knowing the family history, they telephoned Edie as soon as the operation was over to let her know that it had been a success and that Susan was quite safe.

Sure enough, within a couple of weeks Susan was back home again as fit as ever and making her sisters jealous with exaggerated tales of the mountains of jelly and ice cream she'd eaten in hospital. She was a slim, pale child of 7 with soft, curly, fair hair. She was much quieter than the other two. When they called for Terry, Susan was always the one who hung back shyly and it was Susan who lost her tongue when strangers were near. She loved to listen to stories and she was never happier than when she was drawing. While her sisters were playing boisterously on the floor, Susan would sit for hours at the table working away with coloured pencils, her fair hair flopping across her face, the tip of her pink tongue showing between her teeth.

One beautiful summer day, a month or two after Susan came out of hospital, we decided to take the children for a picnic at nearby Denton reservoir. It was a spur of the moment idea, Edie and I cut a stack of sandwiches and filled the flasks with tea for the picnic basket while the men gathered towels and swimming things.

We had a marvellous afternoon. We didn't need money to enjoy ourselves in those days. The children ran races on the grass and darted in and out of the water. Then John and Jack chased in after them and there was a tremendous splashing match, children against Dads, resulting in squeals of delight and showers of water.

Edie and I sat on the bank, dangling our legs in the water and watching them happily. The sun was warm on my face and as I looked up at the cloudless blue sky and then round at the other families scattered across the grass playing ball or running with dogs I couldn't help thinking that this was perfection. The war was over at last and this was what life was all about: children and parents playing together on a summer's day.

The sun was bright, we were all happy and no-one sensed, not even me with my clairvoyant powers, the shadow that lay across the afternoon.

At tea-time Edie and I towelled the children dry and changed the girls back into their cotton dresses and Terry into his shorts. Then we opened the picnic basket, and every sandwich was devoured hungrily. Afterwards there was an unruly ball game, while Susan collected daisies to make a chain.

'What d'you think, Auntie Doris?' asked a small voice as I was stuffing Terry's damp swimming trunks into a bag ready to go home. 'Do I look nice?' and I turned to see Susan standing there, one creamy daisy chain round her neck, another in her hair.

'Like a princess, love!' I told her. 'Go and show your dad.' A flush of pleasure pinkened her cheeks and she danced away to find Jack.

The following Saturday Edie went shopping in town, leaving the girls with her mother who still lived in Turner Crescent – my old street when I was a child. By the time she returned, Susan was complaining that her legs hurt and she couldn't walk. Edie had to piggy-back her home.

Jack called to see me shortly afterwards. 'Could you come and see what you think, Doris? I expect she's only tired but you know how Edie worries.'

When I got there Susan was in bed. She didn't look too bad but her forehead was hot to the touch.

'I think you'd better get the doctor, Edie,' I advised. 'She's running a temperature.'

'That's what I thought,' said Edie anxiously.

I waited while the doctor came and gave Susan some medicine, then I went home to cook John and Terry's tea.

At eight o'clock that night Terry was in bed, the dishes were cleared away and John and I were just settling down to listen to the wireless when there was an urgent knocking on the door.

'Whoever can that be?' I muttered as I got up, but even before I reached the door I knew it was Jack. His hair was dishevelled, his tie had slipped sideways and he looked frightened.

'Would you mind coming again, Doris?' he asked. 'There's something wrong, I'm certain of it.'

An unpleasant thought was trying to gather at the back of my mind but I pushed it away fearfully and hurried out after Jack. Edie met us on the doorstep. She was biting her lip nervously.

'She seems worse now, Doris, but the doctor was only here a couple of hours ago. I don't know whether to bother him again or not.'

I ran up the stairs into Susan's room. The little girl was tossing and turning in the bed, her hair damp on the pillow, her face flushed, her breathing noisy. Automatically I put my hand on her forehead, though it was quite obvious she had a high temperature. As my fingers brushed her skin, a jolt went through me like an electric shock! Susan was going to die. I knew it as certainly as if it had already happened. Horror and pity struggled inside me as I stared down at that thin little figure under the bedclothes. Edie was hovering at my shoulder, wringing her hands in distress.

'What – what d'you think, Doris?'

I couldn't look her in the face. 'You must get the doctor at once, Edie,' I said quietly without taking my eyes off susan. 'She's very poorly indeed.'

The doctor returned, took one look at the way Susan had deteriorated and had her rushed to hospital.

When I got home that night John was waiting up for me. 'It's bad, is it?' he asked, seeing my miserable face. I flung myself into a chair, suddenly feeling tired and old and hopeless.

'It's dreadful,' I said. 'I don't think Susan's going to make it.'

'Oh don't say that love.'

'It's not an opinion, John. I knew almost as soon as I looked at her,' I said wearily.

John and I were both becoming involved in spiritualism by then and my powers as a medium were just coming to light. John knew enough about it to take my premonitions seriously.

'Well let's hope you're wrong,' he said.

'Of course I hope I'm wrong,' I snapped, tired and depressed. But I knew I was right.

The next day I hurried to the Clarks and I was surprised to see a knot of neighbours hovering outside the gate, their faces gloomy yet inquisitive.

'You're not going in there!' someone cried as I approached the door.

I turned. 'Of course I am. Why shouldn't I?'

'They've got polio in there!' said someone else.

'Polio!'

Shocked, my hand went rigid on the knocker. So that was it, polio. Poor Susan. I turned back to the neighbours. 'And what difference does that make?' I snapped angrily and I rapped defiantly on the door.

There was nothing I could do of course. I just wanted Edie and Jack to know I was there sharing the burden with them as much as possible. Joan and Beryl had been sent to their grandmother and Susan was undergoing an emergency trachiotomy to help her breathe. But it was no use. Within 24 hours she was dead.

Poor Susie, poor Edie, poor Jack.

I thought they'd never get over it. For a while Edie blamed herself. If only she hadn't let Susan go in the water that day, if only she'd kept her at home, if only … It's a heart-rending and useless way to think of course, and we pointed out to her time and time again that the others had gone swimming that day with no ill effects. No one could possibly be blamed for what happened to Susan. Yet I understood how Edie felt. I'd been exactly the same after my little John Michael's death.

John Michael died after an emergency operation to remove a blockage of the bowel but the official cause of death was pneumonia. For months afterwards the cruel thought nagged me that the baby in the next cot also had pneumonia, and he survived. That baby was the youngest of nine and compared to John Michael, had been carelessly reared.

If I hadn't been so particular with John Michael. I tortured myself endlessly, he might have had more resistance to germs. But no, my baby had to be spotless. I suppose with John away, a prisoner of war, I had nothing else to do but tend my baby obsessively. Also, my first job after leaving school had been in a hospital where they impressed on me very young the need for high standards of cleanliness and hygiene. It never occurred to me that the standards needed in a hospital where patients were recovering from operations and where infections could be fatal, were not necessarily required in an ordinary home of healthy people. So I washed and bathed my baby continually and nagged my mother. 'Put on a clean apron before you pick the baby up,' I'd insist and though she'd grumble. 'A little bit of dust won't hurt him,' she'd do as I asked.

We lived near a railway station and after he was washed

and dressed I used to put John Michael outside in his pram if the weather was fine. But if he got one speck of black on him from the steam engines, in he would have to come and off would come his things and I'd wash him again. 'Honestly!' said Mother, watching me disapprovingly, but she didn't interfere.

After he passed, the matron in the hospital came to see me and thinking to comfort me, I suppose, remarked, 'We've never had a baby in such perfect condition. There was not a mark on him, not a speck of nappy rash or anything.' But I only sobbed more violently. What was the use of a perfect corpse.

By the time Edie and Jack were suffering their terrible tragedy, John Michael's death had driven me to find out more about spiritualism and recognize my own powers at last. I was taking my first faltering steps as a medium, but I never did do a sitting for the Clarks. Jack wasn't keen on that sort of thing and I was wary of pushing my beliefs onto anyone else. I would have loved to share my peace of mind with them but I had to respect their distaste for the subject. Instead I gave them what comfort I could.

Edie would come and cry in my kitchen and I'd make her tea, put my arms round her and promise her over and over again, 'The sun will shine again, Edie. I know it will.' And, of course, eventually it did. Joan and Beryl grew up into fine, strong young women and presented their parents with healthy grandchildren. Jack and Edie think the world of them, but as Edie said to me recently, 'You never forget do you, Doris?'

And I had to agree, no you don't ever forget …

Chapter 4

I went back to Grantham a few months ago, shortly after the local paper had printed a story about me, and as I was walking down the street an elderly man stopped me.

'It's Doris, isn't it?' he said. 'I don't suppose you remember me, do you?' And though his pleasant open face looked vaguely familiar I had to confess that I didn't. 'I used to be the landlord of the Spreadeagle. Your mum used to help us wash the glasses,' he reminded me. 'Oh, but Doris – that bit in the paper – wouldn't Jenny have been proud of you if only she'd lived to see it? She'd have been so proud about all this.'

I didn't have the heart to tell him that Mum did know all about it because she still keeps an eye on me. It was very nice of him to bother to mention it – but would Mum really have been proud of me, if she was still here on earth? Somehow I doubt it because she always seemed quite incapable of understanding what I did. Whether it was genuine incomprehension or whether she simply closed her mind to it, I don't know, but her complete bafflement was brought home to me, once and for all, the time I took her to a spiritualist meeting.

After meetings in our local hall, the group I was involved with used to sell tea and biscuits for a few coppers to raise money for a visit to another group some distance away. A coach was hired, tea was provided for us by the host group and the occasion was quite a festive afternoon out.

On this particular occasion I had been invited to speak at a meeting quite a long way off. A coach was hired and as it was a pretty journey and I knew Mum loved coach trips I asked if she'd like to come. She wouldn't bother with the spiritualist bit, I realized that, but she'd be given a nice tea afterwards and taken home again, and all in all I thought it would be an enjoyable outing for her.

Mum agreed. 'Oh, yes Dol, I'd love to go,' she said eagerly and immediately started pondering which hat to wear.

Everything went smoothly. The weather was fine. We picked Mum up from her home in Fletcher Street and got her a window seat on the coach. She was thrilled with the route through rolling countryside and once at the hall, she sat most politely through the proceedings. True there was a highly puzzled expression on her face, I could see that even from the platform, and she kept turning round as if trying to see who I was speaking to, but at least she didn't scoff or express loud disapproval as I'd feared she might.

Afterwards she was taken off for tea and by the time I found her again she'd made a couple of friends. She was sitting between two middle-aged ladies, cheerfully sipping her tea.

'All right, Mum?' I asked joining them.

'Oh!' gasped one of the women, staring at me as if I'd just materialized out of thin air, and then turning to the other two as if I wasn't there, she said, 'Isn't she marvellous? I think she's marvellous.'

'Who?' asked Mum.

'The medium, of course,' said the woman in hushed tones.

'Medium?' said Mum. 'What's a medium?'

The woman looked at her in disbelief. 'The medium's the one who's been talking on the platform all afternoon,' she said a little uncertainly as if fearing it might be a joke.

'Well I didn't see any medium,' said Mum firmly, going back to her tea. 'There was only one person up there and that was our Doris.'

I couldn't help laughing. Dear Mum. If she lived to be a hundred I'd never make her understand.

When I was a child, of course, she was quite well aware of my strange 'unnatural' streak and did her best to stamp it out with dire warnings that I'd end up in a mental home one day. But as I grew older and became independent she chose to forget about it and once she made up her mind about something, nothing would shake her. The subject was closed.

She lived next door to a Pentecostal church and she used to make tea for the pastor. He knew I was a spiritualist and we often had friendly but heated discussions about the rights and wrongs of it. This used to distress Mum. She'd follow the conversation backwards and forward for a bit, a bewildered expression on her face and then she'd say, 'Now pastorman's a good man, our Doris. You shouldn't talk to the pastor like that.'

'It's all right, Jenny,' the pastor would reassure her, 'we're not falling out.'

But Mum was quite determined. 'He's a good man, the pastor,' she'd tell me sternly, 'and he's a *pastor*!' and that would be the end of that discussion.

Mum was a living contradiction. Black haired and small – she only came up to my shoulder – she could be timid as a mouse or embarrassingly forthright. When I was in the WRAFs, if I dared linger on the way home for a kiss and a cuddle with a boyfriend and it was after eleven at night, Mum would come to find me, and I was twenty-four at the time. Round the corner she'd appear like a bad dream, her stockings rolled down round her ankles, a broom in her hand.

'You can pack that up, our Doris!' she'd shout. 'It's time you were home.' And she'd stand there, broom at the ready, while the embrace dissolved, quite prepared to beat the unfortunate boyfriend about the head should he refuse to put me down.

She could be very stubborn and she was a push-over for status and labels. Just as she didn't think I should argue with the pastor, because he was a *pastor*, she never really got over my rejecting an officer to marry a sergeant. So incensed was she about my marriage to John, that she refused to come to the wedding and she was cool towards him for many years afterwards. When we adopted Terry, she was totally against it, and declared that she wouldn't allow him under her roof because he wasn't our natural born son. Then a few months later, with one of her

famous about turns, she accepted him so wholeheartedly
that if John or I so much as slapped him for being
naughty, she'd go berserk.

'I'll fetch the police to you,' she'd shout. 'I will, I'll get
the police. Leave him alone, you're not to slap him!' Of
course it didn't take Terry long to learn where to go for
sympathy and sweeties.

She was alone for a long time was Mum, because my
father passed when she was only in her late forties, but she
kept herself busy and everyone liked her. After the initial
shock of father's death, several people tried to persuade
her to marry again. It would have been a good idea, I
suppose, because Mum was hopeless with the business side
of life. Anything to do with money had her wringing her
hands in despair, yet give her someone to clean and polish
for and she was in her element. But she just wasn't
interested in other men.

The only time I can recall her giving in to persuasion
was when her friend Flora Hudson talked her into having
a perm and going out for the evening. I must have been
fifteen or sixteen at the time and I remember being
absolutely astounded at the sight of Mum coming
downstairs in her best dress with her hair a halo of crisp
curls and wearing lipstick for the first time in her life.

'And what d'you think you're staring at, our Doris?' she
asked sharply as she came into the kitchen, but the self
conscious patting of her hair gave her away. 'Well, what
d'you think?' she relented, peering doubtfully at her rigid
hair-do in a tiny handbag mirror. 'Does it suit me or was I
a fool to listen to that Flo?'

'It's very nice, Mum,' I said kindly. 'I was a bit surprised,
that's all.'

And off she went for her evening out, tugging at her
dress and chewing uneasily on the unfamiliar lipstick.

It didn't last of course. Try as Flora might, Mum just
wasn't the type and soon the perm grew out, the lipstick
gathered dust in the drawer and Mum spent her evenings
at home with the wireless.

She might be a bit touchy with us at times but Mum was
really a softie with a heart as big as a bucket. She could

never say no to anyone and consequently she had several little jobs that she did regularly as clockwork because she hated to let anybody down. For a few shillings a week she helped out at the Spreadeagle pub, scraping and cleaning the vegetables and washing the glasses. She took great pride in every task, no matter how small and her vegetables were always spotless, not a mark on them and she polished the glasses until they sparkled like cut crystal. 'I've never had a washer-upper like your mum,' the landlady used to tell me with admiration.

They were pleased with her at the fish shop too. They'd give her her supper and in return she washed their tea towels and carried the takings to the bank. She became a familiar sight trotting through Grantham with the leather bag of money on her way to the bank but no one ever bothered her. It never crossed our minds to think it could be a dangerous journey. It wasn't like that in those days. Mum would never get rich on her little jobs, but then that didn't worry her. As long as she wasn't in debt she was happy and the little she had she was just as likely to give away.

I remember getting cross with her about it one afternoon. I'd popped round to see her and finding her out, I went round the back to wait. There in the yard, I came face to face with a middle-aged woman filling a bucket with coal from Mum's coal bunker.

'What d'you think you're doing?' I demanded angrily.

'Oh, your mother lends me a bucket of coal, you know,' said the woman continuing to heap her bucket.

'Well you just put it back and wait till Mum's here,' I said furiously. John didn't earn much because his war injuries prevented him from holding down a decent job, so I had to go out to work to help support the family and half the time I also paid for Mum's coal because she was always broke.

Reluctantly the woman emptied her bucket and we stood there glaring at each other in silence, until Mum finally returned. I wasn't too surprised to learn that the woman had been telling the truth. Mum did allow her to help herself to coal whenever she needed it. So I had to stand by while she smugly refilled her bucket and carried it triumphantly away.

'Well, you see her husband's not very good to her,' said Mum as the gate clicked shut.

'And what's wrong with her going out and scrubbing floors or something like I have to?' I retorted, but it was no use. You couldn't change Mum and deep down I wouldn't have had her any other way. It did mean that I was frequently called upon to come to her rescue, however, and in those days I'm afraid I was less patient than I am now.

On another occasion I dropped in to see her unexpectedly and found her sobbing at the table.

'Whatever's the matter, Mum?' I cried, rushing to her side. 'What's happened?'

'Oh, nothing, nothing,' she snuffled, wiping her eyes on her apron. 'I just feel so poorly this afternoon, I don't know how I'm going to get through this washing and I've got to finish it today.'

I looked down and for the first time noticed the most enormous bundle of dirty sheets and clothes heaped on the floor.

'Mum, that lot can't possibly be yours,' I said in surprise and then bit by bit the story came out. The woman up the road took in lodgers and for a couple of shillings and a bar of soap, she'd persuaded Mum to do all the washing and ironing for her.

'Why on earth didn't you say no?' I asked in exasperation.

Mum picked helplessly at the hem of her apron. 'I didn't like to. She's got so much to do with the cooking and the house and everything.'

I sighed. It was pointless even asking. 'All right, Mum, leave it to me,' I said wearily and picking up the huge bundle I staggered out into the street. Fortunately the address mum had given me wasn't far away and I knocked boldly on the door.

There was a pause, then a solidly built woman in an apron appeared.

'Are you Mrs So-and-So?' I asked.

'Yes,' she said.

'And you take in lodgers?'

'Yes, that's right,' she said, obviously thinking she had another customer.

'Then do your own dirty washing,' I cried angrily, 'and don't go giving it to my mother to do!' and I'm sorry to say I thrust the bundle at her so hard. I nearly knocked her over.

Before he died, even though I was only thirteen, my father had asked me to take care of Mum and over the years I did my best. I tried to sort out her problems, I visited her regularly, made sure she had enough money and coal and every morning when I was preparing lunch for John and Terry before I left for work, I made up an extra meal for Mum, put it in a covered basin and took it with me. She used to meet the bus and I would hand over that day's lunch and she would return the previous day's basin. That way I knew she had at least one balanced meal a day.

But looking back over the years, I know I did fail Dad at one point and to this day I feel guilty about it. It was in the months following John Michael's death and I'm sorry to say that I was so wrapped up in my own grief I never spared a thought for Mum and what she must have been feeling. During the five months of my baby's life, we lived with Mum and she loved John Michael like her own son. She was so proud of him, she loved to show him off to the neighbours and looking back I realize she must have felt as lost as I did. At the time the thought never crossed my mind. Selfishly I decided I couldn't stay in the house that held so many painful memories so I moved in with my friends, the Webbs, leaving Mum all alone in her grief.

Afterwards I discovered that she and her neighbour Mrs Scothen, used to sit together and cry in the evenings, while I went out with my girlfriends to drown my sorrows.

I was only once knocked out of my selfishness. Early one evening I was getting ready to go out. I was standing at the mirror in the Webbs' kitchen making up my face when the air raid sirens started to wail. I dabbed defiantly at my nose with the powder puff. Well, I wasn't going to the shelter now. Let those Germans do their worst. What did I care if I lived or died anyway? I was still carelessly applying powder when planes whined overhead, and I heard the whistle of falling bombs and then there was the most appalling crash. My whole body jarred, the floor rocked under my feet, the mirror swung on the wall and from somewhere I could hear the sound of shattering glass. Outside guns were chattering at the sky, the planes droned on and the crashes continued like receding thunder.

'God,' I said to my startled reflection, 'that was close!' And as I stared in fascination at the strangely white face and eyes grown huge and dark, I realized that I didn't want to die after all.

I was still standing there muttering stupidly to myself when Stan Webb, who was a special constable, rushed in.

'Doris!' he shouted as he tore up the hall. 'They've fallen on Fletcher Street!'

My heart plummeted. 'Oh my God! Mum!' I cried. The powder compact dropped from my hand and pushing past Stan I raced outside and tore up the road. It was pitch dark because everyone observed the blackout, not a street lamp or lighted window shone and once or twice before my eyes became accustomed to the dark I stumbled and twisted my ankle. I turned painfully into Commercial Road and a haze of dust and smoke seemed to hang in the air. There was a peculiar scorched, burning smell and as I glanced to my left my feet slowed down as if they were moving through toffee. The familiar serrated skyline of rooftops and chimney pots had gone. A row of three storey houses had been razed to the ground. One of them had been the home of an old school chum of mine whose mother was a friend of Mum's. I found out afterwards that the little boy had gone up the passage to look at the searchlights and they never did find anything of him at all.

The full horror of that gaping hole in the night took a few seconds to sink in and then I remembered. 'Mum!' I cried aloud and I took off again faster than before.

Fletcher Street didn't look as bad as Commercial Road. Torchlights were bobbing in the darkness and dazed people were emerging. Mum's house was still standing but the roof had caved in. Shaking with fear I pushed open the door and ran down the dark passage. There were voices. I could definitely hear voices, I realized, and I burst into the kitchen in delight. An amazing scene greeted me. The place was full of people, candles flickered everywhere revealing fallen plaster and cracks in the ceiling and in the midst of it all, hair and eyebrows white with dust, was Mum – making tea. She glanced up from the kettle and saw me standing in the doorway.

'What have you come for? You don't want to be in this lot.'

'Are you all right, Mum?' I asked breathlessly.

'Of course I'm all right,' she said peevishly, shovelling great scoops of tea into the pot. 'You can see I'm all right.'

Rather taken aback I stood there helplessly looking round at the smoking candles and the tightly packed neighbours. I realize now that Mum must have been suffering from shock and she was doing the only thing she could – making tea. Anyone who diverted her from this compulsive task was a nuisance.

'Well, I just came to see if you were all right,' I repeated.

'Never mind me,' she said, 'what about the Burgess family in Commercial Road?'

'I know, I've seen it,' I said miserably.

'Well, you go home, our Doris. You don't want to be in this lot. There's nothing you can do.'

She was right. I hovered a little longer, getting in the way and then I wandered back to the Webbs. On the way I couldn't help reflecting that I'd neglected Mum lately. I'd been so wrapped up in myself I'd hardly thought of her. Supposing her house had suffered a direct hit like the Burgesses'? I'd never have had a chance to make amends. Well, I'd been given a second chance and I decided to make good use of it.

I didn't always remember my good resolution, I have to admit. There were many black days when depression closed in like black fog and I was incapable of doing anything for anyone; but as the months passed I returned gradually to normal, and on balance, I think I kept my promise to Father.

She kept well, did Mum. She lived to 73 and over the years she suffered little illness. The end was sudden and unexpected.

One morning about eight o'clock the doorbell rang and I found a little boy on the step. He was Mrs Scothen's nephew and he'd ridden round on his bike with a note for me. 'Could you come down right away? Your mum's very poorly,' Scottie had written. A knot of apprehension twisted inside. Mum wasn't getting any younger. What on earth could be wrong?

'All right, love, thanks very much,' I told the boy as brightly as I could. 'Tell your Auntie I'll be down as soon as I've got Terry off to school.'

I hurried back indoors and bustled John and Terry through their breakfast. 'I don't know what's wrong, John,' I told him as I collected up the porridge plates, 'but if I'm going to be out for some time I'll send you a message.'

I buttoned Terry into his school mac to save time, though he was quite capable of doing it himself and protested furiously. Then I dragged him to the bus stop, saw him safely on the bus and hurried round to Fletcher Street.

I found Mum in the kitchen, doubled up with pain, her facy shiny with cold sweat. Scottie was there beside her trying to persuade her to drink a cup of tea.

'You'll feel a lot better for a hot drink, love,' she insisted. 'Now come on, just try a little.'

Mum was shaking her head fiercely and declaring she felt sick. No matter what the weather, Mum was in the habit of going out early every morning to fetch Mr Scothen's paper for him so that he could read it with his breakfast. When she hadn't appeared Mrs Scothen had called to see if anything was wrong.

'She's been up all night with pain,' Scottie told me anxiously. Mum didn't seem to hear. 'I'm sorry I haven't been to get Mr Scothen's paper,' she was muttering over and over again. 'I did mean to get it.' She seemed really worried about it.

'Blow Mr Scothen's paper,' I said. 'Let's see what's the

matter with you.' But I knew she was really ill, so I got her into bed, tucked her up with a hot water bottle and went out to phone the doctor.

Some time later after a long examination, the doctor came out of the bedroom with a prescription. 'It may only be a severe tummy bug,' she told me, 'and in that case this medicine will help, but if she doesn't show any improvement, or if she gets any worse, telephone me immediately.'

I fetched Mum's medicine from the chemist, cleaned the house and refilled her hot water bottle. She seemed easier by then and was falling into a doze so I went home to prepare Terry and John's lunch.

When I returned in the afternoon I was shocked at the change in her. Her face was grey, she was soaked in sweat and she was vomiting badly. I could see she was desperately ill.

'Now don't worry, Mumy,' I told her as calmly as I could, 'but I think I'll go and phone the doctor again. She said she'd like another look at you.'

I moved unhurriedly through the house but once outside I flew down to the telephone box. 'You'll have to come straight away,' I told the doctor when I got through. 'My mother's very ill indeed.'

This time there was only a short examination. 'Oh dear,' said the doctor, 'I'm afraid we'll have to get your mother to hospital.'

Mum, however, had other ideas. She wasn't going to budge, she insisted, until she'd had a strip wash. She wasn't going dirty to hospital and that was it. What sort of person did we take her for? Whatever would the nurses think? Although she didn't have a bathroom it was her custom every morning to put a bowl of hot water on the kitchen table and have a thorough wash and woebetide anyone who called before nine o'clock when she finished.

'Get me some hot water, our Doris,' she said firmly, though she must have been in agony because it turned out that she had a strangulated hernia. So I boiled a kettle and took the steaming bowl into the bedroom.

'I'll do it, Mum,' I said setting down soap, flannel and towel beside the bowl.

'Oh, no you won't. I'm quite capable. I'm not in my dotage yet,' Mum snapped but rather weakly. And she hauled herself painfully to the edge of the bed and meticulously scrubbed every inch of her body, only calling me back to help with her feet because she couldn't bend down to reach them.

We took her to hospital then and they operated on her at eleven-thirty that night. When I phoned they told me she'd come through the operation and was as well as could be expected. I was tremendously relieved. I'd had a nasty feeling this would be Mum's last illness and it wouldn't have been surprising, after all, if at her age she had failed to survive the operation.

When I went to see her she was feeling pretty rotten and her chest was bad but she didn't look too poorly. She was obviously depressed, however.

'Well that's it, our Doris,' she announced as soon as I'd shown her the oranges I'd brought. 'I shall have to come and live with you. I can't live on my own any more.'

And much as I loved my mum, my heart sank. Oh no, I thought, it would be a disaster. She could be so difficult at times; reprimanding John and I over the smallest offence, letting Terry get away with murder, digging in her heels stubbornly over some minor detail and yet being amazingly careless over something important. How could we cope? I forced a bright smile onto my face.

'There's no need to worry about it, Mum,' I said. 'We'll always take care of you.'

And of course we would. My mind ticked over the details. We only had two berooms and one living room. Mum could hardly sleep downstairs in that. There was nothing for it but to move Terry's bed into our room and put Mum in his. It wouldn't be comfortable, but we'd manage somehow.

Towards the end of visiting time Mum's eyelids began to droop and I decided to leave her to get some sleep. 'See you tomorrow,' I whispered. 'Have a nice sleep,' and I crept away.

The next morning I was peeling potatoes when there was a knock at the door. Drying my hands on my apron I hurried to open it and came face to face with a uniformed policeman on the step. My heart flipped over and my knees felt watery. It was John Michael all over again. I sagged against the door frame.

'Mrs Stokes?' he asked.

'Yes,' I mumbled, my mouth dry.

'Could you come to the hospital? Your mother's dangerously ill.'

For a moment I didn't know what to say. My brain was racing in confusion and the years turned backwards. Was it John Michael who was ill or Mum, or maybe both of them?

'Mrs Stokes?' The policeman had stepped forward in concern. 'Are you all right? You did know your mother was in hospital, didn't you?'

'Oh yes, yes,' I said and my mind locked into practicalities. John! I must get a message to John. 'I wonder if you could do something for me, officer? Could you tell my husband? He's a gardener and he's working on the green in front of the town hall.'

'Certainly, Mrs Stokes,' said the policeman. 'Glad to help.' He trudged away and I tore off my apron, dragged on my coat and raced round to Edie.

'I've left a stew on,' I told her after I'd explained what had happened. 'Could you give Terry his dinner for me?'

'Of course, Doris,' said Edie. 'You get along to the hospital and don't worry about Terry. I'll look after him. I hope your mum improves.'

I smiled gratefully at her and then I rushed off, buttoning my coat as I went. By the time I got to the hospital John was there. He squeezed my hand quietly and we went into the ward together. We found Mum propped up on a pile of pillows to help her breathe, her chest rasping painfully. Her skin was papery yellow but she was conscious.

'Hello, Doris,' she wheezed. Then she noticed John and her voice sharpened. 'What's John doing here? Is there something the matter?'

I didn't know what to say. 'Well, he thought he'd pop in to see you,' I muttered lamely.

Mum wasn't fooled. 'But they've only just had their dinners. What's he doing here at dinner time? He should be at work.' There was silence as John and I both struggled to think of a plausbile explanation. Before either of us could reply, Mum added, 'Am I going to die then?'

I hesitated. Faced with a direct question like this what could I do? Should I lie? Down the years came my father's voice: 'You must always tell the truth, Dol. You can't go wrong if you tell the truth …' It was as clear as if he'd been standing behind me. That's what he wanted me to do.

'Well it's quite possible, you know, Mum,' I said slowly. 'You've got a bad chest and you've just had a big operation.'

If anything, she seemed relieved. She relaxed back onto the pillows and let out a long sigh. 'Oh well, I'll just go to sleep if I die, won't I?'

'Yes, you will,' I said gently. She lay quiet for a moment, then she looked up at John.

'I'm so sorry,' she said softly but quite distinctly and then she closed her eyes and fell asleep.

Those were the last words she ever spoke and I'm so glad they were to John. For so many years he'd felt unaccepted and even disliked by my mother because she considered he'd 'stolen' me from a man of higher rank. Yet it was John who went to her house uncomplainingly to do little odd jobs for her, it was John who first noticed when she needed new, comfortable shoes and it was John who in the later years cut her toenails for her when she could no longer reach them. He had never shown any resentment about it, but I know it meant a lot to him to hear at the end that Mum had forgiven him and that she realized she'd made a mistake.

I sat with Mum for the rest of the day, only leaving her bedside to phone my half sister, Edna, who was living in London, to break the news and tell her to come at once.

The next day I returned to the hospital and the chair by Mum's bed. She never regained consciousness. The long hours dragged by as if time had been suspended. I never took my eyes off that still figure in the bed. At intervals the kind nurses offered me food but I couldn't touch it. My mind was spinning in confusion.

Of course I knew that Mum couldn't live forever but I

hadn't expected the end to be so sudden. Only four or five days ago she'd been trotting about doing her odd jobs as healthy and fit as a woman fifteen years younger. That was a blessing really, I suppose, but it made her sudden deterioration all the more shocking. I found myself thinking back to my childhood and the time when my father was alive. Those long evenings when I sat at the table drawing endless pictures entitled 'My Family' with a great tall male figure, a tiny little woman tucked protectively by his side and two little girls close by. Every now and then Mum would glance over my shoulder as she cleared away the supper dishes, but we were very quiet, both listening to father who sat by the fire telling us stories as we worked.

How long ago it all seemed now. Yet this time, sad though I was, I didn't suffer the same shattering grief I'd felt over the loss of my father and John Michael, because by now I was a medium, I understood more of what life was all about and I knew that Mum wasn't really dying. She was going on to be reunited with my father. Poor Mum. She'd been on her own for so long, she'd be so glad to be back with her Sam.

Some time during the evening I glanced at the window and noticed it was dark. Edna must be nearly here, I thought, turning back to Mum, and then I gasped. I could see her spirit body poised face down over her physical body and as I watched, it started to rise. I leapt to my feet, hurried down the ward and found a nurse. 'Could you come quickly,' I asked. 'My mother's near the end.'

Without comment the nurse followed me back through the beds to Mother. 'Oh yes,' she said at once, 'I can see she is. We'll move her into a side ward.'

I hovered anxiously while they bustled about in that subdued way they have in hospitals, keeping one eye on the pale spiritual body that was floating away from Mum. They wheeled the bed out of the ward with me at their heels, into a small single room and as they were making Mum comfortable, I glanced up and through the glass partition, I saw Edna in the corridor.

'Edna!' I cried darting outside. 'Come on, Mum's in here!'

Edna was looking pale and harassed, her pretty blonde

hair hastily combed off her face. To my surprise, instead of moving, she hugged her winter coat more tightly round her and hesitated awkwardly. Then I remembered that Edna, like Mum, was squeamish about anything to do with illness or death. Just entering a hospital was very difficult for her.

'You can see Mum from the door,' I said more kindly. 'You don't have to go right in.'

So Edna popped her head round the door and then quickly withdrew.

'You can go and sit in my room if you like,' said the sister who was passing and saw our difficulty. So we trooped up the corridor, settled ourselves in the tiny office and the waiting began.

At one point the sister came back. 'Why don't you go home,' she said. 'There's nothing you can do.'

'Oh, yes. Let's go home,' said Edna half rising from her seat. I shook my head.

'She'll quite possibly go through till tomorrow morning, you know,' the sister added persuasively.

'She won't,' I said firmly. 'I'm staying. You can go if you want, Edna, but I'm staying here.'

Defeated, Edna sank down again. 'Oh well, if that's the way you feel, I'll stay with you.'

The sister went out and hours dragged by again. The hospital was very quiet. The visitors had long gone, the meals were finished for the day and it seemed as if everyone was asleep. Then suddenly, we heard sharp footsteps clacking briskly up the corridor. Tap, tap, tap, tap, tap, they went, coming closer and then they stopped outside our door.

'Oh, my God!' cried Edna fearfully. 'They've come to fetch us!' She jumped up, opened the door – and there was no one there. Puzzled she poked her head out and looked up and down the corridor but it was quite empty.

'I don't understand,' she said coming back. 'I *heard* those footsteps.'

'So did I,' I replied. I was staring at the empty doorway in a fuddled, sleepy way and then with a shock like a dash of cold water my brain cleared. Footsteps ... someone

coming to fetch us – someone who couldn't be seen ...
Mum! I leapt to my feet. 'I must see how Mum is!' I cried
to Edna over my shoulder and I raced back up the
corridor.

The door to the side ward was propped open and as
soon as I walked in I could see I was only just in time. The
silver cord, like an umbilical cord which attaches the spirit
body to the physical one was stretched to its full extent and
my father was there. I couldn't see him but I could feel his
presence in the room. He was standing at the foot of the
bed and he was talking to Mum. 'It's all right, Jen,' he was
saying. 'I'm here. Don't worry. Sam's come to take care of
you. You're all right now.'

I saw a nurse passing down the corridor and I dived to
the door. 'Nurse. My mother's going!'

'Oh no, Mrs Stokes,' she said coming back. 'The doctor
hasn't long been in and he says she'll last the night.'

'I'm sorry, nurse,' I insisted impatiently, 'it's happening
now.'

With a resigned sigh she walked in past me and then
stopped abruptly. 'Oh, my God. I'll get the doctor!' and
she hurried away. But it was too late. Even as her footsteps
echoed down the corridor, Mum sat up, gurgled once, the
cord parted and she was gone.

Mum would have been very pleased with her funeral. It
was a grand affair. Stan Webb, who was an undertaker,
arranged for the passing bell to be tolled. Mum would
have liked that. Whenever she heard the sombre 'dong,
dong, dong' of the passing bell she'd always say,
'Somebody important's passed over then.'

Well it rang loud and clear for her and as the cortège
wound up Commercial Road to St John's church, all the
curtains were drawn in the street. The church was packed.
Even the bank manager and his wife came and quite a few
other 'important' people.

It would have made Mum's day to see all those fur coats
turned out for her – in fact it probably did!

Chapter 5

It was a terrible day. Sleet was falling, the damp, icy cold seemed to step right into your bones and I was huddled over our gas fire surrounded by boxes.

It must have been about the worst possible day we could have chosen to move flats. I'd only just come out of hospital and I was so weak, exhausted and sore, that the most I could manage was to dust our ornaments, wrap them in paper and pack them away. Fortunately our friends and relatives rallied round to help John and Terry move the furniture down the corridor into our new flat.

Matey crouched miserably in his basket. He didn't like all this bustle and fuss, he wanted to stay where he was. I chatted soothingly to him as I worked.

The emptying flat was beginning to look rather forlorn with light rectangles on the walls where pictures used to hang and gaping spaces where furniture had stood for years. We'd had many happy times in this flat and I was sad in a way to be leaving it. I was particularly sorry to be leaving my rose, but it was impossible to take it with us.

It was very strange that rose. A couple of years before, both John and Terry had forgotten my birthday. Now, my birthday comes very soon after Christmas and I know it's a difficult time so I don't expect presents, but cards mean a lot to me. John and Terry had always been very thoughtful in this respect, but for some reason, this particular January, they both forgot.

It had never happened before. I didn't say anything but I felt unloved and sorry for myself. Every time I looked at the bare mantelpiece a pang went through me and in the end I took myself moodily into the bedroom where I wouldn't have to look at it. It's not fair, I muttered; I work

284

and slave for them, see to their every need. How would they like it if I forgot their birthdays? And so I went on, convincing myself I was thoroughly hard done by. After a while I realized it was getting late and with a martyred sigh I went out to start dinner.

As I moved into the living room something bright caught my eye. I stopped and glanced back. It had been something on the wall, something glinting where nothing had glinted before. And then I saw it. Raised from the plain white wall, like an embossed pattern was a perfect, long-stemmed gold rose. My mouth fell open. I had chosen that colour scheme myself. Just plain, bare walls painted white; clean and simple and easy to wipe, the way I wanted it. Gingerly I put out my finger and touched the rose. It felt just like embossed paper. It was as real and substantial as the rest of the wallpaper.

'John!' I called, my birthday sulks forgotten. 'Come and look at this.'

He wandered in from the kitchen. 'What?' I didn't say anything, just in case the rose was my imagination. I simply pointed at the wall.

'Good God!' said John seeing it at once. 'Where did that come from?'

I shook my head. 'I don't know. I'm sure it wasn't there this morning. I would have noticed it when I was dusting. I just came out of the bedroom and there it was.'

John leaned forward and began inspecting the rose closely. He too put out a timid finger and ran it lightly over the flower's raised surface. Nothing happened.

'D'you think it could be a pattern from the wallpaper underneath coming through?' I asked.

'No. The decorators scraped if all off before they put this lot on,' said John. He stared at the rose in wonder. 'I can't understand it.'

I decided a scientific approach was called for so I fetched a knife from the kitchen and carefully scraped away a piece of paper at the side of the rose. Sure enough, the wall underneath it was clean and bare.

There was still one test I wanted to make and a few weeks later I was able to make it. Going shopping one day

I came upon our decorators at work on another flat.
'Excuse me,' I called putting my head round the door.

The foreman came over. 'Yes, madam?'

'I know it's a little while ago now,' I said, 'but do you
remember decorating Flat 55?'

'Yes, very well,' he said cautiously.

'Well, can you remember if you stripped the walls right
down before painting them?'

'Oh yes,' he said. 'We always strip right down to bare
plaster before we put anything else up.'

'So there's no old wallpaper left in the lounge?'

'Not a scrap,' he assured me. 'Why, is anything wrong?'

'Oh no, nothing at all,' I said and went on my way
leaving a very puzzled foreman behind me.

After that my beautiful gold rose became quite famous.
Friends often popped in to ask if they could bring their
friends and relatives to see it and at times my living room
was like a tiny art gallery. I couldn't give my visitors a
proper explanation of my rose, but I like to think it was a
birthday present from the spirit world to cheer me up
when everyone else had forgotten.

The rose didn't fade. It was still there when we left our
flat and I said goodbye to it reluctantly. The chance to
move was too good to miss and had cropped up quite
unexpectedly.

All the flats in our block were to be converted and
modernized with bathrooms installed, but it was a long
slow process. First one empty flat was completed, then a
family would move in and work would start on their old
flat. On completion another family would move into that
flat and the process would be repeated. We were right
down near the bottom of the list and expected to wait well
over a year, but then there was a tragedy.

A few doors along, an old lady lived alone. She was
almost blind, poor soul, but she was unfailingly cheerful. I
kept an eye on her when I could. If I didn't see her for a
day or two and couldn't get an answer when I knocked on
her door I'd alert the nurse. But most of the time the old
lady was in good health. In fine weather she'd toddle
across the landing to see me as I tended the plants we kept

in pots outside our door. She loved a drop of sherry, so I'd go and pour her a glass and she'd sit there happily basking in the sun, sipping her sherry and chatting to me as I weeded.

Then one day when we were abroad, there was a terrible accident. Apparently the old lady got up in the night to put the fire on and caught the hem of her nightie on the bars. The whole garment went up in flames and the poor woman was found burned to death the next day in her smoke-blackened, ash-strewn flat.

We were terribly shocked when we hard the news, but as weeks and then months went by we couldn't help noticing that the flat remained empty. This seemed very strange when there was such a long waiting list for converted homes, but I was amazed to discover that no one wanted that flat. Either they were superstitious about it and felt it was an unlucky place or they were worried it might be haunted. At any rate no one wanted to know, the flat remained empty and we remained near the bottom of the waiting list.

In the end I said to John, 'If nobody else wants it why don't we ask if we can have it? We're not superstitious and I don't mind if the old dear comes back for a visit every now and then.'

John thought this was a good idea. The older we grew the more difficult we found life without a bathroom and the chore of filling the bath in the kitchen was becoming increasingly hard. So I telephoned the secretary of the Foundation and was very pleased to hear that we could have the flat as long as we were prepared to pay for the necessary work and redecoration. In the end it cost us rather more than we'd bargained for, but it was worth it to have a modernized place.

The old lady was quite active in the flat at first. One day I went into the kitchen, partly because I wanted to fetch something but mainly to admire it. I was very proud of my new kitchen with its clean magnolia walls, gleaming white units and smart tiled floor and I stood there beaming round it. Then, suddenly the feel of the room changed and I was conscious that the old lady had come in. There was silence for a few moments and a strong sense of bewilderment, then she said, 'What have you done with my red curtains? They are warm, you know, warm.'

I couldn't think what she meant at first, and then I remembered that before the flat had been decorated I'd found a pair of old red curtains still hanging at the kitchen window obscuring most of the light. I'd taken them down and put up fresh white nets instead.

'Well, dear,' I said as tactfully as I could, 'I like a lot of light and those curtains made the kitchen a bit dark.'

'But red's warm. It's a nice warm colour,' she insisted. Unspoken but strong came the distinct impression that she didn't think too much of my bright, pale decor. Then the feeling faded and I was alone in the kitchen again.

A few days later I came out of the living room and almost bumped into a woman standing in the hall. For a moment I thought John had left the door open and a visitor had walked in without my hearing, but then I saw that it was the old lady. She was wearing the same thick cardigan and tweedy skirt she so often wore as she sipped sherry with me in the sun, and her wispy grey hair framed her face, a little untidily the way it always used to. She seemed to be studying the red carpet and the posters from Australia that I'd pinned to the walls. Then as I watched she wandered towards the bathroom and melted right through the door. I hurried after her but by the time I got there, being forced to go through the door in the conventional manner, she'd vanished. All that was left was an echo of confusion.

I sat on the bath thinking about how it must look to her eyes. I bet she didn't understand it at all. There was the toilet in the same room and same position as before but now instead of blank walls around it there was a shining bath and hand basin. The poor old dear must think she'd come to the wrong flat.

She must have got used to us living there I think because gradually her visits tailed off until the only evidence of her presence was centred around the bedroom, probably because that was the room where her body was found.

One night John went to bed first while I emptied the

ashtrays and plumped up the cushions in the living room. It only took a minute or two and when I came back from the bathroom I noticed that the bedroom door was firmly shut, whereas it had been wide open before I'd gone out. Cheeky devil! I thought, he's forgotten me.

'You needn't have closed the bedroom door!' I called to John. 'I'm coming to bed, too, you know, so don't hog all the electric blanket.'

'I didn't close the door,' John mumbled sleepily as I went in. The blankets were up round his ears, he was dozing off and he certainly didn't look as if he'd risen again after going to bed.

'Well, it must have closed itself then,' I said undoing my dressing gown, but as I glanced back at the door I realized this was most unlikely. Designed for disabled people it was wider and heavier than a normal door and when pushed wide open it had a trick of sitting back on its hinges and staying in place so that it wouldn't swing shut on a wheel chair or slow moving invalid. To close it again required a decisive tug and John, in bed, was too far away to administer one.

The mysteriously closed door became a feature of life in our new flat and in the end I came to the conclusion that the old lady, always one to feel the cold, had been in the habit of shutting the bedroom door every night to keep the warmth in. Our apparent carelessness must have worried her and so she closed the door for us when we 'forgot'.

1980, the year we moved into our new flat, was also the year my first book, *Voices in My Ear*, came out and I don't think I've ever been so busy in my life. The book wasn't coming out until May, so I thought I'd have a bit of a rest until then. Which just shows how little I knew about publishing. Apparently monthly, and even some weekly, magazines publish months in advance, and in order to write about a book appearing in May, they would have to see me at the beginning of the year.

I'd only just come out of hospital, of course, and was still feeling very sorry for myself but with Ramanov, my guide's help, I was sure I'd get through the interviews.

That was something else I had to learn. My interviews
nearly always turned into sittings, but I couldn't blame the
journalists for asking me to work. It's all very well writing
about being able to talk to spirit people, but journalists
tend to be curious and rather cynical people and unless I
could prove to them that I was telling the truth they
weren't likely to believe it.

I did so many interviews/sittings in 1980 I can hardly
remember them, but one in particular, probably because it
was among the first, stands out in my mind.

The interview with the *Tatler* had been arranged for a
date only three or four weeks after I came home from
hospital. Brian Inglis, the book reviewer, was coming
along with the assistant editor who would have a sitting
and there would also be a photographer present to take
pictures.

I'd never seen the *Tatler* before so John bought me a
copy and as soon as I saw it I don't know whether I was
more nervous or excited. It was a glossy high class
magazine, more likely to cover stories of aristocratic
wedding than of ordinary people like me. I fretted about
the state of the flat because I wasn't well enough to look
after it myself and I fretted about my appearance which
was rather the worse for a major operation. By the fateful
morning, however, I'd managed to calm myself and agree
that John was right: they'd have to take us as they found
us.

The photographer was the first to arrive and when he
saw me, his face fell a mile. 'Oh, my God!' he said rather
discouragingly I felt, though I could hardly blame him. I
was perched up on a rubber ring with my legs outstretched
on a pouf.

'Didn't they tell you I'd just come out of hospital?' I
asked.

'No, they didn't,' he said looking even less cheerful than
before.

'Well, I'm sorry, son,' I said. 'I've done my best.' I was
feeling a bit depressed myself by now. I was still so stiff
and sore it had taken me two hours to get myself bathed,
dressed and put heated rollers in my hair. I'd thought the

results were reasonably respectable but obviously I looked worse than I thought.

Anyway John made some coffee, Brian Inglis and the assistant editor arrived and though they looked a bit startled at first sight of the rubber ring they tactfully made no comment and we began the sitting.

I tuned in. Instantly a tiny light swam before me. It was such a faint pin prick that I said to myself, now, am I really seeing a spirit light or is it just a reflection? 'It's a real light, child,' came Ramanov's reassuring voice from a distance. But it's very small, I said silently.

'Yes, he's only just come over,' said Ramanov.

I turned to the assistant editor. 'I've got someone here who's just gone over.'

She shook her head. 'No,' she said.

I stared at the light. 'Yes, it's a man and he's only just passed.'

'No,' she repeated firmly. 'I haven't lost anyone.'

The light still glimmered teasingly before my eyes but I couldn't hear a thing. Brian Inglis and the assistant editor exchanged glances. They were getting impatient and I was getting cross. I knew the man was there. There was no doubt about it but what was the point of coming to me if he wasn't going to say anything. And what a time to choose! Was it some sort of joke?

'For God's sake, don't mess about,' I told him inwardly. 'This is very important to us all. I've got to prove you're here. Give me some clue.'

'My name – is – Clive,' he said with great effort.

The assistant editor looked blank when I repeated this. 'And he's talking about a girl called Tracey,' I added desperately as Clive blurted out more information, but the woman shook her head again.

This is hopeless, I thought, and then I felt Ramanov direct me to the photographer who was sitting on my left and for the first time I noticed he had tears in his eyes.

'You?' I asked.

His face went white. 'Oh, my God,' he said. 'Clive only died at three o'clock this morning.'

'And who's Tracey?' I asked gently.

'Tracey's my girlfriend.'

I breathed a sigh of relief. Clive was genuinely trying to get through to someone after all. He wasn't being mischievous. The difficulty I had experienced was simply due to the fact that he'd only been over a few hours and obviously found it a struggle to communicate.

'You're doing very well, Clive,' I told him. 'It's marvellous that you can do this so soon.'

He was trying to say another name. 'Su – Su – Suzanne.'

'Who's Suzanne?' I asked.

'Suzanne's the one who rang me at seven this morning to tell me about Clive,' said the photographer.

The light was beginning to fade but I felt that Clive was still trying to tell me something important.

'I want to thank him,' he said faintly, 'thank him for taking the trouble – in his busy life – to drive up to see me.'

I repeated this to the photographer. 'Does that make sense to you?'

'Yes, it does,' he said. 'While Clive was ill I used to drive from London to Yorkshire to visit him. I was there last weekend.'

I blinked. The light had gone out. Clive had got his message through and gone. I think the assistant editor found this genuinely interesting but I was suddenly aware that the sitting had been intended for her and she must be disappointed.

I concentrated on her and tuned in. This time there was a response. I got the impression of a man and a sharp pain in my chest.

'There's a man here who passed with a heart attack,' I said.

She nodded at last in recognition. 'My father,' she admitted.

'Tell her I've seen the boy,' he said in a crisp, educated voice. 'She thinks I've never seen him.'

'He says he's seen the boy, love,' I repeated obediently. 'Does that sound right?'

'Oh yes,' she said. 'My son was born after Father's death.'

The man went on to say his name was William but 'Call me Bill, everyone else does. Or you could even call me sir,' he added with a chuckle. I didn't understand this last part, but before I could ask what he meant he took me into a neat, yet lived-in looking sitting room. In my mind I was facing a big window with sun pouring through, then Bill tugged my arm, pulling me to the left so that I could see a photograph on the wall. It showed a squadron leader in full uniform.

'Your father was in the airforce,' I said out loud, 'and there's a picture to the left of the window, in his sitting room of a squadron leader. Am I right in thinking that was him in his uniform?'

'Yes, that's right, Doris,' said the girl in amazement. 'You're absolutely right.'

'No wonder he's telling me to call him sir, then!' I laughed.

Chapter 6

Outside the children's playground Irene MacDonald, mother of the sixteen year old girl murdered by the Yorkshire Ripper, suddenly stopped. She opened her handbag, took out her glasses and bent down to peer at the pavement. She was scrabbling about, examining each paving stone in a preoccupied, distracted way that I didn't understand. I could feel her distress.

'What are you doing, love?' I asked gently, going over and putting my hand on her shoulder.

'I'm just looking to see if the blood's gone,' she said without looking up. 'There was blood all over here, Doris. I just wanted to see that they'd washed it away.'

For a moment I couldn't speak. I just stood there watching that poor tortured woman, busily working over the pavement as if it had been her own kitchen floor, and my heart went over to her. You poor soul, I thought, how this terrible thing has played on your mind.

'Come on, love,' I said helping her up. 'It's all gone now. It's quite clean.'

She came without protest but she still seemed disorientated. 'There was, there were blood stains all over there, Doris,' she kept saying, looking over her shoulder as I led her away. 'You should have seen it. Covered in blood.'

I met Irene quite by chance. In the months before my book was published I found myself caught up in an astonishing blaze of publicity. I'd imagined that all one had to do was write a book, send it off to the publishers and then sit back and wait for it to appear in the shops. Of course it wasn't like that at all.

Tours of Britain, Australia, New Zealand and Tasmania

294

were arranged; there were interviews, television appearances, radio shows; one thing seemed to lead to another.
My feet hardly touched the ground. Of course it was very
exciting and in many ways very helpful. Thanks to the
publicity, I was able to meet many people, people like the
MacDonalds whom I would never otherwise have had the
chance to help.

At first I was delighted. Publicity was marvellous, I
decided, because it created so many opportunities. It was
some time before I realized there was another side to such
exposure. Everything has a price, I suppose, and I finally
discovered with a shock that the same publicity that made
things happen, could also spoil them and leave behind a
sour, bitter taste.

The Yorkshire Ripper story is a case in point. Like
everyone else, I read about the crimes of the Ripper with
horror. As the trail of bloody murders in the North of
England grew, I could understand the anger and the fear
of the people living in the area and I prayed the madman
would be caught. But it didn't occupy too much of my
mind. After all, I was very busy with my own life and the
murders occurred hundreds of miles away. There didn't
seem to be anything I could do to help.

Then one day I was asked to appear on a TV
programme in Newcastle on Tyne. I was getting quite
used to this kind of thing by now and I had my hair done
and packed a smart dress to wear in what was becoming a
familiar routine. John and I went to the studios, they got
me ready, I was introduced to the presenter and then
suddenly, instead of asking me to work with the studio
audience as they normally did, they produced a tape
recorder. 'I'd like you to listen to this tape and see if you
can get anything from it,' said the presenter.

She pushed in the cassette, clicked the switched and the
thick Sunderland voice of a man claiming to be the
Yorkshire Ripper streamed out. The studio fell silent as
the man cruelly taunted George Oldfield, the man in
charge of the Ripper hunt, for failing to find him.

'I'm Jack,' he said slowly. 'I see you are still having no
luck catching me. I have the greatest respect for you,

George, but Lord, you are no nearer catching me now than four years ago when I started.

'I reckon your boys are letting you down. George. You can't be much good can you?'

I'm jack, I repeated to myself and I tried to tune into the voice. There was something odd about it. It didn't sound quite right somehow ...

'The only time they came near catching me was a few months back in Chapeltown when I was disturbed. Even then it was a uniformed copper, not a detective,' the man continued in his slow monotonous drawl. 'I warned you in March that I'd strike again. Sorry it wasn't Bradford. I did promise you that but I couldn't get there.

'I'm not quite sure when I will strike again but it will be definitely sometime this year. Maybe September or October, even sooner if I get the time.

'I'm not sure where. Maybe Manchester. I like it there. There's plenty of *them* knocking about. They never learn, do they, George? I bet you've warned them but they never listen. At any rate I'm going I should be in the Guinness Book of Records. I think it's eleven times up to now, isn't it? Well I'll keep on going for quite a while yet.

'I can't see myself being nicked just yet. Even if you do get near I'll probably top myself first. Well, it's been nice chatting to you, George. Yours the Ripper.'

And at the end of the tape he played a few bars of Thanks For Being a Friend.

I'm Jack, I'm Jack. I repeated the phrase again and again in my mind, turning it round, probing the thing that didn't fit and suddenly it came to me. The man wasn't speaking naturally, it wasn't spontaneous, he was reading a message. His voice was slow and careful at first with all traces of his personality ironed out but towards the end he couldn't suppress little bits of himself creeping in. I got the impression of an intelligent man but very mixed up. I also got the feeling that at one time he could have been a policeman or security man or something similar.

Then over the top of the cassette I heard a woman's voice and she was weeping. She was rather faint because I didn't have a proper link, a sitter to work with, but she said her named was Polly and she'd passed with cancer. I took it that she was probably the man's mother. Anyway, she said the man had been married but was living apart from his wife, his name was Ronnie or Johnnie and the name Berwick featured in his address.

I explained to the presenter and the audience that I had no idea if this information was any use because it is so difficult to get an impression from the voice of someone who's not talking directly to you. Also there was no way of knowing if this man was really the Yorkshire Ripper. Polly had been upset about something but she hadn't said it was murder.

Nevertheless, there were police at the studio who noted it all down and as a result of the broadcast, Irene MacDonald, whose innocent daughter Jayne had been savagely murdered by the Ripper, sent a message asking if I could give her a sitting.

There weren't many gaps in my diary at the time but I felt so sorry for that tragic family that I couldn't refuse.

We arrived in Chapeltown, a run down area of Leeds, on a dull, bleak day in early spring. The MacDonalds were just ordinary working people like John and I and they lived in a neat, square council house on an estate, separated from Chapeltown by a busy main road. Sadness seemed to hang over the house like low cloud and the plants in the wintry garden had a bedraggled, neglected look. They've lost heart, I thought, as I walked up the path and I hoped very much that I could help them.

Wilf MacDonald opened the door. He was a tall, thin man with receding silver hair. He seemed rather uneasy every time his glance met mine. I smiled at him encouragingly, thinking he might be nervous but he only looked away quickly.

'Look,' he said in the end as he took my coat, 'I've got to tell you. I've got no faith in what you do. I only agreed to go along with this because Irene wanted it. I don't believe in it at all.'

'That's all right,' I told him, glad he'd found the courage to speak his mind right away. 'What you believe is your privilege. I'll just get on with my work and you can make up your own mind.'

Hearing our voices Irene came out to meet us and I was immediately struck by the similarity between them. Irene was small while her husband was tall, pleasantly plump while Wilf was thin, and she had thick, springy dark hair while he was grey, but the same haunted look burned in both their eyes making them look like brother and sister.

Outwardly the strain showed more on Irene than on Wilf. Deep lines of suffering ran round her mouth, there were sleepless bags beneath her eyes and her hands clenched and unclenched as she spoke. With Wilf the pain lay under the surface. Irene told me that he'd suffered from nervous asthma since his daughter's murder and it was so bad he'd had to retire from his job on the railways five years early. He wasn't the man he used to be, she confided. Even little jobs around the house got too much for him at times.

Wilf went out to the kitchen to make a pot of tea and watching him go. I realized that there's never just one victim of a murder. The effects of such a senseless, wicked act go on and on, spreading like ripples on a pond, ruining the lives of everyone involved.

A few minutes later Wilf came back, he and Irene drew their chairs close to mine and I tuned in. There was no trouble reaching Jayne. Her clear young voice piped up immediately and I felt she'd been trying to contact her parents for some time.

'Hello, I'm Jayne,' she said excitedly, glad to be talking to them at last.

'I'm Doris, love,' I said. 'Can you tell us what happened to you? Can you remember?'

'My daddy said I had to be in by eleven,' said Jayne slowly.

Wilf nearly shot out of his chair. 'That's right. I did,' he cried in amazement.

'But I missed the bus,' Jayne went on, 'so I walked home with my boyfriend. We thought his sister might give me a lift home but she was out so Steven walked part of the way with me and then I went on alone.'

Her voice seemed to trail off at the end of the sentence

and in its place a picture flashed into my mind. I could see a patch of grass and a set of concrete steps. I stared at them, puzzled. They couldn't be described as a staircase – there weren't enough of them and they didn't lead anywhere. It was just a set of steps, left for some reason on a patch of grass. It made no sense at all. What a peculiar thing to show me, I thought.

'I'm sorry,' I said to the MacDonalds, 'I can't make anything of this but they're showing me a set of steps that don't lead anywhere.'

Irene and Wilf exchanged glances sharply. 'Yes, I know where that is,' was Irene's only comment.

Then I got a name: Sutcliffe.

'Sutcliffe was my maiden name,' Irene ventured.

'They're saying John Sutcliffe,' I said. 'Would that be your father?'

Irene shook her head. 'No – I think we might have had someone way back called John Sutcliffe. Is it him?'

But it wasn't. Instead I heard another woman's voice. She said she was Jayne's grandmother and Irene's mother. Her name was Annie. She talked for a while about members of the family and personal details and then she drew my attention back to the steps. They formed again in my mind. 'They are important,' Annie insisted.

'I don't understand why, Irene,' I said, 'but Annie is going on about the steps too. They are important for some reason.'

'I know what it means,' Irene admitted. 'Jayne's body was found in an adventure playground. The steps were built for the children to play on.'

There was a moment's silence then Jayne came back. 'I wish I'd rung Uncle Jack,' she said wistfully.

'Who's Uncle Jack, love?' I asked.

'Oh he's not our real uncle. We just call him Uncle,' Jayne explained. 'He lives over the back. He's a taxi driver. I wish I'd rung him to pick me up but I thought it was too late to wake him.'

'What happened after you left Steven, Jayne?' I asked. 'Can you tell us anything about the man who attacked you?'

'I didn't see him,' she explained. 'I heard these footsteps coming up behind me and then an arm went round my neck and my chain came off. I think he was wearing something dark, overalls or something like that. Then he hit me and I don't remember anything else.'

Irene didn't know what Jayne meant about the chain, but later she asked the girl who'd called for Jayne the night she was murdered if Jayne had been wearing a chain of any kind. 'Oh yes,' the girl had replied, 'she was wearing a crucifix round her neck.' Irene went up to check in Jayne's jewellery box and sure enough the crucifix was missing.

'What do you look like, Jayne?' I asked, realizing that I hadn't asked her to describe herself.

'I've got shoulder length brown hair with two blonde pieces at the front,' she explained.

At this information Wilf broke down. 'Yes, that's right,' he said. 'And when I went to identify her body, her head was bandaged and all I could see were these blonde bits covered in blood ...'

Jayne couldn't bear to see her father's distress. For a split second she materialized, a fresh pretty young girl with a glowing face and I saw her sit on the arm of her father's chair and lean towards him.

'Wilf, can you feel a pressure down one side?' I asked him. He looked up at me in surprise. 'Why, yes. As a matter of fact I can, and I feel warm all down here.' He waved his arm to indicate an area from his shoulder to his waist. 'How did you know?'

'Because Jayne's sitting on the side of your chair,' I explained. Wilf was speechless but his eyes met mine in wonder and for the rest of the sitting he kept staring at the empty air beside him as if willing Jayne to materialize.

By this time Jayne was getting tired with the effort of making her first communication. She mentioned a few more names including that of Paul Walker. Apparently after the tragedy Wilf could no longer manage some of the household chores he used to do and Paul Walker had come in to help with the tasks that were getting urgent.

Then the name John Sutcliffe came again, as it had come several times during the sitting.

'Well, I suppose one of your long lost relatives must be trying to get through, Irene,' I said, 'but he doesn't seem to be managing it. I haven't heard a man's voice at all.' She shrugged and it was only long aftertwards that, by coincidence, we noticed that the man the police had arrested in connection with the murders was called Peter John Sutcliffe. However, the police assured Irene that he wasn't a distant relative.

At the end of the sitting Wilf went to fetch my coat and Irene told me a strange thing. Apparently the night Jayne died, Irene was out at her waitressing job and when she came home, tired because it was very late, she asked Wilf if all the children were back. He said they were, and that she could lock up.

'What about Jayne?' Irene had asked for some reason.

'Oh yes, she went up to bed a few minutes ago,' Wilf had told her. So they locked the door and went to bed themselves.

The next morning when Wilf woke Irene with a cup of tea he looked worried.

'I can't understand it,' he said. 'I've just been into Jayne's room and she's not there and the bed hasn't been slept in. Yet I know she came in last night. I was dozing in the chair when she came in. She leaned over and kissed me goodnight. I saw her, heard her and smelled her perfume – but she's not there now.'

But as they discovered later, Jayne never did come home that night. By the time Wilf saw her she might already have been killed.

As we stood chatting in the hall ready to leave, someone said, 'Why don't we show Doris the stone steps she was on about? It's not far.'

'Well, if it won't upset Irene I don't mind,' I replied.

'No, I'm used to it by now,' Irene assured me, 'and you might get something else if you go there.' So we all piled into our waiting car and drove to the children's playground.

A damp spring breeze had come up while we were indoors and a few children were chasing each other round the jumble of play objects set out for them. The new grass was just coming through, there were tight buds on the trees and it was difficult to imagine that this place had been the scene of horror and brutality. But then Irene started combing the pavement for blood stains and the tragedy came flooding back.

'They found the blood out here but her body was in there,' Irene explained. 'She must have been dragged right through the playground.'

I looked across and there was the little flight of steps, just as I'd seen it in my mind earlier. I moved towards it and as I did so, I felt Jayne move in close to me again.

'Mum's never been to the grave,' she said. 'Don't go there, Mum, because I'm not there.'

I repeated this out loud to Irene. 'That's right,' she said. 'We've not been back since the day of the funeral. We couldn't face it.'

It had been a long emotional afternoon for the MacDonalds. They fell quiet as we walked around the playground and I know it was a strain for them.

'I'm getting tired. I can't work any more today,' I said after a while. 'Why don't we have another try tomorrow.' They agreed eagerly and I think we were all relieved to leave that sad place.

Wilf and Irene were silent most of the way home and I couldn't help wondering if we'd been any use to them. I needn't have worried. Later Irene phoned to say they'd been so overwhelmed they hadn't been able to take it all in, but afterwards they'd talked it over and even Wilf was impressed. It had made a tremendous difference to them. They even thought that if we carried on with our sittings, we might get some tiny clue, so far overlooked, which might help the police find Jayne's killer.

By this time I was feeling almost as involved as they were in the Ripper case. Having seen at first hand the suffering he caused I wanted to do everything I could to stop this man killing again and destroying another family, so I made arrangements to return to the MacDonald home for another sitting.

This time it was decided that the events should be recorded just in case there was something the police could use. A tape recorder was set up on the table in front of me where it would easily pick up my voice and a brand new cassette tape, fresh from its cellophane wrapper was inserted. Someone switched on the recorder to test it, while I was clearing my mind ready to tune in, and then suddenly, from the blank cassette we all heard someone speak.

'Hello,' said an excited girl's voice, followed by another word that was indistinct, then there was a burst of young laughter and then silence.

'That was Jayne!' cried Irene, her eyes shining and she lunged towards the tape recorder where the cassette was spinning noiselessly, as if she thought Jayne might be hiding inside.

'Now hang on a minute, love,' I said cautiously. 'I know it sounded like a voice but it might have been a noise on the machine. A fault of some kind. Let's play it back and see if we still hear it.'

The tape was rewound and switched on again and Wilf and Irene craned eagerly over it. The little wheels turned silently for an age. The tension grew. We hardly dared breathe lest the noise should drown that brief sound and then, suddenly, there it was again. 'Hello –' the last word was lost in static, then came peals of girlish laughter and then nothing. Just blank tape.

'It's Jayne! I know it is. I'd know her voice anywhere,' Irene insisted. 'She said Hello, Mum! Play it again.'

Back went the tape to the beginning and we played it again and again and again. Irene was adamant that the message was 'Hello, Mum' but I wasn't sure. I never did catch that last world though there was no doubt that the first word was 'Hello'.

The MacDonalds were thrilled and would have sat there happily playing that fragment of tape until they wore it out, but I was still cautious.

'All right, it's definitely a voice,' I pointed out. 'But are you sure it's Jayne's voice? What did she sound like on a tape recorder? Have you got anything we can compare it with?'

Irene looked blank for a moment, then she jumped up.

'Of course we have. The girls were always playing about with the tape recorder. There'll be a tape upstairs.'

She hurried off, rummaged around upstairs and after a few minutes reappeared with a cassette. First we played the old recording and then the new. We tried them several times and I have to admit the voices sounded remarkably similar.

What with the excitement of the recording, we never did get anything of use to the police on tape that day, but one interesting point stands out in my memory. When I finally contacted Jayne she said, 'Mum's been to the cemetery.' I thought I must have misheard because I distinctly remembered her saying on the last occasion we spoke that her parents had never been back to the grave.

'Sorry, Jayne,' I apologized, 'I thought you said your mother's been back to the cemetery.'

'Yes, that's right,' Jayne assured me, 'she has.'

Confused, I turned to Irene. Ramanov, my guide, had always taught me to check a message I was unsure of and if it came back as correct, then to repeat it aloud, however improbable it sounded.

'Well this sounds wrong to me, Irene,' I said, 'but Jayne tells me you've been back to the cemetery.'

Irene blushed. 'Yes, that's right, we have,' she said. 'You see, with all the other funeral expenses we hadn't been able to afford a headstone for the grave but the very same day we did the sitting, a reporter came and said that if we'd agree to be photographed by the grave, the paper would buy the stone for us. We'd felt so bad about Jayne having such a bare grave that we said yes.'

The MacDonalds were very pleased with the results, in fact Irene said I'd changed her life and Wilf admitted that he'd got his faith back. I was fired with enthusiasm to work on the Ripper case. So far, although I'd had very good contact with Jayne, we'd come up with frustratingly little in the way of tangible clues, but if we continued to work on it I felt we'd stumble across something useful.

I couldn't stay in Leeds, of course. I had the flat to look after and a stack of washing and ironing to do but I went home fully intending to carry on with the case from London.

Then one morning shortly after our return, John brought the papers in as usual. I'd finished the hoovering and washed up the breakfast things so I treated myself to a cup of coffee, a cigarette and a five minute read. I sat there with my feet up slowly turning the pages and shaking my head over the more horrifying stories. Then I turned a page and a large black headline leapt out at me: *Doris Stokes Victim*. I almost dropped the paper. Shocked, my hands shaking I read it again. *Doris Stokes Victim*. There was no mistake or coincidence. They were talking about me.

Carefully spreading the page on my knee so I wouldn't drop it, I read the story. Apparently my comments on the so called Yorkshire Ripper tape had been followed up and a man with the name Ronnie or Johnnie who lived in Berwick Street, Sunderland, and whose Sunderland accent matched the voice on the tape had been found. From time to time he even visited the places where the bodies had been found but he insisted he was innocent and the police believed him. However, he'd suffered a great deal of anxiety and suspicion because of me. So much so the paper had dubbed him my 'victim'.

I was absolutely aghast. All I'd tried to do was please the television people and help the police when I'd worked with that tape. I hadn't promised anything. I hadn't said that the Ronnie or Johnnie whose impression came from the voice was the Yorkshire Ripper, and I'd never suggested that this Sunderland man, a complete stranger to me, was the man I was referring to in connection with the tape. Yet, nevertheless, this man was suffering because of me.

I was terribly upset. All day guilt and regret nagged at me. I couldn't settle to anything. No matter what I started to do I somehow found myself back in front of the paper, staring at the photograph of that indignant man and his wife beneath the devastating headline. The words hurt afresh every time I read them. *Doris Stokes Victim*. I hadn't been given my gift for this. My job was to ease suffering not to cause it. With the best intentions in the world I'd failed Ramanov and misused my powers.

I remained in depression for hours and nothing John or

Terry could say would console me. Then during the evening I heard Ramanov's voice gently reproving me for forgetting one of his earlier teachings. 'There is no point in brooding on past mistakes. What's past is past and cannot be changed. It is human to make errors. So learn from them, profit by them and go forward.'

Right, I thought. I will learn from it. From now on, no more Yorkshire Ripper work. I'll leave that case strictly to the police.

It wasn't long, however, before I came up against the double edged power of publicity once more.

Before I left for New York, Mike my American friend had telephoned and asked if I could possibly do anything by phone for a distraught lady who was right there with him in his office.

'Well I don't know, Mike,' I said. 'I'll try. You never can tell with phone contacts, sometimes they work, sometimes they don't.'

'She'd be very grateful if you could just try,' he assured me. There were some muffled clunks as he passed the receiver to someone else and the next minute a young woman's voice said, 'Hello, Doris. I'm Julie Patz.'

'Hello, Julie,' I replied and even as I spoke a strong impression of a child seemed to come to me across the three thousand miles of Atlantic that separated us. 'Julie,' I went on, 'I have a feeling this is about a child. A child who's gone missing.'

'Yes, that's right,' she gasped, her voice breaking. Then in the background I heard a man who spoke with a heavy European accent. 'I'm Hymie. Stanley's grandfather,' he said.

Julie explained that her husband's name was Stanley and his grandfather was known as Hymie. Hymie explained that the child, a little boy of six, had disappeared on his way to the school bus. He never did reach the bus. Tearfully Julie agreed that this was true.

'And I've got an unusual name here,' I went on, 'Aiden or Eiten or something like that.'

'Etan,' Julie corrected me. 'That's him. That's my son.'

Then the voice faded away and in my mind's eye I was

walking up a street. Tall buildings towered on either side of me and I saw a shop with the words 'Mary's Candy Store' painted on the glass. Three doors along there was a laundrette filled with stacks of dirty washing and apartments over the top. Then the picture dissolved and as it faded out I heard someone say 'Ritchie'.

Then I was back in our hall again. Quickly I described the scene to Julie.

'Oh, I know that street,' she said. 'We often took Etan to Mary's to buy candy.'

'That's where he disappeared from,' I explained to her. 'He went from that street.'

The picture appeared to signal the end of the communication. Hymie had gone and nothing else came.

'Never mind, Julie,' I said, 'John and I are coming to New York soon. Perhaps Mike can bring us to see you and we'll try again.'

Naturally I didn't forget the case of little Etan Patz. Julie wrote to thank me for my work over the phone and in her letter she enclosed a picture of her missing son. He was such a beautiful child, I could have wept for his parents. With his big blue eyes, silky blond hair and friendly, wide-awake expression he looked like a child model. I put his picture on my shelf with all the other photographs of spirit children that parents had given me to look after. Not that anyone had told me Etan was on the other side, and I wouldn't have dreamed of saying so to Julie, but privately I thought the Patzes were unlikely to find their son alive.

As I looked at my little gallery of fresh young faces, I couldn't help thinking that it always seemed to be the brightest and most beautiful who pass over young. Why that should be I don't know. It doesn't seem fair – not to the people who love them, at any rate. Or perhaps they are specially privileged to care for such lovely little ones for the short time they have to complete on earth.

I often think that about the parents of handicapped children. It's frequently the case that the parents of such children are the nicest, kindest, most loving of people and one finds oneself feeling especially sad that they are the ones whose children are handicapped. Yet now I wonder whether that is the very reason they have been chosen to undertake the difficult task – because they are special people. Anyone less special wouldn't be able to cope.

So when we arrived in New York the Patzes were among the first we contacted. Julie invited us to visit them in Greenwich village. They had a vast, airy studio flat, open-plan style with the sitting-room created in a wall-less space by the clever arrangements of sofas, chairs and little tables.

Julie had made a pot of delicious, American coffee – a welcome change from the instant stuff John and I drink at home. We chatted while we drank and then I started to work. Hymie came back to talk to me again and told me about the fateful morning Etan went missing.

'He tells me you had another child in the house that morning,' I said.

'Yes,' said Julie. 'I've got two other children.'

'No, not one of yours. Another child.'

Julie looked blank.

'She doesn't know what you're talking about, Hymie,' I told him. 'Can you give us more information?' Back came the reply: Elizabeth.

'Who's Elizabeth?' I asked.

'Oh god, of course,' said Julie. 'I was looking after Elizabeth's baby, that's why I didn't take Etan to the bus like I usually do.'

Hymie mentioned more family details and then I heard a different, young voice. He didn't give me his name and the communication was faint and difficult. It might have been Etan but I couldn't be certain since he didn't tell me his name and so could have been another child connected with the family. Of course I didn't want to upset the Patzes unnecessarily if there was still a slim chance that Etan was alive. The boy, whoever he was, kept talking about a special cap and he went on and on about it as if it was important.

'I know what he means,' said Julie. 'Etan was crazy about baseball and we bought him a cap in a sale which used to belong to a real baseball player. Etan thought the world of that cap. He wore it all the time, even to school.'

The boy went on to tell me many names of people Etan used to go and see. The list made me uneasy: they were all names of men and the child was only six years old.

By the end of the sitting Julie had collected a mass of family information and several bits and pieces about the day Etan disappeared, but of Etan's present whereabouts, there was not a clue. Unless we'd been given a hint but had failed to recognize the information for what it was. I've often found in the past that it's only when a case has been solved and the whole story is revealed that one realizes that a solid clue had been staring one in the face all along.

Julie was pleased with what we'd got so far but naturally disappointed that we hadn't managed to locate Etan. There was still still a lot of work to do on the case. I had a feeling it was going to be a complicated story and I promised Julie I'd work with Etan's photograph whenever I had time.

Over the next few days John and I were rushed hither and thither to be interviewed by this person, to do a sitting for that person, a phone-in for someone else until we hardly knew what day of the week it was. At one point, someone who had heard about my sitting with Julie Patz and the reference to Mary's Candy Store asked if I would agree to be filmed outside the shop to see if I could get any more information from being on the spot. It's sometimes very successful to go to the scene, so I asked, 'Does Julie know about this?'

'Oh yes,' I was assured. 'She thinks it's a great idea.' So I agreed.

A car was sent to fetch us and we drove through a maze of anonymous streets from our hotel until suddenly we turned a corner and I had a strange feeling of *déjà vu*. This was the street Hymie had shown me. I knew it without recognizing anything. The next second Mary's Candy Store came into view. It was like watching a dream turn into reality. The car pulled up outside and I could see the film unit arriving but there was no sign of Julie.

'I wonder where she's got to?' I said to John.

'She'll probably be here in a minute,' John replied. 'It looks as if we're early. They're not ready for us yet.'

We wanted to take some tonic water back to the hotel with us so while we waited we popped into Mary's Candy Store. There was a woman and a little boy behind the counter and as she served me the woman was peering hard at my face.

'Haven't I seen you somewhere before?' she asked.

'I don't think so,' I said, 'unless you've seen me on television.'

She looked quizzical, so I explained I was a medium and that I was visiting the area to see if I could help in the Etan Patz case.

'Oh yes, isn't it a shame about that little boy?' she agreed. She wrapped the tonic water and as she put it into my hand, something made me say, on impulse, 'Do you know someone called Ritchie who lives in the apartments above the laundry?'

'Yes,' she said. 'I know two Richies up there. Which one did you mean?'

Staggered, I could only say, 'Oh, I don't know.'

She looked at me curiously, then she bent and whispered something to the little boy who turned and ran off. We talked for a little longer and then as we left the shop we were surprised to see quite a number of Italians coming out of the apartment building. As they moved up the street everyone scattered and for a few moments, apart from the television crew, the place looked deserted.

'Well, that's odd!' I said to John. 'I wonder what that was all about.'

But there wasn't time to speculate. A reporter came over and started to interview me. I had to explain all over again how I'd become involved in the Etan Patz case and what information I'd come up with so far. The cameras had been rolling for several minutes when out of the corner of my eye I noticed a commotion going on. Turning my head slightly I could see that Julie had arrived and she was having a furious row with someone.

Uncomfortably aware there was something wrong, I lost track of what I was saying and my voice trailed away. Seeing that my attention had gone the reporter brought the interview to a premature close and I was able to hurry over to Julie.

'Oh, Doris, I know it's not your fault!' she cried.

'What isn't?' I asked bewildered. 'What's the matter?'

'All this!' she said angrily, waving her arm at the cameras and the newspapermen. 'Look at them! They didn't tell me you were doing this.'

'But they said you knew! They said you thought it was a good idea. I expected you to be here.'

'They didn't tell me a thing,' said Julie. 'I only found out by accident. I think it's dreadful. My son's missing and they're turning it into a circus!'

I was mortified. I put my arms around her. 'Oh, Julie, I'm so sorry. I had no idea you felt like that. I only did it because I thought you'd agreed.'

'Well, I didn't. I think it's disgusting.' And she began to sob, half in sorrow, half in anger. I felt like doing the same myself. The television crew melted tactfully, or possibly fearfully, away and we were left to comfort Julie as best we could. It was no use. Julie was sickened by the whole thing and wanted no more to do with mediums. For me the Etan Patz case was closed. I was very, very sad about it. Once more, publicity had turned my work sour.

Yet what was I to do? Through the press I was able to reach thousands and thousands of people with the truth that there is no death, and for every painful disappointment like the Patzes and the Yorkshire Ripper case there were a hundred wonderful successes. I knew that, whatever the cost, I would have to go on, but that in future I would have to be far more cautious and far less trusting.

The only good thing I can say about the whole bitter lesson is that throughout it all I remained friends with Irene MacDonald. Poor Wilf never did get over Jayne's murder. His health declined steadily and he died suddenly. This time Irene knew just where to turn. She contacted me and I was able to do a sitting for her. Wilf came through very easily and among the things he mentioned was the fact that Irene had had a fire in her kitchen recently and he was very concerned.

'Tell her to be more careful in future,' he said. 'It was only sheer luck it wasn't a disaster.'

Irene was amazed. 'That's right,' she said. 'I'd left a large cardboard box on the sink next to the stove and it caught fire. By the time I got there it was flaming, but I just managed to get hold of it and throw it out of the door.'

I was a little puzzled because Wilf also kept referring to a pullover. 'Will you take this pullover off?' he kept repeating. When I mentioned it to Irene she was thrilled. 'Those were his last words!' she explained. Apparently she had bought him a pullover in a jumble sale and he hadn't liked it. Just before he collapsed he had decided he couldn't tolerate it any longer and had insisted Irene took it off him.

Wilf also told me joyfully that he'd met Jayne again and they were very happy. But they were worried about Irene. 'She takes too much valium,' said Wilf.

Irene promised to try to cut down as much as possible. 'I'm getting back to normal gradually,' she said bravely.

Looking back over the two cases I have mixed feelings. As far as I know, I've failed to help the police find the Ripper or Etan Patz. On the other hand, I've given the MacDonalds and the Paztes a lot of information, food for thought and, in the case of Irene at least, comfort. In the end that's what my job is all about. I've never claimed to be a psychic detective. My gift was not given to me for that purpose. As Ramanov has often told me, we are here on earth to learn and we must solve our own problems. If the spirit world solved them for us we would learn nothing. But just occasionally, the victim of a murder is so angry about the crime that he is determined to come back and help bring his killer to justice. Sometimes, too, the murderer is known personally to the victim and there are often successful results, but of course, although the police can be told the identity of the killer, there is still no guarantee that the criminal will be caught. If there is no material evidence the police can do nothing.

So, frustrating though it is at times, I have to accept that if I can give comfort to the victim's family, I've done my job and anything more is an unexpected bonus.

I'll let Irene MacDonald have the last word on the subject:

'The last time I saw Jayne she was getting ready to go to her

Saturday job. I know I'm her mother, but honestly she was such a pretty girl and so nice. She was always cheerful and smiling. Anyway, she said goodbye and she skipped off down the road, her whole life in front of her – and I never saw her again. The next thing I knew, she was dead.

'*It's one of those things you always think happens to other people. You can't believe it can happen to you, and then it does. You can't absorb it somehow. I still find it hard to sleep and I'm on valium; Wilf couldn't take it at all.*

'*Everyone was shocked when they heard. I mean everyone loved Jayne. She was very fond of children and one little girl of twelve not far from us came home from school and fainted. They couldn't think what was wrong with her but it turned out she'd just heard about Jayne.*

'*It was awful the way up till then the others that were murdered were prostitutes. People who didn't know Jayne might have thought she was like that too, but she wasn't. She was still a virgin. We were a close family and we talked about it. Jayne used to say "No mum, I'll wait till I'm about nineteen and I've found the man I want to marry," and she meant it.*

'*Wilf and I both lost our religious faith and we were sceptical about Doris at first. We thought she'd be one of these posh television people but she wasn't like that at all.*

'*It was marvellous the things she told us. Little things she couldn't possibly have known, like the bit about our dog. She said she could hear a dog barking and Jayne told her she'd found our dog, whose name was Sam or Sammy. Well, he got called both those names. She even knew how the dog died, he was knocked down and the worst injuries were on his back legs. Jayne said she'd found the dog and his back legs were all right now.*

'*There's no explanation for things like that and it had a big effect on Wilf and I. Wilf used to say he'd got his faith back and he was a changed man, much more cheerful.*

'*The family's still not right, of course. If an ambulance goes down the road they look all round and then say, "Well, we're all here, it's not one of us," and when they walk in the door they see if everything's all right before they relax. My son Ian who's sixteen doesn't like to leave me, even to go to school. "What do you do when I've gone?" he keeps asking and when we go out together he stays by my side.*

'Most of all we miss Wilf but thanks to Doris we know we shall see him again one day. I'm very glad we saw her when we did because as Wilf told one reporter shortly afterwards, "I'm not afraid to die any more because of Jayne — because I know she's there." '

Chapter 7

Looking back over the last few chapters it must sound as if my work is all misery and suffering, an endless procession of murders, tragic deaths and grieving families. Of course, those sort of cases do form the bulk of my work, but there are also light-hearted moments and we mediums enjoy a bit of fun as much as everyone else. Sometimes the spirit messages themselves are funny, sometimes it's the colourful characters of the church officials and sometimes I get myself into hilarious scrapes.

I'll never forget one meeting I did at a church where the president's wife, Vera, was also the secretary, treasurer and harmonium player. Vera was a short, plump little person and like me, very broad in the beam. She was also very fond of her little dog which she took everywhere with her, including the platform during meetings.

I was a little apprehensive about this as I thought the animal might get restless and unhappy, but in the event he behaved beautifully. Throughout the service he curled up on a chair and went to sleep. Then when Vera got up to play the last hymn the dog suddenly woke up, jumped off his seat and sprang onto the long organ stool beside her. Vera, who was already crashing out the opening bars, didn't appear to notice. She bashed away happily, lost in the music, swaying her plump body to the rhythm.

From round the hall under cover of the singing I heard a few titters. What was going on? I looked round and saw nothing unusual on the floor but as the hymn went on the laughter increased.

Puzzled, I stared at the strange little couple on the organ stool, side by side, Vera swaying, the dog wagging its tail, and then I noticed it. Every time Vera swayed to the left, the dog's tail wagged to the right and slapped her ample bottom. And so it went on, sway, slap, sway, slap, until I thought I'd have to stuff a handkerchief into my mouth to stop myself from laughing!

There was another lady, president of a church, who did a lot of good works. She had a ginger cat which used to sleep to top of the fridge in her kitchen, presumably because it was the warmest spot. This lady only had to start singing her favourite hymn, *I need thee, every hour I need thee*, in her not over-tuneful voice and the cat would leap off the fridge onto her lap and start licking her frantically all over the face. We never could work out whether he liked her singing or whether he was trying to get her to stop!

There are quite a few people who put on a 'platform' voice whenever they have to speak in public. It's probably nerves that causes it, but put them in front of more than six people and their normal speaking voice drops away and from nowhere comes a posh, slightly pompous tone, grappling with longer words than they would normally use.

Now this particular lady, who wasn't a bit pretentious or pompous, unfortunately fell into the 'platform' voice habit. Every time I listened to her on a stage, I marvelled at how much her voice could change and how she seemed totally unaware of the fact.

One evening we were doing a service together and the people who looked after the hall had decked the place with flowers and in front of the platform was the most beautiful arrangements of freesias, one of my favourite blooms. Throughout the service the wonderful perfume wafted up to us until we were drenched in it. My friend Rosemary was in the audience and every now and then I looked at her and smiled. Then at the end of the service the president stepped forward to thank everyone for a splendid effort.

I'd only been talking to her half an hour before and she'd sounded quite normal, but now out came this extraordinary voice. In plummy, but mangled tones she congratulated the women who'd made the hall look so nice. In front of me Rosemary's eyebrows rose quarter of an inch. I smiled and looked down.

'... And these *love-ly* flowers,' the president was trilling, 'all these fresians marching across the rostrum ...'

Instantly, a picture of black and white cows trotting over the stage flashed before my eyes and I had to bite my lip very hard. I stole a glance at Rosemary. She was crimson in the face, her shoulders were shaking silently and she caught my eye. That did it. I just exploded and had to press a handkerchief over my mouth to change the giggles into a fit of coughing.

I did manage to do a bit of serious work though. A young girl who used to live in a high rise block of flats came through. She had fallen over a balcony and been killed and everyone had thought it was suicide. It was true she had been depressed, but she came back to tell them that her death was an accident.

'I was in a temper, I stormed out onto the balcony and the sheer force took me straight over the top,' she said. 'It happened so fast I hardly knew what was happening. One minute I was flouncing out of the french doors, the next I was in mid-air.' She mentioned a few more family details to her sister who was in the audience, and then she said cheekily, 'I see my new handbag matches your coat!'

The sister started to laugh with tears running down her face. 'Yes it does,' she said. 'As a matter of fact, I bought the coat to match the bag, because the bag was my sister's.'

The messages often make the sitter laugh. One of the strangest I ever received was for a woman who was introduced to me as 'Bubbles'. She was a widow and her husband came through and explained that her real name ·was Kathleen, but she was nicknamed Bubbles. As he talked, I could hear a strange screeching, squawking noise going on in the background and as soon as I got the chance I had to interrupt to ask what it was.

'Oh that. That's the parrot,' he said. 'Tell Kathleen I've got the parrot with me.'

I'd come across dogs and cats in the spirit world but never parrots. Anyway, I mentioned it to Bubbles.

'Oh yes,' she said, 'it used to belong to my mother and

when she passed over we took it in.'

Her husband was quiet for a few moments and in the silence I distinctly heard the parrot cackle, 'Old Treaclebelly! Squawk, squawk. Old Treaclebelly!' I could hardly believe my ears, but there it was again, 'Old Treaclebelly!' I couldn't help laughing.

'What's the matter?' asked Bubbles.

'Well, quite honestly,' I said, 'I don't know whether you'll be annoyed or upset about this, but I'm certain I can hear the parrot saying Old Treaclebelly.'

And she burst out laughing. 'You couldn't have given me better proof, Doris,' she cried. 'When I was pregnant I had a thing about golden syrup. I ate golden syrup with everything. I was always eating it and my husband taught the parrot to say Old Treaclebelly!'

On another occasion I was speaking at a public meeting in Grantham when the president's husband came through. He described his wife's sitting room and the big stone fireplace which was the centre piece. As he spoke, a picture of the room came into my mind and at the end of the mantelpiece I could see a pair of false teeth, just sitting there all alone, grinning blankly into the room.

Of course, without thinking, I repeated aloud what I could see and the audience roared with laughter. Fortunately the president wasn't embarrassed.

'Yes, I used to get so annoyed with him,' she said. 'After he'd had a meal he'd sit down in the armchair, take out his false teeth and put them on the mantelpiece instead of taking them to the bathroom. But I couldn't change him. He always did it.'

Strangely enough you often come across mention of teeth in spirit messages. I remember being in contact with an old lady who'd passed with a cerebral haemorrhage. She chatted away eagerly but her speech was a little blurred and indistinct. Once or twice I had to ask her to repeat a sentence and in the end she said, 'Can't you understand what I say, dear? You see they sent me over without my teeth.' Apparently, after she'd had the stroke they had removed her false teeth to avoid injury and hadn't put them back again. Her guide must have forgotten to explain how to get them back.

'Just think your own natural teeth back and they'll come,' I advised her.

'Are you sure, dear?' she said.

'Well, that's what I've been told,' I said.

There was a silence filled with deep concentration and then suddenly she was back, clear and precise with no slurring, 'You're right!' she said. 'They've all come back. The full set.'

She was thrilled and thought I was immensely clever but of course it was nothing like that: I was only repeating what Ramanov had told me. I have no idea how it works.

Generally it seems that when a person passes, his appearance returns to that which he had when he was last healthy and strong. If he lost his hair or teeth prematurely he can restore them if he wishes simply by 'thinking' them back. Disabilities and handicaps seem to be corrected automatically. A thalidomide child, for instance, would immediately become whole and perfect, the way he should have been born had nothing gone wrong.

This was proved to me during a sitting in Liverpool. A little boy, no more than 5 years old, came back to talk to his grandma. He spoke perfectly and answered a lot of questions without hesitation but when I asked him his name, he began to stutter.

'Mar, mar, mar, mar …' he kept repeating as if he was trying to say Mark. I couldn't understand this because every other word had been pronounced properly. Surely his name would be easiest of all? Remembering Ramanov's rule, however, I said aloud exactly what I was hearing and the grandmother gasped.

'That's it,' she cried. 'That's exactly the way he used to say it. He was mentally handicapped you see and couldn't speak properly.'

Little Mark was no longer mentally handicapped and he could now speak as well as anyone, but he'd used his old pronunciation of his name to prove to his grandmother it was really him.

Sometimes incidents are only funny in retrospect and these little adventures tend to happen when I'm dashing about from place to place trying to fit far too much into too short a time.

Once I was asked to conduct a service at St Anne's church near Blackpool. The people who ran the church were old friends and I didn't want to disappoint them, but unfortunately I had another engagement the day before and I didn't see how I could reach St Anne's on time. Then Terry came to the rescue.

'Why don't you fly?' he suggested. Terry had always been interested in machines of all kinds. He learned to drive a car as soon as he was legally allowed and now he belonged to a flying club. His greatest dream was to get his pilot's licence.

'But you haven't got your licence yet,' I reminded him.

'I doesn't matter,' he said confidently. 'One of the lads will run you up in no time.'

Though John and I weren't very keen on flying, we did want to get to St Anne's, so we agreed and set off on the appropriate day with Judy, an old friend, for Biggin Hill aerodrome.

'Have you ever flown before?' asked one of the ground crew as we hurried through the gate.

'Oh, yes,' I said more confidently than I felt. 'We've been to the Isle of Man.'

He led us across the tarmac, threading our way between all kinds of impressive machines in an astonishing assortment of shapes and colours, and then unexpectedly the man stopped.

'There you are. That's yours,' he said, pointing at one of the tiniest planes I'd ever seen. It looked as fragile as a dragon-fly. I was just about to protest that there must be some mistake, we couldn't possibly be flying all the way to Blackpool in that, when I noticed Terry and another young man checking the instruments.

Oh, my God, I thought.

'Come on then!' shouted Terry, sticking his head out of the miniature door. 'What are you waiting for? I thought you were in a hurry?'

'It's a bit small, isn't it?' I muttered nervously.

'Nonsense,' said Terry. 'You don't need a jumbo jet for five of us.'

So we gingerly climbed aboard – at least the others did; they had to haul me up since I'm not built for climbing – and we squeezed into the doll size passenger compartment.

'Don't be alarmed if we hit a few bumps,' the pilot told us cheerfully when we were strapped into our seats. 'I haven't flown one of these before.'

.I should have got out then, I suppose, but Terry slammed the door, the engines roared, we lurched off down the runway and lunged clumsily into the sky.

I need hardly add that it was a terrible flight. The little plane hit every air pocket it could find as if bent on suicide. We bounced and rocked all over the sky, dipping and soaring with vibrations fit to tear the cabin apart. The clouds went up and down outside the portholes like waves around a ship and even Judy, a New Zealand girl and a hardened traveller, went green in the face.

The noise was deafening but over the top we could hear the pilot cursing at Terry who was navigating. Towards the end of the flight he was yelling at the top of his voice.

'Well, I'm sorry,' Terry yelled back over the screaming engines 'but I'm navigating properly.'

And then the pilot suddenly clapped one hand to his forehead. 'Oh my god, Terry. I've been reading the wrong instruments!'

If John, Judy and I had had parachutes I think we would have bailed out then. As it was, we shut our eyes and prayed. Fortunately God was looking after us and by some miracle we landed at Squires Gate airstrip in one piece.

I was feeling dreadful. My head was swimming, my ears roaring and the floor was still going up and down under my feet. Dimly I was aware that John and Judy had scrambled out and Terry was squeezing back to give me a hand. He led me to the doorway and pointed out a tiny little steel foot-rest just below the lip of the opening.

'Put your foot on that and jump,' he shouted in my ear.

I looked at the tarmac a long way down and, as I watched it, it rushed up to meet me and then fell dizzily away again.

'There's no way I can jump,' I shouted back and then I

noticed that just beside the door was the base of the wing which sloped gently down almost to the ground. 'I'll get down my way,' I said and before he had time to stop me, I clambered out, perched myself on the wing and slid down. As I whistled toward the ground, my skirt up, my stockings ripping and tearing. I saw the reception committee lined up on the tarmac to meet me and in the front row where the photographers, cameras clicking, recording every second for posterity!

The meeting was worth all the trouble, however. People from miles around packed into the hall and the messages came through with unusual vigour as if my hair-raising journey had somehow strengthened the contact. Perhaps I'd been closer to the spirit world than I'd realized!

One man boldly said he wanted to speak to Nancy from Lytham. He was her husband, he explained, and he'd cut his throat. How can I say that in public, I thought, but the man insisted he wanted to say hello to his wife and the light remained firmly over a pale woman in the middle of the hall.

'Are you Nancy?' I asked looking directly at her.

'Oh. Yes,' she gasped.

'I've got your husband here,' I said. 'He went over very quickly. *Very quickly indeed*,' I stressed.

The woman nodded. 'Yes. That's right.'

'You can tell them I cut my throat,' the man interrupted. 'And my poor wife found me.'

'I can't say that out loud,' I protested.

'Yes you can,' he said and the impression was so vivid I found myself looking at a big double bed, the white sheets all red with blood.

Helplessly, I drew my hand across my own throat. I didn't say anything, I just looked at the woman. She knew what I meant.

'Yes, that's right,' she whispered.

Her husband went on to say that she had moved and was living at a new address and that she had just come back from America. Both facts were correct.

The meeting went on quite successfully for some time and then a lady in the front row stood up. I didn't have any message for her but she said, 'I would like to say something, if I might.'

'Yes, dear, that's all right with me,' I said tolerantly but my heart began to race fearing she was going to complain about something or try to pick a quarrel.

'I'd just like to make this declaration,' she said and then I noticed she was looking past me and in her hand was a white stick. Bless her heart, she's blind, I thought, ashamed.

'Two years ago I went to Lancaster to see Doris Stokes for a sitting,' the woman continued, oblivious of my turmoil. 'She told me I would marry and that my name would be Armstrong. I went away quite convinced she was a fake because I couldn't imagine how on earth I was going to meet a man who would be willing to marry me with my disability. But ladies and gentlemen, I would now like to introduce you to my husband whose name is Mr Armstrong!' The tall pleasant looking man beside her stood up and bowed awkwardly to the audience and the whole place exploded with cheers and clapping. It was a marvellous way to end a marvellous meeting.

We stayed three days with our friends in the North. I told Terry I'd go back by train, but he insisted our problems were due entirely to the size of the plane and promised to return with a larger model. Somehow I let myself be talked into flying again, but Terry was as good as his word. He returned with a chunky, solid-looking machine and the flight was smooth and without incident. Only one person was alarmed. A reporter from the *Psychic News* flew with us to interview me about the meeting at St Anne's. Checking through his notebook he said idly, 'I wonder where we are now.'

'Half a minute, I'll ask Head Office,' I joked but I enquired anyway, and back came a voice saying Birmingham. 'We're at Birmingham,' I told him.

'Oh,' he said indulgently, continuing with his notes, and then suddenly over the intercom came the pilot's voice:

'We are now passing over Birmingham.'

The reporter dropped his notebook like a hot coal and shifted back in his seat to increase the distance between us.

For the rest of the flight he regarded me warily and I think he would have been much happier continuing his journey by train!

I do sometimes forget that some people are easily alarmed and I tend to speak without thinking. I remember when I was packing to leave for Australia last time, Matey was driving me mad. He was circling the flat making a dreadful row and nothing I could do would stop him. I gave him food, milk, water and a cuddle but still he cried and howled. My nerves were on edge in any case about the coming trip and the long flight and I thought if he carried on much longer I would scream.

'What's the matter with the cat?' I asked the spirit world in desperation.

Back came the answer, 'He's got toothache.'

Relieved, I phoned the vet and explained to the helpful receptionist what was wrong.

'That's all right, Mrs Stokes, the vet will be round soon,' she said. 'But how do you know your cat's got toothache?'

'The spirit people told me,' I said thoughtlessly.

There was a pause. 'I beg your pardon?' she said.

Oh, well, I've done it now, I thought. 'The spirit people,' I repeated boldly.

There was a long silence. 'Are you still there?' I asked.

'Eh, yes, yes, Mrs Stokes,' the girl said faintly. 'The vet will be right round,' and she put the phone down.

The vet, however, was made of sterner stuff.

'So you're the lady who talks to spirits,' he said cheerfully as he came into the flat.

'Yes, that's right,' I told him. 'And they've just told me your name is Peter.'

He almost dropped his bag. 'Why, yes, it is. How did you know?' He saw my smile. 'Oh yes, sorry. The spirit people!'

And when he examined Matey he discovered the spirit people had been right about that, too. Matey was indeed suffering from toothache.

Chapter 8

'Now then, Doris, just look into my eyes ... I want you to listen to my voice ... you are getting heavier and heavier. Every muscle in your body is loose and heavy ... you are sinking ... sinking ...'

An overpowering drowsiness was stealing over me: my arms and legs felt so heavy that they would melt through the couch; my head sank on my chest; my eyelids began to droop and a long way off, someone was saying, 'Listen to my voice ...'

Some strange things have happened to me in the past but one of the strangest was certainly my hypnotic regression. While I was still in New York, Dick Sommers who had invited me onto his radio show, asked if I would like to undergo hypnotic regression.

Dick, a very suave young man with piercing dark eyes, was interested in all types of psychic phenomena and he was also an accomplished hypnotist. He explained that under hypnotic trance some people seem able to recall 'past lives' in astonishing detail. Whether this was evidence of reincarnation or simply the brain's ability to store apparently forgotten facts picked up over the years and present them in story form almost like dreams, no one knows but according to Dick quite uneducated people appear to have greater knowledge of life hundreds of years ago than historians who have spent decades studying the subject.

I don't have any firm views on reincarnation myself. I know that occasionally people seem to 'disappear' from the spirit world. You might be in regular contact with them over the years and then suddenly, for no apparent reason, they don't come back any more. Whether they have progressed to a higher plane or whether they have come back to earth in another body, I couldn't say, although Ramanov did mention once that if we didn't learn the lesson we were sent here to learn the first time, we'd only have to come back and do it again, which does seem to indicate some form of reincarnation.

Anyway, I explained to Dick that I found the whole subject confusing but I was quite willing to try the experiment if he was.

So on a crisp morning in spring, John and I presented ourselves at Dick's plush office high up in a skyscraper next to the UN Building. Looking out of the picture windows made me feel dizzy but apart from that the office was extremely comfortable. There were big, green, jungly plants everywhere and soft brown furnishings. John sat down on the sofa, but Dick put me in a big leather armchair, pressed a button and it went back just like a dentist's chair.

'Now there is nothing to worry about, Doris,' he said. 'You just relax, listen to my voice and you'll feel as if you're asleep.'

All the same I found it difficult to relax completely. Although I'd agreed to the experiment, I wasn't completely happy about it. I knew that under hypnosis I wouldn't be in control of myself and that was an uncomfortable feeling ... but Dick was telling me to look into his eyes and as I stared into bottomless brown, and listened to his velvet voice, my mind drifted away and I fell asleep.

I have no recollection of what happened next. Dimly I was aware of someone saying, 'listen to my voice ...' from time to time and once or twice something brushed my face, but apart from that it was as if I was in a deep, dreamless sleep. Dick recorded the session, however, and this is a transcript of what I said:

DICK: *You're going back, back, back ... Now, where are you, Doris?*

DORIS (distressed): *We have to fight ... we have to fight. Please don't let them catch us ... Where are the voices? Why have you deserted? Where are my voices? You held the cross for me through the smoke. I did not betray my voices ... St Catherine give me strength, I will not betray my voices ...*

DICK: *Where are you, Doris? What year is it?*

DORIS: *I am in Paris. It's seventeen-sixty-something. My name is Joan. I'm just a farmer's daughter ... The farm is in the country but I had to go to Paris because my ... France ... Charles has been ravaged ... I know that my voices are truthful. My voices have deserted me, maybe they are right, maybe I'm mad. I know God is on my side. God will look after me. We must fight. We must save France. Are you Pierre?*

DICK: *Who's Pierre?*

DORIS: *He was the man I was going to marry. I had to leave him because the voice told me to. It said I must go and offer myself for service.*

DICK: *What voice, Doris?*

DORIS: *It was St Catherine, she told me. It was St Catharine, she told me in my ear when I was doing the cattle. She said I must go and fight. They laughed at me, a peasant girl, going to court but I did and we fought and we won and when they saw that good was triumphing over evil they took me away ... God, I can see him. He said it was in the name of God ... always blood-red he wore, the colour of blood. I was very lonely, they wouldn't let me talk or see anyone ... All he said was repent, repent ... all the blood he shed. He was a cardinal; I wish I could remember his name.*

It's 1763 ... so cold ... I'm in a cart, wooden wheels and cobbled streets, it throws me from side to side but I have not gone back on my voices ... whatever is to come I will stand firm. Why are the people jeering at me? (voice breaking in distress) *Do you not know it was for you? Why do you have to rope me like an animal? Oh, the voices, do not desert me now! Dear God, do not desert me now! I know what is ahead of me now. Let it be quick.*

DICK(trying to calm things): *Now we are going back to when you were a little girl. Tell me what you can see.*

DORIS: *Mmmmmmum makes the butter; sometimes I turn the handle. I'm so small it lifts me off my feet when I turn the churn with my mum. Grandmère also. We work. Grandmère is very good with needles; she makes not a lot of money. Always we had a little white cap and collar. I am at the farm. I am five; I have two brothers, they are older, François and André. They tease me. We gather apples. Martine is my cousin, she is coming for my birthday tomorrow ... Tomorrow I will be seven. Martine thinks she's very grand because she lives in the city but my hair is just as pretty. I have brown hair, lots of brown hair ... but they cut it all off ... when I was a soldier I could not go to war and fight so I cut it off, but they shaved me ... those men ... in the name of religion, they did it ... I am eighteen.*

DICK: *When did you hear the voices?*

DORIS: *When Martine came I first heard the voice. We'd been to pray, there was a shrine on the hill to our blessed Mary and we'd been to place flowers and I heard the voice that said she was St Catharine and Martine she laughed at me but I did not say. It was my secret. The voices I heard were my voices ... several voices but St Catharine was the only one I talked directly to ... we need more horses ... We have camped outside the city walls. The walls are high, we must scale the walls, Jan. Jan he has made me a sword. Some soldiers laugh at me, they say they will not follow a girl but I know my voices tell me, 'Lead them, Joan. Lead them.' And I did, not for glory, I didn't do it for that but because I loved France ...*

(sobbing) *Dear God make it quick ... The smoke! The smoke! I don't mind the pain, the smoke! I can't breathe! I can't breathe! Please God, make me unconscious. Reach my chest! Let me see the cross! Death is sweet ...*

(calm again) *I am home. Dear St Catherine, I did not fail you. I did not fail you. Forgive me for being weak for a while but I did not fail you. It is over. It is in God's hands now ... Our beloved country. He is just a painted doll and he has our country at his mercy ...*

DICK: *Tell me about heaven.*

DORIS: *Aaaahhhh such magnificence, such flowers, deep blue ... To see the lakes ... such beauty ... But I have been to earth again that is why I'm so confused ...*

(voice changes, becoming flirtatious. A French accent)

I am Odette. I have been to Rome, I have been to Paris, I have been to London I go everywhere ... I am, 'ow you say? – a singer-actress ... when I passed to the other world I was forty-five. I've been over – who knows – over here there is no time ... *I like to think of myself how I was but I came over ... Oh, dear God ...*

DICK: *Doris, now go back as far as you can go.*

DORIS(panic stricken): *Pierre, get the horses, get the horses. Come, come, I beg you. Go forward, go forward. Don't think, just go forward. The voices tell me go forward!*

(long pause – voice changes again, becoming deep and husky)

DORIS: *My name is Zombombie. I am Zombombie. I was born in Jamaica. In our village we were considered to be rich, we had two cows. My father, Buwala, was chief, the beginning of the eighteen dates they tell me to say ... Then one day I was taken away. Men with boats came, long boats not like our boats, big boats and they tied us and took us on big boats. I never saw my family, Buwala, my mother Minetwa, until I came to the spirit world and then I was reunited with my family ... I call my woman Kata. Good woman, we had four ... Don't cut me with the whip ... don't say anything ... I have to, Kata, I can't let them treat us this way ... They've sold my oldest son. Master, I've served you faithfully, do not sell my first-born. My master's name is Bwana Brownlow, sugar, sugar, sugar, is all he thinks about ... But one day our time will come. Our time will come ...*

DICK: *Do you hear voices now?*

DORIS: *Yes, I hear voices. My father say, don't worry, one day our time will come.*

DICK: *Can you go back now before France, before Joan, before Pierre?*

DORIS: *I am going home, I am going home. Up to the top of the mountain: it is Tibet ...*

(voice changes becoming slow, deep and cultured)

I am a lama. I am this child's guide. I am now going to take her to the place that I call home. It is the table of the world. She has often expressed the desire to see my homeland and while she is deep in this unconscious mind I am going to take her for one second so that she can see where I started my last existence.

(Doris' voice comes back)

I am coming Ramanov, I am coming ...

(Deep voice again)

Come, my child, come, feel the peace and the tranquillity, you see you do not need to have a lot. We have milk from goats, we

have grapes from the vines, we have everything, enough to exist
on. Come, come into the quietness, come into the spiritual love
that can surround you. This was my life and a little of this only
can I give you in your lifetime. Sit upon the mountain, let your
spirit soar high. Feel my sun light, open yourself, let your spirit
free, let that almighty power and force flow into you.
(Doris' voice again)
Oh Ramanov, dear Ramanov. I am so sorry I disappoint you so
often. I do try hard.
DICK: *Who is Ramanov?*
DORIS: *Ramanov is my guide and teacher but I have never seen*
him face to face till now. So beatiful, such love, such
compassion; oh, Ramanov, hold me! Let me shrug off all the
pressures of this world. Help me to keep my inner strength.
Help me to find that spiritual level you expect of me …
(Pause – then deep voice again)
And now I'm bringing her back, and to you my son, Shalom!

When I came round it was as if I'd just woken from a
long refreshing sleep. Yet I still felt vague and pleasantly
light-headed. Dick was smiling at me.

'How d'you feel, Doris?'

'Oh, I feel as if I've been asleep for a long time.'

'Can you remember anything about it?'

'No, I can't remember anything.' I stopped. At the edge
of my mind a memory flashed away, like a fragment of a
dream. I struggled to catch it. 'At least – oh, no – that can't
be right. I felt very sad.' And Ramanov, I thought.
Something to do with Ramanov … that he took me
somewhere … oh, it was incredible. It seemed as though it
was the top of the world. The world looked very small,
very insignificant. I think he was trying to tell me to put
things into their proper perspective. Do you think that's
possible?'

Dick thought it was. As he spoke, a sudden memory of
his hands on my face came back.

'Dick, were you touching my face?' I asked. 'What were
you doing?'

'I was wiping away the tears,' he said and showed me the
pile of damp tissues he'd amassed during the regression.

He played the tape of the session, with my permission, of course, over the air. It was disturbing to hear it. I sounded so distressed and panic stricken at times, as if I really was reliving those terrible incidents. The funny thing is my voice changed quite distinctly every time a different person spoke and both Dick and John said that my face changed, too.

I have to admit I don't know what to make of it. Was I dreaming out loud or was I really recalling past lives? I don't suppose I'll find out till I get to the other side myself!

Another strange thing happened when I was staying with my friend Eileen, a singer who lives in a beautiful country house in Stourbridge. I'd gone down to Stourbridge to talk to the local spiritualists but since I hadn't long recovered from my operation for breast cancer and I was still rather low, Eileen asked me to spend a few days resting with her in the clean country air.

I was glad of the excuse. It was always lovely to see Eileen and as she'd only lost her husband, John, eighteen months before I thought I might be able to cheer her up a little.

I had a marvellous time. Eileen spoiled me shamelessly. She put me in John's old bedroom overlooking a green paddock and swaying sycamore trees. It was a striking room with black and white geometric wallpaper, which John, who had been an architect, had chosen himself.

I was not quite as fit as I thought I was. The meeting the first night exhausted me and when I got back Eileen took one look at my tired face and sent me straight to bed.

'Go on, Doris, you get to bed and I'll bring up a pot of tea. We can chat in the bedroom.'

I was thankful to do as I was told and, as good as her word, Eileen came up about ten minutes later with the tea. I was already pretty drowsy and the way I recall it we chatted for a while and then I thought I fell asleep. At any rate I don't remember a thing until I 'came to' about twenty minutes later. I'll let Eileen explain what happened next:

EILEEN: *'It was the strangest thing I've ever experienced and I'm certainly not given to imagining things. Doris wasn't really very well and I was determined she would have a good rest while she stayed with me. I got her to bed early that first night and we were talking over our tea, when suddenly Doris went silent. I thought she must have fallen asleep because she was terribly tired but when I looked at her I saw that her face had changed. It was the most extraordinary thing I've ever seen. It was as if a film had come down over her face, completely hiding her features, and over the top a man's face appeared.*

'The skin was yellowish, the features sharp and clean cut and he was wearing a skull cap. I read a lot, particularly about foreign countries, and I'll swear I was looking at a Tibetan monk.

'I was amazed, absolutely fascinated. I really sat up in my chair wondering what would happen next. Then as I watched, the monk sort of dissolved, the features shifted and suddenly it was my late husband.

'Without a doubt it was John's face. He still looked drawn and ill, the way he did before he died and his hands were plucking at the bedclothes the way they used to. I just couldn't believe my eyes.

' "John, that's not you, is it?" I asked.

'He was in one of his old, slightly querulous moods and snapped, "Who d'you think it is" and before I knew it, we were scrapping again!

' "Don't be cross, John," I said. "I wasn't expecting this."

'We talked for a while about my son, David, and John remarked on the fact that though I'd otherwise kept the bedroom exactly as he'd left it, I'd changed a lamp fitting. I suppose we must have been talking for nearly twenty minutes and then he seemed to go all tired and it was Doris again. The funny thing was she opened her eyes, saw the tea and said "Hello, dear – oh, lovely, you've brought my morning tea." She thought she'd been asleep all night and it was the next morning.

'There's an odd sequel to the story, too. The next morning when I did take Doris' tea in to her, she told me that John had come back to talk to her during the night. John knew a lot about art, his hobby was painting and apparently he spent half the night lecturing Doris on the use of colour.

' "Then he took me to see the painting he's working on at the moment," Doris said. "There was a big painting on an easel and, well, I've never seen anything like it. Great swirling patterns of the most brilliant colours that seemed to pulsate and

absorb you right into the picture. I was drawn right in and out the other side. And when I went through the colours I felt much better."

'I thought it sounded like a marvellous dream, but later on I was talking to an old family friend whose name was also John and who happened to be staying in the room downstairs that night.

' "D'you know, I had a really vivid dream last night. I could have sworn I saw Doris walking through the room in the most beautiful dress of brilliant flowing colours.'

'I can't explain any of these things. I don't know why they happened, or how they happened but, as I said before, I'm not the sort of person to imagine things. It definitely happened and I've seen nothing like it before or since.'

As you can see, the most exciting things seem to happen to me when I'm unconscious and completely unaware of what's going on. It's most frustrating! The lesser incidents are almost as interesting, however.

On one occasion I was visiting a journalist friend, Kay Hunter, at her beautiful seventeenth-century cottage in Suffolk. It was a lovely place, deep in the country, with oak beams and inglenooks. During the visit I popped upstairs to the bathroom.

Like the rest of the house, it had a low ceiling and oak beams but the sink, bath and towels were completely modern. I stood there washing my hands and staring at my hair in the mirror. It was looking really haywire again – I must get to the hairdressers soon, I was thinking, when my eyes seemed to go peculiar and my reflection slid out of the glass.

Shaking my heard to clear it, I turned round in time to see the bathroom fade and another room take its place. I was standing in a bedroom. In front of me was a low truckle-bed covered with a patchwork quilt, and sitting on the bed was an old man.

'My name is George Baker,' he told me. 'You'll find that name in the deeds of the house.'

And then before my eyes, George and his bedroom turned paler and paler until they became transparent and I was back in the bathroom again.

My reaction was annoyance more than anything else.

'Honestly!' I said to my restored reflection in the mirror as I combed my hair, 'I can't even go to the bathroom without them bothering me!'

But all the same I mentioned it to Kay, who said she had long suspected that the bathroom had been converted from a former bedroom.

'It's far too big for a bathroom,' she said, and sure enough when she checked the deeds she found a George Baker.

Another time I was visiting Phil Edwards, our healer friend, who also lived in a beautiful old house. We were sitting in Phil's study, the bottom part of a split-level room, separated from the top by several steps.

Suddenly I looked up to see a baker coming down these steps. He had rosy cheeks as if he'd just come from his oven, there was flour on his face and he was dressed in white with a tall hat, not a small peaked hat like they wear nowadays.

Shall I say something or not? I wondered. I didn't want Phil to think I was one of those mediums who thinks she sees things wherever she goes but the baker just stood there on the steps, beaming round at all of us making it so obvious he wanted to be friends that I couldn't ignore him.

'Phil, you might think me a bit mad,' I ventured, 'but there's a baker standing on the steps.'

To my amazement Phil just laughed, moved back his armchair and said, 'I'm not at all surprised, Doris. You see this part of the house used to be the bakery,' and behind the armchair, he pointed out the original baker's oven which he'd kept in place.

Perhaps I've made it sound as if those sort of things only happen to me. Well of course they don't – I've also witnessed some odd things happening to other people.

Years ago, soon after we had lost our baby and before I realized I was a medium, John and I were investigating spiritualism, desperate to make contact with our son. Someone told us about a trumpet seance that was taking place not far from our home. John and I had no idea what a trumpet seance was but ever hopeful of some word about John Michael, we went along.

We were shown into a large room, bare but for a circle of

chairs arranged around a trumpet on the floor. It was quite an ordinary trumpet that had been painted with luminous paint so that it would show up in the dark. Mediums who did this sort of work needed darkness, we were told.

This sounded like an excuse for trickery to John and I so we inspected the trumpet very carefully but there was no sign of ropes or cords. Then the medium, an ordinary looking middle-aged man, came in and asked if two of the ladies present would volunteer to stitch his jacket. Stitch his jacket? I thought. What's wrong with it? It doesn't look torn to me. So I volunteered out of sheer curiosity.

I was given the strange task of sewing the sleeves of his jacket to the sleeves of his shirt, while the other lady who had stepped forward was asked to stitch his jacket together all down the front. I did my work most thoroughly and when the medium was firmly sewn up he sat in a chair and two of the men tied his legs to the legs of the chair and his arms to the sides of it. This was certainly the most peculiar seance I'd ever been to!

Finally, when the man was trussed up like a Christmas turkey, we all sat down, a quiet prayer was offered, the door locked and the lights turned out. John and I waited in trepidation, wondering what on earth would happen next.

There was silence in the room and all eyes were drawn to the only point of light, the trumpet which glowed ghostly green-white on the floor. As we stared, the trumpet started to rise from the floor, faltered, fell back and then rose again, higher and higher until it was level with our faces.

Slowly it turned in the air until it was pointing at one of the men in the group and from nowhere a voice spoke to him of his family. Round the group it went heralding a message for each one of us, but when it came to me the words were confused. It sounded as if several people were trying to talk at once and I couldn't make out anything clearly. John got a proper message but it wasn't about John Michael. I realize now that we went there in the wrong frame of mind. All we were thinking was we must have our son, we must have our son, and therefore we blocked anyone else who was trying to get through to us. Not understanding this at the time, we were bitterly disappointed.

The seance lasted an hour and a half and when it was over the trumpet fell to the floor again, the lights were put on and there was the medium tied to the chair, but in his shirt sleeves. His jacket lay nearby on the floor next to the trumpet – the stitches still intact. If that was a trick, I remained baffled to this day as to how it was done.

I know much more about this kind of work now. We call it physical mediumship because the medium produces physical phenomena: moving objects, or ectoplasm. You don't see many physical mediums these days, probably because it takes years to develop the gift and in this modern world we don't have the time to spare. I've since learned that physical mediums need to work in the dark or by an infra-red light and also for some reason to metal or electrical objects. If you were to switch on the light while the medium is working, or to produce something electrical, I've been told, you could badly injure him.

I've seen evidence of this myself. John and I were spending a weekend at Stansted Hall, the beautiful Jacobean style mansion in Essex where psychic courses are held throughout the year. Our visit coincided with the appearance of Gordon Higginson, an old friend who is also one of the greatest physical mediums alive today.

Gordon was giving some lectures and a seance at which he hoped to produce ectoplasm which would form itself into the features of the loved one who was communicating. These seances were always very popular and it was difficult to get a place, so John and I, who were both getting over severe bouts of 'flu, decided to let our seats go to other people.

'We're still feeling a bit wobbly,' I explained to Gordon, 'and if we're taken ill half-way through the seance we won't be able to get out.' The doors are always locked during seances to prevent people wandering in by mistake and switching on the light.

'All right, love,' said Gordon. 'I hope you feel better soon.

I'll probably see you in the morning.'

Everyone else was going to the seance, so John and I went early to our room. The lovely old building fell absolutely silent as the seance got under way and I stretched out on the bed, enjoying the peace.

There in the countryside you couldn't hear a sound – not like our flat in a busy London street where cars and lorries roar past day and night.

John unpacked his healing book and settled quietly with that. The minutes ticked by and my eyes started to close. I shall really have to get up and undress if I'm going to sleep, I told myself lazily and was debating whether I could be bothered to move when there was a knock at the door.

'Who can that be?' I asked drowsily. 'I thought everyone was at the seance.'

I got up, smoothing my hair and opened the door. There was no one there. I'd taken a moment or two to answer so I stepped out onto the minstrel gallery and looked over the banisters so that I could see the staircase and the whole front hall. The place was deserted. There was not a soul in sight. Puzzled I went back in. 'That's strange. There's no one there,' I said to John. I sat down on the bed again, about to stretch out once more, when suddenly I froze.

'Something's happened to Gordon,' I cried, hardly knowing what I'd said till the words were out. I rushed to the door and ran out again just in time to hear a commotion downstairs. As I looked over the banisters I saw several men carrying Gordon out of the seance room.

We never did find out exactly what had happened, but apparently Gordon had forgotten he was wearing a metal buckle on his belt. There had been some disturbance during the seance which had caused the ectoplasm to return to Gordon's body with such force, his metal buckle had become red hot and burned him.

I went to see him when his friends had put him to bed. He looked dreadful. His face was crimson and he was too weak even to lift a cup of tea to his lips. Someone had put a plaster over the burn but knowing I was a trained nurse, Gordon asked me to have a look at the wound. Gently I

peeled back the plaster. The burn looked very painful.
The skin round the navel was angry red and bubbling with
blisters.

'It's blistered, Gordon,' I told him. 'It's going to be pretty
sore for a while. Come on, drink your tea and try to get
some sleep. That's the best thing for you.'

As I left him to his painful night I thought to myself I
wasn't a bit surprised that we have so few physical
mediums left today. It's just not worth the risk.

Talking of Gordon reminds me of the time he decided
to test me. He'd always been very close to his mother,
Fanny Higginson, herself a wonderful medium, who
taught him everything she knew.

After she passed, Gordon said to me, 'Doris, I'd like you
to do a sitting for me, because if my mother's going to
come back to anybody it would be to you.'

By coincidence, during the weekend of the funeral I was
speaking at the church in Gordon's village and so he
invited John and I to dinner.

It was a magnificent house standing in extensive
grounds with a front and back drive. We went in through
the large square hall full of plants and flowers and then
Gordon took us into his own room, as he calls it, which
looked to be like a very large lounge with picture windows
and a bar. Gordon himself cooked a marvellous dinner
and insisted on serving us with sherry and wine with
liqueurs afterwards. I'm not used to drinking and I had to
warn him that I wouldn't be able to work if I was tipsy.

'Nonsense,' Gordon protested. 'What's good enough for
my mother is good enough for you, Doris. Oh, by the way,
before you do my sitting I wonder if you could possibly do
a couple of sittings for some friends of mine?'

'Well, I'll try,' I promised.

The curtains weren't drawn and as we sat there chatting
I saw my first sitter arrive, a young girl who walked up the
front drive from the main street. She rang the bell and
Gordon went to let her in.

The girl seemed a little uneasy, and I assumed she had
never had a sitting before but it went very well. Towards
the end I asked 'Who's Gillian?'

'I'm Gillian,' she answered.

Then a few more details came through and I became confused. 'I think I'm talking to Gordon's mother,' I told the girl. 'She's talking about Gordon a lot, perhaps because we're in his house. She's also mentioning Gordon's shop – do you know the shop?'

'Oh, yes,' she said, 'I work in it.'

Then right at the end, Fanny said, 'That's *our* Gillian,' and I suddenly remembered that Gordon had a niece called Gillian who lived in the house with her husband and family. Gillian owned up at once.

'I didn't want to do it, Doris. I felt a bit guilty but Gordon persuaded me. I put on my hat and coat and went out the back door down the drive, along the road and up the front drive so that you wouldn't guess. Gordon wanted to make sure you see!'

I had to laugh. Trust Gordon to be so careful, but at least he was getting real evidence. We went back into the lounge and I scolded Gordon mildly over coffee. Then my next sitter arrived.

She was an older woman and she, too, looked a little apprehensive. I tuned in and we got under way, but after a while I realized I wasn't doing very well. Some of the names that were coming through sounded as if they belonged to the last sitter.

'I'm so sorry,' I said to the woman, 'I think I must be tired. It's quite late and I've just done a sitting. Maybe I'm getting mixed up.' But then without doubt I heard Fanny again.

'That's my daughter, Hazel,' she said firmly. 'And I want you to give my love to our Leslie.'

'That's my daughter,' Hazel admitted.

'Tell her I'm so glad I saw the baby before I came over, Doris,' Fanny went on, 'though I watch over her now.' She also mentioned the name Heather.

'Who's Heather?'

'Heather's my granddaughter,' said Hazel.

Gordon had done it again. Unknown to me he'd brought his sister along for the second sitting. He hadn't wanted a sitting himself at all because he felt that as I knew him so well the information I gave him couldn't be counted as evidence. Now, thanks to his elaborate precautions, he was quite sure that Fanny had come back.

Chapter 9

1980 turned out to be the busiest year of my life particularly the time I spent on my tour of Australia, New Zealand and Tasmania. It was incredibly hard work and it nearly killed me at one point, but I realized that it was all worthwhile. It was meant to be.

Looking back on the tour I find many blanks in my memory. Days blurred into one another, cities became indistinguishable, particularly as I went backwards and forwards on an erratic course, visiting some places more than once. But although the details have faded I am left with a few vivid memories and an overwhelming impression of warmth and love from tens of thousands of people. There were many times when I was so exhausted I didn't know how I could carry on but there were even more times when I was moved to tears by the affection and thoughtfulness of a complete stranger.

I hadn't visited Australia since 1978 and I couldn't help wondering if they would remember me, but the moment we walked into Melbourne airport, I knew it was going to be fine. Limp and bedraggled and seven hours late because of delays on the ground in Europe and Bombay, we were shuffling through immigration when a man looked into my face and said, 'Hello, Doris Stokes. How are you, mate?' and I felt as if I'd come home.

Outside, Tony, a driver from the Myers bookshop chain which was organizing our tour, was waiting with a sparkling limousine to take us to our hotel. 'Doris, will you give me nine numbers for the lotto?' he asked as we drove along.

I assumed this must be some kind of lottery, perhaps the

Australian equivalent of our football pools or premium bonds.

'I don't really do that sort of thing, Tony,' I explained. 'If I could, I'd be a millionaire by now on the football pools.'

'Never mind. Just give me nine numbers,' Tony persisted. 'I've got a feeling.'

Laughing, I reeled off nine numbers completely at random. 'You'd do better with a pin,' I warned but strangely enough the next time we heard from Tony, he told us his numbers had come up. He hadn't won a great deal of money, only about thirty dollars, but he was absolutely thrilled.

The next day our routine began. There were television and radio interviews, phone-ins, live appearances and, most important of all, book signings at Myers book shops all over the country. We drove from store to store within cities sometimes doing three a day and we flew from city to city to repeat the performance. I must admit I had no idea what I was letting myself in for. I had imagined I would visit a bookship, a little place like my local Smiths, autograph a few books and then wander off again. It wasn't like that at all.

The first morning we pulled up in front of an enormous gleaming department store as wide as Harrods and seven storeys high. There were crowds of window shoppers outside and as we walked towards the entrance, they all ran across shouting: 'Hello, Doris. How are you?' and pushed in through the glass doors with us. I think this alarmed the organizers because after that we always went through the loading bay at the back.

I was led through the beautiful store, all airy open spaces and masses of green plants, to the restaurant. I thought perhaps we were going to have a quiet cup of tea before we started to work but instead I was confronted by two hundred people eating scones with jam and cream.

'They've come to have morning tea with Doris Stokes,' someone explained.

I stared at a mass of jammy faces all staring back at me. 'What am I suppose to do with them?' I whispered.

'Just talk to them for a few minutes and walk up and down a bit,' they said.

So I talked and I went from table to table saying hello to as many people as I could. This process was repeated in almost every store I visited and one of the nicest parts about it was the way mothers brought their children along to see me and everywhere I went I was given babies to hold and toddlers to cuddle.

That first morning I came upon a long table with about twenty people seated round it – three generations of one family!

They jumped up as I approached and made a great fuss of me. 'We wrote to you in 1978 and you sent us this,' they explained and proudly showed me a much handled sheet of paper. A lump came into my throat when I saw that it was only one of the standard letters we'd had printed because I couldn't possibly answer personally all the thousands of letters I'd received. On the back was one of my favourite verses: 'God enters the heart broken with sorrow and opens the door to a brighter tomorrow.' Then, before I'd recovered from the letter, they produced a flower. When I'd last toured Australia I was given so many flowers that I handed them out at my live shows to people who had received spirit messages.

'You gave us this in '78, Doris,' they said, 'and look at it.'

I stared down at a faded long stemmed carnation and though it was two years old it hadn't dried up or crumpled. It was still soft and supple and pretty and tears came into my eyes to think that they had treasured this little flower all that time simply because it came from me.

After the restaurant would come the book signing and usually I was led to the book department which had been specially cleared for the purpose and furnished with a little dais completely with table and chair. During my first session a dear little boy of two and a half clambered up onto the dais clutching a bunch of yellow flowers. 'For you, Auntie Doris,' he said, pushing them at me.

'Oh thank you, love,' I said hugging him. 'They're lovely,' and I searched in my pocket for a sweet but was disappointed to find I had none with me. After that I always asked for a bowl of sweets to be left on the table, and of course the children got to know about it. Most of the time I'd be sitting there signing away with children climbing all over my feet.

People would queue for hours to get their book signed. I noticed one boy of about seventeen, patiently shuffling forwards as the queue moved along and when he got to me he said, 'You know, Doris, I stood for four hours waiting to see my favourite pop group but this is more exciting.'

Bless your heart, I thought. 'What, more exciting to come and see an old granny than a pop group!' I teased.

'Yes,' he said solemnly, 'it is, and I've been here since nine this morning.'

Touched, I signed his book, but still he hovered. 'May I kiss you?' he asked shyly.

'Of course you can, love,' I said. So, blushing bright red, he bent, kissed me on the cheek and rushed away.

The next day I returned to the same store and there he was again with his autograph book!

Another time, in a shop in Sydney, the promotions girl on the dais with me touched my arm and said, 'There's a Father Jefferies who'd like a word with you.'

I turned and found a priest standing there. 'I would be very honoured if you would sign my book, Doris. I think it's beautiful,' he said. When I'd signed it he asked if he could give me a blessing.

'I'd like that very much, Father,' I said. So there, in the middle of the store, he gave me a blessing!

At another store on the outskirts of Sydney we were met by a very harassed manager. 'They've been queueing since eight-thirty,' he said. 'We can't take them in the book department or the restaurant so we've had to clear out the furniture department and put them in there.'

We walked in and I stopped dead in amazement. There were hundreds of people as far as I could see and it was obvious they had been waiting for a long time. They were sitting on the floor and mothers were changing their babies' nappies on the carpet. This was another nice thing: they didn't feel I was someone grand for whom they should put on a front. If their baby needed changing, they changed him, and if their baby wanted feeding, they fed him, knowing that it was only Doris and they didn't have to do anything different.

But the length of time people had to queue worried me. I would see young mothers standing for ages with a baby in their arms and another in a pushchair; and old people, crouched on sticks. So I always used to ask the crowd if they would let mothers with babies, old people and any sick people who couldn't stand very well come up first. There was never any fuss. The crowd would always part to let them through with good humour.

Still the little gifts came. One lady came up and put a parcel on the table for me. I'd mentioned in my last book the very special meaning that sky-blue velvet has for me and she'd obviously remembered this.

'Doris, I tried very hard to get some blue velvet for you,' she said, 'but I couldn't so I got the next best thing.'

When I opened the parcel I found a tin of blue velvet talcum powder and of course that set me off crying all over again.

Other people baked us cakes or gave us chocolates and flowers but with all the hotel meals and the constant travelling we couldn't eat them or keep them. I used to give them away and one time one of our drivers, a lovely boy called Paul, said, 'You know it's a good thing my wife's seen you on TV and she knows who I'm with or she'd wonder what I was up to coming home with chocolates and flowers every night!'

Of course I was often aware as I sat there signing till my arm ached and the pages swam before my eyes, that the person standing next to me was desperately hoping for a contact. It would have been impossible to work for everyone, but just occasionally their loved one came through so vividly that I had to repeat what I was hearing.

At other times people had travelled so far in hope, I couldn't refuse to tune in to find some little scrap that might help. One lady told me she'd travelled three hundred and ninety miles. I couldn't turn her away. It was the same at public meetings. At one a man stood up and said he and his wife had come five hundred miles for a message. Hadn't I got anything for them?

It was question time but I couldn't refuse a plea like that. I tuned in. 'You've lost a child, haven't you?' I asked.

'Yes, we have,' he agreed.

'That's odd,' I said. I could hear a little girl's voice but she was giving me a boy's name. It was quite definite, however, so I went on. 'Well, I'm sure it's girl I can hear but she says her name is Bobby.'

'That's right,' said the man. 'That's all we wanted,' and he sat down again.

Question time continued but ten minutes later Bobby returned.

'My *real* name is Roberta,' she explained. We were in mid question at that point but I said, 'Excuse me,' and turned again to the direction where the man and his wife were sitting.

'By the way, Bobby has just told me that her real name is Roberta,' I said. They both burst into tears.

'Doris,' said the man, 'it was worth every mile of the way to know you can tell us we've lost a daughter and her correct name.'

It was all he wanted. Such a tiny piece of information meant so much. It was touching the way so many people were satisfied with so little. One another occasion during question time, two young girls stood up, one supporting the other who was weeping.

'Doris, can you do anything for my friend?' begged the more composed of the two. 'She lost her baby two weeks ago and she's been like this ever since. She's too upset to speak to you.'

I thought of John Michael and my heart went out to the ashen-faced girl sobbing into her handkerchief. There were no words to express the pain and grief she must be going through but I knew, I knew.

In my head a woman's voice said, 'The baby's name is Robin.'

'Is the baby called Robin?' I asked.

'Oh yes, yes!' cried the girl, looking up in wonder.

'Well, don't worry, darling. He's quite safe. His grand-mother says he's with her and she's looking after him for you. He's well and happy.'

And the young mother sat down again, content just to know that her baby was in good hands.

Then there were all the shows – far too many to recall in detail but I started with a radio phone-in presented by my old friend, the cheeky Bert Newton. To my surprise, while we waited to go on the air, a waiter arrived with a china tea service, a silver pot and a plate of sandwiches on a tray. I had to laugh because the first time I went on his show in 1978 I was given coffee in a paper cup.

'What's this in aid of, Bert?' I joked, holding up the silver pot. 'Does it mean I've come up in the world?'

''Course it does,' he said, helping himself to a sandwich. 'Only the best for Doris Stokes. We wouldn't dare do anything else!'

During the programme I was in the middle of a message when another voice cut in. 'There's been a fire,' it said. 'There's five of us. It's only just happened.'

The woman I was talking to couldn't place it at all. 'No, I'm sorry, Doris,' she apologized. 'I don't know anyone who's been in a fire.'

'Don't apologize, love,' I said. 'I've got a crossed wire somewhere. It's not your fault.' But the voice kept coming back during the commercial break and it was most insistent about the fire. I discussed it with Bert.

'I can't understand it, Bert. It seems so positive and they say it's only just happened.'

'It wasn't something you saw in the paper or anything, was it?' Bert asked.

I shook my head. 'We only arrived in the early hours this morning and we came straight to the studio when we got up. I haven't seen a paper since we left London.'

The producer sent out for a paper just in case, and in the next break he passed it to me. There it was. Fire had broken out in a caravan and five people had gone over together.

The next show I did was the Don Lane Show. When we walked onto the set Don was already rehearsing for the night show but as soon as he saw me, he leapt up, as handsome and slim as ever, gave me a big hug and swung me round until I was breathless.

It was so nice to see him again I felt all weepy. You'll have to pull yourself together, Doris, I told myself sternly. The way things were going I'd spend the whole tour in tears if I carried on like this.

Don had got a new set since I had last been on the show. In place of the smart green and tan set he used to have was a beautiful affair of soft violets and greys, but I eyed the graceful steps that wound down the centre of it in dismay. I couldn't help remembering the last time I'd been on his show when I concluded my appearance with a spectacular fall down the steps behind the set, and was obliged to go back to say goodbye with a bruised ankle and laddered tights!

'Don, I haven't got to come down those steps on camera have I?' I asked gloomily, imagining a repeat performance.

'Not if you don't want to, love,' said Don.

'I'd rather not,' I said. 'It takes me all my time not to tread on my dress. I'm sure I'd go flying.'

'That's all right,' Don assured me. 'We'll fix up a curtain or something and you can come straight onto the floor from behind that.'

Relieved, I went off to get ready and when it was my time to appear I was amazed to find they had not only rigged up a special curtain but they had also built a step at the side of the set covered with the same grey carpet for me to stand on while I waited to appear.

Unfortunately my first two contacts weren't promising. I began with a Scottish lady who said her name was McCarthy. Nobody in the audience could place her. She was crystal clear, however, and gave me several more family names but it was no use, nobody claimed her and I had to move on.

Next I got a little boy. He was called Peter and he said he'd passed with leukaemia. I described him carefully but again no one claimed him. 'What a shame,' I said. 'He's only a few years old and he thinks somebody here belongs to him.' But there was no response. Sadly I had to tell Peter we'd had no luck and pass to someone else.

I was getting a bit worried by this time that the

demonstration would be a disaster but fortunately, after Peter, the messages were claimed in the normal way.

After I came off after the show, the floor manager called me over. 'Look Doris,' he said and pointed to a man in the orchestra who was blowing his nose hard on a large white handkerchief. 'It was his nephew, Peter, who died of leukaemia. He didn't like to say anything.'

'Well, thank goodness for that,' I said. 'The little boy was so insistent that he knew somebody in the studio, I wondered what was wrong.'

And the mystery of my Scottish McCarthy was solved a few days later. Don received a letter from a woman who had recently lost her husband. Desperate to believe, she'd pulled up her chair in front of the television set and sent out her love to all her relatives and friends in the spirit world, just as I advised, and straight away my message came. Her name was McCarthy and I'd given her mother's name and the names of her brothers. It had worked even though she wasn't in the studio.

Another memorable show was the John Singleton Show in Sydney. I'd heard a lot about John Singleton. He was a real 'Oker' I was told beforehand which apparently means a real Australian. He was very rich, arriving at the studios in his own helicopter and since it was his show he believed in saying exactly what he thought. John Singleton doesn't mince his words, I was warned. You either love him or hate him.

We drove along through steep hills and valleys and by the time I reached the studios perched on top of a hill with a breathtaking vista of green, I was very intrigued to meet this Mr Singleton.

It wasn't long before I got my wish. We'd hardly got inside the building when we couldn't fail to notice a tall, broad man with corn coloured hair and full evening dress including a dickie bow tie, striding down the corridor.

'Hello, Doris,' he said, taking my hand in his great rocklike grasp and shaking it up and down. 'Come into my dressing room.'

There was much twittering and fluttering in the background over this and I understood that a great honour had been conferred.

We were led into a plush room with enormous black leather armchairs and a settee, and there John Singleton chatted with great courtesy. There was no trace of the difficult, possibly abrasive man I'd been led to expect and throughout our meeting he was charming.

I wasn't allowed to demonstrate on John's show, I was told, because I was already booked to do so on a rival show and for some reason they wouldn't let me do both. This seemed rather unfair to me but John didn't seem to mind. He was content to talk about my book and ask me questions. Then he said:

'Doris, you remember that poem in your book about your baby?'

'Yes,' I replied. How could I forget it? While I was still grieving badly for my little John Michael, I'd heard a voice reciting a poem. That poem had given me so much comfort it was never far from my mind during the thirty years since.

'Do you think you could recite it for us now?'

'Yes, of course,' I said and went straight into those well loved lines:

In a baby castle just beyond my eye,
My baby plays with angel toys that money cannot
     buy.
Who am I to wish him back,
Into this world of strife?
No, play on my baby,
You have eternal life.

At night when all is silent
And sleep forsakes my eyes
I'll hear his tiny footsteps come running to my side.
His little hands caress me, so tenderly and sweet
I'll breathe a prayer and close my eyes and embrace
     him in my sleep.

Now I have a treasure that I rate above all other,
I have known true glory – I am still his mother.

When I'd finished, John invited questions from the audience. 'Excuse me, Doris,' he said, 'you carry on talking,' and he went over to the band and spoke to them for a few seconds. Then he came back.

'I've asked the band to play very softly a piece of music called *No Greater Love*,' he said and even as he spoke the band started to play. 'I wonder, Doris, if you could recite your poem to the music.'

So I recited my poem once more as the music swayed in the background and there was not a sound in the studio. The words and the music combined to create an atmosphere so beautiful that it was difficult to speak and my voice faltered several times, but I struggled on. Finally the last line fell away into dazed silence. For several seconds no one spoke or moved and the programme ended quietly. I was too full of emotion to say much more.

The next day a box almost as long as my coffee table at home arrived at the hotel. I lifted the lid with trembling fingers to find a mass of velvety orchids inside – with love from John Singleton.

There is a lovely sequel to this story. Months later, long after I'd arrived home, the postman delivered a hard, flat parcel to my door. It was covered in brown paper but it must have had 'picture' written on the outside because I heard Terry moan from the kitchen, 'More stuff to dust!'

It was covered with bright New Zealand stamps, however, so I took no notice of him and tore into it excitedly. On a dull, winter's day it was like a little piece of New Zealand sunshine. Inside was one of the most beautiful gifts I've ever received: in flowing black copperplate writing on a gold background with the merest suggestion of flowers and babies on it, and framed in an ornate gold frame with scroll-work at the corners, was a copy of my poem.

The artist explained in an accompanying letter that he'd been so moved by my recital on the John Singleton Show that he'd felt inspired to set the poem down permanently for me. He only hoped he had got all the words correct. He had, and to this day that lovely picture hangs on the wall above the mantelpiece in my flat – a really treasured possession.

Another show that stands out in the mind is Hayden Sarjeant's Show in Brisbane. The Sarjeant Report. Hayden was a former minister, I was told, and likes to cover serious topics, but he allowed me to get on with my work in my usual way. In fact, he had invited so many people to the studio that the seats had to be arranged in stands like a football stadium and even then there were dozens of people sitting on the floor at the front.

The communications were coming through so well that I over-ran my allotted time but no one wanted me to stop. The producer kept saying, 'Carry on, we'll give you an extra five minutes,' and when that five minutes was up: 'Oh well, just five minutes more.' In the end he shrugged his shoulders: 'We might as well get it all in the can and use it later!'

During one of these periods of extra time, I was craning my head in an effort to find my next recipient. She was in the front somewhere, I was informed, but I couldn't see her.

'What's the matter, Doris?' asked Hayden, noticing my difficulty. 'Do you want to be up there with the audience?'

Even as he spoke I saw a light hovering over the head of a lady in glasses.

'No, it's all right. The lady I want is that lady there in glasses – I can see her from where I'm sitting.'

The cameras started to roll, but suddenly I heard Ramanov's voice. 'No it's not her. *Behind* her,' and I stood up abruptly.

'What are you doing? I thought you said it was all right sitting down,' said Hayden.

'Well, I thought it was,' I explained. 'Sorry, dear,' I hastily added to the disappointed lady in glasses, 'it's not you, they tell me, it's somebody sitting behind you, somebody I can't see from here.'

I climbed down and walked into the audience and, sure enough, behind this woman was another lady in sunglasses. As I looked at her I heard a young man saying that his name was Steven. The woman gasped. It was her son.

'I did it myself, you know,' Steven told me. Quickly I

looked up at the cameras all round us. I couldn't say *that* out loud for everyone to hear. So I bent down and whispered, 'Did he take himself over?'

The woman's hands flew to her mouth and she nodded, biting her lip.

The message went on giving several family names and details and then right at the end Steven said proudly, 'I left sixty-three dollars.'

When I repeated this the woman gasped in amazement.

'Oh, my God!' she cried.

'Is that correct?' I asked.

'Yes. Yes it is,' she said. 'We found it in a bottle in his wardrobe. Sixty-three dollars exactly.'

After the programme came to an end, people were milling about asking me to sign copies of the book. I was chatting and scribbling busily but at one point I happened to glance up and I saw Steven's mother deep in conversation with Hayden. A few minutes later Hayden came over.

'That's amazing, Doris,' he said. 'I know Steven's mother – the family are neighbours of mine. But I had no idea they were coming today. They didn't tell me.' The next morning he announced on his radio show that he personally could vouch for the accuracy of my message because he knew the family and everything I told them had been true.

By this time of course the pace of the tour was beginning to tell on me. I'm over sixty, after all, and not as fit as I used to be and, to be fair, I think even a younger person would have found it a strain. We dashed from place to place, from hotel to car to plane and back again, from store to studio to press conference with scarcely a break for meals. At one point lunch was a sandwich and a cup of coffee in the back of the car. The few days off I'd been allocated were rapidly eaten up by interviews, and I suppose I made it worse by being unable to refuse all those desperate eyes. When they looked at me with such hope, I couldn't just keep my head down, scribble *Doris Stokes* and get on my way.

I felt utterly exhausted. My voice was strained and

croaking with all the talking I'd been doing, my right arm, weakened from my mastectomy operation used to swell up like a balloon from all the signing. I supposed I've never known when to stop and I pushed myself on and on trying to meet every demand that was made of me.

At last in Brisbane, after a two hour Press conference, I was led into a store for my second signing sessions of the day in the book department. There was a little dais covered in pale blue carpet on which stood a Queen Anne chair in matching blue velvet. It looked lovely but I noticed wearily that there were about six steps leading to the dais, which meant that once up there, I had to bend almost double to shake people's hands and take their books from them.

I'd already had a hectic day but I gritted my teeth and steeled myself to get on with it. Once up on the dais it was even worse than I had feared. The people crushed below me, at least ten deep and, as always, I found myself thinking, what do they want? What do they expect from me? I can't possibly help them all. Yet I hated to disappoint them. Every time I bent down the floor seemed to swing up and sideways and I could hardly reach the books that were offered.

Then for the first time in ages, I heard my father's voice. Loud and clear, it cut through all the surrounding chatter: 'Dol, get down from there.'

I was in the middle of speaking to someone so I tried to bring the conversation to a close but my father's voice came through again: 'Dol, get down from there *At Once.*' When Father was in that mood there was no disobeying him. Covered in confusion, my head spinning and the room around me a blur, I tried to stand up.

'I'll have to get down from here,' I muttered. 'I must get down.'

From somewhere in front of me a voice said, 'Goodness, what's the matter with Doris?'

'Doris, your face has gone crimson,' cried someone else.

Two men stepped forward, I felt myself half lifted down the steps, the chair was brought down from the dais and I collapsed thankfully into it. A glass of water was put into my hand.

'Are you all right?'

'Yes – I think so,' I mumbled, not really sure. 'I thought I was going to fall.'

A few minutes later, without knowing how it happened, I found myself signing books again. I've no idea what I wrote. I sat there moving my hand automatically across the pages. My head was going round like a clock and I couldn't quite remember where I was.

The next thing I knew I was back at the hotel feeling most peculiar. I wasn't quite so dizzy but there was this out-of-balance, not-quite-there sensation. I could see the room about me but somehow it seemed a long-way off.

'Are you sure you're all right, love?' John kept asking but his voice came from a great distance as if he was speaking down a long tube.

I had a hot bath and went to bed. At least with my eyes closed and the curtains drawn, the room didn't seem so far away.

The next morning I felt a bit better, or at least I thought I did. the point was academic in any case because I had to get up to do a radio phone-in with Hayden Sarjeant. I got to the studio without incident and congratulated myself. I didn't feel too bad really. There was no pain anywhere, just this strange detached feeling as if I only had one foot in reality. There was also this strange inability to take in what people were saying. I gave up trying to follow conversations and concentrated on saying 'Yes' every now and again. No one seemed to notice.

The phone-in went ahead as planned and that was when I noticed another strange thing. As well as not being able to follow other people's conversations, I couldn't follow my own. I heard myself talking but for the life of me I couldn't understanding what I was saying. It might have been complete gibberish for all I knew. I glanced at Hayden to see if he'd noticed anything amiss, but he was talking smoothly into the microphone, his face unruffled.

At last, during the commercial break, I said, 'Hayden, does it make sense to you what I'm doing?'

'What d'you mean, love? asked Hayden.

'Well, half the time, I don't know what I'm saying.'

'Well, you're right on the button,' he assured me. 'That last call was from a woman who had lost her daughter. You told her the girl's name was Caroline, she was nineteen and how she had died. Then the mother said there was one more thing she was waiting for and if you got that you'd save her sanity. You came back with "Caroline says to tell you she's got her teddy bear with her" and the mother burst into tears. Apparently she'd put the teddy bear in the girl's coffin.'

'Oh good. That's okay then,' I said vaguely. I didn't recall a word of it but if it was working it didn't matter. Hayden was staring at me rather strangely now, but the break was over. I fumbled for the headphones and pushed them back over my hair.

Hayden was still looking at me. I opened my mouth to say something to him but somehow I couldn't think of anything to say.

'All right. That's it!' he cried suddenly. 'Take those headphones off. That's it.'

Confused, I looked around. What was wrong?

'Jane!' Hayden yelled into the office behind the studio. 'Doris is ill. She needs a doctor. She's not leaving this building until she's seen one.'

The next few hours are a blur. I drank tea, I recall, and at some point a doctor examined me.

'It could have been one of three things,' he said. 'It could have been a stroke, a mild heart attack or ...' and he mentioned some other complicated medical name that I can't remember. Eventually he came to the conclusion that I was totally exhausted and an artery had closed in my head shutting off the oxygen flow.

'You need a good rest,' he said. 'You must have forty-eight hours doing nothing at all.'

That was a Friday. I spent the rest of the day in my room. Saturday we were put on a plane to Sydney – the next place on our itinerary. I rested for the weekend and by Monday I was ready to work again. Not as well as I might have been but I could cope.

One of the nicest things about Sydney was the fact that an old friend of mine, Alice Chaikovksy, lived there. I'd first met Alice when she was on holiday with her friend, Betty, in England.

Alice had spent three months visiting SAGB, Stansted Hall and other spiritualist places hoping to get a message but had had no luck at all. On her last night, she decided to go to one final demonstration at the SAGB and it happened to be the very night I was asked to take over at the last minute because the advertised medium was ill.

Alice told me afterwards that when it was announced the medium couldn't be there and Doris Stokes would take over instead, she thought, oh no, my last night wasted. But the second person I spoke to was Alice.

'I've got someone here who's speaking either Polish or Russian,' I explained. I don't speak any other languages but over the years I've got to recognize the sound of different languages. This man confused me, however. Part of the time it sounded like Polish and part of the time, Russian.

'That's all right!' cried Alice. 'He's Polish but he speaks Russian.'

'Who's Alice?' I asked.

'That's me!' cried Alice practically jumping up and down.

'Well, I've got Michael here,' I went on.

'That's my husband!'

Michael explained that Alice lived in Sydney, Australia. He told me where he'd left his money and that he wanted a Russian church to be built with it, then he went on to describe an icon he wanted made. He talked about Stanislaus and Swchitz.

'I can't understand this,' I said, 'I thought he said he was a baker or something to do with bakeries but now he's saying it's something to do with the airport.'

'That's right,' said Alice, 'we make all the cakes and things for the airport.'

Finally Michael said, 'Will you tell Alice I've met Edie Turner.'

Alice was thrilled with it all. They don't usually get excited at SAGB but she was standing up and turning round to the audience saying, 'Isn't she marvellous? Isn't she good?'

Afterwards she was waiting on the steps outside and

insisted on paying for my taxi home. We've been friends ever since.

Throughout our stay in Sydney, Alice kept inviting us to her house but our schedule was so tight we had to turn her down, very sadly, every time. Then just as we were about to leave for New Zealand, there was an air strike. We were delighted and packed our bags for Alice's instead.

Alice's house turned out to be very large with a verandah running round it with a big garden, which she called a yard, full of grapefruit, orange and lemon trees. The sight of citrus fruit hanging from the trees never ceased to amaze me and I loved to wander through the garden staring at it. To be allowed to pick a grapefruit was a wonderful treat.

It was marvellous to see Alice and Betty again. They were both confirmed spiritualists by now and Betty had developed a talent as a psychic artist. She's had no art training, she told me, and had never been good at art, but as she became involved in spiritualism she began feeling a tremendous urge to draw on a sheet of paper with coloured chalks. It grew so strong that she went out and bought the materials and, to her amazement, she produced a good picture.

Since then she's never looked back and she showed me some of her work. The detail was marvellous. One picture showed a woman wearing a lace shawl round her head and every whorl and loop of the pattern was as clear and sharp as if it had been real. In another picture of a mother and baby, every crease of the baby's arms and legs is shown in life-like detail.

Betty was particularly glad to see me because she'd been longing to tell me about her house in Spain. I had forgotten but apparently Betty had come to me in London for a sitting and I had told her that she was going to live in Spain in a house on a hill which looked as if it was pink-washed. At the time Betty thought this most unlikely but now she'd bought a Spanish house, standing on a hill. It was white, she explained, but when the sun is setting the walls are bathed in pink light and they look as if they've been pink-washed!

We were very sad to say goodbye to Alice and Betty when the strike ended, but as we drove once more to the airport I began to feel a twinge of excitement. I'd always wanted to visit New Zealand, and I had another wonderful friend there – my old student, almost my adopted daughter – dear Judy ...

Chapter 10

To tell you about Judy I must first go back a few years to talk about my 'psychic evening classes' as they were nicknamed by one reporter.

When I was still working at SAGB in London, I was asked if I would take a teaching class. These classes usually consist of about twelve fledglings, as they're called – ordinary people from all walks of life who have become interested in spiritualism and want to develop their psychic gift.

This is quite possible to do because, as I've said before, everyone has got the spark within them and with practice it can be brought out. This doesn't necessarily mean that the student will become a brilliant medium. After all, you can probably teach most people to play the piano but only a very few would become concert pianists.

The teacher can't teach the student how to use his gift, only his guide knows what he is capable of, but her role is to help build up the atmosphere and give all her power to the fledglings, to tune in to what they are getting and help them sort it out. At first it's difficult to distinguish what's coming from your own mind and what's coming from the other side. The teacher can unscramble the message and help the fledglings reach their full potential.

I'd always believed in training the young. I often felt that if there had been more help around when I was young I could have saved so much time and mistakes instead of blundering around in the dark on my own. Who knows what I might have achieved if I'd started on my way earlier? So now that I had gained knowledge and experience I was only too pleased to do what I could to help the mediums of the future.

There was only one question I asked when a person applied to join the class: why did they want to do it? And I only accepted one answer: because they wanted to serve, they wanted to help other people. I soon got to know whether they were telling the truth or not, but the great majority of youngsters who came to me were genuine, loving people who wanted to help others.

Poor health forced me to give up my regular job at SAGB. I told the class they could join other groups but they begged to stay with me and we ended up hiring a room in Fulham Town Hall, not far from my flat, for our weekly 'evening classes'.

The members of the class were my pride and joy. I was just as new to teaching as they were to learning so I drew on my own mistakes and Ramanov's advice in my efforts to create 'lessons'. I remembered the only teaching class I'd ever attended, years ago, when I'd been told to uncross my legs and hold my hands in a certain position. I'd spent the whole evening concentrating so hard on adopting the right posture I'd completely failed to make any contact at all.

It hadn't worked for me and I was determined not to clutter up my kids' minds with a lot of dos and don'ts. I kept the class as simple as possible. One of them would say a prayer offering ourselves to God in service, then we would join hands round the big oval table and I would tell them to forget the outside world and tune in to each other.

'Just think about the person on either side of you and send out all the love you can.' In this way the circle of love went round the table and this built up the psychic power. You could feel it getting stronger with every passing moment and when I felt it was strong enough I would drop my hands. Not a word was spoken but they would drop their hands around the table and we would get on with the work.

One young man was a yoga fan and he asked if it would be all right if he did his breathing exercises because he felt it helped him.

'Son, you can do whatever you like at long as it's not stupid or intended to draw attention to yourself,' I told him and so he used to sit there very quietly with his hands on his solar plexus doing deep breathing, and before long the rest of us found that we were doing it too! He was right: it did help and it proved to me that we can all learn something from each other. I'd always had trouble making myself relax and that young boy taught me how.

As the class tuned in, they used to tell me that my father was there and he began the lesson by drawing a big letter 'S' in the air above my head. I hadn't told them beforehand that my father's name was Sam as this proved to me that Dad was there, giving a helping hand with my teaching.

Often the students found their messages confusing and I explained what Ramanov had taught me. 'If you're given something you don't understand and the person you're talking to doesn't understand it either, test it,' I said. 'Suppose they are showing you a picture of a man on a black horse and this doesn't mean anything to you. Test the individual details. Say to yourself, it's not a black horse it's white, white. And back will come, it's a *black* horse. So you know the horse part of the picture is correct.'

One boy, Maurice, knew what he wanted to say but he had difficulty putting it into words. I don't know where the idea came from, but one night, watching him struggle, I said silently, 'Write. it on the carpet for him,' and immediately Maurice leaned forward and started reading invisible words off the carpet.

The technique came in useful for other students, too. I used to invite mystery guests along for the evening from time to time because the students got to know each other so well it became even more difficult to judge whether their message came from the other side or their own subconscious. One evening my guest was a journalist called Frank Durham.

'Can you do anything for our friend here?' I asked the class.

There was a long silence. The big old clock on the wall ticked loudly and I could feel the intense concentration round me.

'I hear the name Frances William,' said Alice.

'Well, my name is Frank William,' said Frank.

They gave him a few more bits and pieces, then Frank asked them a question. 'I've been away recently,' he said. 'Could you ask the spirit world where I've been?'

There was another silence. The answer came to me, maddeningly loud and clear but I wasn't allowed to say anything. The silence continued and it was getting painful.

'Show them a picture,' I asked the spirit world silently. 'Put it on the table,' and suddenly Sandra, a schoolteacher, said, 'That's extraordinary!'

'What is?' I asked.

'Well, the table's filled with Flanders poppies,' she said.

Frank Durham nearly fell off his chair. 'That's where I've been,' he cried in astonishment. 'Flanders Fields, to do an article.'

When there were no guests, the class frequently demonstrated their growing powers by giving me evidence. The most striking concerned my old friend Harry Edwards. I mentioned Harry in my last book. He was one of the greatest healers we've ever had in Britain. It was Harry who helped me cure John of cancer – or should I say I helped him – and it was Harry who helped me recover with remarkable speed from my mastectomy operation without the need for radiation therapy.

I visited Harry shortly before he passed over, at his healing sanctuary in Surrey. It was a beautiful old manor house on a hill, with peaceful gardens leading down to open countryside. We strolled in the garden and took photographs, then Harry said, 'Come in here, Doris. I'd like to show you something.'

He led me through the house into a part I'd never seen before, then opened a gothic arched door to reveal a long low room with a vaulted ceiling very much like a church.

'This would make a wonderful church, Harry,' I said, gazing round. There was a great deal of richly carved wood, gleaming with care, and the walls were covered with paintings. Outside of an art gallery, I'd never seen so many paintings in one place. I peered closely at them. They were original oils and they were very good.

'These are beautiful, Harry,' I said, wondering how he

could afford so many lovely things.

'I painted them myself,' he said nonchalantly.

'*Really?*' I examined them even more carefully. 'I didn't know you had a talent like this Harry. They're marvellous.'

Harry put his arm round my shoulders. 'I'll let you into a secret,' he whispered. 'They're all done by numbers!' and we both roared with laughter.

Months later, after Harry had passed, the class was gathered round the large oval table beneath the clock. An intense silence filled the room and I knew that several students had received communications but were struggling to sort out their impressions.

'I get the impression of a man standing behind you, Doris,' said Julie. 'He's got very white hair, a chubby round face and a sweet smile.'

Immediately Harry Edwards sprang to mind. It was a perfect description of him, but I thought I'd better wait for more conclusive proof.

'Can anyone else give me something more definite?' I asked.

'I can see a very large garden,' said one of the other girls slowly. 'It stands very high so I feel as if I'm looking out over the countryside. Now I'm going under a rose arch and there's a fish pond with wire netting over it.'

I knew then, without doubt, that Harry Edwards was trying to get through to them. He had just shown them the grounds of his healing sanctuary.

'Yes,' I said. 'That's very good. I know who it is, but I'm waiting for more.'

'I hear the name Harry,' said Sandra suddenly. 'It's not Harry Edwards, is it, Doris?'

I said, 'Well, I think so, but we need something more to clinch it,' and in my mind I said, 'Give the kids more proof, Harry, so they can be absolutely certain.'

A few moments later one of the girls said, 'I get the impression I'm standing at the door of a church.'

'Well, there's a church in the village,' I pointed out, as indeed there are in most villages.

'No,' the girl persisted. 'I don't think it's that sort of church. I get the impression of a long building and a lot of pictures.'

Instantly the memory of that afternoon when Harry had shown me his special room flashed into my mind.

'And he keeps saying tell Doris about the numbers,' said Sandra in a puzzled voice. 'I'm sure that's what he's saying. Tell Doris about the numbers.'

They'd got it! I knew then without doubt that Harry had made contact with the class.

I was very fond of all my students but the one I grew to love best was Judy. She was a pretty New Zealand girl, tall and slim with fair hair that had a touch of red in it. She wasn't going to develop into the best medium in my class, I knew that, but she was warm and lovable and when I first met her, very depressed.

Many things had gone wrong in her life and I suppose, with most of her relatives on the other side of the world, she was looking for someone to turn to. I was glad to help. We spent many an hour discussing her problems over a cup of tea after the class and gradually a real friendship blossomed.

Judy used to take me shopping and talk me into buying more up to date clothes. If I was ill, my health has always been erratic, she would do my shopping for me and being a great believer in herbal medicines she would also rush round with her health remedies and a list of instructions of what I should take and when. I'd always wanted a daughter and in a way Judy became the daughter I never had.

One morning she was at the flat, terribly upset about something or other and as she was explaining, her voice seemed to fade. I could see her lips moving but the sound was gone and over the top I could hear another voice.

'Judy,' I interrupted her, 'you're going back to New Zealand and you're going to marry a New Zealand man and have two babies.'

For a couple of seconds she was speechless with amazement. Then she laughed. 'Oh Doris, even if I wanted to I couldn't go back to New Zealand. I can't afford the fare!'

'Well, believe me, you will and you'll get married there,' I replied.

As I've told people many times, I'm not a fortune teller,

but occasionally, when a sitter is very depressed and can't see any prospect of life improving, the relatives on the other side will sometimes give them a tiny glimpse of the good things in store to show them that things will get better. When this happens it is always correct and while I was very pleased that Judy was going to get married and have children, I was sorry that she was going away.

Judy took it lightly, however. The months passed and she remained as broke as ever and even if she'd won the football pools I don't think she would have rushed back to New Zealand. She was reasonably happy in Britain and didn't think that going back would improve her life in any way.

Then out of the blue one day she got an urgent phone call. There was trouble at home and she was needed badly. 'I can't afford the fare,' Judy told her relatives, but an aunt sent her the money.

The parting was very sudden. 'I'll be back just as soon as this is all cleared up,' Judy promised.

'You won't, you know,' I told her sadly.

'I will, I will,' she cried, throwing her arms round my neck. 'There's nothing to keep me in New Zealand. I like it in England.'

I didn't want to distress her any more so I just smiled and said nothing. We parted with tears and promises to exchange letters very often.

At first Judy's letters were full of plans for what she would do when she returned to London. Then they became less frequent and finally she wrote to tell me she was marrying a man named McCarthy. Some time later there was a letter with the wonderful news that she now had a little girl called Trinity and later still came news of a son, called Sam, after my father.

That touched me very deeply and when I heard we were going to New Zealand in 1980 I was thrilled because it meant we'd have the chance of meeting Judy and her little family.

The first time I saw Australia I fell in love with it because it was so beautiful. Well, when I went to New Zealand where we were looked after by Sharon and Rolf

Smith as if we were part of the family, I fell in love all over again. It was the middle of winter but everything was still so green and fresh. There were palm trees and even a few flowers in bloom and the air was sparkling clean. You could feel it doing you good every time you breathed. Whenever we got out of doors which unfortunately wasn't as often as we would have liked, John and I took great lungfuls of air to 'set us up' for our return to the carbon monoxide of London.

I'd been a bit worried during the tour because just before we left we'd had a distressed phone call from Judy to tell us her little son was very ill with a breathing problem. John immediately put him on his absent healing list and I concentrated on sending out psychic energy to make him well. I felt sure it would help and as I hadn't picked up any panic from Judy in the intervening weeks I was certain the boy couldn't be any worse. Nevertheless I didn't *know* and until I received definite news I couldn't fully relax.

Then one afternoon I was doing a sitting for a magazine in Auckland when it started to go wrong. I'd been getting a lot of good evidence and then I seemed to go off beam.

'They're telling me about someone called Sam,' I said.

The reporter shook her head. 'No, I don't know anyone of that name.'

I returned the name for checking. Back it came loud and positive, *Sam*. Still the reporter couldn't accept it. My father's name was Sam, of course, and his warning to me to get down from the dais in the bookshop was still fresh in my mind. Was he trying to get through to me again?

'No, not your father,' Ramanov assured me. And the name came through again.

'Sam,' said a voice. 'Sam's better.'

Totally confused by now, I shook my head. 'I've got my wires crossed somewhere,' I told the reporter. 'I'll have to clear the vibration and start again.'

I blocked my mind to Sam and was about to tune in again, when the phone rang. Saved by the bell, I thought with relief. 'Excuse me a moment,' I apologized and hurried to answer it.

'Hello, Doris!' came a dear, familiar voice over the line. 'It's Judy.'

'Judy! How lovely to hear from you,' I cried with pleasure.

'I won't keep you now because I know you're probably busy,' said Judy. 'I just wanted to let you know that Sam's much better we thought we'd come over and see you at your hotel.'

I nearly dropped the receiver. We'd found Sam. Grinning, I went through the arrangements with Judy and then returned to my sitting.

'It'll be all right now,' I assured the reporter. 'I've found Sam. We can get on.' And I was right. The sitting went ahead smoothly with no more mysteries.

A few days later Judy and her family drove for three hours to visit us at our hotel in Wellington. They arrived slightly earlier than expected and they got to the room before I did because I'd had to go to the hairdressers. I was staggered when my door was opened by an attractive man I'd never seen before in my life, who proceeded to throw his arms around me and give me a great bear hug. Then Judy pushed him out of the way and hugged me herself and we all squeezed back into the room laughing and weeping a little.

The children were beautiful. Bright, intelligent and full of life, very like their mother. We had tea and sandwiches sent up and while we sat round eating and chattering, Judy began to unpack a big bag she'd brought.

'You sounded so tired on the phone, Doris, I thought you needed something to buck you up,' she explained and out came her herbal remedies and a list of instructions!

Then someone noticed that Trinity had disappeared and the bedroom door was open.

'For God's sake go and see what's she's doing,' cried Judy to her husband, but I couldn't resist peeping round the door myself. There was Trinity sitting on the bed, gossiping away to someone on the telephone. She'd dialled a series of numbers at random and managed to get a connection!

We had a very happy afternoon and it was even harder

to part this time than it was before, but John and I promised that if we ever get the chance we'll go to stay with them at their home. In the meantine, there are always the letters ...

Of course I wasn't in New Zealand simply to look up old friends and very soon I was immersed in non-stop work. Again, I seemed to be busy every minute of the day, and only a few of those endless shows and interviews remain in my mind.

I remember doing a phone-in in Auckland, where we were staying in the same villa Yootha Joyce used when she was in New Zealand, when a man came on the line asking if I could help. I promised to do my best. Almost immediately I heard a woman's voice. Her accent sounded a little blurred but I thought she said her name was Maddie.

'Would that be short be Madeleine?' I asked the caller.

'I don't think so, Doris,' said the man. 'The nearest I can get to that name is Maisie.'

'Well, it's a similar sound, she might be saying Maisie,' I said. I asked the woman to give me some more information to establish her identity.

'She's talking about the violent death of a young girl and man,' I went on in surprise.

'Yes, that's right. Maisie is the dead girl's mother,' said the man.

I knew I was on the right track then. 'She says it was to do with a property out in the country,' I continued. 'Who's Alan?'

'I am,' said the man.

'Well, Maisie says don't worry, it wasn't Arthur. Arthur wasn't there. D'you know what she means?'

'Yes, I do,' cried Alan in delight. 'Arthur's my son. His name is Arthur Alan Thomas.'

This meant nothing to me but a gasp went up in the studio. I discovered afterwards that Arthur had been convicted for this crime and although he was later pardoned his father wanted to clear his name beyond all doubt.

Suddenly I could smell a strong animal smell, either

sheep or pigs and I was in a room where there had been a terrific struggle. It seemed that I was lying on the floor by the sofa and a young girl was talking to me. She said her name was Jeanette.

'Does the name Jeanette mean anything to you?' I asked Alan.

'Yes,' he said. 'That's the murdered girl.'

Jeanette told me that two men were responsible and they weren't Europeans. One of them wore glasses and they drove a large vehicle, an estate car or a van. It was dark coloured and could have been green or navy blue. They wanted to be cut in on something, she explained and when her husband wouldn't agree to it they'd turned on them.

Then in my mind I was going up a narrow rocky path. 'I don't think a vehicle could get up here,' I said. 'It's not wide enough. I don't think even a wheelbarrow could do it but I think that's where they took Jeanette's body.'

Then Maisie came back. 'Tell Arthur we're sorry for all the trouble he's been through,' she said and the vibration faded and she was gone.

It was as if a spell had been broken in the studio. People started whispering and moving about. Alan on the phone was thrilled. His son had been completely exonerated as far as he was concerned. The broadcast also attracted the attention of the police, who apparently recognized much of what I'd said as correct.

I became involved in another murder case quite by chance during a radio show in Wellington. The city was nicknamed Windy Wellington, I was told, because there's always a breeze blowing, but as we drove to the station I thought Windy Wellington with a hard 'i' would be more appropriate because of the winding roads. We wound up and up through green lanes and rolling hills until we finally reached the radio station on the top.

I was supposed to be doing an ordinary interview but half way through Roger, the presenter, suddenly put his hand in his pocket and produce a photograph. 'Can you do anything with that, Doris?'

I looked at it and saw a pretty young girl with wide, clear eyes and shining hair framing her face.

'This girl's missing,' I said.

'That's right,' agreed Roger.

Once more a picture formed in my mind. I can see a road with trees lining one side of it and heavy traffic moving along. It must a main road of some kind,' I said out loud, my ears full of the roar of cars. 'There's a fork in the road, one road bearing to the left and the other going straight on ...'

Suddenly the picture changed. I was in it myself and I was the young girl. I had a canvas pack on my back and I was inside a vehicle which took the left-hand fork. Then I heard the girl's voice. She told me her name was Mona Blade.

'She says she was on her way home but she never got there,' I said. 'She's written to a girl named Susan.'

Then I was aware of a very deep ravine, damp and rich with vegetation. 'Her pack is down there,' I said, 'and she keeps saying something about a watch. Did you find her watch?'

'No,' said Roger, 'but they found a man's watch.'

Then I mentioned a name, and it turned out that this was the name engraved on the back of the watch.

The programme caused a great fuss in the papers and the police inspector working on the case flew to see me because apparently, out of two hundred and seventy-nine miles of motorway, I'd pinpointed the five miles where she was last seen.

Of all the exciting things that happened on our tour I think the most exciting was the Maori welcome I was given at Rotorua Airport. Ken, who was looking after us at this point, warned me about it beforehand and though I didn't know what it involved I was looking forward to it immensely. It was a great honour, Ken explained, normally reserved only for Prime Ministers and royalty and I was thrilled that they were going to all this trouble for me.

The morning arrived, dull and grey but exciting nevertheless. I sat in our hotel room in Auckland waiting for the car that was taking us to the airport. Our bags were packed, I'd swallowed the tiny amount of breakfast that my nervous stomach would allow and we were ready to leave. The phone rang. John leapt to answer it.

'Car's here,' he cried, dropping the receiver.

There was instant bustle. I grabbed my handbag, jumped to my feet and gasped. The floor swung away from under me and the room spun round. Blindly I groped for something to hang on to and suddenly John was at my side.

'What's the matter? What is it? Here, come on, sit down,' and he guided me back into the chair.

'Oh, no,' I moaned as John fetched a glass of water. It had happened again, the same thing that had happened in Brisbane. Well, I couldn't possibly be ill, not today, not when the Maoris were waiting. Pull yourself together, Doris, I told myself firmly, but my legs were like soft butter and I couldn't stand. I drank the water, crying with frustration.

'Father, Ramanov, *please*,' I begged silently. '*Please* give me the strength to go.'

'You must rest, child,' said Ramanov's voice.

'I know, I know,' I explained, 'but after the Maori welcome. I promise I'll rest then.'

It seemed to me that this internal struggle went on for several minutes. Then the presence of Ramanov and my father receded and my head cleared.

'We should be able to reach them on the phone ...,' someone was saying ... 'not too late ... call it off ...'

'No!' I cried suddenly. 'Don't call it off. I'm going.'

'But, Doris, you can't,' said John.

'Yes I can,' I insisted. 'If you could just help me down to the car, I can make it.'

'You must see a doctor, love.'

'When we get there, I promise,' I said. 'Look, I'm much better now.'

He wasn't happy about it but he agreed. I was half carried to the car and then practically hoisted on to the plane. Despite my protests I really did feel terribly drained and ill and I collapsed gratefully in the big plane seat. I hardly moved a muscle throughout the journey I was so tired.

It seemed as if I'd only just closed my eyes when the plane touched down again and we were in Rotorua. An air hostess appeared at my side.

'Mrs Stokes, would you like to get off first, please?'

How sweet of her, I thought, she must be able to see I'm not well. But when I got to the door, I realized that this was all part of the plan. Below me, great shining puddles covered the windswept tarmac, misty grey clouds almost touched the ground and there in front of the plane, shivering in his bare feet and grass skirt was a Maori warrior.

'Hello, Doris,' called one of the ground crew as I walked shakily down the steps. 'Real English weather this. Bet it reminds you of home!'

It did too, and so did the icy cold air. I smiled at the half-naked warrior. Poor man, he must be frozen. He obviously took my smile as the signal that I was ready because at that moment he walked towards me and placed a small chamois leather bag on the ground not far from my feet.

Ken came up behind me. 'Don't touch it yet, Doris,' he whispered. 'I'll tell you when,' and to my astonishment, the warrior started doing a war dance. He leapt about, his long black hair bouncing, his feet nimble on the cold tarmac. He threatened me with his spear, he turned his back on me, then he turned round again, stuck his tongue out as far as it would go and began pulling faces. All the while the rest of the tribe in garlands, grass skirts, bare feet and goose pimples, waited by the terminal building.

The chief performed another energetic dance and then Ken whispered, 'You can pick up your gift now.'

'I daren't!' I whispered back in anguish. 'My head's so dizzy I daren't bend down.'

So Ken bent down, picked it up and put the little bag into my hands. As he did so the whole tribe started weaving palm leaves and shouting what sounded like 'Teeckla!': Welcome.

Ken told me the word I should shout back, which I did and then he said I must go and rub noses twice with each one of them. 'They have welcomed you into their tribe and you have to acknowledge you belong to them.'

So, giggling happily, I went down the line by the terminal door, carefully rubbing noses with each Maori! I wonder if the Queen does this? I thought. It was certainly one of the most extraordinary experiences of my life.

The welcome over, I was whisked away to the hotel where the doctor was waiting. He gave me a thorough examination.

'Well, Mrs Stokes,' he said when he'd finished, 'there's nothing I can do. You are exhausted. You've got to rest, that's all there is to it.'

'Yes, doctor, I will,' I assured him, silently adding – but there won't be much chance today. A press conference had been arranged, I was informed, as we were driving away from the airport and at this very moment the reporters were assembled in the hotel waiting for my appearance. Then later that evening we were to go to an honorary supper laid on by Rotorua Church. After that I'd rest, I promised myself.

To save time at the doctor's, I'd slipped down the shoulder straps of my underskirt instead of undressing completely and after the examination I hastily pulled my dress on again and rushed out to meet the reporters. Half way across the hotel I was suddenly aware that I felt extremely uncomfortable. Something was tight and twisted across my middle and something else was flapping round my legs. I looked down and to my horror saw that my underskirt was hanging out about five inches below my dress. Goodness, what's happened? I wondered. Has something snapped? Then it dawned. In my haste to get away from the doctor, I'd only pulled up one shoulder strap. To sort it out would mean going back to my room, or finding a ladies' room and getting undressed and then dressed all over again.

Oh well, I thought, it's no good worrying now, I'll just have to get on with it. They can think what they like. And so in I went, my underskirt flapping like a flag.

They couldn't fail to notice, of course, but the reporters were far too polite to say anything and the conference went very smoothly. They certainly couldn't accuse me of putting on airs and graces!

During the conference I couldn't help noticing a Maori
vicar enter the room. He didn't look like a journalist to me
and I wondered what he wanted. In the end I decided he
must simply be curious because he just stood at the back
listening quietly and saying nothing. Then to my surprise,
when it was over, he came and joined me on the sofa and
took hold of my hand.

'Don't you recognize him, Doris?' asked Ken.

'Well, no, I'm afraid I don't,' I admitted a little
embarrassed. How could I forget a Maori vicar, for
goodness sake? 'Have we met before?'

'He's the warrior who welcomed you at the airport!'
chuckled Ken.

'Good heavens!' I exclaimed staring into the beaming
face, and when I looked carefully I saw that indeed it was
the same man.

I had tea with the vicar and then John led me away for a
rest in our room before our special supper.

'I don't think you should go,' John was muttering as I
slipped into bed.

'Oh, John,' I said. 'It's too late to cancel it now. They'll
have got everything ready. I'll be fine when I've had a
sleep.'

It was true. I did feel quite a lot better for my rest and
when we arrived at the little hall I was so glad we'd made
the effort. Never in my life have I seen such a spread!
There was smoked marlin, oysters, trout, sea food, meats
and salads of every possible description. They must have
spent days preparing the meal.

There were about a hundred people present, many of
them children, and they all made a tremendous fuss of me.
The children climbed all over me, the adults tried to tempt
me with the very best delicacies from the table and half
way through the evening John and I were made honorary
members of the church and presented with a diploma
which now stands in our hall at home.

At one point a lady came over shyly and touched my
arm. 'Doris, my husband doesn't normally hold with this
sort of thing but he's seen you on television and read your
book and he's made you these.' She put a little case into my

hands and when I lifted the lid I found a beautiful brooch with matching ring that this man had made himself.

Before I could find words to thank her, someone else tapped me on the shoulder. 'Look, Doris! Look what they've written on the windows.'

I glanced up and there in the steam on the glass, the children had finger-traced the words, 'We love Granny Doris. Come back soon.' I was absolutely overwhelmed. The party went on around me, the people pressed close but I could hardly see them through my tears. What had I done to deserve so much, I wondered, as I groped for a handkerchief and it was several minutes before I dared speak.

We had to leave quite early since I was still under doctor's orders to rest, but I took away with me memories that I shall treasure forever.

There were still several moving moments to come. The next day I was to give a demonstration at Rotorua Theatre. I walked in and the atmosphere nearly knocked me over it was so powerful. There were eight or nine hundred people present and they had been singing hymns while they waited, which built up the atmosphere marvellously. Then, to my surprise, before I started working, two young girls climbed on to the stage and did a belly dance. The Maori drums were beating and the atmosphere charged and charged until I thought the place would explode. It might not be orthodox, but what did that matter? Living and laughing and loving were surely all that counted. It didn't matter how ill I felt, I knew I couldn't go wrong with a power like this all round me.

There was a short break in the middle of my demonstration and when I started again a man stood up with a bible in his hand and started heckling me.

'Where does God come into all this? That's what I want to know,' he shouted.

This kind of interruption doesn't worry me too much because I know mediums have to expect and be able to answer criticism.

'I always start with a prayer and dedicate my work to God,' I explained. 'I couldn't do my job without God's help.'

'It says in the bible you shouldn't dabble with spirits,' he insisted.

'And it also says in the bible you must test the spirits to see if they are good,' I said, 'and I do.'

The argument went on and even the president's wife joined in to try to explain our point of view. The man wouldn't listen. He was intent on disrupting the meeting, and it was quite clear he didn't genuinely want to know the rights and wrongs of our ideas at all.

This thought must have struck the audience at the same time it struck me because just then, in the middle of another tirade, someone started to boo him. Immediately the jeer was picked up and within seconds nine hundred people had turned on him, booing at the top of their voices. 'We came here to listen to Doris!' someone yelled. 'Let her speak.'

It must have been frightening to be on the wrong side of that crowd and the man hastily sat down, rather wisely I thought, and didn't open his mouth again.

The demonstration continued with the evidence pouring through and when it was over the audience spontaneously jumped to its feet clapping. Someone started singing *Now is the hour for us to say goodbye* and nine hundred voices joined in. The children rushed forward and put their arms round my waist, the words of the song soared until the roof must almost have cracked and a tremendous wave of warmth and love from this great mass of people engulfed me. I just stood there with tears pouring down my face, unable to say a word.

It was very difficult to leave and when I finally did reach the airport, there they were again, lined up on the tarmac with a bouquet of flowers and singing *We'll Meet Again!*

After New Zealand we flew to Tasmania and by this time my impressions were getting very hazy indeed. I had done so much travelling, spoken to so many people, made so many communications, stayed in so many hotel rooms and re-packed our cases so many times that every place was beginning to seem just like the last. Only a few memories stand out. In Tasmania I was struck again by the great beauty and freshness of the country and the way everything was so clean and welcoming.

I can't recall any of my work there except that I did a radio show with a young man called Mike Dodds. Mike was very tongue-in-cheek about the whole thing but after we'd recorded sittings with a few people he'd brought along to the studio, he seemed more impressed and even offered to play a record for me on his early morning breakfast show the next day.

'I'd like one of my favourites by Jim Reeves,' I said eagerly. '*May the Good Lord Bless and Keep You* because it says to everyone what I'd like to say and never have the time.'

'Right,' said Mike, 'I'll see if we've got that in our library.'

The next morning during the breakfast show we were already on the road, heading for the next town on our itinerary.

'Oh, could you put on the radio?' I asked the driver. 'There might be a record for me.'

Sure enough the record library had found my Jim Reeves favourite and I listened to it happily.

Then Mike came on again with great excitement in his voice. 'I've got something very exciting to tell you after the next commercial,' he promised enticingly.

'I wonder what's happened?' remarked John. We speculated over whether Princess Anne might have had another baby, or the Queen announced a visit to Tasmania and then Mike came back and to our surprise started to talk about the sitting I'd recorded the day before.

'The tape went down for processing and when it came back we found that there are other voices on it. Voices you can hear when there was absolute silence in the studio and only Doris and her sitter were speaking. Don't ask me how it happened. We've made exhaustive enquiries. Even if the tape had been used before, we have magnetic cleaning processes so that the tape is wiped completely clean. No old material could remain on it. We can find no explanation for these voices.'

Unfortunately Mike didn't tell us what the voices had said and our car soon moved out of the station's range, so we never did find out. I'd love to know.

My other striking memory of Tasmania is of our hotel

room in Hobart. Our hotel was a tall circular building with
thirty-six floors and we were given the penthouse suite on
the top. When they showed John and I to our room our
eyes nearly popped out of our heads. Decorated in red
and gold, there was a huge four-poster bed draped with
red curtains, pink velvet sofas, a well-stocked bar and
pictures of naked ladies on the wall.

It looked out over the sea and it was so high up the
tables and chairs in the sea-side garden looked like dolls'
furniture set on a postage stamp.

We nicknamed it the Sin Bin, and thought it was a
shame to waste it on an old married couple like us!

I did several shows which went off well, and then we
flew back to New Zealand where I did a few more. One I
recall was held in a basket-ball stadium and as the car drew
up outside I couldn't believe my eyes. The queue of people
stretched from the entrance right down the road and
round the corner. It was cold and pouring with rain but
they stood there patiently waiting to get in.

Not for the first time, my legs turned to jelly and my
stomach started fluttering. They'd all come to see me.
Everything depended on me – but what did they want?
What did they expect me to do? If I was able to get
messages for twenty or thirty of them I'd be lucky and yet
there must be thousands expecting something.

The show was supposed to start at eight but I didn't get
on until quarter to nine because they had to put extra seats
in to accommodate the crowd and even then three
hundred were turned away. When I finally walked a little
timidly out into that great arena, such a roar went up that I
nearly turned tail and fled.

I'm told the demonstration went well, though my dizzy
head came on again and I had to be helped off at the end,
the cheering of the crowd ringing in my ears. Backstage
the stadium staff presented me with a bouquet of flowers.

'How sweet of you,' I said feeling overwhelmed all over
again.

'Well, we want to thank you, Doris,' said the manager.
'We've never had the stadium as full as this.'

My last memory of New Zealand is of waiting at the

airport in Auckland for the Australia-bound plane. A young man called Wayne Stevens was looking after us and for some reason I turned to him and asked, 'Have you got a present for your girlfriend, Wayne?'

He looked horrified. 'No! Thank goodness you reminded me, Doris. I'll pop back to the duty free shop. Won't be a minute.'

I dropped into a big, squashy chair in the lounge. Whenever I stopped moving I felt exhausted. Quite honestly I wished I was flying back to Britain and not Australia just then. Not that my love of Australia had diminished, it was simply that I wanted to get back to a permanent bed and a stable routine again after weeks of living like a gipsy.

The minutes ticked by and I glanced round wondering where Wayne had got to. It was then that I noticed the policeman enter the lounge, dressed in a similar uniform to our bobies at home, but with a white helmet in place of our traditional blue. He wandered between the seats staring into faces as if he was looking for someone and eventually he reached me.

'Doris Stokes?' he demanded.

I stared up at six feet of sombre blue and my heart turned over. I thought we were going to be arrested. What had we done? Was some document not in order?

I heard a commotion behind me and turned to see Wayne Stevens dashing across from the duty free shop crying, 'What's the matter? What's the matter?'

The policeman ignored him. Taking off his helmet he knelt down by my side.

'I just want to say thank you, Doris, for coming to New Zealand. I was at your show last night and I thought it was marvellous.' And while I was still speechless with shock, he leant down, kissed me on the cheek, stood up, replaced his helmet and strode quickly away.

'What was that all about? What did you do?' asked Wayne reaching us breathlessly.

But I didn't answer. A pink blush was spreading warmly over my cheeks and I could feel my face breaking into a silly grin.

'Well!' was all I could say.

The excitement still wasn't over. When I arrived in Australia I walked right back into controversy. I was still under doctor's orders to rest because on top of my other problem, which was eventually diagnosed as a slight stroke, I managed to catch a particularly nasty form of gastric 'flu which also felled the All Blacks rugby team.

One morning I was having a late breakfast. I had no plans for the day ahead, and decided I would spend my time flopping about and sleeping. I thought it would be nice to listen to Bert Newton on the radio while I had my breakfast, so I switched it on. I was very glad I did.

Soon I was listening to Bert's guest of the day, a Mr James Randi, a magician whose mission, he said, was to expose fakes like Uri Geller and Doris Stokes. He could duplicate Geller's spoon bending by normal magic tricks, he claimed, and as for me, I was taking the Australian people for a ride. He had seen me in London and I was no good then and I was no good now.

I crashed my cup back on its saucer in anger. Randi? James Randi? I was particularly certain that no one of that name had ever been to me for a sitting in London. I don't remember every sitter, of course, but his voice wasn't remotely familiar. Well, he wasn't going to get away with that!

Furiously I pushed back my chair.

'What are you doing now?' asked John looking at my red face.

'I'm not putting up with this, John – it's not true what he's saying!' I strode to the phone and angrily dialling the radio station I got through to Peter, the producer of Bert's show.

'Peter, it's Doris Stokes here. I've just been listening to Mr Randi and I want to answer him. Will you put me on the air?'

Peter put me on the air.

'Now, Mr Randi,' I said. 'I might not be there in body but I'm there in spirit. You can say to me what you have to say.'

It must have been quite a shock for him but he

recovered quickly. 'Yes, all right,' he said. 'You're conning the people of Australia.'

I struggled to keep my temper. 'You are saying the Australian people are fools, then?'

'No, I didn't say that,' he replied.

'By implication you did,' I insisted, 'because I was here in 1978 and I am back again now, so if I'm conning the people they must be a pack of fools to be taken in twice.'

He huffed and puffed at this and muttered that that wasn't the point in any case.

'Look, there's a quick way out of this, Mr Randi,' I said. 'You say I'm a fake. Well, if I'm a fake it's possible to duplicate what I do. Now, I'm doing a public meeting on Thursday evening at Dallasbrook Hall so I challenge you to come on stage with me and I'll do my thing with the audience – faking, you call it – and then you fake it in the same way and we'll let the audience make up their own minds.'

'Oh no, I have more important things to do,' replied Mr Randi, rather lamely, I thought, but then I'm biased!

'But you said you wanted to expose fakes!' I pointed out. 'Surely there's nothing more important than that? And by the way, when did you say you saw me in London?'

There was a slight pause. 'January,' he said guardedly.

'January this year?' I queried sweetly.

'That's right,' he said.

I must confess to an unworthy feeling of delight. That was the month I had my hysterectomy operation and the only people I gave sittings to, and even then right at the end of January, were a couple of journalists who couldn't see me at any other time.

'Well, it must have been my spirit body you saw then, son,' I said, 'because I was in hospital having a major operation and I've got documents to prove it.'

Mr Randi struggled on valiantly but I think he knew he was beaten.

'Look,' I said more kindly, 'I believe you're a very good magician, I've never seen you perform but I wouldn't dream of coming on to your show and trying to dissect what you're doing because I don't know anything about it.

So what gives you the right to try to dissect what I'm doing when *you* know nothing about it?'

'Oh dear, is that the time?' said Mr Randi. 'I'd love to go on but I've got another appointment and my taxi's ticking away outside.'

And he left abruptly.

That was the last I'd hear of Mr Randi, I thought, but I was wrong. A few days later I stepped off a plane in Brisbane to find television cameras waiting and a knot of reporters who rushed forward the moment I walked through the barrier.

'What do you think about your friend Don Lane?' they asked.

'Why? What's the matter with Don?' I asked in alarm. I hadn't picked up any message that he was ill or had had an accident, but I'd been so tired lately I might have missed it.

'He marched off the set last night,' they said. 'He swore at Mr Randi, swept all his props on to the floor and stormed off. Now he's in trouble with the IBA.'

I was horrified. I had a nasty feeling this was something to do with me.

'Well, I'm very sorry if Don's in trouble,' I said. 'But Don's straight. He must have had a reason for doing it. This man must have said something he couldn't accept. And talking of Mr Randi, let me issue my challenge again. Mr Randi, wherever you are – I'm appearing at such and such a place – come along. Show me up, and if the Australian people boo me off the stage when you've done it I promise I'll go home and never set foot in Australia again!'

This seemed to satisfy the reporters and when we got to our hotel I discovered the airport interview was shown on the six-thirty news and the place was buzzing with the Don Lane Scandal.

Apparently James Randi had appeared on the show and upset Don by implying, or so Don thought, that I was a liar. Don had issued a four-letter word and stormed off. It was the four-letter word which angered the IBA more than the storming off.

I was terribly worried. Suppose poor Don got the sack.

It was largely my fault. If I hadn't retaliated so angrily when Mr Randi spoke on the radio, perhaps he would have been forgotten. Maybe I should have kept quiet and let people believe what they wanted to believe.

I was still turning this over in my mind when Don rang. He had heard I was worried and wanted to set my mind at rest.

'What's up, kid?' he asked cheerfully when I came to the phone.

'Oh, Don, I've been so worried,' I said. 'What with this Mr Randi and the IBA. They said you were in terrible trouble.'

'Now, look, don't you worry about me. I can take care of myself,' he said kindly. 'I've been on the air and apologized to the viewers for that word I used but no way will I apologize to that man unless he can bring me documents or proof that the things he says about people are true.'

'But what about the IBA?'

'I've squared it with them now. They're satisfied with the apology for the four-letter word.'

'Oh, thank goodness for that,' I said in relief and made a mental note to take it as a lesson not to be so hasty in future.

I suppose I did get a lot of mileage out of the James Randi episode, however. He never did take up my challenge to share the stage with me at a public meeting but after that, whenever I appeared anywhere I always started by saying, 'Hello everybody. Where's Mr Randi, then?' and everyone would fall about laughing. At one place a man shouted back, 'If he turns up here we'll lynch him.' So perhaps it was just as well he stayed away.

At last in mid-August the tour ended and it was time to go home. I was sorry to be saying goodbye to so many friends and to a country that has always felt like home to me, but at the same time I was relieved to be able to step off the merry-go-round for a while.

My last memory of the tour is of leaving Perth and being invited up to the flight deck to meet the captain.

'It's all right,' the captain was saying as I squeezed into the glass-ringed cockpit with what looked like great banks of computers on every side. 'Doris is on board, so I know we'll get there!'

He turned and grinned at me. 'Well, it's a bit of a cheek coming on to my aircraft with a Qantas badge on your lapel!'

I looked down at my collar and blushed. During the outward flight with Qantas they'd presented me with a little gold kangaroo badge and the New Zealand Airways had given me a silver kiwi. I'd forgotten to remove them from my coat.

'Well I haven't got anything from British Airways,' I pointed out reasonably.

So he duly presented me with a set of wings, and I finally stepped on to British soil, wearing my British Airways badge!

Chapter 11

'Hello, Mrs Finch – do come in and sit down.'

So this was Mrs Finch. I had spoken to her on the phone, autographed a book for her, but until now I'd never met her. She walked into the flat, a slender, striking woman with delicate bone structure and sleek fair hair brushed back from her face. She perched elegantly on the edge of one of our high-backed armchairs and crossed her long, slim legs.

'Please call me Yolande,' she said.

She looks like a film star, I thought, taking in the expensive well-cut clothes, the good jewellery and the graceful way she moved. Yet I didn't recognize her from any film I'd ever seen and her low voice with its trace of a South African accent wasn't familiar.

Even then I didn't connect her with Peter Finch, the world famous actor who passed over a few years ago – after all Finch is a common name. It wasn't until one of the most vivid sittings I've ever done, including some of the saltiest language I've come across, was under way, that I realized whom I was talking to.

It was October by now, nearly two months since I'd returned from Australia and once again I was supposed to be resting. I was so tired I'd fallen victim to just about every cold and bug around and apart from attending a wonderful welcome home party thrown for me by Wimbledon Church, I'd done very little.

It was strange how Yolande Finch came to have a sitting with me. On the way back from a radio interview about her new book, *Finchy*, on the subject of life with her ex-husband, she discovered that Eddie, the driver of her car, had also driven me a few times. Eddie was listening to a psychic programme on the radio and Yolande thought it was rubbish.

'Switch that off. It's a load of old nonsense,' she said.

Eddie obligingly turned it off but disagreed that the subject was nonsense and proceeded to tell Yolande about me and how I'd once given him an impromptu sitting as we were driving along the road.

'She's written a book an' all,' Eddie added. 'I'll get you a copy. Then you can see for yourself.'

Yolande thought no more about it and the first I heard of it was when Eddie drove me to Covent Garden for some function and asked if I would autograph a copy of *Voices* for him. 'Yes, of course, Eddie. Who's it for?' I asked as I knew he'd already read it.

'Mrs Finch,' he replied. So I quickly scribbled, 'For Mrs Finch, God bless, Mrs Doris Stokes', thinking no more about it than if I'd written for Mrs Smith or Mrs Brown.

Both Yolande and her daughter Samantha read the book and in the end Samantha, anxious to know more about her father, begged her mother to contact me. I was still supposed to be resting, of course, but there was something about this Mrs Finch's voice that made me disregard the doctor's orders. Normally I only did this for women who'd lost children, but something made me say yes to Mrs Finch. It was as if it had cost her a lot to bring herself to phone me and I felt it would be wrojng to dash her hopes now.

I tuned in and immediately a strong male voice was there. He said his name was Peter. 'I passed with a coronary,' he said. His manner was forceful, even arrogant and there was something familiar about his voice. The next second it clicked: this must be *the* Peter Finch. The film star.

'It was a terrible mistake to let you divorce me,' he told Yolande. 'You were the one who wanted the divorce, not me. We should have worked things out. It would have been my salvation.'

'In what way? Why would it have been your salvation?' I asked.

'I used to get very worried and frightened,' said Peter. 'I

was at the top but there was always the fear of slipping. Drink was the only way I could cope, so I turned to the bottle. I didn't realize what it was doing to me. I used to get drunk because I was frightened. I used to live for the drinks cabinet, but I was too young to die. I was only sixty-two.'

At that, another voice chimed in. 'You're lucky. I was only *fifty*-two.'

'Who's that?' I asked. This sitting was beginning to get out of hand.

'Thomas,' replied the man crisply.

'That's my father,' said Yolande in surprise.

'I passed with a coronary just as Peter did,' Thomas explained and would have said more but I got the impression that Peter was elbowing him out of the way.

'I married again after Yolande,' he said, 'and there was another child. Diane.'

Yolande agreed that this was true.

Then a woman's voice pushed in and gave me five names one after the other: 'Sophia, Antonia, Francis, Gertrude and Rose,' she announced, triumphant at having made herself heard above the men.

I was beginning to feel as if my head was a football they were kicking around between them. 'One at a time, please. I can only talk to one of you at a time.' Wearily I repeated the names but Yolande shook her head.

'No, I'm sorry they mean nothing to me.'

'She doesn't know what you mean, dear,' I told the woman.

'Yes she does,' she insisted and repeated the names again. 'And Girly tells me to tell you she gave you her pin.'

Yolande looked completely mystified by this piece of information and I could tell by the look on her face that she was wondering whether I was some kind of crank.

My spirit contact was still quite confident that she was talking to the right person, however. I must be the one that's wrong then, I thought. Have I got the message right, dear? I asked silently. Girly gave Yolande her pin?'

'I didn't say *pin*,' scoffed the woman in a strong South African accent. 'I said *pen*.'

'I'm sorry, Yolande, I got that wrong,' I said. 'It should have been pen, not pin.'

At once a great smile lightened Yolande's face. 'Oh, of course! It's my Great-Aunt Girly. Her name is Gertrude, Doris, but everyone called her Girly. She gave me her pen the day before she died. She was ninety-seven and she only went three months ago.'

Yolande could hardly sit still for excitement now. Leaning forward, eyes blazing, she suddenly recalled that Sophia, Antonia, Francis and Rose were Girly's dead sisters. In fact, Rose was her grandmother.

Then Peter's voice came back, still obviously on the subject of Yolande.

'She was my lover, mistress, wife and friend,' he said. Then he added with a laugh in his voice, 'She used to nag me though.'

'I only nagged you for your own good,' Yolande retorted, stung.

That did it.

'Well, I didn't ask for the bloody divorce, did I!' Peter snapped back and before I realized it we were in the middle of a flaming row. They both seemed to forget I was there and started shouting at each other. At one point Peter's language got so strong I had to ask him to modify it.

'You tell me exactly what he's saying,' cried Yolande angrily.

Peter mentioned his daughter by the nickname that only he used, Sam, and he also talked of his son, Charles.

'Well, why didn't you provide for them if you were so fond of them?' snapped Yolande.

'I did,' Peter protested. 'I made special provision for them in my will – but you know what I'm like with paper work. I didn't realize that by remarrying it was automatically annulled.'

Yolande sighed. 'I know, I know.'

'Accountant, accountant, get an accountant,' Peter went on.

This amazed Yolande because during his life on earth Peter wouldn't hear of accountants. Then she remembered that in order to come to see me she had cancelled an appointment with her accountant.

Things calmed down after that, I was relieved to find, and the sitting ended with Peter expressing his love for his family and his regret that they hadn't managed to work things out in their marriage.

'D'you know, Doris,' said Yolande just before she left, 'while I was writing my book I had the strangest feeling that Finchy was there by my elbow. I thought it was just my imagination at the time but now I'm not so sure. What do you think?'

'I think he was there, Yo,' I told her positively. 'I'm sure he was.'

This wasn't the first time I'd talked to a famous person without realizing who they were. Some years before a young man had telephoned to ask if I could help him. He and a young colleague were writing a book and wanted to contact a pop star called Buddy Holly. I'm ashamed to say that I hadn't heard of this particular singer, but I explained, as I always do, that you can't just nominate whom you'd like to speak to. A lot of people would love to have a chat with Sir Winston Churchill or President Kennedy or Elvis Presley, but they won't come back to a complete stranger. Why should they?

The young man said he understood this but as he thought he had a slight connection with the singer, he'd still like me to have a go.

'All right, son,' I agreed. 'But I can't promise anything.'

Anyway, the sitting started and as I'd feared this Buddy Holly didn't come. Instead I found myself talking to a young man named Charles Hardy something – I couldn't catch the last part of his name. He told me his wife's name and explained that he'd been killed in a plane crash. He also named the people who had been with him in the plane. I asked him what he looked like and in reply I felt him put a huge pair of spectacles on my face.

'He wore glasses,' I explained to the two young men, 'and they were very important to his appearance. He feels that you'll recognize him by the glasses. They were very large.'

Finally William said, 'Paul is buying my music.'

'Paul who?' I asked.

'Paul Mac ...' The end of the name was so fuzzy I couldn't make it out.

'Sorry, love, I didn't catch that,' I apologized.

William tried again but it was no use. I couldn't get it. 'He will be on the television,' William promised at last, 'and then you will know who I'm talking about.'

It was the end of the sitting and I was rather dissatisfied.

'I'm sorry I didn't get the person you wanted,' I apologized to the boys. 'I did warn you.'

'But you did,' they assured me. 'That was him; Charles Hardy, that was Buddy Holly!'

And two days later I was watching the news when a picture of Paul McCartney flashed on to the screen with the announcement that he was hoping to buy some of Holly's music.

My sittings continued erratically throughout the winter, because there were some people I just couldn't turn away no matter what the doctor said.

I remember one couple, Stan and Jackie Ross – how could I tell them I was too tired when they didn't know which way to turn because they had lost their beloved son, Daniel?

During the sitting, little Daniel wanted to tell me about his funeral and he kept drawing something in the air. At first I thought it was an engine, but it had a handle and it was made of flowers. I was absolutely stumped.

'I'm sorry,' I apologized. 'He's showing me this shape,' and I traced it in the air, the way Daniel had done, 'and he says it's made of flowers. I can't think what it can be.'

Then his parents suddenly clapped their hands in joy. 'It's a lawnmower, Doris,' they cried.

Apparently Daniel used to love to mow the lawn and so they had had a wreath made up in the shape of a lawnmower as the centre piece of his funeral flowers.

They were very nice people indeed. A few days later they sent me a photograph of Daniel, to put with my other spirit children, accompanied by a letter and two beautiful bunches of roses – one for me and one for the spirit children because they had noticed the flower beside each

photograph. I'm sure the children knew, because I
explained it to them as I put the fresh flowers beside each
picture.

'Aren't these roses lovely, Daniel?' I explained, placing
his in water first because they were from his parents.
'They're from your mummy and daddy for you, and all
the other children you've met on the other side.' And he
seemed to smile back at me from his photograph, as if he
was very pleased with them.

It is heartrending to lose a child and of all the ways a
child can go, suicide is the hardest for the parents to take.
They torment themselves with guilt and grief and in many
cases they never get over the cruel blow. Their lives are
ruined forever. So when, shortly after the Ross' sitting, I
received a desperate letter from a couple whose
fifteen-year-old daughter had apparently committed
suicide, I knew I would have to see them at once.

They arrived one afternoon, a small pretty woman with
clouds of soft dark hair and a haunted, silent man with
deep blue eyes. Apprehension and scepticism rose from
him like steam from a wet coat, and I knew I would have to
treat him carefully.

'Would you like a drink?' I asked, thinking it might help
them to relax.

'No, thank you,' said the man stiffly. 'We stopped at a
cafe on the way.'

They lapsed into silence again. It was clear I couldn't
ease them into the sitting. I'd just have to begin at once. I
tuned in and straight away a young, girlish voice was
chatting excitedly.

'I'm Linda,' she told me, 'and that's my mummy and
daddy.'

'Can you give me their names, Linda?' I asked.

'My daddy's name is Ray,' she said and there was a long
pause. 'Mummy's name begins with three letters,' she said
at last, a little reluctantly. 'It's a Pa sound.'

'Is it Pam?' I asked going along with the little game.

'No,' said Linda.

'Then if it isn't Pam, it must be Pat,' I guessed.

'That's it, that's right,' Linda laughed. 'It's Pat.'

I asked how old she was when she passed. 'Fifteen and a half,' she told me and as she came closer I felt she had long dark hair swinging round her shoulders and she was a pretty girl, very like her mother.

At the mention of her passing, Linda's voice changed and became upset.

'Can you ever forgive me? Can you ever forgive me?' she cried miserably.

'Will you ever forgive us?' asked Ray, his voice breaking.

'What happened, Linda,' I asked gently.

'There was a boy,' she sniffed. 'He was older than me.'

'Was there something you were afraid of? Did you think you were pregnant?' I probed gently.

She got very annoyed at that suggestion. 'Indeed I wasn't pregnant,' she said indignantly.

'Well, what happened, then?' I persisted, and gradually the whole sad story came out. She was involved with a boy of nineteen and her parents disapproved. They weren't very keen on the boy and they thought he was too old for her. They pressured Linda to give him up. He was possessive and pressured her to stay with him and at fifteen it was too much for her to cope with. As well as this she was jealous of her younger brother, Martin. Martin suffered from asthma and needed a lot of attention. In her depressed state, Linda thought her brother received all her parents' love and she received none.

'I was all mixed up,' she said to her parents. 'You were so busy with your own lives I wanted to scare you. You hurt me so much over the boy, I wanted to hurt you back and I wanted everything to be all right again as well, so I took Mummy's pills.

'What a fool I was. I realize now that you loved me after all. Oh, please forgive me.'

She went on to mention that July and October were two important anniversaries. In July Linda had died and as for October:

'Happy birthday, Daddy,' she said.

'There'll be no more birthdays, now,' said Ray bitterly.

At his words Linda burst into tears.

'Tell him he must go forward, Doris,' she begged. 'And

he mustn't blame Mum as he has done.'

Reluctantly, with tears in her eyes, Ray and Pat admitted that they hadn't been speaking. Ray blamed Pat for leaving her pills lying around and pressuring Linda, and Pat blamed Ray for going on at Linda so often. They promised to try to be more understanding with each other.

'I'm so glad,' said Linda more happily. 'It feels as if a great weight has been lifted from me.'

She went on to talk about Dr Harrison and added that John had been with him. Ray and Pat looked at each other blankly.

'Dr Harrison?' said Pat. 'I don't think she knew a Dr Harrison. That's not our GP's name.'

But they discovered later that Dr Harrison was the pathologist who was called in to perform the autopsy on Linda's body and the mortician who assisted him was called John. Apparently Pat had kept going to the mortuary and begging the mortician to be gentle with her daughter's body. It reduced him to tears.

'I'm glad the inquest wasn't what Mummy was worried about,' Linda said and Pat took this to mean that the verdict of the inquest turned out to be accidental death and not suicide as they'd feared.

'I was afraid people would think I'd committed suicide,' Linda went on. 'Well, I didn't. When I went into the bathroom and took the pills I wanted to make myself ill to hurt Mummy and Daddy, that's all. But by the time they reached me it was too late.'

Linda went on to give much more evidence. She named Beaty and Cathy, two girls she had worked with on her Saturday job. She said her mother had started wearing her blue nightdress which used to belong to her and she also described the blue cardigan her mother wore.

At the end of the sitting Ray and Pat were very quiet, almost dazed. They went away thoughtfully and, feeling rather drained, I went to the kitchen to start the dinner. I was peeling onions when suddenly the doorbell rang. I glanced up at the clock. It was four-thirty. Who could it be at this time of day? Terry wasn't due home from work for a couple of hours yet.

Then I heard Linda's voice again. 'It's flowers from Daddy!' she whispered.

Drying my hands on my apron I hurried to the door, but Ray had already gone. There on the doorstep were eighteen long-stemmed carnations and on the card that accompanied them Ray had written, 'Dear Doris, thank you for the hope and strength you have given us.'

Chapter 12

Since my last book came out, I've received many readers' letters saying how much they enjoyed the philosophy I talked of and expressing an interest to know more. Well I'm not an intellectual and there are many good books available that explain philosophy far better than I could ever hope to. All I can do is talk of the things that have happened in my life and the lessons that Ramanov has taught me.

Sometimes, when I've been agonizing over some difficult philosophical point Ramanov has interrupted with: 'Look, it doesn't matter how much you philosophize and how many hymns you sing, when you come over here what is inside you will show on the outside. It's what you do and what you are that counts.'

So I try to live my life the way Ramanov and my relatives on the other side would like me to because I don't want them to be ashamed of me when I get there, and I leave the finer points of philosophy to the experts.

If I'm in any doubt as to how I should behave, I think of a story that Estell Roberts, a very famous medium before she passed over, used to tell. It came, she said, from her guide, Red Cloud, and I've never forgotten it. It goes like this:

Once there was a lady who owned a big mansion with the most wonderful gardens. So beautiful were these gardens that people used to come from miles around to look at them. Yet she only had one gardener, a man called Joe, but he so loved this garden that he worked on it from dawn till dusk.

Joe lived in a broken-down cottage on the edge of the estate but he never complained or demanded anything else and he was nearer to God than anyone.

Eventually the time came when Joe had to take his transition and afterwards, no matter how many experts and landscape gardeners the lady employed, the gardens never looked the same again because they weren't tended with love as Joe had tended them.

The time came for the lady to go over. When the guide took her there, she was amazed to find her mansion and gardens, just as beautiful as they had been when Joe had tended them. The estate was just the same, right down to the broken-down cottage where Joe used to live.

'How marvellous!' said the lady in delight. 'It's just like it was on the earth plane.'

And the guide said, 'I'm afraid not. Joe lives in the mansion now because he has earned the right to be there. It is your turn to live in the cottage and when you learn to give in love and self sacrifice, as Joe did, then maybe one day you will earn the right to get your mansion back.'

It's not easy to live like that, of course. I do my best but I'm only human and I fail more often than I succeed: I get bad tempered, I complain, and I forget how very lucky I am. But the funny thing is, the lessons are all around us if only we'd recognize them for what they are.

I was reminded of this very forcibly one day when I was convalescing after my mastectomy operation. I wanted to go home but the doctor, knowing what I was like, thought I'd have a better chance of resting if I spent a few days in a convalescent home. I wasn't at all happy about this, and one morning I'd got up to find it was pouring with rain, our breakfast wasn't ready and my plan to go to the hairdressers would have to be cancelled because a new hairdo would be ruined if I went out in such weather.

I stood in the queue outside the dining-room glowering at the window. The beautiful scenery had disappeared under porridgy cloud; sheets of rain were slapping against the glass and bouncing off the path and great brown puddles were appearing on the sodden lawn. The damp weather made my chest ache more than ever and depression heavier than the cloud outside sank over me.

No one was in more pain than I was, I decided; no one

was as miserable as I was. I wanted to go home and I didn't
care if I had to leave in a dustcart; I wasn't staying in this
gloomy place a day longer.

'Doris Stokes? It is Doris Stokes, isn't it?' asked a timid
voice behind me. I scowled at the dissolving garden and
didn't turn round. The last thing I felt like was getting
involved in small talk. Couldn't she see I was ill?

'Yes, it is,' I said ungraciously.

'I thought it was. Is it raining very hard?'

'Absolutely bucketing down,' I snapped bitterly, hoping
to discourage further conversation – particularly conversation of this painfully obvious kind. You only had to
glance out of the window to see how hard it was raining.

'Oh, what a shame for you,' the woman persisted.
'Aren't I lucky, I see only what I want to see, so for me it's a
lovely, bright day out there.'

At this extraordinary piece of logic I turned round and
to my shame I found I was looking at a bent old lady,
painfully holding herself upright on two sticks. There
were callipers on her legs and as she smiled vaguely
somewhere to the right of my shoulder, I realized that she
was completely blind.

Remorse shot through me like a physical pain. How
could I have been so unkind?

'But you're blind, dear,' I said gently.

'Oh, yes, but I used to have sight,' she explained
cheerfully 'and because of that I have lots of beautiful
memories. So, now, whatever the weather, I can look at
what I choose. I think that's very lucky, don't you?'

I stared at her and a lump came into my throat. 'Yes,
dear, I do,' I said humbly.

They say there is always someone worse off than
yourself and it's easy to be smug about such clichés. But
I've found that clichés are usually clichés because they are
true. There I was, feeling sorry for myself, and that poor,
blind, old lady shamed me into realizing that not only was
there someone worse off than myself but that she was
coping with her severe problems much better than I was
with my comparatively minor ones. I was also forced to
admit that once again I'd forgotten all Ramanov's

teachings about giving out love and friendship because I had been so selfishly wrapped up in my own exaggerated suffering.

I'd failed once again. On the other hand, Ramanov always tells me not to feel too bad about failure. As I explained in my last book, he once explained, 'Failure is not falling down. It's failing to get up when you've fallen down.' I took this to mean that it's how you use your failure that counts. If you learn by a mistake and consciously try not to make it again, then you are progressing and that's the most important thing.

Ramanov has always told me to trust and then everything will work out well. Again this is difficult for me to do, particularly as I'm a natural worrier – if I haven't got something to worry about, I'm worried! Yet time and time again he's helped me out of a difficult situation.

When we were still living in Lancaster we had a desperate phone call from Tony Scott, a comedian friend. He was in a terrible state.

'Doris, please help me,' he begged.

'What's the matter, Tony, you sound awful?' I said anxiously.

'My mother's dying,' Tony explained, his voice choked, 'and she's so frightened. I don't know what to say to her, Doris. Please tell me what to say.'

My mind went blank. This wasn't the sort of work I was used to. What could I suggest? Tony needed an answer quickly, but it was a bit late to try to explain spiritualist philosophy to a woman who was on her death-bed. My thoughts raced round, tangling and going nowhere. Then above my confusion I heard Ramanov's calm voice reciting a poem.

'Tony, have you got a pen? Write this down quickly,' I instructed. And I repeated the words of the poem as Ramanov spoke them:

'Gentle spirit, please to come,
My life on earth is almost done.
Appear before my closing eye,
Tell me again I cannot die.

Here is my hand, please hold it fast,
Then with courage I will pass
Across that bridge that's built with love,
Into the summer land above.'

Ramanov's voice stopped. 'That's it, Tony. What d'you
think?'

There was a pause as Tony read it through. 'It sounds
beautiful.'

'Well, read it to your mother and let's hope it helps,' I
said.

Half an hour later Tony rang again.

'Bless you, Doris, bless you,' he said, his voice husky. 'My
mother's gone and the last thing she said was, "read it again,
Tony, read it again!" '

I don't know why I still find it so difficult to trust because
Ramanov has been proved right time and time again. On
another occasion I was doing a phone-in programme for
Monty Moddlin of LBC radio. It was my fourth appearance
on the show and Monty explained that he'd received so
many letters from people without phones complaining that
they were deprived of a chance to talk to me that he had
decided to offer mini-sittings to the first six people who
reached the studios. What did I think of the idea?

'It's all right with me, Monty,' I said, 'as long as you don't
get complaints from the listeners who live too far from the
studios!'

Monty laughed. 'Oh, well, I can't think of everything,'
and he announced the scheme over the air.

It looked as if it would be a success. The first woman
arrived within minutes. The sitting went smoothly and we'd
hardly finished when they told me the next sitter was
waiting outside.

I took a deep breath. 'Okay, send her in,' I said.

The door opened and I was amazed to see two men whom
I recognized. One, a great tall figure with a mexican
moustache, long hair and a gold chain round his neck,
swept in with a sheaf of papers under his arm. It was Gerald
Flemming, a man dedicated to exposing fraudulent
mediums. Behind him was Wally Glower, a small, timid

looking man who had had a sitting with me some months before.

'You want to talk to Doris?' asked Monty, a little taken aback by their purposeful entrance.

'No,' said Flemming. 'I've come to tell you she's a fraud.' I just sighed but Monty nearly dropped his headphones. This wasn't what he'd had in mind at all!

Quietly I stood up. 'I'm not brawling with him over the air, Monty,' I said. 'I'll leave.'

'You see,' said Flemming triumphantly, 'this is what happens when you face them with it. They run away.'

That did it! Furiously I crashed back into my seat.

'Mr Flemming,' I cried, struggling to keep my temper, 'I wouldn't run away from you in a million years. Now, let's hear what you have to say.'

So he began his tirade. I was chased out of Australia in 1978 by the police, he told the listeners. I couldn't hold my tongue at that.

'Then it's very strange that I'm going back again in July, isn't it?' I pointed out.

'I don't think so,' said Flemming. 'I'm certain you're not.' Well, of course I did go that July.

Then he introduced Wally who would talk about the sitting he'd had with me, Flemming promised, and he proceeded to feed Wally with questions. My heart sank as I listened. I speak to so many people over the years that I can't possibly remember the details of every sitting. It's only the unusual ones that stand out in my mind. I was sure Wally had had a successful sitting but, as I couldn't remember it, I couldn't refute what he was saying.

He claimed that I'd told him all sorts of things that were incorrect and had also warned him not to get married. Monty looked at me, his eyebrows raised, but I couldn't answer. I was sure it wasn't true but how could I deny it when I couldn't recall the occasion?

In the end, Monty got fed up with both of them. 'Okay, you've had your say, gentlemen, now will you leave the studio?'

Satisfied, the two men stood up and as they crossed to the door I caught Wally's eye.

'Wally, I hope you can sleep at night,' I said to him quietly. His face reddened, he dropped his eyes and hurried out.

'Are you all right, Doris?' Monty asked, as soon as the door closed behind them. 'Has it shaken you? Will you go on or do you want to call it a day?'

'No, it's all right, Monty. I'll go on,' I assured and the programme continued without further interruption.

But the incident did shake me, much more than I cared to admit. I had to fight to keep my voice calm as my stomach churned over and over. I don't mind criticism. If I stand up in public I have to expect public knocks. I've never pretended that I don't make mistakes now and again and I'm willing to own up to them, but the thought that someone to whom I'd never done any harm should come along and tell lies about me was like a physical blow. Why on earth had he done it? Did he hate me that much?

That night, upset and sickened, I turned to Ramanov hoping for some words of comfort.

'Trust,' he said serenely. 'It will be all right.'

But I didn't feel reassured. The damage was done now, it was too late to undo it. How could everything be all right?

But the months went by and gradually the incident faded from my mind. My work went on as before, no one appeared put off by the remarks and I received several letters of support. I must be prepared for that sort of thing, I told myself. Somehow I must make myself tougher.

I became busier than ever and in the end I'd almost forgotten the whole thing. Then one day, about a year later, I received a letter from Wally. He hadn't been able to sleep at nights, he wrote, and he wanted to ask my forgiveness and to put the record straight. He had told lies, he admitted. He realized now what a rotten thing he had done, particularly as I'd never done anything to hurt him. On the contrary, I had given him a marvellous sitting, even predicting that he would get married and be very happy — which eventually came true. He had also sent copies of this letter to LBC radio and the Psychic News, he explained, in the hope that this would repair any damage his lies had caused.

I read the confession with a glow of pleasure. Of course I forgave Wally, but most important of all Ramanov had been right. I should never have doubted him in the first place.

As I've said before Ramanov has been proved right over and over again. Whenever I worry about bills and rising prices and wonder where the money's going to come from, he has always reminded me to trust, to do my job to the best of my ability and the spirit world will see that I'll never go without. This has always been the case, not only in my life but in other people's.

Phil Edwards, in whose house I saw the baker, attended my teaching class at one time and I told him that he had a marvellous healing power and should use it. Now, Phil was an intelligent, down-to-earth businessman and he wasn't convinced at first, but as more and more people told him the same thing he decided he ought to take it seriously. He was working very hard at the time on his successful garage business but he began to get an increasingly strong feeling that the 'Guvnor', as he calls God, wanted him to devote himself to healing.

The next thing I heard, he had suddenly turned his business over to his son and built a sanctuary with his own hands in the grounds of his beautiful old house in Sussex.

He was soon doing some wonderful healing, but he also had a large family to support and without the money from the garage business, he found it difficult to make ends meet. He was quite convinced, however, that he was doing what his 'Guvnor' wanted him to do and with his wife Sue's encouragement he continued with his work.

Then one day a strange man turned up on the doorstep and Sue thought it must be the tax inspector, but he showed her his card and it turned out he was from the Football Pools. When Phil left the garage Sue had continued to pay their stake in the garage pool's syndicate and now they had had a win. The eight of them would share over a million pounds of prize money the man explained.

It was the answer to all their problems! Phil was able to invest the money and the interest gained replaced the money he used to take out of the business for living expenses. As Phil says, the Guvnor's treated him right.

He treats me right, too. I mentioned earlier that my hysterectomy operation was very expensive and though John and I had a bit put by for new furniture when we moved flats we didn't know whether it was going to be enough. Then one evening, when I was still in hospital recovering from the operation, a nurse came in with an envelope.

'A lady left this for you at reception, Mrs Stokes,' she said. 'We asked if she would like to come in but she said, no, she wouldn't disturb you, and she wouldn't leave a name either. She just put the envelope down and went straight out again.'

'What did she look like?' I asked, my curiosity aroused.

'Well, the receptionist said she was elderly, that's all. She can't remember much about her.'

It could have been anyone, I thought.

'You open it, John,' I said. I was eager to see inside but I was still too weak to lift anything unnecessarily. So John tore across the top of the envelope, pulled out a fat get-well card, and as he opened it up a shower of ten-pound notes spilled onto the bed.

'John! What's this?' I cried in amazement, wondering if I could be hallucinating from the drugs. But it was real!

John gathered up the money counting it as he went. 'There's five hundred pounds here,' he said in wonder.

'Five hundred pounds,' I gasped. 'Who's it from?'

He glanced blankly at the card and then looked inside the envelope again. There was nothing else in there. 'Well, I don't know,' he said, puzzled. 'It just says "from a friend".'

I was overwhelmed. What a kind, sweet, generous thought. Just when we'd been worrying how we were going to meet the bill. But who on earth could have done it? We spent the rest of the evening trying to guess. I wanted to thank them from the bottom of my heart.

'It must have been someone who knew you were having

to pay to get this operation done,' John pointed out. But we couldn't think of anyone who was rich enough to spare five hundred pounds like that.

The weeks passed, I went home and when the bill finally arrived we were very glad of that wonderful gift. Everything was itemized separately: the fees for the room, the surgeon, the anaesthetist, the nurses, the blood. It all added up to much more than we'd thought. I had quite a few visitors during those convalescing weeks and as we talked I dropped the most outrageous hints and scoured their faces for clues – but it was no use. I was no nearer discovering the identity of my mysterious friend than I had been in hospital.

In the end I thought, this is ridiculous, I must ask the spirit world who it is so that I can thank them. I tuned in.

'I know she doesn't want me to know,' I pleaded, 'but I must show my gratitude somehow. Can't you tell me so that I can thank her?'

There was nothing for a few seconds and I thought they weren't going to tell me. Then, when I'd almost given up hope, a young woman's voice came through. It was vaguely familiar and as she spoke I remembered speaking to her some months before, during a sitting with her mother.

'It was my mum who gave you the money,' she said. 'She wanted to thank you for all you've done for her.'

Tears sprang into my eyes. this particularly lady, whose name I can't mention because she says she'll be too embarrassed, was a dear, unassuming soul who had come for a sitting and remained a friend ever since. She never came to see me without bringing some little gift: a cream cake or a bottle of her daughter's favourite perfume. I should have guessed it was her – but how could she afford it? Was she going without now, because of me?

The following Monday when she came to see me I tackled her about it.

'You're very naughty, you know,' I told her as soon as she was settled with a cup of tea.

'Why? What have I done?' she asked innocently.

'You left all that money for me!' I said gently.

She blushed and stirred her tea until the bottom almost came out of the cup, but she didn't deny it.

'I really appreciate it, you know,' I went on to the top of her head, 'but it did worry me. I mean can you manage without it? It was such a lot of money?'

'Oh, yes, it's all right,' she insisted. 'I can afford it. I was left quite comfortable, you know. But how did you find out? I didn't want you to know, that's why I just put "from a friend".'

'Your daughter told me,' I explained.

'Oh,' she said. 'I never thought of that.' But she was delighted with the explanation. It was further proof that her daughter was still with her and aware of everything she was doing.

Some months later my advance for the first book arrived but my friend wouldn't hear of being repaid. 'That money was a gift,' she insisted. 'Whatever next!'

But eventually I found a way of repaying her that I know she would approve of. On a trip to Ireland to appear on the Late Late Show, we had a few hours to spare. Our host had been reading my book and, noticing that John and I had previously worked with the mentally handicapped, he asked if we would like to visit a home for mentally handicapped children nearby. This is just the sort of thing that interests us very much and we accepted the invitation gratefully.

There followed a very happy afternoon at the Marina Clinic in Bray. The staff showed us round and we were able to talk and play with the children. I remember particularly one frail little boy with his legs in plaster who was a spastic, and we could see how nursing techniques had progressed since my nursing days. Finally, with great pride, the matron showed us a wooden trailer which was to be a treatment centre for the six stone deaf children in the home. At present they were holding coffee mornings and jumble sales to raise money for the special headphones that were needed to help teach the children to read and talk.

'We've bought one set already,' the matron told us holding them up, 'and we hope to get another five like these.'

'How much do they cost?' I asked.

'A hundred pounds each, I'm afraid,' she said. 'They're very good but they're not cheap.'

A hundred pounds each – so they needed five hundred pounds to complete the set. It was that magic figure again. I thought of my friend and the operation. She had helped me when I needed five hundred pounds, now what better way could I repay her than by helping someone else who needed the money.

'We'll buy the other five pairs,' I said quickly.

'Oh, Mrs Stokes,' gasped the matron, 'I didn't mean – I mean – I mean I wasn't ...'

'I know,' I said, scrabbling around in my bag for my cheque book. 'But I'd like to do this for the children.' And as I bent across the desk to write out the cheque, my mind went back to the words of that old song: *'If you've had a kindness shown pass it on. It wasn't meant for you alone, pass it on.'* – and I couldn't help thinking, wouldn't it be marvellous if everyone who had received a kindness passed it on? One day my friend's kind thought will lead to five adults able to lead an almost normal life because they can read and write, and if those five adults each passed on that kindness, a chain of love could be created that might eventually stretch right round the world.

When I talk of Ramanov and his teachings, however, I must emphasise that Ramanov explains general principles only, and reminds me of them when I forget. He doesn't tell me what to do or how to solve individual problems because as he keeps pointing out when I get exasperated, he wouldn't want to live my life for me even if he could. I'm here to learn and it's up to me to make the decisions I think best.

Some people find this very difficult to accept. The other day I had a phone call from a young woman who wanted my help. She was in constant contact with her mother in the spirit world and her mother gave her advice daily, but recently her mother had said something about a particular problem which she couldn't understand.

'I'm not sure what my mother wants me to do,' the woman explained. 'I wondered if you could find out for me.'

Whether this woman was really in touch with her mother or only believed she was, it was difficult for me to tell in a brief telephone conversation, but if what she said was true, it appalled me.

'Poor old Mum,' I said to her. 'She brought you into this world, she looked after you as a child and she probably looked after you when you married and now she's gone over you still expect her to look after you! Let your mum go. Doesn't she deserve a rest?'

'Yes, but I need her advice,' the woman insisted.

'I'm sorry, love, I can't help you,' I said. 'You're grown up now. You must work it out for yourself.'

Well, I'm afraid she didn't like that and I was sorry, but a medium's job is to act as a temporary prop to people in the depths of despair not to become a permanent crutch for the rest of their lives.

The other problem I come up against now and then is orthodox religion. Many churchmen are sympathetic but there are still a few who are very much against mediums. A few hundreds years ago I would probably have been burned at the stake as a witch. A hundred years ago I might have been put in prison, but today I'm free to speak, although traditionally the church disapproves of what I do.

I came up against this problem quite recently. A lady called Barbara, distraught over the death of her seven-year-old son, came for a sitting. I have great affinity with bereaved mothers because of my own John Michael and, as often happens in cases like these, the sitting went very well. She left me in great happiness and wrote me a beautiful letter afterwards. She had got on the train to go home, crying and laughing at the same time, she wrote. Since then she had felt a great sense of relief. Part of the problem had been a tremendous feeling of guilt because, since her older son's death, she had felt locked up inside and was unable to give her younger son the affection he needed. But now the floodgates had opened and she felt warmer and more loving towards her remaining son than ever before. Even her mother had remarked on her new serenity.

I was delighted that the sitting had been of such help, so I was very surprised when Barbara phoned me a few days later in distress. Apparently she'd written excitedly to her local vicar, a friend of hers, telling him of her excitement over the sitting. She thought he would be interested. In fact he was alarmed.

'He says I should have nothing more to do with you, Doris,' Barbara sobbed. 'He said that your voices were demons who were impersonating the voices of our loved ones.'

'Yes, it does say something like that in one part of the Bible, love,' I agreed, 'I don't know why. I can only think it's to warn people not to dabble in things they don't understand. Ouija boards are very dangerous for instance; so is witchcraft and black magic and all that kind of thing. But St Paul said, "Test ye the spirits to see if they be of God" and I always do. I always offer myself in service in God's name before I start. I can't believe God would allow my work to carry on if it wasn't right.'

'But another of my friends, a Catholic, said if I came to see you again I'd be struck down dead?'

'What a strange God she believes in to think that He would do that kind of thing to us!' I said. Why would He want to strike you down dead?'

'Oh, I don't know. I'm so confused, Doris,' said Barbara. 'I was brought up a Christian yet my church didn't comfort me. Oh, they tried but it didn't help. You helped me and then the vicar upset me again. I don't know what to believe.'

'Well, I fully understand, Barbara,' I told her sympathetically. 'I'll leave you to sort yourself out. I'm not pushing my ideas onto you and I don't want to make you more confused than you are already. You know where I am if you want me,' and I left it at that.

But other churchmen hold different views. When I was working at the College of Psychic Studies, I was told that a young lady was waiting to see me but wanted to know if I would mind if she brought her vicar in with her because she was frightened.

'Yes, of course,' I said a little surprised. 'I don't mind at all.'

A nervous young woman came in and perched opposite me, followed by a pleasant open-faced clergyman. The clergyman remained quietly in the background and made no attempt to interrupt, but he glanced at his companion from time to time to see if she was all right.

I tuned in and found myself speaking to the girl's husband. He told me his name and that he'd taken his own life. I got the impression of a car parked in a beauty spot in some woods and the smell of exhaust fumes. The woman confirmed that this was correct. The man went on to talk of his children and his family.

Then another voice broke in and I knew the message was for the vicar.

'I hear the name Leonard,' I told him.

'That's my name,' he said in astonishment and I was able to give him a message from his father.

Afterwards he wrote me a beautiful letter saying that I'd done his young parishioner a world of good – in fact, two worlds: this and the next – and that he would be very grateful if I would give a talk at his church. This I later did with great pleasure and we have kept in touch ever since. In fact he still sends his parishioners along to see me when he feels I can give them more help than he can.

Theological arguments are difficult for me to follow. As far as I'm concerned the issue is a simple one. The justification for my work is the effect it has on other people. If I give lasting comfort and support then I must be doing the right thing. Every week I receive hundreds of letters of support. This is a typical example:

Dear Doris,

After a year of suffering, my mother, Ruby Lilian Hill, died of cancer. But just a minute – did I use the word die? Well, let me tell you that you have proved beyond doubt to my father and myself that there is no death, just a natural passing from the earth plane to the astral plane.

When my mother passed over my father was totally devastated. In my vain attempts to comfort him I tried to impart some of the sketchy views I had on the afterlife. But what could I, a kid (his twenty-seven-year old kid), say that could change his views on a subject he just did not believe in?

Shortly after my mother's passing I read Voices in My Ear *which was serialized in a magazine. I thoroughly enjoyed the serial and felt that the honest sincerity imparted, together with the amazing accounts that you related in such easy to understand terms, would make ideal reading for a beginner in the subject. So I bought the book and suggested to my father that he read it. He was very impressed and a seed was indeed sown, but he was not altogether convinced.*

However, I felt compelled to write to you, thanking you for the shred of comfort your book offered to a non-believer and after about a week you telephoned us!

My father answered the telephone and when you said, 'Hello, it's Doris Stokes,' he thought somebody was playing an unkind joke on him and he nearly replied, 'Yes, hello, I'm Tommy Cooper' which is why he probably sounded a bit unfriendly at first.

Then you said, 'I've got Ruby here' and I hadn't mentioned my mother's name in the first letter. You went on to tell us all kinds of wonderful things from my mother including that she was sorry to leave us but she'd been in such terrible pain she couldn't go on any longer. You even gave us the exact location in her body where the cancer was manifest.

The final proof came with the description of our living room. You described the layout of the furniture, the colour of the carpet and wallpaper, commented on the fact that our living room is big because we had a dividing wall knocked down making two rooms into one, you even described where the photographs are – to the right of the fireplace on a shelf!

My father was visibly moved and a great cloud seemed to have been lifted from his shoulders. People are astounded at how well he has adjusted to the loss of my mother after thirty-two years. Some sceptics say, 'oh, well, if you believe in that – fair play to you.' But we know, *because you Doris have proved it to us.*

With love from

Barbara Hill

When I read letters like this I know I must be doing something right. I think: you might grumble Doris, you might get tired, but if, out of ten people, you manage to prove to just one that there is life after death and a better way to live, then you're doing your job properly.

Chapter 13

As we walked through the gate at Dublin airport, the driver waiting to meet us clapped his hand across his eyes in mock alarm.

'Oh no,' he cried in simulated horror. 'You're the one who nearly got us shot last time!'

I couldn't help laughing. I had last visited Ireland to do a ten-minute spot on the Late Late Show and I had made very little impression on the public on that occasion. My most lasting impression had obviously been on this taxi driver – for all the wrong reasons!

He had driven us back to Dublin for our flight home only to find the airport closed because of a strike. We were diverted to Belfast in Northern Ireland.

Until then, having only visited Southern Ireland, 'the troubles,' as they call them, had only been faraway scenes on the television screen but as soon as we saw the soldiers at the border check point the reality began to dawn on us.

We drove through the most beautiful, rolling, green countryside but it was littered with abandoned cars and there were too many boarded-up shops in the towns.

Belfast was a tragedy. An atmosphere of fear and hostility was clamped over the city like a lid. It was Sunday morning and people stood around their gates, but there was a sort of hush over the place. As we went on towards the Falls Road I felt sadder and sadder. Blackened, bombed-out buildings seemed to loom on every side, gaping windows stared blindly down at us, doors were boarded up and every other road appeared to have been hastily closed with old car tyres, crooked posts or police beacons.

The driver was in despair. It was some time since he had

visited Belfast and so many roads were now blocked off
due to bombings or shootings, we soon got hopelessly lost.
We drove aimlessly around for almost half an hour before
we pulled out of a side turning and found ourselves back
on the main road again. In front of us was an armoured
car and in the back sat a soldier with his rifle poking
through the window.

Having been in the forces myself during the war,
without thinking, I did what I'd always done when I saw a
soldier: I raised my hand to wave.

The driver nearly had kittens. 'Oh, Holy Mary, don't
move your hand! Don't move your hand!'

'I was only going to wave,' I pointed out.

'Well, you mustn't move your hand or he'll think we've
got a bomb!' My insides twisted and I thought, poor
Ireland, to have to live like this day after day, when you
can't even wave in case they think you've got a bomb …

Despite my lack of impression on the Late Late Show,
Gay Burn, the presenter, invited me back for another
appearance in January 1981. This time I was given an
hour to work with the audience and the difference it made
was incredible.

The show went very well but only one communication
really stands out in my mind. A boy came through who
had been killed by his brother. He gave the name of his
mother, who was in the audience, and the name of his
brother.

The poor woman was terribly upset but she wanted me
to continue, so I moved away for a few minutes to give her
time to compose herself and then I went back. The young
man told me there had been an argument that had got out
of hand. Suddenly, a sharp pain tore through me and I
knew he'd been shot or stabbed.

'Oh, my goodness!' I gasped clutching my chest.

'Yes, that's right,' sobbed the woman, knowing exactly
what I meant.

It was all in a day's work to me, but the effect was
extraordinary. When I walked off the set, a crowd of
people surged forward and pinned me to the wall in the
corridor. They meant no harm, but the unexpected crush

was quite alarming at first and as I struggled to smile and find out what was going on I heard a voice cry, 'Let me through! Oh, let me through! I just want to *touch* her.'

My blood went icy at her words and a strange fear prickled down my spine. What on earth did they think I was?

'Let her through, please,' I said quietly.

Two seconds later a tiny little woman emerged at the front of the crowd. She gazed up at me with a reverence that was terrifying.

'I just want to *touch* her,' she repeated as if in a daze.

'Now, look,' I said firmly. 'Don't get the wrong idea about me. I'm no one special. I'm just the same as you are. When I get back I'll have a cigarette, I'll probably have a drink and before the night's out I'll probably be swearing. Don't put me on a pedestal. I'm just the same as you.'

But it was no use. The whole place seemed to erupt. The studio was besieged by callers, the phone at the hotel didn't stop ringing and hopeful people waited for me in reception.

The morning after the show I walked into the foyer to find a group of people waiting. I had spoken to five young girls in the back row during the show and got their grandfather back for them, and now they had driven miles to come and see me with their family. I was just on my way out, but when I saw the look in their eyes I knew I would have to give them something. I tuned in and quickly found the grandfather again.

'He tells me he started an extension on the house but he didn't get it finished before he passed.'

'Yes, that's true,' they cried in delight.

'Well, he's telling me it's finished now and you're going to hang some orange curtains in it.'

'That's it,' said the father, 'and when you come to stay with us you'll sleep in the new extension!'

Another family turned up without an appointment having driven a hundred a fifty-nine miles and taken the day off work in the hope of seeing me. I had very little but but I did what I could. I got back their 'daddy', as they call their parents in Ireland.

'Your daddy says you've all clubbed together to buy a new kerb to put round his grave,' I said. 'But he's saying "I wish you'd saved your money because I'm not dead, am I?'

He was also a little indignant with his son. 'I always said you would be late for your own funeral,' he said. 'Well, you were late for mine, and the cortège had to wait outside the gate for you.'

'Yes, that's right,' the son admitted sheepishly. 'I was held up in traffic!'

Most of my time was devoted to sittings with a few really desperate people who had booked beforehand. One of them, a small, dark-haired woman called Teresa, had lost her little boy. He was very anxious to talk to his mummy and came back straight away. He told me he was nine years old and had passed with leukaemia.

As we talked, I saw him for a split second, a thin little lad, almost bald, with just a few tufts of hair left on his head. Then he was gone, and a few minutes later he was back, but this time he had a full head of hair and was much healthier. He rushed up to his mother in his little short trousers and tried to take her hand.

'Look, Mum, look, Mum, I can run, I can jump now!' he cried, dancing round her chair to demonstrate. 'And all my hair's come back! Look!'

But of course his mother couldn't see. He disappeared again, only to return a few moments later with a red rose which he laid on her lap.

'Your little boy has just given you a red rose,' I told Teresa.

She stared sadly down at her lap which to her looked empty. 'I gave him red roses at his funeral,' she said.

'Well, he's brought you one back,' I explained.

The little boy went on to talk of his brother and his daddy who he said drove for a living and he kept mentioning a particular sweater.

'Do you mean your brother's wearing your sweater now?' I asked.

'No,' said the boy and talked of the sweater again, adding the surname, Woods.

'Well, I'm sorry, Teresa,' I said, 'I don't understand this

bit. He's talking about a special sweater and the name Woods. Do you have any idea what he could mean?'

At this poor Teresa burst into tears. 'Oh, yes,' she sobbed. 'We buried him in a sweater that Mrs Woods had knitted for him.' And though she cried, Teresa was smiling through her tears, so pleased to know her son was well again and close by, even though she couldn't see him.

I was able to do another touching sitting for another bereaved mother – a woman called Mary who had lost two children tragically. They came through together, a boy called Robert and a tiny girl called Jennifer.

'It was my head, you know,' Robert, who did most of the talking, explained. 'I was bald there and it did hurt me, Mummy.'

Mary confirmed that Robert had passed with a brain tumour.

Then Jennifer talked of the little girl her parents had adopted after her death. 'My sister's got my teddy now,' she said cheerfully, not begrudging the loss of her toy at all, and Mary was thrilled to hear Jennifer acknowledge the new child as her sister.

Robert wanted to tell me about his mummy's kitchen and in a flash it formed in my mind.

'This is the oven,' said Robert, pointing it out to me, 'and here is the hob and the counter next to it and this is the breadbin and the chopping board. I come back and knock the chopping board down for Mummy to find.'

Mary's hand flew to her mouth. 'My god, they do! I'm always finding it on the floor and wondering how on earth it got there.'

She told me afterwards that she had been to see priests and psychiatrists in an effort to get over the depression caused by the loss of her children, but only now, after the sitting, did she feel any hope for the future.

There were so many people to see that I didn't get many spare moments during the trip, but I was determined to visit the Marina Clinic in Bray before we left, to see how the children were getting on.

We drove up the rise through soft green towards the long, low building and it was as if we had never been away.

Two ponies grazed in the fields, children skipped towards
the car and within moments we were back in that warm,
happy atmosphere, surrounded by splodgy infant paintings and battered toys. I asked after the fragile little spastic
boy I'd met last time.

'Oh, I'm afraid he's not very well,' the matron told me.
'He's in bed with a cold at the moment, but you can come
and see him.'

She led us to the dormitory and there he was, sitting up
in bed looking at a budgie in a cage that his teacher had
brought to show him.

'Now there's someone come to see you,' said the matron
bustling towards him. 'You don't know who this is, do
you?'

The little boy looked up and when he saw me a big grin
spread across his face.

'Yes – it's Granny Doris!' he said, beaming.

I'd brought a big bag of sweets with me and I had to
thrust them into his hands on the pretext of letting him
choose what he wanted, while I turned to wipe away a tear.
If I could have taken them all home with me I would have
done.

On Sunday I was given an official day of rest and
Edward, the young man who was looking after us, invited
us to his home for a traditional Irish family lunch. But first
he wanted to take us for a drive along the coast road
because so far all we'd seen of Ireland was hotel rooms, the
studios and of course the Marina Clinic.

The drive was wonderful. John and I sat with our noses
pressed to the glass, unable to tear our eyes away as each
mile seemed prettier than the last. We sauntered along
past dark, jagged rocks, white sandy bays and a sea that
shone silver grey in the weak January sun. There were
castles on outcrops and tiny whitewashed cottages, and it
was so warm! We'd packed our thick woollies because it
was, after all, the middle of winter and very cold in
London – but we didn't need them.

Finally, towards lunch-time, Edward headed back and
we ended up at his modern house on a smart new estate.
Within minutes the place seemed to be full of people.

There was Edward's Uncle Jack, his father, Chris, and many more friends and relatives. They persuaded me to have sherry before lunch, wine with it and Irish coffee afterwards, and by the time the long, leisurely meal was over I was feeling quite merry. More and more people seemed to come and go and I couldn't keep track of them all. 'We keep open house on Sundays, Doris,' Jack explained, seeing my bemused expression.

They had had strict instructions that I was supposed to be resting and on no account were they to ask me to work, and they were very good about it. But as often happens when I'm in a very relaxed state, the voices seem to come through of their own accord.

Jack was talking to his brother-in-law, Tom, about the loss of his mammy.

'There's only one thing that really bothers me,' Jack was saying, 'and that's that there was no one with her when she died.'

Immediately I heard a voice say, 'Our Paddy was there.'

'Paddy was there,' I said without thinking.

Jack's jaw dropped. 'What did you say?'

'She says Paddy was there,' I repeated.

'By God, so he was!' cried Jack in astonishment.

Well, there was no stopping Mammy then. She talked about a family problem which she disapproved of, she said that Jack still got her handbag out from time to time, and he'd left it just the way it was when she was alive – there was even money in the purse which Anne had given her.

'Yes, that's true,' Jack admitted.

'And there's an unopened bottle of perfume still on my dressing-table,' Mammy went on. 'Give it to our Anne, I'm not going to come back to wear it.'

She was clearly very fond of Edward's father, Chris.

'He's a rash lad, our Chris,' she confided. 'But he's lovely with it. He used to drive a lorry, but not any more.'

Then she talked of the family trouble again. She sat up and folded her arms and bristled because she was very cross. I sat up in the same way to show the family what she was doing.

'Oh God, that's your mother!' someone said to Jack

because by now they had all gathered in a semi-circle round me.

'And another thing,' said Mammy, 'they've redecorated the bedroom in woodchip paper. I don't like it! I don't like it at all.'

A great gust of laughter swept round the group. 'I told you she wouldn't like it,' Chris chuckled.

After a while another voice chimed in. 'My name is Catherine Green,' she told me and her voice sounded more Scottish than Irish.

It was Edward's grandmother and it turned out she was indeed Scottish. She wanted to cuddle Edward and I leaned across and took his hand.

'She's saying this is my baby,' I told him.

'Yes, that's right. She brought me up,' Edward replied.

Catherine went on to describe her funeral which apparently had been a bit of a disaster.

'The undertaker upset the coffin and it went in wrong and so they had to take it out and do it again,' she explained. 'If they'd dug up that privet round the grave when I told them to it wouldn't have happened.'

'What do you mean, love?' I asked. 'What went wrong with the privet?'

'There were gaps in it,' she said, 'where parts of the hedge had died. One of the men slipped between the hedge and the coffin went in sideways!'

And though it was probably very traumatic at the time, the whole family fell about laughing, relieved to know that Catherine didn't mind a bit.

At the end of the impromptu sitting, Jack, who was also a wealthy businessman, reached for his wallet.

'Doris,' he said, 'I'll sign a cheque for any charity you care to name.'

'Are you sure, Jack?' I asked. 'I mean you didn't plan to have this sitting, it just happened.'

'Of course I'm sure. It was worth every penny.'

I bit my lip. Which charity should it be? There are so many I'd like to support. The Marina Clinic had already been helped so I felt someone else ought to have a turn.

'Brandon Lodge,' I said at last. 'It's an old people's home

for spiritualists. They do a lot of good there and they have to rely on donations.'

So while I watched, Jack wrote out a cheque for a hundred pounds. I was thrilled. Mammy and Catherine, aided by the Irish coffee, had achieved a great deal that day.

Chapter 14

When I was still grieving for my son John Michael, I used to have the most marvellous dreams. Soon after I went to sleep it would seem to me that I arrived on a sunny road in the most beautiful place. There were gorgeous flowers on either side and the road sloped gently up to the brow of the hill.

As I stood there basking in the warmth of the sun, my father would appear at the top of the hill carrying my baby in his arms. He'd stride down towards me and I can still feel the indescribable joy that engulfed me as my hands touched baby skin again and I cuddled my son.

In the morning the pillow would be wet with tears but I always woke with a feeling of great happiness and serenity that lasted all day.

Just a dream, you might say, but it was a dream which recurred at regular intervals and I watched my son grow. After a while my father didn't need to carry him any more and a sturdy, apple-cheeked toddler would rush towards me, holding fast to Father's hand. I watched John Michael change over the years into a beautiful child and then a handsome young man. Until at last, when he was 16, he embraced me and told me sadly that he couldn't come to see me any more because he had to go about his Father's work.

As I learned more about spiritualism, I heard of a thing called astral travel. The theory is that while you are asleep your mind can leave your body and float around in time and space, on the astral plane, as we call it. It sounded a pretty far-fetched idea but the more I thought about it the more it seemed to fit into my special dreams. The John Michael dreams were utterly unlike any other dreams I'd

422

had. They were as vivid and real as if they had happened. Had I dreamed continually of my baby as a baby – the way he was then I last held him on earth – the incidents could be more easily dismissed as dreams. But the fact that I watched him change and grow up at the same rate he would have grown up on earth seemed to me to suggest that these dreams should be taken more seriously. Perhaps I had travelled on the astral plane to the spirit world.

I hadn't thought about the subject for years – after all, it's two decades now since my last dream – but reading some of the letters I received after my first book was published brought it all back. Over and over again people would write, 'Yes, it's all very well, but what is the spirit world like? That's what we want to know,' and I couldn't helping thinking they had a point. Spirit contacts often do say a little about their new world but not enough for me to have built up a really detailed picture.

I turned it over in my mind, wondering how I could answer the queries and then it hit me. I would let the spirit world decide. If I really had been there all those years ago to visit my son, perhaps I could go back.

On three consecutive nights, before I went to bed, I asked silently if I could go. Nothing happened. I had my ordinary confused dreams and woke up feeling dissatis-fied. Then on the fourth night, something extraordinary took place.

I was in bed asleep and yet at the same time I knew I was awake and two huge eyes were looking at me. They seemed to fill the room and they were an astonishing shade of violet. Violet eyes, I thought vaguely, John Michael had violet eyes ... And as I watched, a face started to build up round the eyes, until I was looking at a handsome blond man and it was my son. Thirty-six years old but I would recognize him anywhere.

'John Michael!' I cried, almost bursting with pride. This beautiful creature who seemed to glow with light was my son.

'Mother, you asked if we could show you what the spirit world is like, so I've come to take you,' he said and reached for my hand.

Suddenly we were moving. We didn't walk so much as float along effortlessly. The dark bedroom disappeared, I was bathed in bright light and without knowing how we got there, I found we had arrived at a little bungalow and I saw my parents.

'Father! Mother!' I cried, throwing my arms round them. They grinned back at me and I stared at them in amazement. They looked so well. Father looked younger, if anything, than I remembered him.

'Father looks so much younger!' I exclaimed to John Michael.

'Well, you see, Mum, those of us who come over as children grow up normally,' he explained. 'But when old people come over they lose all their aches and pains and the weariness and worry of the world. They simply feel younger and look younger because there are no infirmities, or troubles.'

I stared at my mother. There was something different about her, too, but I couldn't place it. Then I realized.

'Mum you've got two eyes!' I said in delight. She had lost an eye at birth and I had only ever seen her with one.

'But, of course,' said John Michael, 'she's in the spirit world, isn't she? I've told you that the infirmities she had on the earth plane disappear.'

But she was still the same old Mum, bustling and ever-practical.

'That's all very well,' she said to John Michael, 'but how's she going to get back? Will she be able to go back?'

'It's okay, Gran,' John Michael smiled. 'I'll see that she gets back.'

Mum gave him a long look, then, obviously satisfied, she showed me the bungalow. 'It's all on one level, you see,' she said. 'I didn't want any stairs to clean.'

'But surely you don't have to clean?' I exclaimed. I'd hoped that I'd leave housework behind when I passed over!

My father saw I was worried. 'No, not unless you want to,' he said. 'But you know what your mother is. Unless you can eat your meals off the lavatory floor, the house isn't clean!'

'We thought we'd show Dol the hospital, Jen,' Father went on. 'Do you want to come?'

'No, I've got far too much to do,' Mum said, starting to bustle again. 'I've got the house to finish and then I must get on with the garden.'

I smiled to myself. Typical Mum! But I was so glad she'd got her own garden at last, she had always loved plants. I hugged her again and then set off with Father and John Michael. I couldn't get over the way we floated instead of walked and, somehow, without noticing the places in between, I found we were inside the hospital.

At first glance the ward looked quite normal, with rows of beds and people standing round them. Then I noticed that the walls seemed to be made of glass looking out on to gentle rolling hills, shady trees and brilliant flowers. Everything seemed to be twice as big as on earth and I couldn't see the ceiling. I wouldn't mind being ill in a place like this, I thought. There was an extraordinary atmosphere about it. One could feel the healing in the air and it seemed to come not only from within the building, but from outside as well. Healing power seemed to wash in on invisible waves from the idyllic scenery outside the window. Instinctively, I knew that there were no operations or drugs in this hospital, the patients were cured by the atmosphere. But who were the patients?

'John Michael, why do you need hospitals over here if you lose all your infirmities when you come over?'

John Michael smiled as if he'd been waiting for me to ask that.

'Well, you see, when a person leaves his body very quickly, especially through violence or a car accident or a heart attack, they haven't had time to prepare themselves and in that case it's a very traumatic experience for them. Imagine what it must be like to be parted from your earthly body in a split second. So they come here to recuperate, and, surrounded by their loved ones, they sleep until their spirit body recovers from the shock.'

We stood for a while watching the loving people clustered round each bed. Some of the patients were sleeping peacefully but others were sitting up, talking to their relatives, and it was clear that these people would soon be well enough to leave.

'I'm sure Mother would like to see the waiting place, Grandad,' said John Michael. Despite the fascinating scene in the hospital I was still stealing glances at John Michael. I could hardly take my eyes off him. This is my son, I had to keep reminding myself, all grown up and handsome, my son. He caught my eye and as if reading my mind, which he probably could, he put his arm round my shoulders and gave me a look of such love and tenderness I wanted to cry.

'The waiting place?' I said weakly.

'Yes, you'll see.'

We floated out of the hospital and along a little path fringed by flowers and trees. Birds swooped low over our heads and I saw a deer dart away to our right.

A few minutes later we came to a low, round building and the most exquisite woman came out to meet us. She was dressed in white, and seemed to shine, and the love that emanated from her was almost tangible. Perhaps this is where one comes to be judged, I thought, a little frightened even though I knew there was no reason to be. But they took me inside and my eyes grew in amazement. All round the walls were rows of glowing, transparent shells through which little creatures could be seen.

'But they're babies, aren't they?' I gasped. They looked just like human foetus in varying stages of growth.

'Yes, my child, they are babies,' the woman told me. 'These are the babies who didn't fulfil their full term and were sent back before they were born.'

'What happens to them?' I asked, peeping into the little silvery shells.

'They are born into the spirit world and given to spirit mothers who take care of them,' she explained.

Fascinated, I wandered round looking into each little window. Perhaps when I came over I might be given one? I felt something touch my arm.

'Come and see the nurseries, Mother,' said John Michael.

The nurseries were just behind the waiting place and

they were full of laughing children. They raced, they tumbled and played boisterous games and it was hard to remember that they'd died tragically, on earth, and feel sad for them because they looked so happy. There were quite a few adults there, as well, and I was told these were either spirit mothers who brought the children up as their own, or they were relatives.

One elderly lady approached. 'Come and see my great-grandson,' she said proudly and took me to a corner where an angelic little boy was sitting on the floor playing with building bricks. When he saw me he beamed and held out his chubby little arms and I couldn't resist picking him up. I don't know what I had expected, but within seconds I was cuddling warm, solid, human flesh. There was nothing wraith-like about him.

'He came over very tragically at fourteen months old,' his great-grandmother explained. 'Fortunately I was already here so I take care of him. His name is Christopher James.'

Our tour continued. Father and John Michael wanted to show me as much as possible in a short time. We visited a school where lessons were given in thought only, and then went on to a hall of music where one could choose what one wanted to listen to from the variety of pieces coming from the different areas of the building.

We came upon a little room where a young man was playing the organ, totally absorbed in the music he was making. From nowhere I picked up a thought like a voice, 'He couldn't play a thing on the earth plane but this was always inside him, and here he can express it.'

'Isn't that remarkable,' I said to Father and John Michael, 'I've always wanted to make music.'

'When you come over, Mother, you will have the chance to express yourself,' John Michael said, 'and if you want to learn to make music you shall.'

from there we went on to the vast Hall of Learning. I was totally overwhelmed. The walls and pillars shone with colour: rose, mauves and blues swirled into each other over the creamy stone as if it was alive. I thought it would be warm, but when I slid my fingers over the smooth surface, I found it was cool.

Thousands and thousands of people were gathered in the hall. Some sat with their arms folded and legs crossed like buddhists, some slumped comfortably and others lay back with their eyes closed, and yet I knew that they were listening to the teacher with complete attention.

I blinked as my eyes came to rest on the teacher. One moment he appeared very very old, thousands of years old, it seemed, and yet when I looked again he was a young man.

He was communicating to the students in thought. I wonder if I could ask him a question? I thought idly, without realizing what I was doing.

The teacher looked up instantly and turned to me. 'Greetings, my child!'

I jumped, startled. I hadn't said a word. Clearly he had picked up my thoughts.

'I would like to ask you a question,' I said nervously. He nodded encouragingly. 'Well, can you tell me what is happening on our earth plane? We seem to be in a terrible mess.'

'I know, my child,' he said. 'God gave you a beautiful world to live in and you are destroying it by man's inhumanity to man. Until you learn to love one another, then you will continue to destroy the world.'

I must confess I was disappointed. Well, I know *that*, I thought, forgetting that the thought wasn't private, that's just common sense.

'Don't jump to conclusions, my child. Wait until I've finished,' he said gently. 'There comes a time when, if you violate God's law, then you each have to pay for it. Unfortunately, many innocent people, babies and children, get caught, too. Learn to love one another more, feel the love that is in this place. I tell you, child, when these souls came here they were each enveloped in their own individual religion, were each wrapped up in their own material condition, and yet look at them now. Feel the love.' And at this all the students turned to each other and although no words were spoken one could feel the love reaching out one to the other.

'This is what we try to teach you on the earth plane,' the teacher continued, 'but you just won't listen.'

I suppose I was a bit stung by this. 'Well, I try very hard,' I said, a little indignantly.

He smiled. 'We're all human. We've all trodden this path. We know how difficult it is, but think of it as if you had a light within you, that God has given to every one of us that divine light. It's only a small light within you and it's only a small light within the other people you meet, so therefore one light cannot do much good on its own. But, child, if all those lights were joined together, then it would light up the darkness. That is what you have to try to do.

'Do not say in your work, "we have the right way". None of us has the right way. We all have something to learn from each other.'

Then he pointed to the farthest corner of the hall and for the first time I noticed there was a man standing there. He was quite free to move and yet I could sense an invisible barrier around him as if he was in a cage.

'He desperately wants to join us,' said the teacher, 'but he's still hidebound in his own religion, which he thinks is the only way. He hasn't yet learned how to let down the barrier and say, "I am just one of God's children". But he comes every day and soon the barriers will dissolve and he will feel the love.' As he pointed, all the people turned round and sent their love across to the man. At once his face started to brighten with a smile and he took one step forward, then stopped uncertainly.

'Now that is good,' said the teacher. 'He has taken one step. That is enough. He will come in his own time. You must understand that over here no one is pressured, we just give them our love, teach them what we know and what we've learned and they come to us in their own time when they feel their soul is open.

'I have to talk to you as an earthling. Your soul needs the tears. Think of a flower; it cannot bloom and it cannot survive without rain. It cannot blossom out into its full beauty without the sun. So think, if you can, of that divine part of you in your earthly body and when you have tragedy and tears, think of them as the rain falling to feed it, and then when the joyous times come, when something beautiful happens and your heart is full of joy, then that is the sun that is nurturing that fragile flower.'

'What happens if someone who has been very bad comes over at the same time as somebody who has tried to live their life on a spiritual level?' I asked.

'You are as you are,' said the teacher. 'Two people can come over at the exact same second and one will see the most beautiful flowers and blue lakes and mountains with snow peaks. The other soul, who has gone through life treading on everybody because he was determined to get what he wanted out of life and didn't care who he hurt to get it, will see dark forbidding water and trees without leaves. Like attracts like.'

This sounded too much like the old-fashioned ideas of Hell to me.

'Well, where do they go?' I asked John Michael.

'The path of progression is open to every soul,' he said. 'God doesn't close his doors on anyone, but they have to start at the bottom.'

'Do you think it would be possible to see it?' I asked.

'Do you really want to go, Mother? You might feel very unhappy. We feel unhappy. But until these people can put out their hands to their guides who are there, who give up their lives to help them, they can't start on the upward path.'

For a split second he showed me this place and it was dreadful. It was cold and grey and there was a bitterness and ill feeling that could be tasted. I shuddered, and in a flash I was back again.

'We don't like it either, Mother,' said John Michael, seeing my stricken face. 'But don't worry. They don't stay there. They are never left alone and sooner or later the love gets through to them and they start to climb upwards.'

Just before we left, John Michael pointed out two girls and a boy.

'These are my sisters and my brother,' he said.

And before I could answer, one of the girls, a pretty lass with brown hair, came over and kissed me. 'Hello, Mother,' she said.

I didn't know what to say to her. These must be the three babies I lost before birth but I felt helpless with guilt.

They were just strangers to me. I couldn't love them the way I loved John Michael.

When she had gone, I turned to my father in distress. 'I can't love her, Dad,' I said.

'Look, Dol, you didn't know these babies,' Father pointed out, 'so there's no need to worry. The love link is eternal and when you come over the love will be there.

'But for now, the only thought in your head should be your job. We're very proud of you. You're doing your work well, so keep on doing it and we'll do all we can to help you from this side.'

I started to cry because I knew the end of my visit was near and I couldn't bear to leave these two men I loved so much.

John Michael put his arms round me. 'It's time to go back, Mother,' he said. 'I'm busy and so are you. Keep doing your work, Mum, and I'll keep doing mine.'

Then the scene dissolved and I remember no more until I woke up the next morning in my own bed, with tears streaming down my face.

So was it a dream? It was so clear and real and detailed that I can't believe it was only a dream. It is fresh and vivid to me now as it was the morning I woke up. It felt like a real experience. So, people can call me a crank if they like, but as far as I'm concerned I've been to the spirit world, I've seen what it's like and I can say, quite truthfully, that it's beautiful.

INNOCENT VOICES IN MY EAR

Innocent Voices
In My Ear

'Death is nothing at all. I have only slipped
away into the next room. I am I and you are you.
Whatever we were to each other that we are still.

Call me by my old familiar name; speak to me
in the easy way which you always used; put no
difference in your tone; wear no forced air of
solemnity or sorrow; laugh, as we always laughed
at the little jokes we enjoyed together; pray,
smile, think of me, pray for me; let my name be
ever in the household word that it always was;
let it be spoken without effect, without the trace
of a shadow on it.

Life means all that it ever meant; it is the same
as it ever was; there is unbroken continuity.
Why should I be out of mind because I am out of
sight? I am waiting for you, for an interval,
somewhere very near – Just around the corner.
All is well.'

*With thanks to Mandy's mother, Jill,
for the comfort her words have given to
parents over the world*

Chapter 1

The boy appeared almost immediately. He was a small, neat child, maybe four or five years old, with dark brown hair that waved softly round his head and a pointed little face like that of an elf.

He grinned at me and I smiled back, but then my attention was diverted by something his relatives were saying. Moments later a flash of movement caught my eye. I glanced round and there he was – stripping off his clothes. Off came his jumper, off came his jeans, off came his socks, off came his underwear, and as he finished with each garment he flung it to the floor. Finally, when he was naked as the day he was born, he stood in front of me, pink, dimpled and pleased with himself.

I started to laugh.

'What's the joke?' asked the boy's father because, not being a medium, he couldn't see what had happened.

'The cheeky young beggar!' I chuckled. 'He's just taken off all his clothes and thrown them on the floor. He's standing there in the nudie!'

But, to my surprise, the man didn't laugh. He started to cry. 'That's the only evidence I need,' he said. 'Paul was mentally retarded and we used to apologize to guests in advance because if he thought he was being ignored he used to take his clothes off.'

Little Paul had died or, as I would say, passed on some months before, but, although his family could no longer see him, he wasn't very far away. He hadn't changed. He wasn't mentally handicapped any more, of course, but his personality was still the same. He thought he was being ignored when I talked to someone else, so off came his clothes!

I've always been daft about children and I think that's why, even today, my communications with the other side are particularly vivid if there's a child involved. Even as a child myself I loved the little ones smaller than me and I genuinely thought all babies were beautiful. From the earliest age I would beg to cuddle them and change their nappies. Dolls didn't interest me if there was a real live baby around.

'Pol,' young mothers used to say (for some reason everyone called me Polly in those days), 'come and hold our so and so's bottle.'

And I'd stand there beside the pram, barely tall enough to see over the side, proudly holding the bottle until the baby had finished. Then, standing on tiptoe, I carefully wiped its face and mouth.

Even in those days I was getting a helping hand from the spirit world, although I was too young to realize it then. I remember the day I met a neighbour trundling her heavy old pram along the streets of Grantham where I was born. The sight of that pram was like a magnet to me and I was at her side in seconds. The baby was sitting there in his frilly sun bonnet, tiny fists waving, and I'll swear he smiled when he saw me. I skipped along with the pram for a while, shaking his rattle and pulling funny faces to make him laugh, but in the end I could contain myself no longer.

'Oh, can I have a push?' I burst out, and the woman laughed.

'Go on then, Pol,' she said, probably glad of a rest, 'but just mind what you're doing, that's all.'

She moved aside and I took her place on the handle. Proudly, and with infinite care, I manoeuvred the pram over every crack and bump and soon I was bowling along as if to the manner born. It was all going well – I'd even managed the kerbstone smoothly – when suddenly the baby began to cough.

At first his mother smiled and patted him indulgently on the back, but as the coughing grew worse and he turned scarlet in the face, she became seriously alarmed.

'Whatever's the matter?' she cried, unstrapping him and

shooting me an accusing glance as if she suspected it was my fault.

Frightened, I stared at the sobbing child. I was only pushing the pram but could I have done something wrong? What's the matter with him, I wondered guiltily. Instantly, as if a voice had spoken in my head, came the answer. He's got a peanut stuck in his throat.

'He's got a peanut stuck in his throat,' I blurted aloud, without pausing to question how I knew.

The woman stared at me, then put her finger into the baby's mouth. A split second later out came an unchewed nut. Apparently she had been eating peanuts a little while before and, thinking the baby was old enough to cope with them, she'd given him a couple. He must have kept one unchewed in his cheek and forgotten about it until it went down the wrong way.

At any rate, my answer had been right.

'But, Pol,' said our neighbour as she settled the baby back in his place, 'how did ...?' Then she stopped, her expression uneasy. 'Yes, well I think I'd better carry on pushing now,' she finished briskly and sadly I was forced to relinquish the pram.

Throughout my childhood I came to know that expression very well. I would say something quite innocent, intending to be helpful, and an adult face would change from relief to suspicion and then wariness. You could almost hear them thinking, 'But how does she know these things?' Had I not been an ordinary, down-to-earth child, good old Sam and Jenny Sutton's little girl, I think they might have been frightened of me. As it was, they were uneasy but I did have some reassuring saving graces. I was a proper little mother and that they approved of, although my involvement with the little ones didn't always do me any good.

When I was a little older I used to take out baby Hazel Hudson, the youngest of our neighbours' children. I went for long walks with the pram, chattering away to Hazel who couldn't understand a word but who gurgled obligingly as if we were having a proper conversation. So when Hazel's brother and sister, Kenny and Joyce, caught scarlet fever and were sent to the isolation hospital it was only natural that Mrs Hudson should ask me to take Hazel to visit them when she wasn't able to go herself.

I didn't mind a bit. The hospital was outside the town, and it was a pleasant walk. As it happened it was a lovely day in the early spring with the tips of crocus just showing above the ground. It was so nice, in fact, that my sister Edna and her friend Peggy decided to come with me.

It was an enjoyable outing. Hazel was well behaved as usual and the rest of us were in high spirits. We knocked on the door of the hospital to hand in the sweets and comics Mrs Hudson had packed up, then we walked round to the window of the children's ward. We weren't allowed inside, of course, but we waved and shouted to Joyce and Kenny through the glass, and I think we cheered them up.

That should have been the end of my good deed. But the following week I began to feel unwell. My head ached, my temperature soared and, by the weekend, I was being raced back to the isolation hospital by ambulance. As they carried me up the path on a stretcher I pushed the blankets off my face.

'Don't do that love,' said the ambulance man, pushing them back again.

'I only wanted to see if the crocuses were out,' I muttered.

But it was too late. We were through the door and heading for the children's ward where I'd be able to cheer Joyce and Kenny from the inside this time. Of the four of us who'd set out that spring afternoon to visit the Hudson children, I was the only one who caught scarlet fever.

I suppose I picked up quite a few childhood illnesses that way but it didn't deter me. As I grew up I was always surrounded by children and when I eventually married it came as no surprise to anyone that I wanted a baby right away.

Well, I got my wish. I had my baby and that baby was to change my life for ever. As I explained in my first book, *Voices in My Ear*, my little John Michael was taken from me when he was just five months old. Blockage of the bowel, they said. They operated on him but it was no use. He died soon afterwards.

It was the tragedy of my life. When you lose a mother or a father or even a much-loved husband it's bad enough, but when you lose a child it's the worst thing that can happen. That child is part of you and when the child dies part of you dies with him.

Sadly, I was unable to have any more children though I was lucky enough to adopt a little boy called Terry who is with us still. Yet, out of that tragedy something wonderful happened. Inconsolable with grief I drifted from church to church until I ended up at a spiritualist meeting. There, at last, I got proof from the medium that my son was not really dead, that he was happy and well and being looked after by his grandad on 'the other side'.

Naturally, I wanted to know more. My mother had always been very much against 'they spiritualists' and continually warned me about them. I'd end up in a mental home if I had anything to do with them, she reckoned. But they were the only ones who'd been able to offer me any comfort and I was determined to find out what their organization was about.

That's how it all began. Gradually, I realized that I was a natural medium. Hundreds of strange little incidents over the years fell into place and I began to develop my powers. If I hadn't lost John Michael my gift might have remained unused and undeveloped. Though I would gladly have traded all my powers just to hold my baby in my arms again it was nice to think that his life hadn't been in vain. Through John Michael I was able to help hundreds, and eventually thousands, of people all over the world.

Today I work on all sorts of cases, from haunted houses and unsolved murders to public meetings in vast stadiums and private sittings for bereaved relatives. Yet I've noticed that, without exception, over the years my most successful sittings have been with mothers who've lost children.

I am convinced this is because of John Michael. Unless you've lost a child yourself you can't truly understand the complex emotions that tear you apart.

When I got back from the hospital that terrible day the first thing I said was: 'What have I done to deserve this? I must have been very bad somewhere.' You feel you're

being punished. You feel guilty. You think, Was it my
fault? Was there something else I could have done?

No matter how the child died and no matter how
illogical it sounds, you blame yourself.

Of course, everyone tells you that time is a great healer
but the months wear on and the guilt gives way to
desolation and the grief lies like a block of ice right across
your solar plexus. If you smoke, you smoke too much; if
you drink, you drink too much; nothing does any good.
Every morning I woke up thinking it was all a nightmare,
that I'd glance across and see my baby playing happily in
his cot waiting for me to rise. Then I'd remember and it
would hit me all over again. There was no baby, the cot
was cold and empty, and the nightmare was real.

At the time it all seemed so senseless and there were
days when I wanted to die. But now, years later, I know
that it did make sense, there was a purpose to my
suffering. Now, when a sitter walks through my door, I
can tell immediately if she's lost a child and that common
experience strengthens the psychic power. Often I see the
child before the mother's even got her coat off.

This sense of affinity was particularly strong when I met
recently a young woman called Denise. I knew she'd lost a
child, but there was something more than that and it
puzzled me. The feeling nagged as I went into the kitchen
to put the kettle on for our usual cup of tea before the
sitting. When I went back into the living-room I had the
sensation of a baby being put into my arms and I realized
what that something was. Denise, like me, had lost a baby
boy, at five months old. What's more, being particularly
sensitive, she'd had a premonition about his death weeks
before, just as I did about John Michael.

Denise was divorced and looked after her new
husband's three children as well as her daughter from her
first marriage, but, apart from that difference in our lives,
I could have been meeting myself thirty years before.

After the sitting Denise explained what happened
before her baby died. Like me she hardly dared talk about
her fears in case people thought she was mad.

'My first husband died unexpectedly just a few weeks

before Nathan was born,' she said. 'It hit me pretty hard because, although we were divorced, I was still fond of him. Anyway, Nathan was born and I forgot about the shock because there was a lot of worry over him. He was a perfect little boy but he was premature and only weighed three pounds.

'It was a difficult start for him but he seemed to do well. I brought him home and he was settling down and the children were fascinated by him. Then one day a few weeks later I was sitting by the fire when from nowhere the thought suddenly came into my head: "Len had to go so that he could look after Nathan". I hadn't even been thinking about my ex-husband. It sounds crazy but instantly I just knew that this idea was right. I was so certain, I burst into tears, ran in a panic to check Nathan and then when I was sure he was all right I phoned my sister.

' "Nathan's going to die!" I sobbed.'

Denise's sister obviously thought Denise was suffering from the strain and worry of the premature birth. She made soothing noises, pointed out how healthy Nathan had become and told her to calm down.

'I felt I'd been silly,' said Denise, 'but I couldn't get the idea out of my mind. Yet the weeks went by and Nathan was fine. In the end I thought I must have been imagining things.'

Like John Michael, Nathan was an exceptionally good baby. He never cried. He was always happy. He'd let anyone pick him up. He seemed to need an unusual amount of sleep and he rarely woke of his own accord. Most mornings Denise had to wake him for his feed, but when she mentioned this to anyone else they just said she should think herself lucky. With four other children to care for as well, she soon forgot the strange premonition. Or at least her conscious mind forgot.

'Over the next few months I kept having this weird dream,' said Denise. 'Usually I dream in colour but this dream was in black and white, like an old photograph. There was a group of people standing around chatting and laughing as if they were having a lovely time. But as I

446

Innocent Voices In My Ear

looked at them I realized they were all dead. They were people I'd known in the past who'd later died. But as I watched I had this strong feeling of being pulled up – as if they were pulling me up to them to join the party. I shouted out, "I can't come." Then I'd wake up.

'About this time I was looking through a shopping catalogue and I decided to buy a black suit. Now, black is a colour I never wear. I look really dreadful in black and for that reason I haven't got any black clothes. Yet, although I couldn't say why, I was convinced I should spend quite a lot of money on this suit which probably would look horrible. My sister couldn't understand it. "What on earth d'you want that for?' she asked. And I don't know what made me say it but I replied, 'Oh, it'll come in handy for the odd funeral." '

Three months later Denise was driving home from a shopping trip in Shrewsbury when she suddenly became alarmed and stopped the car.

'I felt very strange,' she said. 'The pulling up feeling I'd had in my dream was back and very strong and there was death all around. I know it sounds crazy. Hysterical if you like. I can't explain it but, without doubt, death was very close. I looked over at Nathan but he was sleeping peacefully and I thought it was me who was going to die. It had been snowing and everything was very white and unnaturally sharp as if I was looking through binoculars, and all the time I was being pulled up.

'Death was so close I actually cried out loud, "Oh no, not me. I've got all the children to look after." I don't know whether that helped but gradually the feeling drained away and everything was normal again. I sat there a bit longer feeling shaky and wondering what had happened. Then I remembered the children would be coming home from school so I went back.

'Nathan seemed fine. There was nothing wrong with him at all. It was me I felt the warning was for. That night I put him in his cot as usual and he was quite happy. The next morning I went to get him up and he was dead.'

The doctors told Denise that her baby was a cot death victim. Very little is known about cot death beyond the fact that it is a silent killer which strikes apparently healthy babies without warning. It is more common in premature babies like Nathan than full-term children, they said, and they thought the fact that Nathan slept so much was probably significant, but that was all they could tell her.

It wasn't much comfort and, as the months went by, Denise didn't seem to get any better. She didn't care what happened to her, life didn't seem worth living, and she vaguely realized that she wasn't being fair to the rest of the family. In desperation she wrote to me.

At the time of the sitting, of course, I knew nothing about the whole sad story apart from the fact she'd lost a child. Then as I walked back into the sitting-room and I felt the baby in my arms I looked down and saw that it was a beautiful little fellow, with fairish hair curling into ringlets all over his head. He looked between five and a half and six months old and he was chuckling away. As I admired him a voice told me that Denise had one other child of her own and three of her second husband's children and that this baby, who was their first joint child, had gone to sleep and woken up on the other side.

Denise confirmed that this was right. Then a strong male voice with a Welsh accent interrupted. He said he was Denise's husband and he'd gone over very quickly with a heart attack.

'I still love her,' he told me, 'and for the love we had I have taken her son and made him mine. We couldn't live together but I still love her.' I thought he said his name was Ken but I misheard.

'Len,' Denise corrected.

Len kept going back over the failed marriage. It obviously worried him that he hadn't been able to make Denise understand how he felt for her when they lived together and he wanted to put it right now.

'It wasn't my wish to split up,' he insisted. 'I would have laid down my life for her but I couldn't communicate with her in the end. She always seemed beyond my reach. I thought, whatever she wants I'll agree to, but perhaps I was wrong. Maybe I should have worked harder at it. I shouldn't have let her go.'

He was also worried about the other children. Like many mothers in the same position Denise had sent all her love away with Nathan. She fed and cared for the other children in practical ways but emotionally she'd shut them out.

'Tell her to go home and give Emma Louise a big cuddle and the other three as well,' Len asked. But when I passed the message to Denise she began to cry.

'I can't, I can't,' she sobbed. 'All my love has gone with Nathan.'

This often happens and it's very sad for the children who're left because they don't understand what's happened. Their little brother or sister has mysteriously gone away and won't come back and mummy snaps at them and doesn't smile any more. You don't know what goes through little children's minds. Often they think they must be to blame. Their parents seem to be angry with them so they think the death must somehow be their fault.

'Denise, you must try,' I begged her. 'It's not fair on the other children. You must give them more attention, particularly Emma Louise. She adored her little brother and she misses him terribly.'

Denise dried her eyes and promised that she would try, although she didn't know whether she would be successful.

The sitting went on and her mother, Hetty, came back to talk to her and mentioned the name Lilian.

'That's my real name,' Denise admitted with a smile, 'but I never liked it and everyone calls me Denise.'

As she spoke, a light almost like a torch beam suddenly appeared and started dancing about near her shoulder. I realized that someone else had joined us with a message. It was a man. He'd been over three years, he said, he'd passed with cancer and he belonged to Margaret.

'Margaret's a friend,' said Denise slowly. 'Oh, that must be her husband, Bill. He died three years ago of cancer.' She was puzzled, however, as to why Bill should turn up during the sitting because she hand't known him very well during his lifetime. Why had he bothered to come? It was only afterwards when she met Margaret that it fell into place.

'Margaret said she wasn't a bit surprised,' Denise wrote to

me later, 'because, although I didn't realize it at the time, the day of the sitting was the anniversary of the day he died.'

That special day Bill was obviously thinking of Margaret and when he spotted the communication lines open with one of her best friends he didn't want to miss the chance of letting her know he was all right and he hadn't forgotten.

You often hear people say that grief bring couples together but sadly I've found this isn't always true. Sometimes parents become marooned in their sorrow, isolated from each other and unable to show their feelings. The longer it goes on the higher the barrier between them grows and the more difficult it becomes to break it down.

I was reminded of this soon after Denise's visit when another young mother came to see me. Her name was Theresa and she was a pretty girl with dark curly hair and a look of hope in her eyes. It was only as the sitting progressed that I discovered the real tragedy her looks belied. It was nine years since she'd lost her son and in all those years she and her husband had never spoken of him, nor looked at his photograph. It was as if that child had never existed. Now, that's what I call a tragedy.

The sitting started in a light-hearted way. Two young voices came bubbling through. By the sound of them it was a boy and either a girl or a younger boy with a light childish voice. They were giggling and chattering to each other as well as to me, and they were messing about so much it was difficult to make out what they were saying.

'I've got two voices here,' I explained to Theresa. 'Did two children pass over?'

'Yes, but not both mine,' she said. 'One was my sister's.'

It turned out that they were both boys and, after sending their love to various members of the family, I asked them what had happened. There was much excited interrupting of each other but finally we got it straight. One had been ill and the other had had an accident.

As we talked, a sharp pain exploded across the back of my neck.

'I'm not sure which one it is, Theresa,' I said, 'but the back of my neck hurts.'

'That's my son,' she said quickly.

'Well, he was the one who was killed,' I said as the pain subsided. I asked him for his last impressions. 'I'm falling,' he said, 'and then there's a pain in my neck and nothing else.'

'Yes, that's right,' whispered Theresa. 'He fell from some scaffolding and broke his neck.'

As she spoke I had a fleeting impression of a vivid young face suddenly pressed against hers and her son's arms went round her neck in a quick hug. Theresa was very dark but her son was fair, almost blond, with bright unusually blue eyes. His name was Gary. It was nine years since he'd passed and he wanted to give his love to his father, Tony, and his brother Kevin.

'Mummy could look at me, you know, after it happened,' he explained, going back to the accident, 'because my face wasn't even marked.'

His father seemed to be particularly on his mind. 'I'm very proud of my dad,' he said, 'but he finds it hard to talk about me.'

Theresa agreed this was true, but Gary kept returning to it. 'My mum and dad didn't talk to each other for a long time.'

I hesitated. 'Should you be telling me this, Gary?' I asked.

He seemed to think he should.

'Well, what does he mean, Theresa?' I asked. 'Does he mean you didn't talk about him to each other?'

'Yes,' said Theresa. 'We still don't.'

The whole story came out. Since Gary's accident they hadn't mentioned his name, spoken of him, looked at his picture or displayed a photograph in the house. A stranger would never know they'd ever had another son apart from Kevin. It was one of the saddest things I'd ever heard. I didn't know whether to feel more sorry for Gary or for Theresa and her husband.

'Look, love, you're hurting Gary,' I explained gently. 'He's still your son. He still comes to your home and he thinks of himself as one of the family. But you're shutting him out. When small children go over they are brought back by their relatives to visit their parents and they are hurt if it seems the parents don't want to know them any more. You can't just close the door and think if we don't talk about him it'll be as if it never happened. It doesn't work like that. You've borne your grief individually, you've never had a good cry on each other's shoulders, but it would help you so much if you could share it.'

'But it hurts to talk about him,' Theresa sobbed.

'Yes, but you're hurting Gary too, and I know you wouldn't have him hurt for the world. Get his picture out, no matter what Tony says. It will help. My son John Michael will be thirty-eight years old this year but every night before I go to bed I say "Goodnight, God bless you," and first thing in the morning when I come out of the bedroom I go to his picture and say "Morning, my love. How's all the crowd?" I miss him still, of course I do, and there are times when I say "If only …" but I can enjoy my life because I know he's all right and I'll see him again one day.'

I wasn't just saying this to cheer Theresa. It is quite true. To this day whenever I feel down and I get into one of my 'If only …' moods, a great sense of peace and love will suddenly flood over me and I know that, although I can't see him, John Michael has come to reassure me that he's there.

I wasn't sure how much of this advice Theresa could take in in one go but I felt it was very important to try. I couldn't bear the thought of poor Gary going backwards and forwards for nine years to see his parents, only to find they'd shut him out.

I'm glad to say it obviously struck Theresa in the same light. Soon after the sitting I received a letter from her.

'When I got home from seeing you,' she wrote, 'for the first time in nine years, Tony and I were able to sit down and talk about Gary and get out his photographs …'

So, if I do nothing else this year, I know I've done something worthwhile …

I remember so well, the day I had proof that John Michael still lived, a load was lifted off my back.

If I had had £10,000 to give the medium who told me, it

would not have been enough. There just is not enough money in the world to pay for that wonderful joy and truth. It's given through God's love so it is beyond price.

Chapter 2

I was standing in a house I'd never seen before. There was a bright, well-furnished living-room with a bay window at one end and a view of the garden at the other, but it was the fireplace that drew my attention.

On the wall beside the chimney breast was a large picture of a striking young girl with shoulder-length brown hair and wide expressive eyes with the hint of a smile in their depths. It was those eyes that held me. There was something oddly compelling about them. It was only a picture yet, no matter where you went in the room, when you glanced up those eyes seemed to be looking straight at you. You had the strangest feeling that when you turned your back, the expression on the girl's face changed and that if only you could spin round quickly enough, you'd catch it before it froze into its painted smile once more.

'It's me, isn't it, Doris? D'you like it?' said a voice beside my ear and I realized that Gail Kinchin was proudly showing me the portrait that now hung in her parents' living-room. The portrait that had been painted after her tragic death.

I gazed at it a moment longer, then the scene shifted and crumbled before my eyes, and I was back in my own flat with Gail's mother Josie sitting opposite me. But Gail was still there.

'It's true about my eyes,' she added. 'Mum says they follow her round and they do.'

Josie confirmed that ever since she'd hung the picture she'd noticed this. She had noticed other strange things as well. One evening when she moved Gail's photograph away from the flower that stood in a vase beside it, the flower promptly wilted.

'It was the weirdest thing,' said Josie. 'I moved the photo on to the chair beside me and a couple of minutes later my husband said, "Look at that flower!" And it had drooped right over. Just out of interest I moved the photo back and after a minute or two the flower recovered.'

It was clear that Gail still took a lively interest in her family and wanted them to know that she wasn't far away. She had even appeared a couple of times.

'I haven't seen her,' said Josie sadly. 'I wish I had but on the day before the funeral her friend told me, "Gail's been to me." And I said, "What?" It sounded so peculiar, but she insisted she wasn't imagining things. "She's crying lots and lots of tears," she said, "because you are all remembering her but not the baby."

'And one night later her grandmother saw her. Apparently she asked, "Who's this woman who's having our dogs? You'd better tell her she'd better look after them properly." '

I was not surprised that Gail was so concerned for her family when I realized who she was and the horrifying circumstances of her death. The name had sounded vaguely familiar and, as the sitting progressed, I realized she was the girl who had been accidentally shot by the police a couple of years ago when her boyfriend used her as a human shield during a raid on his flat.

Many people will remember the case but know little of the events that led up to the nightmare. It was only when Josie told me the whole story after the sitting that I understood why Gail wanted me to contact her mother so badly.

'Gail was a real tomboy,' said Josie. 'She was never bothered with the lads. She liked to come out in the evening with her stepfather and me, she was record mad and she loved kids. She and her friend used to go babysitting and after a while Gail started baby-sitting for a couple who lived across the road. They had a little boy she was very fond of.'

The arrangement had been going on for some weeks when Josie began to feel uneasy. She discovered the couple weren't married and although she had nothing against David Pagett to start with her husband, Jim, had never liked him and she began to feel the same way.

'He was very smooth and a good talker and at first, when you had no reason to suspect otherwise, you believed what he said,' Josie went on, 'but after a while I realized it was all talk. He couldn't be trusted to tell the truth. The trouble was Gail, being so much younger, only sixteen, and more impressionable, was very vulnerable, She'd never had a proper boyfriend before, she had no experience of men and I suppose, in her eyes, he was wonderful.'

By the time Josie realized they were going out together secretly, it was too late. Gail was in love.

'He was twice her age and he really impressed her. He used to take her out for meals in nice restaurants and he bought her clothes. But there were also odd bruises beginning to appear on her arms. Well, of course, I didn't like it at all and I tackled Gail about it. We can both be a bit fiery. There was a row and I said, "If you don't stop seeing him you can pack your bags and go." It was just one of those things you say. I never dreamed she'd actually leave – but she did.'

David Pagett's common-law wife had walked out in disgust when she discovered the affair, leaving Pagett with their son.

'He wanted Gail to move in and look after the boy and she was quite happy to. She was very fond of them both,' said Josie. 'I couldn't stop her. I went to the police, I went to the social services, but they said they couldn't do anything about it. Gail was over the age of consent and she needn't come home unless she wanted to.'

As the weeks went by it became clear that the relationship was going wrong. Neighbours told Josie of violent rows between the couple and when she saw Gail, the girl was usually bruised.

'I tried to persuade her to come home, but she never would. One day as I was going out I saw a car pull up opposite and Gail got out, crying and covered in bruises. "Why don't you come home, love?" I asked. "What's this hold he's got over you?" And she said, "You don't know what he's like, mum." And apparently on the night it happened Gail told her friend Marie that he had said, "If you go home I'll get your mum." And she really believed he would kill me if she left him.'

Despite his threats Pagett obviously still feared Josie's influence over her daughter because he suddenly moved his little family to a flat on the other side of Birmingham, well away from Gail's old home. But the contact was not broken. When Pagett was out Gail often phoned her mother and Josie, who had her own car, visited Gail whenever the coast was clear. One day, however, to her surprise, she found Pagett at home and apparently in a civil mood.

'He seemed really pleased with himself,' said Josie. ' "I think you ought to know she's pregnant," he told me. I'm quite sure he got her pregnant deliberately because he thought it would make me disown her. I must admit I was shocked but I was determined he wouldn't see it. "Good," I snapped, "because it won't be born in this hole." Later I told Gail I thought she had more sense but I wasn't really cross. How can you be angry about a new grandchild on the way?

'But I became more and more worried. Gail wasn't going to ante-natal classes because Pagett didn't want anyone to see her bruises. One day his sister came round and said to me, "You've got to get that girl away from him. He'll kill her."

' "Gail, that baby will be born with something wrong with it," I used to plead, but still she wouldn't budge, although I knew she wasn't happy.

'Then one day she rang me and said she couldn't take any more. "Right," I said, "I'm coming to fetch you now."

' "But I can't leave, they've left me baby-sitting," she said.

'Timmy's all right, he's asleep, isn't he?" I said. "I'm getting my coat on and I'll be right over."

'I drove to the flat at fast as I could and when Gail opened the door she was shaking. She hurried to the car and I made the return journey even faster than the outward one. She was still shivering when we got indoors so I ran her a bath and as she climbed in I was shocked to see that you couldn't put a finger between the bruises that covered her body. She was black and blue all over.'

Josie hoped that now Gail was away from her boyfriend the worst was over and at first it looked as if she was right.

'He was very angry when he found out and he was on the phone every night arguing. We wouldn't let him speak to Gail and Jim, my husband, told him to keep away from the house or he'd break his neck. But Gail seemed to settle. We went out and bought everything for the baby, a cot, a bath and a carry cot, everything. She was delighted.

'Then Pagett started phoning during the day while we were at work and I'd come home to find Gail in tears. I spoke to the social worker at the hospital hoping for advice but she only said, "Why can't you compromise? Have her at home, but let her see him."

'I knew that would be a disaster but I certainly didn't want to keep Gail locked up. I encouraged her to go out with her other friends and she did. She seemed to enjoy herself.

'Then one night in June, Jim and I were going to Jim's son's and Gail and her friend were going to stay with the friend's sister. Jim and I dropped them off on our way out and thought no more about it. We must have come home just before midnight which was fairly usual. I went into the living-room to draw the curtains, Jim headed for the kitchen to put the kettle on, when the doorbell rang.

' "I'll go, love," Jim called and went out to answer it. I was just wondering who it could be at that time of night, when there was a great crash. Jim came dashing back, grabbed me and dragged me out into the garden.

' "Quick, he's got a gun!" he yelled.

'But Pagett was right behind us. I turned to see a double-barrelled shot-gun pointing straight at Jim. Without thinking, I lunged forward and wrenched the barrel upwards just as Pagett fired. There was a loud crack and the shot went through Gail's bedroom window. Furiously, Pagett swung round, knocked me down with the butt of the gun and aimed at Jim again, but this time Jim was ready. He leapt towards the garden fence which is four and a half feet high. Another shot rang out and Jim disappeared over the fence.

'There was silence. Had he been hit? Pagett seemed to think so. Was my Jim lying dead in our neighbour's garden?

'There was no time to find out. Blood was pouring from my head but Pagett dragged me up by my hair and marched me out to his car. "Right, you bastard!" he shouted. "Where's your daughter hiding?"

'I wouldn't tell him. I couldn't if I wanted to. My mouth was as dry as a desert. But he kept threatening to shoot me if I didn't answer. He had probably already killed Jim so I didn't doubt that he meant what he said. In the end I gave him the address of another friend of Gail's. I thought he might go there which would give me time to phone the police, but no. He pushed me into the car and took me with him.

' "It better not be the wrong flat, that's all," he snarled.

'Well, of course it was, but the girl who answered the door told him the truth. She didn't have much choice. I got another clout but I didn't mind because I thought at least the girl would have the sense to phone Gail and warn her that we were on the way.

'Well, she did, but unfortunately Gail had hysterics when she heard. Her friends told her to go and hide but she wouldn't.

' "He's got my mum! He's got my mum! He'll kill her," she kept sobbing and she refused to move.

'In the meantime Pagett was driving like a maniac and we got to the flat just as the other girl's boyfriend was arriving. Pagett called out "John!" all friendly, and when the girls opened the door to John, who they thought would be able to look after them, we were right behind him.

'Inside the flat Pagett covered us all with the gun.

' "Get over here," he ordered Gail, but she had seen my head was bleeding.

' "What have you done to my mum?"

'He hit her, knocked me in the ribs with the gun to prevent me going to her aid and threw her down the stairs. She was six months' pregnant. Then he dragged me down after her and pushed us both into the car. There wasn't

much room because Gail was quite big by now, but she sat
on my lap. Pagett jumped into the driver's seat, swung the
car round and it was obvious he was heading back to his
flat. He was driving like a lunatic and all the time he was
hitting Gail in the face with his free hand. I was trying to
protect her and wondering what on earth we could do. I
thought if I grab the steering wheel she'll go straight
through the windscreen.

'Then I looked back and saw a police car in the distance.
I had no idea whether it was just a coincidence or whether
they were looking for us, but Pagett saw it too.

' "I'm going to stop and you can drive," he said.
Whether he thought they might be looking for a car with a
man at the wheel and would be thrown off the scent if I
was driving, or whether he simply wanted his hands free to
shoot at them if they got too close, I didn't know, but I
thought this was our chance of escape. I agreed and he
stopped the car. Obediently I opened the door then I
pushed Gail out as hard as I could and she ran into the
street shouting for help.

' "He's got a gun! He's going to kill us!"

'Pagett was taken by surprise and, while he was off
guard, I grabbed his hair and banged his head against the
windscreen as hard as I could. I wanted to knock him out
but it didn't even seem to hurt him. He twisted round in
rage, threw me out of the car and leapt out after me with
the gun in his hand.

'I was sure then that I was finished. He stood over me
with the barrel of the gun inches from my head, his finger
on the trigger. Then I heard Gail's voice.

' "Don't do it! Don't shoot! I'll do anything, anything you
say, only please don't shoot!"

'To my surprise he hesitated, then lowered the gun and
pushed Gail back into the car. The engine started and they
raced away leaving me on the ground.

'I was really frantic then. I was terrified of what he
would do to Gail when he got her back to his flat. I jumped
up and, as I stepped into the road, I saw a kid on a
motor-bike coming along. The poor boy must have
thought I was mad. I flagged him down, said "Follow that

car!" just like they do in films, and climbed on the back. He wasn't at all happy about it but I don't think he dared disobey me.'

After a short distance Josie flagged down a passing car and they took her to the police station, then to the flat.

'The flat was surrounded by police when we got there and there was an ambulance standing by. "You'd better go in the ambulance," someone said and I thought they were worried about the wound on my head. But that obviously wasn't the idea at all. They locked me in. So that I wouldn't panic or get in the way, I suppose. For two hours I sat there chewing my nails in agony of fear and frustration. Then I heard movement outside.

' "The marksmen have arrived," said the ambulance driver cheerfully, thinking I'd be better for a progress report.

'I was horrified. "Oh, my God."

' "It's all right, they won't shoot," he reassured me but, even before he'd finished speaking, shots rang out.

'The ambulance doors opened and I burst out just in time to see Gail being carried from the flat on a stretcher. "Give me a gun and I'll kill the bastard!" I shouted as I ran to Gail. But I was crying and holding her hand and I knew I couldn't leave her.'

At the hospital, Josie was told that the baby was dead, Gail's chances of survival were slim, and that her husband, Jim, was alive but he might lose his leg. Pagett had wounded him in the thigh.

Gail died a month later. Pagett was sentenced to twelve years' imprisonment.

As Josie finished her terrible story you could have heard a pin drop in the room. How she had kept sane these past two years I couldn't imagine. Sometimes I wonder what on earth is happening to the world, there seems to be so much violence. But at least knowing the background now helped to put the sitting into perspective. One thing that had puzzled me was the way Gail refused to talk about her boyfriend.

'Him!' she'd said emphatically, 'I don't even want to think about him.' She wouldn't even mention his name. I found that odd at the time but, after hearing Josie's story, the reason became clear. Gail loved her family very much and she was distressed at the misery David Pagett had brought them.

She had come through immediately I tuned in and I realized that she was quite a character. She was eager to communicate and very forthright.

'Isn't my mum smart?' she asked me, drawing attention to Josie's immaculate blue suit, shoes and handbag.

Gail wanted to reassure her mother she was all right. Then she said, 'I was so stupid, Doris. Can you forgive me, Mum?' I'm very stubborn and the more they talk at me the more I go the other way. That was my biggest fault. My mother could see it wasn't right and she tried to take me out of it, but I wouldn't listen. Instead, my life was thrown away and he wasn't even free. I've found that out since. My mother wasn't even angered about the baby. She wanted the baby. Mum and Dad had bought me everything for my baby. Even the cot.'

Gail mentioned some family names and asked particularly to be remembered to a girl named Barbara who used to work with her.

Then she sighed and the power wavered. 'It's bloody hard work this, isn't it, Doris?'

'Yes, it is, love,' I agreed laughing. Gail clearly hadn't changed a bit. She'd never been a saint on the earthplane and there was no reason to become saintly on the other side. But she was right. Communicating is difficult for spirit people, particularly the first time they try it.

'You see, I wanted to come home but he wouldn't let me,' she went on. 'He was a swine and I was the only one who couldn't see it, but I saw it that night and all I wanted to do was come home. Me and my baby. And if I had to come over why couldn't it have happened straight away? But they thought I was getting better, that was the awful part. Why couldn't I have come over with the baby? He went first and I lived on for nearly a month.'

Josie confirmed that this was right. There were more family details, then Gail told me that Josie had kept one of her rings.

Josie said this was true and spread out her fingers. She wore several rings on each hand I wondered which one was Gail's.

'No, it's not one of those,' said Gail's voice loudly in my ear. 'She's not wearing it. There's another one and she's not got it on.'

It turned out that Josie had brought with her the cheap little 'engagement' ring Pagett had given Gail. She couldn't bring herself to wear it and on the way to see me she'd almost flung it in a rubbish bin, but at the last minute the thought struck her that it might help the communication and so she slipped it into her handbag.

Gail chattered on, describing the place where her mother worked and the health problems of one of her colleagues. Then she said, 'Give Eric a big hug for me. I miss him. I miss you all.'

I wondered who Eric could be, since Josie had said her husband's name was Jim, but it turned out that Eric and Jim were one and the same person.

'She's the only one who used to call him Eric,' Josie explained.

I kept hearing something about a motor-bike, too, but I couldn't make out what Gail was talking about. It was only afterwards when Josie mentioned flagging down a bike to help her follow Pagett's car that I realized Gail must have been trying to tell me something about that night.

She was very concerned about proving to her mother that she still visited the house and was interested in the family. She told me about that unusual picture on the wall, about a new baby recently born, and the birthday of her little nephew Adam. She even tried to tell me the name of the street where her mother lived but I couldn't catch it. It was just a mumble.

'Come on, Doris, think of trees,' she said in exasperation. But it was no use. 'Oak? Elm?' I tried. She laughed and shook her head.

Afterwards I discovered it was 'wood' – Brandwood. She also insisted that Josie had put something in her coffin with her but Josie denied this.

'It wouldn't have been a flower or anything, would it?' I

suggested, but Josie said no. There was nothing. It was only a few weeks later that she remembered the promise she had made as Gail lay dying.

'She was unconscious and all wired up to drips and things,' said Josie. 'They said she wouldn't last much longer. I climbed on the bed beside her and took her in my arms and even though I knew she couldn't hear me I promised she wouldn't be parted from her baby. And she wasn't. When she died, I had the baby put in the coffin with her.'

It was two years since she'd passed but Gail was still worried about her mother. 'I come and see her at night,' she said, 'and I sit on the bed. She can't sleep. When she closes her eyes she sees that night all over again like a film.'

This really amazed Josie. 'Yes, that's right. When I try to sleep I can't remember nice things any more. It's just that night over and over again, every night. I see every detail in my mind just as if I'm watching a picture on a screen.'

Gail was getting tired now and her voice was fading away but, before she finished, her face, surrounded by a swinging curtain of dark hair, appeared beside her mother's and she said, 'Tell Mum I've got Daniel with me,' and in the last flash of power I had a glimpse of a beautiful toddler with bright auburn hair.

'She says she's got Daniel with her,' I told Josie, and at that she crumbled.

She hurried out of the room to compose herself but when she returned she looked a lot better.

'That's what I was waiting for, Doris,' she said. 'Only Gail and I knew that if the baby was a boy she was going to call him Daniel.'

Well, of course the baby was a boy, and though he was never born on earth, he was growing up with his mum in the spirit world and he was now a little toddler of two.

And Gail, true to her word, had named him Daniel.

Chapter 3

All my life I have been surrounded by children, earth children and spirit children, it makes no difference to me. The only sad thing about spirit children as far as I'm concerned is that, although I can see them, I can't cuddle them or spoil them with sweets. Apart from that they are children like other children.

A few years ago one or two parents started giving me snapshots of their little ones after they'd had a sitting with me. 'I'd like her to stay here with you and John Michael,' they'd say and naturally I would put up the pictures next to the only photograph that was ever taken of our son. Of course, as the months went on other parents would notice the pictures and that would prompt further snaps, until today I have so many photographs I've had to mount them on a special cork board and the way things are going I shall need another board very soon.

I know each of them by name, I try to remember their birthdays and, probably because I have no grandchildren of my own, I like to think of them as my spirit grandchildren. Call me daft if you like, I don't care. They are individuals to me, they have been to my flat to talk and, if they have a message for their parents, they know they can come back and mention it to me whenever they like and I will pass it on.

I try to give them fresh flowers every week, at Christmas I put a tiny tinsel Christmas tree on the shelf for them and when I'm going away I tell them, 'I won't be seeing you for a few days. I'm going to Manchester (or wherever) so I won't see you unless you'd like to come with me.'

And this book is for them, that's why it's called *Innocent Voices In My Ear*. Oh, I know some of them get into bad ways and do silly things that they regret afterwards, but underneath they're still innocent children. There's little Robert who had a tumour on the brain, two-year-old Martin Vosper who was killed by falling scaffolding, baby Oliver Thomas who was shaken so violently he died of brain damage, there's Lilian who made a mistake trying to frighten her parents, there's Careen who took her own life, her sister Charmain who died in a road accident, there's Paul who was killed in a motor-cycle crash and Sandy and Mark and Jonathan and, well, I could go on and on. The important thing is that they're all innocent children growing up strong and happy in the spirit world.

What strikes you forcibly when you look at my kids, and visitors often remark on it, is how beautiful they are. Every single one of them is the sort of child you'd notice in a crowd.

'It's always the best ones who die young,' these visitors often add, and unconsciously I think they have hit on the truth.

Time and time again I hear bereaved parents saying the same things. If they've lost a baby it was no ordinary baby. It never cried, it was no trouble, it would go to anyone, it was unusually forward. Older children are always described as being particularly bright, full of life and somehow extra-lovable. The teenagers are always the kind, unselfish ones who attract friends wherever they go. No one pretends these children were angels, they all had their bad moments, but every parent will say that the child who died was special and somehow unlike the other children in the family.

Now, of course I realize that in these circumstances parents are naturally biased, but often their view is confirmed by people outside the family and it's more than coincidence to hear the identical characteristics attributed to children who have nothing else in common except an early death.

Every time I look at my kids I'm reminded of this and I've come to the conclusion that they are God's special children. They are old souls who don't need to spend much time on earth. They have their useful purpose to fulfil and when they've done their job they have to return to the spirit world. I like to think that the parents of these children, and I'm one of them, have been specially chosen for the task and that we should be thankful that we were allowed to have them, if only for a little while.

I mustn't give the impression that my sitting-room is open *only* to spirit children. There are photographs of living children dotted about all over the place, too, and I've known some pretty special earth children over the years.

As a child, I dreamed of a nursing career but, after my father died, my mother couldn't afford to let me stay on at school and my education wasn't good enough for medicine. Instead, I worked for a time as a ward maid in a large hospital but it wasn't the same. Mother wanted me home and I decided that if I couldn't be a nurse I wanted to be a children's nanny.

Unfortunately, even that seemed impossible. It was a responsible position and you needed experience. How a girl of fourteen going on fifteen gained the necessary experience I had no idea. Neither had Mother but, in her practical way, she told me to put such notions out of my head and get on with the work I *could* do. I was a strong healthy girl, so I was sent to various houses in Grantham to act as a general dogsbody.

In her heart of hearts, though, Mother must have felt this wasn't good enough because, after only a few months, she was not only prepared to listen to an alternative, she actually allowed it.

One day the relative of a neighbour of ours, Mrs Anthony, came to see her. Mrs Anthony had just accepted the position of housekeeper in a household in Bournemouth and she was looking for a maid to take with her.

'Now, your Doris is just the sort of girl I'm looking for,' she told Mother. 'She's wasted here. In Bournemouth she would be working in a properly run household, she'd wear a uniform and she'd learn how to conduct herself. She'd become a properly trained maid. With that experience behind her she could go anywhere.'

Mother was impressed, but *Bournemouth*? It seemed like

the other side of the world. She didn't think she could let me go so far away. After all I was only fifteen.

Here Mrs Anthony played her trump card. 'But Doris is a sensible girl, very grown up for her age,' she said. 'And, besides, I would be with her. I would take care of her.'

The next thing I knew I was off to Bournemouth. I was very excited. There were two new uniforms in my case, a print dress for the mornings and a black dress with a little white apron and cap for the afternoons. I wasn't quite sure why you had to change twice in one day but Mrs Anthony assured me that it was the right thing to do.

'They do things properly in Bournemouth,' she said. 'It's a very genteel place.'

I took that to mean posh and was even more excited.

As the steam train chugged away the miles to the south coast I tried very hard not to wriggle in my seat. Mrs Anthony had said I was very grown up for my age and I was determined not to let her down.

'Now, you just behave yourself for Mrs Anthony, our Doris,' Mother had said as I left, 'or she'll send you home.'

I didn't want to go home. I was going to live by the sea in Bournemouth in a grand house owned by posh people and in a year or two I was bound to work my way up to the position of nanny. Such things happened, I was sure of it.

I don't know what I'd been expecting – some sort of stately home perhaps – but at the first sight of the house my hopes came crashing down. It was a dark gloomy place and the sea could have been fifty miles away for all you could see of it. Across the road was a forest of brooding pine trees and the pungent scent seemed to fill your nostrils wherever you went. At night, as I lay in my tiny attic bedroom, I could hear the wind tearing through the tree tops and the branches creaking, and when the gales blew in from the sea I was sure I'd wake up to find a fallen pine completely blocking the street.

One day in my new job was enough to convince me that my dreams of working my way up to nanny were hopeless. The master and mistress, a colonel and his lady home from India, seemed pretty old to me and, besides that, the mistress spent all her time in bed. She was an invalid, Mrs

Anthony explained. I don't know what was wrong with her but she had a private nurse living in and it was quite obvious that there would be no babies.

I did have a small charge to look after, however – the family parrot. I'd never seen a parrot before, outside picture books that is, and when they introduced me to Christopher I was charmed. He was a magnificent bird with brilliant turquoise feathers splashed with yellow and green. All day long he sat on a perch in the mistress' bedroom, grumbling to himself or preening for visitors, and to look at, he was wonderful.

It was when they explained my duties regarding Christopher that I became apprehensive. Christopher did not spend the night upstairs. At bedtime I was to carry him down to the conservatory and say 'Do your duty, Christopher' before leaving him for the night amongst the potted palms. The next morning I had to carry him back upstairs to his mistress.

It sounded simple enough. But that first night as I approached the perch I noticed what a malicious glint he had in his hard little eyes and how wicked and sharp that cruel curved beak looked. Gingerly, I put out my hand and lifted the perch. There was a loud screech and, quick as a flash, Christopher twisted round to peck my fingers.

Frightened, I dropped the perch.

There was a gentle murmur from across the room. 'It's all right, he won't hurt you. Be firm with him.'

I gritted my teeth and tried again. The same thing happened.

'Now, do hurry up, dear,' said the mistress, sighing. 'He can't stay here all night.'

I scowled at the parrot and the parrot scowled back. It was no use. I had to get him to the conservatory even if I was bitten to death in the process. I took a deep breath, seized the perch, and raced for the door before I could change my mind. All the way down the back stairs (servants weren't allowed to use the front ones) he squawked, flapped and nipped at my hand in protest, but we reached the conservatory intact.

'Right, do your duty, Christopher!' I hissed from a safe

distance and banged the door on him.

It was the beginning of a twice-daily battle. I was scared to death of that parrot and I can only assume the parrot was scared to death of going up and down stairs.

My other duties were easier but not much fun. I got up at six o'clock and cleaned all the grates and lit all the fires before the rest of the household rose. Then I was on call for cleaning and polishing and helping Cook with the vegetables, and at tea time I took a tray up to the mistress. All the time I was learning how to behave properly and trying to carry out the instructions of Mrs Anthony.

I didn't always succeed. One afternoon I was hurrying down the back stairs with the tea tray when the heel came off my shoe. I slipped, the tray flew out of my hands and the china tea things went crashing to the bottom and smashed to pieces on the hall floor.

The silence that followed was awe-inspiring but not long-lasting. Mrs Anthony came running down the passage.

'Doris, whatever have you done?' Then she saw the broken china. 'Oh, you clumsy girl.'

I came limping down the rest of the stairs. 'The heel came off my shoe,' I explained, holding out the culprit, but Mrs Anthony was already on her knees collecting pieces of china.

'Come on, get this cleared up before the mistress wonders what's going on.'

But Mrs Anthony wasn't really cross and I soon discovered why. A little later she called me to her.

'Well, Doris, I must say goodbye,' she said briskly.

My mouth fell open. 'Why, are you going out?'

'No, I'm taking up a new position.'

'A *new* position?' I gasped. 'But what about this one? What about me?'

'You?' She looked surprised. 'Well, you're doing very nicely, dear. As long as you don't have too many accidents like this afternoon's I'm sure the mistress will be well satisfied with you. Just try to remember the things I've taught you.' And with that she went off to pack her things, leaving me speechless.

It didn't stop there. Soon after Mrs Anthony's departure, the cook stopped coming, so I had to cook dinner as well. Luckily, the private nurse was sympathetic.

'You ought to get out more, Doris,' she said, and when I explained that I'd like to but I had nowhere to go, she mentioned a girls' club nearby.

The discovery of the club transformed my stay in Bournemouth. It was a noisy, friendly place, full of girls my own age, and we made our own entertainment with a round of fancy dress parties, concerts and amateur dramatics.

It was through the club that I moved on to my next job. The woman who ran the place was concerned when she found out about my life. She knew I had to work very hard in that depleted household and she said, 'I don't think it's good for Doris to be there. There's nobody young for her to talk to.' So concerned was she that she helped me find another place.

My dreams of working up to nanny flooded back but, once again, I was out of luck. There was less work in my new job but no chance of children. The mistress was an old lady who was stone deaf and the house was run by her much younger companion, an arty type, tall and very thin with a fluting voice and long, trailing chiffon scarves.

The companion was kind but rather eccentric. She played the piano and she liked to pretend the house belonged to her. In the evenings after she'd got the old lady to bed she used to say to me: 'Go to bed, Doris. I'll bring your supper up.' And she would bring me supper on a tray in bed, purely so that she could have the house to herself.

I didn't mind because, if I wasn't going out, I was happy to read in bed, and if I *was* going out the companion didn't mind because she had the house to herself anyway. We got along quite well and, being arty, she took an interest in the theatrical projects of the club. She even helped me make my fancy dress costumes.

After that uneasy start I found I was enjoying Bournemouth very much and I was quite settled when a letter from Mother came. Poor Mother, she could never make up her mind what to do with me. She would send me away to a distant job with what she considered to be good prospects only to find she was lonely without me and wanted me back again. This happened several times and it happened in Bournemouth. I was needed at home, she wrote, she enclosed the fare and I was to come back as soon as I could.

Reluctantly I said goodbye to my new friends and headed north. I wasn't very happy. It seemed I was back where I started when Mrs Anthony had called on Mother. I was no nearer achieving my ambitions. Or so I thought.

Oddly enough as it turned out, I was closer than I'd ever been.

Mother had found me a job at a place called Harrowby Hall. I'm not quite sure what it was, possibly some sort of government training scheme, but there were men from all over the country staying there and this meant an enormous amount of cooking. I was to help the cook as kitchen maid. The potato peeling, vegetable chopping and washing up seemed endless, but people often dropped in for a chat and the hours passed quite quickly.

A local man called Commander Pesani was a frequent caller and one day I heard him talking to the housekeeper.

'So we're desperate for somebody who loves children to come and help out,' he was saying.

The housekeeper nodded sympathetically, then she caught sight of me. 'It's a pity we can't do without Doris,' she said. 'She adores children.'

'Yes, I do,' I added wistfully and, as I walked away, I felt the Commander's eyes on my back.

Later that day as I was taking some rubbish out to the bins I was surprised to see that Commander Pesani hadn't left. He walked quickly across the courtyard.

'Do you really love children?'

'Oh yes, more than anything.'

'And do you think you would like to help out in our nursery?'

I nodded.

'Well, look, come and see Mrs Pesani next week and we'll see what can be arranged.' Quickly, he handed me his card and then hurried away as if afraid the housekeeper would catch him.

And that's how my happy days at The Red House in Melton Mowbray began. The Red House was a large red brick building set in beautiful grounds and when I went to see Mrs Pesani she explained that they were looking for a nurserymaid to assist their nanny. There were three children, Vivienne (five), John (four) and baby Patrick, and they wanted someone to live in, in a room close to the night nursery. It sounded marvellous to me and I was sure I could get Mother to agree. After all, compared with Bournemouth, Melton Mowbray was just down the road.

Once again I was fitted out with a smart uniform, a brown dress trimmed in cream with a cream apron and I set off eagerly to my new life.

Nanny was rather forbidding at first: a thin, prim woman in a smart uniform with a veil down the back of her hat. She was very strict, she told me, and didn't stand any nonsense.

'And I won't allow spoiling in my nursery,' she added sternly, obviously suspecting a weakness in that direction. Rightly, as it turned out.

The children were lovely. Vivienne was a pretty girl with dark, almost black, hair and eyes, John was slim and sensitive-looking with soft wavy hair, while Patrick was a fat, good-tempered baby, a lazy child who would sooner laugh than cry.

The two boys slept in the night nursery, Nanny slept in the room next door. Vivienne in a room on the same landing, and my room was just down the corridor. The day nursery was downstairs and had its own little kitchen and the children's toys – and they had just about every toy imaginable – were kept in an outhouse in the grounds.

The children visited their parents once a week for lunch on Sundays and they said goodnight to them at bedtime. They also saw their mother on Nanny's day off when she helped me bathe them. Apart from that they spent their time with Nanny and me.

My duties were fairly simple. After Christopher the parrot, I reckoned I could cope with most things. I cleaned the nursery, made the beds and mended clothes. I also cooked light meals. Food in the nursery was very plain. The children always had to eat their bread and butter before they were allowed anything more exotic and they only had fancy cakes on birthdays. There was a lot of Marmite on toast and boiled eggs with soldiers and sometimes if they'd had a light tea they were allowed milk and a plain biscuit which was a great treat. Their teeth were absolutely perfect and they had beautiful skins as a result of this diet.

As Nanny had instinctively known, I was a spoiler. If the baby was crying I couldn't resist going to see what was wrong with him. 'What's the matter, darling?' I'd ask, despite Nanny's warnings that he only did it to get attention. And sometimes when the children came out all warm and pink from their baths I'd let them come down to the day nursery in their dressing gowns and give them a biscuit. Of course if Nanny found out I got my head in a sling.

'Dose, will you *not* do that,' she'd say, folding her lips into a thin line.

They all called me Dose. I managed to get through my chores each day so that I had a lot of time left for playing with the children. I used to crawl around the floor with them like a big kid myself. I would get down on all fours so they could ride on my back or we would play hospitals and they would bandage me until I looked like the Invisible Man. They were also very fond of playing shops and I let them take the food out of the pantry and arrange it on the table in front of whoever was shopkeeper. Then we set up a little bell for the customer to ring as he came through the 'door' to make his purchase.

John took this game very seriously as I discovered later when I took him to the children's harvest festival service at the church.

John had never been to a proper church service before and he watched in fascination as the vicar, followed by the choir boys, walked in procession towards the altar. His eyes grew rounder and rounder and when the vicar climbed up into the pulpit his mouth dropped open.

Silence fell over the congregation. The vicar took a deep breath and was just about to start the service when a clear piping voice which carried beautifully through the old stone building said, 'Oh, Dosey, isn't the vicar *rude*! He's got up there with his feeder on!'

Heads turned, there were stifled giggles, and the vicar didn't look too amused. Blushing scarlet, I shushed John and with a sour little smile the vicar opened the service. But John hadn't finished with the vicar yet.

The children's harvest festival was a pretty affair. The church was filled with flowers, and small children clutching baskets of fruit and vegetables packed the aisles. The highlight of the service came when the children filed to the altar to present their offerings to the vicar.

I explained all this to Vivienne and John, adding, 'And afterwards the offerings are taken to the hospital for the sick people to enjoy.'

They seemed to understand and, when the moment came, Vivienne, being the eldest, went first. She used to go to dancing classes and, inspired by her last lesson, she handed over her basket with a charming little curtsey. Everyone smiled and there were murmurs of 'Dear little girl!' I swelled with pride. That was *my* little girl they were talking about. Then came John. He strode towards the vicar, thrust out his basket and then stood there with his legs apart, hands behind his back like a miniature version of his father. The vicar looked a bit puzzled and said something to him but John didn't move.

'John!' I called softly. 'John!'

He didn't budge.

'John. Come back to Dose, John!'

'But he hasn't given me any shillings for it yet,' John wailed for all to hear.

As he knew very well from our games of shop, when a customer was given a basket of food, the shopkeeper was given a handful of 'shillings' in return.

They were well-behaved children generally but, like all children, they loved a joke. Nanny was a bit strict and they weren't sure how she would react to their fun, but the minute her back was turned they were up to their pranks with me.

There was a little table with matching chairs in the nursery kitchen and the seats came out of the chairs for easy cleaning. One of the children's favourite tricks was to remove the seats from my chair and then call me for 'tea'.

'Dose, tea's ready!' they'd call and I would come in and say:

'Where am I to sit?'

Bursting with laughter they'd pull out a chair, spluttering, 'Sit here, Dose, sit here!'

And of course, pretending not to notice the missing seat, I'd sit down and my bottom would go right through. They found this so funny they'd roll about on the floor laughing and laughing. But one day this harmless game almost got us into trouble. I went straight through the chair in the normal way, but this time, being rather plump and perhaps sitting down more heavily than usual, I got stuck. Try as I would, I couldn't get out and when I stood up the chair came with me.

The children found this hysterically funny.

'Come on, you've got to help,' I told them. 'Push, push Dose's bottom.'

Well, they tried but they were laughing so much they didn't do any good and I found I was laughing, too. It seemed to get funnier and funnier and in the end we made so much noise Mrs Pesani came in to see what was going on.

She stood in the doorway, looking from the hysterical children rolling on the floor to me with my behind stuck through the chair, and for one awful moment I thought she was going to explode with anger.

Then her lips started to twitch and she began to laugh.

'You look as if you need some help, Dose.'

I breathed a sigh of relief. It was all right, she wouldn't tell Nanny. I would be in trouble if she did that.

No, the children were rarely naughty but they often got themselves into trouble with Nanny for thoughtless behaviour, particularly if it involved getting dirty.

One afternoon they were going to a party and we'd got them washed and changed and ready to go and Nanny sent them down to wait in the garden while she prepared herself.

I was racing round collecting up the discarded clothes and tidying the nursery before we left, because Nanny couldn't bear to walk out on a disorderly nursery, when something made me go to the window. It was too quiet, I suppose, and I was wondering what they were getting up to. I don't know what I'd expected to see; Vivienne sitting on the grass in her party dress perhaps, or John making mud pies. But the reality was worse than I'd imagined.

There was John with a rusty old kettle in his hand, which he'd obviously filled with pebbles from the drive, standing on tiptoe pouring a stream of little stones on to baby Patrick's head.

Patrick, cheerful as ever, didn't seem to mind. He just sat in his pram smiling away as the pebbles piled up on his clean new bonnet, which by now would be filthy, to say nothing of the condition of John's hands and trousers.

Horrified, I threw open the window.

'John, what *do* you think you're doing?'

Startled, he looked up at me and then down at his brother as if noticing him for the first time. Then he patted him on the head, scattering pebbles all over the pram.

'I'm sorry, but I thought you were the tea-pot, darling!' he said.

How could I be cross? I rushed downstairs with a new bonnet for Patrick and a damp cloth to wipe John's hands, but I couldn't scold him.

John was probably the most imaginative of the three and it was difficult to keep up with him at times. He had a topsy-turvy way of looking at things which was quite logical, as long as you understood his logic.

The Pesanis rented a seaside house in Clacton for a month in the summer and one year, after a glorious holiday on the shore, John, Vivienne and I were driving home with the luggage. It was quite late at night, the sky was dark and the moon was hazy with mist the way it is when it's going to rain.

The children were quiet in the back and I was just thinking they must be asleep when John spoke.

'Look, Viv,' he said, 'there's God in bed.'

Vivienne peered out of the window.

'Don't be stupid,' she said scornfully, 'I can't see God in bed.'

'Dosey, you can see God in bed, can't you?' he appealed to me.

I looked out but, much as I would have liked to, I couldn't see a thing that in any way resembled God in bed.

'No, I'm afraid I can't, John,' I admitted.

Impatiently, John craned his head out of the window and looked up at the moon.

'You are stupid,' he said in disgust. 'Can't you see his bedside light?'

Most children are psychic until the ages of eleven or twelve when the world intrudes, and I looked for signs of it in my young charges. At the time, of course, I didn't know the word to describe the quality I was looking for, and I didn't realize how common it was. I only remembered that when I was about Vivienne's and John's age I had several playmates nobody else could see and I half expected Vivienne and John to have some.

If they did, they never mentioned them to me and never gave any sign that there was more going on in the nursery than Nanny and I were aware of. At the time I decided that this was further proof of my own 'peculiarity'. It was years later that I realized Vivienne and John had no need of spirit friends because they had each other and were never lonely. Invisible friends tend to turn up to play with solitary children, particularly children who have lost a brother or sister.

I was alone a lot as a child and my mother had almost died as a result of a fallopian pregnancy, so I did have a spirit brother or sister growing up on the other side. Our adopted son Terry was in a similar position.

He was an 'only' child to us because we'd lost John Michael and all my subsequent pregnancies ended in miscarriage. As a small boy Terry spent a lot of time on his own, except he wasn't alone. Often when he was playing in his room I'd hear all kinds of thumps and bumps through the wall, sounding for all the world like two boisterous boys having a game. Over the top of it would come Terry's voice:

'Give that to me, John Michael. You played with that yesterday.'

In the summer he spent long hours on the lawn with the toy sword John had made for his 'sword fighting'. He was quite alone, yet if you watched him for a moment or two you realized he wasn't alone. He was aiming blows and receiving blows and concentrating on a fixed spot, just as if he was fighting another boy who could not be seen by us.

I was always very careful not to make a fuss about this or behave as if I thought it was in any way unusual. I knew what I had gone through as a child, forever nagged and hounded for being 'strange', and I was determined Terry shouldn't suffer in the same way. After all there's nothing odd about it, it's perfectly natural.

I was reminded of this when a neighbour in Grantham mentioned that she was having similar problems with her small daughter.

'My mother-in-law says I must do something about Claire,' she sighed. 'She says it's not natural.'

'What's the matter with Claire? She looks perfectly well to me,' I said, for Claire was a picture of glowing health, an apparently happy, well-balanced little girl.

'Yes, but she's got this friend called Roger,' said her mother.

'Oh, and where does Roger live?'

'That's just it. Roger doesn't live anywhere. He's an invisible Roger.'

It all became clear. 'Oh, one of those.'

She looked put out. 'What d'you mean, one of those?'

'One of the spirit children,' I explained. 'Have you ever lost a baby?'

'No,' she said. 'Never.'

'Well, did you ever have a miscarriage?'

She thought for a moment. 'Yes, I did, at four months.'

'Don't you think it's possible that this could be her brother and she can see him and you can't?' I asked.

She stared at me for a moment as if unable to make up her mind whether I was serious or not.

'Well, you must admit it's pretty far-fetched.' Then she stopped. 'Yet, you know, he seems so real to Claire, I almost think she can see him.'

'Anyway, the child is happy,' I said. 'She's obviously in good health. It's not doing her any harm, so does it matter?'

'Yes, you're quite right,' she said. 'I'll tell my mother-in-law to mind her own business.'

And she did. Before they knew it they were accepting Roger as part of the family even though they couldn't see him. When they were going out in the car, Claire would be strapped in her seat and then she'd say, 'Make room for Roger,' and even her daddy would stand back to let Roger climb in beside her. There were practical advantages, too. Before Roger had come along Claire had been afraid to go upstairs in the dark on her own, but now Roger held her hand and she went upstairs quite happily.

I happened to be there one evening at bedtime when this was going on.

'I'd better come up with you, Claire,' said her mother.

'No,' said Claire, 'I'm a big girl now, I can go up on my own.'

'But I'll have to switch out the light when you're in bed,' said her mother. 'You can't reach.'

'It's all right, Roger will do it,' said Claire confidently.

Her mother turned to me in exasperation.

'You see what I mean?'

'Well, never mind, let her be,' I said. 'You can go up and turn it off when she's asleep.'

So we stood at the bottom of the stairs and watched Claire go up. She went into the bedroom, chatting to Roger. She climbed into bed and lay down. And as we stood watching at the foot of the stairs, there was a loud click, and the light went off.

The sequel to this story came years later. On a return visit to Grantham I happened to bump into Claire, now grown up with children of her own.

We chatted for a while then I said:

'Claire, do you remember anything about when you were a little girl?'

She seemed to know what I was getting at.

'About Roger, you mean?'

'Oh, you remember Roger, do you?' I asked.

'Oh yes,' said Claire. 'He was real, you know. I wasn't making him up like everybody thought. It was lovely to have him around. Whenever I was scared I used to say, "Hold my hand, Roger", and he would take my hand and I felt better right away.'

'When did you stop seeing him?'

'I think it must have been when I was about eleven or twelve,' said Claire. 'It wasn't a sudden break. My life became busier and then one day I realized I hadn't seen Roger for a while. I've not seen him since.'

So the world intruded on Claire and Roger when she was twelve years old. But she will see him again one day. When she finally makes the trip to the other side, Roger will be waiting for her, along with her other friends and relatives.

Chapter 4

It was a miserable day. Outside the window the clouds were piled up, grey on grey as far as the eye could see, and the wind whistled through the tower blocks. There were bright flowers on the window-sill and a line of cheerful get-well cards on the table, but today they couldn't lift my spirits.

I was in hospital *again* and it was really getting beyond a joke.

'Surely I've had more than my fair share of ill health,' I grumbled to the spirit world. 'I mean, this is quite ridiculous. I'm either working or ill.'

There was no answer. So they can't even be bothered to reply, I thought crossly.

It was adhesions, or so they said, that had landed me in hospital this time. I needed an operation because of all the other operations I'd had. It sounds crazy, I know, but they assured me it was true. Scar tissue had built up inside my body from past operations and had attached itself to my liver, causing severe pain. In a tricky, time-consuming operation, the surgeon would have to patiently snip it all away and I wasn't looking forward to it one bit.

'Sometimes,' I said out loud to the spirit world, 'I think you've forgotten me.'

There was complete silence from the other side but an unmistakably earth-bound knocking at the door startled me out of my thoughts.

'Come in,' I sighed.

'Hello, Doris,' said my lovely young nurse. 'Here's some more mail for you.'

And she dropped a large envelope on the bed. If the spirit world had forgotten me it was clear my many friends

481

on this side had not. I was touched by the constant stream of
cards, flowers and telephone messages that poured into the
hospital, even Michael Aspel sent good wishes over the air
during his radio show.

Today, however, in my self-pitying mood even this
display of kindness couldn't cheer me. I couldn't be
bothered to open another envelope. I haven't got the
energy, I was telling myself dramatically, when I noticed
that the address was written in the large rounded hand of a
child.

Instantly I melted. I hadn't sunk so low that I could
disappoint a child, had I?

I ripped open the envelope and pulled out a large red
poster, covered with home-made get-well cards and illustrated poems by Katy Beckinsale, eight-year-old daughter
of the actor, the late Richard Beckinsale, and her friend
Amber.

> 'To Dear Doris, We hope you will get better,
> There's not a lot to say,
> We know you can get better,
> Tomorrow or today.
>
> >   Love Katy.'

That was the main card, beautifully coloured in red and
green. Next to it on a frilly-edged sheet patterned by a small
pair of scissors and decorated with red hearts, Amber had
written her poem.

'Oh dear Doris, PLEASE
Call upon my Nanny so fair, her beautiful blue eyes and
    fleecy white hair,
also my grandad so brave, I hope up in Heaven he doesn't
    look so grave,
PLEASE call upon my horses so fair their manes and tails
    is as soft as human hair,
Also my Aunty Lidia who I have never seen,
But I have heard her face is like a moon beam,
And so is yours.

>   With love,
>   Amber XXXXXXXXXX

Next to it, Katy, who had obviously read my first book, had stuck her poem, lavishly illustrated in pink, lavender and purple.

'Your baby doth lieth in Heaven, his violet eyes look down
      each day,
And in your head of love and tenderness, his heavenly
      voice seems to say,
 Mother I wish thee well, and Father and Terry as well,
   Mother please don't be sad, I have only received my
PROMOTION.'

And as I read these words the tears poured down my face. The spirit world had not forgotten me, but it took an eight-year-old child to remind me of the truth.

I first met Katy when her mother Judy came to me for a sitting. She had seen me on the Russell Harty Show and wrote to Russell asking if he could put her in touch with me.

I was a great fan of poor Richard's. I used to laugh and laugh at his television shows, but I knew nothing at all about his private life and I was very surprised to find he had a daughter of Katy's age. Surely he wasn't old enough?

He assured me he was and there were other surprises as well. Far from being a jolly, jokey type, he was in fact very sensitive and concerned. During his lifetime he said he used to think he was a natural pessimist. He was very sorry to leave his wife, the actress Judy Loe, behind and I could see why. Judy was a beautiful girl and very brave. She smiled and laughed, yet deep down in her eyes the loss was there, even though several years had gone by since Richard passed.

Richard was a very good communicator and he came through easily but he was very sad at first.

'I was so frightened,' he said. 'There was always this great fear, not only the night I passed but before. I thought I was a natural doomsday boy, a real pessimist, but I realize now I must have known.'

The night he fell ill, Judy was in hospital. They wanted

another child and she would need an operation to make it possible.

'I was very frightened that night,' said Richard. 'Then I started getting pains in my left arm and in my chest. I rang some friends and they said feel your pulse, but I didn't know what it should have been.'

Later that night he had a heart attack. He was very sad as he talked of those last hours and Judy confirmed that the facts were correct. What's more, later on when she was sorting out his things, she came across several poems and writings that seemed to show that he knew he wouldn't have long to live. She was so moved when she read them that she collected them together and had them published. One short piece seemed to say it all:

> Baby girl widow please take care of my children.
> Baby girl widow will make my dreams come true.

When he wrote those words nobody suspected, least of all Richard, that there was something wrong with his heart.

As the sitting went on, however, Richard cheered up. He sent his love to his Judy Sunshine as he called her.

'Judy was my life,' he said. 'Judy and Kate. My only regret is that I couldn't talk to Judy about my fear. I couldn't make her understand.'

Then he mentioned a girl called Sammy, his daughter by his first wife.

'But, my dear, you're not old enough!' I said in surprise, and he laughed.

'Oh yes, I am. But I was very young when I married and it didn't work.'

He wanted particularly to thank Judy.

'Judy, bless her heart, took my daughter into her heart as well as into our home,' he said, 'and Katy is her sister. I'm only sorry I only had two years to know my daughter Samantha properly.'

As he spoke I suddenly saw him quite clearly beside Judy. I'd always had a mental picture of Richard as he was in *Rising Damp* but he looked different now. His face had filled out, his dark hair was much shorter and those deep shadows had gone from under his eyes.

He sent his love to Ronnie Barker, 'my dearest friend' he called him. He mentioned Katy's birthday and he wanted Judy to be happy.

'Walk in sunshine, you and Katy,' he told her. 'I hope one day you will meet someone who can be a loving companion to you and a father to Katy. I'll always be Katy's father but I wouldn't want you to go through the rest of your lives alone.'

He also talked about his mother, Margaret, and, when she got home, Judy must have told her, because soon afterwards Margaret rang me. She introduced herself and we were chatting when suddenly Richard cut in.

'You don't say Margaret, you say "'Ow's our Maggie then?"' he told me and when I passed this on, Margaret start to cry.

'That's it,' she said. 'Every time he came home he called out "'Ow's our Maggie then?". He never called me anything else.'

Richard stayed very close to his family, particularly to Katy, whom he adored. She was very like him, with the same dark brown eyes that look straight through you and the same perception.

I've noticed before that when there are small children involved, parents who've passed come back frequently to see them and give them a helping hand when necessary. Children of these parents often remark in later years that they always had the feeling their mum or dad was close when they were in trouble, that although they couldn't see their parent, they could feel their presence. This isn't the result of a fertile imagination. It's a real experience.

Parents do come back when their children need them and it makes no difference how humble or exalted that parent was on earth. First and foremost he or she is a parent.

I was reminded of this recently when a sitting with a young girl called Annie suddenly took the most unexpected turn. I'd been introduced to Lee Everett, the healer wife of comedian Kenny Everett, and one afternoon when she came to visit me she brought a friend called Annie.

Afterwards, as they were leaving, I glanced at Annie and suddenly I could see her differently. Instead of the pretty, modern young girl I had seen before I could see great turmoil and confusion.

'My word, you want some sorting out,' I couldn't help saying aloud.

Her jaw dropped and she stared at me in surprise, but Lee said, 'You can say that again, Doris. She does.'

Poor Annie was in a hell of a muddle. She'd got involved in a business project, she'd given up her flat, her job and just about everything she possessed in an effort to get it off the ground, but nothing seemed to be happening and she was drifting from one day to the next not knowing what to do.

She was a nice, kind-hearted girl and I hated to see her in such a state.

'Look, love, I don't know if it will help but would you like a sitting?' I asked. 'Perhaps the spirit people will be able to suggest something.'

Now, as I've said before, I'm not a fortune teller but occasionally the spirit people can see round corners and when one of their loved ones has reached an all-time low they will often let slip just a little of the future to cheer that unfortunate person and help them live through the present. I couldn't promise they'd do it for Annie, but I thought it was worth a try.

The sitting started off in the ordinary way. Annie's brother came through and various members of her family, but in the background I kept hearing a voice say:

'Ask Yoko, ask Yoko.'

Yoko, I thought, that's strange. I only know of one Yoko, Yoko Ono, the Japanese woman who was married to John Lennon. Obviously it was a more common name than I imagined.

Then came the name John Lennard.

'Oh, that's the lawyer who's involved in the business project,' said Annie.

Then another voice interrupted. 'My name is John Lennon.'

I thought I was getting mixed up with John Lennard who was alive and working with Annie, but the new voice was very firm.

'No, I'm John Lennon, I'm over this side,' he insisted. 'She doesn't know me, but my best friend was talking to her on the phone last night. Elton John from New York.'

I repeated this and Annie said, 'Yes. I was talking to Elton last night.'

It turned out that she used to work in the music business and knew Elton John very well, although she'd never met John Lennon.

Nevertheless, John Lennon seemed to know all about Annie's project.

'Why don't they ask Yoko for backing?' he said. 'After all, they named the project after me.'

Annie agreed that this was true. He mentioned a few more details about the business which were confidential, and then he went back to Elton.

'I loved that boy,' he said. 'He's written a song about me you know. It's called Johnny. He played my song all over the world.'

I don't know much about pop music but Annie seemed to think this was pretty accurate. Nevertheless I still wasn't convinced that I was talking to John Lennon. For one thing it didn't sound like him to me. This man had an American accent and I expected John Lennon to sound Liverpudlian.

'Can you give me any proof it's you?' I asked.

'Yoko and I had matching briefs with our initials on,' he said, 'and she has kept four pairs of my solid gold spectacles.'

Then he started talking about a picture with flowers round it and lots of candles, but neither Annie nor I could understand what he meant. It didn't make sense to us.

'D'you mean that Yoko keeps a picture of you with flowers and candles by it?' I asked.

No, he said, that wasn't what he meant at all. He tried to explain again but I couldn't catch it.

'It's no good. I'm sorry, love, clear the vibration and let's try something else.'

It was only later that we solved the puzzle. Apparently, on the anniversary of his death the fans went round Central Park with a flower-decked portrait of John Lennon and they all lit candles.

Next, he showed me the place where he was killed. Instantly a typical New York scene appeared in my mind. Tall buildings and the trees of Central Park nearby. He owned the whole block, he explained.

'And you've been there,' he said.

'Oh no, I don't think so,' I assured him.

'Yes, you have,' he insisted. 'You did a radio programme there.'

And suddenly the picture changed and I saw an image of John and I standing in a magnificent plant-filled hallway waiting for the lift to take us up to the apartment where Lord Fitzgerald and his wife Peggy broadcast their late-night radio show to the wide-awake New Yorkers.

'Oh yes,' I said slowly. 'That was the last time we were in America. So that was your building was it?'

But John Lennon was off again. He seemed a strange boy. He sounded cocky and rather arrogant, I'm afraid, but he was also concerned about helping people. He went back to Annie's project.

'There's plenty of money. I'd like Yoko to back you as long as you devote part of your time to peace.'

I asked him what he was doing on the other side.

'I'm still composing,' he said. 'And I've met two Brians, one who killed himself with drugs and the other who drowned himself in a swimming pool.'

Annie said he must be referring to Brian Epstein, the Beatles' early manager who died of a drug overdose, and Brian Jones of the Rolling Stones who was found dead in his swimming pool.

'What about the man who shot you?' I asked. 'Do you bear him any bitterness?'

John said he didn't. 'After all, he wasn't right in the head, was he?' Then he laughed. 'And if I had to come over I did it the right way, didn't I, in a blaze of publicity!'

He seemed to have a black sense of humour but underneath it he was a caring person.

'There were a lot of things left undone that I should have done,' he said, and his two sons were particularly on his mind.

'I left Yoko you know,' he said, 'but I realized my true happiness lay with my family and I went back.'

He worried that his eldest boy Julian felt unfairly treated.

'He's gone blond now,' he said, 'but the trouble is he thinks he ought to have a lot more and Yoko thinks she's doing the right thing by waiting till he's older.'

And finally he talked about Sean, the younger son. It was clear that Sean had a special place in his heart and he still spent a lot of time close to him.

'I've shown myself to Sean,' he said. 'Sean has seen me.'

Small children are psychic, so it's quite likely that Sean has seen his daddy and he will certainly continue to feel his presence as he grows up.

It's very strange the way so many pop musicians go over young. I know there is a lot of drinking and drug-taking in that profession which would account for some of the deaths, but a surprising number of these young people go over through no fault of their own. John Lennon was murdered, other singers have been killed in plane crashes, electrocuted by their guitars, or like Marc Bolan, been involved in fatal car accidents.

I have done quite a few sittings for the grieving wives, girlfriends and mothers who are left behind in these tragic cases and, from talking to the mothers, I realize that no matter what sort of wild image the young man may have presented to the rest of the world, no matter what sort of bad habits he may have been led into, to his mother he is still her innocent child. Beneath the permissive exterior lies the little boy she always knew.

I realized this when Marc Bolan's mother, Mrs Phyllis Feld, came for a sitting. It was several years since Marc had been killed but I still had a vague recollection of him. Wasn't he the boy with all those long curls down his back and the eye make-up? Being a Jim Reeves fan myself, Marc Bolan wasn't really my cup of tea so I'd never followed his career, but if you'd asked me what he was like

I would probably have said that by the look of him he was one of those couldn't-care-less, rebellious types. Which just shows how wrong you can be. When he came back to talk to his mother, I discovered he was a gentle, kind-hearted young man. He had made mistakes, he knew it and he was ready to admit it.

Mrs Feld had written to me asking for a sitting and I booked her for the only day I happened to have free, but it turned out to be a lucky choice.

As soon as I started working Marc came through singing *Happy Birthday.*

'Why is he singing that?' I asked his mother.

'It's his birthday today,' she explained.

'Twenty-nine,' said Marc.

'Is he twenty-nine today?' I asked.

'No,' said Phyllis, 'but he was twenty-nine when he was killed.'

He then went on to mention his little boy, Rolan, and gave his age, and then he talked of Gloria.

'That's Rolan's mother,' said Phyllis.

'My mum's lovely,' Marc went on. 'She has never blamed Gloria for what happened.'

Apparently Gloria was driving the car the night the accident happened. The Mini went out of control, hit a tree and Marc was killed.

'Gloria was all right,' Marc explained. 'She wasn't unconscious or anything. She kept saying, "Wake up! Wake up, Marc!" But I'd already gone. I think a tyre burst.'

Then, for some reason, he started singing again. This time it was a jolly song called *Tie a Yellow Ribbon Round the Old Oak Tree,* which I found an odd choice. I mean, I'm fond of the song but from the little I knew of Marc's work I didn't think this was his sort of music at all. When he finished the chorus, he muttered something about a girl coming from America on his birthday and tying a ribbon round a tree.

It was double Dutch to Phyllis and me. We couldn't make head nor tail of it.

'We don't know what you mean, love.'

He repeated the message several times but it was no use.

'Let's come back to it later,' I suggested. 'We're not getting anywhere at the moment.'

But a few days later the meaning became clearer. There was a story in the paper about Marc Bolan and it mentioned that his fans still make a pilgrimage every year to the tree where he died. It didn't specifically mention the American girl but since he had a lot of American fans the chances are that an American girl was amongst them.

Marc went on to talk about another Mark. 'But it's his real name,' he said, 'spelt M-A-R-K.' It was only then that I realized Marc didn't spell his own name the same way.

'He has a cousin called Mark,' said Phyllis.

He mentioned other family names and birthdays. Then he gave the name Grace.

Phyllis shook her head. 'I don't know anyone called Grace.'

'No, Mum doesn't know her,' said Marc, 'but tell her I've met Elvis Presley and his mother Grace over here.'

Phyllis didn't think this was unlikely. 'Oh yes, he adored Elvis Presley,' she said. 'He would have wanted to meet him.'

Marc added that his mother was soon going to Los Angeles (which was correct) and Elvis wanted her to phone someone called Prissy and give his love to Lisa.

'Elvis' wife was called Priscilla,' said Phyllis, 'and his daughter is Lisa.'

Then Marc talked about his career. He mentioned several personal financial details which his mother confirmed and he said he was worried about her.

'My mum shouldn't be working,' he said. 'I worked hard and made a lot of money, but I was ripped off. I thought a lot about my music but I was no good as a businessman.

'Fame and money came too quickly. I couldn't handle it. I wouldn't listen to my dad. I thought I was a big star but Dad always said "be careful".'

Phyllis nodded sadly. 'Yes, that's quite true. His dad did worry about him.'

And finally, like John Lennon, Marc's thoughts went back to his son. He was very proud of little Rolan.

'I was writing a song for Rolan just before it happened, you know,' he told me. 'A new song.'

Perhaps one day Rolan will write a song for his dad. Marc would like that.

Chapter 5

It was Halloween night in America. All across the country excited children were scurrying from door to door shouting 'Trick or Treat!', adults dressed as witches and ghosts were hurrying to fancy dress parties and John and I, rather bemused by the eerie celebrations, were on our way to visit friends in Connecticut.

It was a cold night, the sort of night when the wind sighs in the trees, the dead leaves rustle in the gutter and normal objects cast strange, unnatural shadows. A night when even grown-ups hurry to switch on the lights.

Normally such things make me smile. I can understand the tingle of pleasant fear people enjoy listening to ghost stories or playing creepy games, but I can't share it. Ghosts, ghoulies and things that go bump in the night hold no terrors for me. If I see a ghost I simply wish him good day and ask how he is. But this particular Halloween I began to think the atmosphere was affecting me. The nearer we drew to the beautiful old mill house where our friends, the Wiehls, lived, the stranger I felt.

The car pulled into a lush shrub-lined drive, now a mass of heaving black shapes, and I began to feel distinctly weird. There was a hollow, drained sensation in my stomach that grew worse as we approached the house and by the time the car stopped I was feeling definitely ill.

I jumped out, thinking the fresh air would do me good, and then stopped dead. Whatever it was, I'd walked right into it. I was standing beneath a Victorian-style lamp-post from which swung a macabre Halloween pumpkin and the bad vibrations were all around. I wanted to scream and shout and throw things, but somehow I couldn't move.

'Why, Doris, what's the matter? Is something wrong?' It was Pam Wiehl, come to welcome us.

'Oh, no, no,' I stammered, forcing down the urge to scream. 'Let's go inside. I just feel a little, well, odd.'

It's such a beautiful place, I thought, glancing back at the lamp which glimmered on a breathtaking swimming pool. What on earth's going on?

Later, I found out. Pam's nineteen-year-old daughter, Sandy, had leapt up from the breakfast table one morning, rushed up to the roof and thrown herself off into the pool, which was empty at the time. Pam, hearing the crash, had raced outside and seen her daughter broken and dead at the bottom of the pool.

She told me later that she'd stood under the lamp, torn in two, paralysed with indecision. She didn't know whether to rush to her daughter or rush to phone an ambulance and, being pulled in two directions at once, she couldn't move at all. She stood there in agony, and when she opened her mouth to scream, no sound came out.

Strange as it may seem the sheer horror of that moment lived on. So powerful was the emotion Pam felt that morning, the air was still charged with it and any sensitive person would pick it up.

We had been meaning to visit the USA for a long time and our kind American friends pinned us down to autumn 1982. It's amazing how things snowball. On our last trip to New York we met a couple who'd lost their son, Greg, in a car crash. They came to me for a sitting and, as soon as I tuned in, four young people, all nineteen years of age, came bursting in to talk to us. One of them was Greg, and the others were called Sandy, Jamie and Chris. They had all known each other on earth, they explained, and were still friends on the other side.

It turned out that the grieving but enterprising parents had formed themselves into a bereavement circle so that they could exchange help and comfort. Once Greg's parents had been to me for a sitting they were eager to persuade me to visit the rest of the circle and do the same for them.

'Next time you come to the States, come and stay with us

and we'll introduce you to everyone,' they said. 'They'd be so pleased to meet you.'

I felt as if I knew Greg's family home already. During the sitting he had shown me a room which I took to be his parents' sitting-room. I saw a large window and on the wall beside it was a picture of Greg in casual clothes.

His parents, Pat and John, shook their heads blankly.

'No, that's not our living-room.'

'They don't recognize it, Greg,' I told him.

'Yes, they do.' He showed me the scene again but this time from further back so that I could see a red couch facing me. I described it to his parents.

'It's where you watch telly,' I added.

'Oh, our den!' they cried. 'Yes, it's exactly like that.'

Greg went on to talk of his passing. It was early morning just before dawn and a misty rain was falling. I had the impression of a wide open area, and a curve in the road, then a confusion of lights and a bang. Greg said he was killed instantly, his back and neck were broken and his chest was crushed. He was annoyed because his parents didn't receive all his belongings.

'They took my watch and I wanted Dad to have it. I'd just cashed my pay cheque but that was missing, too.'

'Yes, there was only one dollar in his wallet when we received it,' said Pat.

Most of all, Greg was sorry for the way he'd sometimes treated his parents. 'I really socked it to them when I was growing up. But now I realize how much they loved me. Dad was disappointed because I didn't go to college, but I needed time to find myself. I think I was almost there, but then that stupid accident happened.'

Some weeks later, Greg's mother phoned to ask me yet again if John and I would be able to visit them. Within seconds of hearing Pat's voice, Greg was at my side.

'There's been a beautiful wedding,' he told me, 'and I went along. It was terrific!'

His mother gasped. 'Well, that's amazing,' she cried. 'Greg's sister, Debra, got married last week.'

'Did she marry Jean Marc?' I asked, remembering that during the original sitting Greg had mentioned Debra and a young man called Jean Marc. 'They're more than friends!' he told me.

'Why, yes,' said Pat. 'That's right, she did.'

This information made her more determined than ever that we should visit them.

'Sandy's parents are particularly anxious to meet you. After all, you did mention Sandy during the sitting.'

Well, of course, John and I would have loved to go but what with long-standing engagements and spells in hospital it was the end of 1982 before we could manage it. Yet once we arrived we were glad of our timing.

Connecticut in the fall was breathtaking. Never had we seen such colours. The air was crisp and sparkling and we drove down wide, open roads ablaze with fiery trees. Mile upon mile we saw nothing but brilliant trees each vying to outshine the one beside it. There were scarlets and coppers, acid yellows and lime greens, each one setting off the next until our eyes ached from gazing at them. John and I drove for miles without saying a word, so entranced were we with the scenery.

'What a pity you won't see it at its best,' people kept saying to us and our jaws dropped. How could it possibly look lovelier than it did already?

'Why are the colours so much brighter than at home?' I asked John.

'Maybe it's the soil,' he suggested.

Whatever the reason, we were very thankful to have seen it.

As with all my trips abroad, word soon got round and television shows, public meetings and church services were added to my schedule. I ended up visiting New York and Baltimore as well as Connecticut but, unfortunately, on these tours the messages tend to blend into one another in my memory and afterwards I can only remember a few of the more striking ones.

I particularly remember the church service in Connecticut. Quite a few children came back to talk to their parents but after a while I kept hearing an insistent male voice. He wanted to talk to his wife.

I searched round the crowded hall looking for her and

eventually I saw a light hovering around an intimidating, rather wealthy-looking lady. I could tell immediately that she didn't think much of this at all. In fact she told me later that she hadn't wanted to come and after what happened I can't say I blame her.

'I've got a message for that lady there,' I said, waving in her direction.

'Me!' cried the lady, aghast.

'Yes, I've got a man here and I think it's your husband.'

The lady turned pale.

'Tell her to stop being so selfish,' said the crusty male voice. 'Tell her to stop hanging on to things.'

I passed this on as tactfully as I could. I do try to censor or at least modify certain messages especially in public where they could cause embarrassment. But on this occasion he wouldn't let up until he'd made his point.

'She's got two big houses,' he said, 'and now she's bought an apartment. What does she want three homes for at her age? She's hanging on to my clothes when she could give them away to be put to good use, and she's hanging on to me. Tell her to stop.'

This tirade quite took my breath away.

'He says you're hanging on to his clothes and you're hanging on to him,' I explained gently. 'He doesn't like it. He wants you to get rid of the things you don't need and start living.'

The woman looked as if she was going to choke. I must have frightened the life out of her, but fortunately her husband had said what he wanted to say and was willing to let other people take their turn so I was able to move on.

I was worried the lady might be offended, but once she'd had a chance to think about it I believe she felt calmer. She came up to see me afterwards.

'Well, I don't know what to say.'

'I'm afraid your husband was rather frank, dear,' I apologized, 'but he felt it was important you should understand these things.'

'Oh yes, it was typical of him,' she said.

Deep inside, I think it was a relief for her to be able to relax and let go at last. She was hanging on to her husband's things in a desperate attempt to hang on to her husband. Now she knew that she hadn't really lost him, that he was still close, she could relax.

In Baltimore it was a television show called *People Are Talking* that best stands out in my memory.

I was working with a combination of a live audience and unseen viewers who were telephoning the studio. There were two presenters, a man and a woman, and they seemed a bit uneasy with me. They didn't know what to expect and when the recipients of messages occasionally broke down in tears, overcome by emotion, they were rather alarmed.

I explained, as I usually do, that tears are a release and I'm very rarely asked to stop relaying the message, but the presenters were doubtful at first, although by the end of the show I think they'd changed their minds.

'Are you all right?' they kept asking members of the audience. 'Do you want her to stop?'

And time and time again they received the same answer. 'No, no, I'm crying because I'm happy.'

A few minutes into the show a young boy's voice came through. His name was Mitchell and he'd been killed in a motor-cycle accident.

'I went very quickly,' he said. 'My neck was broken.'

'Yes,' sobbed his mother who was in the middle of the audience. One of the presenters rushed over and put an arm round her shoulders but the woman didn't seem to notice.

'Mum said don't go,' Mitchell continued, 'but I went. I'm so sorry. It wouldn't have happened if I'd listened to her.'

'That's so true,' said his mother. 'He wouldn't listen to me. I didn't want him to go.'

But Mitchell didn't want her to be sad. He was an intelligent lad and he was determined to prove to his mother that he still spent a lot of time with her.

'She's been out with Betty,' he said.

'That's my friend,' his mother explained.

'And tell her I was with her when they went to the store and Mum bought a blouse. She paid for it and got as far as the door, then she said. "No, I don't think it's me," and she took it back again. That's typical of Mum. Always changing her mind!'

By this time, the mother's tears had dried up altogether and her eyes were like saucers. She stared at me as if she suspected I'd been following her round the shop.

'That's exactly what happened,' she whispered.

The light moved on shortly after this and I was flitting from person to person when suddenly I got the name Jamie, followed by the name Griffin and the show came to a standstill. Nothing. Nobody could identify either of the names. There was complete silence.

Now I'll be the first to admit that I make mistakes and sometimes I mishear things, but these two names were quite distinct, not the confused blur you sometimes get when several voices are trying to communicate at once.

'Doesn't anyone know Jamie or Griffin?' I asked again.

Still nothing.

'They don't know you, dear,' I told the boy, but I was puzzled. It was so clear there must be a link with the programme somewhere. Perhaps the name was for one of the callers on the phone lines.

As it turned out I was right, except the person concerned hadn't even dialled the number at the time the message came through.

Unknown to me the mother of an eighteen-year-old boy named Jamie Griffin had been watching television when she suddenly heard me mention her son's name. Jamie had gone missing and the police suspected the worst, but Mrs Griffin refused to believe it. Her son was still alive, she was convinced. She believed he had probably lost his memory and was wandering around somewhere, confused and unaware of who he was.

When she heard me on the television she was seized with the idea that I might be able to tell her where she could find her son and she immediately phoned the police officer in the charge of the case to ask if I would be allowed to help. The police had no objections, so they contacted the television station and, almost before I realized what was happening, it was agreed that I would do a sitting before the cameras for Mrs and Mrs Griffin.

As it turned out it was a very difficult project. As soon as the Griffins arrived I found that, like the police, I feared the worst. I kept hearing a young voice, a boy. I couldn't swear it was Jamie, and I wouldn't want to, because as I've said before I can make mistakes, but whoever it was I was getting details of a crime that had taken place.

The sitting started and immediately I was approaching a river bank. Then I stopped abruptly. I couldn't seem to move any farther. In my ear the name was being whispered but it sounded too implausible. I queried it but was given the same name again.

'The name of the river begins with a P,' I said, 'and it sounds like Powder River but that's ridiculous. There's also a waterfall nearby and that's called Powder Falls. I know it sounds ridiculous but that's what they say.'

'I think you must mean Gunpowder River and Gunpowder Falls,' said Mr Griffin.

Apparently the police thought these places figured in the case. Then I got the impression of a body which had been moved twice and I described a location. I was going up a narrow path in wild countryside.

'I've come to a place where the track forks and I can go right or left,' I told them. 'I'm going left and I can see an overhanging rock and a gorge below me.'

The parents shook their heads but Mrs Griffin looked alarmed.

'I don't care what anyone says, my son's alive,' she insisted. 'If you tell me different I won't believe it.'

The poor woman was obviously in a dreadful state.

'I can't tell you anything definite, dear,' I explained gently. 'All I can do is pass on what they tell me from the other side. Now, whoever it is I'm talking to, is giving me a name, a surname.' I mentioned it.

Again the parents looked blank, but I discovered afterwards that my information was correct. The officer in charge of the case phoned me later.

'That name you gave was my undercover name. No one apart from my chief and me know that name. Not even my wife.'

He went on to say that he, too, believed the body had

been moved and they'd found a shallow grave in the location I'd described, but it was empty. He also knew the place where the path forked.

Mrs Griffin, by this time, had had enough. She must have known instinctively that there was no chance now of my telling her that her son was suffering from amnesia.

The person who was talking to me from the other side gave me the nickname of Jamie's grandfather and grandmother.

'A guess. A lucky guess,' said Mrs Griffin wildly.

He also mentioned Atlantic City.

'That's where my car was found,' said Mr Griffin. 'Jamie borrowed it to go to a Unity meeting at the church and he never came back. They found the car abandoned afterwards.'

Then came the name Michael.

'That's the boy who was with him,' said Mrs Griffin.

'They're telling me there was a row,' I explained. 'The boys were on their way to meet a man but there was a row.'

'Yes, but I kept telling you he's got amnesia,' hissed Mrs Griffin.

I stopped. It wasn't fair to continue. This lady had only called on me because she wanted me to prove her theory. She didn't want to know the truth. If I couldn't support her theory then she wouldn't listen. She wasn't ready yet to have an open mind and it wasn't right to force things on her that she wasn't ready to accept.

Of course, if the police found the body of her son, then that would be different. She would have to face brutal reality, but I could offer her no such tangible 'evidence' and it would be wrong to distress her unnecessarily. I thought back to the time years ago when John was missing, presumed dead after parachuting into Arnhem, and I was told by a medium that he was definitely in the spirit world. I had been devastated. What's more, the woman turned out to be wrong.

'I'm sorry, but the power's fading,' I said. 'I'm very tired. I think we'll have to call it a day.'

The cameras stopped, chatter broke out over the set, and people started walking about again. It was as if a spell had been broken.

Mr Griffin stared at me for a long time, then he came and sobbed on my shoulder. Mrs Griffin was quite composed. She patted her hair in case it had fallen out of shape, smoothed her clothes and stood up.

'My son is alive,' she told everyone who approached to offer her sympathy. 'I don't care what *anyone* says. I know he's alive.'

Of the two, I thought it was Mrs Griffin who was most in need of help.

I was all for leaving the case there but afterwards, when the officer in charge rang, he persuaded me to change my mind. I had come up with enough correct information to convince them that I might be of some practical use.

In particular, he was interested in the place I'd described where the path forked and a huge rock overhung the gorge.

'I know exactly where that is,' he said. 'If we took you to that spot, d'you think you might get any more information? We think it could be very important.'

'Well, I might,' I said. 'But I can't promise. Sometimes it works, sometimes it doesn't.'

In the end he convinced me I should try and we made arrangements to meet with the family and go together. But it wasn't to be. Somehow the press got to hear of the plan and contacted the police to see if they could go along as well. The police said no, but that didn't put them off.

'Doris, the police can't stop us. It's a free country, we can go where we like. But it's up to you. If you say you don't mind if we're there, they can't do anything about it.'

It was a terrible dilemma. If I said no, I suspected they'd write nasty things about me, but if I said yes, the police would be upset and so, very likely, would be the family.

I remembered the last time in New York when reporters had led me to believe that the family of a missing boy had agreed to media coverage of my investigations at the scene of the disappearance. The whole thing had turned into a circus and the mother, who it turned out had not been consulted, was almost hysterical. That had been a bitter lesson but I learned it well. I was determined it would never happen again.

What on earth could I do? The problem churned over and over in my mind. In the end it was John who came up with the obvious solution.

'Don't go,' he said. 'It's as simple as that. If you don't go, the press can't accuse you of being awkward and the parents can't accuse you of turning the case into a circus.'

So I didn't go. To those closely involved I explained the truth. To everyone else I had a bout of diplomatic ill health.

Yet, I still haven't finished with the case. The police were so convinced that I could help them, that they sent detailed maps of the area to my home in London so that I could work on them when I returned.

And I must say that one look at those maps was enough to make me very glad I didn't make the trip. The countryside is so very steep and rugged I reckon the journey would have finished me off!

As always, though, my most important work during that visit was the work I did in private. Amongst the pretty white clapboard houses of that north-eastern corner of America there was a lot of grief and tragedy and so many disturbed children. I couldn't understand why these children from beautiful homes with parents who clearly adored them were so mixed up. The ones who hadn't passed in tragic circumstances were receiving psychiatric help. What was the cause of all this confusion?

I asked Ramanov about it one night and he said he thought that the affluence was partly to blame. The parents worked terribly hard, some of them starting at half-past five in the morning and going on till late in the evening. The result was that they could afford a luxurious life-style but they expected their children to achieve the same success. Some children could cope with this but others couldn't and felt under pressure.

At the same time many parents seemed unusually protective of their children. One man kept telling me that he was trying to get his son to go back to school because it would be so much better for him. Yet that son was twenty-five years old, old enough to be a husband and father.

'When they are grown, you have to let children go,' said

Ramanov. 'You have to let them be responsible for themselves because that is what they are here for. How else can they do the work they've been sent to do?'

We enjoyed our visit, but staying in the homes of bereaved parents was a heartrending experience. The children were so close that I kept bumping into them, and seeing them in their family setting brought home just how great a loss their parents had suffered.

In the home of Mark Ernst in New York, for instance, I went to the downstairs powder room and found Mark waiting for me in the corridor.

'Come down here and look at this, Doris,' he said and he led me through a door I hadn't noticed before, down another flight of steps to the basement.

'This is where a lot of my things were kept,' he explained, indicating the typical family jumble, 'but it got flooded one year.'

I'd first met Mark's parents months before when they came for a sitting at my flat in London. They were polite but rather wary of me at first and determined not to give anything away, so when they walked in I said:

'Oh, my dear, you've lost a child.' They denied it. I was convinced they had and that it was a son but, since they didn't want to mention it. I decided to let the sitting take its course and see what happened.

Mark's grandmother and great uncle and various other people came back, but eventually Mark wouldn't keep silent any longer.

He had been found dead in bed, he told me.

'Dad, forgive me,' he said. 'It wasn't me. I was killed. I didn't do it. Honest to God, I didn't do it.'

He was twenty-one and he was already over when they found him, he told me. But he was very concerned because people were saying he had committed suicide.

'They said I took an overdose, but I didn't,' he insisted. 'I was killed. I went to bed but to sleep.' There had been drink and medically prescribed drugs involved but Mark assured me that suicide wasn't in his mind. Unknowingly he had swallowed a combination that proved lethal. But it wasn't suicide. He loved his family and he wouldn't have wanted them to suffer.

'I know what they're doing,' he said. 'My brother Etan has got a new set of wheels. Tell him to be careful.'

'Has Etan got a new car?' I asked.

'No, a new motor-cycle,' said his father.

'Oh, that's what he means,' I laughed and explained what Mark had said.

By the end of the sitting the Ernsts were no longer wary.

'When you come to New York you must promise that you'll stay with us.' They insisted and we promised.

Well, of course, we took them at their word and we had a wonderful time. They looked after us as if we were VIPs. They had a beautiful house and we hadn't been there five minutes when Mark turned up.

One day I noticed his mother looking through a large folder and instantly Mark was at my side.

'That's mine,' he said. 'It's special.'

Sure enough, when I mentioned what he'd said, his mother opened the folder to show me a collection of Mark's old school essays that she'd treasured ever since he was a boy.

At poor Sandy Wiehl's home in Connecticut the vibrations were even stronger but, as I said before, it was in the garden by the pool that you could feel them most.

Her poor parents had been in a terrible state over the tragedy but when I did a sitting and spoke to Sandy I realized that, like Mark, she hadn't intended to kill herself.

She showed me what had happened and I had a swift impression of falling and suddenly halfway to the ground there came the thought: 'Oh no, there's no water in the pool.'

'I forgot the pool had been emptied,' Sandy told me.

It was a desperate gesture, intended to show how unhappy she was, but it had gone terribly wrong. The poor girl was ill, mentally ill.

'If I'd have been in my right mind I wouldn't have done it,' she explained. 'I had every opportunity but I went into depressions. One minute I was on top of the world, the next down on the floor in the flick of an eyelid.

'Nobody could do anything about it. And I was stupid,

Doris. I did stupid things, things I knew I should be doing, just to be like all the other kids. But then afterwards I felt guilty and that made me more depressed. I was so mixed up.'

She was much better now, she said, and she wanted her mum and dad to know that she was very sorry for what had happened.

'What I did to my folks!' she sighed, lost for words to describe her behaviour. 'You see I thought I was grown up, but I wasn't really grown up at all. I must have been such a pain. I moped about the place and sometimes I lost my temper. I shouted at people. I understand now but at the time I was out of my mind.'

She gave her love to her family and talked a lot about Flip. I thought this must be some kind of fish but her parents roared with laughter.

'No, it's her brother Flip. A nickname for Philip.'

I had to laugh. 'I thought it was short for Flipper. I wondered if she had a pet dolphin or something!'

Flip apparently had seen Sandy since she passed but he thought he must have dreamed it. Sandy wanted him to know that it was real. She had also been around when her sister Kim, and Kim's friend Jenny May, had been discussing her in Kim's bedroom.

'They were trying on my clothes and talking about me and I shouted, "I'm here, damn you! I'm here!" but they couldn't hear me. It was so frustrating.'

Then she began speaking in French. She was quite fluent and I couldn't understand a word.

'I'm not showing off, Doris,' she said in English, after I was suitably baffled, 'I just wanted to show you what I was capable of and how much I might have achieved if I hadn't been ill.'

'Yes, she was very good at French,' her mother agreed.

Finally Sandy described a large wooden chopping board that stood on the worktop, or counter as the Wiehls called it, in the kitchen.

'One day I will knock on that board and then Mum will know I'm there,' she said. 'They're teaching me how to do it.'

I think Pam and John found this a little hard to believe but when we went into the kitchen I spotted the chopping board in exactly the position Sandy had described. Everything was quiet, however, and there was no sign of Sandy. It could take her years to learn how to knock, I supposed. I couldn't even guess how long such a skill would take to acquire.

But Sandy was obviously a fast learner. One day when we were gathered in the kitchen, but well away from the work top, we heard a loud rapping noise.

Pam opened the kitchen door. The hall was empty. She went to the window. There was no one there.

The knocking sounded again, hollow and insistent and this time it came unmistakably from the chopping board.

'It's me,' cried Sandy. 'Have you forgotten?'

Pam looked at the chopping board in wonder. 'Well, I never would have thought it possible,' she murmured.

'You might as well get used to it,' I laughed. 'Now she's learned to do that, she'll be knocking all over the place, I expect.'

Quiet, beautiful Connecticut soon became the centre of a burst of activity – or at least that's the way it seemed to us. The bereavement circle was large and we visited home after home.

The Wiehls particularly wanted us to meet Dave and Skip Warren because their daughter, like Sandy, had taken her own life and there could be no doubt that she intended to. Betsy, who was twenty-one, worked in an animal clinic and one day she'd injected herself with a massive dose of animal poison, normally used to putting animals to sleep.

'You can't be right in the head to do a thing like that,' Betsy said when we started the sitting. 'It was a stupid thing to do but I'm happy now. I'm better off out of it.'

Her marriage had failed and she was very depressed.

'I couldn't seem to form relationships,' she said. 'I did try and I worked at it, but things always seemed to go wrong. I used to drink vodka, too. I started drinking in high school and it got worse and worse.'

She envied her sister Susanne because she had a baby,

but these days she was mainly sorry about her mother. Skip had had several cancer operations and was coping very bravely, but Betsy felt that she hadn't offered her the support she should have done.

'I was so wrapped up in my own misery, Doris, I had no time for anyone else. If only I'd been kinder to my mother.'

Skip agreed that this was true. 'Yes, that's right. She had no time for my problems.'

Finally, Betsy was worried about her father.

'He feels guilty, Doris,' she said. 'When I started drinking he used to drink with me and now he blames himself. It wasn't his fault though. Please tell him to stop drinking so much. It's no answer.'

David had been pretty sceptical when the sitting started and, though he seemed impressed afterwards, I wasn't sure whether he would be affected by his daughter's words. But a couple of weeks later Skip rang me.

'And how's David?' I asked.

'Oh, he's being so good, Doris,' she said happily. 'He's cut down on his drinking and he's really trying. I'm so proud of him.'

As I said earlier, guilt is one of the emotions that haunts bereaved parents and it is quite extraordinary how they will go over and over the cause of death until they can find something to feel guilty about. It is no good outsiders getting impatient and accusing them of being ridiculous or of looking for something to make them unhappy. They can't help it and it seems to be a normal, if sad, reaction. I went through it myself when I lost John Michael and I've seen it in just about every bereaved parent I've ever met. It is cruel to tell them to 'pull themselves together'. They need understanding, love and gentle reassurance.

You wouldn't think, for example, that parents could blame themselves for their son's cancer, but the Kreegers did. They, too, were members of the bereavement circle. Their son, Scott, developed a cancerous mole at the age of twenty-one. It was a senseless tragedy for which no one was to blame. Yet Scott's mother blamed herself for giving him the wrong diet as a boy, and Scott's father blamed himself for passing on genes that were clearly faulty.

Scott, of course, blamed neither.

As soon as I walked in the room for the sitting I could tell that his father didn't hold with any of this nonsense, he'd only agreed to it to please his wife. Waves of disbelief and doubt were pouring out of him into the room, making it very difficult to concentrate.

Oh dear, I thought, we'll have to try and sort this out first or we'll never get anywhere. 'Could you tell me something about him?' I asked the spirit world.

'He's an attorney,' came the reply.

I smiled at Mr Kreeger.

'Mr Kreeger, I know you don't think much of this sort of thing,' I told him. 'But I'm getting the message through that you're an attorney. Is that right?'

His face changed and I could see that he was shaken. 'Well, yes, yes, I am,' he floundered. 'But the Wiehls could have told you that.'

I didn't remember them doing so but he was right. They could have done.

Nevertheless the sceptical waves faltered and receded and I felt I'd be able to work more comfortably.

'Well, never mind,' I said. 'Let's see if we can find Scott and get him to convince you.'

I tuned in again and Scott didn't take much finding. He appeared in the room, between his parents, a very good-looking boy with striking colouring. Dark, almost black, hair, pale skin and deep blue eyes.

'What a handsome boy!' I couldn't help saying aloud.

'Yes,' sniffed his mother, 'he was.'

'No,' I corrected. 'He is.'

Scott sent his love to his parents, his sister Lisa and his girlfriend April. He had been very fond of April, he told me. He was a gentle artistic boy and he had been deeply involved in some sort of artistic project.

'Was it a hobby, love?' I asked him.

'No. It was my work.'

He tried to tell me what he did but I couldn't make head nor tail of it.

'I did it with Lisa,' he said. 'I did the designing and cutting out and we took it in turns to paint.'

Whatever could it be?

'Does this make sense to you?' I asked his parents.

'Oh yes,' they said. 'That's absolutely right.'

Well, that was the main thing. As long as they were happy it didn't matter if I didn't understand the evidence.

'There's a single red rose,' Scott continued.

At this his parents shook their heads. 'No, he didn't do any roses.'

'Well, did you give him a single red rose, when he was ill or at his funeral?' I suggested.

Again they shook their heads.

'Sorry, Scott,' I said. 'They can't place the rose.'

He was most insistent that the rose fitted in.

'Yes, but they can't accept it, love,' I explained. 'Maybe they'll think of it later.'

But Scott did not want to change the subject. He was absorbed by his work.

'Ask them to let you have a piece of my work as a memento of today.'

'Oh no, I couldn't do that.'

'Yes, you can,' he said. 'I want you to have something.'

'But I can't say that,' I protested. It would look as if I was taking advantage of his parents in the worst possible way.

'What can't you say, Doris?' asked Scott's mother.

'Well,' I hesitated. 'It seems a dreadful cheek, but ...' and I told them what Scott had said. To my relief they didn't seem offended.

'What a good idea,' said Mrs Kreeger. 'We'd love you to have something to remember Scott by and what better keepsake than a piece of his work?'

'But what did he do?' I asked, wondering what I was letting myself in for. Supposing he carved life-size elephants or something?

Scott laughed at this.

'No, nothing like that, Doris,' he said and tried once again to explain but all I could hear was a 'sk, sk' sound. Sketching perhaps? I wondered. But no. He wouldn't need to cut that out and paint it.

'It was scrimshaw,' said his mother. 'It's a dying craft. An old sailors' craft.'

Apparently, if I understand it correctly, patterns are cut into ivory, painted, and then sealed.

'Some of Scott's work has gone to the museum as an example of scrimshaw,' she continued, 'but there are quite a few pieces left.'

The sitting went on, with Scott giving names of various members of the family and family friends, then he talked about a holiday he'd enjoyed with his father.

'We went to New Zealand,' he said. 'We had a marvellous time, didn't we, pal?'

And at those words his father broke down and went and stood by the window, staring out over the garden. Apparently father and son had been very close and they always called each other 'pal'. That one little word had done more than anything else I'd said to convince Mr Kreeger that Scott was still near.

The sequel to this story came a few days later. Lisa brought it. I found a beautiful pendant on a red ribbon. The medallion was a piece of creamy ivory into which had been cut an exquisite red rose, every petal precise and perfect. Accompanying the gift was a note from the Kreegers.

'When we looked through Scott's things we came across this single red rose,' they wrote. 'This must have been the rose you were talking about and we're sure Scott would have wanted you to have it.'

I deliberated long and hard about what to do with that rose. If I wore it as a pendant it would only be seen on special occasions and would spend the rest of the time hidden way in my dressing-table drawer. Really, it deserved to be on permanent display.

In the end I made up my mind. Now it hangs beside the picture of Scott on my board of spirit children.

One of the nicest things that struck me about all these American children I spoke to was their thoughtfulness towards the people who were left behind, and this was demonstrated once again, just before I returned to England.

I was talking to Lisa Ernst, Mark's sister, on the telephone towards the end of our trip when Mark suddenly joined us.

'Ask her about Malcolm,' he said.

'Do you know anyone called Malcolm, Lisa?' I asked obediently.

'Oh, yes, he was a friend of Mark's,' she said. 'He's English, like you, but he's in hospital at the moment. They don't know what's wrong with him.'

Poor boy, I thought. It's bad enough to be in hospital at the best of the times, but to be in hospital in a strange country thousands of miles from home, far from your family, must be awful.

'D'you think he'd like to hear another English voice?' I asked Lisa.

'Oh, I'm sure he would.'

I jotted down the number of the hospital and when I next had a spare moment I rang Malcolm. The boy was in a terrible state. Apparently he was suffering from some mystery virus, or so they thought, and he'd lost the use of his legs. He was lying there all alone with no family to visit him and the doctors didn't know what to do for the best.

At the sound of my voice he was so overcome he burst into tears.

'Oh, Doris,' he said. 'At a time like this the person you really want is your mother. But if I can't have my mother, you're the next best thing!'

We had a long talk, during which I told him about John's work as a healer.

'We're just about to go back to England,' I said, 'so I'm afraid John won't be able to do anything for you in hospital, but would you like him to put you on his absent healing list?'

John works with this list every night. He writes down the names and addresses of people who're sick, together with details of their ailments, and every night he sits down quietly and sends out healing thoughts to them.

'Well, it can't do any harm, can it?' said Malcolm. 'And the doctors don't seem to know what to do with me.'

So Malcolm went on the list.

A week later we were told he was on the mend, and the last we heard he was walking again and due to come out of hospital any day.

Whether it had anything to do with John I don't know. But I think we can safely say that Malcolm was given a helping hand from his friend on the other side.

Chapter 6

How does that old saying go? Be it ever so humble, there's no place like home? Well, I must admit that after all my travels I've found it to be absolutely true. John and I had a wonderful time in America and we stayed in some magnificent houses with servants to wait on us and vast, manicured grounds.

Yet when we walked through the door of our little flat we both looked at each other and sighed with relief. Home! There was a pile of washing from our trip. Les and George had painted the flat right through and had the curtains cleaned. It was like a new flat. The view from the window was not of gently rolling lawns but the block of flats opposite. Yet it was our place and coming back to it was like swapping an elegant but tight dress for a battered old dressing-gown.

As always, our first priority was sleep. I can never sleep on planes and we'd been up all night on the flight back, but once the jet lag receded I was able to unpack and sort through my memories and mementoes of the trip.

There was a new pile of photographs for my spirit children board. I spread them out on the table in front of me. Scott, Greg, and Mark, Sandy and Betsy. I paused and put Sandy and Betsy side by side, studying their fresh young faces for signs of despair. But there was nothing to see. The torment that ruined their lives could not be captured by the camera.

'You can't be right in the head to do a thing like that,' Betsy had said.

'If I'd have been in my right mind I wouldn't have done it,' Sandy had cried.

Two poor sick girls, whose sickness couldn't be seen and

therefore couldn't be understood by ordinary people.

I think there is probably much more mental illness around, unrecognized and untreated, than people realize. I wonder why it is that we can accept the fact that a body will fall ill with colds, flu or worse, quite frequently through a lifetime, but we can't accept that the mind could suffer similarly.

Perhaps people like little Paul, the boy who took his clothes off when he was being ignored, are the lucky ones. Paul was mentally retarded and it was fairly obvious, so people could see and understand his condition and they treated him sympathetically. No one expected too much from Paul, and when he achieved something they were pleasantly surprised. Paul never felt a failure and his parents, Jean and Steve, adored him.

At the sitting, Paul's grandpa, Joseph, spoke first.

'Paul couldn't talk on earth because he had a convulsion when he was a baby,' Joseph told me. 'And Jean and Steve are worried because he was unconscious when he passed and they couldn't say goodbye.'

I passed this on and Jean and Paul agreed that it was true.

'Well, you mustn't worry about it,' I assured them. 'Because Paul didn't know anything about it and there was no need to say goodbye. He hasn't gone. He's with you still.'

Paul was grinning away while I said this and to prove I was right he piped up:

'Yes, and Sarah's got the pennies out of my money box.'

'Yes!' cried Jean. 'Sarah's Paul's sister. That's the only thing she asked for. Two or three days after he died she said, "Paul won't need his pocket money now Mum, so can I have it?" '

'She's got my teddy in bed with her, too,' Paul added.

Jean and Steve exchanged looks. This too was true and an expression of joy began to spread across Jean's face. But Paul was still chattering away. On the other side he had found his voice and he liked using it. He said his daddy had put a rose in a vase beside his photograph and he liked that. He thought the month of February was important.

'Yes,' said Jean. 'He died on the fourteenth and it would have been his fifth birthday on the twenty-fourth.'

But Paul was off again. 'Look at this. It's our house.' Suddenly I was walking through a front door and upstairs. 'See there's a new stair carpet,' he said as we climbed and when we got to the top we turned right and went into the bathroom. I was confronted by mirrors.

'This is the best room,' said Paul.

Quickly I explained where I was to his mummy and daddy.

'As I got into the bathroom there are mirrors facing me,' I explained.

'That's right,' said Jean. 'The whole wall's covered in mirror tiles.'

'Well, one day,' I told her, 'you will walk in there and see Paul's face reflected in the mirrors facing the door. You'll just see his face smiling at you. Don't be afraid when it happens. Just say "Hello son" and talk to him.'

Jean and Steve looked pretty amazed at this information but Paul seemed so sure he would do this one day, probably with his grandpa's help, that I had to mention it and I'm convinced that sooner or later it will happen. It must have been pretty hard for his parents to swallow at that time, however, but Jean did agree that the bathroom was special to Paul.

'He spent every night of his life in that bathroom,' she explained. 'He loved a bath and he loved to watch himself splashing about, in the mirrors. It was one of his favourite games. We all used to enjoy it because it made Paul so happy.'

'I liked going out in the car, too,' Paul interrupted. 'It was a new car and I used to look at everything out of the windows.'

'Yes, he did,' said Jean, then she turned to her husband. 'You see, I told you he knew we'd got a new car. He was much brighter than people thought. I was sure he could tell the difference between the new car and our old one.'

The sitting went on, more relatives came back to have a word with the young couple and that was when, my attention being diverted from him, Paul stripped off his clothes.

As it turned out, it was the best thing he could have

done. Steven had been sitting there listening to what was going on with an incredulous expression on his face. He had come to the sitting sceptical, what he had heard had amazed him, but he still couldn't quite believe – until Paul took off his clothes in a gesture both typical and unique. There was no way I could have guessed such an unusual habit.

After the sitting, Jean and Steve lingered to talk to me about their son. He was such a happy boy, they explained, and they missed him so badly. It didn't matter a scrap to them that he was retarted. They loved him as much as it is possible to love a child. Any ill-informed person who said that they were better off without him was cruelly mistaken. Paul might have been damaged but he had his own special part to play in the family.

A few days later they wrote to me, thanking me for the sitting and with the letter was a tiny brooch in the shape of a butterfly.

'Please wear this brooch in memory of Paul,' Jean wrote. 'We think of him as our little butterfly.'

As I read the letter tears came into my eyes. What a perfect description of their little boy. Vivid and beautiful, brightening everything he touched and then gone in a flash – just like a butterfly.

There was no question that Paul was a wanted child and Jean and Steve coped well, but other parents aren't so lucky. Some children are so badly handicapped that, although their parents love them, they can't care for them at home. Sadly, there are also other children whose parents reject them almost at birth for the same reason. Yet, in a way, there is no need to be too sorry for these little ones because often they are quite happy in their own little worlds.

You hear a lot of horror stories about the things that go on in mental hospitals. I couldn't say whether or not they are true, all I do know is that when I spent some time working in a mental hospital after I finally qualified as a nurse in my forties, I saw only love, devotion and extraordinary patience.

I'm not saying that the nurses were all saints; far from it.

It was just that those kids, no matter how damaged, were so wonderful in their own special ways, that you couldn't help loving them.

To be frank, there were some really horrifying cases in the hospital. Or at least they were horrifying at first sight. But it was amazing how quickly you got used to them.

I remember the day, not long after I'd started work at the hospital, that I was sent down to help out at the new infirmary. They were short of staff and, despite my inexperience, they thought I might be useful.

The sister was standing beside a cot as I walked in and she was holding a baby in her arms.

I hurried over to her in that brisk nurse's walk that I'd recently acquired. Fast and efficient but with no suggestion of panic.

'Hello, my name is Nurse Stokes,' I said. 'I've been sent down to help you out, Sister.'

She glanced at me and her eyes held mine for a moment or two as she silently weighed me up. Then she smiled.

'Oh good. Well here, hold this. This is Nigel.' She handed me the baby.

By this time everyone knows how I feel about babies and I took the little scrap with pleasure. I should have noticed and been warned that something was wrong by the way Sister didn't move off after passing the boy to me but remained where she was, watching my face. But I wasn't warned. I hardly even registered it.

I was instantly enthralled, the way I always am when I've got a baby in my arms, and I looked down at little Nigel. The most beautiful little face looked back at me and a pair of baby blue eyes stared into mine. My face was folding instinctively into a smile, when I noticed something with a cloth over it next to Nigel's head.

Curiously, I lifted the cloth, and my stomach seemed to fall away. There was another head underneath, with little indentations where the features should have been.

Nigel was one of nature's mistakes.

I bit my lip hard, so as not to pass out and, as the room swung back into focus, I glanced up at Sister. She was watching me gravely.

I took a deep breath.

'What a dear little face,' I said as calmly as I could.

Sister smiled. 'Yes, isn't it? Right, carry on then, nurse,' and she bustled away obviously satisfied that I could cope.

There were more horrors in store. Later that morning one of the other nurses came over.

'You're the new nurse, aren't you?' she said quickly. 'Well, you'll be going in to see the new baby. Take a grip of yourself. I nearly fainted when I went in.'

Before I could question her she was gone. Uneasily, I finished mixing the feed I was preparing. What on earth could be worse than poor Nigel?

I didn't have long to find out.

'Ah, Nurse Stokes,' said Sister, coming alongside me suddenly. 'Leave that for a moment, would you. You'd better come and see the new baby.

This time I was prepared. Grimly, I followed her up the ward to a special room where a single cot stood alone. I steeled myself firmly as I approached it. The warning was a great help and this time I had no fear of fainting, although the poor little mite was a dreadful sight.

She was premature, she had spina bifida and something else had clearly gone wrong, because her head went up into a sharp point and she seemed to have no flesh on her bones. The skin hung in folds from her pathetic, wasted limbs.

I swallowed hard but I had a good grip on myself as I'd been advised.

Nevertheless, I think I went home that night in a state of shock. It seemed so cruel that those poor misshapen children should have been born. Wouldn't it have been better for them to pass over at birth than linger in this way?

I couldn't understand it. I still don't understand it, although now I know there must be a reason and that those innocents must have a part to play, no matter how obscure it seems to us. All I can say with certainty is that they are not unloved and I believe they are not unhappy.

Within days I found I didn't notice Nigel's deformity. I didn't even see it. When I looked at him all I saw was that lovely face. To me he was a beautiful baby.

It was the same with the new baby in the special room.

Before the week was over us nurses were falling out about those voices she recognized and who she liked best. Of course, looking back I don't suppose she recognized any of us, but we liked to think she did.

Some of the sick children on the ward did know us. There was Geraldine who'd been in a car crash. She wasn't marked at all but she couldn't see and she couldn't sit up. Yet she was a cheerful little thing and she knew your voice.

Every morning I used to tickle her and say 'Who's a pretty girl then, Geraldine?' And she'd gurgle away with pleasure.

Then there was Anthony. He was about four or five but he had water on the brain which left him with a great swollen head and a tiny undersized body. Nevertheless, he knew when he was wet or cold or hungry and when you talked to him he'd smile up at you.

You soon got to love them, those poor little children and, despite everything, the ward was a happy place.

Not all the children were as severely handicapped as Nigel, Geraldine and Anthony. Often they were capable of far more than anyone believed possible. That's what made working with them so rewarding.

You weren't supposed to have favourites but you couldn't help it and one of mine was a spastic girl called Patsy Kelly. She couldn't walk and she had to have her hands tied up in an apron because for some reason she kept putting them down her throat and making herself sick. Despite this, she was a lovable character.

'Who's a bad 'un?' I used to pretend to scold. 'I'll give it to you. Who's a bad 'un?' and she used to rock herself in delight and laugh till the tears rolled down her cheeks. She may not have known what the words meant but she recognized them and understood that they were spoken with love.

One day we were getting the children ready for a walk in the gardens. It was quite a laborious procedure because they all had to be taken to the lavatory before going out. We used to round them up and change them one by one and sit them in the corridor to wait until everyone was ready.

This particular morning I thought I'd finished when I discovered that little Sharon had had another mishap and her knickers were soaking wet.

I whisked her up, took her back and laid her on the changing table again.

'Who's a bad 'un!' I was saying to her as I worked. 'I'll give it to you! You wet these knickers and I'll have your guts for garters!'

Sharon thought this was a tremendous joke. She was giggling and I was laughing and I suppose my voice must have been louder than I realized because outside in the corridor, Patsy Kelly, who couldn't walk, suddenly got to her feet and, beaming all over her face and rocking like a boat, she tottered towards the door from which she could hear those familiar words.

'Who's a bad 'un!'

The incredible event was the talk of the hospital for weeks and Sister never got over it. Such things didn't happen after all ...

One day Sharon, as well, shook me rigid. She was a pretty girl of five with brown curly hair and blue eyes. She had been in hospital all her life. We were the only family she'd ever known. She had never spoken and we all assumed she couldn't.

Then came the time when she caught German measles along with several other children. This was serious, as it could lead to an epidemic in the hospital from which some of the patients might not recover. Great precautions were taken which involved a lot of extra work for the nurses.

Sheets were wrung out in carbolic and hung in lines across the ward. The doorknobs were covered in carbolic and the nurses had to wear rubber gloves.

Inside the isolation area the children just lay in their beds with nothing to do. I felt sorry for them. It seemed boring to me to have to lie there all day so, when I was on duty. I used to sing to them to liven things up.

I'm absolutely tone deaf and not by any stretch of the imagination a singer, but nevertheless I enjoy singing and those children, who after all knew no better, seemed to enjoy listening to me. I used to go from cot to cot singing each child a different song and for some reason I chose a jolly little tune called *He Wore a Tulip*, for Sharon.

'He wore a tulip, a bright yellow tulip and she wore a red red rose,' I used to sing and her eyes would widen and she'd listen to this with rapt attention. After a few days she began coming to the end of her cot when I started to sing and she'd pull herself up and look right into my eyes and if I stopped singing she rubbed my face until I started again.

She never tired of this game and for me it became a routine. Then one day I started off in the same old way:

'He wore a tulip, a bright yellow tulip and she wore a ...'

'Wed wed wose,' interrupted a strange little voice.

I stopped dead and stared at Sharon. Surely that wasn't her? She couldn't speak.

'He wore a tulip,' I began again cautiously. I was probably imagining things but I might as well put it to the test. 'A bright yellow tulip and she wore a ...' I paused.

'Wed, wed wose,' Sharon finished.

If the bottle of baby lotion in my pocket had suddenly offered an opinion on the weather I couldn't have been more surprised.

'There's a clever girl, Sharon!' I cried and I tried it again. Each time I sang the song, Sharon finished it for me.

'Sister, come and listen to this,' I called when her head appeared round the carbolic sheet. 'Sharon's just spoken.'

'No!' said Sister, coming over to the cot. 'She's never spoken in five years.'

'Well, listen.' I launched into another rendering of *He Wore a Tulip* and she always came in at the end.

It wasn't just the nurses who found the children surprising, sometimes they amazed their parents as well. There were some parents who never visited, some who came every week, and some who could only get to the hospital every now and then.

It was the irregular visitors who got the most surprises. I remember one little girl called Sylvia who was in a shocking state when she was brought to us. I don't know what happened to her mother, but her father had to go away to work and he'd left Sylvia in the care of an elderly relative who could hardly look after herself let alone a backward child as well.

By the time the social workers heard about Sylvia she was a mess. I'll never forget the day they brought her in. I'd never seen a child in such a state.

She was filthy, her hair was so matted and unwashed it looked like an ancient dog blanket, and she was thin and under-nourished. We could only guess at her former life-style from her behaviour with us.

The first thing to do with her was to give her a bath, but she was obviously a complete stranger to washing. She was terrified of water. She screamed and kicked and yelled and it took two of us to get her in the bath and even then she wouldn't sit down. We had to wash her standing up.

Finally after a good half hour's truggle, a thin, bedraggled little creature emerged from the bathroom, rather sorry for itself and resembling a drowned rat, but clean.

'Come on, love,' I said taking her hand. 'Let's get you something to eat.' That was when we discovered more about her former life. Faced with the meal table Sylvia was totally at a loss. She'd never sat at a table before and she'd never eaten proper food or, if she had, it was so long ago she couldn't remember it. The old lady had existed on bread soaked in sweet tea and so had Sylvia.

In those first few weeks life with Sylvia was hard work. She had been happy enough with the old lady and she couldn't understand why she should change. But gradually she settled down and, as a proper diet, regular washing and plenty of sleep began to take effect, we realized that she was a very beautiful child.

Her hair, which had been lank and lacklustre, grew thick and glossily black, her skin which had been pale and delicate turned creamy pink with health and suddenly you noticed that her eyes were enormous and the deepest shade of blue I'd ever seen.

The months passed and then came the news that Sylvia's father was coming to visit her. I'd grown very fond of Sylvia by this time and I wanted her to make a good impression so I went to the store and found her a pretty

blue dress the colour of her eyes. Then on the great day I
rushed down to the city before going on duty and bought a
length of blue ribbon to match the dress.

Back at the hospital I brushed Sylvia's hair until you
could practically see your face in it, dressed her in the new
dress and tied the ribbon into a bow. She looked
wonderful.

'Who's a beauty then?' I said taking a step back to
admire her. 'Don't you look nice? Good enough to eat.'
She dimpled with pleasure.

Hand in hand we went downstairs and I tapped on the
nursing officer's door.

'I've got Sylvia here for visiting,' I said, putting my head
round the door.

'Right. I'll be there in a minute, nurse,' said the nursing
officer, collecting up the papers on her desk and, thinking
she meant she'd be following us, I walked on with Sylvia to
the visitors' room.

There was a man standing in the hall as we passed but I
didn't give him a second glance. I assumed he had an
appointment with someone.

Anyway, when we reached the visitors' room it was
empty. Oh no, I thought, don't say he's not going to come.
But I didn't want Sylvia to sense my disappointment so I
sat her on my knee and started telling her a story.

A few moments later we heard voices in the hall.

'Where's Sylvia?' asked the nursing officer in surprise.

'I don't know,' answered an unknown male voice. 'I
haven't seen her.'

'But Nurse Stokes has only just brought her down,' said
the nursing officer with a hint of impatience creeping into
her voice. 'Didn't she take her into the visitors' room?'

As she spoke, we could hear footsteps crossing the hall,
the door opened, and the nursing officer and the man
we'd passed in the corridor appeared in the doorway.

'Why, yes. Here she is,' said the nursing officer.

The man's mouth just fell open as he took in his
daughter. She looked so beautiful he hadn't recognized
her.

The sequel to that story is that Sylvia turned out to be a

talented artist. Years after I left the hospital she sent me a beautiful picture which I still treasure and to this day she paints the most fantastic oil paintings.

It is amazing how much the children do remember. There was a blind girl called Geraldine, for instance, who came to us when she was very small. At first, she was a bright little thing who chattered away and helped us look after the tots. The only problem with her was that she kept hitting herself in the eyes. Whether it was in frustration because she couldn't see, we didn't know, but to prevent her harming herself she had to have her hands fastened behind her back all the time.

It used to break my heart to see her like that and I used to think, poor little girl your arms must ache. So when I undressed her ready for bed I used to untie her arms and stretch them over her head and to the sides. To distract her from hitting her eyes during these exercise sessions I used to say to her:

'Tomorrow I'm going to bring you a parcel and what will be in it?'

Geraldine would say, 'An apple!'

I'd say, 'And an ...'

'Orange!'

'And a piece of ...'

'Chocolate cake!' Geraldine would cry.

She began to look forward to our parcel sessions at bedtime and all the time she was making good progress. Eventually she was judged to have improved so much she was allowed home.

We never did find out what happened or what went wrong but somehow Geraldine deteriorated and she was sent back to us. She never spoke again.

The years went by, I left the hospital and long afterwards I went back for a visit. As I walked through the grounds I noticed a group of patients sitting in a circle on the grass and a scattering of the nursery children skipping round them.

The children spotted me first and came running up shouting, 'Nurse Stokes! Nurse Stokes!'

I was busy saying, 'Hello, love, hello, love,' to each one

individually when suddenly I heard one of the adult patients say:

'Would you look at her!'

I glanced up to see Geraldine, in the adult wing now, coming towards me. She was blind, but her sense of hearing was so acute she knew exactly where I was. She came straight over, put her head on my chest and started to cry. And I thought, they do remember, they do.

Afterwards I made my way from the gardens into the hospital and arrived at one of my old wards just on bath time to see one of my other favourites, Jenny Lee.

'Hello, Jenny,' I said going up to her.

'Hello,' said Jenny impassively as if she'd never seen me before in her life.

'I've brought you a pat of chocolate!' I whispered.

She beamed all over her face and took it eagerly.

'You took me to the pictures, didn't you, Nurse Stokes?' she said as plain and distinct as anything, 'to see my sister.'

I was amazed. It must have been three years ago or more since I'd taken her to the hospital cinema to see her sister, Frances Lee, in a film. Yet, despite the fact that I wasn't in uniform and she didn't know I was coming, Jenny remembered both me and the occasion.

Sometimes, of course, it was heartbreaking. We knew that many of the children had short life expectancies but knowing that didn't make you stop loving them and didn't make it any easier when they passed. Although I wasn't working as a medium while I was nursing I couldn't switch off my psychic powers, and therefore I always knew when a child didn't have long to go. Yet knowing in advance was probably harder to face than not knowing, because I felt so helpless.

When Patsy Kelly's time was close I was frustrated to find that I'd been sent to work on a different ward, the adult ward, so I had hardly any time to be with Patsy. That was probably why I was transferred. Yet it's amazing what can happen.

One afternoon I was asked to take a message to the sister of the nursery ward, whose office happened to be close to the room where Patsy lay unconscious with a nurse at her side twenty-four hours a day.

I obediently delivered the message but afterwards, instead of going straight back to my work, I couldn't resist looking in to see how Patsy was.

To my surprise the nurse on duty seemed to be expecting me. 'Stokes, an amazing thing just happened!' she said excitedly. 'When you were talking to Sister just now I'll swear Patsy could hear your voice. She's been unconscious all this time yet as soon as you started talking she opened her eyes, grinned all over her face and tried to sit up.'

I looked down at Patsy, now as silent and unmoving as she had been the last time I peeped in, and it seemed very hard to believe.

'Hello, Patsy,' I whispered. 'How's my bad 'un then?' There wasn't a flicker and in the distance I could hear the murmur of spirit voices come to take her home. My eyes filled with tears.

'It won't be long now, nurse,' I said, my voice wobbling and I turned and hurried away. It wouldn't do to be caught sobbing on duty.

A few hours later Patsy passed over. She was fourteen years old.

Later I went to visit her in the chapel and when I saw how lovely she looked I knew that it was selfish of me to wish her back. I would miss her infectious laughter on the ward but she was happier now with her relatives on the other side.

'Well, you're at peace now, Patsy,' I said aloud as I left her for the last time.

But, unlikely as it might sound, there was more fun and laughter than tears. After tea when I was on duty I organized hilarious games of hokey-cokey in the ward and during the day when the weather was fine, we played 'Here We Come Gathering Nuts in May' on the field outside.

The children varied enormously in intelligence but this didn't cause any problems. We put the brightest next to the most handicapped and they helped each other. It was wonderful to see how patient the children were with each other and how they looked after the least able. A child who was blind need never fear the teasing you might expect from normal playmates. There was always someone there to see they came to no harm.

Some of the children, particularly the epileptics, were extremely intelligent. We used to keep a record of the number of fits each child suffered and if they went for two years without a fit we used to have a party.

They took great interest in the recording of fits and they knew how long they had to go before their party. Those who achieved the two years were ecstatic. They came rushing into the ward, their faces alight with pleasure, shouting:

'I'm out of the fit book, nurse. I'm out of the fit book.'

Others were so clever you wondered why they were in the hospital at all. One woman had been there as long as anyone could remember, so long, in fact, that I couldn't find anyone who knew why she'd been admitted in the first place.

Perhaps years ago she'd had an illegitimate baby at a time when women who got into trouble were sometimes hidden away so as not to bring shame on the family. Anyway, whatever the reason, this woman was so settled in the hospital she wanted no other way of life and it would have been cruel to push her into the outside world.

She was happy and she ran the private ward. It was unofficial, of course, but she knew how it worked far better than any of the nurses and whenever a new nurse arrived she would take her under her wing and show her how everything was done.

Other patients weren't so obviously intelligent but they were very talented in other ways. I've still got an exquisite work basket made for me by one of the patients and there were two girls who could knit beautifully. No matter how intricate the pattern it presented no problems to them. It reached the stage where if any of us nurses got into a muddle with our knitting we'd take it to them. They could look at it, spot what was wrong, pull it apart and put it right, in minutes.

Of course there were plenty of other patients who gave

no trouble but who were harmlessly eccentric. One of them was a little girl called Emily. Emily was a sweet, gentle girl who had an obsession with hats and handbags. She was devoted to her collection and I used to beg all the hats and handbags I could get hold of to help her increase it. Emily gave offence to no one and she said very little. All she wanted to do was put a hat on her head, a handbag over her arm, and walk up and down the corridor. After about ten minutes she's go back to the ward, change her hat and handbag and repeat the process.

She would cheerfully play this solitary game all day long and nobody could persuade her to do anything else.

Emily's obsession was unusually deep, but all the children, even the most handicapped, were very attached to their few possessions. They all had to have something that was theirs, even if it was only a carrier bag with a postcard in it. They would take these possessions everywhere with them, even to bed.

Entertaining people with such mixed abilities could have been difficult, but the hospital had an enlightened attitude. Facilities were provided and the patients benefited from them in different ways, according to their capabilities.

On Good Friday, for instance, there was a religious service followed by a film about the crucifixion. Some patients enjoyed it in the normal way, others had no idea what was going on but liked to hear the singing and watch the moving pictures.

The vicar had to be ready for anything. One year the religious service seemed to be dragging on longer than usual and the children were shuffling a bit, wondering when the film was going to start.

Unfortunately the vicar didn't seem to be aware of the restlessness of his flock and he launched into another lengthy prayer. He didn't get far. Two lines into the prayer a little boy near the front of the hall piped up:

'Oh bloody 'ell, our men!'

There was a stunned silence. Then the vicar said, very quickly:

'In the name of the Father, the Son and the Holy Ghost,

Amen,' missing out the whole of the middle section of the prayer and brought the service to a swift end.

There was no point in scolding the boy. He didn't understand what it was all about. All he knew was that when he said 'Our men' the picture would start.

There were quite a few mongols at the hospital and they were delightful, so cheerful and affectionate. They used to wash our cups out for us and rub our feet after a long day on the ward. They loved music and had regular dancing lessons. Once a month the older ones had a proper dance with a band from outside.

This was the highlight of their days. The girls used to make long evening dresses to wear and the nurses would make up their faces for them. They thought it was marvellous. Out on the dance floor they'd bow and curtsey to each other and then swing round the room beaming at the nurses as they sailed past as if to say, 'Look at us!'

There were usually few nurses in attendance but we took part in the fun and, if we were asked to dance, we danced. The boys would be very offended if we refused.

Many of these older ones were allowed out into the town on their own and, like small children, they were innocently determined to enjoy themselves and were quite uninhibited.

Often John and I would be quietly shopping in a crowded store when suddenly a great yell would ring out, startling shoppers.

'Yoohoo! Yoohoo! Nurse Stokes! Mr Stokes! Yoohoo!'

Heads would turn and John and I would look up to find we were being greeted from the other side of the store by a merry bunch of waving patients who were quite unaware of the disturbance they were causing.

These patients became highly independent and this was encouraged. A large house was bought for them just up the road from the hospital and the rooms were beautifully fitted out, two beds to a room, with matching bedspreads and curtains and good quality carpets on the floor.

There was one nurse and a sister on duty but the patients more or less took care of themselves. In the early days the staff used to walk them backwards and forwards to the main hospital for school or classes or to work in the laundry, but after a while they put in a petition asking for the right to make the journey unaccompanied.

They went down to the town without an escort, they said, so why couldn't they be trusted to go to the hospital on their own?

Initiative was rewarded and they got their permission.

In the evenings they ran their own club and this was an entirely private affair. Strictly no admittance to nurses without an invitation. It was all very innocent. They spent the evenings concocting weird meals and dancing to the music on the radio. John and I were invited one evening and they cooked us a feast of bacon and onions. It arrived swimming in grease but we had to eat it. We wouldn't have hurt their feelings for the world.

They all stood round, bursting with pride as they watched us eat, saying:

'Isn't it good? Isn't it good?'

And, smiling through the grease, we assured them it was delicious.

I don't want to give the impression that working with the mentally handicapped is all joy and fun, because it isn't. It's exhausting, demanding and very hard work. There are difficult patients and some can turn violent. I should know because I had to give up nursing after being injured by one. But I would like to stress that in my experience mental hospitals are not all gloom and misery.

Of course, patients have their off days. Don't we all? But most of the people I worked with were content and secure, happy to stay in a protected world where no one expected more from them than they were capable of achieving.

Chapter 7

'Oh, eh, hello Doris. I hope you don't mind. I've brought my friend with me.' There is a slight pinkening of the cheeks and the eyes fall to study my shoes. 'Well, you see I was a bit scared to come on my own.'

This is the nervous sitter. I know her well.

'That's all right, love. I don't mind a bit,' I say. 'Come on in.' And I take her inside, knowing that after a few minutes she'll be quite relaxed.

It's amazing how many people are frightened when they arrive for their first sitting. They think I'm going to fall into some terrifying trance, or draw the curtains and condemn them to darkness and supernatural shadows.

In fact, we merely settle ourselves into armchairs and have a chat, in broad daylight unless, of course, it's winter when I might have to turn on the electric light.

Afterwards the sitters unanimously agree that there is nothing remotely scarey about the process. Yet people who have never experienced it still frequently ask:

'But what *happens* at a sitting?'

So for all those who are still curious I thought it might be interesting to record a sitting in full, as it happened.

Below is a transcript of a sitting I did with Susan Otter and her husband in early 1982, omitting only some personal details that are private to the couple and some irrelevant conversation.

DORIS: I think by the size of his light that Simon hasn't been over a year yet, has he?

SUSAN: March.

DORIS: Now he's talking about someone called Bill. Do you know a Bill?

SUSAN: No.

DORIS: That's funny. I thought he said Bill. It can't be right then. It's not Bert, is it?

SUSAN: Yes, that's my father.

DORIS: That's it. He said you'd been talking to someone about him but I thought he said Bill. Oh, he's saying 'No I didn't, I said Bert. I speak English, don't I?' He's a cheeky young thing.

SUSAN: Yes, he was.

DORIS: He said they all cried and I had some flowers and me Grandad Bert said why couldn't it have been me?

SUSAN: Yes he did say that.

DORIS: But I'm all right, Mummy. It was very quick. He went out and never came home.

SUSAN: No.

DORIS: And I never saw me daddy. I saw him the night before.

SUSAN: Yes.

DORIS: I feel as if I was thrown. As if something hit him very quickly and he was falling into unconsciousness.

SUSAN: Yes, the disease hit him very quickly.

DORIS: And he never came round again. The back of his head hurt.

SUSAN: It did. It was a brain disease.

DORIS: That's the only indication he can give me. Call me Granny Doris, love, all the other kids do. I've got two grannies already, he's saying. Well, I'm an extra one, darling. But he said it happened within twenty-four hours, love. Incredible. From being a healthy little boy he got very hot and he felt sick and I fell asleep then.

SUSAN: Yes.

DORIS: He said you took a sweater out and you kissed it and put it back. Didn't you, love?

SUSAN: Yes, I did.

DORIS: You see, he was there then when you did that and he saw you. He hasn't gone away. He's round the house still.

SUSAN: Yes, I know, I can feel it.

DORIS: Now, who's Philip he's talking about.

SUSAN: That's his dad.

DORIS: That's what I've been waiting for. I said to him, I
know he's your daddy but what's his name?
Right, so that's your daddy. Now, are you going to let
anyone else speak? No, no he's not going to let anyone
else talk ... I can see him so plainly ... He's talking about
the police for some reason.

SUSAN: They came to take statements for the inquest
reports because he'd only been in hospital twenty-four
hours.

DORIS: I see, because he was saying, the police came, you
know. I was very important ... I expect you were, darling.
Now, who's Anne ... A ... A no it's not, it's Alan.

SUSAN: My brother-in-law.

DORIS: He says Alan was in our house, Granny Doris. He
came back so I did a bit of good.

SUSAN: Yes, we hadn't seen him for years.

DORIS: Now, who's Rose ... R ... R it's an R ... sound. Hold
it, hold hold it, don't get yourself fussed, lovey. Well, I am
listening, Simon, honestly I am, but you keep bobbing
about, first to your mummy, then to your daddy ...
Richard it is! Richard!

SUSAN: Yes, next door.

DORIS: He said, Richard, will you listen. I used to play with
Richard, he was my best friend when we weren't falling
out!

SUSAN: Yes!

DORIS: He used to say I'm not friends with you any more,
but do you know, Richard cried and he brought me a
little bunch of flowers.

SUSAN: Yes, he did.

DORIS: 'Cos they stand and watch. He says there were so
many people there. Margaret was there. Who's
Margaret?

SUSAN: Richard's mummy.

DORIS: He says yes, they all cried. Richard was my best
friend and we used to take it in turns on my bike. So you
only had one bike between you, did you?

SUSAN: Yes, in our garden.

DORIS: And Margaret cried and do you know what she said
to my mummy? She said, It could so easily have been me.

SUSAN: Yes, that's what she said.

DORIS: Now, there's somebody called George on the spirit side ... I think he belongs with your father, love.

SUSAN: Oh, his brother George.

DORIS: George is here when he can get a word in with young Simon. He's telling me there was a great hoo-hah and they still haven't been able to find a satisfactory answer as to why it happened, but he says it doesn't really matter, now, does it. Simon's here, he's happy, he's full of joy ... Who's Betty?

SUSAN: Aunty Betty.

DORIS: Betty loves me, he says she's got a picture of me and she puts roses by it.

SUSAN: Yes, she does.

DORIS: She puts them down and says those are for you Simon ... Now, George is saying he knows what the problem is. You are worried because you felt you couldn't say goodbye to him. And you blame yourself, love, we all do it, believe me. There's not a parent comes into my house, including me, that doesn't ask themself was there anything I could have done? Should I have noticed anything? Should I have insisted on having another doctor? Should I have done this, should I have done that? We all go through it, love. But there was nothing you could have done ... He was one of God's special children ... Now, March the seventeenth's important.

SUSAN: March sixteenth was the day he died.

DORIS: Why they are telling you this is that when March sixteenth comes round you're not to say it's a year since our Simon died. You must give him some flowers and say happy anniversary, love. Because it'll be the anniversary of the first year of his new life ... Who's Tony? It's a T sound. Tony, Terry, Tommy ... No, you've missed it Simon. Now hold it. What are you showing me? He's taken his shirt off and here, on his shoulder blade he's got a little mole.

SUSAN: Yes.

DORIS: I said you're not going to strip off, are you? And he said no only my shirt to show Mummy that it's me ... Now there's a J ... Jamey ... no, Jenny.

SUSAN: That's his friend's mum.

DORIS: What about a caravan, love? I've just been talking about a caravan but you know a caravan too?

SUSAN: Yes, his grandpa's caravan. He lives in a caravan. We've just been there.

DORIS: Well, he went with you ... You see, for a child like Simon who was eight when he went over, to suddenly find himself having to live somewhere else with people he didn't know before was a great shock, so they let him come back and see you and join in with what you're doing. And he says we went to the caravan, you know. We did. And I, I-I-I-I ... He stutters when he gets excited.

SUSAN: Yes, he did.

DORIS: He's getting so excited his tongue trips over itself. At the caravan there's four steps, you know, and we've been going there since Mummy had to lift me down but now I'm a big boy and I walk up and down them myself.

SUSAN: Yes, we've been going there since he was very small.

DORIS: And he says he still goes and cuddles his teddy.

SUSAN: No, we put the teddy in with him.

DORIS: Oh, I see you've got your teddy with you ... I thought you meant you came and played with it ... And you've got that other ... elephant, is it? Funny-looking thing. I don't know what you call that? Your Wopple?

SUSAN: Womble.

DORIS: Now he's saying something about a guitar. I thought he said his daddy promised him a guitar when he's a big boy.

SUSAN: He always loved guitars. He had a little wooden one. Mark's got it now.

DORIS: I was going to have a proper one when I was a big boy, he's saying.

SUSAN: Yes, he used to talk about playing in a pop group.

DORIS: There's Mark his brother, then there's someone called Michael and someone called Nicolas.

SUSAN: His friends.

DORIS: Yes ... and ... Wait a minute, darling, wait a

minute, Simon, love, off you go again, I can't keep up with you. Tell me again. Yes, you had your teddy with you, yes and you had your womble. Now, what are you telling me? He's putting my hand over, like that. So you put something in his hand. Did you say a photograph?

SUSAN: Yes, I put a photo of the two boys in his hand.

DORIS: That's it, because he folded my fingers over and said it's a picture ... And he twists his hair round. All the time he's talking to me he's twisting his hair ... Do you drive for a living, Philip?

PHILIP: No, but I drive a long way to work.

DORIS: Oh, 'cos he said I drive with Daddy, you know. A long way we go. So that's what made me ask if you drive for a living. Oh, he's saying no, Daddy's got a big machine, he's ever so clever.

PHILIP: Yes, I work in a factory.

DORIS: Now ... slowly, slowly, Simon. He won't let George do it. He will do it himself. Now, you know your sitting-room. It used to be two rooms.

SUSAN: The house where he was born was like that.

DORIS: And then the wall came down. Now, where you live now I'm facing a glass door and there's a picture on the right of him and a picture on the left, too.

SUSAN: There used to be a picture on the right but I took it down and now there's just the one on the left.

DORIS: Had he just had a watch?

SUSAN: Yes, just before Christmas.

DORIS: It's a proper watch, he says. Mark's got that now. He's talking about Christopher.

SUSAN: Christopher sat next to him at school.

DORIS: And there's a little chair that he used to take out in the garden.

SUSAN: Yes, a fold-up one.

DORIS: He says I used to go and sit in the garden with Mummy and I had my own little chair ... Oh, you didn't! Now, just a minute, let the grown-ups show me a picture, darling ... You've got me a bit lost now because you get very excited. Now, there are kitchen units and they look like pale olive green.

SUSAN: That's Lynne, next door but one.

DORIS: That's where he's taking me and there's a chopping board or a tray or something, on these units. He said I knocked it down.

SUSAN: Yes, he did.

DORIS: He's done it since he's been over to let you know he's there.

SUSAN: She blames it on Gary.

DORIS: No, it's Simon. He says it makes ever such a bang. And then he's talking about a dog.

SUSAN: Poppy.

DORIS: The dog can see me but they can't see me. That puzzled him ... You know when he was born, the cord wasn't round his neck, was it?

SUSAN: It was round Mark's.

DORIS: Oh, that was Mark, was it. He says the cord was round his neck and he nearly died, but then he didn't and it was me ... Now he said he had a money box and that's been opened and d'you know how much was in it? There was nearly £4.

SUSAN: Yes, he was saving for his Lego fire station.

DORIS: I only wanted two more pounds then I could have had it.

SUSAN: Yes, he could.

DORIS: £6 was it. You see they don't forget. He's still your child even though you can't see him ... Oh, he's disappeared now. I don't know where he's gone ... It's all right, he's back. No, I'm here, he said and I asked where he'd been and he said I've been to fetch Elsie.

SUSAN: Elsie lived over the road. She's only just gone.

DORIS: Did she have a stroke? Because Simon says she had a head thing too.

SUSAN: Yes, she did.

DORIS: Elsie says to tell you that your little boy is more beautiful than ever. She used to see him every day. He used to go down to post a letter because there's a letter box at the end of the road.

SUSAN: Yes, there is.

DORIS: Now they're talking about someone called David.

SUSAN: Yes, he lives next door.

DORIS: Then there's Mark and Lesley and Geoffrey.

SUSAN: His cousins, but he didn't know them.

DORIS: He does now ... And he used to love pink blancmange I heard him say ... Now, who's Maisie? Think of your mum. Is there a Maisie or Mabel connected with her?

PHILIP: Yes, Auntie Mabel.

DORIS: Somebody called Arthur.

SUSAN: That's my side.

DORIS: And somebody's got a van, I thought he said.

SUSAN: We've just got a funny little car. A Panda.

DORIS: It's not a van, love, it's a Panda. Oh, I thought it was a van, he says. It's not like the other cars we had.

SUSAN: No, it's not. It's square, like a little box van.

DORIS: Now, that's Irene or Eileen living. I have to give you both because they sound alike to me.

SUSAN: Irene.

DORIS: Then there's Kathleen.

SUSAN: Katy. It should be Kathleen but we call her Katy.

DORIS: His birthday's just gone, there's another one in August and one in October.

SUSAN: Yes mine.

DORIS: Now, what is it you're telling me? Just before you went to the spirit world you had a new red sweater?

SUSAN: Yes, he had a new red sweater. He was buried in his favourite red shirt.

DORIS: You can ask me about it, he's saying, I don't mind because I'm here. They've told me about it. It's only like a garden in memory of Simon. There's a tree there, and roses planted.

SUSAN: Yes.

DORIS: When Mummy and Daddy go there I try to tell them please don't cry because it's only my garden. I'm not there. Can you tell me where you come from? All I've got written down in my book is 'child' ... I thought he said Chester.

SUSAN: Winchester.

DORIS: December the ninth, I think he said. No? Could it have been September, November. No, I'm guessing at it. Let it go Simon, love. I think you've done extremely well. Do you think I look like my daddy, he's asking. Yes

I do, love, and your mummy too. He's got your eyes, Susan, that's for sure ... Well, I've got to get washed and changed now, love. You've done extremely well.

I know it was a terrible blow to you, love, losing him so quickly. But at least it was over in a few hours. He didn't suffer. Not like some of these parents whose children have leukaemia and they have to watch them suffer for years ...

Anyway, I'll make you some more tea ...

Well, as you can see, there is nothing eerie about a sitting. It's just a three-way conversation filled with trivial little bits of family information. Not much in themselves, but important to the people concerned because they are things that only the loved one could have know, described in the language that he used to use.

There is such a difference in the way sitters arrive and the way they leave. Particularly the parents who've lost children. They walk in droopy and desolate, hope almost gone. And you should see the way they go out. Heads held high, the spring back in their step because suddenly they can face the future.

Chapter 8

It was cold, very cold, and all around me the world was exploding. Smoke blurred my vision, there were voices shouting, great flashes lit up the sky and crashes like thunder shook the ground under my feet.

Half-deafened and confused, I stumbled about, then there was a tremendous bang and everything went blank. I had a last vague impression of pulling something over me, of covering myself and then there was silence.

So began one of the strangest cases I have ever worked on. I have no real explanation for it even today. Yet it happened and I faithfully recorded every detail. It puzzles me still.

The above scene was shown to me as the last impression of Philip Alan Williams, a young soldier missing, presumed dead in the Falklands War. His parents had attended a memorial service for him in their local church and they were invited to the official memorial services at St Paul's Cathedral. But still they grieved and in desperation they wrote to me.

I had a very busy schedule but they sounded so unhappy I went against my normal family rule and agreed to see them on Sunday afternoon. Usually I try to leave weekends free unless I have church work to do because the older I get the more rest I seem to need. Psychic contact seems to be very physically draining.

Anyway, the Williams's arrived and I was glad I'd broken my weekend rule. We had a marvellous sitting. Philip Alan came through and gave a mass of information about his family, along with quite a few private, personal details that no one, apart from his closest friends and family, could have known. He described the place where

541

he was last seen, the people he was with and the terrifying events going on – all with great accuracy as we discovered afterwards.

Yet unknown to us, as his parents were speeding down the motorway to London, halfway across the world in the Falklands Philip was walking into a house in Goose Green. He was cold, half starved and exhausted. he was given a meal and put to bed by the kind family and, at the time of our sitting, he was not on the other side, but in a deep, exhausted sleep.

So how did it happen? I've got no definite answer. My only theory is that the part of us that lives on after death, the spirit, is naturally present within us when we're alive and in some circumstances it can leave the body during deep sleep, travel about and return to the body before the sleeper wakes. These travels are sometimes remembered afterwards as a dream.

I realize this might sound far-fetched but it would explain the many cases you hear about where a person 'dreams' of going to visit a close relative or friend and finds them ill, only to discover the next day that that person really is ill.

I believe that in Philip's case he was anxious about his parents, knowing that they must have feared the worst, and when he slept, his 'spirit' restlessly came in search of them to give them reassurance.

The psychic 'pull' must have been very strong when you consider that the three of us, his mother, father and me, were sitting there concentrating all our energies on contacting Philip, willing him to come and talk to us. The power generated must have shone out like a beacon on the astral plane and guided him straight to my living-room even though it was half a world away.

I cannot prove this theory of course but one little remark after the event makes me think I'm right. During the sitting Philip mentioned something about his father having bought a new car. Now, he would not have known about this in the normal way because his father didn't get it until after Philip had sailed for the Falklands. Yet the person I was talking to mentioned the car. Very puzzling.

Then when Philip finally arrived home from his ordeal his father proudly showed him the car but Philip didn't seem surprised.

'It's funny, Dad,' he said, 'but while I was away I had a funny dream. I can't remember it all but I remember I dreamed you'd got a new car – and you have.'

To me, that proves Philip was able to reach out to his parents from thousands of miles away even though he dismissed the experience as a dream.

That's my theory anyway but I'll put down the whole story and you can make up your mind whether you agree with me.

The Williams's arrived, as arranged, having driven hundreds of miles for a one-hour sitting. The poor things must have been worn out so we put the kettle on to make them some tea, but even as I was crossing the hall I heard the name Goose Green.

Anyone who followed the Falklands War will know that Goose Green figured very heavily in all the reports about it, so I could be accused of guessing. Nevertheless, I heard the words so clearly and distinctly I was sure they were significant.

'You son didn't go missing at Goose Green, did he?' I asked the parents.

They shook their heads. 'No. He wasn't involved in that, Doris,' they said firmly.

I was puzzled. I knew this wasn't a mistake because it was too clear, but if they said the boy hadn't been to Goose Green, then he hadn't.

It was only the next day we learned that even as we were talking Philip had turned up in Goose Green.

Anyway we sat down in the living-room, tea-cups within reach and I was about to tune in, when an odd feeling began to nag at me. There was something not quite right here.

'Are you quite sure your son's been killed?' I asked them.

'Oh, yes,' they said. 'We were invited to the memorial service at St Paul's and everything.'

'He couldn't have been taken prisoner?' I queried.

'No,' they said firmly. 'We were told there were no prisoners.'

I bit my lip. It was quite wrong of me to go on like this. I could be planting cruel seeds of hope in their minds when there was no sense in hoping. The Army were quite sure Philip was dead and they should know. The parents seemed to have accepted the fact and that was the best thing for them. It would be very wrong to unsettle them now. And yet ...

Firmly I stamped on this rebel instinct and tuned in. I was instantly reassured. A young, male voice came straight in and gave the name Philip Alan. Called Alan for his Dad.

'Yes, that's Philip,' said his mother.

He gave his father's name, his sister's name and the name of a great friend of his.

'They've had a letter from Jimmy,' he said. 'And Stewart came to see them and they talked about me.'

His parents were astonished.

'Yes, that's true.'

Then he told me about himself. He chuckled and said he was a handsome lad, he had fair hair and he was trying to grow a moustache.

'Oh, I don't know about the moustache,' said his mother.

But Philip, if Philip it was, was adamant that he was trying to grow one.

He mentioned more family names and friends and asked to be remembered to various people, but he seemed unusually confused about which side some of his family were on. Occasionally a person making his first communication gets a little mixed up but in Philip this confusion was very strong. He would talk of people he'd met as if they were on the other side. Yet his parents would assure me that while these names were correct the people concerned were very much still with us.

Albert and Kitty were a typical example. He said something about meeting Albert and Kitty.

'But he couldn't have done,' said his father in dismay. 'Albert and Kitty are still alive. I was only talking to them the other day.'

'Philip, love, d'you mean you met Albert and Kitty or

your father met Albert and Kitty?' I asked. He mumbled
something about his father meeting them.

'Well, you must make it clear what side they're on,
darling, or we'll get in a right mess. I thought you meant
they were with you on that side.'

There was a strange scrambling of the vibration and a
strong sense of confusion. Philip couldn't seem to understand what I meant. Abruptly he changed the subject.

'I didn't want to go you know,' he said. 'When I joined I
never thought there'd be a war. On the way out we were
laughing and joking but underneath we were scared ...' I
can't print the word he used but let's just say that Philip's
language was just as rich as it always had been.

His mother nodded sadly. 'No, he didn't want to go,' she
said. 'That's quite true.'

But he hadn't finished. He wanted them to know that,
although he had been frightened at the beginning, he
hadn't been a coward.

'At least mum and dad can be proud of me. I found me
guts in the end. When it came to it you don't have time to
think, you just go straight in.'

Then another voice interrupted, a young woman's voice.

'I'm Barbara,' she said. 'You mustn't worry about Philip.
We're looking after him. He's all right.'

'That's his aunt,' said Mrs Williams.

Barbara said she was only in her thirties when she passed.
She had been ill for some time but at the end it was very
quick.

'I just went to sleep and woke up over here,' she said.

But Philip wasn't going to let Barbara take up much time.
In the background I could hear organ music and Philip
wanted to talk about his memorial service.

'They played *The Lord is My Shepherd* and lots of people
came,' he said.

'I gave our Gareth a watch before I went away and he's
still got it.'

He was also concerned about the pay still outstanding for
the time he was in the Falklands. He wanted his father to
chase it up.

'I earned the bugger,' he said, 'so you might as well have it.'

But Barbara was back. 'Don't you worry,' she said again. 'He'll be all right.'

Then yet another voice came in.

'I'm Elizabeth,' she said.

'That's his grandmother,' said Mrs Williams.

And she too was anxious to reassure them. 'Don't worry, we're looking after him.'

Listening to the tape afterwards I was struck by this constant reassurance. Relatives often like to let parents know that they are caring for the lost child who is now happy and well on the other side, but I have never heard it stressed so often during one sitting.

'Don't worry. He's all right. We're looking after him.' I heard it again and again. At the time I supposed that Mrs Williams must be particularly worried about Philip because his body had never been found and she didn't know he had died. Afterwards of course I realized that Philip's aunt and grandmother were not merely reassuring us but trying to tell us what was happening. They certainly were looking after Philip and he *was* all right. There was no need to worry.

Philip was not going to let his grandmother have any more of a say than his aunt. Back he came again as soon as Elizabeth finished speaking. He mentioned the new car, then he said, 'Dad's been talking to Joe Bailey. He works with him.'

Mr Williams nearly fell off his chair.

'Joe Bailey. Yes, that's right. I have,' he said. But then he remembered what he most wanted to know.

'Can you give me your last impressions, Philip?' I asked. Again there was that strange scrambled sensation. A feeling of confusion and bewilderment. Then came the nightmare battle scene and a name.

'Temple something,' I said. 'Tem, tum ...'

'Tumbledown,' said his father. 'That's right.'

Philip was getting agitated. 'There were all these explosions and then boof! That was it.' It sounded as if he had probably stepped on a landmine or been caught as one exploded.

'Chalky White was there and Anderson ...' he added.

'Yes,' cried Mrs Williams. 'We had a letter from Sergeant White's widow, and Anderson *was* there too.'

'I was in the Guards,' said Philip.

His parents confirmed that he was indeed in the Scots Guards.

'How old are you, love?' I asked.

'Almost nineteen,' he replied.

Again this was correct. Yet suddenly that peculiar feeling was back, something was not right. What on earth was it?

'Well, I don't know,' I said aloud. 'If it's not Philip I'm talking to, how does he know all these things? It must be him.'

His parents were quite convinced of it. The way he talked. The occasional swear words he used and the information he gave were absolutely in character.

Yet the very next morning the news came through that Philip was alive. He was safe and well after living rough for several weeks. When he arrived home he was dressed in Chalky White's clothes, his own having been in an appalling state after weeks in the wild. He had also grown a moustache.

There had been a terrific explosion, he said, and he didn't remember any more until he found himself wandering alone in the bleak Falklands countryside. Thinking he was behind the Argentine lines and would therefore be taken prisoner if he was caught, he laid low until, at last, the bitter winter weather forced him to seek help.

His parents were overjoyed and when they phoned to tell me the good news I was delighted for them. But I was also mystified. If Philip was alive then who had I been talking to during the sitting? Could it have been one of the other young men who was killed that day? But no, the details were too personal to Philip. Could it have been Barbara? Again I had to dismiss the possibility. Barbara had turned up later in the sitting and was definitely a new voice. What's more Barbara's voice was unmistakably feminine while the person I'd thought was Philip was unmistakably a young man.

The only conclusion I could come to was that somehow I had been talking to Philip, even though Philip was not dead.

So how did it happen? Well, as I've said, I've got my theory but I wouldn't insist it was right or force it on anyone else. I'll leave you to make up your own mind.

Philip Alan Williams however wasn't my only contact with the Falkands War. Soon after my sitting with his parents another set of distraught parents telephoned me. Marion and Don Pryce had lost their son, a Fleet Air Arm electrician, when his ship the *Atlantic Conveyor* had been hit by an Exocet missile.

Soon after the disaster, the Pryces' daughter, who was a nurse, accidentally knocked a book on the floor when she was looking for something else at the hospital where she worked. Irritably she picked it up and saw that it was called *Voices in my Ear*. Something about the cheerful yellow cover attracted her interest and although she was in a hurry she turned the book over and read the little introduction on the back.

It was enough to convince her that the book might contain something that would help ease the terrible sense of loss the whole family was suffering, so she took the book home. It was passed rapidly to every member of the family and when they'd finished it they went out and got the sequel, *More Voices*. At the end of that Marion phoned me.

I was still feeling bewildered over the Philip Williams case but I couldn't refuse the Pryces'. Something in Marion's voice told me I had to see her. The Pryces were a very close family, it turned out, and all five of them arrived on my doorstep. Mother, father, and three pretty daughters. It was a pleasure to see such a lovely family and, though our small sitting-room looked rather overcrowded, I enjoyed it immensely.

I'd always wanted a big family myself and though it wasn't to be I still enjoy the company of other people's families.

We chatted for a few moments then I felt the presence of a young man. He was a tall, slim lad with thick hair and the sort of friendly, open face that immediately attracts people and invites their trust. As he hovered close to me I felt compelled to touch my hair with my fingers.

Marion gasped. 'That's our son! That's what he used to do. He used to touch his hair just like that!'

'I'm Don,' said the boy. 'And there are two Dons over here now. Me and my grandad.'

At that an elderly male voice interrupted.

'Yes, he was named after me, not his father. We used to be called the Three Dons.'

I asked the youngest Don what had happened to him. Immediately I could smell fire. I could see flames licking around and I could hear a lot of shouting.

'I was helping some of the others to get overboard,' said Don, 'and I think my life jacket caught fire. When I jumped into the sea it went down.'

He was drowned very quickly, but at least he didn't suffer for hours in the icy cold waters of the South Atlantic.

But Don didn't want to dwell on the war. He changed the subject and talked instead of his friend Danny and his girlfriend Sarah.

'I think I would have married Sarah,' he said, 'if it hadn't been for the war. Just before I went, you know, Mum took me out to buy me some new things. She bought me some underpants.'

'Yes, that's true, I did,' said Marion.

He went on to give more family names and he said that his sister had some pictures on the wall over the fireplace which he had given her, that his parents had a crucifix on their bedroom wall and that he'd given his youngest sister a soft toy. He also mentioned Mr Bond, his scoutmaster.

'Oh yes, he was a very keen scout,' said Don senior.

Then the grandfather came back.

'I died of cancer of the lungs,' he said, 'but there's no need to be sad. It was a happy release to go.'

'Is Don happy with you all over there?' I asked.

Don's voice came back. 'Not yet,' he said sadly, 'I miss you still.'

The power was fading but with a last effort he muttered something about 'Flowers and a message of love'.

There was a pause. 'Roses,' he added.

This didn't mean much to his family.

'Did you give him roses by his picture or at the memorial service?' I suggested.

But no, the Pryces couldn't think of anything that seemed likely. However the day of the sitting was 4 August. Afterwards they discovered that on 30 July their next-door neighbour had dropped a wreath made of silk roses from his helicopter into the sea around the Falklands with a message of love for Don and all those who had lost their lives there.

I never thought I'd live long enough to see Britain involved in another war or that I'd one day work for parents and wives who were suffering the way we suffered in World War II.

I know from bitter experience about the tragedy of war. There were the weeks of heartache when I was informed my husband was missing, presumed dead at Arnhem. Then the anxious months when I discovered that he'd been found but he was a prisoner of war and seriously injured.

Long before that I lost the boyfriend I hoped to marry when his plane was shot down. I'd met John Stewart at a dance. He was a rear gunner in the Air Force, a tall fair-haired boy from Scotland.

He was kind and thoughtful and he was the first person to buy me an Easter egg. It was a big one with roses on it and I was thrilled. It was typical of John.

We had been going out together for eighteen months when we decided to make it permanent. He was stationed in Huntingdon at the time and I was in Wales and he wrote to ask me if I would meet him at Grantham so that we could visit my mother. Afterwards he said we could travel up to Scotland to meet his parents and buy an engagement ring.

I thought this was a wonderful idea and I dashed off to apply for a forty-eight-hour pass. Yet as I handed over my request a voice seemed to say in my head.

'You're not going to go.'

This sobered me up a bit. Oh, I suppose they'll turn me

down, I thought. I was convinced that if I wasn't going it was because something my end would prevent it.

The pass was granted, however, and I forgot all about those warning words. Then on the Thursday before we were due to leave a bulky packet arrived for me. It contained the letters I'd written to John, with a note to say that he had been killed.

The terrible thing about war is how quickly it can flare up. In the case of the Falklands conflict it was over very quickly too, yet for hundreds of people those few weeks changed their lives for ever and they will never be completely happy again. They will carry sadness in their hearts – for as long as they live.

Violence isn't confined to war. It seems to spill over into everyday life and I get an increasing number of these cases involving ordinary people who've met violent senseless deaths.

I've asked Ramanov about this and he says it's because we don't love each other enough. That until we learn to love each other more and not to expect more from people than they're capable of giving, then these things will happen.

I expect that's true but I still don't understand what makes one person lash out at another. I mean what makes a man beat the woman he's supposed to love so savagely that he smashes her bones? It doesn't make sense. All I can do is try to comfort the other victims, the ones who are left to grieve when the violence goes too far.

The case of Shirley X (I won't give her full name because she doesn't want her children to know the whole story) is a particularly horrifying example. Her mother came to see me because she was desperate to know more about what had happened to her daughter.

Shirley came through quickly enough but she was full of regrets. She couldn't settle until she'd told her mother how sorry she was for the mess she'd made.

'I threw my life away at thirty-three,' she said, and as she came close my whole body seemed to ache and there was a burning pain in my stomach.

'I suffered very badly,' she said. 'I couldn't have taken much more. I tried so hard to stay but it was no use.'

'Shirley, can you give me your last impression, love?' I asked. She said she went under and then I felt a falling sensation as if I'd been thrown. It was difficult to make out what was happening.

'I wasn't killed outright,' Shirley explained. 'I suffered.'

At first I couldn't see her, but I could feel that her hair swung down round her shoulders. Then she appeared by her mother and I realized she was a strikingly beautiful girl, with film star looks.

'Now, how can I describe your hair, Shirley?' I asked. 'You're not blonde and you're not auburn.'

'You could say sandy, I suppose,' she replied, but she was being modest. Her hair was a lovely natural golden colour.

'We used to call it honey blonde,' said her mother.

She mentioned the names of her ex-husband and her two children who lived with him. She talked of her grandad and dozens of other relatives and friends.

Then she mentioned a man's name.

'That was the person who was supposed to be her friend who lived in the same block of flats,' said her mother.

'Hah hah,' said Shirley when she heard this. 'Friend!'

She sighed. 'I didn't want to say because I didn't want to upset Mum, but it was him. He threw me and belted me and I hadn't got a lot left to make me look nice after the divorce but all I had was taken. My jewellery, rings and watches, everything was taken.'

'Yes,' said her mother, 'he stole them.'

'And now he's walking free,' Shirley added bitterly. 'You see, my mum and dad helped me so much over my husband and I'd been a real trial to my parents. I've got to be honest about myself, and then I made another big mistake and I was too bloody proud to go and say I've made a mistake, can you get me out of it. It cost me my life. Can you understand why I couldn't go to them when I should? I'm very proud, an arrogant young bitch and I couldn't face telling them.'

'That's the way she speaks,' I added hastily, in case her mother thought I was being insulting.

'Oh yes, that's all right. I know.'

Shirley went on to tell me she promoted things for a living.

'Yes, she did a lot of demonstrations,' said her mother.

'I made a very good living but I was so stupid, I always fell for the takers, not the givers. He was very cruel to me. He was evil, yet he had a fascination for me.'

She was worried about her sister who had had a nervous breakdown over the tragedy, and she was full of remorse.

'I lived in a slum and it was a slum, Doris,' she said. 'I came from a good home, a good clean home yet I just couldn't … I don't know. I'm so sorry for all the heartache I caused my parents, but my kids will be all right. As far as they're concerned I just died and that was it, but please God they never find out about the rats and the state my body was in.'

Her mother explained that Shirley had been dead for three months when she finally got the police to break into the flat and her body was a mass of fractures and broken bones.

'My ex-husband was upset when he heard,' said Shirley. 'There was no real bad feeling between us, we were just not compatible. He wanted a home bird and I was never a home bird. That was the main problem. Now he's got a wife who's content to stay at home.'

In the end her life was so unpleasant Shirley said she was glad to have gone to the other side.

'I was scared stiff of him,' she said. 'He wouldn't let me out of the flat. Before the last beating he fractured my femur and I never did get to the hospital. I was glad to be out of it.'

Afterwards her mother told me that they tried everything to get Shirley away from this man but she would never come. They even paid for a taxi and sent it to the door but it returned empty. Letters and phone calls went unanswered and when they tried to visit her this man wouldn't let them in. She was ill, he would say, the place was a mess and Shirley didn't want to see them.

Eventually they were able to convince the police that this wasn't merely a family dispute, that they felt there was serious cause for alarm, but by then it was too late. Shirley had been dead for three months, this man had pawned her jewellery and withdrawn the money from her building society account. He spent a short time in a mental hospital but there wasn't enough evidence to convict him of murder.

I came across another dreadful case like this quite by chance. I'd been asked to take part in a radio phone-in on Capital Radio.

It was the sort of show where listeners ring the studio and I try to get a few details for them over the phone line. This is more difficult than working with the sitter close to you but sometimes you get very good results.

The phone was going non stop and the programme was flowing the usual loving messages, when a male caller was put through to me. At once I heard the name Susan, which turned out to be the name of his daughter, then there was a terrible pressure round my neck. I was choking for breath. Shocked, I realized that this girl had been strangled. But how could I say that over the air?

'This girl should not have died,' I croaked, my throat still dry from the unpleasant experience. 'She went over very quickly. It shouldn't have happened. Do you understand what I mean?'

The man assured me he did. There were a few more family details and then I was urged to move on to the next caller. Reluctantly I had to leave the bereaved father but I hoped he would contact me privately.

He did. Soon after the show I got a phone call asking if I could possibly see Mr and Mrs Chalkley, whose daughter, Susan, had spoken to them through me on the phone-in.

Apparently the case had been in the papers while I was away in Australia. Susan had been strangled by her lover who then set fire to the house in an effort to get rid of the body, even though Susan's small daughter was still inside.

Susan couldn't rest because she was so angry about this and because she was upset by the things that people were saying about her. She didn't mind for herself but she couldn't bear to see what it was doing to her parents.

'It was the first time, Mum, I don't care what anyone says, it was the first time. Believe me,' she cried.

'I was living apart from my husband and I was going to get a divorce and then this had to happen. I know my parents worry that I suffered a lot but I didn't. I was unconscious almost immediately.'

The gossip that always surrounds such cases was still on her mind. 'I know what people have said but I didn't keep a bad house,' Susan sobbed. 'It was the first time, before God, on my baby's life, that I'd ever gone to bed with somebody.

'I don't know what I was thinking of. I was lonely and fed up and look what happened. But I wouldn't want them to think badly of me. We were brought up decently.'

She mentioned a few family names and remembered her grandmother and her two sisters' birthdays.

'I was the middle one of the family,' she explained. Yet she was still sad.

'There's been so much aggravation since it happened over my baby,' she said and her mother nodded. 'He didn't want to know about our Mandy before, so what the hell does he want to start now for? Now I've gone and my sister and my family have stepped in and said they want her, he's suddenly said he wants her.'

I paused for breath. Susan was getting very cross, and it was difficult to keep up with her.

'Presumably she's talking about her husband,' I said.

'Yes,' said Mrs Chalkley. 'That's right, but Mandy is very happy and well looked after by her father.'

Susan calmed down at this.

'Oh, she's beautiful, my little girl,' she told me. 'She's got big eyes and a fringe across her forehead ...' Her voice changed again. 'You see it was in the bedroom. Then there was the bathroom and Mandy was in the room next to the bathroom. The bastard set a fire, you know. Thank goodness the bathroom was in between my bedroom and where Amanda was. The bastard ... You see I used to go out, I won't pretend I didn't, but I didn't bring men home to sleep with me.'

She was starting to upset herself again, so to change the subject I asked her for some more details about her family.

She mentioned the boy who used to run errands for her,

she talked of Whitley Bay where she'd spent many happy holidays as a child and then she spat another name.

'Dickinson.'

'That's the name of the man who did it,' said her father.

Finally as the power faded, she made a last effort to help her mother.

'Mum, you're going to stop taking those tablets now, aren't you?'

Mrs Chalkley crumbled. 'I've already tried to stop but I can't,' she sobbed. 'I go down so much.'

'Oh, tell her she must,' Susan begged me.

'They're not doing you any good, love,' I said. 'Susan does so want you to stop. She tells me you still feel guilty inside but it's not your fault. You think if you'd taken a bit more interest, maybe she wouldn't have got married when she did, or maybe the marriage would have worked. But there was nothing you could have done. She is a very strong-willed girl and she'd made up her mind.'

Susan of course, had not changed a bit. She hadn't become a little angel now she was on the other side. She was still strong-willed and she was still angry about what had happened to her.

This is often the case. Possibly after years on the other side people learn saintly forgiveness and tolerance, but those who feel rushed over before their time remain angry for quite a while.

Stephen Peace, for example, was only nineteen when he was killed in a motor-cycle accident. He was a very good rider and had passed an advanced motor-cycling test, yet his skills couldn't help him escape a fatal accident. He was very sad because it happened at an exciting moment in his life.

'Julie and I were going to get engaged,' he said. 'On Julie's seventeenth birthday. I loved her very much, as she loved me, and I still love her.'

Everything was going well for him when one day he rode down Market Street he said, near his home.

'I was riding down the road when this woman pulled out in front of me. She did a U-turn without looking. I tried to avoid her, I turned the bike hard, but it was no use. I went into her sideways.

'And do you know,' he added furiously, 'that bloody bitch got away with it!'

He was anxious about Julie.

'She can't forget me,' he said. 'But I want her to be happy. I want her to go out with other people. She's so pretty. Her hair comes down to her shoulders and it flicks up at the ends. She always wears T-shirts. Even in the winter.'

Fred and Pat Peace, Stephen's parents, agreed that all he said was true and, hearing them, Stephen seemed to calm down. I've noticed that the one thing that helps these angry people is to get their grievances off their chests.

'Oh well,' he finished. 'Mum always said "That bloody bike, it's a bloody death-trap." If only I'd listened to her.'

Chapter 9

Early one spring morning in 1982, Waiter 25 clocked silently into the Pizza Inc Restaurant in Swallow Street, London.

He punched his number into the special clocking-in device on the till, which automatically recorded it, along with the date and the time. It was 20 March and the time was 6.54 a.m.

But when the owners, Richard and Barbara Possner, arrived an hour later at 8.00, the place was deserted, the doors were still locked and bolted just as they were left the night before, the burglar alarms were undisturbed and the till was switched off because the Posners possess the only key to switch it on.

Of Waiter 25 there was no sign. But then that didn't surprise them. They don't have a Waiter 25.

'The thing is, Doris,' said Richard Possner when he telephoned me several weeks later, 'it's just not possible. I mean, without the key you can't record anything on the till. It just won't work. There is only one key, which Barbara and I keep for security reasons, and it was with us that morning in our flat.

'What's more, forgetting the key for a moment, we know someone must have been in the restaurant at 6.54 a.m. but how did he get in and out without setting off the alarms or breaking any of the locks?'

It was a mystery all right but this incident alone hadn't driven them to seek help. It was only when strange things were happening with such regularity that the staff were getting uneasy that the Posners realized something would have to be done.

There was the burglar alarm, for instance. The bell was

situated inside the restaurant high up on a wall where no
one could reach it without a ladder. So, when during a
routine test the Possners discovered it wasn't working, they
called in a specialist.

'When he opened up the bell he found a stone wedged
inside it, breaking the circuit,' said Barbara. 'He said in all
his experience he'd never seen anything so clever and he
was used to dealing with the work of professional
criminals. But even if a criminal had thought up the idea,
how would he have got in to tamper with the bell? Richard
and I keep the keys to the restaurant and you couldn't
help noticing a man on a ladder messing about with the
alarm.'

Then there was the clock. On the wall they had mounted
a handsome station clock powered by an electric battery so
that it didn't need winding. It was a lovely clock. Everyone
admired it, but within days of coming to the restaurant it
went wrong. No matter what anyone did, it would not go
past twelve midnight. At midnight it stopped dead. In the
end the Possners had to get rid of it.

But they couldn't get rid of everything. They needed
the gas oven, for instance. Yet after a while even this
became faulty. For no apparent reason the gas kept
blowing out and nothing could be cooked. The engineers
were called in and although they solved the problem, they
deepened the mystery.

'They said they couldn't understand it at all,' said
Richard. 'They said a hidden screw deep inside the oven
had come unscrewed, but it wouldn't have done so on its
own. Yet unless you were an expert on these particular
ovens you wouldn't even know the screw was there, let
alone know what it was for. You certainly couldn't see it by
looking through the oven door.'

When they opened the freezer and found all the meat
defrosting because the switch had apparently turned itself
off, they weren't even surprised so hardened had they
become to the peculiarities of the restaurant.

The 'ghost', they told each other, had a weakness for
gadgets. They began to feel they understood how his mind
worked.

Well, they shouldn't have said that. Not aloud anyway. Because then he changed his tactics. One afternoon Richard walked into the restaurant and noticed a strong smell of gas. Several people complained about it and everyone could smell it.

Naturally assuming they had a leak, Richard telephoned the gas board. The emergency engineers arrived almost immediately. One sniff was enough to confirm that there was indeed a very bad smell of gas. yet when they set up their instruments they could find no trace of a leak. After an exhaustive search of the area they were forced to give up, quite baffled.

It was around this time that Val, one of the waitresses, happened to be alone in the bar polishing glasses ready for the lunch-time customers.

'Val!' called a male voice.

She looked up, but no one was there. The restaurant and bar were quite empty. Impatiently she put down her cloth and went into the kitchen.

'Yes? What d'you want?'

The chef looked blank. 'Want? I don't want anything.'

'But you just called me, didn't you?'

'No, not me,' said the chef.

Puzzled, Val returned to the bar but there was no one there. She searched the store rooms and cupboard for signs of colleagues playing a joke, but found nothing. It was odd, that's all, and she would probably have forgotten about it had it not happened again, not once but several times.

Soon she was hearing her name called softly whenever she was working alone. It was always the same male voice but since he only said one short word, she couldn't get any clues to his identity. Age and accent were impossible to guess. At first Val found it merely irritating but as the weeks passed she began to get edgy. She wasn't frightened exactly but the place was beginning to give her the creeps.

It was some time before she mentioned it to the Possners. She felt a bit foolish, as if they would think she was going mad. But in the end it was so obvious there was something wrong she had to tell them. And of course they didn't laugh.

By now after six months at the restaurant they were

convinced the place was haunted and they were beginning to take the ghost seriously.

They were both young, down-to-earth people, hard-working types who had never given such things a thought before, but this was different. It had reached the stage where the business they'd dreamed of for so long might be at risk.

'Could you come as soon as possible, Doris?' asked Richard. 'This afternoon if you like.'

I laughed. 'Oh dear, I'm afraid I can't come now, I've got somebody coming. What about Monday?'

'Okay. Monday,' said Richard.

And that's how, despite the fact that I was up to my eyes with cases involving children, I came to be sitting drinking tea the following Monday afternoon in a London restaurant.

It was a welcome relief from the pressure of work. These days I get so many thousands of requests for sittings that I have to turn away more than I can accept. For this reason I devote most of my time to bereaved parents because, rightly or wrongly, I believe they are the ones most in need of help.

The trouble is, this kind of work is the most emotionally draining of the lot and so, just occasionally, it's nice to get my teeth into a good old impersonal ghost.

Pizza Inc turned out to be a very nice, very unusual restaurant. The minute I walked through the door I could tell that there was nothing evil here. There was a warm, pleasant atmosphere and it felt, and looked, relaxing. The air of tranquillity might have had something to do with the fact that the place appeared to have been furnished with items discarded from churches.

There was stained glass in the windows, pews had been made into bench seats, there were bits of screens and altar rails and even a pulpit.

'Oh, isn't it lovely!' I exclaimed as we walked in.

'Glad you think so,' said Richard, looking pleased. 'We like it anyway.'

'Did all this stuff come from a church?'

He explained that it had been gathered from all over the

place but a lot had come from old churches. He went off to get us a pot of tea and I stretched out in my chair.

'Well, this makes a change, doesn't ...' I stopped and stared in amazement as a monk in a long brown robe walked past.

For a moment I thought they might be extending the ecclesiastical theme to the waiters and waitresses by dressing them as monks and nuns, but then I realized that this was a real monk and he'd passed over long ago.

As I watched he turned, and seemed to glide back past us but, as he drew level, he raised his head and gave us a smile of great serenity. Then he was gone.

Well, I thought to myself, there is a ghost here but he's not doing any harm, he's certainly not fiddling about with switches and making trouble. The monk is responsible for the feeling of peace and tranquillity. He likes to see his old things put to good use and cared for.

All the same I was very surprised to have seen him. These days I rarely see adult spirits, I only see children. Occasionally an adult will appear, but hardly ever during a sitting. It's usually when I'm not tuned in and when I least expect it.

'Well, there's a monk here, I can tell you that,' I said to Richard as he came back with the tea. 'But it's not him. He's happy to come back now and again to see what you're doing with his stuff. No, there must be something else.'

But I could feel there was something complicated about this case, so I tuned in first to see if Richard's relatives could help. It was Richard's father, I think, who came through. He said how proud he was of Richard and that he had no need to worry because the restaurant was going to be a great success.

'Some of these incidents,' he said, 'are nothing to do with us. They are man-made. There is jealousy at work,' and he went on to name one or two members of staff who had recently left.

'These people had something to do with some of the incidents,' he said.

Richard agreed that he'd always been uneasy about one of the people named and was glad he'd gone.

However, even though some of the mysteries were of earthly origin, it was clear that others weren't. The next step was to find out where the spirit was operating from. Once we'd located him, we could talk to him.

In all these cases, the presence of the spirit is betrayed by a patch of freezing cold air. You have to walk slowly across the floor until you find the cold spot and, no matter how good the central heating, a cold spot will be there if there is a spirit present.

'Now,' I said to Richard and Barbara, 'I'm going to walk round the room and I want you to follow me, putting your feet in exactly the same place that I put my feet. All right?'

They thought it was rather funny but, laughing and chattering, we formed a little procession and wound slowly through the restaurant.

Richard had a feeling the problem might come from the kitchen, so we went there first.

Carefully I padded over every inch of the floor but there was nothing. The temperature was quite even.

'No, it's not here, Richard,' I said. We moved on to the store cupboard. Again, though it was chilly, it was the natural chill of a cool room not the unmistakable sensation of a cold spot in an otherwise normal room.

We backed into the restaurant again and I stepped carefully along the strip of lino behind the bar. Halfway along I stopped.

'I think I've found it.' The room was warm but just here, close to the beer taps, cold waves were rippling over me. Then I realized I was standing next to the ice bucket.

I laughed. 'No. It's probably a false alarm. I'm beside the ice bucket!'

Was it just the ice bucket? I wondered, or was there something else there? I couldn't be sure and unless I was certain I wouldn't say anything.

I returned to the main body of the restaurant. It was fairly large and we patiently pigeon-stepped up and down the aisles. At last, at the far end, I felt another wave of cold air. I stood still. Yes, definitely cold air.

'Barbara,' I said turning round, 'come and stand just here and tell me what you feel.'

I moved aside and Barbara took my place. She paused for a moment, head on one side.

'Yes, it's cold. Just here. It's peculiar.'

Then Richard glanced up.

'Hey, you're standing underneath the fan!'

I followed his gaze. There on the ceiling was one of those big old-fashioned blade fans.

'Oh dear, would you turn it off, Richard.'

Richard obligingly went to the switch. The fan stopped and I moved back to my original position. The cold was still welling up like bath water. The fan had made no difference.

'All right, Barbara,' I said, 'come back and we'll try it again.'

Barbara fitted her feet once more into the place I'd indicated.

'Yes, it's still here. It's the strangest thing.' Then she stopped. 'It seems to be going.'

'Going?' I echoed.

'Yes. Now it's gone.'

Quickly we changed places and I realized what she meant. The cold spot had gone and now the area was the same temperature as the rest of the room. This was very odd. Of course spirit entities can move around but since the aim of causing a disturbance is to draw attention to themselves they usually want to be found and they don't whisk about playing hide and seek.

'That is strange,' I said, but time was running out and we couldn't spend hours chasing an invisible ghost. The restaurant would be opening soon for the evening customers and I had to be finished by then.

'Well, never mind, let's see if he'll come and talk to us.'

We returned to our table from which the tea things had been cleared and I tuned in. There was a confusing sort of scuffle as if several people were trying to communicate at once, then a male voice seemed to elbow the others out of the way.

'I was killed,' he said gruffly. 'I was killed here.'

Now we were getting somewhere, I thought with satisfaction.

'Here?' I said. 'What happened?'

Immediately I felt a rushing, falling sensation as if I was falling through the air and my neck and head hurt badly.

'I went right down the stairs,' said the man. 'From top to bottom. That's what did it.'

'Which stairs, dear?' I asked, because we'd just walked round every inch of the restaurant and hadn't come across a flight of stairs.

The man sighed as if I was being unusually dense. 'I'll show you,' he said.

Immediately in my mind I was standing at the top of a flight of steep, narrow stairs with an arch over them. They descended down somewhere gloomy and would need artificial light over them all the time. They were so steep that I could well believe it was dangerous to fall down them.

'I see what you mean,' I told the man. 'But are you sure the stairs are here? I haven't seen any.'

'Of course they're here. Right in this building,' he insisted.

I turned to Richard and Barbara. 'Can you think what he means?'

They exchanged glances. 'Well,' said Richard, 'there's a bar under the restaurant. It's nothing to do with us but it's in the same building and it has its own separate entrance down a flight of stairs just like the ones you described.'

'Do you know if anyone has fallen down them and been killed?'

He shook his head.

'Well, see if you can find out. I'm sure there has and I'm sure it was a man.'

Having no love link to work from made talking to the man very difficult because he had no special desire to talk to Richard and Barbara and as soon as he grew bored he wandered away. Nevertheless we persevered. He mentioned quite a few names. Some of them meant something to the Possners, most didn't. Then he said Derek, or Eric.

Richard shook his head.

'They don't know him, dear,' I said. But shortly afterwards, as if he felt they really did know, he said, 'In connection with Derek – Bentley.'

Again the Possners couldn't place it. Neither Derek nor Bentley meant a thing to them.

But the vibrations were getting muddled again and I thought I heard another voice come in.

'I was killed, you know,' he said.

'Yes I know, you told me,' I replied, thinking I'd made a mistake and the first man was still talking.

'No, I didn't. This is Billy,' he said loudly. 'I was killed and it wasn't an accident.'

As he spoke I had a brief picture of a young man with flaming ginger hair standing behind Barbara's chair and there was a strong sweaty smell of gymnasiums.

'I was a waiter, you know,' he said, 'and I was killed.'

'This place didn't used to be a gym, did it, or have anything to do with gyms or boxing?' I asked.

'Not as far as we know,' said Richard, 'but we've only been here six months and I don't think the people before us stayed very long. There's no knowing what it was ten or twenty years ago.'

But then the first man was back with more names. They meant nothing to the Possners and I could see Richard looking at his watch. It was time to bring the sitting to a close.

'Now about these things that have been happening,' I said to whoever was listening. 'It's got to stop. You're worrying these young people and it's not fair.'

There was more scuffling then a voice said, 'Didn't mean to do any harm … sorry,' and faded away.

'Well, I don't think you'll have any more trouble,' I told Barbara and Richard. 'He says he's sorry.'

They seemed quite happy and we gathered up our things ready to leave as the first customers came through the door.

'Oh, before you go, Doris, would you like to see the staircase you mentioned?' asked Barbara.

I said I would. She led me out into the street and there next to the restaurant was another door. Barbara tried it but it was locked.

'Oh, what a shame,' she said, 'the stairs are behind that door. They're terribly steep.'

I stared at it for a moment or two.

'Would they finish at a point just below your bar?'

'Yes, I suppose they would.'

Immediately I thought of the cold spot I'd felt when I stood behind the bar, the one I'd blamed on the ice bucket. Also the fact that Val had heard her voice when she was probably standing near the same place. I was just about to mention this to Barbara when a band of writing over the top of the door caught my eye. It was the details of the licensee of the bar and his name was written up there, small but clear. Mr Derek Bentley.

'That's the Derek!' I cried in triumph.

Excitedly Barbara came to see and she called Richard. Derek Bentley, as plain as plain, the name that had come through during the sitting.

'I'll be right back,' said Richard. 'There's someone I can ask.' And he darted off up the road.

'Some of the people round here have been in the area several years,' Barbara explained.

Minutes later Richard was back, a big grin all over his face.

'Derek Bentley is dead,' he said. 'He died one night after falling down those stairs.'

Well, that seemed to settle it. John and I headed back to Fulham pleased with the afternoon's work.

But as it turned out, that wasn't the end of the story. Weeks later we heard that though the name calling and trouble with clocks had stopped the mechanical problems were still going on.

Lights kept switching on and off. The stereo kept breaking down, a blade myseriously flew off a machine landing only inches away from the chef and within an hour of laughing and joking about the ghostly Billy, three of the boys who helped in the restaurant all suffered minor but unpleasant accidents.

This puzzled me until I remembered that if the cold spot behind the bar hadn't been caused by the ice, then there were two cold spots in the restaurant. This would explain why I'd contacted two different men, Derek Bentley and the mysterious Billy. At the end of the sitting when I'd asked them to stop messing about only one voice had agreed and sent its apologies. Looking back I think that voice must have belonged to Derek Bentley. Billy refused to commit himself and it seems Billy is still making his presence felt.

So who is Billy? At the moment we don't know. Richard and Barbara haven't yet found anyone who's lived in the area long enough to give them a clue.

I can see that one of these days I'll have to go along and have another word with Billy.

Around this time I seemed to go into a phase of spontaneously seeing spirit adults. I can't think why this should be unless it's doing so much work with children that's caused it. Maybe because I always see spirit children and I've seen so many of them lately, my psychic eye is getting so highly tuned that it's picking out spirits all over the place.

What with the monk and the flame-haired Billy at the restaurant in Swallow Street I felt sure I'd seen my quota of adults for the year. It's been a long time since my days as a young medium when I was so full of undisciplined psychic energy that I was seeing things all over the place and our homes were full of knocks and bangs and objects flying about. Yet suddenly here it was starting to happen all over again.

I was still rather run down after my operation and was wondering how I was going to get through the string of engagements looming ahead, when Lee Everett offered to give me some healing. Now John is a healer and he was already treating me himself, but I've always believed that every little helps and I accepted gratefully.

As usual Lee arrived with a companion. Not Annie this time but her sister.

'I hope you don't mind,' she said.

'Not a bit.'

I led them into the living-room and Lee's sister and I sat down on the sofa, while Lee sat opposite by the window. We were chatting away and Lee brought me up to date with the latest news, when a sudden movement caught my eye. I glanced up to see a man had appeared in the room.

My sofa is a three-seater. I was sitting at one end and Lee's sister sat at the other. To my amazement the man crossed the room and plonked himself down on the vacant seat between us. My eyes widened ... I glanced quickly at the other two but they didn't seem to have noticed anything unusual. Lee was in mid-sentence and her sister was listening attentively. So, too, was our unannounced guest.

He wasn't doing any harm so I decided to leave him be. If he wanted to drop in to listen to a bit of conversation I couldn't blame him. He looked so real and solid he had probably not been over long. Perhaps he missed our company.

'Well, I suppose I'd better start the healing, Doris,' said Lee suddenly. 'Change places with me, Bren.'

Obediently Brenda stood up but as she did so the man laid his hand on her knee.

'Don't go, Bren,' he said sadly.

But of course Brenda couldn't hear him or see him. He failed to stop her and, as she stood, his hand went right through her knee. The man disappeared.

Yet the sadness in his voice touched me. The man hadn't dropped in for a chat. He belonged to Brenda and he wanted to see her. Therefore I felt I must say something.

'Look, Brenda, I don't know what to do about this,' I said slowly, 'but it's so definite I must tell you. There's a man been sitting between us and as you got up to go he said, "Don't go, Bren."'

One look at her face told me I was right to mention it.

'Oh dear, it's your husband, isn't it!' I added.

She nodded, her eyes full of tears. 'He only passed last Friday,' she whispered.

Well, what could I do? After the healing session Brenda and I had a sitting and her husband was able to return with messages of love and reassurance.

Shortly after this there was a small gap in my diary and since the weather was fine, John suggested it would be a good idea if we went down to our caravan for a few days.

For a long time we've been dreaming about moving out of London. John would like to have a garden to potter in and I must admit it would be nice to live somewhere where you could hear the birds singing and when you walked out of your front door you breathed lungfuls of fresh air instead of traffic fumes.

We've finally had to face the fact that it would never happen. I need to be in a central position for my work, or people wouldn't be able to find me, and we can't afford anything else in such an area. It looked as if we would have to give up our dreams for ever. Then someone told us about caravans. Apparently you could buy them on country sites complete with furniture and some of them even had little garden plots attached. It sounded ideal for us.

'We could do with a bolt hole,' said John. 'This place drives you mad at times with the phone going non-stop.'

He was right. Often the phone rang all day and although we don't give out our full address people find us and come to the door on spec. It would be marvellous to have somewhere quiet to escape to now and again, where we could rest well away from the pleading eyes which were so difficult to refuse.

Terry was just as enthusiastic about the idea, and he kept bringing us advertisements of suitable places. Eventually we picked out a place in the middle of nowhere about an hour's drive from the flat.

Terry took us down to see it one weekend and we were all thrilled with it. It was in a small, green park surrounded by fields and it had two bedrooms, a bathroom, kitchen, living-room and a little garden. When you stood still and listened you could hear nothing, nothing but silence and birdsong.

'Oh, John,' I sighed, 'I don't care if we go bankrupt. Let's have it.'

So we did.

Soon John was pottering happily in the garden, I could sit out in a deckhair and watch him when the weather was fine and Terry was making lots of new friends. We all enjoyed it for different reasons.

Down in the country I tried not to think about my work at all so I was very surprised when I walked into our sitting-room one morning to find a strange lady sitting in the chair by the window, waving through the glass at the passers-by.

For a moment I wondered if I could have wandered into the wrong caravan by mistake, it was still so new to us. Then I realized that it was our chair she was sitting in and those were our flowers in the vase on the table.

Maybe she was one of our new neighbours. I took a step closer and she heard me. She turned and gave me a lovely smile.

'Hello, dear,' she said as if she'd known me all her life.

'Hello, dear,' I replied and then blinked. She disappeared like a puff of smoke.

Even though I'm used to such things it's always a surprise when it happens because spirit people look so real. Often they look no different, no less solid than the people you pass in the street. I don't know where this idea of ghostly being drifting about in long white sheets comes from but it's certainly not inspired by real contact with the spirit people.

'D'you think she could have had the van before us?' I asked John later when I'd explained what happened.

'Probably,' he said, 'but the neighbours are bound to know. We can ask them.'

'We'll be careful how we put it though, John. They don't know us from Adam and if we start saying there's a ghost in our caravan they'll think we're crackers!'

John laughed but he took the point. We made our enquiries as discreetly as we could, but even so it was rather difficult to get the phrasing right.

'You wouldn't know if a lady ever passed over in this van?' I asked our neighbour soon afterwards.

He nearly choked on his tea.

'What makes you say that? I've been here two years and I've not heard of anyone dying.'

I'd obviously not handled the subject very well.

'Oh I just wondered that's all – about who had the van before us, I mean.'

'Oh, I can tell you that,' he said and launched in to a description of the previous owners who were very much alive and kicking.

Nothing more was said and it seemed as if the identity of our elderly visitor would remain a mystery.

Then on another visit a few weeks later we met the people whose garden backed on to ours. They had been away on holiday when we were last down so we'd not had a chance to talk to them. We soon put that to right. Not long after we arrived we were chatting over the fence like old friends.

'Of course, old Mrs So and So died in the bedroom there,' said the woman suddenly.

I was instantly alert. 'You mean in our van?'

'Oh yes,' she said.

'Tell me, did she used to sit by the lounge window waving to people?'

The woman stared at me in amazement. 'Why, how did you know? She was in a wheelchair and she used to wave to me when I took the dog for a walk.'

So that was it. The van used to belong to her and she'd come back to have a look at us and see that we were taking care of it.

Incidentally, if anyone who has read my last two books wonders what we did with our cat, Matey, while we made our jaunts down to the van, I have to explain that we didn't leave him behind and we wouldn't have dreamed of leaving him behind. Sadly, he passed over before we got our country retreat, which is a shame because he would have loved the garden.

One day he simply disappeared. He didn't come in for his meal as he normally did and when he hadn't turned up by nightfall I was fearing the worst.

'He's probably got shut in somewhere,' people suggested to cheer me up. Or, 'It's spring. He's probably having a last fling on the tiles.'

But the next day there was still no sign of him. John and I searched the walkways and the courtyard around the flats and found nothing. Matey seemed to have vanished into thin air.

That afternoon I felt terribly tired.

'I think I'll have a lay down, John,' I said yawning and, unusually for me, I was asleep in minutes. But it wasn't a restful sleep. Dreams came almost at once and in my dreams I saw a very tall man holding the body of a ginger cat in his arms. I couldn't see the man's face but the cat was Matey and I'm pretty sure the man was my father.

When I woke up I knew I'd seen the truth.

'We can put away Matey's bowls,' I told John. 'He won't be coming back. My father's taken him. He's on the other side now.'

We never saw him again.

It's sad because Matey missed his garden when we moved to London and he would have enjoyed stalking about in our little plot at the van. On the other hand I know he's got all the space he wants on the other side, because animals live on just as humans do and we shall see our pets again one day.

It wasn't many weeks before we discovered that even deep in the country we couldn't escape entirely. Word got round in that mysterious way it has and some people were arriving unannounced. I discovered too that, even in the country, I wasn't to escape the lessons Ramanov wanted to teach me.

One evening I was watching television and John had gone round to our neighbour to take back a clothesline we'd borrowed, when I heard a commotion outside. I lifted up the corner of the curtains and saw a lady, a man and two youngsters all coming down the lawn.

'Perhaps they think the place is still for sale,' I thought. Oh well, they'd soon realize their mistake. I went back to my programme.

A few minutes later John came back.

'Hey, love!' he said putting his head round the door. 'There's a lady outside and she doesn't want to bother you but she wondered if she could have a look at you just to make sure it was you.'

'What d'you mean, make sure it's me?' I asked.

'Well somebody told her you were staying down here and she said she wouldn't believe it unless she saw it for herself. She says she doesn't want to be a nuisance, but could she just look at you for a moment.'

Well, what could I do? It was vain but I couldn't resist it.

Up I got and out I went onto the verandah and, despite the fact that I was wearing an old sun dress, slippers and no stockings, I stood there feeling like the Queen. My admirers gathered round to gaze at me in awe and I have to admit it was very flattering.

I enjoyed myself thoroughly and granted them much longer than a minute or two. And what was the result of my vanity?

As I stood there on the verandah holding court like the Queen, a mosquito bit me three times.

The next day the bites swelled into hot red lumps that kept me itching and scratching for days. And as I rubbed away at the blazing skin I couldn't help smiling.

Well, that'll teach you, Doris, I said to myself. What does Ramanov say? 'Your gift is for helping others not for your own self-aggrandisement.'

That's what comes of being vain!

Chapter 10

'Rawlinson,' said a voice.

Startled, I looked up to see who had spoken but even as I did so I realized my mistake. Despite the fact that I wasn't tuned in, it was a spirit voice I was hearing.

'Rawlinson,' it said again. 'Rawlinson.'

The car was speeding along the motorway, engine roaring, tyres loud on the tarmac, yet above the noise I could hear the quiet voice distinctly.

I was on my way to a public demonstration in Maidenhead and, as the Berkshire countryside flashed past the window, the name was repeated again and again. It was quite obvious to me that Rawlinson, whoever he or she may be, was going to be important at the coming meeting.

All right, I told the voice in the end, I understand. I'll see what I can do when I get there. I've sometimes wondered in the past how much comfort people can get from mass meetings. I know they are very useful in awakening interest and getting people to ask themselves questions that might never have occurred to them before but can you give much help to individuals? Is it better to give a lot of people a little or a few people a lot? In Maidenhead I got my answer, with the Rawlinson case.

As with all the answers I get in one form or another from Ramanov it was vaguely disconcerting. I was to stop bothering about things I didn't understand, do my job and leave the rest to the spirit world. How much or how little help I thought I was able to give was irrelevant because my messages weren't an end in themselves, but just another link in the chain the spirit world was building.

As far as I was concerned, I wasn't able to give the

Rawlinsons much time, but the spirit world was already at work with them and the information they got from me, on top of the things that had already happened, was all part of a process that was to change their lives.

When I went on stage at Maidenhead I chatted to the audience for a few minutes and told one or two jokes to help them relax. Then as the laughter died away and I could feel a general loosening up all round, I reckoned it was time to start work.

'Now, before I begin,' I said, 'is there anyone here by the name of Rawlinson or who knows anyone called Rawlinson? I've been hearing the name all the way down here so I know it's important.'

There was a stunned silence for a moment, then a man raised his hand.

'I'm Rawlinson.'

Immediately the voice came back, a young man's voice eager to communicate and clearly delighted to have got through first. The names tumbled from him so fast it was difficult to keep up.

'He's talking about someone called Margaret.'

'That's my wife,' said Mr Rawlinson.

'And Joe, or is it John?'

'My daughter's called Joanne.'

'Then there's Paul,' I continued. Then I stopped. The man nodded, yes he knew Paul, but he was clearly very upset. The young man came close in and I realized there was a great tragedy here. He was only nineteen, he said, and there'd been a car crash. In the background other voices were clamouring to be heard. I didn't want to start the evening on too sad a note and I didn't want to embarrass Mr Rawlinson.

'I'll have to move on, I'm afraid,' I told him. 'They're all trying to get through, but don't worry. I'll come back to you.'

As it turned out though, I didn't. There were so many spirit people determined to talk to their friends and relatives in the audience that our time ran out before I was able to return to Mr Rawlinson.

Wearily I left the stage and headed for the kitchen

where my customary cup of tea was waiting. I felt rather bad about Mr Rawlinson but I have to go where the spirit voices lead me and that night his son, for I was sure it was his son, had not led me back to his father.

What I hadn't realized, of course, was that Glen, as I later discovered his name to be, was doing it the other way round. He was leading his father back to me.

I was deep into my second cup when suddenly the kitchen door opened and there stood Mr Rawlinson. He hesitated in the doorway obviously unwilling to disturb me.

'It's Mr Rawlinson, isn't it?' I said, motioning him to come in. 'I'm sorry I didn't come back to you but it was too sad. Your son tells me he was only nineteen and he was in an accident. He was coming round a bend, he says, and there was a head-on collision. Two people went over and three ended up in hospital.'

Mr Rawlinson look dumbfounded. 'Yes, that's right. My son and the other driver were killed and three passengers were taken to hospital.

Glen was back now, loud and clear. 'I was killed instantly,' he said. 'I didn't suffer but I'm so sorry it happened. I shouldn't even have been there. I wouldn't have been there if it hadn't been for Kevin.'

Mr Rawlinson nodded. 'Yes, he was giving Kevin a lift home to Cookham.'

'I'm so sorry for the upset I caused just when I was doing what Dad wanted me to do,' Glen went on. 'Now they're shattered, especially Mum, because I didn't say goodbye.'

'Yes, that's what upset her the most,' said Mr Rawlinson. 'He always said goodbye when he went out but that night she was upstairs and for some reason he didn't call out to her.'

Glen was worried about his mum. 'She's falling apart and she's got to stop because I'm all right. I'm alive and I'm happy. Oh, and tell her Margaret, called Maggie, is looking after me.'

This was gratifying because apparently one of the things that most worried Mrs Rawlinson was that if there was an

after life, Glen would be alone because very few of his
relatives had gone over. The only one was his
grandmother, Margaret, nicknamed Maggie.

On a lighter note Glen added, 'Tell Mum there's lots of
sunshine here because she is a great sun fanatic, and tell
her that I spend a lot of time in the halls of music. Not just
with pop music, good music too.'

Mr Rawlinson drew in his breath. He recognized the
phrase. 'In his spare time Glen was a DJ,' he said, 'and he
always said, "I don't just play pop music, you know. I play
good music." '

Glen went on to give more family names, then he
returned to the accident. 'I wouldn't have minded,' he
said, 'but I'd only sold a house that morning.'

Apparently Glen was an estate agent and the day of the
accident he was particularly happy and excited because
he'd just sold his boss's house and he was going on holiday
to the South of France the following weekend.

That was about all I was able to do that night and it
seemed little enough to me. I was particularly sorry that
Eric Rawlinson's wife Margaret wasn't there. Apparently,
Glen had only passed a month before and the grief was so
strong she felt she couldn't face a public meeting.

What I didn't realize was that the whole family was to
experience a real change and a new world was opening up
to them quite literally.

My communication, while not much in itself, fitted
neatly into what they were finding out, and was further
confirmation of the truth.

Several months later Eric and Margaret explained what
happened.

'Glen was something special,' said Eric, a property
developer and insurance broker. 'He was a positive, lively
young man who was great with people. So many people
loved him. In fact afterwards, when we were looking
through the old photographs, it was difficult to find a
picture where Glen didn't have his arm round someone.

'It was impossible to have an argument with him because
he always apologized and put his arm round you. He gave
out so much love. We're still finding out about the things

he did for people and at the hospital where he was a DJ in his spare time, they are putting up a plaque in his memory because they were so fond of him.

'After his death the family were devastated. He was such an extrovert that there was a great void in our lives. Even today nothing can fill it.

'Yet some incredible things have happened. Four days after his death I had the most incredible spiritual experience. I've never known anything like it in my life. It is very difficult to put into words. All I can say is that on Thursday afternoon after the accident I was sitting in the kitchen in a terrible state. I was so distraught, so unhappy.

'Then suddenly the kitchen started to fill with light, a tremendous light like coming out of the fog into bright sunshine and I heard Glen's voice say, "You have to die to be born."

'All at once everything fell into place. Life, death, everything. I knew. I understood. Yet if you ask me what I knew, I couldn't tell you. At the time I felt uplifted, tremendously elated. I've never been so happy in my life. I wanted to rush out and open bottles of champagne.

'I turned to Margaret and she said, "Yes, I know. It happened to me last night." But when I mentioned it to a friend later, thinking he'd understand, he thought I was going out of my mind.

'I wasn't. I've never been saner. I'd seen the truth. Suddenly I understood what all those old clichés like "seen the light" really meant. The elation didn't last. The next day I was depressed again, but the truth remained.

'I don't believe any more. I know.'

The experience caused Eric to read as much as he could on spiritualism and philosophy and everything he read seemed to confirm his feelings. Although he'd never read these subjects before, he instantly recognized what they said. Even the philosophy was familiar.

In the past he'd been a forceful, down-to-earth businessman with little time for such matters. He didn't even know that the spiritualist church existed. Yet when the family came back from a holiday Eric had taken them on to get over the shock of the accident, he found two tickets for the meeting at Maidenhead waiting for him.

'A neighbour got them for me,' he said. 'She had read *Voices in My Ear* and *More Voices* and she thought that seeing Doris might help. There was never any question in my mind that I shouldn't go. I knew I had to go and I knew Glen would contact me. When Doris called out my name I was shocked but somehow not surprised, if you see what I mean.'

Of course, as I found, and as every parent I've ever spoken to has found, Eric discovered that you never get over the loss of a child, but you do learn to live with it. He also realized that it helped to talk about it, and the more he talked the more he became aware of a dimension he'd never noticed before when he was deep in his money-making schemes.

'People are embarrassed to talk about their beliefs,' he said, 'but once you make it clear that you understand, they come out with the most amazing stories. I've discovered that about sixty or seventy per cent of the people I've spoken to are spiritually motivated.

'One man I've known for years wasn't at all surprised by my experiences. "I know you're right," he said, "because of what happened to my brother."

'Apparently his brother had been extremely fond of their grandfather, but while he was away in the Navy, the grandfather died. When the brother's ship docked, the whole family went to meet him and once the greetings were over their mother said, "I'm afraid there's some sad news as well."

' "If it's about Grandad, I know," said the brother. "I know he's gone. He came to me on board and told me."

'The family were astonished but the brother stuck to his story. "He appeared to me on the ship and said goodbye," he said.

'The strange thing is,' Eric added, 'I've heard dozens of stories like that ever since.'

Margaret Rawlinson knows exactly what he means. Although she didn't feel able to attend the Maidenhead meeting, she, too, was learning and discovering.

'That meeting was too soon for me,' she said. 'I was still

in the depths of grief. Yet I'm glad Eric went because the things he was able to tell us afterwards helped the whole family so much. We knew nothing about the subject at all. We were feeling terrible, then suddenly there was this joyous news. It brought us such comfort to know that the person we loved was still there and that we'd meet again one day.

'We've been reading books ever since and talking to people and we have been told the most amazing things. One woman from the village told me that she knew there was life after death because she'd been to the other side. She had been involved in a terrible accident and she had "died" for several minutes. She says she can remember what happened in great detail. She said she was in a tunnel and there was a bright light at the end and she could see all these loving people waiting for her. She was moving along the tunnel towards them and she knew that once she reached the light she would be "over". Then suddenly she was pulled back again and the doctors revived her.

'She also believes she has visited her grandmother – in a dream that she is convinced wasn't a dream. She was very sad because her grandmother died and she hadn't said goodbye. One night she "dreamed" she met her grandmother in a beautiful place. Her grandmother was looking much younger than she remembered her and they hugged and kissed and said goodbye. Most people would say it was a dream, but this woman is quite convinced it actually happened.'

For Eric Rawlinson the tragedy has had far-reaching effects.

'The most important thing that has happened to me since the accident is that I'm no longer afraid of dying. I used to be terribly afraid. I used to wake up in the night in a cold sweat imagining black eternity and vast, endless space. For years I'd been living in terror of death. Now I don't fear it at all. Quite the opposite. I know that death is simply rebirth on a higher level, to a world of beauty and love.

'But it isn't something you can get over to other people. Before all this happened, if you had told me this I wouldn't have believed it. I wouldn't have listened. You can't tell people. It's something they have to experience for themselves. Because of what's happened to me, I know.'

What's more, the experience has made Eric question his values and way of life. He is a successful businessman with a talent for raising money and now he would like to use his talent to help other people.

'I suddenly realized that in his short life, my son had achieved more than I have done in the whole of mine,' he said. 'Now I would like to do something worthwhile for others. In fact, I know I will. When the time is right it will all fall into place and I will see what I have to do.'

After talking to the Rawlinsons I will never again doubt the place that my little snippets of information have in the overall scheme of things and I have been going to public demonstrations with new enthusiasm ever since.

I'm often invited to speak at the Spiritualist Association of Great Britain's headquarters in Belgrave Square, and the last time I was there I had some very vivid communications. At one point I glanced up and saw a little girl dancing round the feet of a woman in the audience. It was quite clear from the way she moved and the way no one took any notice of her that she was a spirit child.

'My name's Helen,' she told me, giggling. 'And this is my mummy.'

Then she skipped up to the platform and got hold of the necklace I was wearing.

'Look round Mummy's neck. Look round Mummy's neck,' she instructed excitedly.

But I was too far away to see her mother's neck or what she was wearing. Helen wasn't going to give up though. After the meeting she accompanied her mother to the front to see me and round her mother's neck I noticed a chain from which hung a tiny picture of Helen.

During the same meeting two young people, a boy and a girl, came to say hello. They were called John and Lorraine, and John's mother was in the audience.

'What happened, love?' I asked John and in reply he gave me what I took to be two contradictory sensations. I could smell gas very strongly but I was also surrounded by water, lots of water. That confused me. Were they gassed or drowned, or was one gassed and the other drowned?

John's mother explained. 'They were on a boat, Doris, and one of the gas bottles was leaking.'

'I tried to get help,' said John, 'but I couldn't make it. I collapsed. It's a good thing Mum didn't look at me afterwards. We were strawberry coloured.'

It was horrifying, of course, yet these two lovely young people were still together and happy.

You hear so many tragic stories on these occasions yet, strangely enough, there is usually a lot of laughter as well. I remember when I gave a similar demonstration shortly afterwards in Hitchin, Hertfordshire, one lady was astonished when I was able to tell her she'd got £42.50 tucked away in a tea caddy. The audience rocked and her face was a picture.

'Yes, I have,' she gasped. '£42.50 exactly!' And she stared at me with great suspicion as if she thought I'd been peeping through the window.

When I was working with a live audience on the Granada television show, *An Evening With Doris Stokes*, we hardly stopped laughing all night. An elderly man with a walking-stick came along to talk to one lady and I could hear his stick tap-tap-tapping in the background.

'He used to use a stick, didn't he?' I said. 'For walking and getting in and out of chairs.'

'Not just for that, either,' she replied tartly. 'He used to whack things with it as well.'

Everyone laughed but the man who had a strong Yorkshire accent wasn't put off.

'When's she going to get rid of that blue hat that's been standing on the wardrobe all these years?' he said. 'She gets it out and puts it back. Why doesn't she throw it away?'

'He's right,' the woman chuckled. 'It's still in its C&A hat bag.'

Then there was the dear old lady who had relatives halfway across the world.

'You've got relatives in Australia, in Melbourne, and relatives in Christchurch, New Zealand,' I told her.

'Yes I have,' she agreed happily.

'And next year they're all coming over to see you for a special celebration.'

'Are they?'

At this there was an irritated hissing in my ear.

'It's a surprise. A surprise,' said a voice. 'You weren't supposed to tell her.'

'Oh dear, I wasn't supposed to say that,' I apologized. 'It's a surprise.'

'It's all right,' the old lady beamed. 'I didn't hear a word.'

The animals got a look-in as well. A little later in the middle of something serious I had to break off and turn to someone else.

'There's a dog called Barney just turned up,' I said to a lady with tight dark curls. 'Do you know Barney?'

'Barney? why, yes, I do,' she said in surprise. The last contact she'd expected was from her dog.

That was all for the time being, but a few minutes later I was dragged back to her. Oh no, I thought, when I heard what the voice wanted me to tell her. That sounds ridiculous. But the voice insisted.

'All right,' I said in defeat. 'Well, you know Barney, well, with Barney was there a parrot? They're saying something about a parrot and Barney.'

A great hoot of laughter filled the studio and even the woman giggled.

'A stuffed parrot, yes,' she said. 'Over Barney's basket.'

There were sad cases as well, of course. There was a little boy no more than four or five running up and down the aisle. His name was Anthony he said and he had leukaemia. His parents weren't in the audience but a friend of theirs was. Anthony wanted his parents to know that he was all right now and his hair had grown back.

Then there was the baby girl who was a cot death victim. She'd gone over leaving behind her identical twin, Collette, and the seven-year-old girl whose mother had put a rose and a teddy bear into the coffin with her. Even Barney's owner was there for a more pressing reason than contact with Barney. She had been waiting for twenty-one years for news of her daughter who had never recovered from an operation to repair a hole in her heart.

There were warnings too. One woman was told of her relative's great concern over the cellar steps.

'He's very worried about these steps,' I said. 'Something about a door at the top and a child falling down. He wants you to put a bolt on the door as soon as possible.'

Another woman, there with her young daughter, was warned of a motor-bike.

'There's something about a motor-bike,' I said. 'There's a boy here who was killed on a motor-bike.'

The woman shook her head. 'No, I don't know anyone.'

'No, it's something to do with your daughter. Do you know anyone who was killed on a bike?'

She said she didn't.

If I hadn't been so certain this message was meant for them I would have thought I'd got the wrong contacts. As it was I knew it fitted in somehow.

'Who wants a motor-bike?' I asked.

'I do,' said the daughter.

'She's always on about it,' said her mother.

That was it. No, they were saying emphatically on the other side. No, and they pointed to the boy who had been killed.

'No way,' I said. 'She mustn't get a bike. They've brought this boy back as a warning of what could happen. She mustn't have a bike.'

The girl looked distinctly fed up as if she wished she had stayed at home.

'I shan't be allowed to have one now,' she muttered gloomily.

I felt a bit sorry for her but I wouldn't take back what I'd said. I've seen the parents of so many children who've lost their lives on motor-cycles.

Last year I was also invited to appear on the *Russell Harty Show*. Russell was a lovely boy but he seemed a bit nervous at first and he tried to rush me round to too many people in the audience.

That's the trouble with television. Producers don't like it if you stay too long with one person or if the messages are not evenly distributed round the audience. I can see their point but unfortunately I have to go where the voices take me and I can't force or hurry them.

I was a bit disappointed with my work that night for this reason. I didn't feel I had time to establish a rapport with the audience before Russell was rushing me again.

'Now,' he said, 'we have a surprise mystery guest here tonight. We thought it would be a bit of fun if Doris could discover her identity.'

Well, I was certainly surprised. I'm a medium not a mind reader, after all, but I hate to refuse a challenge.

'I can't promise anything,' I said slowly, 'but I'll have a go.'

The mystery woman was sitting in another room speaking to the studio by telephone. We only had a couple of minutes but soon I was listening to a warm Irish voice.

I've been to Ireland a couple of times and the accent sounded identical to me to the accents I'd heard on my travels, yet something made me wary.

'It's not genuine,' Ramanov whispered. 'Be careful.'

'I don't think this lady usually speaks with an Irish accent,' I said slowly. But, even as I was talking, spirit voices were drawing close, hoping for contact with her. One of them muttered something about the stage.

'I think this lady is something to do with the stage,' I said.

Then I heard the name Minnie.

The mystery woman said she knew someone of this name.

Next came the name Pat.

'And I'm getting the name Pat. Do you know anyone called Pat?'

There was a tiny pause as if she had taken a deep breath before answering.

'Yes, I know a Pat,' she admitted.

I began to relax. The contact was there. It would be all right.

'Well, I'm sorry, Doris,' said Russell Harty, so suddenly I jumped, 'but that's all we've got time for. And now here is our mystery guest.'

I was brought so swiftly back down to earth my mind

was spinning and before I fully realized what was happening, the actress, Pat Phoenix, was walking towards me. I was thrilled. Pat was one of my favourite characters from *Coronation Street* and I never missed an episode if I could help it.

'Hello, Doris,' she said, smiling in such a friendly way I felt as if I'd known her for years. But then I suppose in a way I had. She'd been coming into my living room twice a week for as long as I could remember.

'You know, if you'd have had more time you would have got me,' she said. 'You were getting so close.'

She was just as nice and natural as I'd always imagined and we became friends. To this day Pat regularly phones to see how I am and she gave me an autographed copy of her book which has pride of place in my bookcase.

Yes, my work does take me all over the place and into some very unlikely situations, from large halls to television studios and radio phone-ins, as well, of course, as my own living-room which has to double as a 'sitting' room, since it's our only reception room. When I'm working, poor John and Terry are banished to the kitchen!

Perhaps one of the loveliest aspects of my work is when I'm asked to be the medium at a naming service. This is the spiritualist version of a baptism, I suppose, but we don't baptize our children with water, because water is supposed to wash away sin. We believe that every newborn child is pure. They come straight from God or the spirit world and therefore they know no sin.

We name them with white flowers as a symbol of their purity. The other unusual feature of this service is that the child receives two names. The name his parents have chosen for him and his spirit name. This is the name he was last known by in the spirit world before he was born. To find out this name, a medium has to be present to tune in and ask.

This service isn't only for children, adults can take part too and I was 'named' myself in a lovely ceremony on the Isle of Man. It is not essential but I thought it would be a nice thing to do, a sort of public affirmation of my faith. The medium told me my spirit name was Lena, and John was given the name Samuel. Quite a coincidence that, since my father, who still helps me, was called Sam.

I took part in a very moving but informal naming just a few weeks ago, but it came about most unexpectedly. We have known Del Robinson, president of the Wimbledon Church, for years. When we came back from Australia last time it was Del who arranged a wonderful welcome home party for us. So naturally we were very excited for him when he told us he was about to become a grandfather for the first time.

The event was very close when Del's partner, Reg, happened to be visiting us. We were changing our car and he had brought the new one down to us. Anyway we were standing in the kitchen having a cup of tea when he asked if he could make a phone call.

'Jackie's been taken into hospital today, you see,' he said, 'and I wondered if there was any news.'

'Help yourself, love,' I said. 'You know where the phone is.'

He turned and went out into the hall but before he reached the phone, Rose, Del's mother, came bustling through.

'He needn't bother,' she said proudly. 'I can tell you. It's a fine big boy. A *big* boy. It's here. He's been born,' and I thought she said they were going to call him Alec.

'Reg,' I called, 'phone by all means, but Rose has just told me the baby's here and it's a fine big boy.'

A startled look crossed Reg's face as if he didn't know whether to believe me or not.

'Well, I'll just check, if it's all the same to you,' he said with a sheepish grin.

I laughed and went back into the kitchen as he began to dial. It was 1.40 by our kitchen clock.

Reg was connected immediately and his voice floated in from the small hall. We could hear him getting more and more incredulous with every word until John and I had to put our hands over our mouths to stop ourselves from laughing out loud.

'Already ...' said Reg. 'What? A boy ... Really? That's a big one ... and when ... half past one? You mean ten minutes ago? Well, I'm blowed.'

This went on for some time. Then there was a click and a bemusmed Reg came back to the kitchen.

'You were right,' he said reaching for his tea. 'It's a boy. Born ten minutes ago and he is a fine big lad too, nine pounds, seven ounces.'

There was just one thing wrong. I thought Rose had said he was going to be called Alec. But he wasn't. It was Ashley.

The story didn't end there. Del Robinson was so delighted he asked us to go to see the baby.

We had a marvellous time. The little flat was full of white flowers and Ashley was the sweetest little fellow you ever saw, with smooth creamy skin, a tiny button nose and a few thistledown tufts of fair hair. I took him in my arms and tuned in.

Rose came over immediately for another look. 'Isn't he lovely? My great grandson,' she sighed.

Then another, firmer, voice took over and I realized I was dealing with someone on a much higher plane. He spoke with kindness and yet there was authority in his voice, too. It was the sort of voice you obeyed instinctively.

'I am the baby's guide. My name is Clear Water,' he said. 'His spirit name is John.' Then he was gone.

I passed this on to the parents and as I spoke I could hear cameras clicking away. The proud grandparents wanted to make sure that every event in Ashley's life was well documented.

We moved on to the tea and sandwiches and I kept Ashley on my knee for as long as Jackie would allow.

'Isn't it strange?' I said to Del. 'Ashley's spirit name is the same as my baby's earth name.' And because of this I felt a strong bond with him.

There was another surprise in store. A couple of weeks later the photographs were developed and Del noticed something strange about the picture that was taken as I named Ashley. There was me, quite clearly in the foreground with Ashley in my arms, but up near the ceiling to my left was a large ball of white light and if you looked closely you could make out the face of a baby in it.

The light was hovering in front of the dark brown curtains and Del couldn't understand it at all. There was no glass or mirror anywhere near that could have caused a reflection.

He asked the photographer for an explanation but the photographer was equally baffled.

Since then we've shown the picture to many people and without telling them why we ask them what they can see, if anything, in the light. Most of them say without hesitation 'A baby' although some look at it for a long time twisting it this way and that before at last it falls into place.

'Oh yes, I can see it now,' they say. 'It's funny once you've seen it, it jumps out at you and you can't understand why you couldn't see it before.'

What's the explanation? I don't really know. My own guess is that John Michael was present and showed himself in the form that I would best remember him – as a baby, not much bigger than the one I was holding in my arms.

The spirit world loves babies and I often get news of them before the parents know themselves.

When I was working on the Granada programme, I was talking to one of the men connected with the show and I said, 'You've got two children, haven't you?'

He laughed. 'No, only one, Doris,' he said.

'Well, they're telling me two,' I said. 'If you've only got one at the moment, you're going to have two soon.'

He shrugged it off. Anyone can say that. But a week later his wife told him she was pregnant.

In Australia they were tickled pink because I was able to tell them that the Princess of Wales was pregnant before the official news came out.

It was on 6 October 1981 and some Australian reporters had come to interview me. The royal wedding was still in everyone's minds and they were talking about the young couple.

'When d'you think they'll start a family?' asked the reporters.

'Well,' I started to say, 'I think they'll wait until ...' but then I stopped. That was just Doris Stokes guessing, but over the top of my opinion came something more substantial from the spirit world.

'No, I don't think,' I corrected myself, 'I know. She's pregnant now.'

As I said it I nearly had kittens, because I don't go round predicting things and I don't profess to be a fortune teller. But this came through so spontaneously I had to say it.

Well, of course, it caused a great stir. The Australian papers splashed the headline all over the place. 'Doris Stokes says Princess Di is Pregnant!' and the Sydney *Sunday Telegraph* reported, 'Mrs Stokes, who predicted the marriage of Prince Charles and Lady Diana Spencer ... predicts the birth of a Royal babe about July next year.'

It frightened the life out of me. Supposing I was wrong?

Boy, was I relieved when a few weeks later Buckingham Palace released the official news.

And what did the Australian papers do? Across the front pages: 'How Doris Stokes Knew Before the Queen!'

Chapter 11

In the distance I could hear a train coming.

It was dark and cold and the noise was getting louder and louder. Beneath my feet the rails were vibrating, the whole line singing with the approaching train. Suddenly lights filled the night, a blast of air shook my body and my senses were drowned in a terrible roar.

I had a brief glimpse of a motor-bike with a crash helmet placed neatly on the saddle. Then the picture went out as if a bulb had blown.

It is always a tragedy to lose a child but the worst tragedy of all is to lose that child through suicide.

All parents suffer guilt, but the parents of children who have chosen to die face unimaginable torment. For the rest of their lives they will be tortured by endless questions. 'Why?', 'Why did he do it?', 'Why didn't I realize?', 'How could he have been so unhappy without me knowing?', 'Where did I go wrong?', 'Was there something else I could have done?'

The questions never stop because there is no answer.

Other parents can find comfort in the thought that accidents will happen, illness strikes anywhere. But the parents whose children commit suicide have only the knowledge that the life they gave was deliberately thrown away because it became intolerable. Their love just wasn't enough ...

Or at least that's how it seems to them. If only they could understand that they are not to blame. Neither are the children. The children who do these terrible things are as sick as they would be if they had leukaemia. This is understood on the other side where they are not punished but nursed back to health. And when they are well again these children are horrified at the suffering they have caused.

Nigel Cox was a loving, apparently happy boy who one night stepped in front of a train. When he realized what he'd done he was so distraught he couldn't rest until he received his mother's forgiveness.

In addition to her grief Betty Cox was haunted by an impression of Nigel standing behind her, sobbing. She thought she was going out of her mind. In fact the bond between mother and son was so strong she was simply sharing his anguish.

It was Betty's friend, Lois, who first contacted me. She was afraid for Betty, she explained. Since the tragedy she'd been unable to get over her grief and they were afraid of what she might do. She so loved Nigel that she felt her life was not worth living without him.

It was obvious that Nigel was a special child – well, listen to Betty's description:

'He was a wonderful baby, Doris. He was so contented. He never cried. He grew up to be a happy lad with a great sense of humour. We had a lot of fun together. I miss the laughs. He was very generous even to the point of being taken for granted, but he enjoyed helping others. The last two years he loved to help his friends with their bikes and they loved him so much that over a hundred of them came to his funeral.'

Nigel was there as soon as I tuned in and it was clear his grief was as strong as his mother's. He was sobbing and all I could hear was, 'Forgive me, forgive me.'

Until he heard his mother say the words I couldn't get anything else out of him.

'Of course I forgive you, Nigel,' Betty said at last when she realized the problem. Immediately the atmosphere changed. A weight had been lifted from Nigel's shoulders.

'I'm so sorry for what I did,' he told me. 'I must have had a brain storm.'

As we talked, he explained that he had everything to live for. A loving family, lots of friends and the prospect of a good job when he finished college. Then things started to go wrong. One evening he went out on a recently acquired motor-bike and he was stopped by the police. He didn't have an MOT certificate for it and he was very worried that they would take him to court over this.

Had he been his normal self this wouldn't have been an unsurmountable problem but he wasn't his normal self. A few weeks before he had been attacked in a disco and he had suffered a broken nose and concussion.

'Everyone thought I had recovered from the attack but I hadn't really,' Nigel told me. 'I changed after that. My personality changed.'

'Yes, he's right,' said Betty, 'he did change. He used to shout a lot over little things which wasn't like him.'

'But Nigel, why did you do it, love?' I asked. 'What happened that night?'

He sighed. 'I don't know why. It was like a brain storm.' Suddenly everything seemed too much for him. That terrible scene at the railway track flashed into my mind. Nigel rode to the railway line. Stood his beloved bike beside the track, placed his crash helmet on the saddle and walked in front of a train.

'Why didn't they do a post mortem on my head?' he cried. 'They would have found a blood clot in my brain. That's what did it.'

But he was all right now, he wanted to assure his mother. The only thing that made him unhappy was her unhappiness. He was being looked after by his grand-mother and he often visited his family at their cottage in Leicestershire. He knew about his sister's wedding and he wanted her to know that he would be there.

By the end of the sitting both Betty and Nigel seemed calmer and afterwards Betty wrote to me:

'Lois and I were on cloud nine coming back from London, so excited by the marvellous contact. Lois said I was looking different, the strain of sadness gone from my eyes. Funny that, for my friends at work today said I looked happier ...

'Now I feel at peace that Nigel is safe with my mother and all the family. I am content to wait to join him when only a few weeks ago I felt I could not live without him ...'

Margery Foden-Clarke was in a similar state to Betty

when she came to see me. Her son, David, went out to the kitchen one Sunday afternoon to make a cup of tea, or at least that's what he said he was going to do. Instead, he hanged himself.

It seemed so senseless. He was surrounded by loving people, his mother, his sister, his wife and his two beautiful daughters. He had a nice home and a good job. What's more, he was a considerate man. What on earth could have made him bring such distress to his family and horror to his wife who found the body?

It was a question that whirled round Margery's head endlessly. She sat in my living-room fiddling with her teacup explaining the things that most bothered her about the tragedy.

'Well, let's see what David has to say,' I said and tuned in.

At once I heard a man's voice, very warm and loving yet there was tension underneath.

'I tried very hard, you know,' he said. 'I tried so hard with my life … but there was something at the back of my mind. I thought I had a brain tumour.

'I was ill. I wasn't kidding. Sometimes I felt as if my head would burst. I used to hold my head in my hands, but I couldn't make them understand.

Margery agreed that David had been worried about his health but the doctor could find nothing wrong with him.

David went on to give more family names, then he returned to the day of the tragedy.

'I was going out to make some tea and then suddenly it was all too much for me. I said I feel like ending it all, and I thought someone said, 'Why don't you?' The pain came back so I took some tablets and I don't remember much more.' That's when he hanged himself.

'I just wanted peace and quiet,' he said, 'and I wanted the pain to stop but it didn't work out like I thought. I was still alive. I went to hospital over here and I slept.'

When he woke again on the other side the pain had gone and he had time to realize what he had done to his family. He seemed happy in the spirit world but he wanted his family to be happy too.

'I wish my wife well,' he said. 'I hope she meets some nice man who will look after my children. Could you ask my mother to go out and do some voluntary work or something? She gets very lonely. She lives alone with just her little dog.'

Like Nigel he was sorry for what he had done.

'Can you forgive me?' he asked his mother. 'I'm afraid I left a lot of chaos behind ...'

I still see Margery from time to time. She has her bad days, of course, we all do. But she feels close to David. He often makes his presence felt in the house and she knows that whenever she needs him, he's not very far away.

Chapter 12

Edinburgh
1 September 1982

Dear Doris Stokes,

Last night my daughter and I went to the Assembly Rooms to see you.

Whilst we were waiting in the queue to get in I said to my daughter, 'If all these spirits are lining up to give messages your father will be saying, After you, After you. He's so bloody polite he'll either be last or miss it altogether.'

Well, I was the last person you spoke to. The one who lost a wallet with £25.00 in it and who has an anniversary coming up this month. And then you said I must finish now. Oh, the frustration of not being able to hear more!

Anyway, my daughter and I were both so thrilled at the little you told us we came away from the town hall feeling so happy.

Is there any chance of a private sitting? I'm keeping my fingers crossed.

Yours very hopefully
Mrs Miller

Edinburgh
6 September 1982

Dear Mrs Stokes,

Because of the way you coped last night in what must have been very difficult conditions I must thank you and Ramanov.

You got through to me (I was in a blue dress seated on your 'actor's' right) through 'someone in a brewery'. This

597

was my father who died in the 1914 war along with three of my mother's brothers. A whole family of young men slaughtered.

The other name, Duncan, amazed me so I thought immediately of Frank Duncan (you gave me Frank later) but I remembered after I left the hall how when I was very young, Isadora Duncan, the great dancer, was brought through as a guide. You also gave me Louise and as we have French ancestry this is likely.

The two wedding rings was right and the necklace.

I intend returning tonight. I have never had my Dad come through before.

Much love to you
Jean Bruce

Edinburgh
9 September 1982

Dear Doris,

I attended two of your meetings in the Assembly Rooms this month. I have read both your books and look forward to the one you are writing at the moment.

I listened to you speaking to the young woman whose mother had passed on with leukaemia. It was a privileged experience. Then just after that you had us laughing heartily about the couple who had been left to look after a very spoiled pussy cat!

Thank you for coming to Edinburgh.

Yours

Mary Sleight

Strathclyde
10 September 1982

Dear Doris,

I had to write to you. I was the lady whose little girl was there Monday and Tuesday night. Thanks a million, Doris. I was too full to speak much. I would love you to have a photo but I cannot part with the one I have.

I see my little one often. I am one of the fortunate ones

who have seen spirit in body.

Oh, Doris, thanks a million. I tried for a reading but I know the ones who were lucky are the people most needing comfort. Please remember my wee one at your Christmas party.

God bless you
Rose Keenan

Dumfries
11 September 1982

Dear Doris,

It was so nice to meet you and you looked much younger than the picture on the books.

I will never meet anyone who could reassure me more that I will meet my darling Morag again. I'm sorry I was so dull and upset. I need the drugs to help me through my days and work.

A lot of the names you gave me meant nothing at the time but afterwards I remembered a lot of them. Derek is Fiona's boyfriend. I wondered what Morag would have said about that.

You will see from Morag's photo that she is just as you described. How I wish the accident never happened and we could all be struggling on together, but at least I know that one day I can put my arms round her again.

I am so grateful that someone like you, Doris, has been given this gift.

God bless you,
Moira

One of the most exciting things I did last year was to take part in the Edinburgh Festival and these letters are just a handful, chosen at random from the hundreds I received after my visit.

Now what, you're probably wondering, was I doing at the Edinburgh Festival amongst all that ultra-modern culture and talent? I can only say I often wondered the same thing myself.

The place was full of weird people. Very nice people, as it happened, but definitely weird to a lady of sixty-three like me.

I couldn't understand it at all. Take the frog, for instance. What would you say to a frog who approached you in the restaurant as you were quietly sipping your morning coffee? There I was, just back from the hairdressers, all nice and relaxed after a soothing spell under the drier and I looked up from my coffee to find a frog standing there. Well, it wasn't a real frog. Underneath, I think there was a young girl but her feet were painted green, her hands were painted green, she was dressed in a brown baggy suit and she was wearing a great papier mâché frog's head over her own.

I think I put my cup down with rather a clank at this extraordinary sight, but the girl didn't seem to notice anything unusual. Making no reference at all to her appearance, she said:

'I just wanted to tell you that I saw your show the other night. I thought it was marvellous. When I saw you sitting here I just had to come over and speak to you.'

'Oh,' I said. 'Well, thank you very much.'

Somehow my eyes remained fixed on this great papier mâché head and I couldn't think of anything else to say.

She smiled, at least I think she did under that mask; if she didn't, her voice certainly smiled, and wished me luck. Then she was off to wherever she'd come from. I looked across at John but for once I was lost for words.

There were many other strange sights that fortnight but gradually we got accustomed to them. When I walked into the foyer and saw two girls dressed from head to foot in black, patiently painting each other's faces with multi-coloured squares, triangles and circles, it hardly even struck me as unusual.

Edinburgh was a beautiful place. The wind was freezing and there were steep, cobbled streets that were a bit difficult at times but one look at that great rugged castle all floodlit on its rock and you forgot the cold. And I must say the bracing air certainly did me good. Despite the fact that I was working hard, I went home without the dark circles under my eyes that had been there for so long I thought they were a permanent feature of my face.

It would be much nicer this time if we stayed in a self-contained flat rather than a hotel, John and I thought. That way we needn't worry about bothering people for meals at odd hours and we could come and go as we pleased. So we asked some friends to find us a flat for the fortnight.

I must say they did us proud. The place they found belonged to a Mr Wong and you could have put our flat in London into the sitting-room and still have had space to spare.

When we walked in for the first time we just dropped our suitcases and gaped. One wall was covered entirely with mirror tiles. Another was orange with curtains to match and on another wall was a full-length picture of Gordon Jackson dressed as the butler from *Upstairs Downstairs*. As for the kitchen, it was so smart and modern I reckoned you'd need a pilot's licence to operate the gadgets. Wouldn't it be lovely if I could take it home with me, I thought.

We were certainly comfortable, the city was beautiful and the atmosphere in the streets was friendly and exciting. Nevertheless, I was apprehensive.

I couldn't see how I fitted into this modern young festival. Surely the sort of people who came to see all this experimental theatre and dance wouldn't be the sort of people who would be interested in a granny like me. Supposing nobody came to the demonstrations? I'd look a proper Charlie then.

Ramanov must have been grinding his teeth in frustration to hear me doubting again. He had always told me to trust. If I would only trust I would have no worries. And, of course, I should have known it would be all right. The spirit world would not have sent me to the festival if they didn't think it was important.

That first night I had to work hard to get a rapport with the audience and then when I did, I seemed to be getting the wrong messages.

A young girl came through. She said her name was

Morag and she gave me a Scottish surname as well, but I've been asked not to mention it. She said she was looking for Moira and that she had Robert with her. This information caused a great silence to fall over the audience. Nobody could place a Morag.

'Sorry, love,' I said. 'There's no one here who knows you.'

Reluctantly Morag went away and after that the other messages flowed.

The next night, however, Morag was back. She was a persistent girl. She seemed to think Moira ought to be present, but still no one claimed her and I had to send her away without making a contact. Again the sitting went well after she'd gone.

Soon afterwards, however, a lady who said her name was Moira telephoned me. Someone had told her about the unclaimed message and she thought it might be for her. Her daughter's name was Morag and Morag's father, Robert, was also on the other side. It sounded pretty conclusive to me and she asked if she could have a private sitting.

'All right, love,' I said, flicking through the crammed appointments in my diary. 'Could you manage next Friday at twelve?'

She said she could.

In the meantime the public demonstrations were attracting quite a following. I remember one at 5.00 in the afternoon when the rapport was so good I couldn't seem to stop and the mood changed from happiness to sadness and back again with every message that came through.

A young mother who had gone over at an early age with leukaemia came back to talk to her daughter. She gave several family names and then she said that one of the girl's sisters, Donna I believe it was, was getting married.

'Would you ask her to put one small rosebud in her bouquet for me?' she asked. 'And say "That's mum. Mum'll be there."'

At this the girl suddenly broke down in tears and as I glanced up, pausing to give her a moment to compose herself, I saw that the audience was a forest of handkerchiefs. Even the men were crying.

Five minutes later there was a complete contrast. The spirit light bounced over to two old ladies sitting side by side. They were sisters, alike as two peas, and a voice told me their names and various personal details.

Every time I said something that was right, they dug each other in the ribs, almost knocking each other off their chairs, and they were laughing so much they could hardly speak.

Suddenly whoever was talking from the other side said, 'And tell them we know they've got the big ginger cat and they're having to look after it.'

There was a gasp at this and more tremendous digs. Then they went off into hysterics.

'Is that right?' I asked. 'The cat belongs to your sister and she's gone off to Australia?'

'Yes,' spluttered one of them. 'She has and she's left me the cat to look after and blooming expensive it is, too. She didn't tell me it was on a special diet!'

Well, the place was rocking so much heads kept appearing round the door to see what on earth we were doing.

During a later meeting I kept hearing something about a sum of money. £50 it was.

'You've paid it out for something,' I said to the woman I'd been talking to, but no, she couldn't understand what I meant.

I moved on, but halfway through a message for someone else I had to stop and go back. The £50 wouldn't stop coming until we'd pinned it down.

'I'm sorry,' I said, 'but this £50 is for you and it's something to do with a gas cooker.'

The woman gasped and clapped her hands to her mouth.

'Oh, my God. She's only been over two weeks and I bought her gas cooker. I did pay fifty pounds for it.'

We'd got there. A feeling of satisfaction flooded out from my houseproud contact on the other side.

'She's got a bargain there, too,' said the voice. 'It was nearly brand new.'

'Yes, it was,' agreed the woman. 'Thank her very much.'

Word spread about what was going on and soon other performers would slip into the hall after their own shows and sit quietly on the steps or stand at the back. Little presents started arriving at the theatre for me just as when I was in Australia. One lady gave me a crystal vase just big enough to hold flowers for my spirit children. Someone else brought me a brooch with feathers in it and one lady gave me some lovely mother-of-pearl shells, all cleaned up and polished. I've put them in my cabinet.

Some people clearly had mixed feelings to start with. I came out of my dressing-room one evening and almost bumped into a woman who was standing determinedly outside the door. She had had no intention of coming she told me. She'd read about my work and thought that if God was going to give anybody a gift like mine he would have given it to priests and nuns not to ordinary housewives.

Yet at the last minute she changed her mind. Something had made her come along to the theatre to see for herself and after the show she was so impressed she felt compelled to come and talk to me. As we chatted I heard a young man's voice in the background. It turned out to be her son who had been killed.

Well, what could I do? I could hardly turn her away so I gave her a quick private sitting. As soon as I tuned in I got a falling feeling as if I'd been thrown and then I landed on the floor with my fingers across my neck. Apparently it was a car accident and the boy's brother had been driving. Someone called Donald had gone over at the same time.

I wasn't to leave Scotland, however, without stirring up a bit of controversy. It seems to be getting a habit these days, although I don't do it on purpose.

Quite a few reporters came to interview me for the Scottish papers while I was there and during one of these interviews I was asked how I felt about God.

'I mean I don't believe in God,' said the girl turning a fresh page in her notebook. 'Do you?'

'Oh yes,' I said. 'Without God I couldn't exist and I certainly couldn't do my work.'

The girl frowned. This was obviously not what she wanted to hear.

'Well, how do you stand on the question of Jesus?'

And I told her what I believe. I don't ask anyone else to believe it. I'm not saying it's a hundred per cent right. It just happens to be my view, that's all.

'Well, I think Jesus Christ was the greatest medium and healer who ever lived and that he was put to death for political reasons by the people in the church,' I said. 'They were afraid of him because they realized he had something that the church couldn't offer.'

The girl was scribbling furiously. 'So what about the crucifixion?'

'Well, it happened,' I said, 'but I don't believe that because Jesus was crucifed he can me wash free of sin. He can't take responsibility for what I do. Only I can do that. If I do something wrong I just can't walk into church and have the slate wiped clean and go out and do it again. I am responsible for my actions and if I do something wrong I have to pay for it.

The reporter seemed quite satisfied with this and after a few more questions she packed up her things and left. But when the paper came out, blazed across the column werew the words: 'Doris Stokes Doesn't Believe That Jesus Was the Son of God.'

This upset a lot of people and in particular it upset one of my sitters. For three months before the Festival a certain gentleman had been writing to the promoter's office regularly to arrange a private sitting. Then as the Festival drew near he began ringing every few days to check that the booking was still all right. He was assured it was. His appointment was for 12.00, Thursday.

The day of the sitting happened to be the day this newspaper story came out. I was feeling irritable because I'd been misunderstood, but when the doorbell rang at 12.00 I made myself calm down. It wouldn't be fair to take it out on this poor man who had been waiting so long for a sitting.

John went to the door but was surprised to find a young girl standing there.

'I've come to see Doris Stokes,' she said.

'No, I'm sorry there must be some mistake, dear,' he said.

'She's expecting a gentleman any minute now.'

'Oh, he's not coming,' said the girl. 'He's given his booking to me.'

Apparently this man had been so angry at what I was supposed to have said in the paper that he refused to come, but since this girl was curious about what I did he said she could go in his place.

John doubtfully let the girl into the hallway and came to talk to me. Rightly or wrongly I was furious when I heard. I thought of all the desperate people in Edinburgh whom we'd had to turn away because all the bookings were taken. All those people who had lost children, or husbands, or wives, and were craving for reassurance. people who would jump at the chance of a cancelled booking, and he thought it would be all right to send someone who was merely curious.

'No,' I said to John, 'I won't do it. I'll save my energy for someone who actually needs help.'

Unhappily John went to relay this message to the girl in the hall. By the time the front door had slammed behind her I was already regretting my harsh words. Maybe I was being unfair. After all, it wasn't the girl's fault. Perhaps I had been too hasty.

Miserably I began leafing through the paper with that unpleasant sensation in my stomach that's caused by a bad conscience. The doorbell rang again. If it's that girl back maybe I should see her I was thinking, when John put his head round the door.

'It's Moira,' he said, 'she's got the date mixed up. You said Friday at 12.00 but she wrote down Thursday at 12.00.'

I sighed with relief. I had done the right thing after all.

I got up and went to the door.

'Never mind, love,' I said. 'You come in.'

I was very glad I was free to see Moira that day. She had travelled a long way to meet me in Edinburgh and she was so heartbroken at the loss of her daughter that she had thought about taking an overdose.

When Morag came to talk to me I felt myself flung violently into the air then there was a pain across my throat. Apparently Morag had been travelling in a car when the door came open and she was thrown out. She hit the pole of a bus stop and was killed instantly. During the sitting she gave the names of her brother and sister and her sister's boyfriend. She also mentioned a photograph that her mother had.

'The jumper I'm wearing in the photo is the one Mum took out of the drawer and held to her face,' she said.

She was very concerned about her mother because of the pills she needed to keep her going in her grief. 'Please don't, Mum,' she kept saying. 'Please don't.'

She was so distressed her mother promised to try to cut down although she didn't feel she could do without them entirely.

Strangely enough while I was in Edinburgh I got the chance to help someone who was normally to be found working only ten minutes away from my home in London.

The producer of the *Jimmy Young Show* had been ringing all round Edinburgh in a desperate attempt to find me. Apparently Jimmy was supposed to be leaving for a publicity tour to publicize his new book but at the last minute he refused to go.

Two incidents had convinced him that he would be in danger. A medium had rung the BBC to say that she had seen a black cloud hovering over Jimmy Young and she thought it was a warning. Then a friend of Jimmy's had gone to a healer and the healer had told him he could see a man connected with him in a plane crash. He saw a small plane and a man slumped inside with a gash on his head.

Jimmy put these two messages together and came to the conclusion that his small plane was going to crash as he travelled the country on the tour. The publishers were desperate. Would I be able to help put his mind at rest?

'Well, I'll talk to him,' I said, 'but if I feel he's in danger I'll have to say so.'

'Well, yes, of course,' they said, 'we don't want anything to happen to him after all. We just wondered if he might be over-reacting.'

I was quite excited as I waited for Jimmy Young to come on the phone. I've always liked his prog, as he calls it, and he has some interesting people appearing. I was sitting there with the receiver in my hand daydreaming about whether I should ask him to play a Jim Reeves record for me, when a bright breezy voice suddenly crackled in my ear.

'Hello, Doris? How are you?'

It was Jimmy and sounding exactly like he does on the radio. He explained in more detail about the warnings and how he felt about them.

'Some people might think I'm crazy, Doris,' he said, 'but I don't want to take the risk.'

'Well, just a minute. Let's see if we can find any of your relatives on the other side and ask them,' I said.

I tuned in and after a moment or two I contacted Jimmy's father.

'Tell him not to take any notice,' said the father. 'He'll be all right. I'll be with him and he won't come to any harm.'

I passed on the message along with several other bits and pieces and the result was that Jimmy went on his book tour and afterwards flew on to Australia as well. He sent me an autographed copy of his book as a souvenir.

People still have some strange ideas about our work. When I returned to London I got a letter from a woman who said her vicar had told her she was wicked to read such evil books as mine. I have had quite a few letters like this over the years. The writers are usually upset about the unsympathetic attitude of the clergyman but determined to carry on reading nevertheless.

'I don't care what he says,' they often write, 'nobody else has been able to give me the comfort I've found in your books.'

It's a pity but at the moment the orthodox church can't make up its mind about mediums. Some clergymen regard us as servants of the devil, while others think we're wonderful. On many occasions I've shared the platform with vicars and I even gave the Bishop of Southwark a sitting in Southwark Palace.

Yet funnily enough that incident illustrates the confused attitude of the church to spiritualism. A friend of mine, the Rev Terry Carter, had taken me to meet Mervyn

Stockwood who was Bishop at the time. Terry was due to appear on stage with me at our Easter service.

We drove through the enormous gates of Southwark Palace and we were led through beautiful rooms to see the Bishop. I don't know what I expected, but Mervyn Stockwood was certainly no disappointment.

He was sitting on his ornate Bishop's throne in a splendid purple robe and I felt as if I was meeting the King. I was rather nervous to start with but nevertheless we had an interesting sitting and afterwards we fell into general conversation.

Terry Carter had told the Bishop about his plans to conduct the Easter service for us but there was one point on which he needed advice.

'Do you think it would be all right if I wore my collar, Bishop?'

The Bishop thought for a moment or two. 'Oh, I don't think so,' he said doubtfully. 'No, I don't think it would do.'

He wasn't actually forbidding it but his reaction made me cross.

'Well, I think you're a hypocrite,' I burst out before I could stop myself.

The Bishop raised his eyebrows. 'Why do you say that, Doris?' he asked politely.

I'd done it now, I thought, so I might as well have my say. 'Well, look at you,' I said. 'There you sit in all your purple with your Bishop's ring on while I give you a sitting and yet you say Terry shouldn't wear his collar to conduct a religious service. I think that's hypocritical. It ought to be left up to Terry to decide for himself.'

I think he was rather surprised at this outburst but the Bishop was very good about it. He agreed that I had a point and that Terry should let his own conscience guide him on the matter.

And on Good Friday as we prepared ourselves for the meeting at Brixton, the Rev Terry Carter climbed bravely on to the platform wearing his dog collar for all to see.

Chapter 13

The last time I was in hospital an Irish friend came to see me.

'You always seem to be in hospital, Doris,' he said. 'How many operations have you had now?'

Briskly I totted it up on my fingers.

'It must be twelve now,' I said. 'I've had my boob off, my thyroid out, my gall bladder out, my ovaries removed, a hysterectomy and seven other minor operations.'

My friend listened to this impressive list with awe.

'Well, you know what it is, don't you?' he said at last.

'No. What is it?'

'They want you over on the spirit side but they can't have you because you're too busy so they're taking you over piece by piece!'

Well, I just roared with laughter. It was the funniest thing I'd heard in ages. I laughed so much I had to make my friend promise not to crack any more jokes – it was too much for my stitches.

Yet afterwards it set me thinking. At my age and with all the operations I've had I couldn't help wondering how much time I'd got left. Was this operation going to be my last? I asked Ramanov.

'Ramanov, can you tell me how much time I've got left?'

There was a long silence. Then came one of his typically enigmatic answers.

'You will have enough time to do the work God wants you to do.'

So I wasn't to know. Well, it didn't really matter. I'm not afraid to die. I know it's a great adventure I've got to look forward to and though I'm not in a hurry to leave John and Terry and all the people I love on earth, I'm happy to

610

think that one day I will see my John Michael again. I will be able to take him in my arms and we will never be parted again.

So to all those parents like me who have lost children, I would just like to say, please don't leave your child's room as a shrine. Please don't turn away from those who are left.

Put his toys and clothes to good use. Hug the children who remain, and thank God for the joy of that special child lent to you for a little while, in the sure and certain knowledge that one day when your work is done you will see him again.

Do not stand at my grave and weep …
　　I am not there – I do not sleep,

I am a thousand winds that blow,
I am the softly falling snow,
I am the gentle rains that fall,
I am the fields of ripening grain.

I am in the morning hush,
I am in the graceful rush
Of beautiful birds in circling flight,
I am the starshine of the night.

I am in the flowers that bloom
I am in a quiet room.
I am in the birds that sing,
I am in each lovely thing.

Do not stand at my grave and cry –
　　I did not die …

Mary E. Frye
1932

WHISPERING VOICES

Whispering Voices

Chapter 1

It was a hot summer day the first time I saw the house.

'Come and look at this Doris,' said Laurie and I walked up the road, puffing a bit because the heat was bouncing off the paving stones and making the air go swimmy and what I really longed for was a shady chair to rest my back and a long cool drink.

But then I saw it and for a moment the heat melted away.

Set back from the road and on a slope so you looked down at it, the house was blue and white with tiny lattice windows that glinted in the sun and a strip of garden ablaze with roses. There were matching blue gates folded neatly across the sloping drive and a pretty cottage-style front door.

'Oh it's gorgeous!' I cried in delight, and then with a pang I realized that a house as lovely as this would be far too expensive for me. 'Oh Laurie,' I said, suddenly disappointed, 'I wish I hadn't seen it. I could never afford that.'

But Laurie's not one to give up easily. He just shrugged and grinned his unstoppable grin. 'Well let's go and see shall we ...'

It was a strange feeling, this house hunting for the first time at my age. In the past John and I had always been very grateful for whatever rented accommodation was offered to us. It might not look like something out of a glossy magazine but we filled it with our bits and pieces, put our pictures on the walls and made it home. Now, suddenly to be given a choice was a bit bewildering. And this business of walking into someone's home and wandering about inspecting the decoration – well I just couldn't get used to it. It always seemed so rude somehow to say no.

Yet it had to be done. It was the answer to a problem that had been worrying me for months. When John and I came to London we'd managed to get a flat in a block for disabled ex-servicemen because John is a disabled veteran of Arnhem. It wasn't a palace – in fact some people said the blocks were ugly – but it was comfortable and convenient and we soon had it looking cosy. We even made a miniature garden outside the front door with rows of plants in pots along the balcony and on summer evenings John and I could sit there in deck-chairs amongst our geraniums and busy-lizzies and pretend we were in the country.

In 1982 things got even better. As flats fell empty, the management began putting bathrooms into them. Until then we'd used a tin bath in the kitchen, but after a long wait, John, Terry and I were moved up the corridor to one of the converted flats. We paid a bit extra and had a shower installed as well and after a couple of weeks we couldn't imagine how we'd managed without it.

The improvement was so great that the blow that fell soon afterwards was doubly unexpected. The whole site was going to be completely redeveloped, the tenants were told. Our block was to be demolished to make room for a garden. The other blocks were to be modernized and in many cases two flats were going to be made into three.

We had a choice. We could live on a building site for the next five years while we waited for a flat in one of the other blocks to become available – though they couldn't guarantee we'd get another two bedroomed place – or we could find another home.

Now the spirit world has always told me not to worry – just to trust and we shall be provided for. But I couldn't help worrying. How could I do my sittings with the noise of building work going on all day? And how could we turn Terry out if at the end of five years we were only offered a one bedroom flat? The mobile home we'd bought as a country retreat might be a solution, but it was tucked away in a quiet little backwater near Ashford in Kent. Lovely for holidays but it would be very awkward to carry on my work from there.

I lay awake at night wondering what on earth we were going to do, and all Ramanov my spirit guide would say was 'Trust, child.' Which was all very well for him but for me it was easier said than done.

John, who's not a worrier like me seemed to be just as unconcerned. 'Don't worry yourself love,' he used to say soothingly. 'It'll work out. You'll see.'

But I didn't see. The months went by and nothing seemed to happen except that I developed a very bad back. London became very hot and dusty the way it always does in summer and John and I were very glad when our holiday came round and we were able to go down to the van for some fresh air.

And then when I least expected it, the spirit world stepped in. It was an overcast day and my back was playing me up badly so when John said he thought he might go out for a bike ride I told him to go because all I felt like doing was sitting about with a hot water bottle. Yet no sooner had John pedalled away than I was bored. I'd finished my book the day before and I'd got nothing else to read. There was no one around to talk to and nothing on TV.

Dejectedly, I fiddled around with the remote control buttons. Terry had got us linked up to the Oracle and he was always looking at it, but I'd never used it. I wonder if I can get Russell Grant's stars? I thought. I always enjoy horoscopes. I pressed a few buttons and sheets of information began flashing across the screen but half of it was double dutch to me and there was nothing that resembled a horoscope.

Impatiently I pressed more buttons and then suddenly one of the bright pages caught my eye. It was nothing to do with Capricorn. It was a list of properties for sale at a London estate agents, and one of the houses in South London had three bedrooms and was surprisingly cheap.

I did a quick bit of mental arithmetic. If we sold the van and added our life savings I reckoned we could afford the house. It would be the answer to all our problems.

Excitedly I dialled Laurie's number. I don't think I've introduced you to Laurie. He's the latest addition to our team. To say he's my manager sounds rather grand and it's not really like that. In the last couple of years my work has snowballed so much that what with personal appearances, radio and TV, as well as my normal sittings, I couldn't cope with all the organizing. People kept saying you need a manager Doris but it sounded so official I dithered. Then one day I was introduced to Laurie O'Leary, and we hit it off straight away. Laurie had actually given up a management career for a more peaceful life but when he saw what a mess I was in he decided to go back to management to help me. So now Laurie looks after the bookings, sees to the travel arrangements and all the other bits and pieces that take up so much time. He's much more than a manager. He's like one of the family.

Anyway, on the phone that morning I told him I'd read about this house I thought I could afford.

'Okay, Doris,' he said, 'I'll come and fetch you tomorrow and take you to see it.'

Well John wasn't bothered. 'If it suits you, girl, it'll suit me,' he said. But he didn't want to interrupt his holiday to go trailing through a house. He'd much rather potter about with his roses in the garden at the van. And in truth I knew he'd feel like a spare part – after all women are much more interested in that sort of thing than men.

Instead, Nancy our good friend and neighbour from the flats, said she'd come with me. As it turned out the first house wasn't right. A young couple lived there and they'd worked very hard on it but it was too arty for me. There was a bare white room with one sofa in it and flash shelves. They'd stripped down the doors to bare wood and built a big stone fireplace. It was beautifully done and would have been perfect for a young couple but not an old fashioned sort like me.

I wandered about making polite noises but Nancy, bless her heart, is a bit forthright.

'Well, that'll have to come out for a start,' she said shaking her head at the fireplace. And, 'Oh no you don't like those doors do you, Doris? They'll have to be painted.'

It was obvious we'd have to spend a fortune on decorating to get it to our taste and I don't suppose the young couple were too pleased at the thought of us tearing out all their improvements. I think it was a relief all round when I explained it wasn't quite us.

The area was very nice however: convenient for the shops and central London but green and open with trees and flowers in every garden and the countryside an easy drive away. Laurie checked with another estate agent and this time we were in luck. The first house we were sent to was very nice but somehow it didn't feel right.

'We'll think about it,' I promised. My back was killing me by this time and I was quite prepared to go home again but that was when Laurie called me to look at the blue and white house he'd found.

I fell in love with it on the spot.

'Come on then, let's have a look inside,' he said ignoring my protests about the expense and the fact that we didn't have an appointment.

A tiny little lady opened the door and when she saw me her eyes flew wide in astonishment.

'Oh Doris Stokes!' she gasped. 'I never ever thought I'd meet you.'

Her name was Hilda and she led us round chattering brightly. The house was as lovely inside as out. There was a beautiful kitchen with work tops all round – no more trying to balance half-a-dozen plates on the kitchen table – there were patio doors looking out onto the garden and a spacious bathroom. The bathroom was a bit of a problem though because it was downstairs.

'There's no way I'll get down stairs with my legs crossed first thing in the morning!' I said doubtfully.

'Don't worry about that, Doris, you could have a loo put in the bedroom,' said Laurie.

The other problem was that with my bad back I could hardly lift one foot from the ground let alone tackle those stairs. Never mind, said the others, they'd look at the bedrooms for me.

They clattered away and Hilda and I stood chatting in the hall. It was a particularly nice hall. Square and airy with a rich blue carpet and sunshine streaming in through the windows on either side of the front door.

'I do like this hall, and such a beautiful carpet.' I was saying, when out of the corner of my eye I saw a blur of movement. Someone else was heading up the stairs to the bedroom. It was a frail old man, taller than Hilda and rather stooped and by the way he hauled himself from step to step, pulling heavily on the handrail, I guessed he had difficulty walking. A flash of intuition told me that this was Hilda's husband and substantial as he looked – he was a spirit person.

'Excuse me, love,' I said suddenly to Hilda, 'but was your husband an invalid?'

'Well, yes he was,' she said in surprise.

'I thought so,' and I glanced back at the stairs. They were quite empty. The man had vanished. So I was right. He'd passed over but came back from time to time to visit his wife and his old home. Well that was alright by me. I've never minded sharing a place with spirit people as long as they don't make a nuisance of themselves.

There was a lot of clumping overhead and then the others, unmistakably of this world, came thudding down again.

'The bedrooms are lovely, Doris,' said Nancy, 'and the one at the front looks right over that little green outside.'

But still I hesitated. I'd love the house. I didn't need to go upstairs to know I'd be happy here but I wasn't at all sure we could afford it.

Hilda must have read my mind. 'Look, Doris,' she said, 'I'd like to think you lived here. As it's you I'll bring the price down.'

'She'll take it!' said Laurie instantly.

On the way home of course the doubts set in. Oh dear what have I done? I kept thinking. Our life savings and I haven't even been up the stairs. I hope I'm doing the right thing. Our friends in the mobile home park thought we were mad. There they were selling their houses to move into mobile homes and here we were selling our mobile home to move into a house. At our age! But then John and I have always been impulsive. We married a week after we met and they all thought we were mad then. In fact I couldn't convince my family it wasn't a joke. When they discovered after the wedding that we were only too serious they shook their heads disapprovingly and said it wouldn't last. Yet here we are 40 years on, still going strong.

You know you're doing the right thing when everything goes smoothly, however, and soon it was obvious that the spirit world wanted us to have this house. The legal side went through without any bother and just when we were trying to decide on a moving date, another piece of good luck came along. I was talking to *Woman's Own* magazine on the phone one day and I told them I'd let them have my new address as soon as possible.

'I've got my house at last!' I said happily.

'Oh wonderful,' they said, 'you will let us design it for you, won't you?'

Design it for me? The idea of having a house designed had never crossed my mind, but the more I thought about it the more exciting it seemed. It was true that Hilda's colour schemes wouldn't go very well with our furniture, but I haven't a clue about decorating. As long as a place is clean and comfortable I'm happy. But if someone else would sort out the paint charts and wallpaper ... well, yes, it *would* be very nice to have everything matching and colour co-ordinated, as they say these days.

Well the house became legally ours by the end of the summer but we put off the moving date until December to allow time for the decorating to be done. In between we went down again with Deborah, nicknamed Dobs, from *Woman's Own*, to discuss the colours. Dobs had great plans. I couldn't quite picture what she meant half the time but she seemed to know what she was talking about so I thought it best to let her get on with it. At this point, though, I still hadn't been up the stairs and Dobs was very insistent that I should.

'Come on, Doris, you'll have to come upstairs,' she said. 'I must show you what I have in mind.'

My back was still twinging and I hadn't had any stairs for twelve years but it did seem ridiculous, so I held my breath and took a run at it. I flew up those stairs as if I was on a wire and when I got to the top I turned round and saw everyone was killing themselves laughing.

'You went up those stairs like a two-year-old!' giggled Dobs.

I couldn't help smiling. 'Yes well I didn't dare stop,' I confessed. 'If I'd run out of steam half way up I'd have been stuck.'

The planning stage didn't take very long, because John and I were about to leave on the publicity tour for my book *A Host Of Voices*. We were going to be away three weeks and when we came back we were going straight into our new home. Terry was going to organize everything he said. He'd pack up all our things and arrange the whole move. I must admit I was a bit apprehensive. I was afraid I'd never be able to find anything again, but Terry told me not to fuss. He was quite capable of managing.

Well John and I set off on the tour, but back at the house things were far from tranquil. The first we knew about it was when Steve, the electrician, refused to work in the place on his own. He wouldn't say much about it but we gathered he heard strange noises when no-one was there and his tools were always being moved about. He could never find them where he left them.

Laurie was the next one to realize something odd was happening. He and Steve left the house together one evening and before leaving they turned the lights off at the mains, as an additional safety measure. They banged the front door shut, went out to the car and as they glanced back they noticed that the light was on in the loft.

Bewildered, they went back and checked. But the electricity was still off at the mains. Puzzled, Laurie went up to the loft and switched off the light. Then they locked up again and went outside. By the time they reached the car, the loft light was twinkling brightly. Back they went, rather nervously by now and switched the light off once more, and this time they headed for the car at a near run.

'Come on, Steve, let's go for goodness sake,' said Laurie, 'or we'll be here all night.' And they sped away without looking back.

About an hour or so later Terry called at the house on his way home from work. Afterwards he phoned Laurie.

'Did you know you left the loft light on?' he asked.

Finally Terry discovered for himself what they meant. Arriving first at the house one morning, he went in, locked the door behind him and wandered into the living-room to see what the decorators had done. But as he stood there admiring the paint work, he heard the front door bang again. Thinking it was Laurie he stuck his head into the hall to say hello but to his surprise the hall was empty. The front door was wide open and no one was in sight.

Crossly Terry closed the door and was just walking into the kitchen when there came a great crash from upstairs. A portable light on a long cable had disengaged itself for no apparent reason and come smashing down onto the floorboards.

On later visits to the house with Laurie and Steve, the three of them were startled by further unexplained crashes and even the sound of footsteps crossing the boards above when everybody was downstairs.

In the end it became a joke. They christened their unseen visitor George and when he became particularly troublesome Terry would say, 'Oh pack it in George, or I'll turn the old woman on you!'

Funnily enough, since John and I moved in George has been quite peaceful. Occasionally a door will open silently and close again when there's no-one visible and we say, 'Hello, how are you.'

Recently I decided it was time we had a chat to get things straight, so I waited until the sitting room door opened all by itself and then I tackled George.

'Your missis doesn't live here any more,' I told him because I was certain it was Hilda's husband, and in case he was confused I explained where she'd gone. 'It's our house now,' I added gently.

He said his name wasn't George but Edward, nicknamed Ted, and the house used to belong to him. He couldn't understand why we were here stripping off his wallpaper and knocking things about. Once I'd explained he seemed quite happy.

'We don't mind you popping in whenever you like, Ted,' I said, 'but don't move things about. It makes life so difficult.'

And there have been no problems since. Ted wanders in from time to time but he doesn't bother us at all.

Not long ago we had another spirit visitor as well. I don't think we are particularly unusual in this. I think that probably most houses are visited by previous occupants and people who were closely linked to the building, it's just that most people aren't aware of it, or dismiss strange noises and unexplained draughts as the wind, or the people next door.

Anyway on this particular occasion we'd had some bricklayers in building a garden wall and I put a strip of plastic down in the sitting-room to protect the carpet from their muddy boots. I was sitting there by the fire winding down before going to bed when I heard footsteps quite distinctly walking across the plastic. Everyone else was in bed and the sound definitely came from just a few inches away. What's more one foot came down much more heavily than the other so I knew this person walked with a stick or a pronounced limp.

'Who's that?' I asked.

'Reggie,' said a man's voice and then the steps faded away and he was gone.

Reggie? I thought. How odd. I was sure the man who used to live here said his name was Ted. So the following day when our next-door-neighbour Margaret came in, I asked her about it.

'Did the man who used to live here walk heavily on one side?'

'Oh no,' said Margaret, 'he was an invalid. You never saw him walk. He was either in a chair or in bed.'

'That's strange,' I said, 'I heard a man walk across my sitting-room and he came down very heavily on one foot so he must have had a limp or walked with a stick. He said his name was Reggie.'

To my amazement Margaret burst into tears. 'That's my husband,' she whispered dabbing at her eyes. 'You've just described my Reggie.'

So now we know that Margaret's husband has been in to have a look at us to check that we're the sort of people who'll be nice to his wife.

It certainly was marvellous to come back from our tour to a lovely new house. Terry had done very well with the move and, though there are still one or two things I haven't found yet, practically everything was safely in one piece. Dobs had worked wonders and for weeks I kept wandering around reminding myself that this magnificent place really belonged to us and we wouldn't have to leave it soon and go home. It still seems a bit unreal.

Dobs' *pièce de résistance*' was my bedroom which was done up like a beautiful birthday cake in pink and white with mirror doors on the wardrobes all along one wall to make it look twice as big. When she'd suggested the mirrors and all the other bits and pieces I hadn't the faintest idea what it would look like and I must say when I saw the end result I was staggered – in the nicest possible way!

I sat there in my pink chair with the frill round the bottom and looked at myself in the mirrors, all thirteen-and-a-half stone of me and I said, 'Sixty-five! You could have done with this girl when you were twenty five! All these frilly pillows and scatter cushions and pink satin bows on the pictures, and all they've got to look at is Doris in bed with no teeth in and her indigestion pills!'

I was appearing on TV AM with Derek Jameson not long after this and I couldn't help telling Derek about my beautiful bedroom and the mirrors. Derek's an earthy straightforward man with a great sense of humour and I knew he'd enjoy the joke.

'Well you know, Doris, twenty-five years ago those mirrors would have done your sex life a bit of good,' he chuckled, and of course I was in fits again.

A few weeks later on our wedding anniversary the delivery man came to the door with two packages. One was a single red rose in a long flat box with a card saying: Happy Anniversary, John and Doris, from Derek Jameson. The other was a square box which said: Happy Anniversary, John and Doris and the wardrobes. Also from Derek Jameson.

And the wardrobes? I said to myself. What did that mean? Intrigued I tore off the wrapping paper. Inside was a crimson box with two black tassels on the top. What on earth could it be?

'D'you think it's an orchid?' I wondered aloud.

Laurie who'd just popped in suggested it might be

stationery. John hadn't got a clue.

So I opened the box and inside was a black lace suspender belt, a pair of black silk stockings and a tiny wispy object that Laurie explained was a G string. The black tassels I'd thought were for opening the box were in fact to go on your boobs!

What a sight for the wardrobes that would have been, if only I'd been able to get them on!

Chapter 2

It was a very eventful summer that summer of '84 before we moved into our new house, and quite by chance we found ourselves caught up in a tragedy that moved the whole country.

The weather was very warm that year and so John and I, who're not well suited to the heat, tried to escape to our mobile home whenever we could. I was always glad when I could work from the van instead of our stuffy flat in London, and one particular week the van proved specially convenient because I was doing a demonstration at Tunbridge Wells – just up the road.

The show went well and afterwards I felt very drained, the way I always do, and I sat in my dressing-room drinking tea while the clamour of spirit voices faded away and the ordinary day to day world re-established itself in the forefront of my mind. There were a lot of people milling about nibbling sandwiches but I didn't notice anyone in particular until Laurie came up.

'Doris, I'd like to introduce you to an old friend of mine, Ted Roffey.'

Ted was a slim, dapper man, he lived in the area and Laurie had sent him tickets for the show. He seemed to have enjoyed himself and he was very kind. He'd never seen anything like it, he said, fascinating. Certainly made you think. Then he steered a young couple in my direction.

'They're dying to meet you, Doris,' he said. 'This is my nephew Tony and his wife Janet.'

They were a lovely couple. Very young, dark and a little shy and Janet of course was heavily pregnant. A pregnant woman is a wonderful sight I always think, so full of hope for the future, and yet when I looked at Janet it was as if a cloud passed quickly over the sun. There was a sudden coldness and I felt afraid for her for no reason I could put a name to. I looked at her carefully trying to work out what was wrong and noticed that she was wearing high heeled shoes.

'You want to get those shoes off, love, and put flatties on,' I said. 'You've only got to go over ...'

Tony who was standing slightly behind, put his arms round her. 'I'll buy her some flatties tomorrow, Doris,' he promised and as he said it he leant forward and kissed the top of her head and there it was again. That quick pang of fear. There and gone again, before I could identify it.

'That's right. Give her all the love you can,' I said without realizing what I was saying. 'She's going to need all the love you can give her in the next few months.'

They just smiled at each other, so young and so very much in love, and Tony brushed her hair with his lips again. They didn't realize how seriously I meant it. But how could they? I didn't really know what I meant myself. All I knew was that every time I looked at Janet I wanted to go and put my arms round her and support her in some way. I was sure there was something wrong somewhere. Yet she looked the very picture of health and Ted said the doctors were very pleased with her.

Oh stop being fanciful, Stokes, I told myself sternly. You're imagining things. What you need is another cup of tea. And I went to fill the kettle, pushing that shadow firmly to the back of my mind.

Half an hour later as she left the theatre, Janet stumbled on an uneven paving stone and went straight over. Fortunately there was no harm done, but Ted and Tony, remembering my warning, made her take off her shoes then and there and walk the rest of the way to the car in her stockinged-feet. In a way I was relieved. Perhaps it was just the potential danger of her high heels that I'd picked up.

Weeks passed and at last came the news that the baby had been born. Janet had had a little girl and they were going to call her Hollie. Mother and baby were doing well we were told. It was good news, of course, but it didn't banish the feeling that there was something wrong somewhere. Every day, when I thought of the Roffeys and little Hollie that shadow seemed to grow stronger.

Well I'm not going to ring up and worry them, I told myself, you're just being over-imaginative because of John Michael. And it's true that after losing my own baby at 5 months, I've always mentally held my breath over other people's babies until they're a year old. It might seem illogical but I tend to feel that anything can happen in the first 12 months of life. Once a baby has reached a year I let out a sigh of relief and feel that he's safely on his way.

Then one day I opened the paper and there was a story about the baby who was to become the world's youngest heart transplant patient. It was a baby girl and her name was Hollie Roffey. The paper slipped from my fingers and with a cold sinking feeling, I realized that this was what I'd sensed from the start. Apparently at birth, Hollie had appeared quite normal and healthy but as the days went by her colour didn't look quite right and she was taken off for tests. The day Tony and Janet hoped to bring her home the results came through. They were told that the left side of Hollie's heart was missing. The defect was too drastic to attempt a repair. Hollie's only chance of survival was a heart transplant – if a suitable donor could be found.

Everybody worked very hard to save little Hollie. By the time I phoned Ted, a donor had been found and the family were at the hospital pacing the corridors and drinking strong coffee while the operation took place. Ted's son, Simon, answered the phone.

'Simon, I don't want to intrude,' I said, 'could you just tell your dad that I rang and that we're praying for Hollie.'

I don't know how the Roffeys got through the next few days. It was such a tense time. Little Hollie's plight touched the whole country. The newspapers, radio and television carried regular stories about her and her brave struggle for life melted the coldest hearts. Amazingly for such a fragile little thing she hung on for 17 days after the operation. She was a born fighter.

At one point she seemed to rally, she started to suck and all the signs were hopeful. The whole nation held its breath. The length and breadth of the country people were rooting for Hollie.

Tony and Janet had spent every day at the hospital but at last Hollie's condition was so encouraging they were persuaded to go home for a rest. Tragically, while they were away their baby took a turn for the worse and before they could get back to the hospital she was gone.

John and I were at the van when we heard the news. I wasn't surprised, yet at the same time it was a shock and I felt desperately sorry for poor Tony and Janet. I knew exactly how they must be feeling. It was the story of John Michael all over again.

I know some people back away from tragedy. They don't know what to say so they don't say anything at all and you even hear of people who will cross the road rather than face someone who's suffered a bereavement. Yet the strange thing is, if you do face it, the words come and it means so much to the bereaved to know that people care.

It didn't even occur to me not to get in touch. Sadly, I dialled Ted's number.

'Ted, I'm so very sorry,' I said when he answered.

At the sound of my voice he seemed relieved.

'Oh Doris. Tony and Janet are here with us now. Can we come? Can I fetch you?'

How could I refuse? Scarcely half an hour later Ted arrived and whisked us back to his home. I think he was very glad that John and I happened to be in Kent that day because he was finding it difficult to comfort Janet and Tony.

They were in a dreadful state as anyone would have been. I put my arms round them both, then I sat them down and tried to talk to them. I don't know how much of what I said actually got through but we talked for about 3 hours.

'Listen, darling, Hollie's not dead,' I said. 'And she's done more in her short life than all of us put together could do in ninety years. She's paved the way to show that these operations can be done on tiny babies. Thanks to her, who knows how many lives will be saved. Just be proud you were chosen to be her parents.'

It's odd how in times of tragedy people often focus on one tiny detail which seems to take on an importance out of all proportion to the greater horror of what has happened. With Tony it was his baby's hair. Distraught as he was he was particularly upset because they'd shaved Hollie's head.

'She was so beautiful, Doris,' he sobbed, 'but they shaved her head. Why did they have to cut off her hair?'

He didn't really want a medical answer, of course, though doubtless there was one.

'Look Tony it doesn't matter,' I said, 'she's beautiful again now. She's got all her hair again on the other side. That wasn't Hollie you saw when you went back to the hospital, just her old overcoat.'

I didn't even attempt to do a sitting for them. It was too soon. Grief is natural, it's part of the healing process and I think it's better to let it out and adjust a little to the loss before contacting a medium. In the Roffey's case though the spirit world wanted to clear up that one small point.

Suddenly as I was speaking I felt a small jolt as something was put on my lap. I looked down and there was Hollie. Now I love babies and they all look beautiful to me, but Hollie was one of the most beautiful children I've ever seen. She was gurgling happily to herself and her head was a mass of tiny red gold ringlets, glossy as a new conker.

'There, isn't she lovely?' said a woman's voice. 'Tell Tony he can take it from me that she's got all her hair back now and I'm looking after her.'

It was Tony's grandmother and I gladly passed the message on. Only one thing puzzled me. The red gold hair. Both Tony and Janet were dark and I'd have expected Hollie to be dark like them or else baby fair with the kind of hair that darkens as the child grows. Yet Hollie's hair was bold and distinctive and quite unlike her parents.

It was only a few days later when I met Tony's brother that I discovered the answer. As soon as I saw his deep copper head coming towards me I realized that the colour ran in the family, and for some reason had bypassed Tony.

But the Roffeys' ordeal was far from over. The baby's body was taken to the undertakers and Tony and Janet had arranged to see her there. They told me about this and they kept hovering round until at last I realized what they'd left unsaid.

'D'you want to ask me to go with you?'

They exchanged relieved glances. 'Would it be imposing too much to ask you?' said Tony.

'Not a bit, love. Come and pick us up when you're ready.'

Well, it was an experience I'll never forget. I couldn't believe it. We drew up outside a bike shop, and at the side was a window, bare but for a vase with a few dusty artificial flowers in it. In we went and a man emerged from the shadows at the back.

'We've come to look at our baby,' said Tony painfully while Janet clung to my hand.

'Oh yes,' said the man. 'Follow me.' And he led us out through the back of the shop, across a yard filled with old bikes, to a desolate little room at the end.

'In there,' said the man standing back.

Tony and Janet, quite numb, didn't move. 'Would you go in first, Doris?' Janet whispered.

'Yes, all right love,' I said and I'm very glad I did. The first thing I saw as my eyes adjusted to the light was a tiny white box no bigger than a shoe box, and a dead carnation lying on the top. Fortunately before we left the van that morning I'd cut a white rosebud, just starting to open and, quick as a flash, I whipped off the carnation and laid the rosebud in its place. And then there were those two poor kids standing beside me, Tony repeating, 'It's not fair. It's just not fair', over and over again while Janet sobbed her heart out.

There was nothing to be done, of course, there never is, and at last I kissed the poor cold, uncomprehending little face and touched Janet's arm.

'Come on, love,' I said gently. 'It's only her old overcoat. She's not there you know. She's safe and happy.'

And, finally, we persuaded them away from that dismal place and took them home.

There was still the funeral to be got through and I was dreading it. Tony and Janet wanted us to be there and we wouldn't let them down for the world, but the whole sad episode was bringing back such vivid memories of the loss of John Michael that I found it very painful. After all, one heartbreakingly small white box looks very like another and day and night I found myself reliving the worst moments of my life.

'Now look,' I told Tony and Janet just before the funeral. 'The worst part is when you see that little box disappear into the earth. Just keep telling yourselves that's not Hollie. Hollie's safe.'

But it was a heart-rending affair nevertheless. There was a terrible moment when two hefty men came into the chapel with this pathetic little white box carried on a canvas sling between them. There was something ludicrous about two such burly figures sharing such a tiny burden. Why couldn't one of them have simply carried the coffin in his arms I wondered? At John Michael's funeral we had a little fair, curly-haired boy carrying my baby's box in his arms. It was simple, touching and appropriate. You don't need pomp and ceremony for an innocent little baby.

Yet although it was sad, that funeral underlined what a special child Hollie was and how in just a few short days she'd won the affection of so many people. The church was packed and magnificent floral tributes poured in from all over the country. Hollie's grave looked as if it was set in a carpet of flowers and to that blazing sea of colour John and I added our own little contribution. We'd cut every bud from every white rose bush in our garden, wrapped them in a white doily and added a little card. 'To Hollie. You didn't know the world but the whole world knew you.'

Afterwards, back at Ted's home, Janet and I strolled in the garden as she tried to calm herself. It was a warm day and crowds of mourners drifted outside for some air. We walked slowly back and forth and suddenly through the chatter I distinctly heard:

'I don't care what you say. Hollie's not there. Read Doris Stokes' books. I'm telling you …'

I couldn't help smiling. How nice to know that my words hadn't fallen on deaf ears. I moved towards the speaker, a pleasant-faced, middle-aged man to thank him for his recommendation but just as I reached him he noticed me. His words died away, his jaw dropped and his skin went a little pale under his tan.

'B-b-b-but it's her. It's Doris Stokes. Where did you come from?' he stammered for all the world as if he thought I'd just materialized out of thin air.

'I came to the funeral,' I said, 'I'm a friend of the family.'

He looked relieved and his healthy colour returned. 'Well, Doris! how lovely to meet you. Come and talk to us.'

Janet and I joined the group and although I hadn't intended to work, the day had been too emotional already, I found that the man's wife had arrived unseen from the spirit world and wanted to send him her love.

'And give my love to our Mary,' she said, 'and as for him, tell him to talk to Mary. They haven't spoken for years.'

Apparently there had been some sort of family disagreement and the man had fallen out with his sister-in-law. As the years passed it became harder for either of them to break the ice and although they sometimes went to the same functions, they behaved as if they'd never met. It turned out that Mary was at the funeral too and the prompting from the other side was all they needed. Before the afternoon was over that man was crouched beside Mary's chair, sheepishly making up for years of silence.

Once people find out that I'm a medium they're usually full of questions and after a while one of the other men in the group, Micky Dallon who'd been listening quietly, finally plucked up the courage to raise a subject that must have been bothering him for some time.

'When my mother was dying I sat with her holding her hand,' he said, 'and at one point I wanted to jump up and shout for the doctor, but at the same time I didn't want to leave her. In the end I stayed with mum and she died. Ever since I've been wondering if I did the right thing. If I'd got the doctor then, perhaps we could have saved her.'

I shook my head vigorously.

'No, love. You were right to stay and comfort her. It wouldn't have made any difference who you called. If it was your mother's time to go over she had to go and no one could have prevented it.'

Micky seemed satisfied and the conversation moved on but I couldn't concentrate on what they were saying. A woman had joined us and she was bending forward to whisper to me.

'Give my love to Micky,' she murmured.

'Who are you?' I asked.

'It's Lilian,' she said and she was gone.

'Sorry to interrupt,' I said quietly out loud, 'but I just got something for Micky. It's not much. Lilian sends her love, that's all.'

It was the tiniest of messages but the effect was amazing. The colour just drained from Micky Dallon's face and he went so white I thought he might faint.

'It's such an unusual name ...' he blurted through pale lips, 'you could never have guessed my mother's name was Lilian ...' and he blundered away to get a drink to steady his nerves.

There are two sequels to the story of Tony and Janet, one rather strange and inexplicable, the other perfectly explicable and down to earth but just as wonderful.

The first occurred during that same long hot summer. The Roffeys spent quite a lot of time with us in our mobile home and naturally the subject of Hollie came up frequently. Tony seemed to be particularly anguished. He couldn't come to terms with the tragedy at all.

'I believe you, Doris,' he said time and time again. 'I believe everything you say but if only they could give me a sign that my baby's all right, then I could rest.'

His words used to tear at me because I wanted to help but there was nothing I could do. I'm only human after all. I could pass on messages I heard, and tell him what I knew about life on the other side but as to signs that he could see for himself, well that was out of my hands entirely.

'Well, Tony, be patient,' was all I could advise. 'If they think you need a sign, perhaps they'll send you one. Who knows?'

A week or two later when my back was less painful I decided to get on with some housework around the van. I pulled out our nest of tables and was giving them a good polish when suddenly I dropped the duster in surprise. There on the table we used most, the pattern of the wood had re-arranged itself, that's the only way I can describe it – into the face of Jesus complete with beard and crown of thorns. The little picture was about four inches long and in the opposite direction to the grain and what's more it had certainly not been there before. I blinked, look away, and looked back again but it was still there.

Quickly I went into the bedrookm where John was hoovering and touched his arm. 'Switch it off and come and look at this and tell me what you see.'

Puzzled he followed me into the living-room. Without saying a word I pointed at the table. John looked, then frowned, looked away and looked back, just as I had done.

'It's the face of Jesus,' he said. 'That's what it looks like to me. But I've never noticed it before.'

It's very easy to let your imagination run away with you in cases like this and John and I are so closely attuned I couldn't be sure I wasn't influencing him, so we decided to call in other opinions.

'If anyone'll know what that table used to be like it's Phyllis and Doreen,' I said.

Phyllis and Doreen were two of our friends on the site who used to air the van and give it a quick going over before we arrived if we'd been away for some time. We invited them in and without mentioning what was going on we asked them to look at the table. Both spontaneously saw the picture of Jesus.

'Well I've polished these tables I don't know how many times,' said Phyllis, 'and I've never seen that before.'

Finally, when we'd heard enough exclamations of astonishment to know we weren't seeing things, we told the Roffeys. They came, looked, and Ted was so impressed he took the table away to be photographed.

'Well, Tony,' I said, 'I'm not saying it is – but you did ask for a sign ...'

Several months passed before the second sequel. I was very busy with the arrangements for moving and with the tour and so quite a few weeks went by before I saw the Roffeys again. Then, just before Christmas I did a very exciting demonstration at the London Palladium (more of that later) and afterwards, to my delight, Tony and Janet walked into the dressing-room. They both looked well and much happier than the last time I'd seen them and I was instantly reminded of my parting words in the summer.

'Well this time next year I hope I'll be able to come and have a drink with you at your christening.'

Janet was still as slim and agile as ever and yet there was something about her ...

'Yes the baby's on its way,' whispered a voice in my ear and I beamed at the kids.

'I'm still keeping the summer free for the christening,' I joked.

Tony laughed ruefully. 'No, Doris. I'm afraid you'll have to wait a bit longer. We've had no luck yet.'

I stared at him in surprise. 'But I'm sure they ...' then I saw Janet frantically signalling behind his back and I stopped. 'Oh well never mind, love,' I finished lamely, 'it'll happen in good time.' And I left it at that. I didn't want to spoil Janet's surprise.

Sure enough, a few days later on Christmas morning, Tony came downstairs to find a plain white card amongst his brightly wrapped parcels.

'Dear Tony,' it said. 'Sorry you'll have to wait another 33 weeks for your present. Love Janet.'

Tony, who must have been celebrating rather freely the night before, didn't get it. 'Thirty-three weeks?' he said puzzled, 'why will I have to wait thirty-three weeks?'

'Because I'm pregnant you idiot!' cried Janet and the next second he was swinging her round, very gently, in delight. It was the best Christmas present they could have had.

Chapter 3

The garden of the mobile home was looking lovely as I showed Lady Michaela Denis Lyndsay round and all about us was the scent of roses. Roses are my favourite flower. We'd planted dozens of bushes when we bought the van and now they were all out and blooming like mad.

It was so beautiful that Michaela and I quite forgot the cameras whirring away in the background recording every move and we drifted towards the seat beside a glorious 'Blue Moon', chatting as if we were alone.

'Oh look!' I cried as we sat down. 'There's Minnie the mongoose!'

The late Minnie had been a very special pet of Michaela's and now I saw her as plain as I saw my roses, snuggled on the bench against Michaela's leg, a little blur of fur with a pointed face and bright eyes.

'Oh yes,' said Michaela in delight, 'I see her. She's often with me you know.' And she stroked Minnie's head fondly. I reached out to pat Minnie myself and as I did so I smiled up at the cameramen. This must make a lovely scene for them, I thought, what a bit of luck, and then I noticed that far from smiling back, they had turned distinctly white and nervous and were staring at the seat uneasily.

That was when it clicked. Of course, Minnie was invisible to them. They must have thought we'd gone stark raving mad, patting and talking to a patch of thin air!

I bet they won't forget that particular edition of *Forty Minutes* in a hurry! I was tremendously flattered when BBC2 rang to ask if they could make me the subject of the programme. As most people probably know the programme takes its name from the length of screen time allotted to it but it takes a great deal longer than forty minutes to make.

The documentary team seemed to follow me round for weeks filming everything, until in the end they became like members of the family and I hardly noticed the cameras at all. They filmed in our flat, in our mobile home, at public demonstrations and church services and even in Bert Weedon's garden. Bert Weedon of course is the guitarist who wrote and played the background music on my LP. They couldn't use half of what they'd filmed, of course, because they must have recorded hours and hours of material, but I was very impressed with the finished programme. They'd made an interesting, intelligible documentary out of a great hotch-potch of different topics.

They said they wanted to cover just about every aspect of my work and beliefs and they certainly did. To explain my spirit guide, Ramanov, they decided to focus on the name plate of the mobile home which we'd named in his honour and then show me explaining the origin of the name to Michaela.

I've known Michaela for years and since she happened to be in England at the time they thought it might be nice if she appeared. A lot of people remember the wonderful wild life programmes she used to make with her first husband Armand. When he passed over she married Sir William Lyndsay which is why she is now a titled lady. Sir William, too is now on the other side and these days Michaela lives alone in Kenya surrounded by her beloved wild animals. What few people realize though, is that Michaela is also a medium and every year she comes to London to attend the SAGB dinner dance and visit her spiritualist friends.

Michaela and Minnie did eventually reach the screen but many other scenes did not. At one point the producer got quite excited about the news that I could do sittings over the telephone.

'D'you think you could do one for us this afternoon?' he asked. 'If we pick a letter from your post bag could you phone them and do it straight away?'

'I can try,' I said.

So one of the team delved down my huge pile of letters and came up with a note which included a phone number. To make doubly sure that I knew nothing of the contents she even dialled the number herself and then passed me the receiver as the phone was answered.

'Hello,' I said to the woman at the other end. 'This is Doris Stokes. I believe you wrote to me asking for a sitting.'

'Oh yes,' she said.

'Well,' I explained, 'I can do one on the phone for you if you don't mind the BBC recording it. They're here now making a documentary.'

'Oh,' she said, 'what time?'

The producer signalled impressively.

'It's got to be half-past-one.'

'Oh dear,' said the woman, 'couldn't you make it four-thirty. I go to bingo at half-past-one.'

But the producer was adamant and the woman seemed reluctant to miss her bingo so another letter was drawn from the bag. This time I tuned in as they were dialling the number and instantly I heard the name Doug.

'Look I don't want to know what's in the letter,' I whispered, 'but just tell me, is the name Doug mentioned?'

They skimmed through it. 'Yes.'

Thank goodness for that. I'd contacted the right person and not someone connected with the TV crew. It's so easy to get crossed wires when there are a lot of people about, because their friends and relatives in spirit are often so close to them.

This time we were in luck. The woman on the line was only too delighted to help and 1.30 suited her perfectly. It turned out that Doug was her husband. He was only fifty-four and he'd died suddenly of a heart attack.

'Who's Jenny?' I asked.

'My daughter-in-law,' said the woman.

'Doug tells me that you were with Jenny when it happened.'

'Yes I was,' she agreed.

'They were out Christmas shopping,' said Doug. 'They were in Marks and Spencers' buying me a sweater when I passed. I tried to tell them not to bother because I wouldn't be needing it but I couldn't make them hear.'

The woman was dumbfounded when I told her what her husband had said.

'That's exactly what we were doing,' she gasped when she got over her astonishment. 'We were in Marks buying him a sweater! Oh I'm so glad he knew.'

Unfortunately Doug and his sweater never did reach the final programme, there simply wasn't time, but I'd like to let him know that he's not forgotten!

The demonstration I gave at Poplar fared better on the screen. I can't say that every message I gave was shown on the programme but a good proportion did make it. There was a lot of laughter that night and one message in particular tickled the audience. A pair of women were standing together at the microphone and one of their relatives – I think it was their father – was chatting away in my ear.

'And when they knocked the wall down it all went wrong,' he tutted.

'Are you doing some building work at home?' I asked them. 'He's saying something about a wall knocked down and everything went wrong.'

The women looked at each other and giggled.

'Yes!'

'What a mess,' the man went on. 'And when they got the tiles for the floor, there weren't enough!'

I passed this on and by now the women were practically in tears of laughter.

'Yes, but it wasn't the tiles, it was the glue we ran out of!' they corrected.

'Oh well, tiles, glue whatever, they ran out and had to rush off to the shop to get some more,' said the man. 'And at home they daren't move till the glue arrived. What a mess! I cleared off till it was all finished.'

There were the usual moments of confusion too, which I've learned I just have to put up with when I'm working with a big audience. I can normally tell who a message is intended for by the light I see shining close to them, but often there are so many spirit people eager to talk to their loved ones that the place is packed with lights. What's more the theatres are usually so crowded, with the seats packed so close, it's impossible to say exactly which person I'm looking for.

That night in Poplar, a woman called May told me she was looking for a young lady in a red dress. There was a light hovering near a woman in the front who seemed to fit the description.

'Yes that must be me!' she shouted eagerly hurrying forward.

But I wasn't certain. Something didn't seem quite right. In the background someone gave me the name Fred.

'D'you know someone called Fred, spirit side?' I asked.

She shook her head. She was the wrong contact. As soon as I mentioned the name Fred, Fred himself came in drowning May altogether.

'It's my daughter I want,' he said, 'and she's wearing red.'

Suddenly I was aware of a hand waving frantically near the back of the hall.

'I know a Fred,' she called.

'Are you wearing red, love?' I asked because, dazzled by the lights, I couldn't see the back.

'Yes I am,' she called and came running down to the microphone.

I wanted to make absolutely certain however that I'd

found the right person so I asked for further identification. 'Mention working for the Co-op,' he said.

'Who worked for the Co-op?' I asked.

'My father,' said the girl in wonder, 'he was a milk lorry driver.'

I breathed a sigh of relief. We'd found Fred's daughter.

'Tell her that Eva's here with me,' he said.

The girl gasped. 'That's my mother! They're together? Oh I'm so glad.'

'She's our baby,' said Fred and you could hear all the love and affection in his voice. They must have been very close. 'And she's wearing her mother's ring. She's got it on tonight.'

His daughter's smile was dazzling. 'Yes I have.'

All at once the crowded hall faded and before my eyes I saw a glorious lilac bush. Not the spindly insignificant little tree that you see in so many gardens, but a really lush, magnificent shrub. Then the picture was gone. Now why had Fred shown me a lilac bush I wondered.

'You haven't got a lilac bush in your garden have you?' I asked the girl.

'Why yes. A really beautiful one.'

'That's it,' I said. 'They've just shown me a beautiful lilac bush and they're saying when the lilacs are out in the spring cut a spray and say Mum and Dad's here.'

'Oh, thank you, I will,' she assured me her face lit with joy.

All evening the spirit people came flooding through. Some were marvellous communicators, others quite overcome by the excitement. One grandmother was so thrilled to be able to tell her daughter that she had seen the grandchildren she'd never lived to meet on earth that all she could do was babble their names over and over again. 'Rachel and Rebecca! Rachel and Rebecca!' she kept telling me in delight.

Another young lad who was killed in an accident seemed to think that the name of his favourite pub was all the information necessary to convince his sister that he was really there.

'Just mention the Green Man,' he said confidently.

And some messages seemed puzzling to me but made perfect sense to the recipients. At one point I got the name Proctor and not one, but two ladies claimed it. It turned out they were the Proctor sisters, a bubbly duo full of fun.

'Well, this is very odd,' I told them, 'I've got a lady here, I'm sure it's a lady, but they're calling her Henry.'

The sisters collapsed into each other's arms all laughter and dimples. 'Yes that's right. It's Henrietta but Father always called her Henry.'

'And now I've got another lady but they're calling her George.'

The sisters could hardly speak for mirth. 'That's right,' they spluttered, 'Georgina!' and the whole theatre laughed with them.

The Proctor sisters were obviously enjoying themselves immensely. So much so that the next day when they were on a day trip to Clacton they decided to buy me a present. They'd read in my books that I'm specially fond of gold roses and passing a florist's they saw the very thing they were after. A pretty arrangement of roses in the very shade I described. The only snag was that the shop was shut but the Proctor sisters weren't going to be defeated by a tiny detail like that. They went all the way back to Clacton the next day and bought it.

Soon after the Poplar demonstration the Forty Minutes' team followed me to Deal where I was doing a church service. I try to attend a church as often as possible because I think it does me good. It reminds me what my work is all about. The big theatres and the assorted messages are only a small part of it. The rest is as much about living your life now, as life after death.

I must say our services are usually quite lively. We have hymns and prayers, of course, like other churches but it's all very informal, not a bit holier than thou. Then when the religious part is over there's a short demonstration.

It was lovely to visit Deal. A pretty little town on the South coast with the salt tang in the air you always get by the sea and a fresh breeze blowing. The church was bright and welcoming and full of flowers and the congregation was squeezed in so tightly it's a wonder they had enough breath to sing!

After a relaxed service I did a demonstration. This was the time when I was suffering with my back and the actual details of the demonstration have faded, all I can recall is the dull ache that I hoped didn't show on my face. One thing does stand out though. A boy came through saying that he was connected with the navy and that he'd taken himself over. He was claimed immediately by a woman in the congregation but once again it seemed slightly off key. Many of the details didn't mean a thing to her and though she was eager for the message to be hers I had an uneasy feeling I was talking to the wrong contact. But my back was aching, the heat was increasing and other spirit voices were jostling to be heard. So instead of working at it and trying to sort out the confusion as I normally do, I passed on to the next message. I might have known, however, that Ramanov wouldn't let me get away with such sloppiness.

After the service I noticed out of the corner of my eye a woman and a young man approach the producer. They stood talking to him for some minutes and then he brought them over to me.

'They were so disappointed, Doris, not to get a message,' he said and the woman pressed a photograph into my hand.

'That's him, Doris,' she told me pleadingly.

She was a handsome blonde with clear, creamy skin but the expression in her blue eyes told me she'd lost a child. I looked at the picture. A smiling, suntanned young man looked back at me and as I stared I realized that he was with us.

'I'm here,' he said, 'I've been trying to get through.'

'What do I call you, son?' I asked silently.

'Stephen,' he said.

'I hear the name Stephen,' I told the couple and the other boy clutched the woman's arm.

'That's him. That's my brother!' he said.

'He's wearing all my jewellery and stuff,' said Stephen, 'but I don't mind. It's no good to me now is it?'

'That's right I am,' cried the brother.

The woman's face lit up. 'He's been waiting for that for a year,' she said. 'He used to be frightened of spirits and things but he's read your books and he felt sure you could help.'

The case was not a clear one though. Around Stephen's passing I could sense a great deal of mystery and confusion. It wasn't the sort of thing to be tackled in five minutes before lunch I felt.

'Look,' I said impulsively. 'I think there's a lot to be gone into here. I've got a day off tomorrow. Why don't you come and see me at the van and we'll see what we can do.'

They agreed eagerly and when we got started on the sitting I was very glad I'd asked them to come back.

As soon as I tuned in, the feeling of confusion swept over me more strongly than ever. This was no ordinary accident victim or sufferer from an illness. This poor mixed up boy had taken his own life.

I chose my words carefully in an attempt to spare the mother's feelings.

'There's a great deal of mystery and confusion here,' I said, 'Stephen wasn't killed, he was found.'

His mother bit her lip. 'Yes, I found him.'

I caught a fleeting glimpse of a teenage bedroom.

'You found him on his bed?'

She shook her head. 'No, on the floor in his bedroom.'

So that was why he'd shown me the room, but Stephen wasn't quite ready yet to discuss the details. He was still ashamed to have caused his family so much pain and he kept shying away from the subject whenever I brought it up.

'Don't forget to remember me to Gary,' he said ignoring my question.

'Who's Gary?' I asked out loud.

'One of his best friends.'

I tackled Stephen again. 'Now look I know it's difficult love,' I told him silently, 'but I do need to know your last impressions. Can you just give me some idea what happened?'

All at once the confusion swamped me and there was an uncomfortable feeling in my head. My head hurt and my chest felt constricted.

'I feel as if I've got something over my head,' I said thinking aloud, 'and I can't breathe. Did he take an overdose or something?'

His mother shook her head. 'No he shot himself.'

I was surprised. The strange feeling in my head was a very strong impression. I don't deny that I sometimes make mistakes but when spirit people give me a clear impression it's never wrong. My interpretation of it may be way out but the impression itself is always correct.

'Well this feeling in my head seems very definite,' I insisted.

'It's funny you should say that Doris,' said Stephen's mother, 'because for a couple of weeks before he died he'd been complaining about his head.'

'I'd got it into my head there was something wrong,' said Stephen, 'I must have been mad. What a stupid thing to do. But it felt as if the top of my head was coming off. I thought I was ill.'

Then he gave me the name Joan.

'Who's Joan?' I asked.

'I am,' said his mother beaming.

Stephen went on to tell them that he played the guitar on the other side, which pleased them very much.

'He always wanted to play the guitar,' said his brother, 'he used to stand in front of the mirror and pretend.'

Stephen also started talking about a dinner service

which puzzled me rather because young men aren't usually bothered about things like that. It wasn't at all clear though and I wasn't sure what he meant.

'Why's he talking about a dinner service?' I asked. 'He's saying it's connected with work. You know plates and things, he's saying.'

His brother was thrilled. 'I think he means me. I've just started work as a steward. I work with plates and things.'

Finally, right at the end of the sitting I realized it had been Stephen trying to get through during the service in Deal with the message about the navy. He was talking about his funeral and he wanted to thank his family for the anchor of flowers they'd given him. It turned out that his father was in the navy. I'd found the right contact at last!

Not long after the *Forty Minutes* documentary, I had another phone call from the BBC, but this time it was from BBC Radio 2. Would I like to do *Desert Island Discs?* they asked.

For a minute I thought there must be some mistake, because surely they only have highbrow people on *Desert Island Discs*? But no, they said, they were quite certain they wanted Doris Stokes the medium. All I had to do, they explained, was pick out eight of my favourite records, records which meant something special to me, and talk about them.

Well it seemed easy enough and I love music. But when it actually came to narrowing down my favourites to just eight tunes it turned out to be more difficult than I'd imagined. Just when I thought I'd been really ruthless and pruned down my list as far as I could go, I'd suddenly think of a really lovely piece I'd forgotten that I couldn't manage without.

It took me days. I got through pages of my writing pad with lists, revised lists and endless crossings out. But at last I settled on eight lovely tracks.

Presenter Roy Plomley, and producer, Derek Drescher, were lovely men. They invited John and I out to lunch to plan the programme but I explained that we don't really feel comfortable in posh restaurants.

'We just can't manage a big meal in the middle of the day,' I told Roy. 'We'd really much prefer tea and sandwiches in the office if it's all the same to you.'

So tea and sandwiches it was and we spent a lovely hour listening to all my discs and picking out the bits they were going to play because, of course, they can't play the records right the way through. Then it was time to record the programme with me talking to Roy between the music.

'I warn you I can woffle,' I told them but they thought I was joking.

'I'd sooner have a woffler than someone who doesn't say a word,' said Roy and away we went.

We started on a light note. Roy asked if I played a musical instrument and I explained that I didn't, though I'd always wanted to and I was hoping to learn in the spirit world.

'What will you play?' asked Roy. 'A harp?'

My first record was *One Day At A Time Sweet Jesus*. I go for the words every time and this song sums up how I've learned to live my life since I had cancer. Next was *I Love You Just Because* for John, because he's always there and when I'm tired or ill I don't always remember to let him know how much I appreciate it. *Morning Has Broken*, because it's such a beautiful song and it captures the pleasure I feel to see each new morning. Then there was *Mother Kelly's Doorstep* which always makes me smile because whenever I hear it, it reminds me of the time Danny La Rue came on stage at Birmingham Odeon to help me hand out flowers and got me singing a duet with him of *Mother Kelly's Doorstep*. Now I can't sing a note, there's no two ways about it but the audience loved it. I think they treated it as a comedy routine!

After that there was Freddie Starr singing *Have I Told You Lately That I Love You* because whenever he phones, he serenades me with this song. Then I changed the mood completely and played *May The Good Lord Bless and Keep You*. Some people might think my reasons for choosing this rather sad but I don't. When I pass over I'm going to be cremated and I'd like this song played for my family because I'll be all right. I'll be away and happy with my loved ones on the other side. It's the ones who're left behind who will need help and comfort.

Finally I ended with *My Way* followed by my own reading of the poem that was given to me when I was mourning the death of my baby John Michael: *In a Baby Castle*. The words brought me such comfort at the time that I like to pass them on to every mother grieving for a lost child, in the hope they'll do the same for her as they did for me.

And then suddenly it was all over. The programme was recorded and I realized I'd been enjoying myself immensely.

Derek Drescher's head appeared round the door. 'That went on a bit too long, Roy,' he said.

I laughed. 'Well I did warn you I can waffle.'

And Roy, bless him, just grinned and leaned across the desk. 'Ah, but such magical waffle,' he said.

I seem to have been involved in a lot of programmes lately but with one of the most recent, *Glass Box*, which is only shown in the Granada TV area, I wasn't sure if I'd make it on to the screen at all.

Glass Box is recorded at the TV studios in Liverpool and it's a sort of visual *Desert Island Discs*. The idea is that you select a number of film clips that you particularly enjoy or that remind you of some special moment in your life and instead of taking them to an imaginary desert island, you seal them into a glass box to preserve them for ever.

I'd met the presenter, Shelley Rohde, before and we got on well and after enjoying *Desert Island Discs* so much I knew I'd enjoy *Glass Box*. I was looking forward to it. The choosing of the film clips had not been so difficult for me because films somehow don't seem to have such sentimental associations. There were some clips from the *Dambusters* to remind me of my airforce days, a piece from *Yield to the Night* with Diana Dors to remind me of our friendship and everyone else what a wonderful actress she was, some beautiful ballet because I've only recently learned to appreciate it and finally a scene from a horror movie because horror movies make me laugh so much. The whole thing would be great fun, I was sure.

Unfortunately, though, Liverpool went wrong from the evening we arrived. Some time before, a little girl of ten had written me a touching letter. She'd lost her Daddy she told me and she knew I could speak to him because she'd read my books. Could her Mummy bring her to see me because she wanted to tell her Daddy she loved him? I saw from the address that she didn't live too far from Liverpool and I realized that we might be able to combine a meeting with the *Glass Box* trip, so I asked Laurie to see if he could arrange for her to come and see me at the hotel.

This he did. 'But do remember to be there by six o'clock,' he said, 'because Doris has to go out at half-past-seven.'

We were meeting the producer of *Glass Box* to plan the next day's show and it was something that couldn't be put off.

Well we waited and waited. Six o'clock came and went and there was no sign of the little girl and her mother. At six-thirty I was convinced.

'They're not coming, Laurie, I'm certain of it,' I said.

'But they must be, they were so keen,' he insisted. 'Perhaps they're stuck in traffic somewhere.'

We waited until seven o'clock and then I had to get changed.

'Give me a shout if they arrive and I'll see if I can do something quick,' I said, 'but I've got a feeling Laurie. They're not coming.'

By half-past-seven even Laurie was forced to admit I was right. And it wasn't until the next night that we discovered what went wrong. They'd got the dates mixed up and come a day late. By the time they arrived in Liverpool I was almost home. I felt so sorry for that poor little girl. She'd been looking forward to talking to her Daddy and it had ended in disappointment. I'm still hoping we can meet one day.

The mishaps continued. That evening, no sooner had the meeting ended than Laurie hurried away to bed. It's most unusual for Laurie because normally he's a night owl, but his face was pale and drawn, despite the fact that he was complaining of the heat.

'Aren't you feeling too good, Laurie?' I asked, 'you don't look well.'

'Oh I'm fine, fine,' he insisted because he hates to admit to being ill. 'I only need a good night's sleep.'

'Looks like the 'flu to me,' said John when he'd gone.

'But it came on so suddenly,' I pointed out. 'He was all right at the meeting.'

We fully expected to find no sign of Laurie at breakfast the next morning but there he was, as bright and cheerful as if nothing had happened.

'Yes I'm fine now,' he said. 'But oh did I feel rough last night. At one point my legs just went to jelly. I could hardly stand up.'

Well, apart from shaking our heads over the peculiar bugs that go around these days we thought no more about it. Liverpool was like the North Pole that day with a wind that must surely have been blowing from a glacier and the weather was the main topic of conversation.

Earlier Laurie had taken a short stroll to the studio to check one or two points. It was only up the road from our hotel but the cold was so intense he couldn't face the walk back and had to take a taxi instead!

'Well if it's as bad as that I'm certainly not walking.' I said, 'I'll be blue by the time I get there!'

So at mid-day we climbed into our immaculate limousine for the two minute journey. They were very kind at the studio and had laid on a beautiful lunch in the directors' dining-room. Everyone tucked in hungrily except Shelley Rohde and I. Neither of us could eat a thing before working so we just pushed our food around on our plates and watched the others.

Then at last the meal was over and I was taken away to be made up. But half way down the stairs I went all dizzy and I swayed towards the make-up girl who was leading the way.

'I'll have to hold on to your shoulder, love,' I explained. 'I've come over a bit dizzy. I expect it's the heat.'

For it was very warm in the studio after the icy weather outside.

And settled in the comfortable chair in front of the big make-up mirror I felt fine. The girl soothingly combed my hair and put in heated rollers and then she put my face on. I did look a bit pale I thought but the foundation cream soon cured that.

At last, five minutes before I was due on the studio floor, I popped into the ladies. I was all ready. I've only got to slip into my dress and I can go on I was thinking, when suddenly without warning my legs went to jelly and my head spun. Anxiously I grabbed at the wall to steady myself. I was so dizzy I didn't think I could stand upright let alone walk coolly into a TV studio and talk intelligibly for half an hour.

Panic rising, I waited for the attack to pass, but it didn't. My God, I thought, here I am with my make-up on and everything and I'm not going to be able to do it. They'll be calling me any minute and I don't think I can even get out of the loo.

In desperation I sent out a prayer to the spirit world. 'Please spirit friends just see me through this bit. Just see me through this hour. I don't mind what happens afterwards if I can just get this show done.'

And as always they turned up trumps. Even before I'd finished the prayer my head started to clear and my legs felt a little stronger.

By the time they called me to the studio I was wobbly and going hot and cold, but I was upright and walking and I got through that show as if there was nothing wrong with me.

The only one who had any idea was Shelley Rohde.

'You're not feeling very good are you, Doris?' she said afterwards.

'Oh dear, was I dreadful?' I asked.

'Not at all, it went marvellously,' she said. 'No one else noticed a thing. It's just that we're old friends and I could tell.'

And in fact when I saw a tape of the show afterwards I was relieved to see she was right. I don't look my best I'll admit. I look rather tired and drawn about the eyes and despite the make-up my colour's not good. But I don't think anyone would know that only five minutes before the cameras started rolling I could hardly stand up, let alone make light-hearted conversation.

The mystery bug hadn't finished with me of course and the journey back to London was pretty miserable but I couldn't complain. I'd asked the spirit world for the strength to see me through the show and they'd given me exactly what I'd asked.

People often comment about how frequently I seem to fall ill. Well all I can say is I'm as fed up about it as anyone I can tell you! I can't understand why I seem to be so unlucky in that respect. I can only think it's the spirit world's way of forcing me to slow down when I'm doing too much.

Yet ironically when I appeared on the Wogan show it wasn't me who was ill – it was Terry Wogan!

I was filled with trepidation when I first received the invitation to appear on the show. After all Terry can be a bit, well not sarcastic exactly, but cheeky with his guests and I thought I might be an ideal target. Nevertheless I've always had a soft spot for Terry Wogan. I think he's a gorgeous man and so I couldn't help but agree to go on his show just to get the chance to meet him!

I'd been keeping my fingers and toes crossed that I

wouldn't get a cold or anything before the show and I was in luck. But when I arrived at the studio poor old Terry was all flushed and snuffling and struggling to get through the show despite a nasty bout of 'flu.

He gave me a terrific build up – psychic superstar and goodness knows what else – and then when I walked on he took both my hands in his and kissed my cheek. Well, even at my age it sent shivers up my spine!

'Terry,' I said when we sat down, 'before you start I must say that I think you're gorgeous – and I'm old enough to be able to say it!'

He looked at me with that wicked twinkle in his eye but he was very good. He asked me sensible questions and let me answer them. He was tickled to death when I told him about the Sod It Club – the club I'd formed with fellow cancer sufferers with one aim in mind – to say sod it, I'm not going to have it, to the dreaded 'C'.

Terry rocked back in his chair when I explained that Sod It didn't stand for anything, it simply meant sod it.

'I thought it was to do with psychic things!' laughed Terry.

Our interview lasted fourteen minutes I'm told and I enjoyed every second of it. Afterwards we met Terry in the hospitality suite and I realized that he wasn't at all well.

'Why don't you spend the weekend in bed love?' I asked.

'I wish I could, Doris,' said Terry, 'but I've got to work.'

It was a very happy evening. What I particularly liked about the programme was that every guest had a person to look after them throughout. They met you at the door, took you to your dressing-room, then on to make-up. They took you to the set, waited for you to come off and then took you back to the hospitality suite. It really made you feel they were pleased to have you on the programme.

All that and Terry Wogan too!

Chapter 4

The demonstration was going well. I was standing on the
stage at Birmingham Odeon, the audience seemed to be
enjoying themselves and the voices were coming through
thick and fast. Once again, though I'd been tired earlier in
the evening, energy seemed to flow from nowhere and I
was skimming along on a wave of psychic power getting
through more work than I'd have thought possible a few
years ago.

'I'd like to ask a question,' said a neat little lady at the
microphone on the floor below me.

'Go ahead, love,' I told her.

'I'm a widow and I'd like to know if my husband knows I
go to the graveyard every week and that every time I go
there's a little robin. If he's not there when I arrive, he
comes soon afterwards and I take him something to eat.'

I was just about to tell her that I was sure her husband
knew, because our loved ones stay close to us and continue
to take an interest in all our activities, when a scornful
Brummie voice interrupted my thoughts:

'Does she think I've come back as a bloody *bird*?' he
asked.

Well I burst out laughing and when I explained why, the
audience roared. The woman giggled too.

'Yes but I'll tell you something strange,' she said as the
laughter subsided. 'Before he went over we used to discuss
things and I used to say when I go over I'm going to come
back as a bird so I can poop on all the people who pooped

on me in my life!' (Sorry about that but that's exactly what she said.)

Anyway the audience fell about and the atmosphere which was already happy became almost euphoric.

Well I like to share everything that happens with the audience and I thought this story was fun, so the following night when I was appearing at the Odean again, I told them about the robin, only I thought I'd better clean up the punch line a bit.

'... and she said, "I'd like to come back as a bird so that I can **** on all the people who **** on me in my life," ' I quoted.

As I expected, the audience roared, but as the commotion died away I saw a neat figure waving wildly from the front row. It was the little widow.

'I'm here, Doris! I've come again!' she shouted. Then she turned round to the rest of the audience: 'It's quite true. Every word – only I didn't say **** I said "so that I can poop on all the people who *pooped* on me!" '

And of course the theatre practically exploded.

Yes we have a lot of fun one way and another. I think people who come along to demonstrations for the first time are quite surprised. They expect gloom and doom and instead they get jokes and laughter. There are tears as well, of course, but they are tears of joy and emotional release, not sorrow.

Sometimes it's the spirit people who say funny things. During one demonstration I'd been talking to a man on the other side for some time when suddenly he said rather mischievously, 'Mention the mountain goat.'

I thought my powers were going peculiar.

'Mountain goat?' I queried silently. 'Did you say mountain goat?'

The man assured me that he did.

It was one of the unlikeliest messages I've ever been asked to pass on but he was insistent, so feeling a bit of a fool I took a deep breath.

'Well I don't know if this means anything to you, dear,' I said, 'because it sounds strange to me, but he's saying something about a mountain goat.'

To my surprise the girl just fell apart. 'You couldn't have given me better proof,' she said. 'That's what we used to call my father-in-law – the mountain goat!'

Sometimes the messages leave me tongue-tied because they're so forthright. I stand there dithering and stalling while I try to translate them into a tactful phrase. After all I don't want to embarrass anybody.

'Will you tell my daughter to make up her mind,' said one irate mother. 'She's living with two men. One's on nights and one's on days.'

Well how could I say that out loud in front of hundreds of people?

Just as often though, it's the people who're still with us on this side who provide the fun. Not long ago we did a book signing session in a big Midlands store. Afterwards we ran through the rain to the car and as I got in I noticed a very pretty blonde lady beckoning to John.

He went over to see what she wanted and she took his arm and walked him up the car park. The next thing we saw, she had her raincoat open and John had his head inside.

Laurie and I exchanged glances. 'What on *earth* is my husband doing!' I exclaimed.

A few minutes later John came trotting innocently back. 'She's got a cut-out under there!' he said climbing into the car and grinning from ear to ear.

'You dirty old man!' said Laurie.

John looked puzzled. 'Why? What have I done now?'

'We saw you with your head in her coat,' teased Laurie, 'and now you tell us she had a cut out dress.'

'Cut out dress?' said John in surprise. 'She didn't have a cut out dress. She had a cut-out of Doris.'

And he looked so wounded we couldn't help laughing. Back at the bookstall we'd noticed a few large cardboard cut out photographs of me on a stand and this lady had obviously whipped one and smuggled it out of the shop under her coat.

We were still laughing as we swung out of the car park. We rounded a bend and there on a traffic island in the middle of the road was the blonde and a few of her friends, waving this cut-out over their heads and chanting, 'Doris Stokes! Doris Stokes!' just like a football crowd. They waved merrily as we went by and we all waved back.

What they made of our car I don't know. Since Laurie has been looking after us we've taken to travelling long distances in grand style. We often have to travel hundreds of miles to an appointment and in the past when we had to go by train and taxi I've arrived so exhausted by the journey I've not been sure whether I'd have enough energy left to work. Laurie changed all that.

'You can't do your job if you're worn out by travelling,' he said, 'you need to travel in as much comfort as you can.'

And he promptly hired us a grand midnight blue Daimler, complete with TV, telephone and cocktail cabinet for our next long journey. We've used it on our tours ever since. It's the most beautiful car you've ever seen and I feel like the Queen rolling up at theatres in it. I suppose we must look very impressive as we bowl along the motorways, but what other motorists don't see is that we're sitting there with our shoes off and our feet up, eating tuna fish sandwiches, drinking tea out of paper cups and singing our heads off. It's the only way to cover the miles. If we didn't have a laugh and a sing-song we'd go mad.

'You don't drink *tea* out of paper *cups!*' said one horrified friend. 'You should have champagne in a car like that.'

But we'd sooner have tea than champagne any day and we're not interested in the car as a status symbol. It's simply the next most comfortable thing to my armchair at home. Mind you, although I'm not out to impress anyone, I had to laugh at the reaction of an old cousin of mine recently.

We happened to be in my home town of Grantham, and

this cousin I hadn't seen for years, came up. We chatted for a while catching up on old times and when it was time to go he walked out to the car with us.

The sight of the limousine nearly took his breath away.

'Ee, is this what you came in, Dol?' he asked.

I assured him it was.

He walked round it a couple of times, ran a reverent hand over the gleaming bodywork and peered through the window for a look at the palatial interior.

'I say, Dol, is that a TV you've got in there?'

I nodded.

'And is that a telephone?'

I had to agree that it was.

The information took a second or two to sink in and even then he clearly found it difficult to believe.

'Ee,' he said at last, shaking his head, 'bloody 'ell you could live in there!'

Yes the last few years have brought a great deal of fun but it wouldn't be true to say the growing fuss hasn't brought problems as well. I find the letters very worrying. Every week I get literally hundreds of letters. Soon after we moved to our new house I breathed a sigh of relief because there had been no mail that morning. But I spoke too soon. Minutes later there was a knock at the door. It was the post girl.

'Could I possibly have a drink of water,' she said, 'I've almost finished then I'm going home for the pram.'

The pram? I thought. Surely she wasn't going to bring a baby out in this weather. It was bitterly cold and there was a freezing wind.

'Oh no,' she said, 'it's for your post. There's so much I can't carry it all so I'm going to put it in the pram and wheel it round.'

You can see the problem. I get pram loads of mail every day. If I spent each day doing nothing but answering letters I still wouldn't finish them and the next morning there would be another batch. It's impossible to deal with.

What's more, the letters themselves are heartrending. Each has a tragic story. Every correspondent starts by saying they know I'm very busy and that I can't see everyone and then goes on to explain why they should be a special case. The trouble is, I know everyone's a special case but I can't see everyone.

Sometimes it makes me despair. There's so much sadness out there and I want to help but I feel as if I'm trying to empty the ocean with a tea cup.

Even more of a worry are the people who get fed up with waiting for a reply and come calling instead. A couple of weeks ago I had my first day off in two months. It was a wonderful luxury. Our glamorous hire car might seem like the height of good living to some people, but for me there is no greater luxury than sitting at home with absolutely nothing to do.

Right, I thought, that morning. I'm not going to do a thing. I'm not going to talk to anyone, tune in to anyone, I'm not even going to open a letter. I'll just sit in my chair and watch a bit of television. But I must have been more exhausted than I knew, because no sooner had the programme started than I fell asleep. John woke me up with a sandwich at lunch time but afterwards I drifted off again.

All around me I was vaguely aware of the sounds of the house, but they could have been a thousand miles away. Then at some point in the afternoon I heard a bell ringing.

'Oh, it's the phone,' I thought sleepily. 'John'll get it.'

But it wasn't the phone, it was the front door and I was abruptly woken by John leading a complete stranger into the room.

'I thought you'd better see her, love,' he said. 'She's come a long way.'

Apparently this lady had set out from Hertford early that morning determined to find me despite the fact she didn't have my address. She'd read in the books that I lived in some disabled ex-servicemen's flats and she was under the impression they were in the Kensington area, so she went to Kensington and walked the streets looking for the flats and asking if anyone knew of them.

At last a newsagent told her he thought the place she was looking for might be in Fulham and he told her which bus to get because Fulham is quite a distance from Kensington. But the lady was too impatient to wait for a bus. She ended up walking all the way to Fulham and after more tramping about she found the flats. Now there are a great many flats in the complex where we used to live. There are several long blocks, each block four storeys high, but undaunted, she started knocking on doors until she stumbled across one of the three people who knew my new address and persuaded them to give it to her. Then she caught two trains and walked another fair step, until she reached my door.

What could I do? I was not at all pleased, but after such a long journey I felt I had to give the poor woman a cup of tea. The one thing I wouldn't do though was give her a sitting. There was a time when under similar circumstances I'd have relented but not any more. Now I realize that it wouldn't be fair to all those people patiently and politely waiting, some of them for two years, on the waiting list. So I chatted to this lady, gave her tea and let her phone her family because they'd had no idea what she was up to and she'd be very late home and then I gently explained that we were about to start our supper and she would have to go.

I felt a big guilty about it afterwards but also annoyed. Why should someone make me feel guilty about having a day off? It wasn't fair. Even vicars are allowed time off. I'm sixty-five years old now and surely I'm entitled to a rest now and then.

The great ocean of grief all around is just too much for me to handle so I've had to be sensible. Now I concentrate on mass demonstrations because I can give a lot of people a little comfort in the time it used to take me to comfort one. As for private sittings, I still do a few, but I let the spirit world guide me. They let me know which people are most in need of help which people I must see. Sometimes I'm going through a sack of mail and one letter will literally leap into my hand. Occasionally the feeling of urgency is so strong that I immediately drop what I'm doing and phone the sender right away, although it's not always clear to me why speed is so important. Sometimes the sender will be a distraught mother almost out of her mind with grief over a lost child, but other cases are less straightforward.

One morning I was sifting through the mail as usual when a small envelope addressed in a round childish hand almost flew into my lap. It was from a sixteen-year-old girl in Scotland who'd recently lost her much loved Nanna. A sad but not unusual story you might think but there was more to it than that. From the other side there was a great rush of urgency and I got the impression of a woman trying to push me to the phone.

I looked at the signature on the letter. The girl's name was Cheryl and she obviously needed help. I put down the rest of my postbag and dialled the number she'd printed beneath her address.

Cheryl herself answered the phone and once she'd got over the surprise, the sad story came pouring out. Brought up chiefly by her grandmother she'd been devastated when the old lady died. Now she was unhappy at home. She didn't get on with her step-father and to comfort herself she'd started eating vast amounts of food.

'She always was a big girl,' said a strong Scots voice in my other ear, 'but now she's gone up to nineteen stone and she won't go to school. She won't leave the house. It's such a waste.'

Cheryl admitted it was true. 'I can't go to school. The other kids laugh at me because I'm so fat,' and she started to cry.

I realized that if something wasn't done quickly there could be another tragedy.

'Now, Cheryl, listen to me,' I said, 'you're making your Nan very unhappy. She's here now and she's telling me you're such a beautiful child she can't bear to see you letting yourself go. If only you'd lose some weight and make yourself smart, everyone would want to know you and you wouldn't want to hide away at home.'

'If you'd just stop buying sweets and biscuits and nibbled at an apple or a carrot when you were hungry you'd soon lose weight. If you do that, I promise you that before the year's over you'll be having a wonderful time. You're only sixteen for goodness sake. Your Nanna wants to be a great-grandmother and she's not going to do that if you're shut up in the house ...'

Cheryl sniffed and sobbed but eventually she agreed to try a diet.

'It's not easy, Cheryl,' I said, 'I've got thyroid trouble and I'm sixty-five and I have to be really strong with myself or I'd be twenty-one stone. But your Nanna says there's nothing physically wrong with you – it's just insecurity. So if you could just stick to a diet for a few months you'd see the weight roll off.'

Cheryl promised to do her best and I gave her my phone number so that she could ring me with progress reports or just for a chat if she felt desperate.

'And remember, Cheryl,' I added at the end of the conversation, 'when things get difficult just put out your hand and your Nanna will be there to help you. She's not far away and she's watching over you.'

Afterwards I could only pray that I'd got through to that poor child and helped her back on the path to a normal life. The spirit world had done their bit, I'd done mine, and now it was up to Cheryl to find the strength to pick up the pieces.

Occasionally, however, my post bag brings me news of even more disturbing matters. Another of the letters that forced itself to my attention contained a very alarming story. It was from a woman whose hotel business was almost ruined despite the 'advice' I'd been giving her for so long through a 'mutual friend'. She wanted to thank me for the work I'd done on her behalf, but she'd now sadly come to the conclusion that the business was beyond redemption.

Horrified, I skimmed through the letter again. I had never heard of this lady or her hotel and the name of our 'mutual friend' meant absolutely nothing to me. What on earth was going on? This time I didn't need the spirit world to prompt me. I was instantly on the phone.

'Oh thank goodness you phoned,' said this poor woman when I explained who I was and that I was quite mystified by the whole thing. 'It was my daughter who suspected there was something wrong. She read your books and then she read your predictions and she said you know Mum these sound as if they were written by two different people. There's just no comparison.'

'Predictions?' I asked more alarmed than ever. 'What predictions? I don't make predictions I'm not a fortune teller.'

'Oh yes this friend says she knows you and that she regularly visits you to discuss people's problems and that you make predictions about what they have to do. Just a minute, I'll read you some.'

She went away and came back with a piece of paper.

'It says here, "I, Doris Stokes, do hereby declare ..."' and she went on to read out the worst load of rubbish I've ever heard. It included instructions to sweep up the leaves from the hotel yard, put them in a jar and keep them in the bathroom. This utter nonsense was apparently signed with my name and these so called messages from me had been arriving almost every month for some time.

'I feel such a fool now,' said the poor woman, 'but she was so plausible. She described you and your home. She even said things like, "d'you like my dress? Doris Stokes gave me this." We followed all her instructions thinking they came from you and now we're just about ruined.'

I was appalled. 'But I've never met this woman in my life,' I said. 'She's probably seen me and my flat on television or in pictures.'

There was little I could do to help save their business. I could only sympathize and suggest they throw away the dead leaves in the bathroom and anything else I was supposed to have instructed them to collect. Finally I asked for the address and telephone number of our 'mutual friend'. She must be stopped. How could people be so wicked? And how many other people was she ruining in my name?

Furiously I dialled the number and got through right away. My 'old friend' sounded quite taken aback to hear from me.

'Now look,' I said, 'I've never met you, I've never spoken to you and you've never been to my home.'

'Eh. Well. No. But we have met,' said the woman faintly.

'Where?' I demanded, 'I don't recall ever meeting you.'

'We met in a previous life,' she insisted, but I think it sounded ridiculous even to her.

Well I'm afraid I told her what I thought of her. I told her that her friend would probably lose the hotel and that what she'd done was quite wicked.

'And how many other people have you been sending predictions to?'

She hesitated. 'Eh, well, not many. I only do it to comfort them you know. I didn't mean any harm.'

I was too angry to think straight at that, so I brought the conversation to an end intending to ring back when I'd cooled down. From then on, however, the phone was permanently engaged. In the end I had to be content with sending a strongly worded solicitor's letter forbidding her to pass on any more messages in my name.

The lengths people will go to and the nonsense they are prepared to come out with constantly amazes me. Why they do it I can't imagine. Perhaps they're trying to get attention, perhaps they've got problems, but whatever the reason they've got no right to take advantage of gullible people looking for help.

A newspaper rang me recently to ask if I could help with a reader's query. This woman had written in to say that her husband had gone missing and she'd consulted a medium to find out if he was dead or alive. The medium had taken her money and told her that the husband was definitely on the other side but that he couldn't talk to her because he'd been killed by a blow to the head and he was delirious. The newspaper wanted to know if this was possible! Now I ask you? It would be funny if it wasn't so serious.

Another woman sent me a tape recording of a sitting she'd had with a so called medium who had spent most of the time singing hymns.

'I was so upset and felt so dreadful after that sitting,' she wrote, 'that I felt like coming out and throwing myself under a bus.'

As I read the letter I heard the name Mark, very clearly, so I phoned her straight away.

'I'm so sorry you had such a bad experience,' I said, 'but as I was reading your letter I heard the name Mark and I knew it was important.'

'Yes, that's right. That's what I was waiting for. Mark's my son.'

'Well, love, he took himself over didn't he,' I said because Mark had just told me he was very ashamed of what he'd done.

'Yes he did,' she admitted in astonishment.

'And he tells me he did it away from this country.'

'Yes.'

'Tell them I'm sorry,' Mark begged me, 'I hadn't been married very long.'

'Only four months,' sobbed his mother, but despite the overwhelming emotion she was pleased. 'That's all I wanted,' she said. 'That's why I went to a medium in the first place. I didn't want to bother you because I know you're busy, but I felt so dreadful after this other sitting. It was awful. All I wanted to do was get out. I felt sick.'

She was quite content with the few scraps I was able to give her but I felt very sad that she'd been treated so badly, especially by a person who called herself a medium.

Sometimes I just don't understand people at all.

I suppose the most depressing reading of all though, comes through the letter box every morning in the shape of the newspaper. Is it just my imagination or is the news getting worse? Every day people seem to think of new and more horrible ways of being nasty to each other. But at least now I have a little money behind me I sometimes get the chance to put right, in a very small way, a few wrongs.

Some months ago I was upset to read about a poor little boy who was set upon by louts who smashed his expensive hearing aid. How they could be so cruel to a child who has enough problems to contend with anyway. I don't know, and my heart went out to the little boy. He must be so confused and disillusioned with life.

Impulsively I sat down and wrote him a note. I promised to buy him a new hearing aid and added: 'Just to tell you there aren't all nasty people in the world – there are some nice people too, people who love you and want you to be happy.'

I couldn't undo the pain and misery he'd gone through but perhaps I could cheer him up a little, and help restore his faith in human nature.

It's worth all the hard work and tiring journeys to be able to make little gestures like these and I know my dad would be pleased. As he used to say to me when I was a girl: 'If you want to keep love, Dol, you have to give it away.'

Chapter 5

Diana Dors was unmissable. There she was, large but glamorous in a sleeveless black dress, her blonde hair falling round her shoulders, her long, long, eyelashes almost brushing the glass in her hand and her infectious laugh brightening everybody in the room. The place was packed and all the guests had dressed up, yet it was Diana you noticed. The slender figure of the fifties sex symbol might have disappeared for ever but Diana was still every inch a star.

John and I were a bit over-awed to tell the truth, so we just said a polite hello as we passed and moved on to mingle with the other guests. It was certainly a splendid do. Robert Maxwell who owns the company which publishes my books had invited all his authors to a reception at his beautiful home, Headington Hill Hall near Oxford. It was a magnificent house, built like a castle with a massive staircase and a minstrel gallery, and the Maxwells had gone to endless trouble over the arrangements. A toastmaster announced the guests as they entered the solid oak door; there were waiters circulating with trays of champagne and wine and there was a bar for those who wanted something different. Outside there were two bands playing, one by the swimming pool and one by the marquee and the buffet lunch, spread out on huge tables, was quite dazzling.

Feeling slightly overwhelmed by it all, John and I decided that the first thing we'd better do was cool down with a drink and since neither of us touches alcohol we had to make our excuses to the waiters and I went up to the bar for fruit juice.

'Two orange juices, please,' I said and as two glasses tinkling with ice appeared on the bar a deep voice at my shoulder said, 'Are you on the wagon too?'

I looked round. It was Diana's husband, Alan Lake. 'No, it's just that we can't drink,' I explained. 'It doesn't agree with us.'

But Alan wasn't listening. He was staring at me as if he couldn't quite place the face. Then his frown disappeared.

'You're Doris Stokes, aren't you! I did enjoy your book. Do come and meet Diana.'

And that was how John and I became friends with Alan and Diana. We never did get around to visiting each other's homes, but we bumped into each other at functions and TV stations and when we heard that Di had cancer, the dreaded C as we called it, I rang her regularly.

Diana was a great fighter and at first it looked as if she'd won. As anyone who's had cancer knows, you have to keep going back for check-ups and no matter how healthy you feel, it's a worrying business. It can easily play on your mind and so to boost our morale at these difficult times, Diana and a couple of other friends and fellow sufferers, Julie Goodyear, the actress from Coronation Street, Pat Seed, who wrote the lovely book *One Day At A Time*, and I formed the Sod It Club. We used to get on the phone, have a good laugh and advise each other to say: 'Sod it! I'm not going to have it!' I don't know whether, medically speaking, laughter and defiance is the best way to react to the dreaded C, but it certainly made the four of us feel a lot better. In the nerve-racking days that surrounded the regular check-ups and tests those phone calls were like a tonic.

Diana seemed to blossom again. She went on a diet, exercised every day and swam in her pool and the pounds fell off. I bumped into her at TV AM one morning towards the end of her diet and I could hardly believe my eyes. Glamorous as ever, she was half her former size and she looked sensational.

'You make me want to spit!' I joked when I saw her because we'd both been fighting a losing battle with our weight for months and now she put me to shame.

Diana laughed, delighted. 'You're never too old, Doris! You're always telling me that! You could do it too if you tried.'

'I never stop trying!' I wailed. 'And look where it gets me!'

They were a devoted couple, Alan and Di. They were always together. At parties and receptions they didn't split up and talk to people separately the way some couples do. They preferred to move round as a pair, Alan was dark and handsome with the cravat he always wore, and Di bubbly and full of fun, the silvery blonde hair bouncing when she laughed.

They'd had their problems, of course. Alan was an alcoholic and at the height of his illness he became very violent but Di stood by him.

'They always turn on the one they love,' she said and knowing that she stayed and helped him to beat his addiction. She was a very wise lady. Diana was the strong one in that partnership and, as the old saying goes, she really was his mother, lover, friend and wife. For his part, Alan worshipped her.

The last time I saw Di was at Robert Maxwell's. The annual reception had come round again and it was beginning to be a regular date in our diaries. There was no sign of the Lakes when we walked in this time, but as we loaded our plates at the buffet table they appeared.

Alan, charming as ever, was at my side in an instant to help me to the food.

'Caviar, darling?' he asked lifting a dish of what looked like miniature black ball-bearings.

'Oh no thank you, I don't like it,' I said.

He replaced the dish and tried another, 'Smoked salmon?'

'Oh no thank you, I don't like it,' I said again and at my other side Diana roared with laughter.

'It's no good, Alan. Doris and John only have cold chicken and a tomato!'

And I had to laugh because she was right. With all that rich food to choose from John and I invariably came away with just a bit of chicken and salad on our plates and possibly a bread roll to keep it company. The shame of it is that all this grand living has come too late for us. We'd never had the chance before to get used to caviar and smoked salmon and we're too old now to get started on that sort of thing. Apart from not liking the taste, we'd probably end up with dreadful indigestion!

Lunch was as merry as ever but for the first time I felt uneasy about Diana. She looked absolutely beautiful and yet something seemed to have happened to the figure she'd dieted so long to achieve. Her tummy looked enormous. Of course Diana enjoyed her food as much as the next woman but there was something about her shape that wasn't quite right. It didn't look as if she'd been on an eating spree, it seemed more serious than that.

As we moved away I said to John, 'There's something the matter with Di, I'm sure of it.'

Shortly afterwards we heard she'd gone into hospital with a stomach complaint. I was on tour at the time and dashing about from place to place with scarcely time to draw breath but between appointments I phoned the Lakes' home in Berkshire to find out where she was, and sent flowers to the hospital.

Then we were whirling off to the next town and by the time I caught up with the news, Diana was back home. Thank goodness, I thought to myself. It was a false alarm.

The weeks passed and then came the day I discovered I'd have to go into hospital again to have another lump removed. Of course I feared the worst the way you always do and I longed to talk to someone who'd understand. I didn't know if Diana was away or not but I rang her home on the off chance and she answered.

'Oh Diana, I'm so glad I caught you ...' I said and soon I was pouring out all my troubles.

Diana was wonderful. She listened sympathetically to all my worries and when I'd finished she said, 'Oh sod it, kid. Just say you're not going to have it!'

And I couldn't help laughing. Thank goodness for the Sod It Club. And all the time I was moaning on to Di she knew that she herself was going to have to go back into hospital and the chances didn't look good – and she never said a word. What a wonderful lady.

My little operation was over quite quickly and I was up and on the road again when I picked up the paper one day and saw that Diana was back in hospital. I'd been feeling quite cheerful until that moment, but suddenly depression swept over me.

'Look at this, John,' I said pointing at the story, 'I think she's going to have a job to make it this time.'

There wasn't a moment to lose. I rang the hospital and after a short delay Alan came to the phone. They'd operated, he said but Di was too weak to talk at the moment. A cold feeling settled lower and lower in my stomach.

'We're thinking of you both, Alan, and praying for you,' I told him but as I put the receiver down I knew.

'I have an awful feeling about Di,' I told John, 'I don't think she's going to make it.'

A couple of days later we were having breakfast in our hotel room when the news came on the radio that Diana had passed. Even when you're expecting it the actual announcement is always a shock and my heart went out to poor Alan. I would miss Diana, of course, but I was relieved for her sake that it was over so quickly and she didn't have to suffer. She would be happy now with her family and her new life on the other side. It was Alan who needed help and sympathy. How was he going to manage without her, I wondered? She had been his crutch in life. Would he find the strength to stand alone?

I can't honestly say that I was seriously afraid for Alan. I was worried about him of course and I felt desperately sorry for him but it didn't cross my mind that he might be suicidal. He and Diana were devoted to their fifteen-year-old son, Jason, and I never dreamed that Alan's despair would reach such a pitch that his need for Diana would over-ride his fatherly instincts. He was a good father and my first thought was thank goodness for Jason, he'll be the saving of his dad.

Not long after the announcement, Diana came through to me quite spontaneously, 'Tell Alan I'm only a whisper away,' she murmured in my ear, 'and that Minnie met me.'

Her voice was faint because she hadn't been over very long and it was difficult for her to communicate, but as always her concern for Alan was so great she felt she had to pass on some words of comfort.

I rang Alan immediately. There was a long pause. 'He's not taking any calls at the moment, he's too upset,' said the housekeeper, 'but seeing as it's you, Doris, I'll tell him you're on the line.'

The seconds ticked by and at last a distraught Alan came to the phone. 'Alan, I don't know what to say. There's nothing I can say to you,' I said gently, 'except, never forget, she's only a whisper away. I've spoken to her and she wanted you to know that Minnie met her.'

'Minnie's my mother,' he said brokenly, but he seemed relieved to know that Diana was all right and she hadn't been alone.

I didn't go to the funeral. I try to avoid conventional funerals whenever I can because spiritualists believe that a funeral should be, as far as possible, a happy occasion, when you celebrate the fact that the person who's passed on has taken his 'promotion' as we call it, and is free at last of all pain and suffering.

So I didn't go to the funeral but afterwards I phoned Alan every week, on Sunday mornings when he came back from Mass, to give him what support I could. The months went by and my life became ever more hectic, yet somewhere at the back of my mind it registered that Alan wasn't recovering from his grief the way he should. He put on an act when he first picked up the phone, but good actor though he was you could tell. Then suddenly he'd break down and the phone would go dead.

To be honest I don't think anyone could have prevented the tragedy. A lot of Alan's friends blamed themselves for not realizing how ill he'd become and I felt guilty myself because the Sunday before it happened I hadn't phoned him. It was one of those things you regret for ever. I've already mentioned the bad back that plagued me that summer and by this stage it had reached such a pitch that the doctor decided to send me to hospital to have it looked at.

I was going in the next day and that Sunday I was in agony, but struggling to cook lunch, get my case packed and leave everything organized for John and Terry. All day I kept thinking I must ring Alan, I must ring Alan, but somehow I didn't get round to it. In hospital the next day it was the same. I'd taken the phone number with me and I fully intended to make the call but I was wheeled here, there and everywhere for tests. There were consultations with doctors, a stream of visitors and phone calls and all at once it was bedtime and I hadn't phoned Alan.

'Oh well, I'll definitely phone him tomorrow,' I said to myself. But Tuesday was the same.

Then on Wednesday, John switched on the television in my room just in case there was something on and then left it babbling to itself the way he often does. No one was taking much notice, when suddenly there came a news bulletin that stopped me in my tracks. Alan Lake had shot himself that morning at his Berkshire home.

I felt absolutely sick. If only I'd made that call – perhaps things would have been different. Why hadn't I paid more attention to that nagging in my mind? It was so persistent I recognized it now as the spirit world's attempt to alert me to Alan's plight but I was so bogged down in my own problems I couldn't see it at the time. And what would happen to poor Jason? The more I thought of him the worse I felt. Poor boy to have lost both his parents so tragically and in such a short space of time.

It went round and round in my mind and by the end of the day I was in a right old tangle and inclined to blame myself. Fortunately, Ramanov came that night to talk some sense into me.

'Don't worry yourself, child, about things that can't be changed,' he said when I'd all but given up hope of getting to sleep. 'It is a waste of energy. There was nothing you could have done. It would have made no difference in the end, whether you made that phone call or not. Learn from this and go forward. Don't look back.'

And of course he was right, as I was to learn from Alan himself later.

It's strange how one chance meeting on a summer's day can lead to so many others. Just before Christmas I was invited by *Woman's Own* to their special Children of Courage service at Westminster Abbey and who should I bump into but Jason.

He was a beautiful child. Very like Diana but with light brown hair rather than blonde, yet when he moved you could see Alan in him.

After the service he came up to me and I noticed that his shirt collar was all frayed and I thought his mum would go mad if she saw it. But that's what kids are like. They have their favourite clothes and they won't stop wearing them.

'I'm going to America, Doris,' said Jason, 'what d'you think?' He had a stepbrother in America from an earlier marriage of Diana's.

'Well, love, you go,' I said, 'and see if you feel happy living with Gary. But if you don't, come back because there are plenty of people here who'd like to give you a home.'

I was very impressed with Jason. The sadness was there at the back of his eyes but he was so brave and so mature you'd have thought he was nineteen rather than fifteen. He wasn't at all bitter against his father as some boys might have been.

'I was angry at first,' he admitted with that steady gaze so like Diana's, 'but I don't blame Dad now. He was hopeless without Mum.' And then he was a child again needing reassurance. 'They are still with me, aren't they, Doris?'

'They are,' I said firmly, 'and what's more your Mum in particular is watching over you and she's going to be helping you every step of the way.'

And suddenly over the hub-bub around us Diana's voice came chiming in. 'You'd better believe it.'

My contact with the Lake family didn't end when Jason went to America, however. Not long afterwards, to my amazement, I received a phone call from comedian Freddie Starr. Apparently Alan Lake had been his best friend and ever since the tragic suicide he'd been haunted by the feeling that Alan was trying to get in touch with him. Could I possibly help?

I looked through my diary doubtfully. It was booked up solid for months ahead. The only spaces occurred on Sundays, my day off. Now, as I've said, my Sundays off are precious to me. I can't do my job properly unless I have free time to recharge my batteries and of course I like some time at home with my family like everybody else.

Yet Alan and Diana were good friends to me. Diana in particular had always spared the time to listen and to cheer me up when I needed the support of the Sod It Club. If they were really trying to get through to Freddie and they needed my help then surely I owed it to them to see him. I picked up my pen.

'Well, Freddie,' I said, 'I'm afraid I only have Sundays free.'

'That's all right I can make Sundays,' said Freddie writing down the address. 'Now which garden can I land the helicopter in?'

I thought I was hearing things. 'Did you say helicopter?'

'Yes,' said Freddie, 'I was going to pop across in my helicopter.'

I laughed. 'Freddie, where d'you think I live? There's no room to land a helicopter in my pocket handkerchief garden. I'm afraid you'll have to come by car.'

But Freddie was so keen to set his mind at rest that the inconvenience didn't bother him. I'll let him explain for himself.

'Alan was my best friend and ever since he died I've had this feeling that he was still close to me. It was as if he'd left something unfinished between us and there was something he wanted to say to me. I had this feeling all the time but most strongly of all when I passed the graveyard where he was buried. It was like a magnet pulling me to the grave.

'Once I stopped the car at three o'clock in the morning and got out and went to the grave because it felt as if he was calling me. Yet no matter how hard I tried I couldn't hear what he was saying. It had been like that for months ever since the day he died, but after I found myself at the grave at three o'clock in the morning I knew I was going to have to do something.

'The next day I phoned Doris.'

Everyone thinks that Freddie Starr is just a zany comedian without a care in the world, but in fact he's a very sensitive, loving man. Just before he died Alan visited Freddie's home and when he left, he said goodbye and walked away through a garden gate. Freddie never saw him again and from that moment on he couldn't bear to look at that garden gate. It caused him so much pain that in the end he had it bricked up.

But, of course, before our first meeting I didn't know how nice Freddie was and I was a little apprehensive. I didn't know what to expect. Yet at four o'clock on that Sunday afternoon there was a knock at the door and in walked a compact, slimly built man with blond hair and the most beautiful blue eyes I've ever seen on a man. I've heard it said that some comedians are really very serious men and not at all funny off stage. Well I don't know whether that's true or not, but all I can say is that Freddie had us in stitches.

I didn't realize it then but he's a brilliant ventriloquist and hardly had he sat down when the bottles of drink we keep on the trolley for visitors began to talk. I glanced up in surprise and I distinctly heard a bottle of rum say:

'I don't need your ear, Doris, I'm a spirit!'

Well! It was definitely not a message from the other side, that was certain, but had I finally flipped as my mother always predicted? I looked round anxiously to see if the others had heard it too and then I noticed the mischief sparkling in Freddie's eyes.

'Freddie!' I gasped. 'It's you!'

'I'm a spirit, I'm a spirit!' insisted the rum while Freddie sat motionless, his lips not moving. But then he burst our laughing and gave the game away. Undaunted the other bottles started chattering too, and John and I laughed till we had to beg Freddie to stop because we were aching so much.

But of course Freddie had come for a sitting so the afternoon wasn't just confined to fun. There was work to be done too. Yet the work wasn't difficult because Alan was there immediately I tuned in. Freddie was right. Alan was anxious to talk to him. He wanted to explain to his old friend why he'd felt driven to take his own life and to reassure Freddie that nothing could have prevented it.

'It's Alan, darling!' he said straight away as soon as I began concentrating and his voice was as deep and rich as I remembered it. 'Tell Freddie about the black cravat. He was looking at the black cravat.'

I was puzzled but then I'm often puzzled by things the spirit people tell me so I just passed the message on to Freddie.

He looked blank at first but then he smiled. 'Last night I got Alan's photo album out and I was looking at a picture of me and Alan together,' he said. 'I noticed that Alan was wearing the black cravat that he wore all the time after Diana's death.'

'Well Alan must have been with you last night, love,' I said.

'Can he hear me now?' asked Freddie.

'Of course he can.'

'Right, Alan,' said Freddie to a point over my shoulder. 'I was so mad at you for what you did. Did you know that? I was so bloody annoyed.'

. 'Look, Freddie, speak truthfully,' said Alan, 'if you'd been in the same boat and it had been Sandy you'd lost – could you have gone on?'

Tears sprang into Freddie's eyes and he looked at the floor. 'No, I don't think I could.'

'I hadn't planned to do it,' Alan went on, 'but I saw no future without Di. I never went back to the sauce (drink) but I'd started smoking again and I was so depressed.'

Then despite my protests he insisted on telling me what happened. Apparently out of the blue one morning he'd just decided he'd had enough. He didn't want to go on any longer. He just couldn't face it. He got his gun, rested the butt on the floor between his legs, leaned over, put the end of the barrel in his mouth and pulled the trigger.

'I felt a pain in my jaw, then blood came into my throat and that was it,' said Alan.

He told Freddie that since then the family Cadillac had been sold but the red car he used to drive was still there.

'We're together now,' he went on, 'but I got a tongue-lashing from Diana when I first got here. She was furious about Jason.'

Then there was a weakening in the vibration and a woman's voice cut in. It was Diana.

'I was so angry,' she spluttered, 'I was livid. What was he thinking of leaving Jason like that? I told him he was a selfish bastard. After all I had no choice, but *he* did. But then I realized that Jason's probably better off this way.

Alan's so weak he might have gone back on the drink and that would have been worse for Jason in the long run. Now at least he can remember his father as he was.'

And then she added, woman to woman, just the way she used to, 'I don't know. I'm still mothering him. I was mothering him then and I'm mothering him now, but mind, I love him.'

Other voices were crowding in now and I got an impression of a whole group of people jostling and eager to talk to Freddie.

'I'm Richard but everyone calls me Dick,' said a man loudly.

'That's my father,' said Freddie.

'Will you ask him to forgive me,' said Dick. 'He thought I didn't love him because I wasn't very demonstrative but I did. The trouble was I could never work out whether our Freddie was mental or whether he was a genius.'

Freddie laughed. 'Well I'll settle for half of that. I'm a mental genius!'

Dick went on to mention Jack, Freddie's stepfather and to say how pleased he was that Freddie's mother had married again and to tell her not to feel guilty about it because he wanted her to be happy. He also mentioned Muriel.

'That's my Auntie Muriel,' said Freddie in surprise, 'I've not seen Auntie Muriel for about twenty-five years.'

'Well Dick says that Muriel's been in hospital recently,' I said.

Freddie shook his head. 'I wouldn't know. I've not seen her for so long.'

But in fact Freddie checked with his mother the next day and it turned out that Auntie Muriel had had an operation only the month before to improve her hearing.

Dick also remarked that he enjoyed Freddie's shows and that he'd been with him to Barbados and to Canada.

'I hope he paid!' said Freddie.

Then, towards the end when the power was failing, Alan

came back to say he was sorry for what he'd done and to thank Freddie for looking after Jason.

Afterwards, although it had been lovely to talk to Alan and Diana again, I felt drained. It had been an emotional sitting particularly since they were personal friends, and Freddie seemed to sense my fatigue. He sat on the rug by the fire and talked quietly.

'What d'you think God is, Doris?' he asked suddenly.

It was a big question but he was quite sincere.

'Well I can't visualize God as a person,' I said. 'To me he is a divine power. That's the only way I can put it in words.'

Freddie was silent for a moment then he said. 'You know they spell it wrong. It shouldn't be G-O-D. It should be G-O-O-D because everything good is God.'

I thought that was beautiful.

In all Freddie stayed five hours. Although he arrived at four o'clock with the intention of staying half an hour or so, he didn't leave until nine o'clock at night. And being Freddie, the serious mood soon passed and it wasn't long before he had John and I in fits of laughter again. I don't think we've laughed so much in years. Freddie certainly did us more good than any medicine the doctor could prescribe.

As he was leaving, he put his arms round me and gave me a big hug.

'I'm going to give you a gift,' he said, blue eyes sparkling in that teasing way he has.

'Oh how lovely,' I said. I adore flowers and people often give me flowers after a sitting. Thanks to my sitters the house is always filled with the scent of fresh flowers.

'Yes,' Freddie went on, 'I'm going to give you a race horse.'

I nearly fell out of my chair, the placid response strangled somewhere in the back of my throat.

'A race horse?' I gasped half choking. 'Freddie, you're winding me up.'

'No I'm not,' said Freddie, his face going serious again.

'We've just had two foals born and I'd like to give you one. I'll keep it at my place for two years then you can choose your colours and put it with a trainer.'

I was overwhelmed and to tell the truth I couldn't believe he was serious. I mean whoever heard of an old lady in a London semi owning a race horse?

Yet Freddie meant it – as I discovered a few weeks later when he invited us over to see the foal.

It was a wet and windy Sunday morning, the sort of day when you look at the weather and wonder in a depressed way if spring is ever going to come. Yet for once the weather didn't bother me. I was as excited as a child on Christmas morning about meeting my foal. Although I must admit I was a little nervous too because I've always been a bit frightened of horses.

We splashed for miles through the dripping Berkshire lanes and at last turned in through a neat brick entrance. On either side all I could see were paddocks with horses and acres of lawn and trees. The drive seemed to go on for ever, and then suddenly there was a beautiful mansion in front of us and Freddie waving at the door.

He led us through into the hall and before I'd even unbuttoned my coat, two small blonde heads came charging towards me.

'Hello, Doris!' cried the little girl throwing her arms around me. This was Donna aged nine.

'Hello, Doris!' cried the little boy, Jodie aged five, doing the same.

They were lovely children. They'd just come back from a holiday in Spain so they had healthy brown faces and their father's bright blue eyes that shone even bluer against their tanned skin.

We sat down for a cup of tea, enlivened by Jodie's display of break dancing, then we all put on wellington boots and tramped up to the stables to meet my foal.

Jodie danced at my side as we squelched through the mud.

'I've got a horse too,' he told me, 'but not as big as yours, Doris.'

'Is my horse big?' I asked, alarmed, 'I thought it was only a baby.'

'Oh yes,' said Jodie. 'Bigger than mine.'

And in fact the horse *was* larger than I'd expected. When Freddie had said it was a foal, I'd imagined a tiny, fragile little creature staggering after its mother on matchstick legs, but the animal the groom led out into the stable yard was as tall as me. Nevertheless he was obviously very young, and nervous, and quite lovely. His coat was a beautiful reddish brown, he had a white diamond on his forehead and one white sock and when I stretched out my hand to stroke him, he put a nose into my palm that was as soft as velvet.

'Aren't you *lovely*!' I told him, 'I'm going to call you Stoksie.'

Freddie walked him round to calm him and then turned him loose into a paddock to play. He was a joy to watch. He galloped about revelling in the grass and the rain and kicking up his heels like a spring lamb.

'Freddie, he's the most beautiful gift,' I cried in delight. 'I love him.'

But the fun wasn't over. Freddie and his wife Sandy went to a great deal of trouble to give us a lovely day. I'd told Freddie not to bother about organizing a lunch.

'Sandy doesn't want to be working on a Sunday,' I said, 'a sandwich will do.'

But Sandy had laid out a delicious spread that included *vol-au-vents* and smoked salmon and must have involved as much work as a roast dinner.

Afterwards Freddie showed me the house. It was absolutely magnificent. The guest bedrooms alone were like hotel suites and one of them came complete with bed, bathroom, sofa, piano, TV and video. Freddie's own personal bathroom was all red and gold and columns and things like some impossibly luxurious picture in a glossy magazine, and his bedroom was lined in red pleated silk. I'd never seen anything like it. It really did take my breath away.

'You should have all this, the work you do, Doris,' said Freddie as he led me back downstairs again.

I shook my head. 'Freddie, it would scare me to death,' I told him and it would too. I'm grateful for my three-bedroom semi. I couldn't cope with a grand mansion.

Back in the sitting-room little Jodie was jumping about and exchanging meaningful glances with his father.

'Can we start now, Dad? Is it time?' he kept whispering.

Freddie evidently decided it was because we were requested to take seats and father and son disappeared to return a moment later with guitars. There they stood, father and son, Freddie with his guitar and beside him like a miniature replica, Jodie with his tiny guitar. Then Freddie started playing and singing and Jodie strummed away at one chord. Freddie went down on one knee and Jodie went down on one knee and all the time the little lad kept looking up at his father to check he was doing the right thing.

We all clapped heartily at the end of the performance, but Jodie hadn't finished yet. His tiny drum kit stood in the corner and when the applause died away there was an official announcement.

'Ladies and gentlemen, there will now be a cabaret in honour of Doris, performed by Jodie Starr.'

Grinning eagerly, Jodie bounded to his drums and gave us a very spirited rendering of something modern. I don't know what it was but it was very good and afterwards Jodie jumped down and gave a solemn bow and we all had to clap, then he ran off through the kitchen door and came back to take an encore. It was magic. Absolute magic.

We went home that evening, happy, full of food and convinced that the Starrs were one of the nicest, most unspoiled families you could wish to meet.

Chapter 6

At first there was nothing but a feeling of horror. Stark, terrifying, pure horror. Then a confused series of images. Bumping along in a car, then a dimly lit room and all the time the horror was growing until suddenly the impressions were shattered by a child's piercing scream. The pictures went blank and there was nothing but the terrible cry, 'I want my Mummy! I want my Mummy,' echoing round my head.

Cold and shaking, I lit a cigarette. A medium's job is not a cosy one. Every person who comes back to talk from the other side, describes the manner of their passing and not everyone is lucky enough to go gently in their sleep. I hear of illness and accidents, suicide and murder. I've spoken to young boys who've shot themselves and little children who've been stabbed to death, but nothing I've encountered so far, prepared me for the case of Lesley Anne Downey – one of the victims of the notorious Moors Murderers, Ian Brady and Myra Hindley.

No other case has left me with such a sick, cold feeling as if my tummy was filled up with ice. At the end of it I was mentally and physically exhausted and despite the central heating and the fire going full blast, it was hours before I felt really warm again.

I'd had no idea when I got up that morning, what I was letting myself in for. My diary said I had a sitting with a Mrs West who'd lost a child. Apparently a newspaper reporter had rung Laurie and asked if we could possibly see this lady because she was absolutely desperate. He gave us no other details and I was booked up for months ahead, but something told me it was important to see this mother. When the spirit world nudges me like that it's very unwise to ignore it so we did a bit of rearranging and juggling with dates and we made an appointment for Mrs West.

Just before she was due to arrive, I tuned in and immediately I heard the name Lesley, followed by a fleeting glimpse of a fragile, dark-haired little girl. A pretty little thing. Then the bell was ringing and I hurried out to the hall to open the front door.

Mrs West absolutely rushed in, there's no other way of describing it. She flew into the hall and gave me a big hug that spoke of years of pent up emotion.

'I can't believe it,' she said, 'I can't believe I'm actually here.'

You poor soul, I thought, my heart going out to her. You've been searching for a long time, and I prayed very hard that I'd be able to help.

She was an attractive woman was Anne West, with nice clothes, carefully blonded hair and beautiful eyes. Yet when you looked into those eyes you could see a great well of despair and emptiness. There was such a bleak quality to her unhappiness that I knew her daughter's passing had affected her very badly.

'Well come on in,' I said leading them into the sitting-room 'and let's see what we can do.'

The reporter who'd brought Mrs West had a tape recorder and afterwards he very kindly gave me a transcript of the sitting. This is how it went:

DORIS: I can't promise you anything, my love. But I know you have come here with all this love in your heart and I only hope I can do something to help you. All I know is that your name is West and one of your little children passed over tragically. I started to tune in this morning and I got the name Lesley but her other name was not West.

MRS WEST: No, it was Downey. I married again.

DORIS: Where do I get the number ten from? Was it ten years ago when she passed?

MRS WEST: She was ten years old when she died.

DORIS: She will come back first as a child and later as the grown woman she is now. She tells me there's been four passings. She's telling me I'm not on my own because Mum has had other tragedies. Who's Terry?

MRS WEST: He's my son. My eldest son.

DORIS: She's talking to someone. I think it's Alice, Annie, Alan. She's telling me you haven't got it right, Doris. Listen. Yes, my love. It's Alan.

MRS WEST: Alan's my husband.

DORIS: She's talking about Alan. I thought she was talking to someone on the other side and she's told me to listen carefully. She's telling me he's very good to Mum. I love him for that. Who's Bill?

MRS WEST: My Dad.

DORIS: She's saying Bill's this side Doris. Try again love. Was that Millie. Molly. No it's Mary. Do you know a Mary on your side? No? We won't take it, love. We haven't got it right, love? Forgive me she's talking about Myra. She's saying don't upset yourself Mum over what you read in the papers about her being paroled. It's not going to happen because that woman will never reform. She's just play-acting. She's bad, Doris, really bad. They were taking you where, love? They made you go with them? We were going for some fish and chips. Two of us went with them to show them where the chip shop was. We never went home again, Doris. Don't relive that, love. Your mum has had to live with this for years. Who is Vickie, love?

MRS WEST: My grand-daughter.

DORIS: Mum's got a red rose by my picture frame – thank you for that Mum. Alan thinks as much about me as my Mum, you know. Edward wants to say hello because no one ever talks to him. I'm ever so glad you came Mum because I wanted to tell you everything was all right.

I spend my time among the children Mum. The children and the babies who have been taken back because no one wants them. But I love them and I spend all my time with them. I never had the chance to have babies of my own but I have lots of them to love here. Bill's here, Mum. And Jim wants to say hello.

MRS WEST: My brother.

DORIS: She's grown into a beautiful girl, love. Auburn hair, or brown with touches of auburn. A beautiful woman. I have fulfilled my life, Mum. She's asking about a locket you wear with her picture in it.

MRS WEST: I usually wear it. I left it at home today.

DORIS: She's talking about Elsie.

MRS WEST: That's my sister.

DORIS: She's getting so excited and bubbling over. It's difficult love. John. He went over tragically. He should not have gone over.

MRS WEST: John was my nephew. He died three years after Lesley when a simple operation went wrong. They were devoted to each other.

DORIS: Are you all right, darling? Yes, I know it's difficult. No Lesley, you're talking to your Mum and I can't catch you. Mill Street?

MRS WEST: That's the police station where we first reported her missing. We went at four-thirty in the afternoon and they didn't want to know. Told us to go back later if she hadn't come home. It was ten-thirty before they started looking for her and there had been a fall of snow in between. That wrecked any chance they had of finding her.

DORIS: I met a man called Frank here. He used to be a policeman at Mill Street.

MRS WEST: Yes. Frank Rimmer. He was a sergeant.

DORIS: He helped when it happened to me and he is over now. I was able to say thank you to him for trying to help. He said he only wished they had been able to stop it. But they did try, Mum, didn't they?

I see my Mum a lot, Doris. I was listening when they were talking about going to Spain.

MRS WEST: We were trying to work out whether we could afford a holiday in Spain because Alan is about to lose his job. That was only two nights ago in the kitchen at home. We haven't even mentioned it to anyone else.

DORIS: I was listening, Doris. I was saying go on Mum and Dad. Do it. Life is too short to miss anything. Look how short mine was.

She's talking about a caravan holiday she really enjoyed.

MRS WEST: Yes. She went away with the Sunday school to Wales, three months before she died.

DORIS: Best holiday I ever had. I did have a good time then this had to happen. Now I'm grown up I realize you must get through to kids they must never go off with strangers, but you just don't think when you are a child. You trust everyone.

Don't go on with that love. It's only upsetting your Mum and you as well.

What are you laughing at, love? A pub? The Green Man? Tell them I was with them in the Green Man, Doris. With Alan and Tony.

MRS WEST: Tony is Alan's brother. We had a night out with them when we came from Manchester to London to visit them.

DORIS: Don't worry Alan. Everything will work out. I can see from this side. Live your life, Mum, you've suffered enough. Be happy and do the things you want to do. I'm okay. I'm happy. When we came we were in hospital. They nursed us back. I had a spirit Mum for a while until I grew up and grand-dad came. So don't worry that no one looked after me. I know you were afraid I was on my own but we are not. Nothing hurts spirit children. They are innocent so they are loved and taken care of.

I wish you'd stop laughing, lovey. I'll shake them. She's talking about a baby called Emma Louise.

MRS WEST: I don't know anyone like that.

DORIS: She's probably not born yet. Auntie Mo.

MRS WEST: That's Alan's sister.

DORIS: Well the baby's connected with Auntie Mo. She's talking about a stone in a graveyard. It's shaped like an open book.

MRS WEST: It's a grave by Lesley's. The book is open and the message of remembrance is carved into its pages.

DORIS: I often go and look at it when Mum's having a little weep over my grave, Doris. That's where they buried my body but of course I'm not there. I had a terrific funeral, Doris. There were so many people there. Mum gave me a big heart of flowers and she put a single red rose in the grave. It's been such a long time, Mum, but I've always wanted to say thank you for that. You gave it to me with love, Mum, and I brought it back with love. Mum has a single red rose by my picture at home, Doris. It's lovely.

MRS WEST: Yes it's a silk rose in a tiny rose glass by her framed picture in the lounge.

DORIS: She's really cheeky you know. She's talking about divorces in the family. Three of them.

MRS WEST: I can only think of two.

DORIS: Lesley says don't forget your own, Mum. Don't forget that one.

Bill's coming back. He's trying to tell me something, he's saying just say Rutland Street, love, and she'll know what I mean.

MRS WEST: Rutland Street was round the corner from where we lived when I was a child. My dad, Bill, used to drink at a pub called Joe Daleys' there.

I pray every night, Doris, that Lesley will one day appear to me. But it hasn't happened yet.

DORIS: You're trying too hard, lovey. Relax. It might happen. She says Mum still sees me as I was at the end. Wipe this out of your mind, Mum. We were cleaned up in hospital.

She says she played with someone called Claire. She lived next door. She's grown up now and is married. I used to play with Claire all the time, Doris. If I had been playing with Claire when it happened I would not be here now.

DORIS: What's that love? M what? You really loved her.

MRS WEST: Muriel, a Sunday school teacher on the caravan holiday. I was talking to her at Lesley's funeral and it was only then that she told me right through the holiday Lesley couldn't wait to get back home. She kept telling Muriel she loved me and missed me.

DORIS: She's talking about a tape. Something about a tape. No not those awful tapes at the trial. I mean the one Mum wishes she had kept. The one with me singing on it which got lost.

MRS WEST: It was a tape Lesley's brother Terry made of her singing her favourite song – *Bobby's Girl*. We had a stereo record player with a tape deck and he made the recording. Then he asked me if he could swap the set for a guitar and he gave the tape recording away as well. It didn't mean much at the time. But two months later Lesley was dead. And that was the only recording we had of her voice. It has broken my heart ever since that we didn't keep it.

DORIS: She's talking about someone called Edward. Edward is here and he wants to say hello. Because no one ever talks to him. He wants to say thank you. No one visits him.

MRS WEST: It's Edward Evans, another victim of Brady and Hindley. He is buried only a few feet from Lesley. It looks as if his grave has not been touched since he was buried. We try to keep it tidy. Tidying the grass and keeping the weeds down.

Lesley also mentioned the name Lillian, which Anne West couldn't place but afterwards it came back to her.

MRS WEST: What she was talking about was the day she had

her waist length hair cut when she was about eight. She came home and Alan told her she looked like a boy and he was going to call her George. Lesley came right back at him and told Alan, if you're going to call me George, I'm going to call you Lillian!

There were a few things that Lesley told me which I didn't repeat out loud during the sitting for fear of upsetting her mother but I discovered afterwards that Anne West knew of them already. Most disturbing of all was the fact that rats had eaten the child's body before it was found. Anne confirmed that this was true and that she'd not even had a complete body to identify.

The story was a nightmare in every way. It was back in the early sixties when an apparently harmless young couple named Ian Brady and Myra Hindley began to look for victims on the streets of Manchester. To their family and neighbours they were a quiet, devoted pair. They worked together, lived together and were always in each other's company. They didn't seem to have many friends and they weren't interested in noisy parties or going dancing like so many people. Instead they were content to drive about in Myra's little van making frequent trips to the moors. Great country lovers were Ian and Myra.

What nobody ever suspected was that Ian and Myra buried bodies on the moors and then went back to picnic on the graves.

Three children were murdered before they were caught, John Kilbride, aged 12, Lesley Anne Downey aged 10 and Edward Evans aged 17. John and Lesley were both buried on the moors and Edward would have probably ended up there too, had the murderers not been arrested before they had the chance to move his body. Who knows how many children would have died if Myra's brother-in-law hadn't called the police when they tried to persuade him to help them move Edward Evans' body.

Poor little Lesley had been so happy before it happened.

The last her mother saw of her was when she skipped out the door on Boxing Day 1964 with her two younger brothers and three little friends from up the road, for a trip to the special Christmas fun fair round the corner.

By all accounts they had a wonderful time. In fact Lesley enjoyed herself so much that when it was time to go she couldn't tear herself away. She asked her friend Linda to take her little brothers home while she went back for one last look at the roundabouts.

Her family never saw her alive again.

The world has become a more violent place since the early sixties and these days child murders seem to be getting ever more common, yet people still recall the Moors Murders with particular horror.

It wasn't just that the children had been killed, but that they'd been tortured before they were killed and Lesley Anne Downey's suffering was recorded on tape, presumably for the evil couple's gruesome enjoyment later. During the trial of Brady and Hindley the tapes were played to an appalled courtroom and afterwards the judge said:

'None of us are likely to forget them for a very long time.'

The memory of those anguished cries will probably haunt the listeners for the rest of their lives.

I don't believe in harbouring bitterness but I must say that I could understand how Anne West felt, particularly over the rumours that Myra Hindley was coming up for parole and might even be released from prison soon. If Lesley had been my child I would have found it almost impossible to put Romanov's tolerant principles into action.

'It's the hate that keeps me going,' said Anne West quietly and with deadly sincerity. 'I will live until Myra Hindley dies.'

Her words made me shudder involuntarily. I believed her ...

Chapter 7

If I close my eyes and concentrate I can hear the music now. Da da, da da da. da da da … The distinctive opening bars of *Sunday Night At The London Palladium*. Every Sunday the sound of that familiar tune brought us hurrying from whatever we were doing, to our places in front of the television for a night of glamour, big names and good old fashioned entertainment.

Like millions of other families we sat glued to the set as Bruce Forsyth, or Norman Vaughan or even later I think, Jimmy Tarbuck, introduced act after act and the glittering Tiller Girls, all long legs and flashing head-dresses, high kicked their way round the famous revolving stage.

Sunday Night At The London Palladium was the highlight of our week and for the stars who appeared, it was the highlight of their careers.

I've lost count of the number of hours we must have spent watching those old variety shows and all I can say is thank goodness I'm not a fortune teller. If one night I'd glanced up and seen myself standing on that stage I'd have thought I was going mad. The idea that one day I might appear at the London Palladium would have seemed totally impossible and also quite terrifying. It was about as likely as John and I moving into Buckingham Palace.

Yet unknown to me, the years were gradually winding me towards the stage. Without realizing where I was going, I slowly progressed from draughty church halls to larger assembly rooms, from tiny provincial theatres to larger theatres, until at last in 1984 I was asked if I'd consider appearing at the Palladium.'

The *Palladium*! Well I nearly had kittens.

'Oh, Laurie, I don't know,' I said. The very thought brought me out in a cold sweat. 'It's one of the most famous theatres in the world. I mean the Beatles have been on there and just about every other big name ...'

I mean Lewisham Town Hall was one thing, but the London Palladium ...

'But Doris you've done the Dominion in Tottenham Court Road,' said Laurie at his most persuasive. 'That was no bother. The Palladium's very similar.'

Not in my mind it wasn't. I thought of all those plush balconies, the red velvet, the Royal Box. No, the Palladium was quite paralysingly different.

'We'd never fill it Laurie,' I said, stalling.

He grinned. 'Well let's give it a try and see.'

At that point I didn't really believe I'd actually do it. Even when Laurie said everything was fixed for December 16th I just nodded and humoured him. I didn't think it would really happen. You've still got the tickets to sell, my lad, I thought to myself. And when you can't shift them we'll have to cancel and forget all about it.

The day the tickets went on sale I was still convinced we'd have to call the whole thing off – until Laurie phoned that is.

'Doris, it's fantastic!' he cried, sounding so elated I thought he'd won the football pools.

'What is it, Laurie?'

'I've just heard from the Palladium. The tickets have sold out in an hour and a half. They say it's a record!'

I stared at the receiver blankly. 'Are you sure someone's not pulling your leg, Laurie?'

'Positive. They've gone. Everyone of them's gone in an hour and a half.'

I should have been beside myself with excitement, of course, but all I could think of was 'Oh heavens – that means I've got to do it. I've really got to go on at the Palladium!'

As December 16th drew near I hovered between excitement and panic. I tried on all my dresses, bought a couple more and still couldn't make up my mind which one to wear. Worse still, my hair was a mess, I decided, and my nails were breaking up all over the place. But the fuss over details was only to cover the real panic going on inside. I was intending to get up on stage at the Palladium, in front of a sell-out audience, without an act, without a script, without the ability to sing, dance or act, without anything definite at all and I was going to stand there and hope for the best. From thin air I was hoping the means would come to entertain the audience for two hours. Now this surely was madness.

My mother had always said I'd end up in a mental home. Was she proving right at last? Had I finally flipped? Supposing nothing happened? Supposing when I tuned in all I heard was the sound of my own thoughts? How on earth would I cope with those tiers and tiers of blank faces growing more hostile by the minute?

It was enough to give you nightmares.

'Trust,' Romanov told me over and over again. 'Trust.'

And I pushed the doubts very firmly to the back of my mind. After all wasn't this the same problem I faced every time I did a sitting or appeared in any theatre? Yet while I was busy not thinking terrible thoughts, small decisions suddenly became overwhelmingly difficult. I swished through my wardrobe for the umpteenth time. Now should it be the pink, the blue or maybe the turquoise …?

At last on December 16th I was sitting in the wings in a pretty dress of soft peach, waiting to go on and trembling from head to foot.

John Avery, the manager, came past and smiled at me kindly. 'Don't be so nervous, Doris,' he said, 'but then you wouldn't be a star if you weren't nervous. All the big stars that come here are just the same when they're waiting to go on.'

I wondered if Roy Castle could possibly feel as bad as I

did. It was hard to believe. He always seems so relaxed when you see him on television. I was thinking of Roy because I'd been given his dressing-room. Six days a week he and Tommy Steele were appearing in *Singing in the Rain* and Sunday, their day off, I'd moved in. I hoped he didn't mind. I was very careful not to touch any of his things. There were good luck telegrams and cards all over the place and cuddly toy mascots and the dressing-room itself was beautiful. Lovely and warm, with soft carpets and the ceiling all draped in pleats like a dome. It was a far cry from the church halls where I started, where you changed into your dress in the toilet because the only room back stage was full of people drinking tea and gossiping.

I always try to relax quietly for a few minutes before I go on so that I can tune in and hopefully get a name or two to give me a start. So sitting there in Roy Castle's dressing-room I closed my eyes and concentrated. I was in luck. After a moment or two I heard a young boy's voice. He wasn't very old, no more than fourteen I'd have said.

'My mother's coming tonight,' he told me, 'her name's Rita.'

'And what's your name, lovey?' I asked him.

'I'm Stewart,' he said.

And that was it. But it was a start. Something to get my teeth into when I stood there in front of that audience.

Then all at once, the show had started. Tony Ortzen, the editor of *Psychic News*, had introduced me and I was walking out on to the stage at the Palladium. There were the tiers and tiers of balconies that I remembered from the television show, the chandeliers and the acres of red velvet and there on the stage, standing on a piece of carpet and flanked by flowers, were the chairs from the Royal Box. Nervous as I was, I couldn't help thinking goodness me, the Queen's probably sat in this as I sat down. It was a weird feeling.

I did my little gossip at the beginning, as I always do to

relax people and reassure them that I'm just like them and I'm not going to swing from the lights or wave my arms about or do any of the peculiar things that people unfortunately associate with mediums. Then I told them how I'd tuned in earlier.

'I got a little boy called Stewart who's looking for his mother,' I said. 'She's called Rita, or it could be Anita. They both sound similar to me. Is there a Rita or Anita here with a little boy called Stewart?'

There was an expectant silence, which grew and grew and my stomach started turning somersaults. Surely I hadn't mucked up my very first message?

And then, just as I was getting seriously worried, a woman stood up and walked, half-stunned to the microphone.

'I'm Rita and my son was Stewart,' she said faintly. We were under way.

After the weeks of anxiety, the evening seemed to fly past for me. Stewart talked about his family and the milkman, Philip. He was fond of Philip because he used to help him on the milkround. He raised a laugh when he said that a baby would be born and to ask Philip about it, and a few tears when he described how he was killed in a cycling accident.

Then there were various friends and family members who came to talk to Margaret who worked with mentally handicapped children and had the potential to be a medium herself. There was the mother who was worried because her son and his girlfriend were happily expecting a baby but had no plans to get married. Another tragic mother who had been buried with her dead baby and wanted to reassure her orphaned children that she was with them still and wanted them to enjoy their Christmas. There was the son looking for his mother, Jane Jones, and the father who'd been sent over without his teeth in. And so it went on and on.

Once or twice there were a couple of loud, unexplained

bangs and out in the audience a light blew out for no apparent reason and I remembered that the Palladium is supposed to be haunted. The resident ghost didn't put in an appearance though and I had enough on my plate with all the spirit people who wanted to talk to the audience without trying to contact anyone else.

Then, suddenly it was all over. We handed out the flowers I like to give to people who've had messages, there were cameras going off all over the place and at last I could escape to the dressing-room for a long cup of tea.

It was only when I sat down that I realized how exhausted I was. My hair and my back were wet with sweat and I felt too drained even to talk. Up the corridor in Tommy Steele's dressing-room they were having a party but I couldn't face it. Making conversation with all those people no matter how nice they were was too much of an effort. All I wanted was to get home to bed and so John and I crept out to the car and left them all to it.

'Hey, don't forget this, love,' said John as I stole away.

I looked back. It was the large box the doorman had brought in during the evening. It was marked 'fragile' and had been handed in for me at the stage door earlier. I make a point though of never looking at letters left at the theatre before I go on, and I was too tired now even to be curious.

'Oh. No. Could you bring it love, I've got my dress to carry.'

John picked it up. 'It's heavy,' he said in surprise. 'I wonder what it is?'

Back home he could contain himself no longer. Before he'd even got his coat off he was out in the kitchen with the box, sawing through the string with a knife.

From the sitting-room where I'd collapsed into my armchair I heard a low whistle.

'You'd better look at this, girl.'

I groaned to myself. 'Can you bring it in here, John?'

There was a pause and then out he came with the most

enormous birthday cake tied in yellow ribbon, decorated with yellow roses and piped with the words, 'Happy Birthday Doris.'

I was so touched that tears sprang into my eyes. It was from a boy called Pat and he'd made it himself. Apparently he'd read in one of my books how John and Terry are apt to forget my birthday, coming as it does right after Christmas and how the spirit world once left me a gold rose outlined on the wall to cheer me up. This year he wanted to make sure my birthday wouldn't be forgotten so he'd send me my very own birthday cake.

What's more the spirit world had even arranged a Christmas present for me through that same kind young man. The Palladium evening had come right at the end of a three week tour around the country and on top of moving house. Now here I was a week before Christmas and feeling so tired I could hardly move. I'd rashly invited a few friends over for Christmas dinner a day early on Christmas Eve. It had seemed like a good idea at the time. I could get all the cooking over with on Christmas Eve and relax on Christmas Day with nothing to worry about but a cold buffet. But now I was having second thoughts. I hadn't so much as unpacked my dinner service yet. It was still stashed away in a crate somewhere and frankly I didn't feel up to anything more strenuous than opening a tin.

This problem was still bobbing around in my mind the next day when I rang Pat to thank him for the lovely cake. We chatted for quite a while, and then the conversation got round to Christmas. What was I having for Christmas this year Patrick wondered.

'D'you know, Pat, I'm too tired to care,' I said. 'What I'd really like is for some caterers to come and do the whole thing for me. That would be better than any present.'

'I'll do it,' said Pat immediately.

'But Pat you're not a caterer are you?' I asked. I'd assumed that cakes were some sort of hobby for him.

'No I'm a chef,' he said.

'Well look it's very sweet of you,' I said, 'but I wasn't serious. It was only wishful thinking. I haven't even got my dinner service unpacked yet or anything.'

'Don't worry,' said Pat, 'I'll bring mine. Now don't you bother. I'll see to everything.'

And he was as good as his word. On Christmas Eve he arrived with a dinner service, coffee service and silverware. He even brought a candelabra. Then he sent me off to put up my feet while he cooked the turkey, vegetables and Christmas pudding. The meal was delicious and afterwards Patrick cleared away, and washed the dishes. I didn't have to lift a finger. It was the best Christmas present I could have had.

But the Palladium connection didn't finish there. Not long after Christmas, Rita Broadfield, whose son Stewart had come through right at the beginning and started the evening off, came for a private sitting. This time she brought her husband with her.

'Quite honestly I've come because I was afraid for my wife,' he told me sternly and I could see that he was deeply suspicious about the whole thing. He was probably afraid his wife was going to be taken in by some sort of weirdo.

'That's alright love,' I said. 'There's nothing to be afraid of. Just send out your love to Stewart and we'll see what we can do.'

As before, Stewart came along as soon as I tuned in. This time I could see him standing in my sitting-room beside his parents. He was a tall boy with fair hair and a lively face. It turned out that he was 13 and not 14 as I'd first thought.

He told me more about the accident.

'There were four of us at first,' he said, 'then two went off and there were just the two of us left. I was going up the bypass and then bang ... It was the back of my head got hit ...'

He talked of the heart of flowers his parents had given him at the funeral, the extension they were building at home and even Wilson School – the school he'd attended before the accident.

Then, right at the end, just as we were finishing sitting and the power was at its lowest ebb, Rita Broadfield said sadly, 'He never mentioned his sister.'

Stewart was at her side in an instant.

'Does she mean Caroline? I wouldn't forget Caroline.'

And that did it for his father. The pent up emotion he'd been supressing since the previous August when the tragedy happened came spilling out and he cried.

'Doris, there's no way you could have known all that,' he said afterwards. 'It was marvellous.'

Appearing at the Palladium has got to be the peak of anyone's career and once the big day was over I thought things would die down. Strangely enough though the reverse seemed to happen. If anything the fuss went on building.

Extraordinary news came from my home town of Grantham where tickets had just gone on sale for a show in a hall built over the exact spot where I was born. One Wong Row which in Chinese means Fresh Fields. Apparently there was a bit of a riot. The queue went right round the leisure centre where I was appearing, so that the end met the beginning and there were minor dust-ups over the number of tickets some people were allowed to buy. To add insult to injury ticket touts walked up and down selling tickets for £10 and £15 each.

Ticket touts! I thought in amazement. Anyone would think it was a pop concert. Perplexed, I put it down to the fact that it was my home town and probably a lot of people were curious to see what had become of the local girl.

But even stranger news came from SAGB, The Belgrave Square headquarters of the Spiritualist Association of Great Britain. I still try to give demonstrations there as often as I can, just as I used to in the early days when I first came to London and this particular week I had a free evening. The day the tickets went on sale however I had a desperate phone call from the chairman Tom Johannson.

'Doris, I don't know what I'm going to do,' he said, the panic rising in his voice. 'They've been sleeping out all night in sleeping bags. There's a thousand turned up and I've only got room for 180 and they're blocking the pavements so much I've had the police here.'

When I eventually arrived the place was like a refugee camp. There were people packed into every tiny space. They were sitting on boxes in the aisle, they were crammed standing, along the back wall, they were even overflowing on to the platform at my feet.

It was a daunting prospect and not for the first time I felt vaguely frightened. 'What do they want from me?' I wondered anxiously. 'What are they expecting? I can't perform miracles.'

Nevertheless it was a happy evening. There were a lot of animals. We had a dog called Barnaby back, a cat called Doodie and another cat called Candy. I thought at first they were talking about a girl, but no. Candy turned out to be a cat!

I also got two Andrews that night. The first belonged to a family from Wisbech near Cambridge.

'I've got a young man called Andrew,' I explained, 'and he's something to do with the police.'

'Yes,' said his father, 'he was a policeman.'

Then another man stood up. 'Our son's Andrew too. We've got an Andrew.'

And before he'd finished speaking the other Andrew came in loud and clear and it turned out that he too had a connection with the police. His father was a policeman.

I was so pleased, because it turned out that the parents had come all the way from Cheshire. They'd left home at two o'clock in the morning, arrived in London at four o'clock and joined the queue.

We were in the depths of a very bad winter at this time and I'd cut my touring down to the barest minimum. I didn't have to be idle though, just because the weather was awful. I was able to use the time to do some private sittings – children wherever possible – and soon the sad cases were pouring through my door again.

There was something about one particular letter asking for a sitting that worried me and I asked the couple to come along. I'm very glad I did because during the sitting their son Alan told me that his father's hobby was shooting and that in moments of despair they'd talked of committing suicide. The father intended to shoot his wife and then turn the gun on himself. Alan of course was horrified by this idea. He begged them to promise that they'd never ever consider it again.

'Tell them I'm alright. I'm happy and I'll be there to meet them when their time comes,' he said. 'But that's not yet. They mustn't bring themselves over. They've got their lives to lead.'

Afterwards Laurie who'd organized the meeting received a lovely letter from them with a beautiful cameo enclosed, as a gift for me.

'Doris really helped Alan and I so much in bringing our son back to us,' wrote his mother. 'It was unbelievable. He was speaking to us nearly all afternoon.'

There were many other similar stories. There was the boy who'd suffered from a blood disease. Twice he thought he'd beaten it and then it started up again. He was only seventeen but he hadn't lost his sense of humour.

'Tell Roger I've seen Sue and I think she's a bit of alright,' he told me with a roguish wink.

Roger was his brother and Sue was Roger's new girlfriend. He also knew that Roger was wearing his ring, that his parents had planted a rose bush on his grave and that the old man in the end bed of his ward, old Walter, had since passed over and they'd met on the other side.

Then there was the young soldier only nineteen years old who was killed in Germany when the army vehicle in which he was travelling rolled over.

'There were three of us,' he said in disgust. 'And I was

the only one who passed over. We were going home. Only forty-eight hours stood between the accident and when I should have gone home.'

He'd been bitter at first he told me. He was engaged, looking forward to getting married and then this had to happen.

'I've settled down now,' he said, 'but I was angry at first. I thought why did it have to happen to me.'

Then there was Sarah, an air hostess who went down too deep when she was scuba diving. She came and stood beside her mother as we were talking and I saw that she was the most beautiful girl with long blonde hair turned under and huge eyes.

'Yes I was attractive and I knew it,' she said. 'It was my own bloody fault. I was always a dare devil. I always had to go one better than anyone else.'

She struggled to give me an impression of what happened. Suddenly there was water all around me and she was putting something over my nose. I got an impression of swimming around looking at things, then there was a booming sound in my ears and nothing more.

'Yes she came to the surface too quickly and was incoherent,' said her mother. 'She was trying to pull off her mask. Her friend tried to pull her to the boat but she was too heavy and she was drowning him. He let her go and she slipped off the reef.'

But Sarah too could still laugh at herself.

'I'd just had all my dental work done. I had all my teeth crowned. If I'd known this was going to happen I'd have saved my money. It cost me a bomb!'

Afterwards Sarah's mother confessed that she'd been living with the fear of losing a child for a long time.

'I've always known I was going to lose one of them,' she said. 'I kept thinking it was a wicked thing to think but somehow I just knew. And I thought if it had to happen, let it be quick.'

Well it had been very quick. Sarah was enjoying herself,

then suddenly she lost consciousness and knew nothing more about it until she woke up on the other side. That was one small comfort I could offer her poor mother. Sarah didn't suffer at all.

After sittings like these it's difficult not to feel sad. When you meet the grieving parents and speak to the young people, lovely children every one, it's hard not to feel a sense of waste. Yet I know that young as they are, they've done their time on earth and now they are happy and fulfilled in new lives on the other side.

We shouldn't weep for them because nothing can hurt them now.

Chapter 8

They were making a valiant effort at the estate agents'. There was a big board nailed over the window and the neat rows of photographs of houses for sale had been taken down, but the name of the shop was still boldly outlined over the top and inside it was business as usual.

Set in a comfortable, suburban area amongst news-agents and grocery shops you'd have thought that the owner, doing particularly well, was simply having the place smartened up. In fact this ordinary looking estate agents, apparently no different from any other, was reputed to be haunted.

A number of disturbing events had worried the staff and the strange goings on had already attracted the attention of the local paper.

From what I could make out, there had been a series of unusual accidents, interspersed by small, but inexplicable incidents. First, during a spell when the electricity supply was off, workmen had come to install mobile gas heaters, and in a freak accident, one of the gas cylinders blew up, injuring one of the men. Not long afterwards a water pipe burst, flooding the shop and no sooner had they got the place dry than there was a terrible commotion outside and a car careered across the road, mounted the pavement and crashed straight through the estate agents window, missing the owner by inches.

As if this wasn't bad enough, less dramatic but equally worrying things were happening almost every day. There was a room at the back of the shop where there was a definite atmosphere – almost as if an unseen presence was watching and a dog belonging to one of the staff refused point blank to enter this room.

One day the owner was sitting there attempting to work when the strange atmosphere suddenly built up around her. She ignored it for as long as she could but in the end it became so oppressive that she had to run out of the room and slam the door behind her. So shaken was she by the experience that she couldn't bring herself to cross the threshold again until the next day.

In the outer shop objects were frequently moved about, the closed sign on the front door was often mysteriously turned around to read 'Open' when the shop was shut and one morning the staff walked in to find a house brick in the middle of the floor. It had not been there when they'd locked up the night before, no one else had been in the shop and there was no sign of forced entry and yet, somehow, the brick had found its way into the centre of the carpet.

It was the sort of story that papers love to print and readers love to read but not nearly so fascinating for the people involved. By the time the Thames News picked it up and decided it might make an amusing little item for the tea time show, the people in the shop were beginning to feel desperate. Most of all they wanted to know what was going on.

The first I heard of it was at 2.00 one afternoon when Thames News rang to ask if I could do an urgent job for them.

'Well when did you have in mind?' I asked uncertainly. The photographer from the publishers' had arrived and we were in the middle of doing the pictures for the cover of my new book.

'Straight away,' they said. 'We'll send a car for you.'

'I'm sorry but I don't think I can.' I explained, 'I've got the photographer here and we're doing a photo session'.

There was a hurried exchange at the other end of the

phone, then the researcher came back. 'How long will you be?'

'I don't know, just a minute I'll ask.' I put my hand over the mouthpiece, 'How much longer will it take?' I called out to the photographer.

It had already taken longer than I'd thought because I'd had to change. I'd worked so hard to make myself look nice. I'd put on a new navy blue dress with spots, navy blue stockings and navy blue shoes and I thought I looked marvellous, a real thoroughly modern Millie. And the first thing the photographer said when I opened the door was, 'Oh. Haven't you got anything lighter?'

So we trouped upstairs and looked through my wardrobe and he picked out an old pink dress that I've worn dozens of times before! So much for thoroughly modern Millie!

Anyway, by the time I'd changed and tidied my hair again we could have taken a whole roll of film.

Fortunately the photographer was a good-natured man and he didn't mind being rushed. 'Seeing as it's you Doris we'll get it done in an hour,' he promised.

I told the television people to collect us just after three o'clock and we galloped through the picture, then I dashed upstairs to change again, because the photographer had put me in a long dress and the viewers might think it strange to see me gallivanting round an estate agents' in evening dress at tea-time.

By now I was feeling distinctly breathless. What I didn't realize was that the peculiar jinx affecting the estate agents had now extended to include the TV story as well. And if you think jinx is too strong a word for it look what happened.

First of all, the driver the company used happened to be at home in Essex when the call came through and it took him some time to reach us. By the time he arrived the rush hour traffic was building up and ahead of us was one of the worst journeys you can make in London. I live in

South East London and the shop was in North West London and separating us was a whole city of jammed, exhaust-fogged streets where the cars crawled at walking pace. Not surprisingly the journey seemed to last hours and by the time we arrived, the producer was getting rather anxious about his chances of finishing in time for the programme that evening.

'I don't like to rush you Doris,' he said, 'but we really do need to start filming at once.'

'That's alright love. You start and I'll do my best.'

But the cameras had hardly started rolling, when they stopped again.

'Sorry, Doris. The batteries have gone down on the sound.'

We took a break while the batteries were changed then we were off again, but a few minutes later the same thing happened. By now the producer was quietly distraught. The situation was practically unheard of he told me as he hurried off to phone the studios and get fresh batteries sent out by messenger.

In all three lots of batteries went down before we managed to start filming and then the crew announced that they finished at 6.30 and they were going home. I thought the poor producer would have a stroke but instead he looked resigned.

'Well we've no chance of catching the news now,' he said. 'There's no point in panicking.'

We sat down to wait for the new crew to arrive but when they turned up, our driver, who had been hanging around throughout all the disasters, suddenly told us that he had a date and he couldn't wait any longer. He was off. He climbed into his car, accelerated away up the road and that was the last we saw of him. John and I looked at each other and burst out laughing. You had to see the funny side or you'd go mad.

Fortunately the sitting went better than the filming. When we'd first arrived the owner took me into the room where the atmosphere was sometimes oppressive. She believed the trouble stemmed from this room and I felt she was probably right. I walked carefully round, checking for a presence. This must look rather strange to people who don't realize what I'm doing but in fact you can tell if there's an entity present by the cold spot. This is a place in an otherwise warm room which is freezing cold for no apparent reason. It's a strange sort of cold which creeps up from the floor and chills you to the bone. Once you've felt it, you'd never mistake a cold spot for an ordinary draught again. The sensation is quite different.

Well I walked around, pacing every bit of that room and nothing happened. The warmth was uniformly spread over the floor.

'He's not here at the moment,' I said at last, but as things turned out we had plenty of time.

When filming eventually started I went back to the room and this time I felt it straight away. Walking past the desk a stream of icy air suddenly flowed up from the floor freezing my right side. I stopped and as I did so the room shifted, swung before my eyes and somehow rearranged itself. The desk was different. I saw a dictaphone, two telephones and an in tray on the top and beside it a big swivel chair.

'This is how it used to be when it was my office,' said a man's voice.

The image held for a moment longer, then it disolved and I was back with the camera crew. I described what I'd seen and the new owner gasped.

'That's right. We've got a photo of it like that,' she said.

We were in business. The man wanted to talk. Apparently he'd run the estate agents some years before and got himself in a bit of a mess. Eventually he'd taken his own life.

'I went into the garage and did it in the car,' he said.

Now his main concern was for his wife. He hadn't been married very long and he wanted his wife to know how sorry he was for the misery he'd caused.

'There were two children,' he said, 'my wife had one and I

had one. I'm afraid I treated her quite badly because I was worried.'

He had been moving things about at the shop he admitted because he was trying to attract attention. He wanted to warn the new owner about a possible business problem and most of all he wanted a message passed on to his wife. Could they buy her some flowers as a token of his love and tell her he was sorry?

As further proof that he really had been one of the previous owners of the shop, he told me that he used to keep the keys in a very unusual place.

'I'll say,' said the new owner, 'he kept them behind the radiator.'

The one thing he wouldn't do, however, was claim responsibility for the accidents that plagued the shop. They were simply accidents, he insisted, and the fact there had been so many was unfortunate coincidence.

'And as for the last one, the car coming through the window, I'll tell you what happened there. The woman was pulling into the side of the road, went to put her foot on the brake and hit the accelerator instead. She lost control of the car and it shot across the pavement straight through a window. But don't let them blame me. I wouldn't do a thing like that. Someone could have been killed.'

By the end of our chat the man seemed much happier. We promised that the message would go to his wife and he said he'd leave the shop in peace.

At last filming finished. We'd long ago missed the early evening news but the producer said they'd keep the story and use it another night. It had been a very long day. By the time we got home it was nine o'clock and I hadn't even started the dinner. I just hoped I'd been of some help at the estate agents because a medium can't always put a stop to such 'hauntings'. I can't force a spirit person to do something against his will. I can only find out what's troubling him, attempt to put it right and endeavour to persuade him that it's time he accepted that his earth life is over and it's time he moved on to higher things. But spirit people don't have to take my advice any more than people here do.

People have some very funny ideas about 'ghosts' and 'hauntings'. In fact 'ghosts' never 'haunt' a place in order to scare people – or at least I've never come across one like that. They tend to cling to places they have known either because they refuse to accept that their earth life is finished, or because they are desperately trying to communicate with someone and can't rest until they've done so. They very seldom drift about for nothing.

One of the most extraordinary and poignant 'hauntings' I've come across in recent years was brought to my attention by journalist Michael Hellicar. He had written an article about life after death for the *Daily Mirror* and afterwards one of his readers rung him in desperation. This poor man thought he was going mad because he kept seeing his wife who'd died only a few days before. Michael phoned me and asked if I could help save his sanity.

Well I did a sitting and I remember I picked up the wife very easily because she was hovering so close to her distraught husband. It seemed to go well but as far as I was concerned there was nothing particularly remarkable about the case. It was a tragic affair, but sadly I seem to hear so many similar stories these days. It wasn't until long afterwards that I heard the whole story from Michael Hellicar and then I realized I'd been involved in something very unusual indeed. I'll let Michael explain it to you the way he explained it to me.

Michael Hellicar: 'I had quite a big response to my story on life after death but the strangest of all was a phone call from a man whose wife had committed suicide the week before by jumping off a tower block near their home. Apparently her death wasn't entirely unexpected because she'd had a history of mental illness, but she was only twenty-seven, had left a young family and he was very upset.

'The reason he was phoning me was that he feared he was going mad. Apparently after he'd talked to the police, identified the body and gone through all the gruesome formalities, he went home, walked into the bathroom and there she was. Solid and real wearing the dress he liked her in and her usual perfume. He reached out and touched her and his hand didn't go straight through. Her flesh was warm and real and what's more she talked to him. She said how sorry she was for what she'd done, but that she couldn't explain why she'd done it. Then she went on to give him advice about how to bring up the children.

'The man was totally confused. His senses told him one thing and his mind told him it wasn't possible. Could this really have happened, or was he mad?

'Now I must admit at this point I thought he'd been temporarily deranged by grief. But I've been a journalist for 30 years and by now I can tell whether I'm talking to a crank or not. The peculiar thing was that this man seemed completely sane. What's more as he continued his story, it became stranger and yet oddly more plausible.

'The next day he'd woken convinced that he'd dreamed the whole thing and that grief had made the dream particularly vivid. He put it out of his mind and set out to break the news to the family. On the way though, he bumped into a neighbour and stopped to tell her that his wife had died the morning before.

' "Oh no," said the neighbour when she'd got over the shock, 'it couldn't have been the morning. You must be mistaken. I saw her at the window yesterday afternoon watching for you to come home the way she always did."

'Puzzled the man assured her that his wife had definitely died in the morning. Later at his parents' home he was sitting at the table breaking the dreadful news when he saw his younger brother pass the window. His brother waved and a few minutes afterwards put his head round the door.

' "Hello," he said. "Where's Jan?'

'Everybody winced and the parents gently told him that

Jan was dead.

' "Don't be silly," he said, 'I just saw her sitting with you when I looked through the window," and he described the dress she was wearing. It was the dress she'd been wearing in the bathroom the night before.

'More confused than ever the husband went home to find his wife's perfume filled the house and the dog refused to go upstairs. He walked into the bathroom and there she was again. This time she begged him not to brood about why she'd done it but to get on with his life and marry again.

'Shortly afterwards the phone rang. It was his in-laws. "You won't believe this," they said, "but we saw Jan last night. She came to the house and sort of melted through the wall."

'It was at this stage the man phoned me. After reading my article he thought I must be an expert on such things. Was he going out of his mind he wanted to know, and if he wasn't, what had happened to his wife? He didn't like to think of her just floating around.

'Well I met him and I was very impressed by how straightforward and normal he seemed. His story was incredible but he didn't seem to be unbalanced or lying. The only problem was that I couldn't answer his questions and I felt that if the situation went on much longer he'd have a breakdown under the strain. In the end I phoned Doris and asked if she could help. I didn't give her the details. I just told her this man had lost his wife and thought he'd seen her after her death …'

Well, although I hadn't heard this extraordinary story it was quite obvious that this man's wife was anxious to talk to him. She was there the moment I tuned in and she told me her name was Jan and that she'd jumped off a roof.

'He's quite right when he feels that I'm close to him,' she said. 'Last night he was very clumsy and broke a teapot and today he went out and bought another one. It's a pretty yellow one. I like it.'

The astonished husband agreed that this was quite true.

Jan went on to say that she felt better now than she had when she'd first gone over. She was still full of guilt for leaving her family but she felt easier in her mind.

'At first I didn't want to tell him why I did it. I didn't want to cause trouble,' she said, 'but now I know that he needs to know and he won't rest until he finds out.'

And she went on to explain that there'd been a row with her mother and sister. Apparently in the heat of the moment they'd told her that she wasn't bringing up her children properly because she was always in and out of mental hospitals.

'They'd be better off without you,' they'd said. And Jan, in her disturbed state, promptly went out the next day and threw herself off a roof.

'But please don't blame them,' she begged her husband. 'It wasn't their fault. I was sick in the mind. I would have done it sooner or later anyway.'

She gave a great many family names, thanked her husband for removing the ear-rings in which she died and replacing them with her favourite pair and finally she mentioned a little surprise she'd been planning.

'I'd saved £15 to take the kids out to the seaside for a treat,' she said, 'it's hidden under a pillow in the cupboard over the wardrobe. Please give them a good day with my love.'

The husband promised that if he found the money he would. By now the power was growing weak. Few people realize that it's as difficult and tiring for spirit people to contact a medium as it is for a medium to contact them, especially when the spirit person has not long passed over. Jan was getting very tired and her voice faded.

'Tell him not to feel guilty if he meets someone else,' she said. 'I want him to be happy,' and then she was gone.

The sitting was over. Michael and the husband stayed on a little longer, drinking coffee and I was pleased to see that the man looked much happier.

'So I'm not going mad, Doris,' he said, 'I really did see her?'

'I'm sure you did love,' I answered him, 'She's very close to you. It's only her old overcoat in that coffin.'

And of course it's not unusual for people to see loved ones who've passed over. It depends how psychic they are and how hard they are trying. Children are more psychic than adults and they see spirit people much more frequently but either they don't say anything for fear of ridicule or their parents don't believe them. As for adults I'm sure it's no coincidence that we see spirit people when we least expect it. Time and time again bereaved mothers or widows will tell me they keep trying to see their husband or child but nothing happens. It can only conclude that it doesn't work when you try too hard. Perhaps your conscious mind swamps the psychic part and drowns any psychic messages struggling to get through. I know that when I'm trying desperately hard to do well at my work I've often been disappointed with the results and yet at other times when my mind's not fully on it for some reason, if I'm not feeling too good or I'm thinking about something else – I've been astonished how clearly the messages have come through.

Anyway, Michael Hellicar and his reader eventually left and that was the last I thought of the matter. Michael Hellicar however, had become very interested in the case. He gave the husband a lift home and out of curiosity went inside with the man to see if the message I'd given them about the money hidden in the wardrobe was correct.

'We went into the bedroom and I saw that there was a bridging unit between two wardrobes,' Michael told me. 'The husband opened the unit and inside was a pillow. He lifted the pillow and underneath was £15 just as you told him. It was amazing.

'But that wasn't quite the end of the story. A couple of weeks later I rang him again to see if the sitting had done the trick. He sounded much better.

'Apparently after the sitting he'd found a note in his wife's handwriting on the dressing-table, yet it had not been there before. It read: "I'm sorry but now at least you understand."

And since then she'd not been back and the dog was quite happy to go upstairs again.

'I'm quite happy now,' he said. 'I know my wife's alright and that she wants me to get on with my life.'

And as far as we know, that's exactly what he did.

Chapter 9

'Doris,' said the woman at the microphone, 'can you help me?'

It was question time at Fairfield Halls, Croydon and she'd been patiently waiting her turn in the queue. A fragile little woman but she held her head high and she spoke out bravely.

'I'm living in agony because I know I'm not long for this world. I'm not frightened of death but I'm frightened of waiting for it,' she paused and swallowed hard. 'And ... and I don't want to leave my family behind.'

My heart went out to her. Poor woman. She had cancer, of that I was sure and I knew how she must be suffering. I've been there myself. I've been lucky so far but I've had a glimpse of what it must be like for those poor souls who can't be helped by modern medicine. What could I say, in just a few moments, to comfort her?

'Well, darling,' I said gently, 'you can't take your family with you, can you? But remember you're only going into the next room. You are only a whisper away. To me death is nothing to be afraid of. I don't want to go just now I admit because I've only just got my house and I'd like to have time to enjoy it. It would be just my luck to pop my clogs just when everything's going well!'

The atmosphere lightened and the woman smiled.

'But seriously, death is a great adventure,' I went on, 'I just hope you don't have any, pain ... Besides, how do you know how long you've got? Miracles do happen. Until the time comes I don't believe I'm going. Why don't you join our Sod It Club? Whenever I'm going in for tests I say sod it, I'm not going to have it!'

Little by little the tension went out of the woman and after a few minutes she was laughing. Afterwards I got Laurie to give her my telephone number so that she could telephone me for moral support whenever she felt down, and that's how I got to know Ros quite well. It turned out we were both going into hospital for tests at the same time and afterwards I rang her to see how she'd got on. It was bad news. The cancer had spread and there didn't seem to be much hope.

'What about you, Doris,' she asked, 'have you had your results yet?'

And the words stuck in my throat. How could I tell her I was all right after she'd had such bad luck.

'Ros, I don't know how to say it. I feel dreadful after your news. But I've got the all clear.'

'Oh Doris, I'm so pleased,' she said warmly and the relief in her voice was so sincere it brought tears to my eyes. In spite of her own turmoil and tragedy she could still feel glad for me.

She was such a brave lady. That morning she said, she'd been talking to her young window cleaner whose wife had gone off and left him with a three-year-old son.

'Doris, I thought what's the matter with the world,' she said. 'There's that girl with everything to live for, a nice husband and little child and she goes away and leaves them. And here's us, such a close family and I'm being forced to leave them.'

And yet, she could still feel for that boy and sympathize with his unhappiness. That's what happens when you're getting near the spirit world. You seem to find acceptance of your own fate and a new understanding and compassion for other people.

I didn't know what I could do to help Ros so in the end I

sent her a poem which had been sent to me, in the hope it would give her strength:

He Walks The Wards

If Christ came to this world again
Would He sit with those in pain?
Would he walk the hospitals at night
With tender steps so soft and light
Would he pause by each bed and pray
Hoping that He might hear you say:
'My pain is easier to bear, Christ
Now that I know you're here.'

Well, Christ is there my friend with you
He walks the ward the whole night through
He pauses by each bed to pray
So if you can, I beg you say
Your pain is easier to bear
Because you know that He is there.

Do you think that He who suffered so
Would stand aside and let you go
Through all those hours that you have passed
Pain-racked and faint yet holding fast
To life with all your bravery?
Why Christ is always there.

He knows the fight you've had to wage
He alone your heart can gauge
He knows those moments when you feel
That nothing but your pain is real
He knows and lends His hands to you
To hold on till you get through.

So don't give in, you mean so much

Don't ever feel you're out of touch
With life and all the folk outside
For none of them are satisfied
Unless they too can with you say
Christ passed along my life today.

And in your ward and by your bed
Those words are very truly said
For Christ will ever linger near
All those who live close to a tear
And He will dry your eyes and give His Strength
   to you
So you may live within His Heart
And living there will make your pain much less to
   bear.

It makes me cry to read that poem. I think it's so
beautiful. In fact I'm sent a lot of lovely poems. The most
inarticulate people are suddenly touched by the spirit world
and words pour out of them. Here are some of my
favourites:

Mother

You always used to watch us
Anxious if we were late
In Winter by the window
In Summer by the gate.
And though we mocked you tenderly
Who took such loving care
The long road home would seem more safe
Because she waited there.
Her thoughts were all for us
She never could forget
And so I think that where she is
She must be waiting yet
Waiting till we come to her

Anxious if we're late
Watching from Heaven's window,
Leaning on Heaven's gate.

Age

Age is a quality of mind
If you have left your dreams behind
If hope is cold
If you no longer plan ahead
If your ambitions all are dead
Then you are old.

But if you make of life the best
And in your life you still have zest
If love you hold
No matter how the years go by
No matter how the birthdays fly
You are not old.

It doesn't seem so long ago
We came to say goodbye,
We held your hand and kissed your face
And had our private cry.

You looked so peaceful lying there
It was hard to realize
That when you left us here on earth
You simply closed your eyes.

So if it's true what people say
We have no cause to fear
For God will take you by the hand
And ever keep you near.

We wouldn't wish for you to stay
And suffer day by day
So when God took your hand in his
It was as if to say
No need to suffer any more
So let's quietly slip away.

Mrs Blanche Lloyd

Send Them To Bed With A Kiss

To Mothers so often discouraged,
Worn out by the toils of the day,
You often grow weary and cross and impatient,
Complain of the noise and the play,
For the play brings so many vexations,
But Mothers, whatever may vex you,
Send the children to bed with a kiss.

The dear little feet wander often,
Perhaps from the pathway of right,
The dear little hands find new mischief,
To try you from morning till night,
But think of the desolate mothers,
Who would give all the world for your bliss,
And as thanks for your infinite blessing,
Send the children to bed with a kiss.

For some day the noise will not vex you,
The silence will hurt you far more,
You will long for the sweet childish voices
For a sweet child's face at your door
And to press a child's face to your bosom,
You'd give all the world just for this,
For the comfort 'twill bring you in sorrow,
Send the children to bed with a kiss.

Shado's Poem

So small was he, so fat and round
His tummy nearly touched the ground
He stood on my hand with room to spare
Regarded me with brown eyes so aware,
Sized me up, then adopted me this special pup.

He grew in size, in wisdom too
Always seeking things to do,
The children were his special babes
None dare touch them, they were his
Love and licks and always a kiss.

Football was his special love,
Be it on the beach, on grass or on TV
He knew it all, but oh the referee
Never knew the furore he caused
When the ball was held more than a pause!

He knew his Dad was ill and tired
So kept a vigil at his side,
Those wise brown eyes so more than we
Who waited for the inevitability.

He stayed by me throughout the time
That dragged on endlessly,
Then suddenly he needed his rest,
His time had come, my special chum,
He deserved the best.

I can still see him now on that lovely plain
He'll yawn and stretch, find no more pain
That well loved voice will say to him
'Well done my son – where's Daddy's boy?'

Enjoy your new life my lovely lad,
Go walks, play games with beloved Dad,

You gave so much love to everyone,
For you the best is yet to come.

When my time to roam is over
My heart will be so happy to discover
The two of you there to wait –
One wagging his tail, one leaning on the gate!

My lovely poems may not be worthy of Shakespeare but they bring tears to my eyes just the same. You can tell that every one is written from the heart and springs from the suffering and courage of personal experience.

Shado's Poem was accompanied by a moving letter from Cathie Cluff:

Dear Doris,

Thank you for all the comfort your books have brought to me ever since my beloved husband David passed over last year.

I was one of the many who were lucky enough to have a contact through you at the Usher Hall in November 1984. David was the cheeky one, in RAF Bomber Command. You were puzzled at the connection with Guy Gibson until I explained that David had flown on that Squadron. As you said 'I was Guy Gibson's driver so I know you have no connection with him – yet there is a connection!' How right you were. Right away you said 'Lancasters'.

Well, Doris, I know you occasionally like poems so hope you like this one. You see Shado adored David, never left his side towards the end and was distraught when David passed over. I had to get the vet in to him The vet to the dog and the doctor to me – you can imagine what it was like!

I was convinced that Shado was left with me this past

year to help me, too, in fact he kept my sanity. The years of nursing were taking their toll. In January of this year Shado was telling me his time had come. Arthritis had taken his rear quarters badly. So I was there too when Shado passed over. A strange thing this, Doris, don't ask me how but I know David and Shado are together again. They are company for each other and to that end, two days after Shado died, I found myself writing Shado's Poem. Thought you might like to see it.

Hope John is keeping well. I understand what hell he went through at Arnhem.

Love

Cathie Cluff.
Edinburgh.

People who sneer that a pet is 'only an animal' obviously have no idea how much comfort and love they bring, and how much sorrow the owners feel when they pass. I think a lot of readers must have been surprised to discover from my past books that animals too live on, because I get a lot of letters on this subject.

Chatham,
Kent

Dear Mrs Stokes,

I was given one of your books recently – A Host of Voices – following the death of my dog three weeks ago. Although he was only an animal, to me he was more a member of my family – a child almost, and it was a great loss when I had to have him put to sleep through throat cancer.

Reading your book gave me great comfort, not only for this loss but also for the loss of a very dear friend

who committed suicide last year – and for other deaths
which I must surely come up against in the future. I feel
confident now that one day I will see them both again
and that in the meantime my dog has got all the fields to
run in he could ever want. I still say goodnight each
evening because after reading your book I know he is
still around.

Once again, many thanks for your help and comfort in
your books. I realize that my grief must be small
compared with most people's losses, but I'm glad to have
found the opportunity to discover Spiritualism.

Good luck in your work and may God bless you.

Mrs B. Edwards.

Matlock
Derbyshire

Dear Mrs Stokes,

A little note to say a very big thank you. I went to the
City Hall, Sheffield, on 27 November last year with many
friends, and you have changed my whole life.

On 4th March our darling Rupert (cross fox terrier/
poodle) passed over. I just thank God that although he
was nearly 15 years of age he had a wonderful life with
quality. He was so very much loved and I long to put my
arms around him and cuddle him. He loved his cuddle. I
know he is only a whisper away.

Yours sincerely

Mrs V. Kembery

She is absolutely right of course. Our pets do live on and
it was proved to me yet again only a couple of weeks ago.

I've mentioned Patrick who baked the beautiful

birthday cake for me and then cooked my Christmas dinner – well Patrick and I have become great friends. He pops in regularly and when he does, he always brings a little gift – a plant for the garden or some flowers for my spirit children or sometimes another cake.

'Patrick you mustn't feel you have to bring something every time you come love,' I said after a whole string of gifts had arrived. 'It's just nice to see you.'

But he insisted it gives him pleasure. He lost his mother not long ago and he likes to think of me as a substitute mum. Anyway, one particular Saturday while he was visiting me his mother came through with news that was going to be difficult to break. Apparently Patrick's beloved dog Sally was about to pass over. Oh dear, I thought. How am I going to tell him that. He loves that dog like a child.

'Patrick, love,' I said gently, 'you've got to be very brave. Your Mum's just come through and she's told me she's waiting to welcome Sally into the spirit world.'

The colour drained from Patrick's face. 'Oh no, surely not. She doesn't seem too bad.'

Sally was after all sixteen-and-a-half years old and her health was variable.

'I'm sorry Pat but that's what your mum says and if they're preparing a place for Sally it must be right. I think she'll pass over either tomorrow or Monday.'

Poor Patrick didn't know what to say. He'd known for a long time that Sally was a great age for a pekinese and couldn't last much longer, but he'd tried to pretend it wouldn't happen.

Well that night, he told me later, Sally didn't seem too bad, but the following morning she was obviously ill and by the afternoon Patrick realized she was going. Distraught he phoned me.

I tuned in straight away and his mother was there, all ready to collect the dog.

'It's her time to come to us,' she explained.

'Now Patrick be brave. You've got to let her go,' I said.

'Your Mum's come for her and it's only your love that's holding Sally back.'

Naturally Patrick was upset but he realized the poor dog was ill and it wasn't fair to try to keep her any longer.

'Pick her up in your arms,' I said, 'and say, "here you are Mum. Take her with love." '

There were some muffled sounds as Patrick put down the phone and reluctantly did as I suggested. Nothing happened at first but then he whispered, 'Go on Sally. Go to Mum.' And as he said the words Sally went limp in his arms and I had a sudden mental picture of a little honey brown dog bounding away across a sunlit meadow towards a woman who was standing with open arms.

'It's all right, Patrick,' I said when he returned speechlessly to the phone. 'She's safe over. I've seen her. She's racing around, happy and as lively as a puppy.'

The saddest letters, of course, are from parents who've lost children and it gives me special pleasure to know that I've been able to give them a little comfort in their grief.

East Lothian
Scotland

Dear Doris,

I hope you don't mind if I just call you Doris but you don't feel like a stranger to me, more like a trusted friend.

Our beautiful wee boy Craig passed over. I and my husband knew our wee boy was very ill, only we kept hoping and praying that it was all a bad dream and we could wake up and take him home to us, away from the hospital and just love him and look after him. Craig was only nine days old but we treasure all the beautiful memories of him and the happiness he brought to everybody.

I've always believed that when we die there is something more, that someone is looking after us. I was given your book and it seemed to lift me and reassure me in a way I can't explain very well.

The poems are beautiful and I try to remember them when the awful black despair closes in.

We love our wee boy so much. I pray we can meet him again, cuddle him and never have to part again.

You have given me the strength to really believe this.

Mrs T. Johnston.

Cullompton
Devon

Dear Doris,

I expect you receive many letters like this, but I would like to say thank you so very much for making life easier for my Mum and I after having lost our little Jessica of three months in a cot death. Even though she was so young we found there was a great hole in our hearts. Twelve months have now passed but it seems like yesterday.

Until I read your books death frightened me even though I am a committed Christian. Many friends have told me it is wrong for Mum and I to believe in what you do and stand for – yet you were the one who brought comfort to our grief stricken family, knowing Jessica was being well looked after.

May God bless you both, thank you once again for being such a comfort and friend.

C. Ruttey

Yarmouth
Isle of Wight

Dear Doris,

Today I listened to your Desert Island Discs programme which has very much moved me.

Forty-three years ago today, my husband of 24 years was shot down and died over Germany, flying with Bomber Command.

The child I was carrying was born in July '42 and brought all who knew and cared for her much joy, and to me much comfort. She was taken into spirit two days before her 11th birthday, 1953 after falling into an empty lift-shaft. Although I had by then other children and a fine husband I prayed to die, we had been *so* close, and I loved her *so* much.

Since then, but not at the time, I've learned much and truly believe her short life was completed and she is with her dear father.

But for years, before my eyes I saw that white coffin going into another deep black hole.

I have passed your books to my sister who is Catholic and whose life has been transformed. Also to friends in hospital.

I can hardly see to write, having two cataracts, not to mention tears! God bless you, my dear, and give you the strength you need for your glorious mission.

Mrs B. Pense

The bulk of my letters though, are about grief in all its different forms, because of course there is not one of us who escapes grief.

Tintagel,
Cornwall

Dear Mrs Stokes,

I feel I have to write to you after seeing and hearing you on the Wogan Show last evening. Having read your books, your thoughts and experiences have given me the extra courage to face the world since my beloved husband slipped quietly away from me two years ago.

When you said you and your friend belonged to the Sod It Club how could you know that for the past 20 years or so it was my beloved's favourite expression. Oh how through the years it has relieved the tension over so many traumatic times.

Even our vicar uses it now! As indeed do all my friends.

Yours sincerely

E. Kiness

Leigh on Sea
Essex

Dear Doris,

Until I saw you on TV last year I'd never heard of Doris Stokes. I was overwhelmed with what I saw and very soon after I bought one of your books, read it and quickly bought and read the other three. I can't put into words the impact they had on me. You took away any fear I had of death, you explained so beautifully the continuation of life when we pass over and the more I read the more you became a personal friend.

Shortly after this wonderful happening, my mother passed over and immediately I knew she was with her loved ones who she'd earlier lost. When I left the cemetery I knew I wasn't leaving mum behind, and in the visits to her grave since, they have only been out of respect, for I know she's not there. Mum's with me when-

ever I want her to be, she's in my home, she's any beautiful flower, she's the brightest shining star in the sky.

You've given so much love and happiness to so many
people that it makes me so happy just to write and tell you
so.

Paul Russo

Bolton,
Lancs

Dear Doris (please forgive familiarity!),

I feel I must write to you after hearing your selection on
Desert Island Discs yesterday morning. It was my
birthday and my dear husband passed on two years ago
last February and I miss him so much, especially on such
anniversaries.

I was very weepy but I cannot tell you how your record
selection touched me so much, for each record you
picked Doris (with the exception of your own lovely
verse) had a very special place for Tom and me.

I wrote them all down when you started with Lena Mar-
tell's One Day At A Time – a *special* favourite of Tom's –
and then I could hardly believe my ears at all the rest of
your choice. It was wonderful. Just as if dear Tom was
sending me a birthday message through you.

Thank you so much. I've been so unhappy since he
went but my heart was lifted for a best ever birthday
present.

Yours sincerely

Mrs J. Norris

I also receive letters from children and I find it very
touching to think they've struggled through my books and

understood them. This is the letter from the little girl I was hoping to meet in Liverpool:

Withington
Manchester

Dear Mrs Doris Stokes,

I am writing to you because my Daddy has just died I am age 10 one time I watched television and my mummy said that you were very good and Mummy said that she would take me to see you at your house if you would let me becouse I love my Daddy ever so much and I would like to know if he is happy or sad becouse I keep on crying all the time for my Daddys love

All my love

Gale

Finally there are my 'tonic' letters. Like everybody else I get tired and fed up from time to time and when it's bitterly cold and I've got to struggle into my dress and travel miles to some theatre instead of sinking into my armchair by the fire for the night, I think to myself what are you doing Doris? You must be mad.

Well I'm lucky. Because when I feel like that I've only got to read a few of my tonic letters and I know that the effort is all worthwhile.

Perranporth
Cornwall

Dear Mrs Stokes,

I felt I just had to write and thank you for such a wonderful evening last Saturday at St Austell. Having read all your books and any magazine article I could find, it became an ambition of mine to see you 'live' at one of your meetings. I found the reassurance and comfort you gave to those fortunate enough to have a sitting with you so marvellous and I'm sure most people like myself sat there spellbound!

My husband came with me on Saturday and beforehand was quite sceptical and so sure he would be able to 'see through' you. However he came away a total believer!

So thank you once again for a wonderful evening and for all the marvellous work you do.

With best wishes

Jayne Moon

A Midlands vicarage

Dear Mrs Stokes,

I am an Anglican priest and had almost lost my faith when I read your books earlier this year. You have helped me greatly and given me much more confidence in the realities of the spiritual world.

With all good wishes
(I will not embarrass him by
publishing his name)

Kingsbridge
Devon

Dear Mrs Stokes,

I have just been listening to Desert Island Discs and I feel so strongly to say what a comforting feeling it gave to me. I do so staunchly believe in a better life to come but, Doris, you made it all so clear, bless you.

My eyes aren't so good now but I read two of your

books a few years ago and now, to hear you in the flesh is
something I will never forget.

Yours most sincerely

Mary Winterburn

Dormansland
Surrey

Dear Doris,

I came to your evening at Croydon and I can't stop
thinking or talking about it. You gave so many messages
not only to those to whom you were talking, but to many
others present as well. The evening was a very happy one
despite all the tragedies we heard about.

I have never been to a more packed theatre and the
audience on leaving were very animated – hundreds of
people were converging on to the car park – all talking at
once.

Something happened to me during the day prior to
coming to see your show. I was convinced that it was my
mother's doing. Almost towards the end of your show
you were talking to another spirit called Bert – you said,
'Just a minute Bert, I have a Violet coming in.' Nobody
claimed Violet. Violet is my mother's name. You carried
on speaking to Bert for a minute or two. Then you said, 'I
have a Violet looking for Pat.'

I am Pat. I was so overcome that I just couldn't move to
speak or come down. You carried on talking to Bert
again. Then you said. 'I have someone here who died of
cancer of the lung.' So did my mother. Someone did
claim that their father died of cancer of the lung and this
message may have been for them but it did seem a
coincidence.

I said to a friend that if something else happened the

following day – which did seem very unlikely to both of us – then I would be convinced that the Violet you heard was my mother. This did happen so I am convinced.

Thank you Doris for all the comfort you have given in your books and also for giving us the experience of sharing in your incredible gift. It was a truly marvellous evening last Monday and one I shall never forget.

Yours sincerely

Pat Hearn

Chapter 10

Half way through the sitting Terry put his head round the door.

'Sorry to interrupt but I'm looking for that letter from Lincoln. It's very important. Have you seen it?'

I looked at the shelving unit beside me, every surface overflowing with mail. 'Yes – well it's here somewhere.'

And I was just rummaging through when a voice from the spirit world said: 'No. It's back here,' and my hand was pushed back to the shelf behind my chair.

'Oh. No it's not,' I corrected myself. 'They've just told me it's on this shelf back here.'

I reached back and sure enough, the first letter I put my hand on was the important one from Lincoln.

'By God that's useful,' said Pat Coombs, my sitter, 'I wish I could do that. I've lost a photo album and I'm very sad about it. I wish my mother could tell me where it is.'

Her mother had been talking to us before Terry came so I tuned into the same vibration and asked. Back came a message about a garage and a chest that used to be kept there.

Pat shook her head. 'No, I've looked in the garage and it's not there.'

But her mother was insistent.

'She's really certain, Pat,' I said. 'It's in a chest that belonged to your grandparents and it was always kept in the garage. You're not to worry about it because you're going to find it very soon.'

I could see Pat was a bit sceptical about this but the

sitting went on and more and more evidence came through. Her mother brought back Pat's old cat, Pip, and then she kept going on about Tiddy. I thought this must be another pet, but no, it turned out that Pat's mother's nickname was Tiddy May. She mentioned other members of the family and then suddenly a man's voice cut in. A very domineering voice.

'I was in the army,' he said.

'Oh, what rank?' I asked.

'Well you would have had to call me sir,' he chuckled. 'I was a major.'

'Yes, Tom's with me.' Tiddy May confirmed in case Pat was in any doubt that her father had arrived.

'I was always very strict and military,' he said, 'but I went peculiar towards the end. I'm glad I came over before I got incontinent. I didn't approve of Pat going into acting at first,' he added, 'but afterwards I was so proud of her. I used to say Coombs is my name. Pat Coombs' father.'

By now a great many of Pat's family and friends had come to say hello. Some of the names, however, she couldn't place. I kept getting the name Lillian which meant absolutely nothing to Pat. Back it came again and again and I was getting myself into a bit of a mess, when Ramanaov took pity on me.

'It's not Lillian,' he said, 'it's Lally.'

Pat recognized it at once. 'Lally Bowers! An old actress friend of mine.'

There was also an answer to a tragic mystery. A young man called Nicholas joined us, bringing with him a feeling of confusion.

'My nephew,' said Pat.

He mentioned Kings Cross in Sydney, Australia, where he'd lived and also talked of Brighton. Brighton, Australia? I queried. 'No. Brighton-on-Sea, England,' he said.

'That's quite right,' said Pat, 'we used to live there and he came to visit us.'

Nicholas should not have passed over when he did he kept telling me. It shouldn't have happened. There was a great deal of confusion surrounding his last hours on earth. There was something about a car.

'I was thrown,' he said, 'that's the last thing I remember. I was thrown.'

'Nobody knows what happened,' said Pat. 'His body was found beside a road in Australia. He had head injuries but apart from that there wasn't a mark on him.'

From what Nicholas said it sounded as if it wasn't an accident. The poor boy was an epileptic and it may have been that he started to have a fit and the occupants of the car, thinking he was turning violent, opened the door and pushed him out.

By the end of the sitting Pat was even more fascinated than she'd been when she arrived and she stayed on chatting for most of the afternoon. She was particularly pleased by something that sounded almost like a prediction from the other side, although I always stress that I don't tell fortunes.

I heard the name Agatha Christie very strongly and at the same time I got a very clear impression of Pat moving away from comedy.

'Pat, people associate you with comedy,' I said, 'but from what they're telling me, you could do much meatier roles. I'm getting the name Agatha Christie.'

'Oh God, I'd love to do Agatha Christie,' Pat agreed.

'Who's Michael?' I asked suddenly.

'He's a writer friend. He adapts things.'

'Well I think Michael might have something to do with you appearing in Agatha Christie. You'd make a wonderful Miss Marple,' and as I said it a vivid picture of Pat as Miss Marple with a battered hat, a bicycle and a cat round her ankles flashed into my mind.

'Let's hope you're right, Doris,' said Pat, 'I'd love to play Miss Marple. I really would.'

Most extraordinary of all the things she'd heard from

the spirit world as far as Pat was concerned though was the affair of the photo album.

When she got home that afternoon she phoned her sister to tell her what happened.

'But when I got to the part about the photo album she went very quiet,' Pat told me afterwards. 'It turned out she'd found the album that very morning in a sort of treasure chest that belonged to our grandmother. The chest was under her bed but before it passed to her it probably had been stored in the garage for years.'

People are often astonished by the accuracy of the spirit world, even more so where figures are involved. I'm not quite sure why. After all, all the messages that I hear quite distinctly are correct, so why some truths should seem more impressive than others I don't know. I remember once at a public demonstration the spirit world remarked that a woman in the audience had just bought a new oven and she'd got £130 off the recommended price. The audience were amazed when this turned out to be absolutely correct. Yet when another woman was told that a relative had just had a baby and was given the correct name, the audience seemed almost to take it for granted. I couldn't help feeling puzzled. Surely both pieces of evidence were equally good?

Something similar happened recently. A couple who'd lost their much loved daughter, Sarah, came for a sitting. The wife seemed very keen but the husband was highly sceptical and I got the impression he was only there on sufferance to please his wife. Throughout the conversation with Sarah, he sat there looking perplexed, as if he knew there was a catch somewhere but he couldn't work out where. Then towards the end, Sarah said that she'd left £28 behind to buy her brother, Chris, a present.

'Well we can soon settle that,' said her mother, 'I've got her pay packet here. I've not opened it yet.'

And she opened her handbag, brought out a battered envelope, tore off the top and shook out the contents.

Onto her knee fell several notes and some loose change. She counted it. There was exactly £28.20.

At this the father shook his head in wonder.

'There was just no way you could have known,' he said. 'Even we didn't know …'

Even Laurie, who sees these things happen all the time, is sometimes shaken. Not long ago we were talking about Marc Bolan. I'd once contacted Marc on the other side during a sitting and it turned out that Laurie knew Marc on this side and that his brother used to work with him.

'He was such a nice guy,' said Laurie, 'd'you know he even left Alphi £5,000 in his will. Unfortunately when it came to it there wasn't enough money in the estate to pay out so Alphi didn't get anything, but it didn't matter. He was really touched to know that Marc remembered him.'

I was just about to agree what a nice thoughtful boy Marc was, when suddenly Marc himself arrived.

'He's had the money now, Doris,' Marc assured me, 'and he got £6,000 not £5,000.'

'Laurie, Marc's just told me Alphi's had the money,' I said quickly, 'and it was £6,000.'

Laurie shook his head. 'No, love. You're wrong somewhere. This was years ago and there wasn't enough money to pay Alphi. He didn't get a thing.'

Well I didn't pursue it. It wasn't important and Alphi's affairs were none of my business. I didn't even give it another thought until a couple of days later, Laurie phoned me in great excitement.

'You'll never guess, Doris, I've just had a call from Alphi. He wants to take my wife and I out to celebrate. The money from Marc Bolan's come through and he did get £6,000. Marc left him £5,000 but the interest has been building up all these years and it's £6,000 now.'

Laurie himself has never had a sitting with me. Night after night at theatre demonstrations he meets so many people desperate for a sitting that he feels it would be wrong to ask me to use up my psychic energy to satisfy curiosity when there are more urgent cases out there than I could ever hope to get through in a lifetime. Nevertheless I sometimes come out with little bits without realizing it.

One morning when he called in, I asked him if he'd mind taking a bundle of clothes we no longer wear down to the Oxfam Shop or the Salvation Army for the old folk. Laurie didn't mind at all and we were just stuffing them into large carrier bags, when a woman's voice suddenly said: 'Tell him to take them round to Issy's.'

'You're to take them round to Issy's, Laurie,' I repeated out loud.

Laurie stopped dead, a pair of trousers poised in mid-air.

'What did you say?'

'It's your Mum, love,' I explained, 'she's just come over and said you're to take the clothes round to Issy's. What's Issy's?'

Laurie looked flabbergasted. 'I can't believe it. When we were kids in the East End my Mum used to take us to Issy Goodyear's in the Roman Road to buy second-hand clothes. I've not even thought about Issy's for years. The place must have been knocked down thirty years ago!'

He was so thrilled to hear from his mother that he phoned his wife, Iris, straight away to tell her the news.

'I couldn't have better proof that my old Mum was there,' he said. 'No one else would ever have known of Issy's.'

Yes, it's certainly true that occasionally the spirit world can help you find things or give you information that you want, which as Pat Coombes said, is very useful, and it's for this reason I'm sometimes asked to work on police cases. When I was in New Zealand last, I was asked to help find a missing girl. She gave her name, Susan, and she described the landscape she remembered in her last moments, but it was wintertime and the whole area was covered by snow. Later when the snows had cleared the police went back and searched the place and sure enough they found the body. I had pinpointed within 500 yards, the motorway where she was picked up and last seen alive.

But I must stress that it doesn't always work. Sometimes the messages are too confused, sometimes the significance of the information doesn't dawn until after the case is solved – like the time I was given the name Sutcliffe during a sitting with the parents of Jayne MacDonald, one of the victims of the Yorkshire Ripper. Mrs MacDonald said it was an old family name and we thought no more about it until the Ripper was caught and he turned out to be a man called Peter Sutcliffe – and sometimes the spirit world deliberately withholds information if it would do more harm than good.

I remember recently the police brought a man to see me whose seventeen-year-old daughter had been raped and murdered. Naturally they were after any clues they could get to the identity of the killer but I just couldn't help. The distraught father sat there on the sofa willing me to come up with a name and all I could feel was hate and the desire for revenge. The poor child came back and tried to talk to her father.

'I was a good girl, you know,' she kept saying. 'Tell him I was a good girl.'

But I didn't feel he was properly listening. He didn't so much want contact with his daughter as a name to pin on his hatred.

The violence of the atmosphere washed over me in wave after wave until I eventually faltered.

'Ask her who did it. Ask his name,' insisted the father, knuckles white, teeth clenched. 'Who did it, who did it?'

But from the spirit world there was only silence.

'It's no good,' I said at last, 'they're not going to give me his name because if I tell you I know what you'd do. You'd get up from that sofa, get in the car, find that boy and kill him.'

'Yes, that's right. I would,' said the father.

Many fathers in similar situations must have threatened the same thing but this man really meant it. These were no empty words.

'Well,' I said, 'the spirit world won't help you do it. What good would it do? What would happen to your wife and children with you in prison? Because that's what would happen to you.'

He wouldn't listen. 'I'll worry about that,' he said. 'Just give me his name.'

But his relatives on the other side had more sense. They refused to be a party to his plans and although they probably knew the answer, they said not a word.

'I'm sorry,' I apologized to the policeman at the end of the sitting. 'I can't help you. It might work with another member of the family but I'm afraid the father's blocking it.'

In desperate circumstances of course I try to help because there's always the chance that the tiniest scrap of information might lead to the capture of a killer and prevent another murder, but I stress strongly that I can't guarantee anything.

Not long ago I received a telephone call from the *Sevenoaks Chronicle* asking if I could help find a missing person. I explained the problems but they were still keen to try. I didn't know the details and I didn't want to but I gathered the case was something of a mystery and the normal channels had failed. I was a last resort. We could well be dealing with a murder, I realized, so I agreed to do what I could.

The reporter came along with a tiny, nervous looking middle-aged lady who was clearly at her wits' end with trying to solve the puzzle. They set up a tape recorder, the reporter got out her notebook and once we were all settled in armchairs with a cup of coffee close by, I tuned in.

At once my head was full of a German voice. I don't understand German but I knew instinctively that German was the language I was hearing.

'I hear German being spoken,' I began uncertainly.

'That's right,' said my sitter, 'I'm German.'

And in fact she did have a faint trace of an accent but her English was so good it was impossible to say where she originated from.

Oh well, I thought, I suppose I'll have to ask Ramanov to translate the whole thing for me, but to my surprise the atmosphere changed and the rest of the evidence came spontaneously in English.

Now I could understand what was said but it didn't seem to make any sense.

'Yugoslavia,' said a distant voice and I got a confused image of mountains. Now why, when we'd just established the German connection, was I getting information about Yugoslavia, I wondered.

'I'm hearing something about Yugoslavia, mountains and things,' I said, 'so there must be a connection there.'

'Yes, that's right,' said the woman.

Then I was surrounded by darkness and I didn't know what was going on. Out of the black the man's voice came again.

'Anna,' he said.

'That's me,' said the woman eagerly.

'And who's Willie?'

'That's my husband.'

Instinctively I understood that it was her husband who was missing and I was pretty sure it was Willie I was talking to on the other side, although he hadn't said so in so many words. I was very reluctant to come right out and say that he's definitely passed over, however – I always am in cases like these. I will never forget the war years when John was missing, presumed dead and a medium had told me that he was definitely on the other side, when in fact he was wounded and lying in hospital in a prisoner-of-war camp.

We can all make mistakes and sometimes the voices are muddled and indistinct. There are times when you might think you've made contact with a particular person when in fact you're tuned in to a member of their family who's talking about them.

I find it best to keep an open mind, repeat what I'm hearing and leave it to the sitter to decide if it sounds like the person they've lost.

'Anneliesse,' said the voice in my ear.

'Who's Anneliesse?' I asked.

'That's my full name,' said the woman, 'but everyone calls me Anna.'

It was sounding more and more as if it was indeed her husband I was talking to.

'I feel there's a grat mystery and a lot of confusion,' I went on. 'I feel as if I'm falling. I feel as if he was walking in the mountains and you weren't with him.'

Willie was getting agitated. 'I left everything behind in the hotel,' he said. 'Some people say it must have been planned, but how could it? I left everything behind. My clothes, everything.'

Once more there was an impression of darkness and then a drop. I struggled to keep hold of the vibration. It was really frustrating. The impressions were so confused I could hardly make head or tail of what was coming through. From somewhere a long way off came a hard 'k' sound. A name.

'Carl ... Kurt ...' I tried.

'Kurt,' said the woman, 'he lives in Sevenoaks. He's worked very hard to try to find Willie.'

But I hardly heard her voice. Suddenly I was on a rocky path and very loud I could hear the sound of rushing water. Not far away there was a waterfall.

Now at last we were getting somewhere. This, I felt sure, was significant.

'I can hear water rushing,' I explained out loud, 'and there's a drop close by and a waterfall. And this man who's talking to me, he has a very loving voice. He isn't the type to just disappear. He says he had only been there three days and if he'd wanted to disappear he would have gone on the first day. He just went out and never returned.'

'Katarina,' said the man emphatically.

'Who's Katarina?' I asked.

'She's a Yugoslav girl who was there,' said the woman.

She too was important. The man was obviously anxious to prove that he hadn't planned to run away, neither had he been suicidal.

'Ask Katarina,' he said, 'she will tell you I was perfectly all right. I wasn't depressed.'

And then there was the rushing water again. The sound was in the background the whole time. If I closed my eyes it would have been difficult to believe I was sitting in my own armchair in my own sittingroom. I felt as if I was high on a mountainside beside a stream. And there was the waterfall again. There was something about that waterfall …

'He's saying you go up the path before the fall, then there's a drop,' I said slowly. 'And it's a big fall …'

But my contact couldn't seem to hold the impression steady. I was getting the sounds all right but the pictures kept going. The rocky path disappeared and instead I got a name.

'Wolfgang.'

The woman gave a little gasp. 'That's Willie's real name – but nobody knew. Everybody called him Willie.'

The man was getting agitated again. He had a very orderly mind and he seemed to feel that the search hadn't been thorough enough.

'He gets very impatient,' I explained. 'He can't understand why they are so lax. He says they only have to go five paces and they would find him. He seems to think they've stopped bothering in Yugoslavia.'

Another impression flickered before my eyes. I was bending down to look at something interesting, some plant I think and then something hit me on the back of the head. The sound of running water continued but in addition I got a fleeting glimpse of caves.

'He was climbing just before the waterfall and stopped to look at something that interested him,' I said out loud. 'Further up the mountain there are caves ... I don't think the caves have been searched properly.'

The sitting went on. There were more names. The man mentioned Derek, his son, and Jenny the cat and he even asked about his white car. I was pretty certain from the way he was talking that he was the missing husband and he'd been killed in suspicious circumstances. I couldn't think why but there seemed to be some sort of cover-up somewhere.

'Well, what do you think, love?' I asked Anneliesse when the power eventually faded. 'D'you think we've been talking to your husband.'

'Oh yes,' she said. 'It sounded just like him.'

Afterwards the reporter filled me in on the story. Apparently the couple were called Mr and Mrs Bleyberg and they had been going to Yugoslavia on walking holidays for the past twenty years or so. They always went to the same area and they knew the hotel and locals quite well. They could even speak some of the language.

Willie was a respected science teacher in Sevenoaks, Kent, and the couple lived a quiet, ordinary life. Then in July 1984 when the time for their holiday came round again, Anneliesse's mother was ill and she had to stay behind to look after her. Anneliesse wasn't keen on her husband going away alone but he seemed to have his heart set on this holiday so reluctantly she agreed.

The morning he disappeared was fine and bright and Willie breakfasted at the hotel and set out for his walk straight afterwards. He left his personal belongings behind in his room and gave every indication that he would be returning for dinner.

Later in the day two locals saw him on the mountain alone but cheerful, and an hour or two afterwards they bumped into him again. He'd tried one particular path he told them but it was too difficult so he was going to set out in a different direction. Off he went with a good-natured wave and was never seen again.

The extraordinary part of the story was that Anneliesse wasn't informed that her husband was missing until five days later. The area was searched but nothing was found, and to add to her distress, Anneliesse realized that without a body she couldn't prove that her husband was dead and all his financial affairs would be frozen until a death certificate was issued – which couldn't be done, of course, without a body.

The muddle and the uncertainty, added to her natural grief, was proving almost too much for the poor woman. The only consolation was that the evidence from the sitting might be enough to persuade the authorities to reopen the case and call for another search.

Yes, the spirit world does often help us find things – but it's not a one-way affair. Sometimes they want us to help them!

I was doing a couple of demonstrations in Bridlington not long ago and I had been looking forward to it. After the long cold winter and several doses of 'flu, a breath of sea air was just what I needed. We were staying in a nice seaside hotel and that first night I was hoping for a long refreshing sleep.

Well I had the refreshing sleep all right, but it wasn't very long! Early in the morning, just as the dawn chorus was starting up, I heard a voice talking to me.

'It's Paul. I hung myself,' he said.

Half asleep, I thought I was having a nightmare. I peeped out through slits in my eyelids and saw that I was quite safe in my comfortable hotel room. I'm dreaming I said to myself and turned over for another hour or two.

'I hung myself,' said the sad voice again. And this time I realized it was no use. I couldn't pretend. I wasn't asleep and I wasn't dreaming. The voice was real.

I sat up. 'You what, love? What did you say?'

'I hung myself,' said the boy. 'Can you tell my Mum I'm

sorry? She's so upset.'

'Well how am I going to find your Mum, love?' I asked. There was no telling where he came from or anything.

From the other side I could feel a great effort being made. The lad couldn't have been over very long and he was having difficulty keeping the power going.

'Paul,' I heard again. Then, 'Plane Street.'

There was silence for a long time and then just when I thought he'd gone there came the name 'Hewson', very faint.

'I was twenty,' he added. 'Shane's got my things.'

That was it. Well it wasn't much to go on. How on earth was I going to find Paul's Mum. I had part of an address but Plane Street on its own wasn't much use without a town to go with it.

Luckily later that day I had an interview booked with a reporter from the Hull *Daily Mail*. Perhaps she might have heard something. After all if it had happened recently it might have been in the paper.

When she arrived I explained what had happened.

'I got the name Paul, and Hewson and Plane Street,' I said. 'He said he hanged himself and that he was only twenty. Does that ring any bells? D'you think Plane Street could be in your area?'

She shook her head. 'No, it doesn't mean anything to me, Doris. I don't remember a story like that, but I'll check with the paper if you like.'

She rang through to her office and we waited while they flicked through back copies of the paper. Then ten minutes later they found the item. On the previous Saturday a boy named Paul Hewson hanged himself. He lived in Plane Street. They couldn't confirm whether there was anybody in the family called Shane, but Paul was only twenty years old. Now all I needed was the Hewsons to be present at my demonstration that night and I could do as Paul had asked.

Well it didn't work out quite as neatly as that but it

wasn't bad. Mrs Hewson wasn't in the audience that night but her cousin was. I gave her some flowers to take home to Paul's Mum and I explained that if Mrs Hewson would like to come to the demonstration the following night, we'd arrange it. Thank goodness we were doing the two nights in Bridlington!

Sure enough, Mrs Hewson wanted to come and during the second half of the demonstration Paul came back, clear and strong. His practise the morning before had obviously helped him get the hang of communicating.

Mrs Hewson came to the microphone as the message began and gradually she was joined by more and more people.

'He's talking about Shane,' I said as we began.

'Yes, Shane's his brother,' said Mrs Hewson.

'And he tells me he's being buried at three o'clock on Friday.'

'That's right.'

'Who's Donna?'

'His girlfriend.'

Dabbing quickly at her eyes, a very young girl came to the microphone. 'Donna and I were going to get engaged you know,' Paul said proudly.

'Yes, we were,' she sobbed.

Then Paul spotted someone else he knew. 'There's Dave. There's my mate!' he cried in delight. 'He's in my group.'

It turned out Paul was a drummer in a pop group and his friend Dave had been very close to him. Dave stepped forward to join Mrs Hewson and Donna.

'We were doing so well with the group and Donna and I were going to get engaged. I must have been mad. I must have been off my trolley to do it,' Paul went on.

'Apparently he had words with someone, Dave, about a gig,' I explained. 'He was a very likeable boy but very sensitive and someone upset him.'

But Paul didn't want to dwell on the unhappiness. 'My guvnor's here tonight as well,' he confided, 'Frank.'

Sure enough, Frank was there and grinning bashfully he came out of the audience to join the little crowd round the mike.

'I'll always be with Frank in the car,' said Paul. 'When he's out in the motor tell him to think of me and I'll be there.'

'Yes we were often together in the car,' said Frank, 'I used to run him around.'

Most of all though, Paul was concerned about his brother Shane. I couldn't quite work out what he meant. He seemed to want Shane to have something that belonged to him but I couldn't catch what it was and Mrs Hewson couldn't think of anything that seemed likely.

'Well I don't know quite what he means,' I admitted, 'but I know he's very concerned about Shane. He says it frightened Shane badly.'

Mrs Hewson nodded. 'Shane hasn't broken down yet, you see,' she said. This was a bad sign. When people don't cry it means the pain and bitterness turns inwards and can make them ill. No wonder Paul was worried.

'Well give him something of Paul's and tell him that Paul wants him to have it with his love,' I said. 'It might help.'

And, finally, right at the end Paul told me that they were having a beautiful set of drums made in flowers for his funeral.

'Thank them for that, I shall enjoy it,' he said, 'but tell Mum not to spend too much money.'

I couldn't devote the whole evening to Paul's people, of course, because it wasn't a private setting and other families wanted a turn too. I had to move on. But at least Paul had been able to prove to his mother that he wasn't dead, that he was still taking an interest in the family and above all that he was sorry for the heartache he caused.

Chapter 11

It was spring, though you'd never have guessed it from the weather, and there we were back on our travels, gliding down the motorway in our posh limousine heading for Cornwall.

The rain was streaming down the windows, the wipers slapping like mad but our voices drowned out the storm as we sang along lustily to *Sing Something Simple*.

Maybe it was the flat countryside we were passing through or maybe it was the tune I was croaking, but suddenly my memory did a backward somersault – the years rolled away and I was bowling along in the battered old Morris E with running boards on the side that we'd bought for £32. Terry couldn't have been more than four in those days and we couldn't afford holidays, but it didn't matter.

On fine summer Sundays we used to get up at the crack of dawn, load the Morris and head off to Skegness, our nearest seaside resort – sixty miles away. We'd drive as far as our empty stomachs would allow, and then when we couldn't stand it any longer, we'd pull up in a pretty spot, get out the little spirit stove and I'd cook breakfast at the side of the road. Later, on the beach, we paddled with Terry, and John took him in swimming. Then at the end of a long happy day we'd drive back, singing along to *Sing Something Simple* at the top of our voices.

I sighed and wiped condensation from the window. Here we were forty years on swanning round in a Daimler and staying at the best hotels, yet we'd never been so happy as those days when we rattled off to the seaside in our £32 Morris and had to stop and think twice about whether we could afford to buy an ice cream for Terry.

There's something about travelling that sparks off memories and when I'm anywhere near Lincolnshire, the floodgates really open. Grantham, of course, is my home town and although it's changed a lot since I was a girl it's like stepping into a time machine when I go back.

The last time I was there I met my long lost cousin Ron Sutton and when he walked in my stomach did a sudden flip, because these days he looks so much like my father it was as if Dad had come into the room. You can certainly tell Ron's a Sutton all right.

He's a great character is Ron. Everyone in Grantham knows him. Sixty-nine years old, he jumps fences like a two-year-old and races around on his moped in his leather jacket and crash helmet. The effect is a bit spoiled by the fact that Ron doesn't wear any teeth, but when people ask where they are he says: 'I left them in a jam jar when we lived in Norton Street. I suppose they were still there when they pulled the houses down.'

He's not at all bothered. 'I can eat whatever I like. Pickled onions, anything,' he insists and he can as well. He must have very tough gums.

In his time Ron has been known to do a bit of poaching – just like my father. When I was a little girl my father once disappeared for a week and I was told he'd gone to Lincoln. This was quite true, but I didn't find out until I was older that he'd actually been sent to Lincoln prison for poaching.

In those days we were very poor and it was quite common for people to do a bit of poaching to make ends meet. My father was quite open about it.

'Yes and I'd go to prison for 7 days again rather than see my family go hungry when Lord Brownlow's got all those rabbits running wild on his land,' he used to say.

It all came back as Ron stood grinning in the reception

of the George Hotel, his crash helmet dangling from his hand.

'I've just been to the sales,' he told me. 'By – there was some good stuff going for little or nothing.'

And once again it could have been my father talking. Dad loved auctions and what we called 'the stones' in the market. Grantham is an old market town and on Saturday the farmers used to bring all their produce in. There was cattle one side, then all the pets, puppies and kittens and caged birds, then the big furniture and then the small stuff laid out 'on the stones' – small areas enclosed by railings with tables full of boxes in the centre.

Dad used to gravitate towards the stones and what he was after was clocks. He had a thing about clocks. We had so many clocks in our house it was incredible. You must have heard the place ticking like a time bomb from right up the street. When I look back now I think why on earth didn't we keep them? They'd be worth a fortune now. There were chiming clocks and grandfather clocks, you name it and we'd got it. Dad used to get them cheap if they didn't go. He fiddled until he got them working and then, as often as not, if someone admired a particular clock he said, 'Well you can have it.'

He gave them all away.

But no matter how many clocks we had, Dad just couldn't resist the market. In fact he loved it so much that he carried on visiting from the other side, as I happen to know.

Like everyone else in Grantham, John and I used to do our shopping in the market on Saturday. There was an old saying in Grantham that if you wanted to meet any of your old pals you haven't seen for years, go down to Grantham market on a Saturday and sure enough, somewhere or other you'll bump into them.

Well John and I with Terry in tow used to shop and chat then we'd wander up to the auctions on the stones for a look round. One particular day we were standing peering through the railings when I noticed a large cardboard box standing on the table inside. You weren't allowed to examine it, you were expected to bid and hope for the best. It seemed crazy. I mean who'd bid for a cardboard box without knowing what was inside?

I was just shaking my head at such madness when I heard my father's voice clear as clear.

'Bid for that box, Dol,' he said firmly.

And I didn't hesitate. When my Dad used that tone of voice you did as you were told – even if it was over thirty years since he'd passed.

'I'm going to bid for that box, John,' I announced loudly.

John stared at me as if I'd been out in the sun too long. 'Don't be a fool. You don't know what's in it.'

'I know, but I'm going to bid for it,' I insisted, and I went right ahead.

There were obviously quite a few people as reckless as me because the bidding went up and up and eventually it reached ten shillings, which was a lot of money in those days. Ten shillings! I thought with the first pang of anxiety. But Dad had told me to do it and he must have seen something in that box that was a bargain.

I shot my hand up. 'Yes ten shillings!' I called in case they hadn't noticed my hand.

And miraculously everyone else dropped out and the box was mine. John shook his head in disbelief, quite speechless at such extravagance, and I must admit I had a few qualms myself.

'Suppose it's full of old clothes or plaster ornaments,' I thought in horror. But I held my head high and handed over my ten shillings as confidently as if I knew for a fact that the box was full of treasure. All the way home I had a nasty fluttery feeling in my stomach and I raced inside as soon as John opened the door.

Down went the box on the kitchen table and rapidly I tore open the top and ripped out the newspaper packing.

Then I relaxed and a great big grin spread over my face. Good old Dad. He hadn't let me down.

'John, look at this!' I called and I pulled out of the box a silver Queen Anne tea service, followed by a set of silver cutlery with beautiful carved ivory handles.

That box was a godsend. It went under my bed and whenever we were really hard up I rummaged through for a piece of silver to sell. My silver got us through quite a few difficult times.

I'm sure Dad continued to go to the sales with us because a year or so later the same thing happened again, only this time it wasn't a cardboard box but a sealed jewellery box he told me to bid for. When I got it home I discovered it was filled with pretty pieces of jewellery.

I don't suppose they were worth a fortune but they brought in a shilling or two when I was at my wits' end and I didn't know how we'd manage till the end of the week.

Ron and I had a wonderful time catching up on the old days. There was a time when his house had been like a second home to me and Ron's mum, Aunt Aggie, was very good to me when I was a little girl. She had a thing about lace did Aunt Aggie and she had lace draped over her pictures and mirrors and lace draped along the mantelshelf. In fact anywhere you could drape lace, Aunt Aggie draped it.

She was very kind. The first thing she said when you crossed the threshold was, 'Are you hungry? Have you eaten girl?' And there was always something to eat even if it was only a piece of bread and dripping. And when I was fourteen and just started work and came home with my hands all chapped and bleeding from scrubbing floors, it was Aunt Aggie who rubbed them with vaseline and bandaged them up for me.

So I was astonished when I came out of the hotel, climbed into the Daimler and waved goodbye to Ron one day, when a lady said to me, 'How on earth did you get a relative like Ron Sutton?'

I just stared at her in amazement. I come from a poor background and I'm not ashamed to admit it. I'm proud of being a Sutton, just like Ron. It's made me hard-working and self-reliant. Years ago when he came home from Arnhem with a head wound, John found he couldn't work in the factory. The noise of the machines was driving him mad. He needed peace and quiet and the open air, so he took a job as a gardener at a private school just outside Stamford.

Accommodation was provided and I was to do a bit of everything – cleaning, standing in for matron, a little cooking now and again. At the interview we'd been shown a pleasant little flat inside the main building, but when we arrived with our furniture, having given up the house we'd been renting, the owner announced that she couldn't allow a man in the place with the girls, so she was putting us in the coach house.

Well we couldn't believe our eyes. The place had previously been used as a stable. There were rats as big as cats and no proper cooking facilities. Another woman might have turned right round and gone straight back to Grantham and who could blame her – but I was a Sutton and Suttons, I decided, stuck it out. We'd burned our boats in Grantham. Factory work was making John ill. We'd just have to make the best of it.

I scrubbed the place from the top to bottom. I made do and I learned how to make Yorkshire puddings in a frying pan on an upturned electric fire. We survived and we stuck it out for six months until John found something better.

That was the way I was brought up and Ron too and no matter what material things we collect along the years we're still the same people. So why on earth shouldn't I have a cousin like Ron Sutton?

Yes travel does send me off down memory lane but that's not to say that the present isn't every bit as interesting as the past. Cornwall turned out to be just as pretty as people told me it would be. The hedgerows were full of buttery primroses, there were daffodils in every garden and the little thatched cottages really did look like chocolate box lids come to life. It was a pity about the rain but through the flowing windows you could tell it would be beautiful when the sun came out.

There had been a bit of difficulty booking a hotel. Laurie had found a conveniently situated place but when he phoned they sounded doubtful.

'Are you a group?' asked the receptionist.

'I suppose so,' said Laurie, 'there are four of us.'

The receptionist wasn't sure this counted. 'You'll have to ask the manager,' she said.

The manager wasn't too encouraging either.

'Doris Stokes,' he said. 'Never heard of her.'

Nevertheless, he agreed that if Laurie sent in written confirmation it would be all right. Well Laurie wrote his letter but just before we left some niggling doubt made him phone the hotel again, just to make sure.

It was a good thing he did, because the rooms had been let to other people.

Perhaps it was a simple mistake, but I got the feeling that the manager didn't want the likes of us staying there. Maybe he thought I'd bring ghosts into the hotel, or hold weird seances in my room!

Undaunted Laurie found us another place in Newquay, but I was a little anxious about the reception we'd receive. Perhaps we wouldn't be welcome in Cornwall.

It just shows how wrong you can be. They couldn't have been nicer at the hotel in Newquay. The manageress herself came to greet us, apologizing profusely because her hands were grubby.

'I've just been potting up some plants in the greenhouse,' she explained. Then she peered at our tired faces, bleary from the seven hour journey. 'You look as if you could do with some tea,' she said. 'Come and get settled and I'll bring you a pot. I've put Mr and Mrs Stokes in the villa because we've got a wedding tonight and it'll be quieter away from the main building,' and she led us outside, chatting as if we were old friends come to stay.

The villa turned out to be a pleasant little house in the grounds and we'd hardly put down our suitcases before the manageress was back with a tray of tea.

'Now don't forget. If there's anything you want just call.'

It was a hectic visit. We'd travelled to Cornwall to do a charity show in aid of the Save the Children Fund at a school hall in St Austell, where we were also to be presented with a cheque for the same cause. There were a frantic few moments when Laurie found that the man who'd organized the whole thing and made all the arrangements couldn't be reached at the telephone number we'd been given. We had panicky visions of having come all this way for nothing, when Ramanov stepped in with some sensible advice.

'Get in touch with the radio station. They will find him.'

'Brilliant,' said Laurie and sure enough little more than an hour after the SOS went out over the local radio, the organizer phoned us.

While we were in Cornwall there was one sitting I had to do. Apparently there was a girl who'd been trying every way she could think of to get a sitting. She'd even written to *Jim'll Fix It*. I didn't feel I could turn her away after that, particularly as I was going to be in the area, so I invited her to come and see me.

Well three of them turned up, Phyllis, who'd written the letter, and two other girls, Pat and Nicola. It was a right old mix up, with spirit people wanting to talk to all of them, but we managed to sort most of it out. It turned out that Phyllis' husband, Peter, had died suddenly of a heart attack while he was playing badminton and Peter was related to Pat.

'That's my sister,' he told me.

Peter's parents, Bertram and Ivy, came back too, to say hello and then I kept hearing a strange word. It sounded very like 'Catshole'. I tried to ignore it but they kept sending it back to me. Well I didn't know what to make of it. It sounded a bit rude to me but they were so insistent, I decided to risk it.

'Look I don't know what to make of this,' I admitted, 'but I'm hearing something like Catshole. I don't know what it means ...'

'Yes Catshole!' exclaimed Pat in delight. 'It's a place. We used to live there!'

They seemed quite pleased with the sitting but there was no time to hang around, we had to be off to St Austell. I changed into my long dress, climbed back into the car and we set off down tiny lanes with steep green banks on either side. It was still raining. If it carried on like this I'll need flippers not a long dress, I said to myself. I'd long since given up worrying about my hair. In damp weather it goes just like a gollywog and I must have looked like something the cat dragged in. But in St Austell it didn't matter a bit. We had such a wonderful evening, there was so much love generated in that school building that if you could have connected it to the national grid we'd have lit up Cornwall!

They'd gone to a great deal of trouble with the stage and it looked magnificent. They must have emptied six flower shops. There were tubs and tubs of daffodils and great baskets of flowers for me to give away. It glowed bright gold even with the lights turned down and when the spotlights came on it was radiant.

Nobody was left out. As the audience came in they were presented with white carnations and I was given a beautiful spray of yellow roses.

The atmosphere was wonderful from the start and the voices flowed. One in particular stands out in my mind because it was a lesson for all of us.

A boy named Richard came through, very distressed because he'd taken his own life. He was looking for Lynne he said and Stephen went with Lynne.

A woman came forward at once.

'I'm Lynne,' she said, 'Stephen's my son and Richard's my son in spirit.'

'Richard's very distressed,' I began tactfully.

'Yes, Doris,' said the woman, 'he shot himself.'

She seemed quite composed so I went on.

'He's got a girl with him.'

'Yes that'll be my daughter, she drowned.'

I paused unable to quite believe all the tragedy I was hearing. 'And there's another young person just joined them who's just gone over and ... Oh dear, don't say he took himself over as well ...'

'Yes,' said the woman, 'that's my nephew, Kevin. He took his own life three days ago.'

The horror grew. More and more names came through and the woman recognized them all, reeling off their sad stories one by one, 'Oh yes he took himself over, she did it ...' Until in the end I was almost speechless. What tragedy some people suffer, I thought, and yet this lady's face was serene and she managed to smile.

'Well like you, Doris, I take one day at a time,' she said, 'there must be a reason for it.'

I had to admire such courage. What a marvellous attitude. She was absolutely right of course, but in the same situation I don't know if I would have had the strength just to trust and believe that everything happened for a reason.

There was great love and unselfishness that night. Later I got the name Maria.

'Who's Maria?' I asked.

'I am,' said an Italian woman walking down to the microphone.

I got her son back and as I was talking to him I felt something cool and knobbly put into my hand. It was a rosary.

'He's put a rosary into my hand,' I said, 'so I know you must have put one in with him.'

Maria broke down. 'That's it, it's all I wanted to know,'

she sobbed in relief, quite content to move aside and let someone else have a turn now she'd got the one piece of evidence that proved to her her son was still close.

The same unselfish attitude touched everyone. They held a raffle for a beautiful doll during the evening and later when I was having a cup of tea in one of the classrooms, the winner asked if she could come and see me. She came in, tears streaming down her face, the magnificent doll in her arms.

'Doris, my little girl's only sixteen months old, too young for this,' she said, 'I'd like you to have it for the Save the Children Fund.'

The doll was exquisite, all done up in silver organzine but, I thought, a child would sooner have a doll she can undress. So when we got home I asked a clever friend to make a set of clothes and underwear that could be taken off and put on again, so that I could give the doll to the bone marrow unit at Westminster Hospital for some frightened little girl to play with.

There were more lovely surprises at St Austell. When the demonstration was over, two little children came on stage carrying a giant £2,000 cheque between them, just like the giant pools cheques you see on television. They presented it to me for the Save the Children Fund, then off they went, only to return with Tracey, a little girl staggering under the weight of a huge box of Cornish goodies and Stephen the little boy, carrying a breakfast set of Cornish pottery. Gifts from Cornwall for me to keep.

Then a man stood up and said he'd written a poem specially for me. His name was Basil Thorne and he came on stage to read it. It went like this;:

Cornwall's mystic and magical charms,
Welcome you Doris with wide open arms,
We need your gift to strengthen those,
Within whose breast, doubts still repose.

We wish to know more of the power from within,
That you can receive from our kith and kin,
We believe very strongly and know that it's true,
That Spirits transmit their thoughts through you.

Our gifts are many, varied and free,
All different branches of the very same tree,
We must all make the most of the gifts that we
   have,
And use them to strengthen the weak and the sad.

One thing is certain, we don't always choose,
The right road to take – our gifts best to use,
We hope that your visit will help in some way,
To clarify things for our people today.

And now dear Doris, let's hasten to say,
It's lovely to have you with us today,
We've waited so long so listen we pray,
We hope the next time you come here to stay.

Then he presented me with a copy, all beautifully written on thick creamy yellow paper. But that wasn't the end. When Basil left the stage two young girls, Karen Retallick and Norma Arthur came on to sing me a song they'd written and composed themselves. It was a special welcome song and the chorus went: 'Welcome from us Cornish folk to the land of pasties and cream.'

By the time they finished, my eyes were so full of tears I could harldly see the stage. I felt quite overwhelmed. The journey had been long and tiring but the love they'd shown me in St Austell made it worth every mile.

And just as I was walking out of the hall, a man leaned over from the audience and said, 'How about the *Don Lane Show*, Doris?'

I stopped in surprise. The *Don Lane Show* was so far from my thoughts I felt sure I'd misheard.

'I beg your pardon?'

'The *Don Lane Show*,' the man repeated, 'the last time I saw you Doris was in Australia!'

I couldn't help smiling. What a small world. I'd come all the way to Cornwall to be reminded of the day all the fuss began – when I appeared on the *Don Lane Show* in Australia.

When we got back to our hotel the manageress had seen that the lights were on in the villa, the table was laid up with cold meats and salad and there were hot water bottles warming our beds. It was the perfect end to a perfect evening.

To cap it all, the next morning as we were leaving, the rain actually stopped and the sun came out. The bay was all blue and glistening as we drove away and I could see what looked like black and white penguins bobbing about in the water.

Penguins? I thought, In Cornwall! But when we got closer they turned out to be little lads in black and white wet suits surfing!

We seemed to spend a lot of time on the road that Spring and I dread to think how many miles we covered. We crossed and recrossed from one end of the country to the other and as well as the charity evening in St Austell, I was asked to speak at a literary dinner in Yorkshire.

We drove up and up into the moors until our ears were popping and I hardly dared look out of the window because I'm scared of heights.

'When you said Yorkshire, Laurie,' I said as we passed another sheer drop, 'I thought you meant a town somewhere.'

'So did I,' said Laurie.

But we ended up at a beautiful old world hotel deep in the moors. It was a lovely place, all beams and great log fires and there was time for a nap in our rooms before dinner.

At seven forty-five we went downstairs to the bar where

everybody was meeting and we couldn't believe our eyes. The people were crammed in, shoulder to shoulder and extra tables were being carried into the dining-room. How they squeezed so many people in I don't know, but Robbie who drives our Daimler was wedged in so tightly he could only use his left hand! He was able to trap a carrot or two as they went by he told us later, but that was about all!

Johnny Morris was the other guest that night. We'd expected him to tell some animal stories but instead he sang the *Floral Dance* which certainly made a change. You don't associate Johnny Morris with singing.

Then it was my turn. Earlier as I was getting ready I'd heard the name Cocklin and though I didn't know what the literary dinner people were going to make of me, I asked if there was anybody present who knew the name.

'Yes that's me,' called a woman in surprise. 'I'm Mrs Cocklin.'

She was there with her husband who apparently had come with the greatest reluctance.

'Well I'll go for an evening out,' he'd said, 'but it's a load of old balderdash.'

Well I was chatting away to Mrs Cocklin when suddenly a woman's voice interrupted us.

'Oh by the way,' I said, 'I've got a lady here called Lizzie and she wants your husband.'

The man beside her, a little flushed from the wine and the heat all those people had generated, stood up, a bemused expression on his face.

'I just don't believe this. I said to my wife on the way here, if there's any chance of my mother coming back she'd come back, but there isn't. And here you are getting through to her. Nobody ever called her Elizabeth. It was always Lizzie.'

We were under way. A boy called Ashley came back to his mother. Then there was a Mrs Turner.

'Who's Ronnie, living?' I asked.

'Ronnie's my husband,' she said in such a surprised voice

I think she suspected Ronnie of passing me a note under the table or something.

It went on and on and it was nearly midnight before we were able to slip away to our room. I'd hardly taken my shoes off though when there was a knock at the door. It was the organizer.

'I'm sorry Mrs Stokes but you're supposed to be signing books. There's a long queue.'

So back I went and signed books till one o'clock in the morning. It was the longest dinner I've ever had!

A month or two later there was another lovely trip in the diary, this time to Portsmouth. Unfortunately I was very tired by the time we got there – but it was my own fault.

The Portsmouth visit happened to coincide with the *Psychic News* dinner dance. Now as a rule, apart from work, John and I hardly ever go out. We do so much travelling and attend so many functions in the line of duty as it were, that we like to spend our free time flopping at home. The last thing we want to do on our nights off is climb into our fancy clothes and go out on the town!

The *Psychic News* dinner dance though is the one exception of the year. It's the chance to meet up with our old friends, have a good gossip and let our hair down if we feel like it and we never miss it. This year in particular was going to be fun I knew, because Russell Grant was going and Derek Jameson was guest of honour and would be making the speech and knowing Derek's sense of humour, it was bound to be hysterical.

Well we had a marvellous time. I danced every dance and we didn't leave till the end, even though we were driving straight down to Portsmouth afterwards. My feet were killing me by the time we came away. It was my own fault entirely, of course, but as I told the audience the next day, when handsome young men come and ask you to dance at my age, you have to get in when you can!

Had we been able to set off there and then though, it wouldn't have been too bad, but it was at that point I discovered I'd left my pills behind. My pills are vital. I have to take them every day of my life because my thyroid gland was removed after I was injured by a patient when I was a mental nurse.

For a moment we thought we'd have to go all the way back home to fetch them, but then Laurie had a brainwave.

'Let's call in at the hospital. They'll let you have some, Doris.'

The hospital was just round the corner and they said yes, it would be quite all right, but I would need to see the doctor. So in we went in all our finery, me in my long dress and John in his smart suit and we sat in casualty for half an hour. It was long past midnight by now but we were so exhilarated by the dancing we were wide awake.

At last the doctor called me in.

'Actually I didn't really need to see you,' she confessed, 'but I've heard you on the radio and on TV and I wanted to meet you!' But she organized the drugs for us and at last we were off.

Oh well, I thought, another one and a half hours and we'll be tucked up snug and warm in our hotel. Which just goes to show how wrong you can be even if you're psychic! Not far out of London we came upon a bad accident on the road and we sat there for over an hour while we waited for ambulances and breakdown lorries to clear it up.

Oh dear some poor soul's got it tonight, I thought. You couldn't grumble. You just sat there thankful to be safe.

We eventually got to our hotel at four in the morning. Almost staggering with tiredness John and I let ourselves into our room to be greeted by a great welcoming basket of fruit and a letter addressed to Doris Stokes.

'Heavens above who knows I'm here?' I said to John. 'We're only here two nights.'

But it wasn't a heartrending letter imploring me for a sitting, it was just a little note from the Chief Accountant thanking me for the books because he'd enjoyed them so much.

As expected we paid for our adventurous night by feeling particularly sluggish when we got up. Well it serves you right, Doris, I told myself. If you will go dancing all night like an eighteen-year-old what do you expect! But as the show drew nearer it stopped being funny.

I just don't know how I'm going to do it, I thought as I went off reluctantly to get ready. But when I started to tune in, in the bathroom as I always do in the hope of a few scraps to get the ball rolling at the theatre, a little boy walked in. He was about ten years old, fairish, and he was wearing a t-shirt with writing across the front.

'Hello, love,' I said drying my face.

'Kittiwick,' said the boy, and, 'Sylvia,' and a bit later, just as he was going, 'Brent.'

I couldn't make out if it was a place or a name but when he vanished I put my head round the bathroom door and called John.

'Can you help me remember, love? It's for tonight. Kittiwick, Sylvia and Brent.'

'Kittiwick, Sylvia and Brent,' repeated John. 'It doesn't sound like much.'

'No I know, but it was a little boy and I bet his Mum's in the audience tonight.'

Driving to the theatre that evening we pulled up at traffic lights and a red car drew alongside us. There were four youngsters inside and when they noticed us, they started shouting 'Hello Doris!' and waving their tickets at us.

The lights changed, the red car shot ahead and suddenly in the back window appeared a big sheet of paper saying:

'We love you, Doris!' and still waving and shouting, the kids led us to the theatre.

After such a warm welcome I was surprised to find the theatre manager a little cool. I couldn't understand it. I'd been to Portsmouth before and everything had gone well then but this particular manager hadn't been there at the time so perhaps he didn't know. Or perhaps he was simply annoyed at having to work on a Sunday. Whatever it was I felt he didn't seem all that pleased to see us.

Fortunately the audience didn't seem to share his feelings. When I walked on stage they didn't just clap, they stamped their feet and cheered. What's more, Sylvia was in the audience and the meaning of the little boy's visit became clear.

Sylvia lived in Kittiwake Close, she'd lost her ten-year-old son, Matthew, and his friend was called Brent. I got Matthew back again when I tuned in and the whole tragic story came out.

Sylvia had been going shopping and Matthew begged to be allowed to stay behind to play with his friend. Some time after his mother had gone, Matthew decided he wanted something from the house, and impulsively tried to climb through one of the small open windows at the top of the main window.

'Oh I was so naughty. So naughty,' said Matthew, repentant now. Somehow he'd slipped with his head caught in the window and broke his neck.

'Mum's not been back home since,' Matthew told me, 'but she's got all my pictures up.'

I didn't understand how this could be, but Sylvia confirmed it was true.

'Oh yes. A friend went and fetched them for me,' she said.

When I came off after the first half the manager was a changed man. He put his arms round me and gave me a big hug.

'That was marvellous,' he said, 'the last time we had anyone like you here it was embarrassing and I thought tonight would be the same, but what a difference. That was marvellous.'

And out came the silver tea service for my intermission cup of tea and everything was all right. I was in.

The rest of the evening went just as well. Throughout

I'd been rather puzzled because I kept hearing the name Daisy but no one claimed it. Then during question time a little old lady came up to the microphone to ask a question about her sister Maisie.

Instantly I got it.

'That wasn't Daisy, I was getting, it was Maisie!' I exclaimed and immediately Maisie was back.

'I came over with a brain tumour,' she said, 'and now my sister's got the same thing.'

The sister was worried about the suffering she might have to go through but Maisie soothed her fears.

'Don't worry, it's as easy as slipping on butter coming over here,' she assured her, 'and I will be there to take your hand.'

The little old lady's face lit up. 'I'm not worried now. Not if Maisie's with me.'

The other nice surprise was that Joan Scott Alan was in the audience, unknown to me. I'd never met Joan but I'd given a message to her daughter during a demonstration in Nottingham last year. I'd given the daughter Joan's full name, the fact that she nursed the mentally ill and that she wrote beautiful poetry inspired by the spirit people.

Her daughter Pauline was so impressed she phoned her mother the next day and Joan wrote to me enclosing a tape of some of her poems. They were certainly beautiful and I printed one of my favourites in my last book.

Somewhere in the back of my mind I suppose it had registered that Joan lived near Portsmouth but I hadn't heard from her for some time and I never gave her a thought when I walked on the stage. I was absolutely delighted though when a message came through for her and she walked to the microphone and we were able to meet for the first time.

'Joan, they're telling me you've retired now from nursing,' I said.

'Yes, Doris, I have.'

'But you're still writing the poems.'

Joan smiled. 'Yes I am, in fact I've brought some with me tonight to give you. There's a special one I've dedicated to you.'

But the spirit people weren't finished.

'They tell me you must concentrate on the poetry but forget the music,' I repeated. It seemed rather a shame because Joan had previously set her poems to music but perhaps she was using vital energy on the music when the important part of her work was the words.

'Oh, I see,' said Joan, perhaps a little disappointed.

Nevertheless afterwards she left me a whole sheaf of poems and as ever they were absolutely beautiful.

This is the one she dedicated to me:

The Interlude

My brief encounter on the earth
Was bitter sweet – I had to search
I could not bear the grief and pain
I knew I'd give but not in vain.

The sacrifice I had to make
To help this soul her path to take
The wretched pain the silent grief
So many souls through her would speak.

I made my journey to the earth
All alone she gave me birth
I clung in love against her breast
In sweet serenity to rest.

Her mother love engulfed the air
She washed and tended me with care
No greater love could ever be given
To a tiny soul sent from heaven.

She proudly put me on display
My Gran would laugh – then walk away
You'll spoil that child she would often scold
Mum's reply was a tighter hold.

Her love emitted from her soul
The mother love you can't control
I knew the pain she'd have to bear
When I was taken from her care.

She sang me lullabies at night
I clung to her with all my might.
I knew the interlude was brief
Forgive me Mum – I kiss your feet.

For many months she walked alone
With heavy eyes and heart of stone
Her anguished soul cried out in pain
John Michael please come back again.

Her cries were heard her sorrows shared
The people here did really care
But they all knew that one day soon
The gifts she had would fully bloom.

I met her in her dreams at night
To show her that I was all right
I crept beside her, watched her sleep
Her lovely face made me weep.

Dear Mother I'm so proud of you
All the loving things you do
So many souls you comfort bring
The heavenly choirs for you do sing.

So please may I be forgiven
For leaving you to go to heaven

The Father's works we have to do
And some are the specially chosen few.

When your earthly job is done
You're more than welcome to my home
You'll have the time to stand and stare
And understand just what we shared.

Until that day dear friend, dear mother
I watch and guard you like no other
Your earthly life will always be
A path of love and serenity.

Before I go I feel so sad
For I have not included Dad
The part he plays and love he shares
Is not forgotten over there.

My Mother you will always be
A true companion to me
The love you gave in my interlude
Is being repaid back to you.

And now my story has been told
Go in peace till you are old
You have helped the Kingdom come
And I am proud to be your son.

I wish I could tell Joan how much that poem means to me. I read it over and over again till the tears streamed down my face. It's the story of the loss of my baby John Michael, told from John Michael's point of view and if I can live up to the words of that poem then I'll be very pleased with myself. Joan has captured perfectly the way I try to live my life, so that my family on the other side will not be ashamed of me when I arrive. I often fail of course but at least I try.

One of my other favourites in the batch she handed me shows great compassion for the parents of handicapped children:

A Parent's Lament

Ring out the bells
Aloud from the hills
A child is born
Our hearts are filled

With love and pride and joys untold
What perfect beauty to behold

We watch her grow
With hearts so full
Of love and caring
But she's no fool

The moment we both creep away
From that nice cradle where she lay
A cry rings out

An icy hand grips both our hearts
That cry is something quite apart
A different ring – what can it be?
Our little child is almost three

We watch her play
Why can't she walk?
All other children seem to talk.

With heavy hearts we take advice
And find this soul will pay the price
For we are told in gentle tones

This child can never be left alone.

Oh God our hearts cry out in pain
What did we do to upset you
That we should rear a child in vain?

The dear Lord heard our cry and said
Hush now, take your child to bed
Then listen to what I say – let me explain
These children are my precious gifts
It's not meant to bring you pain.

If you just stop and think it through
My special gift I've sent to you
To teach you simple things of life
And most of all she's saved from strife.

The world is such a greedy place
Where man fights man
And hate meets hate.

Our worldly goods we proudly show
But when we pass where do they go?
To be passed down?
And so it goes
NO that is mine NOT for Aunt Rose.

Have you heard all this before?
Well now I knock upon your door

My special gift to you I give
That you may learn from her to live.

A life that's full and very sweet
With face upturned sat at your feet
With love that melts the hardest heart
Take this child set apart

Watch her try to talk and sing
And then, thank God for everything.

Jean's poems are always a great joy to read and they brought a lovely evening to a close for me. As the demonstration ended the audience went mad. There was so much clapping and stamping and waving of handkerchiefs they almost pulled me off the stage. I looked up at the swaying rows of cheering faces, all 2,000 of them, and it didn't matter how fagged out I'd been earlier I knew I was doing the right thing. I was on the right track, doing the work I'd been made for.

Chapter 12

I couldn't believe my eyes when I opened the paper. BATTLE OF THE PSYCHIC SUPERSTARS said the giant headline strung across two pages and beneath it was a report of demonstrations given by myself and medium Doris Collins as if we were arch rivals fighting for supremacy.

It was annoying because it's so untrue. Doris Collins and I have known each other for years. We once even shared the *Psychic News* award for Spiritualist of the Year. Doris is a very good medium and I respect her. Our styles are different just as any two people working in the same field will bring their own different personalities to the job, but there's certainly no need for us to 'battle'. There's more than enough work around to keep us, and goodness knows how many other mediums as well, fully occupied for the rest of our lives.

More than anything the story was a disappointment. The reporter had come along to a public meeting at Fairfield Halls, Croydon and we'd had some marvellous evidence. I got two lots of twins back including a pair who'd gone over after a premature birth. The poor mother had gone into labour unexpectedly on holiday in Greece and she'd lost both babies.

'You're grieving, love, because you left them in Greece,' I said. 'You came home and you left your babies there.'

'That's right,' she sobbed.

'Well, you didn't leave them, love, because they're here

with you now. Two little girls and I'm getting the names Amy and Donna.'

'That's what I called them!' she cried and her whole face became radiant.

Not long afterwards I heard the name Stephen.

'I want a little boy named Stephen,' I said. 'Our side of life.'

And to my surprise a little boy, no more than eight or nine years old came racing down to the stage.

'I'm Stephen,' he cried, while behind him, his mother struggled to catch up.

It was a young man I was talking to and since the woman didn't look old enough to have a grown up son I felt sure it must be Stephen's father.

'It's a man's voice, love,' I told her, 'a young voice.'

'Yes, that's right. I lost my husband when Stephen was only six months old,' she said.

'Does my Daddy know me, does my Daddy know I'm here?' asked Stephen bouncing up and down.

'Yes he does, darling,' I assured him and to prove it his father said, 'Tell him I know about Simon. He's a big bully.'

'Yes he is,' Stephen agreed. 'Actually he gave me a black eye last week.'

'Well stand up to him, son,' said his father, 'and if you can't hit him, kick him. You only have to stand up to a bully once.'

Stephen stood there taking it all in, his head on one side. He was a dear little soul, very old-fashioned and well spoken.

'He likes Tim, though,' the father went on.

'Do you know a Timothy?' I asked. 'Your father says you get on well with him.'

'Oh yes he's a good chap,' said Stephen.

Then the father began to talk about other members of the family. He mentioned Kitty, but before Stephen's mother could answer Stephen jumped in again. 'He's talking about Auntie Kit, Mummy.'

'Kitty's very good to him,' said the father.

'Well actually I don't see her very often,' said Stephen 'but when I do see her she's very good to me.'

At the end of the message I said to Stephen, 'Because it's a very special occasion because you've never seen your Daddy, I'm going to give you the big centre piece of flowers to take home. Your Daddy tells me your Mummy's got a car so she'll be able to manage it.'

So Stephen came up on the stage and staggered off with the flower arrangement that was nearly as big as he was.

I thought that was the last I'd seen of Stephen but after the demonstration was finished, when I was relaxing in the dressing-room, there came a knock on the door. It was Stephen bringing me a single flower from the spray.

'This is to tell you I love you,' he said.

I put my arms round him. 'I love you too,' I said. And suddenly there was a great flash and I looked up to find the photographer for the newspaper was still there, taking pictures.

'There's a photographer taking pictures of us,' Stephen whispered.

'Yes I know,' I said, 'we're going to be in the *Sunday Mirror*.'

Stephen's eyes widened. 'Oh really. Are we? How spiffing!'

He was thrilled by the idea and so looking forward to the day the paper came out. I too waited eagerly to see the pictures of the two of us and the single flower.

But when the day came there was no mention of Stephen and no photograph. Instead just this battle of the psychic superstars nonsense. It was such a shame and I could imagine how disappointed Stephen must have been.

Mind you, to be fair, the newspapers are mostly very kind to me and I've had some lovely write ups. It's odd to see yourself as others see you and some of the descriptions make me laugh. John Slim from the *Birmingham Evening Post*, was very nice and he had an amusing turn of phrase ...

'She emits a sudden, chesty laugh which hits her hotel room like a quick half hundred weight of bucketed gravel ...' he wrote, 'Doris Stokes ... is a motherly mixture of humility and good humour who carries her ample poundage with the implacability of a benevolent battleship ...'

John and I were in stitches over that one.

'When people start describing you as a battleship, it really is time to go on a diet!' I sighed.

One interview I'd been anxious about was with Jean Rook of the *Daily Express*. She'd seemed very friendly on the phone but I'd heard she can be very sharp about people in print, and I couldn't imagine what she'd say about me. If you wanted to I suppose it would be quite easy to do a mickey-taking piece about spooks and ghosties.

Jean had a very tight schedule and what with one thing and another she ended up coming to interview me in my hospital bed. I'd had to go into hospital for a couple of days for tests – as I have to regularly since I had cancer and Jean obviously didn't think much of my chances because she wrote afterwards:

'Mrs Stokes was lying in bed, pale as her cream satin négligée. And looking too close for my comfort to the Threshold she professes to cross as casually as most of us move from room to room.'

The one thing Jean didn't want was a sitting. She put up a great barrier and was most emphatic that she didn't want to talk to anyone. It was strictly an interview. Nevertheless she was a great friend of Diana Dors and while she was there Diana popped in.

'Jean's very good at tennis you know,' she said.

That shook Jean a bit I think. It turned out that Diana had never known Jean played tennis and in fact has become so keen on the game that she's having a tennis court built at her home.

After that I stuck mainly to the questions, but sometimes

things happened that I couldn't help. Jean stayed a long time and she even waited while I went off for one particular test. On the way back to the ward I sensed Diana with me.

'Oh Di – could you go and look at the results for me?' I asked because this was the test I'd been worried about.

She zipped off and a few moments later she was back. 'It's all right, kid. You're clear,' she said.

Back in my room I smiled at Jean. 'It's all right. I can relax and have a cup of tea now. I'm clear. Diana's just told me.'

Jean looked rather doubtful and made no comment but later on the doctor looked in.

'It's all right, doctor, I know the results already,' I told him cheerfully, 'I'm clear.'

He grinned. 'Yes you are.'

Then just as she was leaving, I did it again. Earlier I'd heard the name Eileen, and it came back suddenly connected with a man who passed very quickly with a heart attack.

It meant nothing to Jean, but the photographer turned pale.

'My mother's name is Eileen and my father died of a heart attack seven months ago,' he said shakily.

'Well tell your Mum your Dad's fine now, love,' I told him.

After that I couldn't think what Jean would write and I was a bit jittery until the paper came out. But I needn't have worried.

This is what she wrote:

Medium rare

I make a pig's ear of it when the spirits are all trying to talk to me at once, says Doris Stokes

Even for sceptics, Mrs Doris Stokes is the ultimate psychic phenomenon.

Few people in this world – even with one foot in the next – can pack the London Palladium with its capacity 2,000 audience, plus standing room. And not a dry eye in the sobbing, cheering, rapturous house.

Mrs Stokes is a built-in telephone exchange to the Other World. She claims to speak to the dead. She plugs them in to their living relatives. Takes messages from the Great Unknown like an answering service.

For grieving multitudes, this 65-year-old spiritualist is the antidote to death's sting. She is Victory, in a £100 beaded evening dress, over the grave.

Whether or not you believe a word she claims the dead tell her, her delivery is stunning. She dismisses all candlelit hocus and gloomy pocus. All the audience gets is a well-lit, plump, grey, permed housewife, talking on an imaginary phone to their loved ones who are not lost.

She gives the distraught parents of a 17-year-old, who died of a heart attack, all the chat they want to hear: – 'Change that coloured photograph you keep of him, lovey – he doesn't like it, he says his hair doesn't look right.'

Stokes is the thoroughly modern medium. She will appear for three Sunday Nights at the Palladium this summer – already sold out.

Comfort

Even Frankie Goes to Hollywood causes no more stampede for tickets than Doris Goes to the Other Side and Back.

When we met last week in London's Guy's Hospital for a rare 'private sitting', Mrs Stokes was lying in bed, pale as her cream satin negligee. And looking too close for my comfort to the Threshold she professes to cross as casually as most of us move from room to room.

She has survived 13 cancer operations. 'When I told

Dick Emery I'd lost a breast, my thyroid, my womb, a large chunk of intestine and my right ovary, he joked: "Doris, they want you over the Other Side but you've too much work to do so they're taking you across bit by bit".'

She added: 'I'm not worried about today's tests. I took Diana Dors down to the X-ray unit with me, and she's already checked on the results and told me I'm clear. So we can have a ciggy now, and relax,' she said, lighting her Menthol.

Did Mrs Stokes know it was the eve of the anniversary of Diana Dors' own death from cancer? (my first slip – don't feed the medium information). Did she know I'd come to ask her to raise Diana (slip two – don't show the medium your hand and give her something to grasp at).

Right out of the blue she claims is heaven, Mrs Stokes fixed me with her unnaturally huge, cloud-grey eyes and said: 'Diana says you're a terrifically good tennis player.'

Diana, though the closest friend in life, didn't even know I played tennis. And nobody but my family and the building firm knows I've just paid a deposit on a hard tennis court.

Game to Miss Dors and Mrs Stokes.

May I see Diana? 'No and I can't,' said the clairaudient (as opposed to voyant) who can only hear the dead. 'I can hear her in this room as clearly as the evening she died, when I didn't even know she was in hospital.'

How did Di take the news of her death?

'She was angry when she first got there, like Noele Gordon two weeks ago – they'd fought so hard to stay down here. Diana was angry too when Alan committed suicide (Diana Dors's husband Alan Lake shot himself five months after her death).

Laughed

'They came together to me and she told me how he did it – put the shotgun between his knees and balanced it under his chin. She kept saying: "How could you leave our baby? (their son Jason, now 16). Why didn't you have the guts to stay with him?" You know how straight out with everything she was.

'When he told her "I was like a bird without wings without you it was hopeless," she forgave him everything.'

What do you wear on the Other Side? 'Anything you fancy. You certainly don't wear wings or a white sheet and go "oooh!" and frighten folk to death.'

'To WHAT?' I said cunningly. A slip of the psyche, laughed this Grantham-born daughter of a Romany who 'lived across the road from the Prime Minister.'

'Margaret got awfully upset one night because she heard some kids outside church whisper: "There goes Creeping Jesus" – she thought they meant her Dad, who was a lay preacher. I told her not to worry, as they meant me.

'I worried though. I tried to hide what I could hear *and* see – because when I was young I could do both. I can still see spirit children – because I've lost four and love them so much.'

When her longest surviving child, John Michael, died at five months, she and her healer husband, John, accepted her unwanted gift. 'I really DIDN'T want to know, I wanted to be normal and ordinary. Sometimes I still tell the spirits to "push off" if they start whispering to me at a party.'

Do the blue lights which is all she can see of the spirits flickering above her audience, ever glow angry?

'Oh, they do, dear, they tell me to "get on with it, woman" when I get my wires crossed, and I do make mistakes when they're all trying to talk at once,' said the psychic whose greatest strength is admitting weakness, even to desperate parents, with: 'No, I'm guessing. Don't take that. I'm making a pig's ear, don't believe what I'm saying.'

'And they sometimes get cross with This Side. The nastiest case I had was a widow all in black, sobbing "that's my husband Jim, he only passed over last week," and Jim yelling in my other ear: "The bloody hypocrite, she's sitting next to the boyfriend she was carrying on with when I was in hospital." '

Chatting

Six years ago, she began to raise huge audiences from her soirees with the spirits and massive money from her four autobiographical books. 'I like the money. I just bought a new house,' she said.

I grabbed at her grasping flesh. Nothing materialized but a modest £50,000 semi-detached.

Her much talked-about limousine is hired: 'Because I have to stretch out my body to ease the pains.' Her £1,000 cut of an expensively staged Evening with Doris Stokes goes to charity.

'Who's Pepe?' she said. 'There's a dog barking!' 'Peri,' I said. My long-lost poodle, dead 15 years. 'No not dead, dear, jumping about all over the place.'

She had now been chatting, almost non-stop, for two hours. And not always to me and the photographer, alone with her in the room.

'Who's Eileen?' she'd asked, an hour before. Now she said: 'I've got someone here who died very suddenly of a heart attack. He's connected with the Eileen I asked about earlier.'

My photographer, Barry Gomer's father, died of a heart attack seven months ago. His mother's name is Eileen. Even I didn't know until 10 minutes before we left the office, which photographer would be going with me. Or his mother's name.

'Well, tell your mother he's fine, lovely,' she said. There was a long silence. For startled Barry it wasn't dead.

My spirits sank. Which is where I intended them to remain. 'You've a barrier built up against me, lovey,' said the woman who, in one of her rare sightings, alleges she watched Tommy Cooper rise from his body when he slumped, dying, on live TV.

I have an electrified fence, I thought silently (maybe she reads your mind, like a palm). When my beloved father died, 16 years ago, he made me swear on everything but the Bible I'd never try to contact him.

'Why do I get a conservatory?' she suddenly said. She knew she'd cracked it. How many journalists have a 'conservatory' as opposed to a greenhouse, or cloche?

And why did my mother pick this week, after 40 years in our Yorkshire family home, to have my father's treasured, but now disintegrating Victorian conservatory restored?

'I'm sure I could make contact at a sitting at home,' beamed Mrs Stokes, now lit up like the sun shining through glass, brightly. 'But I'm only the bridge, I can't do it if you're not willing and he's not willing.'

'We're not,' I said, speaking up before Pa weakened and had a word with Mrs Stokes.

I'd prefer to speak to him quietly, myself. And much as I still adore him, at some later date.

Daily Express
Monday May 6 1985

Yes, generally I can't complain. The papers have been very fair with me. Only one article has made me really angry and that wasn't about me at all. It was about Diana Dors and Alan Lake. It was a very nasty piece full of insinuations that Diana and Alan didn't love each other. That Alan was off with other women and Diana was having an affair in the last year of her life.

I was furious when I read it. How could they say such terrible things about two lovely people who weren't here to defend themselves. And what about Jason? Hadn't he suffered enough without reading such terrible things about his parents?

The more I thought about it the angrier I became. I couldn't believe it. Diana was far too ill in the last year of her life to be interested in an affair and as for Alan – he was a flirt, that's the way he was made, but he didn't mean anything by it. He worshipped Diana.

I got so upset by the whole thing that I couldn't eat for two days and in the end Ramanov gave me a talking to.

'Child, this won't do,' he said sternly. 'You are wasting your energy and making yourself ill. You have work to do and others that depend on you.'

He was right, of course, but then Ramanov always is.

He has been spending quite a lot of time with me lately. We've been going through a difficult patch with Terry and though the crowds wouldn't think it from my smiling face on stage, life at home has been very hard at times.

Last year Terry had a dreadful accident. He could have been killed but he was lucky and escaped with severe concussion. He seemed to get over it very well, but then just after Christmas he began to look ill. He developed violent headaches, he had no energy and suddenly for no reason, he'd fly into terrible tempers.

There were quite a few unhappy scenes at home before we discovered the problem. The shock of the accident had brought on sugar diabetes and his body was completely out of balance. In the meantime though, my nerves got very bad and I sometimes fled to my room in tears. But I wasn't alone. Ramanov was always there.

'Why does this have to happen now?' I sobbed one night. 'Just when everything's lovely and we've got this beautiful house. Why does it have to be spoiled?'

'I never promised you sunshine all the way did I?' said Ramanov. 'Learn from it. There are many lessons here.'

Well I tried and I think I've learned to be more tolerant. I've tried to understand why Terry gets these violent moods and bit by bit we've guided him through. As long as he sticks to his diet he should be all right.

I don't want it to sound as if Ramanov runs my life for

me because he doesn't. The spirit world won't do that. If you have a problem you have to try to solve it yourself, but if you've tried everything you can think of and nothing's worked, then a prayer to the spirit world will usually be answered.

Many times I've turned to Ramanov in despair and said it's no good, I've tried and tried and I'm at my wits' end. Can you help? And the next morning I've woken up with a new idea in my mind that turns out to be the solution to the problem. But you do have to help yourself. It's no good saying 'I need £1,000. Please God work a miracle.' They will only help if they can see you've genuinely done your best.

Mind you, although he doesn't run my life, Ramanov certainly lets me know if I'm straying from the path. If I start to get too materialistic he steers me back and shows me where I'm going wrong.

Now I have got a little money for the first time in my life it would be so easy to go wrong. I used to be a great idealist. I used to say that material things don't matter – and they don't really – but in spite of that, it is nice to have a beautiful bedroom to relax in and a lovely house to come home to and I'm not going to pretend it's not.

I'd be telling a lie if I didn't say it's nice to have a house with nice gardens and to be able to look out of the window and say this belongs to us.

People at the mobile home park say they can't understand it. Why on earth are we saddling ourselves with all this at our ages. But I say, you've already had it love. You've had your beautiful house, you know what it's like. I never have. I've always lived in ex-servicemen's flats or prefabs or rented houses where I've had to ask permission to hold sittings or have people in. Now I can do what I like. Maybe it's late in life but at least I can say I've done it.

One thing I thought was lovely was that when the article about my house appeared in *Woman's Own*, I didn't have one letter begrudging my good fortune. Everybody wrote to say how beautiful it was and that I deserved it. I think I do too! I've worked very hard and I've known what it's like not to have two pennies to rub together. I think I deserve a little comfort now.

Of course it's no good being the richest body in the cemetery, as Ramanov keeps reminding me, so I do as lot of charity appearances and give away as much as I can and it gives me great pleasure to do so. It's so nice to be able to help people out in a practical way at last.

I do get tired and fed up with work at times and wonder if I'm mad gallivanting around the country at my age, but Ramanov finds lessons for me in the smallest things.

One day in early spring the builders cleared away a pile of rubbish beside the drive of our house and when I went to look I saw a group of tiny crocuses that had been buried by the bricks. They were bruised and battered but they'd struggled up through all the rubbish and were flowering bravely. And as I admired them I heard Ramanov's voice in my ear.

'See what I've been telling you for so long,' he said. 'As long as you keep the spark alive, no matter how bruised and battered you may be you can survive, just as these fragile little flowers have managed to struggle through the bricks to give beauty to the world.'

His words often come back to me when I'm moaning about being tired, and also when I'm talking to someone who is stricken by grief. The human spirit is battered and bruised by grief just as the crocuses were battered by bricks, yet if we can just keep that spark of love alive we'll come through it. And you know grief isn't a bad thing. It's God's healing gift to us, because it enables us to cry. Without crying the bitterness would stay inside and make you ill.

I know it's easy for me to say, but truly no one can escape grief – not even a medium who knows that loved ones live on and talks to them every day. The tears flow because you can't touch them any more. It's the physical presence we miss.

Although I know with certainty that there's another world, if anything happened to John I would go through exactly the same thing. I would weep and weep because I couldn't put my arms round him any more. That's grief and nobody can bear that cross for us. But if we know that God or our guide is there to hold our hand, we can get through it.

Ramanov comes along at the most unlikely moments. On May 8th 1985 we were celebrating the 40th anniversary of VE day and it was an extra special occasion for John and I because it was also the day he came home from the prisoner-of-war camp. He got a beautiful new leather jacket out of that!

Anyway there we were toasting each other in tea, when Ramanov interrupted.

'This is all very well,' he said, 'but while you are celebrating peace, there are wars going on all over the world. Until you learn to live as brothers and love one another you won't have peace.'

It made me stop and think. I mean people are always saying, if there is a spirit world why don't they do more to stop wars and violence, but my Mum and Dad couldn't run the country when they lived here, so why should they be able to run the country now, just because they've been sent to the spirit world. And after all, it's the people here now, who're making wars.

As Ramanov's said before. 'God gave you a beautiful world to live in and look what you're doing with it.'

It's no good us complaining. We've made the problems and we must solve them.

When I came back from St Austell I brought a poster with me which reads: 'Any act of kindness no matter how small, is never wasted!' and I've got it up on my wall. It's so true. If everyone followed that advice, the small acts of kindness would lead to greater acts of kindness and we'd be well on the way towards loving each other.

I know that it is true – just as the reverse is true. Small acts of unkindness can have a ripple effect and do far more damage than the original mean act.

I remember doing a demonstration at SAGB not long ago and as soon as I walked onto the stage I could feel there was something wrong. Well it was a terrible night. I gave the wrong messages to the wrong people and I couldn't understand it. I've not had a night as bad as that for years.

This happened about the time we were having difficulty with Terry and I wondered if the traumas at home might be affecting me. Whatever it was, I knew I'd been dreadful and I apologised to the people there. They were very sweet and said it was fine, but I knew they were just being kind. It was not fine and I knew it.

Then two days later I had a note from a woman who'd been in the audience. She said how sorry she was that I was unhappy with the evening. We weren't hostile to you, it was the man on the door, she said. Apparently the doors had opened at five-forty-five even though the demonstration didn't start till seven and this man was shouting at people and telling them to shut-up and refusing to let them leave their seats to go to the loo or get a drink. Naturally they didn't like it, the hostility and anger built up and the evening was spoiled for everyone.

That one small act of unkindness ruined things for over one hundred and fifty people and many of them probably lost the chance of making contact with loved ones – a chance they'd been waiting for for months.

I've been doing a lot of public demonstrations lately and at most of them, I'm happy to say, the atmosphere's been marvellous. It makes such a difference. It's the love in the air that brings the spirit people close and the more love that's generated, the more contacts we get.

Some extraordinary things have come through. One night at Woolwich I was talking to a mother on the other side who was trying to comfort her husband and daughter who were grief stricken. She gave me a number of names and family details and then the daughter explained how they came to be attending the meeting that night.

Her mother had been to see me last year at a demonstration in London and had obviously been impressed.

'The Saturday before she died, she said if I'm going to come back through anybody it will be Doris Stokes,' said the daughter. 'She made me promise to buy tickets for this show and to come with Dad.'

'We bought the tickets for her,' said the bemused father, 'and she's come.'

On a lighter note, I was talking to a young boy who'd been killed in an accident. He was chatting away to his sister who was quite happy and regarded it all as perfectly natural.

'And there was a Mr Barns or Burns,' said the boy, 'he was a right pig.'

The sister laughed, 'Oh that'll be the coroner. Yes he was!'

But his next words were drowned out by the squawking of a parrot.

'Good boy Joey. Good boy Joey. Who's a pretty boy then?' it screeched and I couldn't hear a word anybody else was saying.

'Could you keep the parrot quiet a minute?' I begged the spirit people. Then I turned to the audience.

'Does anyone recognize a parrot called Joey?'

A young girl came forward at once. 'It's my mother's parrot.'

'Well she's brought it back with her, love.'

'Have a Guinness, have a Guinness,' muttered the parrot in my ear and I burst out laughing.

'Oh they never taught him to say that! He's saying have a Guinness, have a Guinness!'

The girl nodded. 'That's right. Dad used to come in drunk and that's what the parrot would say.'

The audience, of course, loved it.

I must say my theatre visits have been much more enjoyable for me lately because of a marvellous shop I heard about in Forest Hill, London. Some years ago, as I tell everybody, I had a masectomy and until you have something like that you don't realize the problems it causes.

For instance, you're like a bird with one wing, particularly when you're my size and it's very easy to over balance if you're not careful because your weight is no longer evenly distributed. You have to think twice about all kinds of everyday things, like climbing into the bath. Climb in from the wrong side and you're likely to go flying – as I did a few months ago. To make matters worse we didn't have any grab bars on the sides of our bath, so I couldn't get out again. I just lay there with my legs in the air not sure whether to laugh or cry!

Going on stage was another problem. The false boob they'd given me at the hospital weighed a ton and was very hot to wear, particularly under spotlights. When I got home my muscles would be aching and I found I'd perspired so much it was soaking wet.

I'd more or less resigned myself to the fact that I'd got to learn to live with it, when someone told me about this girl in Forest Hill who was going to have to close down her shop beause she couldn't make a living wage. Apparently she stocked special bras for ladies like me and she has special lambswool pads to go inside them.

She sounded just the person I was looking for and I discovered she runs a wonderful service as well. Sometimes she tries on as many as seventy bras to make sure she gets the fit absolutely right. She measured every little part of me and if it fitted in one place and not another, she'd take it off and try another. She spent ages, altering a piece here and a piece there. What a difference from the hospital where they simply put a tape measure round you and give you a bra, a bag and a piece of foam filled stuff to put inside, and that's it.

What's more this girl doesn't charge for the service, only for the articles she sells. And when any of her ladies are going to a wedding or a special function, they take all their clothes to the shop, dress, shoes and everything and they try it all on with the bra to make sure it looks right.

Now that's what I call doing God's work and it'll be a tragedy if she has to give it up for lack of money.

Chapter 13

'Doris,' said the young man at the microphone, 'just before my grandad died seven years ago, we had a blazing row. I told him to drop dead. And he did. It's been playing on my mind ever since. Do you think he blames me?'

It was question time. The short spot that opens the second half of my public demonstrations, and this lad had obviously been waiting all evening to ask the question that had been worrying him for seven years.

'Oh you poor soul,' I said. 'Of course he wouldn't blame you. He wouldn't bear any malice. We all say it when we're young don't we. He's just come through and he says, "I was a bit of a nagger." But he's watched over you ever since and he says you've been right down on the floor and he's picked you up and you're doing all right now. That row doesn't make a bit of difference. He still loves you.'

I get asked all sorts of things at question time but the same subjects do occur again and again, so I thought it might be helpful to collect a few examples of questions and answers from recent demonstrations. These are the sort of things people want to know:

Q. My friend's still got her Dad's ashes and she doesn't know where she should put them. What should she do?

A. We've been asked some rum things before! He says, 'I don't care a damn, love, I'm here.' If it'll make you happy I think he liked rivers, you could spread them on water. But let him go free with love and he will come back with love.

Q.   My question is about senility. If people are senile before they pass, do they remember what happened to them when they get to the other side?

A.   No, because they are not responsible for their actions. When they get to the other side they go into hospital and are nursed back with love. They don't remember the details of their passing. When they come back they usually say: 'I got very difficult towards the end.'

Q.   If a murderer goes on to a different plane on the other side what happens to someone who commits suicide?

A.   They are sick in the mind so they go into a special hospital where they are nursed until they're well. The person you're talking about was in a car wasn't he love?

Q.   Yes.

A.   He's here and he just told me: 'I was in the car under some trees and I was found,' he said. He'd had words with someone and wanted to frighten them.

A.   Well he's here now love and he's better. He's fine now. He's not in hellfire or anything like that.

Q.   My little girl died when she was two. Who looks after her? Does she still play?

A.   Yes. She's happy, love. They don't let anything hurt the spirit children. They even keep them away from our grief. A spirit mother looks after them. You have a grandmother over there and she is looking after your little girl. When there are no close relatives on the other side a girl who's gone over without knowing the joys of motherhood will be given the child to look after.

Q.   Is it possible to see someone if they have died? I did

several times and I was told I was imagining it. I
think I upset him because I told him I couldn't take
any more and I haven't seen him since. Did I do the
wrong thing?

A. If it was wrong, love, they'd have left me years ago
because when I was young I used to get so fed up
with the spirit people I used to say, oh push off –
leave me alone. I think they are giving you time to
adjust and if you have psychic ability you must use it,
love. If it happens again say: Hello, how are you
doing?

Q. My friend lost her husband in 1983. He died from a
rare disease. Now they want to open him up. Is it the
right thing to do?

A. He's just come in. I think it was something to do with
the brain wasn't it because he says, 'I went like a
baby'.

Q. Yes that's right.

A. He says it doesn't matter a bit what they do with his
body and if it will help someone else let them get on
with it.

Q. I lost my little boy about two years ago. I moved
from that flat but people say the little girl who
moved in keeps pointing when there's nothing there
and things are being moved. Could it be my little
boy?

A. Yes. The little girl will see him. Children are psychic
until ten or eleven. He just wanders in and out to see
what's happening in his old home.

Q. Last year my sister went over. Just before she died
she had a row with my brother and we wonder
whether she's forgiven him.

A. Of course she has. She went very tragically, very
quickly, didn't she? It was a virus and it was all over

in 48 hours she tells me. Don't cry she says because she's all right and of course she doesn't bear any malice. We all fall out now and then but it doesn't mean anything.

Q.   You seem to pick up people who haven't passed long ago. Does that mean it's harder for people to come back if they passed a long time ago?

A.   It's not harder love it's just that when someone has just passed their relatives are still grieving and they want to reassure them. They stay close to comfort them. But the other night I had a girl whose mother passed over when she was three and she came back to talk to her daughter twenty-seven years on!

Q.   If you carry a kidney donor card and leave parts of your body to someone on earth, does it hinder your progression into spirit?

A.   Oh no, love. Blimey I hope they've got my parts parcelled and labelled! I've had so many bits and pieces taken away, love. Whether I'll be any good to anyone now I don't know but John and I have put in our will that anything that can be used, can be used. It doesn't make any difference to us over there. My mother only had one eye. She lost it at birth but when I saw my mother on the other side I couldn't understand what was different about her at first — then I realized she had two eyes.
     They can put me in the dustbin when I've gone for all the difference it'll make to me. I'll be away.

Q.   You never seem to talk to foreign people in public meetings why's that?

A.   I do. The other night I had a woman from Cyprus, but I agree I talk to more British people in public demonstrations. I think it's because I have trouble getting my name round foreign names and it takes up so much time, it's better to save them for private sittings when I have longer.

Q. If a child is not born on earth what age does it grow up to in the spirit world?

A. The age it should have been had it lived here. It will grow up and be brought back to see its mother and when she goes over she will recognize him or her immediately, even though she never saw her child on earth.

Q. If you lose a baby what happens when the person looking after it gets too old to look after it?

A. They don't, love. There's always someone there to take care of them and when you've reached the age you were meant to reach you don't grow any older.

Q. I was waiting to adopt a baby when my nan passed over. Does she know I've got my son now?

A .Of course she does. She comes to see you regularly.

Q. The evening my grandmother died I was in the bedroom and she said there was someone else in the room and she didn't want them there. Who was it?

A. Someone from the spirit world come to get her. The minute you see that you know you're about to pop your clogs! Your gran probably would say take him away, because she didn't want to go just then.

Q. If you have more than one husband, who do you end up with?

A. If you loved them both equally you'd go to both because there is no jealousy. But if you didn't get on on earth you probably wouldn't want to see each other again so you wouldn't. You go where the love is.

Q. How do you develop psychic power?

A. Everyone has a psychic spark but in some it's stronger than in others. Sometimes it is inherited and sometimes you get interested in psychic things and it just happens. Join a good developing circle – you'll hear of one through your nearest spiritualist church. Or if that doesn't suit you sit with two or three friends in love and harmony and offer yourself in service.

Q. If you have an animal put down, are you held responsible even if it was for the good of the animal?
A. No, love. I hope someone would do the same for me if I was suffering and never going to get well. But animals live on too and they are fit and healthy on the other side. You will meet your pets again.

Q. Do they celebrate birthdays on the other side.
A. Yes. They are lucky. They have two celebrations, the day they were born on earth and the day they arrived in the spirit world.

Q. Can I put in a request now to work with animals over there?
A. Oh yes, love. There are always poor animals that are put down because they're unwanted or are killed in accidents and they are nursed back on the other side too. They tell me you've got a dog called Sammy now.
Q. Yes and I love him to bits!

Q. If they watch you from the other side, do they come into the room or do they watch you from somewhere else?
A. Are you worried about your privacy, love? There wouldn't be any babies born if everyone thought like that. No, they respect our privacy. They come when you send out love. If you think, isn't this lovely I wish so and so could be here to see it – they come.

Q. If we are all here to learn, what have the people in Ethiopia got to learn?

A. I'm afraid I can't answer that, love. I've often wondered myself. It's the people at the top who're to blame. But the rest of us can learn from the suffering people in Ethiopia. Look at Bob Geldoff. He went there and was touched by what he saw. It will have changed him for the better.

Q. Have we all got a spirit guide?

A. Yes, every single one of us. Someone on the other side volunteers to give up their progression in the spirit world to guide us even before our bodies are conceived. They are waiting and our spirit is waiting to come to earth and when we go back the guide goes back. You might call it your conscience or your instinct or a hunch, but it is your spirit guide trying to lead you onto the right path.

Q. I lost my daughter last year and I want to know if I live to ninety, will she still be there when I go over or will she have gone on?

A. No darling it takes hundreds of years. It doesn't matter how old you are she'll still know you are her mother. It doesn't matter how long we have to wait, we'll see our kids again. The love link is eternal.

Q. I have been grieving badly for eleven months now and I wonder if that grief will stop the person from progressing in the spirit world?

A. Well yes, I'm sorry to say it'll make it more difficult. You have to let them go free with love so that they can come back with love. We all have to go through a grieving period, but it makes them sad to see us unhappy.

Q. Is healing hereditary?

A. Well I inherited my gift from my father who was a Romany Gypsy so I should think healing might be inherited too. You only have to want to help people and if the gift is there, it will come.

Q. My mum didn't have a very happy life but I have a very very happy life and I want to share it with her a bit more but I'm frightened.

A. Well it scared me at first, love, but really there's nothing to be afraid of. It's as natural as breathing. Your mum will be close to you, just say hello to her and put a flower by her picture with your love.

Q. I lost five relatives recently and I wonder if they are together. Also does it hurt my dad because I love him so much?

A. They will be together and it hurts your dad to see you unhappy. You can't live with your daddy in the spirit world can you, love? You've got your own life to lead and your own family to think of. You mustn't send all your love with your daddy. He's happy in his new life but your grief is making him sad.

As you can see, the questions come in all shapes and sizes and every question time is slightly different but these are the types of questions I'm most often asked. Perhaps yours is amongst them.

Chapter 14

The other day I was going through the mail as I do first thing every morning when I shook one envelope and out fell a faded snapshot. People often send me pictures of their spirit children for my wall, but I knew immediately that this was something different. It was old and blurry, not a bit like the glossy colour photographs we take today.

Curiously I picked up the magnifying glass to have a good look and suddenly the face of my dear old Mum leapt out at me. I gazed at the picture in delight. It showed three ladies dressed in the style of the twenties or thirties walking along a street in Skegness and I knew them all; Winifred Webb, Florrie Hodson and Mum. Mum and two of her friends were obviously enjoying a holiday, or possibly a day trip to our nearest seaside resort.

People often ask me why I've printed pictures of my father in previous books but not my mother. Well it's not that I loved mum any less – it's just that there are hardly any pictures of her in existence. You see Mum had only one eye, she lost the other at birth during a forceps delivery and she went through life wearing an ugly old shade. She was always a bit self conscious of it and consequently when anyone got a camera out, Mum would head off in the opposite direction. She was extremely reluctant to have her picture taken to say the least and now there are hardly any photographs to remind us of her. That's why I was so thrilled to receive the Skegness snapshot and since then we've had it blown up.

You can tell just by looking at the way Mum's hat is pulled down low on her forehead how much she hated that eye shade and tried to hide it. Yet when I saw her in the spirit world she had two eyes, good as new. We lose all our infirmities over there and Mum had got rid of that patch for good.

Memories of my family have been crowding in lately because I've just come back from Lincoln which is very nearly home ground. Actually it should have been home ground proper, but we had such difficulty over the arrangements for a demonstration at Grantham that we moved the whole thing down the road to Lincoln. I mentioned earlier the trouble there was over ticket touts and some people getting twenty tickets while others had none. Well in the end there was so much bad feeling I couldn't work in that sort of atmosphere, so we laid on coaches and ferried all those who wanted to go to Lincoln and back, and the proceeds of the evening went to the mentally handicapped.

We had a lovely room in Lincoln overlooking the cathedral which is floodlit at night – a very beautiful sight. The only trouble was people kept climbing the fire escape next to our room to take pictures of it. The first morning there I woke up in alarm, convinced a crowd of people had come into the room. Fortunately the room was empty, but when I drew back the curtain I hastily let it fall again. Some particularly enterprising tourists had climbed over the fire escape onto the flat roof outside our window and were clicking away at the cathedral from there! I had to creep about with the curtains closed until they'd gone!

After all the kerfufle with tickets and coaches and change of venue I was a bit apprehensive about the evening but the spirit world didn't let me down. When you're worried about something they always come up trumps. In the bathroom – where I always go for a bit of privacy! – I heard the name Maisie Bolton from The Pastures, Barrowby. It was Maisie's Mum.

'I was a medium like you, Doris,' she said. 'My guide was called Topsy.' She wanted to wish her daughter happy birthday she said, because it was her birthday the following week.

Well when I got on stage and tried to find Maisie Bolton from The Pastures, Barrowby, I discovered her Mum had miscalculated Maisie – or Mavis as her name turned out to be, I'd misheard – wasn't there. She'd fallen ill and given the tickets to a close friend.

Her mother was quite put out. She told me her name was Doris like mine and she folded her arms and settled down for a good chat and wouldn't let anyone else in for some time. In the end she agreed to let other spirit people have a turn on condition that Mavis' friend took some flowers to her for her birthday.

'And tell her it's true what I used to say about the after life,' she added as a parting shot, 'I'm here now and it's just as I said.'

Once Doris cleared the line they all came through; a husband who'd left a trilby hat in the wardrobe and was complaining because he'd splashed out on a new suit just before he passed, the mother who knew that her daughter had got a new car and £250 knocked off the price and who worried about her grandson, a lovely boy who 'wouldn't apply himself', a young girl who passed with leukaemia and knew that her sister was wearing her favourite blue sweater but hadn't managed to get into her shoes because they were too small, a mother who complained her family had put artificial flowers beside her picture instead of fresh ones, a little boy who'd left behind £4.75 in his building society account and so it went on ...

At one point I got a contact for the Richardson family. They were all sitting there in a row, about twelve of them, and I got practically all their names; Donna, Diana, Deborah, Peggy, Alan ...

It was marvellous. A wonderful evening for me and for the mentally handicapped.

The next day we set off for Bridlington where we were doing two shows and a very lively time we had! The weather had changed at last and we glided through the Lincolnshire countryside, bathed in warm sunshine. I'd forgotten how pretty Lincolnshire can be. We passed whole fields of shining gold which I took to be mustard, but later Tony Ortzen who was introducing me on stage said, 'Did you see all those fields of rape?'

'Of what?' I asked, horrified.

'Rape,' he grinned, 'that's what it's called.'

'Well we always called it mustard,' I told him, 'I think that's much nicer.'

And as we skimmed through the country lanes I suddenly saw a name that sent the years rolling back. Scampton. My very first station when I was in the WAAFs.

'Oh Robbie, slow down a minute,' I said to the driver. 'There's my old station. I wonder whether they'd let us have a look round and drive down to dispersal.'

This was the place where one cold dawn long ago I'd heard a young airman whistling *The Lord's My Shepherd* as he climbed into his plane and I'd known with absolute certainty that he wasn't coming back. Yes Scampton was the place where I'd come to terms with my psychic power for the first time. It made my heart beat faster just to look at it.

It had been modernized, of course, but the old married quarters where we'd been billeted were still there. We slept under canvas in those days but we used to go to the married quarters to get undressed and get ready to go out and to wait for the buses that took us to our tents for the night.

Robbie stopped the car. 'I'll go and ask them if we can look round,' he said and strode away to the guardroom but sadly it wasn't to be. Apparently you had to write in and make an appointment. I often wonder if I'd thought to ask myself whether it would have made any difference. After all having been in the forces myself I know how to put the question and who to ask for. But there you are I didn't think of it at the time and when I did it was too late.

Disappointed we continued on our way, but the magnificent Humber bridge almost made up for it. It was such a wonderful sight, rolling out and out across the brown water. An incredible feat of engineering.

At our seafront hotel in Bridlington, the lady on the desk was thrown into confusion by our arrival.

'What terms do you want?' she asked.

'Terms?' said Laurie. 'What do you mean?'

'Well, do you want dinner or just bed and breakfast?'

'Oh I don't think we'll want dinner tomorrow night,' I explained. 'We'll be at the theatre, but tonight ...'

'Surely Doris Stokes can order what she wants,' Laurie interrupted.

'Oh, well, yes – if you like,' but the lady looked a little crestfallen as if she'd much prefer to get things straight in advance.

We were in the area of the great trenchermen of course and when they served you a meal, boy, they served you a meal. No wonder food is the first thing they ask you about.

Oddly enough though, we didn't even see a Yorkshire pudding, not that I'm allowed to eat them these days. But when I was a girl, Yorkshire pudding was a great filler up. We had Yorkshire pudding and gravy before the main course on a Sunday. Then a tiny scrap of meat surrounded by a mound of vegetables and finally to finish, Yorkshire pudding again with jam or sugar and vinegar. It was a good filling meal and I expect the older people still eat it like that.

We phoned the theatre soon after we arrived just to check the arrangements and found the manageress highly perplexed.

'We've had a call from two vicars,' she said. 'They asked if we wanted them to come into the theatre in case anything happened. I didn't know what to say. What do you think? Do you normally have vicars there?'

'No, love, not unless they've bought tickets,' I said, 'but don't worry. Give me the phone numbers and I'll sort it out.'

Well the first vicar was on holiday, so he couldn't have been too worried but the second vicar was at home.

'Hello,' I said, 'it's Doris Stokes here. I understand you've volunteered to come to the theatre. Do you mean you want to come on stage with me?'

'Oh no,' he said, 'I meant did they want me to come and clear out the evil influence afterwards.'

'Evil influences!' I echoed. 'What on earth are you talking about?'

'Well, sometimes, it's happened when we've had people like you here before, it leaves evil influences in the place and we have to go in and clear them out.'

'I can assure you there'll be nothing like that with me,' I said firmly. 'But if you are really so concerned why don't you come on stage with me and warn the people and let them make up their own minds.'

Well he didn't fancy that either but it turned into quite a discussion. He quoted the Bible at me and I quoted the Bible at him, but we weren't really getting anywhere.

'Look,' I said at last, 'I'll tell you what I'll do. I'll give your name and telephone number out so that if anybody is in trouble after seeing me, they can ring you for help.'

There was a small pause. 'Oh, eh – I don't think that would be a very good idea,' said the vicar.

'No? Well that's what you're talking about isn't it? Or do you just want the glory of going into the theatre and doing the whole blessing bit? I thought you were concerned about the people.'

'I am.'

'Well I'll give them your number then,' I said. And I did as well.

But I felt a bit sad as I put the phone down. Why they feel it's wrong to bring joy and strength and comfort to people I don't know. After some demonstrations the love in the air is so thick you can almost see it. How can that possibly be evil?

There wasn't time to dwell on it though because we'd promised to do an interview for Radio Humberside. I'd hesitated at first because I was afraid it might be a long distance to travel, but no they said, they had a studio in Bridlington, we could do it from there.

Well it turned out to be the funniest broadcast I've ever done. The address we'd been given was on the seafront and we pulled up at a strange little building like a cross between a broken down café and a nissan hut. Next door was a funfair and right beside the building a giant swing boat lunged backwards and forwards full of wildly screaming people.

'This can't be right,' said Laurie surveying the place in amazement.

'Well I'm sure this is where they told us to come.' There was a girl at a little tourist information kiosk outside so I asked her.

'Oh yes,' she said, 'there's a studio here. You can go through. I'll give you the key.'

'The key?' I queried my voice going into a squeak. 'Isn't there anyone there?'

'No,' said the girl.

Well we couldn't believe our eyes. We opened the door on a do it yourself studio. It really was radio by numbers. There was a list of instructions: One. Sit comfortably. Two. Pick up the telephone. Three. Dial this number ... Four. Place yourself in front of the microphone ...

We were in hysterics. Almost crying with laughter I dialled the number and a young girl answered.

'Oh hello, Doris,' she said. 'The power's by the door. Right, now press that button. Put on the headphones ...' and so it went on.

The place was double-glazed and absolutely sweltering that day so we propped the door open with a bucket to get a little air and somehow through our giggles we started the broadcast. Half-way through there was a great clatter. A girl outside had kicked the bucket away.

'Sorry!' she called, 'but we want to use the phone in the other room and we aren't allowed to when this door's open.'

Laurie almost fell off his chair. 'I don't believe this,' he gasped. 'It's *Candid Camera* isn't it? It's not real!'

And over the top of it all, even with the door closed, came the screams from the swing boat.

I don't know what the programme was like but all I can say is I've not had such a good laugh for ages!

On a sadder note it was while we were in Bridlington that the news came of Roy Plomley's passing. We were getting ready to go to the theatre and the television was playing away in the next room, when suddenly I recognized Roy Plomley's voice.

'Roy Plomley's on the television,' I called to John and drifted out of the bathroom to watch. But it was only a recording and afterwards they announced that Roy had passed that morning.

I was very sad because he is such a gentle, loving, man. A real old world gentleman. When they showed the list of stars who had been on *Desert Island Discs* I felt very humble and very proud to have been invited. In fact I was one of the last guests on the show. Roy will be sadly missed, not only by his family but by his millions of listeners and by his colleagues at the BBC. He knows now that what I was talking about was true and I hope he has a happy life on the other side. Well I know he will because he was always such a considerate, lovely man.

There was more fun and games when we got to the theatre that night. The dressing-rooms and everything else backstage seemed to be in the basement and when you opened the door from the street, instead of walking forward you went straight down, down these narrow winding stone steps without a handrail. Frightened the life out of me, of course, and I was sure I'd break my neck but I managed it.

Talk about Casey's Court. When it was time to go on stage, there was me holding my long dress up at the front and John holding it up at the back, struggling one in front of the other up these steep steps like some kind of broken down pantomime horse! And when I got on stage and sat down, I nearly shot into the audience! Laurie is a stickler for cleanliness and he'd given the leather seat that had been put out for me, an extra good polish. It looked lovely but it was as slippery as glass and I had to spend the whole evening with my feet braced hard against the floor to stop myself sliding out onto my bum into the auditorium!

Both Bridlington shows were a success thank goodness. I've already mentioned in an earlier chapter Paul Hewson who came to talk to me in my hotel room, but there were many other good contacts. There was a husband who mentioned the £79 his wife had won at bingo. There was ten-year-old Susie who'd been killed in a road accident. 'It was 4.30 and I'd been running, then bang ... It wasn't fair. I'd only just been to the dentist and I hate the dentist's. I needn't have bothered ...' There was also a puzzling message about something being rolled up in the toe of a sock.

'Did you find some money in the toe of a sock, or did she use to hide money in a sock. It's something to do with a sock,' I explained.

'I know what that means,' said the young woman at the microphone. 'When I was little we were very very poor and I was hoping for something for Christmas. They got an old sock, filled it with bits of screwed up paper and old hair brushes and things for a joke!'

I also met up with two previous sitters, only one of them was now talking to me from the other side.

'It's Barry,' said a man's voice, 'and I know you.'

I realized then that he must have been for a sitting but I meet so many people I didn't recognize his voice. Barry said he was with Amanda and looking for Margaret. Well when Margaret came to the front I recognized her face.

Hers was one of the *Forty Minutes* sitting that didn't ever reach the screen. She'd come with her husband Barry hoping to contact her daughter Mandy who was in the spirit world. But now it seemed as if fresh tragedy had struck, because Barry was also in the spirit world.

'Oh no, he took himself over, darling,' I said in horror. 'He just wants to say he's sorry. I'd upset her two days before and she sulked a bit,' he said, 'but that wasn't it.' And he went on to explain that he was afraid of being made redundant. 'I was redundant once before then I got another job and I thought I was about to lose that as well. I hadn't got the guts to face it ...'

Most of all he wanted his wife to know that it wasn't anything she'd done, and he still loved her.

During question time a dear little lad came up. He was only two pennyworth and he looked up at me on the stage and said I've read your books and I would like to ask is there room for everyone up there or do we move on?

Well I explained that it takes hundreds of years to move on and there seems to be room for all and he trotted back to his seat, but at the end of the show he came back again with his book to sign and they hoisted him up onto the stage so that I could give him a big hug.

That night they gave me a standing ovation and through the cheers and shouts I detected a familiar chant: 'Doris Stokes ... Doris Stokes ...' I looked up at the balcony and there was the girl who'd shown John the cardboard cut-out she'd pinched from the book signing all those months ago. She'd come with a great bunch of friends plus the cut-out and they stood there waving it above their heads as they chanted. Gradually the rest of the audience took up the chant until the whole theatre was swaying to the rhythm of 'Doris Stokes! Doris Stokes!'

It was the most magical moment.

As it turned out I was to have a more lasting reminder of Bridlington and that wonderful evening than my own memories. When I got home there was a letter waiting for me from Kathy Nicholson who'd been in the audience:

> Dear Doris, I just felt that I wanted to write to you to say thank you from the bottom of my heart for bringing my little boy Steven to talk to me last night. Everything you said about his accident and how he was put onto a machine to help his breathing, and the fact that he would have been a cabbage if he'd lived, were all so very accurate. His personality came through so very real and I feel so much love towards you because of what you did for me. I would just like to say Doris that right at the beginning of the demonstration you gave us a 'Mrs Roberts' then at one point you said 'Kathy' or 'Katharine' and then later you said 'Caravan' but then you said 'Oh I don't know what all that is about' and there was a group of ladies gathered at the front acknowledging your messages.
>
> I didn't stand up at the time because I was a little confused but I firmly believe now Doris that my Dad, Arthur Roberts, was trying to talk to me. He passed over almost 18 months ago and I have always looked for comfort in the belief that Steven and his Grandad were together in the spirit world because they were very close.
>
> My name is Kathy and at the moment we live in a caravan until we move into our new home. I would be very pleased if you would accept a little gift from me. The cassette enclosed is one I recorded last year. You see I play the trumpet and my Dad was very proud of me and I dedicated my cassette to him. He never got to hear it whilst on the earth plane and I *know* now that he knows all about my recording the cassette and also that he and Steven enjoy listening to it in the spirit world.
>
> God bless you, Doris.

My sincerest best wishes to you and to your dear
husband, John,

Yours sincerely
Kathy Nicholson (née Roberts)

Well I played the cassette and it's absolutely beautiful.
Kathy is a very talented girl and her music has given me
great pleasure. What's more, when I close my eyes and
listen to *Danny Boy*, and all the other old favourites, I'm
back on that stage in Bridlington surrounded by a great
wall of love.

Readers who've got this far will realize that all kinds of
wonderful things have happened since my last book! The
most exciting of all, however, was being presented to
Princess Anne, when she opened the new Bone Marrow
Unit at Westminster Hospital.

As I mentioned in a *Host of Voices, Woman's Own*
magazine launched an appeal to build the unit as part of
their support for the Save the Children Fund. Well they
raised over a million pounds I believe, and I was able to
contribute £12,000 from my own charity shows which was
marvellous. The unit was built and on June 6th it was
opened by Princess Anne who is president of the Save the
Children Fund.

Naturally I'd been looking forward to the ceremony for
months and months. I'd got my clothes sorted out. I was
going to wear a mandarin style dress in spiritual colours of
swirling blues and mauves.

Then just the day before the ceremony I had a slight
stroke. I was horrified; not so much by my physical
condition as the fact that I might miss the presentation and
also two appearances I was supposed to be doing in
Brighton immediately afterwards. My right arm was
clumsy and almost useless and when I tried to speak it
came out as a terrible stammer.

'There is no way you can stand up on a stage and talk to

people,' said my wonderful doctor when I finally stuttered out what was worrying me. 'You are not to do any work whatsoever. But I don't see why you shouldn't go to the presentation. It'll do you good because you'll enjoy it and you won't have to do any work. Afterwards, though, I want you in hospital for a check-up.'

Sadly, I had to cancel my Brighton appearances but I did struggle along to Westminster Hospital and I'm so glad that I did.

They looked after me marvellously. Professor Hobbs met me at the door and arranged for a nurse to be with me throughout. Then they took me into the boardroom and let me sit there in a chair intended for a lady-in-waiting, until Princess Anne arrived.

She looked breathtaking. I don't know how to describe her: chic, elegant, immaculate – nothing quite captures the way she looked. She was wearing a cream skirt with a navy blue jacket and her hair was swept up and topped by a cream hat with navy blue spots.

She really is a lovely girl. Very slim and upright with a serious expression until she smiles, and then it's like magic. Her whole face lights up with such radiance that you can see how beautiful she really is.

I was last in line to be presented. In front of me were other fund raisers: Miss Jackie Berger, Pauline and Brendan McAleese from Northern Ireland and then me.

I was terrified I might fall over or do something stupid before she got to me, and as she moved along the line my heart was crashing in my ears so loud I thought everyone in the room must be able to hear it. And then, there she was.

'May I present Doris Fisher Stokes, ma'am, who is a medium, writes books and who has worked unstintingly for the Save the Children Fund,' said Iris Burton editor of *Woman's Own*, while I tried to do a little bob.

The Princess looked directly into my eyes so that the rest of the room disappeared.

'Have you lost any children with this?' she asked, referring to the blood diseases that would be treated.

'No, ma'am,' I said, 'I lost four children when I was young but I just love kids, so I try to do what I can.'

She smiled, 'You look a little bit tired.'

She was observant too. 'Well I don't work as hard as you, ma'am.'

'Oh it's a little bit different for me!' she said giving a lopsided grin as if to say it's all laid on for me. I don't have to work like you do.

And then it was over and she was moving towards the platform for the speeches. I think perhaps I didn't pay quite as much attention to the speeches as I should, because we were standing the whole time. The chairman offered, Princess Anne a chair but she said, 'No I will stand,' and so everyone else had to stand up too.

It seemed endless. I braced my back against the wall and I didn't know whether to stand with my legs pressed together or apart to balance myself. It went on and on and the room grew very hot yet Princess Anne never moved once. Everyone else got a bit fidgety and even the man on the platform was fanning himself discreetly with his programme behind the Princess's back. Princess Anne, however, didn't move a muscle, she didn't perspire. She simply stood relaxed, attentive and as cool as if there was a pleasant breeze blowing.

I looked at her and I thought, my God, that's breeding, that's royal training for you. You can't buy what that girl's got.

The ceremony moved on. The Princess unveiled a blue and gold commemorative plaque and she was presented with a bouquet of flowers and a plate by a little girl and a little boy.

The boy turned out to be Mark, the first boy to have had a successful bone marrow transplant. He'd been at the Dorchester when we launched the appeal and he remembered me. Down came the blue rope that separated us and he came over to give me a hug.

'Did I do it right?' he asked. He'd been told to bow and he'd given a quick duck of his head.

'You did it beautifully,' I told him.

Afterwards we went off for a buffet tea and dear Professor Hobbs had arranged for a table to be carried in for me with my own waiter and waitress to bring me the goodies so that I wouldn't have to stand in the queue.

Mr and Mrs McAleese from Northern Ireland were at my table and I thought they were a wonderful couple. They'd lost their little boy before the unit was built but they'd gone ahead to help raise money so that other children could be saved. And they'd managed it all despite the fact that Brendan was unemployed.

I wasn't supposed to be working of course but while we were chatting I suddenly heard the name David and a little boy's voice said something about his sister.

I didn't want to jump in until I was sure so I asked Pauline innocently if she had any other children.

'Oh, yes, a little girl,' she said.

That was it, I must be talking to her son.

'Who's David?' I asked.

'Why that's my little boy's name!' she said.

'He tells me you got a red sweater out of his drawer the other day and buried your face in it.'

She looked stunned. 'Yes I did, two days ago. But nobody knows about that. I didn't even tell Brendan.'

'Well David was with you love,' I said.

I had to be careful not to go into a sitting of course but I was able to give her a few more words of comfort including the fact that David knew his sister was staying with her Auntie Marie while her parents were in London.

Strangely enough we were joined by a very nice young man who'd raised a lot of money in Germany. His name was Flight Leutenant John Foster who worked for the Ministry of Defence. When I told him about my visit to Scampton he said what a pity it was that he hadn't met me then.

'I could have got you in,' he said. 'Just let me know if there's anywhere you'd like to go and I'll arrange it,' and he left me his telephone number.

They were a cheeky lot on our table. They wanted to smoke so they shouted, 'Doris Stokes wants to smoke!' And immediately an ashtray was brought.

Then a bit later somebody wanted to go to the loo. They went out and found they weren't allowed through because Princess Anne was coming down the stairs. So back they came and said: 'Doris Stokes wants to go to the ladies' room!'

'That'll be all right,' they said.

Of course I had to go then but this blonde lady tucked on behind me.

'What did you do that for?' I asked her, 'I could have waited.'

'Well I wanted to go, too,' she said, 'but nobody knows me. Everybody knows you!'

After tea Professor Hobbs came to take me up to see the unit. I'd read in my programme that the unit contained seven special cubicles, five of which are laminar flow cubicles, each with its own filter system bathing the patient with germ free air. There was also a sterile kitchen and utility room.

It sounded very impressive but it was even more impressive when you saw it. There were all these filters and big germ free bubbles.

'Put your hand just there, Doris,' said Professor Hobbs and when I did as he asked I felt a great rush of sterile air pushing against my hand.

There was one little boy in the unit who had already had his transplant and didn't need to be kept in isolation.

'This is Matthew,' said Professor Hobbs.

'Hello, Matthew darling,' I said. He was a dear little boy of about three who was lying on his bed with his head on his Daddy's knees. His hair was just begining to grow back like a little haze of fur all over his head.

'Tummy's going down now isn't it Matthew,' said Professor Hobbs. 'He had a big tummy a little while ago.'

'Aren't you lucky,' I said, 'I've got a big tummy and mine's not going to go down!'

There was a photographer hovering about and he asked if I could get on the bed with Matthew for the picture.

'Yes that's all right,' said Professor Hobbs.

'Can I sit on the bed with you, Matthew?' I asked.

'Yeth.'

'Can I give you a big hug?'

'Yeth,' he said again, so, of course, I did.

It only remained for me to present the doll from Cornwall, now named Anne and resplendent in a red velvet dress and bonnet with underclothes and panties and shoes and socks that all came off and then it was time to go.

I suddenly realized I was exhausted but I wouldn't have missed it for the world.

So here I am in my hospital bed, a bit battered and bruised and playing Kathy's tape to cheer myself up. The doctors shake their heads and tell me I should slow down but I'm busy doing my arm exercises and singing away to get my voice back. I'm determined to be on my feet again soon.

I'm not getting any younger, of course, and I don't know how much longer I've got, none of us does, but I've got a strange feeling that there's still something else I have to do. I can't think what it can be because I've done private sittings, public demonstrations, television, radio and newspaper interviews. Yet I still feel there's something I must do.

No doubt the spirit world will show me what it is in their own good time – and when I find out – you'll be the first to know!